£32.99

PostgreSQL

DEVELOPER'S HANDBOOK

SAMS 201 West 103rd St

PostgreSQL Developer's Handbook

Copyright © 2002 by Sams Publishing

International Standard Book Number: 0-672-32260-9

Library of Congress Catalog Card Number: 2001094252

Printed in the United States of America

First Printing: December 2001

05   04   03   02   4   3   2   1

Trademarks

Warning and Disclaimer

Acquisitions Editor
Patricia Barnes

Development Editor
Scott D. Meyers

Managing Editor
Charlotte Clapp

Project Editor
Anthony L. W. Reitz

Copy Editor
Nancy Albright

Indexer
Becky Hornyak

Proofreader
Jody Larsen

Technical Editors
Luke Welling
Vince Vielhaber

Interior Designer
Gary Adair

Cover Designer
Aren Howell

Page Layout
Michelle Mitchell

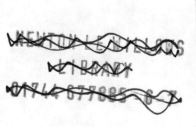

Contents at a Glance

Table of Contents

About the Authors

Ewald Geschwinde

Ewald Geschwinde was born on June 21, 1976 in Vienna, Austria. After primary school he attended the high school for economics in Oberpullendorf. During this time he dealt with computers and even extended the work in his favorite field while studying at the Technical University in Vienna.

A few months later he started working at the computer center of CA (an Austrian bank), where he was responsible for writing data converters and network solutions for backup systems.

In February 1999 he joined Synthesis, where he focused on monitoring the development of unemployment and generating reports using C, EFEU, LaTex and Perl. In his spare time he developed a database solution for business consultants.

After focusing on Oracle databases he left Synthesis to found Cybertec Geschwinde & Schönig OEG—a company providing commercial support, training courses, tuning, and remote administration for PostgreSQL.

Hans-Jürgen Schönig

On August 9, 1978 Hans-Jürgen Schönig was born in Knittelfeld, a small town 125 miles southwest of Vienna. After primary school he attended a private school in Seckau. After the high-school final exam he started studying Economics of Information at the Technical University and the University of Vienna. Just for fun Hans started working on various projects and was finally employed at Synthesis (an Austrian research company focusing on forecasting the Austrian labor market), in September 1998. There he was responsible for the scientific analysis of data provided by the Austrian social security insurance system (all together dozens of millions records). During the time at Synthesis he worked with Unix systems and automated text production, using EFEU, LaTex and Perl. Additionally, he taught Unix classes in an adult education program once a week.

In 2001 Hans and Ewald left Synthesis to found Cybertec Geschwinde & Schönig OEG (www.cybertec.at) and focused entirely on PostgreSQL and Unix databases.

Dedication

*This book is dedicated to our girlfriends, Christina and Etschi, who had to
stay in bed alone during all those nights we spent writing this book.*

Girls, this one's for you.

Acknowledgments

We want to say thank you to all the people who contributed to this book and who
made it possible for our dream to come true.

We thank Erich Fruehstueck (the maintainer of the EFEU package and our long-time
colleague and mutual friend at Synthesis), who was our Unix teacher for almost two
years. Without him, there would be no Cybertec company.

Special thanks goes to the entire team of Sams Publishing for all the wonderful
support and professionalism in the past few months. During the whole process, we
worked with a very professional team, people who gave us all the information we
needed and a lot of encouragement to complete our work successfully.

We thank Patricia Barnes (our acquisition editor), who gave us the chance to write this
book and who accompanied us through the entire process in an extremely reliable way.
Although we have never seen each other, we feel that we can rely on her 100%.

A special thanks also goes to Etschi Bruckner for doing all the basic proofreading for
us here in Austria.

Last but not least, we want to thank all the open source developers out there who
provided all the wonderful software we used to make this book come true. We want to
thank not only the PostgreSQL development team, which provided a lot of newsgroup
support during the last few months, but also all those programmers who implemented
the other tools and software packages we needed (KDE, GCC and all other GNU
tools, Gimp, vi, SGI's XFS, Perl, and Xfree—to name just a few).

Thanks to all of you.

Tell Us What You Think!

As the reader of this book, *you* are our most important critic and commentator. We value your opinion and want to know what we're doing right, what we could do better, what areas you'd like to see us publish in, and any other words of wisdom you're willing to pass our way.

You can email or write me directly to let me know what you did or didn't like about this book—as well as what we can do to make our books stronger.

Please note that I cannot help you with technical problems related to the topic of this book, and that due to the high volume of mail I receive, I might not be able to reply to every message.

When you write, please be sure to include this book's title and author as well as your name and phone or fax number. I will carefully review your comments and share them with the author and editors who worked on the book.

E-mail: webdev@samspublishing.com
Mail: Mark Taber
          Sams Publishing
          201 West 103rd Street
          Indianapolis, IN 46290 USA

Introduction

When we were little boys, we both wondered how people could write hundreds of pages about a certain topic. How could one person manage to keep all those things in mind, and how long does it take to write one of these voluminous books?

We never imagined that only a few years later we would be among those people ourselves, writing a real book that other people can buy and read all around the globe. Somehow, a dream has come true, and now that the book is ready, we are really proud of it and hope that it will be one of the books other people use to build their database applications—just as we have read books written by others that were essential for our work.

It's a strange feeling to be one of these authors and to contribute documentation to the PostgreSQL community we have dealt with in the past few years.

It was back in 1996 when we first heard about Linux. Both of us remember it very clearly. It was during a C training course at the University of Vienna when, all of a sudden, the entire group was in the middle of a discussion about whether it is better to use Emacs or Vi. At that time, we hadn't heard of either of these two programs so the entire situation was somehow a little bit strange for us. We had only dealt with DOS and Windows. During this session, someone was also talking about Linux—an operating system we had never heard of. Back then, the idea that someone had developed an operating system that was completely free seemed very strange, but also very interesting, to us. Knowing that something interesting was going on out there encouraged us to pay the data processing center of the Technical University of Vienna a visit and download Slackware (a famous Linux distribution). The entire system could be stored on a 100MB zip-media. It was interesting to work with the system, although we had no previous experience with Unix. We did it just for fun and it was great to have a really powerful command line instead of a boring graphical interface.

Things changed rapidly, and we soon began to work extensively with Unix. During our time at Synthesis (a research company dealing with the Austrian labor market), we got more and more in touch with Unix. We did not know about PostgreSQL yet, but we had the pleasure of working with the EFEU package (`http://efeu.cybertec.at`), created by Erich Fruehstueck, to perform all basic database operations for the company. Because we had to deal with dozens of millions of records on comparatively weak machines and very complex algorithms for transforming the data, it was impossible to work with "ordinary," commercial databases. Erich had to implement every operation manually, so we learned a lot about Unix (AIX and Linux) and the philosophy of Richard Stallman's Free Software Foundation (FSF). A year-and-a-half after we had started working at Synthesis, whether to switch to a commonly used database system was discussed. We started dealing with relational databases very extensively and learned about Oracle and other databases.

One day, we set up a new server environment in cooperation with a Linux company situated here in Vienna. We had a lot of in-depth talks with the engineers of that company and during one of the discussion one of them said, "Why don't you use PostgreSQL?" I remember thinking, "What is PostgreSQL?"

We started dealing with the subject matter and it got more and more interesting. In a way, PostgreSQL was fascinating and that's what it still is.

A few months later, we left Synthesis and founded the Cybertec Geschwinde & Schoenig OEG here in Vienna (`www.cybertec.at`). From the beginning, PostgreSQL played a major role in most of our projects. The database had finally become some sort of friend, and we used it frequently. The more we found out about the database, the more interesting the topic turned out to be.

In December 2000, when my co-author Ewald Geschwinde (we call him Epi) and I were on a skiing trip in the south of Austria, on a chair lift Epi suddenly said that it would be interesting to provide commercial support for PostgreSQL. At that time, we had already dealt with PostgreSQL extensively and felt qualified enough to launch such a project. I guess that was the best and most far reaching decision in the history of our company—it actually was some sort of enlightenment.

On February 22nd, 2001, I was reading the logfile of our Web server to see what had happened in the past few hours—not knowing that this was the most important entry in the logfile I have ever seen:

```
macmin.mcp.com - - [21/Feb/2001:16:32:55 +0100] "GET / HTTP/1.1" 200 2290
```

A little later, I received an e-mail starting with

"Dear Webmaster—could you forward this e-mail to your director of marketing?"

All of us here at Cybertec were extremely amused, because we are only a small company and something like a director of marketing doesn't exist. Since then, addressing each other as the director of marketing became some sort of a running gag for us. At first, we did not know how to react, because this offer was one of the things we had always dreamed of. The e-mail said that Sams Publishing was looking for an author or a co-author for a book about PostgreSQL. We started preparing a table of contents (the first version of the table of contents was actually ready after about 45 minutes, because all of us were extremely enthusiastic) and we sent it over to Sams.

When we started to write the sample chapter, all of us were extremely curious if our work was good enough to satisfy the high quality demands of Sams Publishing. We were also wondering whether we would be able to write such a voluminous book about PostgreSQL. After more time had passed and more work had been done, our confidence grew, and we started to believe that we would finally achieve our target—the vision to be the authors of a book about PostgreSQL, our favorite database system. The reader will decide if the vision of being the designers and authors of a really good will finally come true. We have done our best to make this book fit your demands.

We have tried to make this book suitable for people who have never dealt with relational databases, as well as for professional developers. In the first 10 chapters, we will cover the basics of SQL database administration, including backup and recovery, PostgreSQL's extensibility, and software related to PostgreSQL. Chapters 11 through 20 present some real-world scenarios and solutions for common problems. We also want to present ideas and hints as to how you can use PostgreSQL efficiently and which software is best to use in combination with the database.

This book is not designed to be a complete reference of PostgreSQL, but we have tried to extensively cover all aspects of the database from the user's point of view. All the sample code presented in this book has been tested, and we have tried to avoid code fragments.

PART I

PostgreSQL

CHAPTER 1

About PostgreSQL

PostgreSQL is an object-relational database management system (DBMS). Its initial implementation started in 1986, and PostgreSQL is now the world's most advanced Open Source database system available. PostgreSQL's predecessor was Ingres, a database developed at the University of California at Berkeley (1977–1985). From 1986 to 1994, Michael Stonebraker led a team that focused on the development of an object-relational database server called Postgres (*post* is the Latin word for *after*; PostgreSQL came after Ingres). The code was then taken by Illustra and developed into a commercial product.

Illustra Information Technologies merged with Informix, which is now a global player in the database business (in 2001, Informix was bought by IBM).

The developement of Postgres officially ended with version 4.2 in 1994, because the maintenance of such large amounts of code took too much time—time that should have been devoted to database research.

Two graduates of Berkeley, Jolly Chen and Andrew Yu, added SQL support to PostgreSQL in 1994 and 1995. This project was called Postgres95. Chen and Yu left Berkeley, but Chen continued maintaining and developing Postgres95. Even an active mailing list existed.

Postgres95 was completely implemented in ANSI C and had some major enhancements beyond Postgres 4.2, such as a GNU readline interface, a TCL frontend, and support for GROUP BY clauses.

A team was formed to continue the development. Jolly Chen stated: "This code needs a few people with lots of time, not many people with a little time." At that time the source code included about 250,000 lines of C code; it seems that Chen was right.

The core development team consisted of four people: Marc Fournier in Canada, Thomas Lockhart in Pasadena (California), Vadim Mikheev in Krasnoyarsk (Russia), and Bruce Momjian in Philadelphia (Pennsylvania).

In late 1996, it became obvious that Postgres95 was not the right name for a database of the future, and PostgreSQL was chosen. PostgreSQL reflects the relationship between the old Postgres system and the SQL capabilities of PostgreSQL. The version number was set to 6.0, which represented the real number in the sequence of PostgreSQL development.

The main target for the PostgreSQL developers was to enhance PostgreSQL and to add new features:

- The locking system (only table locking was implemented at that time) was replaced with multiversion concurrency control.

- Datatypes for geometric operation were added.

- The speed of the backend was increased significantly.

- ANSI SQL92 features were added.

- Subselects, triggers, defaults, and constraints were implemented.

More than a dozen developers are currently working on PostgreSQL, and the number of PostgreSQL users is constantly growing around the globe.

License

PostgreSQL is distributed under the terms of the Berkeley license and can, for that reason, be used, copied, and modified without a fee.

Open Source means that the source code of PostgreSQL is open and distributed with the package.

The BSD license is very similar to the GPL license; for further information about the GPL license, check out the following Web site:

`http://www.gnu.org`

Here is the text of the license:

License

PostgreSQL is subject to the following COPYRIGHT:

PostgreSQL Data Base Management System

Portions copyright (c) 1996–2000, PostgreSQL, Inc
Portions Copyright (c) 1994–6 Regents of the University of California

Permission to use, copy, modify, and distribute this software and its documentation for any purpose, without fee, and without a written agreement is hereby granted, provided that the above copyright notice and this paragraph and the following two paragraphs appear in all copies.

IN NO EVENT SHALL THE UNIVERSITY OF CALIFORNIA BE LIABLE TO ANY PARTY FOR DIRECT, INDIRECT, SPECIAL, INCIDENTAL, OR CONSEQUENTIAL DAMAGES, INCLUDING LOST PROFITS, ARISING OUT OF THE USE OF THIS SOFTWARE AND ITS DOCUMENTATION, EVEN IF THE UNIVERSITY OF CALIFORNIA HAS BEEN ADVISED OF THE POSSIBILITY OF SUCH DAMAGE.

THE UNIVERSITY OF CALIFORNIA SPECIFICALLY DISCLAIMS ANY WARRANTIES, INCLUDING, BUT NOT LIMITED TO, THE IMPLIED WARRANTIES OF MERCHANTABILITY AND FITNESS FOR A PARTICULAR PURPOSE. THE SOFTWARE PROVIDED HEREUNDER IS ON AN "AS IS" BASIS, AND THE UNIVERSITY OF CALIFORNIA HAS NO OBLIGATIONS TO PROVIDE MAINTENANCE, SUPPORT, UPDATES, ENHANCEMENTS, OR MODIFICATIONS.

The Basic Concepts of PostgreSQL

As mentioned earlier, PostgreSQL is an object-relational database server. The main goal of PostgreSQL development is to be 100% ANSI SQL–compatible, and PostgreSQL is close to achieving that goal. SQL92 compliance offers many advantages over proprietary functions and features: Applications can easily be ported to or from PostgreSQL to other systems, and new users can easily use their knowledge of SQL when switching to PostgreSQL.

Relational databases are often not suitable for modeling complex scenarios. Object-relational databases, such as Oracle or PostgreSQL, offer powerful features to enable more complex software design than would be possible with relational databases.

Here are the key features of PostgreSQL's object-oriented data model:

- Classes

- Inheritance

- Function overloading (supported by PL/pgSQL)

You will take a closer look at object orientation in Chapter 3, "An Introduction to SQL."

PostgreSQL is an extremely modular piece of software; you can easily insert functions or design programming interfaces. A huge number of datatypes is supported, and you can easily design and implement your own datatypes. PostgreSQL's modularity enables users and advanced programmers to achieve a goal quickly. Programming interfaces for PostgreSQL are available for all important programming languages, such as C, Perl, Python, Tcl, Java, and PHP.

PostgreSQL not only provides external programming interfaces. With a powerful language called PL/pgSQL (which is similar to Oracle's PL/SQL), you can make packages that can be integrated directly within the database. PL/Perl, PL/Tcl, and ECPG are additional easy-to-use interfaces for PostgreSQL.

One advantage of PostgreSQL is that it can easily be handled. PostgreSQL fits perfectly well into UNIX systems, but can also be used on other platforms, such as Microsoft Windows. An increasing number of graphical user interfaces is already available, making PostgresSQL administration even more comfortable. Web interfaces especially seem to be the standard for doing administration work.

Software Architecture

Before you get deeper into PostgreSQL, let's look at a brief overview of PostgreSQL's software architecture. Knowing the basic concepts and facts makes using the database much easier and gives you a deeper insight into what is happening.

PostgreSQL uses a rather simple client/server model, with one process per user request. Unlike Apache, PostgreSQL is not a *preforking server*, which means that a process is started when a SQL query has to be executed. No spare servers have to stay in memory—every process is a working process.

The system consists of three major components:

- Postmaster
- Backend
- Frontend

The Postmaster

The *postmaster* is the supervisor daemon and has to be up and running if someone wants to access the database. One postmaster daemon can handle various databases. If a request has to be processed, the postmaster starts a backend process. The postmaster also manages the shared memory pool of the database server.

Usually one postmaster is running per machine, but you can run multiple postmasters. In that case, every postmaster has to use its own port and data directory to work correctly.

The Backend

The *backend* is used to execute a SQL query. If many queries have to be executed simultaneously, many backend processes are started by the postmaster.

The maximum number of backends allowed can be defined by the database administrator.

> **NOTE**
> Currently the postmaster and the backends have to run on the same machine.

The Frontend

With the help of the *frontend*, users can connect to their PostgreSQL database server. Frontends and backends need not run on the same machine. You can use psql, for example, to connect to a database running on a remote machine.

When a user wants to connect to a PostgreSQL database, the connection is established by the frontend. The postmaster starts a backend process, and from then on, the frontend communicates with the backend without the help of the postmaster.

Limitations of PostgreSQL

PostgreSQL has some minor restrictions. The size of a database is actually unlimited and depends only on the amount of available HDD space and RAM the system has.

The size of a table is restricted to 64 terabytes (TB) on all operating systems; single rows can have unlimited size (since 7.1). Single fields can be up to 1 gigabyte (GB) (since 7.1). This is especially important when working with binary large objects (BLOBs).

The number of rows in a table is unlimited; a table can have up to 1,600 columns.

You can see that PostgreSQL is capable of handling large amounts of data. When building really big databases, consider that PostgreSQL's limitations are not the only ones a developer has to face. Many file systems can't be as big as a PostgreSQL table. Check out the documentation of the file system you are using when building a large database. If a table becomes very big, PostgreSQL splits the table in multiple files.

We have worked with databases larger than 30GB and PostgreSQL was stable even when performing complex queries. If 64TB per table is not enough for your application, feel free to split the table.

CHAPTER 2

Preparing

Before you get to the installation process of PostgreSQL, let's take a look at the basic software and hardware requirements of PostgreSQL databases. PostgreSQL is a very slim database system and therefore does not require a lot of system resources.

Hardware Requirements

In contrast to many other databases, such as Oracle, PostgreSQL is designed to run even on very slow machines that provide only a few megabytes of memory. This does not mean that PostgreSQL does not perform well on strong machines. Depending on the machine you want to run PostgreSQL on, the database system can be tuned very effectively to reach maximum performance.

The minimum amount of memory available cannot be evaluated because it is hardware- and compiler-dependent. Different compilers generate different code on every system, and therefore the core binaries that the database has to keep in memory are not always the same size. In general, the more memory you have, the faster your system will work and the more queries can be run simultaneously.

There is also no minimum clock frequency your processor has to provide. The faster your processor is, the more performance can be achieved (depending on the quality of your compiler, of course). PostgreSQL is available for a variety of different microprocessors and for a lot of operating systems, such as Linux, Solaris, and Microsoft Windows.

PostgreSQL has been written in C, so the source code is portable. Table 2.1 lists all the systems PostgreSQL has been tested with. "Tested" means that PostgreSQL can be compiled successfully and that all regression tests can be executed without any problems. Table 2.1 is taken from the PostgreSQL Web site.

Table 2.1   *Systems with Which PostgreSQL Has Been Tested*

OS	Processor	Version	Remarks
AIX 4.3.3	RS6000	7.1	See also doc/FAQ_AIX
BeOS 5.0.4	x86	7.1	Requires new BONE networking stack
BSD/OS 4.01	x86	7.1	
Compaq Tru64 UNIX	Alpha	7.1	4.0–5.0, cc and gcc
FreeBSD 4.3	x86	7.1	
HP/UX	PA-RISC	7.1	32- and 64-bit on 11.00; see also doc/FAQ_HPUX
IRIX 6.5.11	MIPS	7.1	32-bit compilation model
Linux 2.2.x	Alpha	7.1	
Linux 2.2.x	armv4l	7.1	
Linux 2.0.x	MIPS	7.1	Cobalt Qube
Linux 2.2.18	PPC74xx	7.1	Apple G3
Linux	S/390	7.1	
Linux 2.2.15	Sparc	7.1	
Linux	x86	7.1	2.0.x, 2.2.x, 2.4.2
MacOS X	PPC	7.1	Darwin (only) Beta-2 or higher
NetBSD 1.5	Alpha	7.1	
NetBSD 1.5E	arm32	7.1	
NetBSD	m68k	7.0	Mac 8xx
NetBSD	PPC	7.1	Mac G4
NetBSD	Sparc	7.1	32- and 64-bit builds
NetBSD 1.5	VAX	7.1	

Table 2.1 *(continued)*

OS	Processor	Version	Remarks
NetBSD 1.5	x86	7.1	
OpenBSD 2.8	Sparc	7.1	
OpenBSD 2.8	x86	7.1	
SCO UnixWare 7.1.1	x86	7.1	UDK FS compiler; see also
doc/FAQ_SCO			
Solaris 2.7-8	Sparc	7.1	See also doc/FAQ_Solaris
Solaris 2.8	x86	7.1	See also doc/FAQ_Solaris
SunOS 4.1.4	Sparc	7.1	
Windows NT/2000 with Cygwin	x86	7.1	With Cygwin toolset, see doc/FAQ_MSWIN

Some platforms are not officially supported by the PostgreSQL developers team. However, it has been reported that some platforms not listed in the table are capable of running PostgreSQL. In some cases, there is no official guarantee that the latest version of PostgreSQL can be run; but the fact that previous versions of PostgreSQL worked indicates that you have a good chance to run PostgreSQL on one of them. These platforms are listed in Table 2.2 (also taken from the PostgreSQL developers Web site). The column labeled *Version* tells you which version of PostgreSQL has already been run on the platforms listed in this table.

Table 2.2 *Platforms on Which to Run PostgreSQL*

OS	Processor	Version	Remarks
DGUX 5.4R4.11	m88k	6.3	6.4 probably OK
MkLinux DR1	PPC750	7.0	7.1 needs OS update?
NextStep	x86	6.x	Bit rot suspected
QNX 4.25	x86	7.0	Spinlock code needs work; see also doc/FAQ_QNX4
SCO OpenServer 5	x86	6.5	7.1 should work, but no reports; see also doc/FAQ_SCO
System V R4	m88k	6.2.1	Needs new TAS spinlock code
System V R4	MIPS	6.4	No 64-bit integer
Ultrix	MIPS	7.1	TAS spinlock code not detected
Ultrix	VAX	6.x	No recent reports—obsolete?
Windows 9x, ME, NT, 2000 (native)	x86	7.1	Client-side libraries (libpq and psql) or ODBC/JDBC, no server-side

Software Requirements

In general, any modern UNIX-compatible system should be able to run a PostgreSQL database. PostgreSQL is also available for Microsoft Windows, although most people run PostgreSQL on UNIX platforms. UNIX platforms offer some significant advantages over Windows because the system is highly command-line–oriented. In recent days, Cygwin (a compilation of UNIX tools on Windows) has become very popular; consider installing Cygwin when running PostgreSQL on Windows.

PostgreSQL cannot be run without GNU Make. Keep in mind that PostgreSQL works only with *GNU* Make—other versions of Make will not work.

To find out whether the right version of Make is installed, use this command:

```
[hs@notebook hs]$ make --version
GNU Make version 3.79.1, by Richard Stallman and Roland McGrath.
Built for i386-redhat-linux-gnu
Copyright (C) 1988, 89, 90, 91, 92, 93, 94, 95, 96, 97, 98, 99, 2000
        Free Software Foundation, Inc.
This is free software; see the source for copying conditions.
There is NO warranty; not even for MERCHANTABILITY or FITNESS FOR A
PARTICULAR PURPOSE.

Report bugs to <bug-make@gnu.org>.
```

> **Note**
> GNU Make is included with all Linux distribution and is also very widespread on other UNIX machines (Sun, AIX, and so forth). PostgreSQL is not the only software that requires the GNU version of Make.

If your version of Make displays a significantly different output, try typing gmake instead of make.

You also need an ISO/ANSI C compiler. PostgreSQL can be compiled with a variety of compilers, but developers recommend the GNU C compiler. gzip and tar are required to extract the PostgreSQL source archives. For adding some comfort to PostgreSQL, the GNU Readline library should be installed on the system. GNU Readline is responsible for some wonderful features, such as using the cursor keys to go back to the previous commands. If you want to build PostgreSQL from a CVS tree, Flex and Bison are required for building the parser. Building PostgreSQL from the tar archive does not require Flex and Bison because the components generated by Flex and Bison are pregenerated. To compile PostgreSQL on Windows machines, Cygwin and cygipc are required. For further information, please check out the

FAQ_MSWIN file, which can be found in the doc directory of your PostgreSQL source tree.

Installing PostgreSQL

In this section, you take a closer look at the installation process of PostgreSQL on various platforms.

Installing on UNIX Systems

In contrast to Windows systems, UNIX systems can have many different faces; therefore the installation process on various UNIX systems can differ significantly.

Many Linux systems, such as RedHat and Debian Linux, provide package management software for simplifying the installation of PostgreSQL binaries or source code. This section provides an overview of how PostgreSQL is installed on UNIX systems.

Installing on RPM-Based Systems

Package management has always been a very desirable feature on Linux systems. With the help of the RedHat Package Manager (RPM), Linux offers a simple and efficient way to manage software packages on Linux systems. The RPM has been developed by RedHat and is available under the terms of the GPL. Packaging software means that files belonging together are compiled into an archive. But archiving files is not the key feature of a package manager; software products can be installed and uninstalled easily with the help of a simple shell command or GUIs available on the Internet.

It is also possible to assign rules to a package. Imagine a software product A that needs a library called B to be compiled correctly. If somebody wants to install the RPM package of A on a system, it seems logical that it can be installed only when package B is also available. RPM takes care of details such as that and makes sure that no packages can be installed or uninstalled that are still needed by other software components. RPM keeps information about all packages installed in a small database, so it is an easy task to find out whether a package is installed on your system. If you want to find out whether PostgreSQL is installed on your machine, try the following command:

```
[root@notebook hs]$ rpm -qva | grep postgres
postgresql-libs-7.1.2-4PGDG
postgresql-python-7.1.2-4PGDG
postgresql-7.1.2-4PGDG
```

```
postgresql-test-7.1.2-4PGDG
postgresql-perl-7.1.2-4PGDG
postgresql-docs-7.1.2-4PGDG
postgresql-tcl-7.1.2-4PGDG
postgresql-odbc-7.1.2-4PGDG
postgresql-devel-7.1.2-4PGDG
postgresql-server-7.1.2-4PGDG
postgresql-contrib-7.1.2-4PGDG
postgresql-tk-7.1.2-4PGDG
postgresql-jdbc-7.1.2-4PGDG
```

The `rpm -qva` command lists all packages found on the system. You find out all packages related to PostgreSQL by using a simple `grep` command. On most Linux distributions, such as RedHat or Suse, PostgreSQL is already included and you do not have to install it manually.

> **Tip**
>
> It is possible that you won't find all packages, because some—such as the PHP's PostgreSQL package—do not contain the string `postgres`. Try searching for something like `pgsql` as well.

If no packages are found on the system, PostgreSQL is not installed. If you don't have the packages on one of your Linux CDs or if you want to upgrade your PostgreSQL installation, you have to download the sources from a mirror near you. To find the best mirror for downloading the files, check out `www.postgresql.org`. After finding the best mirror site for your location, click Software. Choose an FTP server near you and go to the binary directory of the FTP server. There you will find several subdirectories, where you can find the appropriate binaries for your system. Usually, binaries for x86 CPUs and the most widespread Linux distributions are available. If you do not have an x86 compatible processor (Intel Pentium or AMD, for example), you might have to compile the sources manually. To download the software, use a simple FTP client, a Web browser such as Netscape, Konqueror, Opera, or Internet Explorer. `wget` is another tool for downloading software and is included in most recent Linux distributions. `wget` is a powerful command-line tool for downloading and enables the user to start downloads as background processes (in combination with `&`).

Now that you have downloaded all RPM packages on your machine, you can start installing the software. To install the database you use a simple command (assume that your current directory contains only PostgreSQL binaries):

```
[root@notebook hs]$ rpm -Uvh *rpm
postgresql-tk          ##################################################
postgresql-test        ##################################################
```

```
postgresql-tcl            ################################################
postgresql-server         ################################################
postgresql-python         ################################################
postgresql-perl           ################################################
postgresql-odbc           ################################################
postgresql-libs           ################################################
postgresql-jdbc           ################################################
postgresql-docs           ################################################
postgresql-devel          ################################################
postgresql-contrib        ################################################
postgresql                ################################################
```

If no packages are missing, the installation is ready—everything is done by RPM automatically. Updating packages that are already installed on the system works the same way as installing packages.

Uninstalling the software is as simple as installing the packages. Use this command:

```
 [root@notebook hs]$ rpm -e postgresql postgresql-jdbc postgresql-tk postgresql-
contrib postgresql-server postgresql-tcl postgresql-devel postgresql-odbc
postgresql-perl postgresql-test postgresql-docs postgresql-python postgresql-
libs
```

If no errors are displayed, the packages have been uninstalled correctly. Sometimes uninstalling does not work because PostgreSQL is needed by other packages. In that case, you either have to uninstall those packages related to PostgreSQL or leave everything on the server.

Installing on Debian-Based Systems

Debian is a Linux distribution that is not based on the RPM. Debian's package management tool is called dselect and can be compared with RPM. Both tools support a simple interface for installing packages from the command line.

To install a PostgreSQL package for Debian on your Debian system, use the dpkg:

```
[root@debian deb]$ dpkg -i *deb
```

This command installs all Debian packages in the current directory and is equal to the following:

```
[root@debian deb]$ dpkg -install *deb
```

If you cannot find recent Debian packages of PostgreSQL, you can easily convert RPM files to DEB files by using a program called Alien. To find out more about Alien, check out http://kitenet.net/programs/alien/.

Installing the Source Code

Some people prefer to install the source code themselves instead of relying on precompiled software packages. This has significant advantages because you know what is inside the binaries and what you have done. Compiling PostgreSQL manually is also necessary when you want to install the most recent version of PostgreSQL, because there might be no binary packages available for your system and CPU yet. Before you get to the installation process, you have to download the sources from a PostgreSQL mirror near you. The easiest way to download the source code is to use wget:

```
[hs@notebook hs]$ wget ftp://ftp.postgresql.org/pub/postgresql-x.x.x.tar.gz
```

To unpack the source, you use gzip and tar:

```
[hs@notebook hs]$ tar xvfz postgresql-7.1.2.tar.gz
```

If the z flag (which automatically unzips the archive) is not supported by your version of tar, the package can also be extracted like this:

```
[hs@notebook hs]$ gunzip -c postgresql-7.1.2.tar.gz | tar xv
```

This command creates a subdirectory containing the PostgreSQL package, so you need to install the database. The first thing to do when installing PostgreSQL is to run configure. The configure script has a lot of options that you can use to configure PostgreSQL exactly to your needs. Here is an overview of PostgreSQL's configure script:

```
[hs@notebook postgresql-7.1.2]$ ./configure --help
Usage: configure [options] [host]
Options: [defaults in brackets after descriptions]
Configuration:
  --cache-file=FILE       cache test results in FILE
  --help                  print this message
  --no-create             do not create output files
  --quiet, --silent       do not print `checking...' messages
  --version               print the version of autoconf that created configure
Directory and file names:
  --prefix=PREFIX         install architecture-independent files in PREFIX
                          [/usr/local/pgsql]
  --exec-prefix=EPREFIX   install architecture-dependent files in EPREFIX
                          [same as prefix]
  --bindir=DIR            user executables in DIR [EPREFIX/bin]
  --sbindir=DIR           system admin executables in DIR [EPREFIX/sbin]
```

```
  --libexecdir=DIR          program executables in DIR [EPREFIX/libexec]
  --datadir=DIR             read-only architecture-independent data in DIR
                            [PREFIX/share]
  --sysconfdir=DIR          read-only single-machine data in DIR [PREFIX/etc]
  --sharedstatedir=DIR      modifiable architecture-independent data in DIR
                            [PREFIX/com]
  --localstatedir=DIR       modifiable single-machine data in DIR [PREFIX/var]
  --libdir=DIR              object code libraries in DIR [EPREFIX/lib]
  --includedir=DIR          C header files in DIR [PREFIX/include]
  --oldincludedir=DIR       C header files for non-gcc in DIR [/usr/include]
  --docdir=DIR              doc documentation in DIR [PREFIX/doc]
  --mandir=DIR              man documentation in DIR [PREFIX/man]
  --srcdir=DIR              find the sources in DIR [configure dir or ..]
  --program-prefix=PREFIX prepend PREFIX to installed program names
  --program-suffix=SUFFIX append SUFFIX to installed program names
  --program-transform-name=PROGRAM
                            run sed PROGRAM on installed program names
Host type:
  --build=BUILD             configure for building on BUILD [BUILD=HOST]
  --host=HOST               configure for HOST [guessed]
  --target=TARGET           configure for TARGET [TARGET=HOST]
Features and packages:
  --disable-FEATURE         do not include FEATURE (same as --enable-FEATURE=no)
  --enable-FEATURE[=ARG]    include FEATURE [ARG=yes]
  --with-PACKAGE[=ARG]      use PACKAGE [ARG=yes]
  --without-PACKAGE         do not use PACKAGE (same as --with-PACKAGE=no)
  --x-includes=DIR          X include files are in DIR
  --x-libraries=DIR         X library files are in DIR
--enable and --with options recognized:
  --with-includes=DIRS      look for additional header files in DIRS
  --with-libraries=DIRS     look for additional libraries in DIRS
  --with-libs=DIRS          alternative spelling of --with-libraries
  --enable-locale           enable locale support
  --enable-recode           enable character set recode support
  --enable-multibyte        enable multibyte character support
  --enable-unicode-conversion  enable unicode conversion support
  --with-pgport=PORTNUM     change default port number [5432]
  --with-maxbackends=N      set default maximum number of connections [32]
  --disable-shared          do not build shared libraries
  --disable-rpath           do not embed shared library search path in executables
  --enable-debug            build with debugging symbols (-g)
  --enable-depend           turn on automatic dependency tracking
```

```
--enable-cassert          enable assertion checks (for debugging)
--with-tcl                build Tcl and Tk interfaces
--without-tk              do not build Tk interfaces if Tcl is enabled
--with-tclconfig=DIR      tclConfig.sh and tkConfig.sh are in DIR
--with-tkconfig=DIR       tkConfig.sh is in DIR
--with-perl               build Perl interface and PL/Perl
--with-python             build Python interface module
--with-java               build JDBC interface and Java tools
--with-krb4[=DIR]         build with Kerberos 4 support [/usr/athena]
--with-krb5[=DIR]         build with Kerberos 5 support [/usr/athena]
--with-krb-srvnam=NAME    name of the service principal in Kerberos [postgres]
--with-openssl[=DIR]      build with OpenSSL support [/usr/local/ssl]
--enable-odbc             build the ODBC driver package
--with-odbcinst=DIR       default directory for odbcinst.ini [sysconfdir]
--with-CXX                build C++ modules (libpq++)
--with-gnu-ld             assume the C compiler uses GNU ld [default=no]
--enable-syslog           enable logging to syslog
```

As you can see, the number of options you can define is nearly endless. Before you start compiling the software, let's take a closer look at some of these options:

- cache-file=FILE makes configure.cache the results of a test run in a file defined by FILE. Normally results are cached in config.cache. If the file generated by the test run contains test results you don't want, the file can be edited or removed. Using --cache-file=/dev/null disables caching because the output is sent to the electronic trash can.

- version displays the version of autoconf that is currently used on the screen. If --version is passed to configure, no testing will be performed. Only the version is displayed on the screen.

- prefix=PREFIX defines where to install architecture-independent files. If no other options, such as --bindir or --libexecdir, are defined, the entire system is installed in PREFIX.

- exec-prefix=EPREFIX installs architecture-dependent files in EPREFIX. If this option is not defined, PREFIX is used.

- sbindir=DIR defines the directory in which to define system administrator executables. If DIR is not defined, EPREFIX/sbin is used.

- libexecdir=DIR determines that program executables will be installed in DIR. If this option is not defined, EPREFIX/libexec is used.

- `datadir=DIR` defines the directory in which to install the system-independent data (database templates—not the actual databases yet). If this option is not defined, `DIR` is set to `PREFIX/share`. If this option is not defined, `PREFIX/etc` is used.

- `libdir=DIR` tells the system where to install the libraries. The default value is set to `EPREFIX/lib`. Knowing the exact position of your modules might be important if you are planning to install additional software, such as Perl's PostgreSQL module (DBI + DBD module).

- `includedir=DIR` defines the location in which to install the C header files. When installing PostgreSQL binaries on Linux systems, the location of header files is usually set to `/usr/include` or `/usr/include/pgsql`. The default value is `PREFIX/include`.

- `oldincludedir=DIR` sets the location for C header files for non-gcc compilers. The default value is `/usr/include`.

- `program-suffix=SUFFIX` indicates that `SUFFIX` will be appended to the end of the name of every program.

- `program-transform-name=PROGRAM` will be run to change the names of the programs that will be installed. Use this option very carefully.

- `x-includes=DIR` defines the position of the X include files. On most Linux distributions, the files can be found in `/usr/include/X11`.

- `x-libraries=DIR` defines the location of the X11 libraries. On most Linux distributions, such as Linux RedHat, the files can be found in `/usr/lib/X11`.

- `with-includes=DIR` indicates that if additional header files are required for compiling PostgreSQL, header files can be added by defining a colon-separated list. If you have things such as GNU Readline installed in an unusual directory, this option is essential for you.

- `with-libraries=DIR` is often used in combination with `--with-includes` to add additional libraries to PostgreSQL.

- `enable-local` enables local settings for PostgreSQL. The problem with local settings is that they decrease the overall performance of your server.

- `enable-recode` was formally known as "Cyrillic recode support." This flag makes PostgreSQL support all types of single-byte character-set recoding.

- `enable-multibyte` enables multibyte characters. For languages such as Japanese, 1 byte is not enough to store a character. To deal with multibyte character sets, the `--enable-multibyte` flag has to be set at compile time. Multibyte characters can also be used with regular expressions and other functions provided by PostgreSQL. Several multibyte character sets are available: SQL_ASCII (ASCII), EUC_JP (Japanese EUC), EUC_CN (Chinese EUC), EUC_KR (Korean EUC), EUC_TW (Taiwan EUC), UNICODE (Unicode), MULE_INTERNAL (mule internal), LATIN1 (ISO 8859-1), LATIN2 (ISO 8859-2), LATIN3 (ISO 8859-3), LATIN4 (ISO 8859-4), LATIN5 (ISO 8859-5), KOI8 (KOI8-R), WIN (Windows CP1251), and ALT (Windows CP866). To use one character set as the default one, you have to define it at compile time. Here is an example:

```
./configure --enable-multibyte=SQL-ASCII.
```

If `--enable-multibyte` is used with no parameter, `SQL_ASCII` is assumed.

- `with-perl` adds Perl support to your PostgreSQL server. PostgreSQL's support for Perl consists of the Pg module, which you can use in your Perl scripts, and PL/Perl (an embedded version of Perl used for writing functions, which can be used in SQL). On some systems (RedHat 7.1 with PostgreSQL 7.1.2, for example), PL/Perl cannot be built in combination with Perl 5.6.

- `with-python` tells the system to build the Python module for PostgreSQL. You will have a closer look at this module later in this book.

To continue the installation process, you create a group and a user called `postgres`. The user does not have to be called `postgres`, but people normally use that name for running the database server. To add the group and the user, you use these two commands:

```
[root@notebook postgresql-7.1.2]$ groupadd postgres
[root@notebook postgresql-7.1.2]$ adduser postgres -g postgres
```

You want the PostgreSQL binaries to be installed in /usr/local/postgresql; the database should be located in /data/postgresql. Both directories can be created by using a simple `mkdir` command. The two directories should be owned by the `postgres` user, so you have to change the permissions of the directories with the help of the `chown` (change owner) command. Now that precompilation is finished, you can write a small shell script. Using a script has many advantages: On the one hand it documents how you have compiled the server, and on the other hand you can easily use the same script for updating PostgreSQL. Documentation is important and can save you a lot of headaches. Here is a simple script called compile.sh:

```
#!/bin/sh

# configuring the PostgreSQL server
env CFLAGS='-O3' ./configure --cache-file=/tmp/postgres_test.txt \
     --prefix=/usr/local/postgresql --enable-multibyte\
     --datadir=/data/postgresql --with-maxbackends=128 \
     --with-tcl --with-perl --with-python --enable-odbc \
     --with-CXX

# building the binaries
make

# installing the binaries
make install
```

Let's have a closer look. First, you call `configure` with the parameters you want PostgreSQL to be compiled with (Perl, Python, multibyte support, and so forth). You also pass an additional compiler flag to the script by using `env`. The `-O3` option does everything `-O2` does, and also turns on `-finline functions`. Passing compiler options to configure is not necessary; don't use it if you don't know exactly what you are doing.

To show you an easier way to compile the server, here is another script:

```
#/bin/sh

./configure --prefix=/usr/local/postgresql --datadir=/data/postgresql --with-tcl \
        --with-perl --with-python --enable-odbc --with-CXX
make
make install
```

Let's get back to the more complex installation script—we will use it for the rest of this section. To execute the script you add execute rights to compile.sh by typing the following:

```
[root@notebook postgresql-7.1.2]$ chmod +x compile.sh
```

Now that the shell script is ready and the correct rights are set, you can start the installation process by executing your script:

```
[root@notebook postgresql-7.1.2]$ ./compile.sh
```

Configuring and compiling the server takes some time, but when the script is ready, you can go on with the installation process. In the next step, you initialize the database templates that you will need to work with PostgreSQL. Therefore, you have to use the initdb command, which can be found in the bin directory of the database server. Here is an overview of the command's syntax:

```
[postgres@notebook bin]$ ./initdb --help
initdb initializes a PostgreSQL database cluster.

Usage:
  initdb [options] datadir

Options:
 [-D, --pgdata] DATADIR      Location for this database cluster
  -W, --pwprompt             Prompt for a password for the new superuser
  -E, --encoding ENCODING    Set the default multibyte encoding for new databases
  -i, --sysid SYSID          Database sysid for the superuser
Less commonly used options:
  -L DIRECTORY               Where to find the input files
  -d, --debug                Generate lots of debugging output
  -n, --noclean              Do not clean up after errors

Report bugs to <pgsql-bugs@postgresql.org>.
```

Now you can initialize the database:

```
[postgres@notebook bin]$ ./initdb -L /data/postgresql -D /data/postgresql/data
```

-L defines the directory containing the input (template) files for your database (defined by --datadir in compile.sh).

> **Note**
> The extension of the template files is .bki. Some more recent PostgreSQL distri-
> butions store the template files in a subfolder of datadir; the extension of the
> templates will help you find the right directory.

-D defines the location where your databases are going to reside, the place where all the data you will insert will be stored by PostgreSQL. Initializing a new database should, in most cases, work without any problems. The database has successfully been installed now and you can start the PostgreSQL daemon.

Installing on Windows

Windows differs from UNIX-based operating systems, but PostgreSQL is a flexible piece of software. Like most open source programmers, the PostgreSQL developers have implemented a software that is capable of running on various platforms—one of those platforms is Microsoft Windows.

The easiest way to install PostgreSQL on Windows is to use Cygwin, a UNIX-like environment that provides all tools commonly known under UNIX (for example, Bash, gcc, and so forth).

With the help of the Cygnus tools, it is easy to install PostgreSQL under Windows. To install Cygwin on your system, check out http://sources.redhat.com/cygwin/ and press the Install Cygwin now button to download a file called setup.exe. This file contains the installation process for the software. Start setup.exe and you will be guided through the installation process.

A binary version of PostgreSQL is included in the Cygwin distribution, so you do not have to worry about installing PostgreSQL separately.

After installing Cygwin, you have to initialize a PostgreSQL database. Therefore, you have to install the cygipc package available at:

```
http://www.neuro.gatech.edu/users/cwilson/cygutils/V1.1/index.html)
```

This can be done by extracting the `tar` archive containing the software in the root directory of the Cygnus environment. Installing this package is necessary to run the server because PostgreSQL needs System V IPC system calls. `ipc` is a common kernel entry point for the System V IPC calls for messages, semaphores, and shared memory. If the package is not installed, PostgreSQL can't initialize the database.

Now that the software is installed, you have to add the bin directory in the Cygnus environment to the environment variable `PATH` of your Windows system; otherwise, cygipc won't be able to find the DLLs it needs for starting.

First you install the daemon as a service:

```
ipc-daemon --install-as-service
```

Then you start the daemon:

```
net start ipc-daemon        # NT/2000 or
ipc-daemon &                # 9X/Me
```

After that you can go on with PostgreSQL by initializing the database with the `initdb` command:

```
initdb -L /usr/share/postgresql -D /data/postgresql
```

`-L` defines the location of the templates PostgreSQL must use it to generate the system databases. `-D` defines the directory in which to store the files of the database you want to generate using `initdb`. Keep in mind that the directory specified by `-D` must be empty or nonexistent.

Starting the Server and Creating Databases

Usually, RPM packages of PostgreSQL contain scripts for starting and shutting down PostgreSQL properly.

Using a Startup Script

First you check whether the postmaster is running. On UNIX systems, this can easily be done with the following command:

```
[root@duron /root]# /etc/rc.d/init.d/postgresql status

postmaster (pid 4114 4089 4086 4085 4083 4082 4081 4080 4079 4075) is running...
```

This command works for RedHat 7.1 systems with PostgreSQL RPM packages installed. In the example, you can see that the postmaster is up and running. You can also check whether PostgreSQL is running by using a command like this one:

```
[hs@duron hs]$ ps ax | grep postmaster

 4075 ?        SN      0:00 /usr/local/postgres/bin/postmaster -i -D /data/postgres

14111 pts/0    S       0:00 grep postmaster
```

Simply pipe the process table (try ps ax on Linux) to the grep command by using your favorite UNIX shell.

> **Note**
> grep commands can differ slightly on various UNIX versions, such as IBM's AIX or Sun Solaris. Many UNIX systems require a hyphen (-) before the option (for example, ps -ax). Check out the man pages for further information about grep on your system.

To start the server, you can use this command:

```
[root@duron /root]# /etc/rc.d/init.d/postgresql start
```

Shutting down the server can be done by using stop instead of start.

Using pg_ctl Directly

If you don't have init scripts installed on your machine or if you want to have a more flexible way for starting your server, you can use pg_ctl directly.

Here is an overview of the command's syntax:

```
[root@athlon /root]# pg_ctl --help
pg_ctl is a utility to start, stop, restart, and report the status
of a PostgreSQL server.

Usage:
  pg_ctl start   [-w] [-D DATADIR] [-s] [-l FILENAME] [-o "OPTIONS"]
  pg_ctl stop    [-W] [-D DATADIR] [-s] [-m SHUTDOWN-MODE]
  pg_ctl restart [-w] [-D DATADIR] [-s] [-m SHUTDOWN-MODE] [-o "OPTIONS"]
  pg_ctl status  [-D DATADIR]

Common options:
  -D DATADIR           Location of the database storage area
  -s                   Only print errors, no informational messages
  -w                   Wait until operation completes
  -W                   Do not wait until operation completes
(The default is to wait for shutdown, but not for start or restart.)

If the -D option is omitted, the environment variable PGDATA is used.

Options for start or restart:
  -l FILENAME          Write (or append) server log to FILENAME.  The
                       use of this option is highly recommended.
  -o OPTIONS           Command line options to pass to the postmaster
                       (PostgreSQL server executable)
  -p PATH-TO-POSTMASTER  Normally not necessary

Options for stop or restart:
  -m SHUTDOWN-MODE     May be 'smart', 'fast', or 'immediate'

Shutdown modes are:
  smart                Quit after all clients have disconnected
  fast                 Quit directly, with proper shutdown
  immediate            Quit without complete shutdown; will lead
                       to recovery run on restart

Report bugs to <pgsql-bugs@postgresql.org>.
```

Let's try to start PostgreSQL. Use -D to define the directory where your PostgreSQL databases can be found:

```
[root@athlon /root]# pg_ctl -D /data/postgresql/ start
postmaster successfully started

"root" execution of the PostgreSQL server is not permitted.

The server must be started under an unprivileged userid to prevent
a possible system security compromise. See the INSTALL file for
more information on how to properly start the server.
```

You can see that an error has occurred, because the PostgreSQL daemon must not be launched as root.

For security reasons, you should create a user called postgres that is used solely by the PostgreSQL daemon. Switch to user postgres and try to start the server again—this time you use some additional parameters:

```
bash-2.04$ pg_ctl -D /data/postgresql/ -o "-i" -l /tmp/postgresql.log start
postmaster successfully started
```

As you can see, the server has successfully been started. This time you have also passed some additional options to pg_ctl. -o tells the server to pass -i to the backend process. -i makes PostgreSQL backend processes listen to remote hosts so that the database cannot be used only locally. Don't forget this flag or there will be no way to make PostgreSQL listen to remote requests, even if you add entries to pg_hba.conf. (You take a close look at this file in Chapter 6, "Database Administration.") -l defines a file PostgreSQL will send the logging information to. Using -l is recommended because you might need it for debugging purposes.

Creating Databases

You create databases with the createdb command. Here is an overview of its syntax:

```
[hs@athlon hs]$ createdb --help
createdb creates a PostgreSQL database.

Usage:
  createdb [options] dbname [description]

Options:
  -D, --location=PATH          Alternative place to store the database
  -T, --template=TEMPLATE      Template database to copy
  -E, --encoding=ENCODING      Multibyte encoding for the database
  -h, --host=HOSTNAME          Database server host
  -p, --port=PORT              Database server port
```

```
-U, --username=USERNAME       Username to connect as
-W, --password                Prompt for password
-e, --echo                    Show the query being sent to the backend
-q, --quiet                   Don't write any messages
```

```
By default, a database with the same name as the current user is created.
```

```
Report bugs to <pgsql-bugs@postgresql.org>.
```

If the postmaster is up and running, you can log in as user postgres and type createdb
name, with name being the name for your database in your UNIX shell:

```
bash-2.04$ createdb name
CREATE DATABASE
```

If your result looks like the preceding line, you have successfully created a new
PostgreSQL database. If you received a result like this, it didn't work:

```
[root@duron /root]# createdb name

psql: FATAL 1:  SetUserId: user 'root' is not in 'pg_shadow'

createdb: database creation failed
```

In this example, user root doesn't have the privilege to create databases because there
is no user called root in the system tables. You will learn how to set permissions for
your PostgreSQL box later in this book.

The name of your PostgreSQL database can be up to 32 characters long. The first
character in the name has to be an alphabetic one. You can choose any name for your
database, but it's wise to use one that describes what the database is being used for.

Sometimes it is necessary not to use the standard character set. By default,
PostgreSQL uses SQL_ASCII; in some cases this won't be the right character set, and
you have to tell PostgreSQL to use a different one.

This example shows how to create a database that uses UNICODE as the default
character set:

```
[hs@athlon hs]$ createdb --encoding=UNICODE myunicode
CREATE DATABASE
```

To see whether the database has been created successfully, you use this command (psql
-l lists all databases that are currently available on the system):

```
[hs@athlon hs]$ psql -l
        List of databases
  Database   | Owner | Encoding
-------------+-------+-----------
 db          | erich | SQL_ASCII
 myunicode   | hs    | UNICODE
 template0   | hs    | SQL_ASCII
 template1   | hs    | SQL_ASCII
(4 rows)
```

As you can see, the database myunicode uses UNICODE instead of SQL_ASCII.

Login

If you have successfully created a new database, you can connect yourself to it. Become user postgres and type psql name, with name being the name of the database you want to connect to, into your UNIX shell:

```
bash-2.04$ psql name

Welcome to psql, the PostgreSQL interactive terminal.

Type:  \copyright for distribution terms
       \h for help with SQL commands
       \? for help on internal slash commands
       \g or terminate with semicolon to execute query
       \q to quit
name=#
```

If your screen now looks something like this example, you have successfully connected to your PostgreSQL database. If you get an error, you have possibly tried to connect to the database as the wrong user or you haven't created your database correctly.

Let's try a simple query to see whether PostgreSQL works:

```
name=# SELECT 1+1;
 ?column?
----------
        2
(1 row)
```

1+1 makes two—it seems the database works correctly so far.

The User Interface

PostgreSQL offers an extremely powerful and comfortable user interface called psql. psql is the frontend of the database. It can be used to connect to local or to remote databases and offers many additional functions. Unlike Oracle's SQL plus, psql offers a very comfortable readline interface, which means that the user can scroll back to previous commands simply by using the cursor keys. Let's take a closer look at the psql command-line flags first (you can get the list by using `psql --help` in your favorite shell):

```
This is psql, the PostgreSQL interactive terminal.

Usage:
  psql [options] [dbname [username]]

Options:
  -a                 Echo all input from script
  -A                 Unaligned table output mode (-P format=unaligned)
  -c <query>         Run only single query (or slash command) and exit
  -d <dbname>        Specify database name to connect to (default: postgres)
  -e                 Echo queries sent to backend
  -E                 Display queries that internal commands generate
  -f <filename>      Execute queries from file, then exit
  -F <string>        Set field separator (default: "|") (-P fieldsep=)
  -h <host>          Specify database server host (default: domain socket)
  -H                 HTML table output mode (-P format=html)
  -l                 List available databases, then exit
  -n                 Disable readline
  -o <filename>      Send query output to filename (or |pipe)
  -p <port>          Specify database server port (default: hardwired)
  -P var[=arg]       Set printing option 'var' to 'arg' (see \pset command)
  -q                 Run quietly (no messages, only query output)
  -R <string>        Set record separator (default: newline) (-P recordsep=)
  -s                 Single step mode (confirm each query)
  -S                 Single line mode (newline terminates query)
  -t                 Print rows only (-P tuples_only)
  -T text            Set HTML table tag options (width, border) (-P tableattr=)
  -U <username>      Specify database username (default: postgres)
  -v name=val        Set psql variable 'name' to 'value'
  -V                 Show version information and exit
  -W                 Prompt for password (should happen automatically)
  -x                 Turn on expanded table output (-P expanded)
  -X                 Do not read startup file (~/.psqlrc)
```

```
For more information, type "\?" (for internal commands) or
"\help"
(for SQL commands) from within psql, or consult the psql section in
the PostgreSQL manual, which accompanies the distribution and is also
available at <http://www.postgresql.org>.
Report bugs to <pgsql-bugs@postgresql.org>.
```

You can see that psql is indeed very powerful and flexible. Here is an example of how you can use these flags:

```
psql yourdb -h 192.168.1.2 -p 5432
```

This command establishes a connection to the database yourdb stored on 192.168.1.2 using port 5432. If the postmaster on 192.168.1.2 is correctly configured, you have successfully connected to the database.

psql opens the door to a huge pool of information and online help. Information about syntax or datatypes can easily be found by using the \? command. Here is a complete list of all available commands:

```
\a                          toggle between unaligned and aligned mode
\c[onnect] [dbname|- [user]]  connect to new database (currently 'xy')
\C <title>                  table title
\copy ...                   perform SQL COPY with data stream to the client
                            machine
\copyright                  show PostgreSQL usage and distribution terms
\d <table>                  describe table (or view, index, sequence)
\d{t|i|s|v}                 list tables/indices/sequences/views
\d{p|S|l}                   list permissions/system tables/lobjects
\da                         list aggregates
\dd [object]                list comment for table, type, function, or
                            operator
\df                         list functions
\do                         list operators
\dT                         list datatypes
\e [file]                   edit the current query buffer or [file] with
                            external editor
\echo <text>                write text to stdout
\encoding <encoding>        set client encoding
\f <sep>                    change field separator
\g [file]                   send query to backend (and results in [file] or
                            |pipe)
\h [cmd]                    help on syntax of sql commands, * for all
                            commands
```

```
\H                          toggle HTML mode (currently off)
\i <file>                   read and execute queries from <file>
\l                          list all databases
\lo_export, \lo_import,     large object operations
\lo_list, \lo_unlink
\o [file]                   send all query results to [file], or |pipe
\p                          show the content of the current query buffer
\pset <opt>                 set table output  <opt> =
                            {format|border|expanded|fieldsep|null|recordsep
                            |tuples_only|title|tableattr|pager}
\q                          quit psql
\qecho <text>               write text to query output stream (see \o)
\r                          reset (clear) the query buffer
\s [file]                   print history or save it in [file]
\set <var> <value>          set internal variable
\t                          show only rows (currently off)
\T <tags>                   HTML table tags
\unset <var>                unset (delete) internal variable
\w <file>                   write current query buffer to a <file>
\x                          toggle expanded output (currently off)
\z                          list table access permissions
\! [cmd]                    shell escape or command
```

You can easily imagine that all the information that can be accessed with the simple psql help commands makes daily life easier. Imagine that you would have to check your documentation every time you want to know the correct syntax of an SQL command. psql does the job for you. Learn the most important commands in this list, because they will save you a lot of time.

CHAPTER 3

An Introduction to SQL

Structured Query Language (SQL) is a database query language that was adopted as an industry standard in 1986. A major revision of the SQL standard, SQL2, was released in 1992. Its successor, SQL3, also contains object-oriented components. Currently, ANSI SQL92 is the most important standard.

This language enables you to pose complex questions to a database. It also provides a means of modifying databases. SQL is widely used. Many databases support SQL, which means that if you learn how to use SQL, you can apply this knowledge to MS SQL Server, DB2, Oracle, PostgreSQL, and countless other databases. SQL works with *relational databases*, which store data in objects. An object can be a table, for example. A *database* is a collection of tables and functions. A *table* consists of a list of records; each *record* (*row*) in a table has the same structure and each has a fixed number of *fields* (*columns*) of a given type. SQL can be used to communicate with a database and its components.

Every database has a slightly different version of SQL implemented, so it can sometimes be very hard to port applications from one database to another. For that reason, ANSI SQL92 has been developed. ANSI SQL92 is a standard that should be understood by every database supporting SQL.

Unfortunately, many commercial database developers don't implement fully ANSI SQL92–compatible SQL engines in their databases.

PostgreSQL developers are working hard to make PostgreSQL 100% ANSI SQL–compatible. Therefore, PostgreSQL applications are portable and easy to understand.

For further information about the ANSI SQL92 standard or any other ANSI standard, check out `http://www.ansi.org`.

Relational Databases and Their Components

The relational database model was conceived by E. F. Codd in 1969. The model is based on branches of mathematics called *set theory* and *predicate logic*. The main idea is that a database consists of various unordered tables called *relations* that can be modified by the user. Relational databases were a major improvement to traditional database systems, which were not as flexible and sometimes hardware-dependent.

Relational databases consist of various components. This chapter provides basic insight to those who have not dealt with relational databases, and is not a tutorial about the theory behind relational databases.

Tables and Keys

Tables are the key components of relational databases. A relational database consists of one or more tables used to store information. A table consists of rows. Every row is divided into fields (columns) that have a certain datatype.

Assume you have a table used to store names and salaries (see Figure 3.1). A row containing this information consists of two fields: one for the name and one for the salary. If information from various tables has to be collected by a query, a *join* is performed by the database. Joins are covered extensively later in this chapter (see the section "Joining Tables").

Primary Keys

Every table should have a *primary key*. In this case, the name would be a useful primary key if the names are unique. Primary keys have to be fields that contain unique values—a primary key is the identifier of a record (row).

Keys have a significant impact on performance, but are also needed to guarantee data integrity.

id serial	name text	gender chart(1)	salary int
1	Paul	m	2900
2	George	m	1860
3	Clara	f	3200
4	Pat	f	2850
.	.	.	.
.	.	.	.
.	.	.	.

We have a table with four columns.
Every column must have a datatype.

Figure 3.1

A simple table with four columns.

Foreign Keys

Foreign keys are keys "taken" from a different table. Imagine a database with two tables. In one table, we store information about companies, such as the name and the location of each company. In the second table, we store information about the employees of the companies stored in the first table. We use a foreign key to make sure that the second table cannot contain information about employees who do not work for one of the companies listed in the first table. The behavior of PostgreSQL when dealing with foreign keys can be defined for every table. It can be defined, for instance, that all employees in the second table are removed when a company is removed from the first table. Rules defining PostgreSQL's behavior are called *integrity constraints*.

Foreign keys are extremely useful when working with complex data models and are usually used to protect data integrity. See Figure 3.2 for an example of two tables connected with a foreign key.

Datatypes

Every column in a table must have a datatype. The user's job is to find the best datatype for storing a certain piece of information in the database. Let's assume that we want to store the name of a person. Names are character strings of undefined length. A suitable datatype for names would be varchar(50). In this example, 50 is the maximum length of the field. A varchars is stored efficiently in the database, because only the actual length of the field—and not the maximum length of the varchar— is used to store the text.

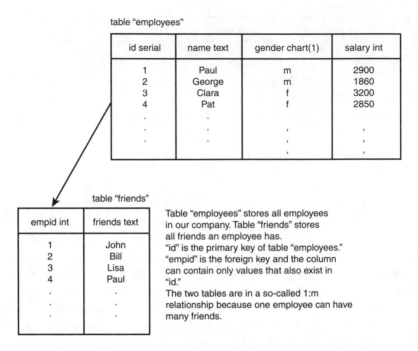

table "employees"

id serial	name text	gender chart(1)	salary int
1	Paul	m	2900
2	George	m	1860
3	Clara	f	3200
4	Pat	f	2850
.	.	,	,
.	.	,	,
.	.	,	,

table "friends"

empid int	friends text
1	John
2	Bill
3	Lisa
4	Paul
.	.
.	.
.	.

Table "employees" stores all employees in our company. Table "friends" stores all friends an employee has.
"id" is the primary key of table "employees."
"empid" is the foreign key and the column can contain only values that also exist in "id."
The two tables are in a so-called 1:m relationship because one employee can have many friends.

Figure 3.2
Connecting tables using a foreign key.

PostgreSQL offers a variety of datatypes. Here is an overview of all datatypes available in PostgreSQL 7.0.3:

```
xy=# \dT
```

```
List of types

     Type    |                        Description
-------------+---------------------------------------------------------------
  SET        | set of tuples
  abstime    | absolute, limited-range date and time (Unix system time)
  aclitem    | access control list
  bit        | fixed-length bit string
  bool       | boolean, 'true'/'false'
  box        | geometric box '(lower left,upper right)'
  bpchar     | char(length), blank-padded string, fixed storage length
  bytea      | variable-length string, binary values escaped
  char       | single character
  cid        | command identifier type, sequence in transaction id
  cidr       | network IP address/netmask, network address
```

```
circle     | geometric circle '(center,radius)'
date       | ANSI SQL date
filename   | filename used in system tables
float4     | single-precision floating point number, 4-byte storage
float8     | double-precision floating point number, 8-byte storage
inet       | IP address/netmask, host address, netmask optional
int2       | -32 thousand to 32 thousand, 2-byte storage
int2vector | array of 16 int2 integers, used in system tables
int4       | -2 billion to 2 billion integer, 4-byte storage
int8       | ~18 digit integer, 8-byte storage
interval   | @ <number> <units>, time interval
line       | geometric line '(pt1,pt2)'
lseg       | geometric line segment '(pt1,pt2)'
lztext     | variable-lengthstring, stored compressed
macaddr    | XX:XX:XX:XX:XX,MAC address
money      | $d,ddd.cc,money
name       | 31-character type for storing system identifiers
numeric    | numeric(precision, decimal), arbitrary precision number
oid        | object identifier(oid), maximum 4 billion
oidvector  | array of 16 oids, used in system tables
path       | geometric path '(pt1,...)'
point      | geometric point '(x, y)'
polygon    | geometric polygon '(pt1,...)'
regproc    | registered procedure
reltime    | relative, limited-range time interval (Unix delta time)
smgr       | storage manager
text       | variable-length string, no limit specified
tid        | (Block, offset), physical location of tuple
time       | hh:mm:ss, ANSI SQL time
timestamp  | date and time
timetz     | hh:mm:ss, ANSI SQL time
tinterval  | (abstime,abstime), time interval unknown     |
varbit     | fixed-length bit string
varchar    | varchar(length), non-blank-padded string, variable storage length
xid        | transaction id
(47 rows)
```

You can see that PostgreSQL offers powerful datatypes for nearly any purpose you can imagine. Thanks to PostgreSQL's modularity, new datatypes can easily be added to this list. The CREATE TYPE command can be used to add a datatype.

The most important datatypes are covered extensively later in this chapter. You will learn how to use these datatypes efficiently in real-life scenarios.

Indices

Indices are used to speed up searching. Let's assume you have a telephone directory containing 1,000,000 records consisting of two fields. The first field contains the name of a person, and the second field contains the phone number. If someone wants to know the phone number of a certain person, the database runs a *sequential scan*, which means that every record is scanned for the requested name. On average, a query such as that needs 500,000 (1,000,000 divided by 2) steps to find the result. If tables are large, the performance of the database system decreases significantly.

In this case, an index can be defined on a column. An index is, in most cases, a tree, and the leaves of the tree point to a data object.

Before you look at PostgreSQL's implementations of indices, let's explore the basic idea of indexing using B-trees.

B-trees are an efficient data structure for retrieving values in tables. Trees provide the data sorted so that values can be accessed much faster. In a *B-tree*, the tree consists of nodes, with up to two children. A child can be a node for up to two more children. *Nodes* are values in the data that are the parents of other values. A child that has no children is called a *leaf*. The data structure looks like a tree, but it's upside down.

B-trees are used to search efficiently for a value in a data structure. If the number of values stored in a tree doubles, the time to search for a value doesn't double—it takes *one* additional step. If the number of values stored in a tree is 1,024 times higher, it takes only 10 additional steps to find a value, because 1,024 is the result of 2^{10}.

Imagine 1,048,576 (unique) datasets. It would take 20 (logarithmus dualis: 20 = ld 1,048,576) steps to find the right value. In this example, you can see how an index can speed up your query; if no index is used to find the right value out of 1,048,576, the database needs 524,288 steps (1,048,576 divided by 2) to find the result.

> **Note**
> This works only as long as the B-tree is 100% balanced (see Figure 3.3).

In databases, B+ trees are usually used instead of B-trees, because B+ trees guarantee higher performance in real-world scenarios. The Reiser Filesystem (a Linux Filesystem) is also based on balanced B+ trees.

PostgreSQL supports three types of indices:

- B-tree

- R-tree

- Hash access

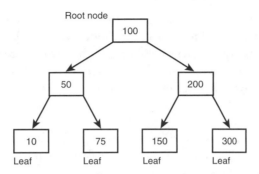

Figure 3.3
A balanced B-tree.

B-Trees

As mentioned in the last section, one way of indexing a column in PostgreSQL is to use a B-tree. PostgreSQL doesn't use "ordinary" B-trees for indexing because some additional features are required that can't be implemented with ordinary B-trees. One of the problems has to do with index locking. Assume that one user adds data to an index while a second user does an index scan. User two needs a fixed and persistent "image" of the index while performing the query. This problem can be solved with the help of a Lehman-Yao high-concurrency btree. This kind of tree is a super-high–concurrency solution at the expense of a little extra complexity in the data structure. The following changes have to be made in the data structure:

- Use a B+ tree (sometimes called a *B* tree*).

- Add high keys to each page.

- Add right links to each page.

- Scan index from top to bottom and left to right.

- Insert from bottom to top.

This ensures that *no* locking for reading is required and lock coupling for writes is rare.

R-Trees

R-trees use Guttman's quadratic split algorithm and are a dynamic index structure for spatial searching. Traditional indexing algorithms are not suitable for computer-aided design or geo-applications. Because PostgreSQL offers many datatypes that can be used for spatial calculations, R-trees can be a powerful method of speeding up your applications.

To understand spatial queries, imagine a situation where you want to find all countries that have land within 100 miles of a specific location. R-trees can be used to solve the problem for the database efficiently. R-trees are highly balanced trees and can be compared with B-trees. PostgreSQL offers a variety of operators for working with geo-data. In most cases, the user does not need to care about the details.

Hash Access Methods

The linear hashing algorithm used by PostgreSQL was developed by W. Litwin for disk-based systems with one processor. Linear hashing allows dynamic reorganization of a hashed database when records are inserted or updated. The possibility of accessing one record with one-bucket access should be maintained. Linear hashing enables the hashing function to be changed while the database is changed; only a small part of the database is affected when the hash function is changed.

Concurrent linear hashing adds a locking protocol and allows simultaneous access.

Sequences

Sequences are a comfortable method for building lists that are numbered consecutively. A sequence can be used in the entire database (if all users have access to the sequence). Every time a user accesses the sequence, the value of the sequence is incremented. It is guaranteed that a certain number is used only once. Sequences can therefore be used to create unique numbers. The user does not have to care about transactions when dealing with sequences, because the database makes sure that every value is used only once internally.

Triggers

Powerful and comfortable applications can be built with the help of *triggers*, which are used to start certain functions after certain events. Triggers are defined for tables and have to be associated with an event such as INSERT or UPDATE.

In real-world scenarios, triggers are used to perform operations automatically, but triggers are also used for many purposes by the database internally.

You will explore triggers extensively in Chapter 5, "Understanding Transactions," which is about PL/pgSQL.

Objects

Object relational databases consist of objects. Object orientation is an extension to the relational database model and is, in the case of PostgreSQL, a very powerful feature. Objects offer important core features, as explained in the following sections.

Classes

A *class* is a named collection of object instances. Each instance has a unique object identifier (OID).

> **Note**
> Each OID is unique in the entire system.

Classes can be created using the CREATE command. Various versions of a class are called *instances*. In case of object relational databases, an instance can be a row in a table.

Inheritance

Inheritance means that a class can inherit functions or attributes from a class that is "higher" in the hierarchy. If a new class is derived from one of those upper classes, it inherits all information from the upper class. It is now possible to implement additional features for the new class.

> **Note**
> Features defined for a derived class are not visible in the parent class.

Here is an example of how to make the inheritance process clearer:

Imagine a table containing information about cars. We define a class that stores all information about a car that is common for cars, such as the color or the year the car was built. Now we define a class for a specific type of car that is used to store additional information, such as technical data about the air conditioning. The class defined for the specific type of car inherits all information from the parent type storing information about ordinary cars.

You learn how to query derived tables later in the book.

Function Overloading

Function overloading is a key feature of object-oriented systems. In *function overloading*, many versions of a function can exist. The difference between those functions is the number of parameters that can be passed to it. Assume a function called sum() used to sum numbers. Summing can be useful for 2, 3, or more values. With function overloading, you can implement functions for each of the cases.

PL/pgSQL supports function overloading, and you will soon recognize it as a powerful and easy-to-use feature. Function overloading can also lead to dangerous bugs that are sometimes very hard to track down, because the programmer has to find the correct version of the function that was used before looking for the real error in the source code.

Views

If you want to look at your data from a broader perspective, views might be a good choice. A *view* is a virtual table that contains information from other tables. A view is nothing else than the result of a SELECT statement presented as a virtual table by the database system. Views can be used to simplify SQL statements.

Procedures

Procedures are functions that are stored directly within the database. Many database systems offer embedded languages. Oracle databases, for instance, offer a language called PL/SQL. PostgreSQL offers a language called PL/pgSQL, which is similar to PL/SQL and also very powerful. PostgreSQL offers even more programming interfaces, but PL/Tcl and PL/Perl are the most important ones to mention here. Writing procedures will be a major part of the chapter about PL/pgSQL.

Aggregate Functions and Aggregate Expressions

The capability of performing aggregations is an important feature of SQL. It enables the user to perform tasks on more than just one record.

Aggregate Functions

Aggregate functions are used to perform data calculations, such as maximum, minimum, or average. Aggregate functions can easily be added to PostgreSQL by using the CREATE AGGREGATE command. Many functions are already included in the base distribution, but it can be extremely useful to add your own features.

Aggregate Expressions

Aggregate expressions are used to perform operations with multiple lines returned by a SELECT statement. The DISTINCT command is a good example of an aggregate expression. If multiple rows contain the same data, DISTINCT returns multiple entries only once. Assume a query where you want to retrieve all names from a table and you want each name to be returned only once. The DISTINCT command is the solution.

Building a Database

In this section, you will learn to build simple PostgreSQL databases. PostgreSQL supports a lot of functions and features to make the definition of a data structure easy. In addition, data can easily be inserted into tables using simple SQL commands.

Building Simple Data Structures

The core component of every data structure is a table. Tables are used to store the data, and most database operations are based on tables. Defining and removing tables correctly are essential steps when working with databases.

Creating Tables

In this section, you learn how to create tables with the help of SQL commands. If you want to create a table, you can use the CREATE TABLE command.

If you want to create a table called emp for storing names and salaries, you use the following command:

```
name=# CREATE TABLE emp(id serial, empname varchar(50), sal numeric(9,2));
```

The display is the following:

```
NOTICE:  CREATE TABLE will create implicit sequence 'emp_id_seq' for SERIAL
column 'emp.id'
NOTICE:  CREATE TABLE/UNIQUE will create implicit index 'emp_id_key' for table
'emp'
CREATE
```

You can check to see whether the table has been created by using the \d command—in this case, \d emp:

```
name=# \d emp
Table "emp"

 Attribute |     Type     |              Modifier
-----------+--------------+------------------------------------- --------
 id        | integer      | not null default nextval('emp_id_seq'::text)
 empname   | varchar(50)  |
 sal       | numeric(9,2) |
Index: emp_id_key
```

The table has successfully been created and contains three columns. The first column is used as a sequence; every record will have a unique id. If the datatype serial is used for a column, a sequence will implicitly be created by the database. The second column will be used to store the name of the person. Because a name has no fixed length, you use the datatype varchar() with a maximum length of 50 characters. The third column will be used to store the salary. Salaries are usually decimal values. In this case, the salary can have up to 7 digits before the comma; 2 digits can be used after the comma. PostgreSQL automatically creates an index on the first column if no special primary key is defined.

Here is a second, slightly different CREATE TABLE command:

```
CREATE TABLE emp2 (id serial,
        empname varchar(50) UNIQUE,
        sal numeric(9,2) NOT NULL,
        currency varchar(4) DEFAULT 'USD');
```

The following is displayed:

```
NOTICE:  CREATE TABLE will create implicit sequence 'emp2_id_seq' for SERIAL
column 'emp2.id'
NOTICE:  CREATE TABLE/UNIQUE will create implicit index 'emp2_id_key' for table
'emp2'
NOTICE:  CREATE TABLE/UNIQUE will create implicit index 'emp2_empname_key' for
table 'emp2'
CREATE
```

We have created a table called emp2, but the column named empname can be used to store only unique names. This can be useful because it is extremely confusing to have two people with exactly the same name but with different salaries in the database. If someone tries to insert a name twice, the database will report an error. NOT NULL means that a correct salary has to be available. If no salary for a particular row is inserted into the table, an error will be displayed. The fourth column is used to store the currency of the salary—the default value is set to USD. The default value will be used if no value is inserted into the field.

If you don't know the syntax of the command by heart, you can simply use the \h CREATE TABLE command. The following lines will be displayed:

```
name=# \h CREATE TABLE
Command: CREATE TABLE
Description: Creates a new table

Syntax: CREATE [ TEMPORARY | TEMP ] TABLE table ( column type [ NULL | NOT NULL
] [ UNIQUE ] [ DEFAULT value ] [column_constraint_clause | PRIMARY KEY } [ ... ]
] [, ... ] [, PRIMARY KEY ( column [, ...] ) ] [, CHECK ( condition ) ] [,
table_constraint_clause ] ) [ INHERITS ( inherited_table [, ...] ) ]
```

Using Temporary Tables

Temporary tables are an extremely powerful feature of PostgreSQL. They can be used to store session-specific information in a comfortable way. Temporary tables can be created with the CREATE TEMPORARY TABLE command, which works like the CREATE TABLE command.

The difference between ordinary and temporary tables is that temporary tables are visible only while the session is active. If users quit the session, all temporary tables they have created will be deleted by the database.

If two users log in simultaneously, both users can create temporary tables with the same name because the temporary tables of one user can't be seen by the other user. This feature makes temporary tables easy and safe to use.

The DROP TABLE Command

The DROP TABLE command can be used to delete tables. Here is an example:

```
DROP TABLE emp2;
```

The table will be dropped immediately and no ROLLBACK can be performed. You will learn about ROLLBACK and transactions in Chapter 4, "PL/PGSQL."

Be careful when using DROP TABLE. DROP TABLE can also be used to drop multiple tables at once. If you want to drop more than one table, add a comma; the name of the table you want to drop to the statement and two tables will be deleted (as long as you have the permission and the tables are available).

DROP TABLE does *not* automatically drop sequences that are implicitly created when you use serials in a table. This is extremely important when you want to create a table with the same name and structure you have just dropped, because the sequence won't be overwritten. For solving the problem, use the DROP SEQUENCE command manually.

The ALTER TABLE Command

The ALTER TABLE command can be used to perform multiple operations. ALTER TABLE can be used to add columns to a table. The following example adds a column called currency to table emp (the one we created in the CREATE TABLE section):

```
ALTER TABLE emp ADD COLUMN currency varchar(4);
```

The new column is a varchar and can be up to 4 characters long. If we want to set the default value of that column to USD, we have to write a second SQL statement:

```
ALTER TABLE emp ALTER COLUMN currency SET DEFAULT 'USD';
```

The default value is set to USD, but ALTER TABLE can also be used to rename tables. Here is an example where the table emp is renamed to oldemp:

```
ALTER TABLE emp RENAME TO oldemp;
```

Columns can also be renamed:

```
ALTER TABLE emp RENAME COLUMN sal TO salary;
```

In the example, the column sal is renamed to salary. The ALTER TABLE command is indeed powerful and useful. Here is the complete definition of the command's syntax (try \h ALTER TABLE):

```
Command:     ALTER TABLE
Description: Modifies table properties
Syntax:
ALTER TABLE table [ * ]
    ADD [ COLUMN ] column type
ALTER TABLE table [ * ]
    ALTER [ COLUMN ] column { SET DEFAULT value | DROP DEFAULT }
ALTER TABLE table [ * ]
    RENAME [ COLUMN ] column TO newcolumn
ALTER TABLE table
    RENAME TO newtable
ALTER TABLE table
    ADD table constraint definition
```

You can see that setting or dropping default values and adding constraints can also be done easily.

> **Note**
> Renaming tables can sometimes be very tricky and can lead to confusion. We have renamed the table emp to oldemp, but what about the sequence used in the first column? It is still called emp_id_seq. If the number of tables and sequences increase, this can become a complicated and confusing issue.

Creating and Dropping Indices

Indices are used to speed up queries. PostgreSQL normally uses B-trees for indexing a column. It is also possible to create a single index for multiple columns, but let's look at the syntax of CREATE INDEX first:

```
persons=# \h CREATE INDEX
Command:     CREATE INDEX
Description: Constructs a secondary index
Syntax:
CREATE [ UNIQUE ] INDEX index_name ON table
    [ USING acc_name ] ( column [ ops_name ] [, ...] )
CREATE [ UNIQUE ] INDEX index_name ON table
    [ USING acc_name ] ( func_name( column [, ... ]) [ ops_name ] )
```

Let's create an index:

```
CREATE UNIQUE INDEX idx_oldemp_empname ON oldemp (empname);
```

In this example, we create an index called `idx_old_empname` on `table oldemp`. The index is used to store unique values, which means that a name can appear only once in the table. The index is defined for the column `empname`. PostgreSQL uses B-trees for indices by default. If you want to use R-trees or hashes, the SQL command has to be modified slightly:

```
CREATE INDEX idx_oldemp_empname ON oldemp USING HASH (empname);
```

> **Note**
> Hashes and R-trees cannot be created on tables in combination with the UNIQUE constraint. It is also not possible to use T-trees for certain datatypes. If you try to, the following error messages is displayed:
>
> ```
> name=# CREATE UNIQUE INDEX idx_oldemp_empname ON oldemp USING HASH (empname);
> ERROR:  DefineIndex: unique indices are only available with the btree access method
> ```
>
> ```
> name=# CREATE UNIQUE INDEX idx_oldemp_empname ON oldemp USING RTREE (empname);
> ERROR:  DefineIndex: unique indices are only available with the btree access method
> ```
>
> ```
> name=# CREATE INDEX idx_oldemp_empname ON oldemp USING RTREE (empname);
> ERROR:  DefineIndex: opclass "varchar_ops" not supported by access method "rtree"
> ```

Indices can also be defined for multiple columns; here is an example where one index is used for two columns:

```
CREATE INDEX idx_oldemp_salcur ON oldemp (salary,currency);
```

If you want to drop the index, use the following command:

```
DROP INDEX idx_oldemp_salcur;
```

You should use `idx` as a prefix or postfix for the name of your index (it helps you execute larger projects).

Inserting Data

Inserting data into your table is usually done with the `INSERT` command. Let's assume that you want to insert an employee named `Alan Cop` with a salary of `20000 USD` into the table called `oldemp`:

```
INSERT INTO oldemp (empname,salary,currency) VALUES ('Alan Cop',20000,'USD');
```

The first variable to be specified is the name of the table where you want to insert the data. The names of the columns where data is going to be added have to be in parentheses. In our example, we don't want to add a value in the column called id because this column will get the value from the serial used as the primary key. All fields that are not listed in brackets will be NULL or default values after the INSERT.

Importing Large Datafiles and Using Pipes on UNIX Systems

If large amounts of data have to be imported into a PostgreSQL server, INSERT statements are far too slow for that purpose.

In this case, other methods, such as files and pipes, are far more effective. You can use the COPY command to import data directly from files. PostgreSQL supports reading both binary and ASCII data, which can be quite useful because working with binary data can sometimes be much faster.

Suppose you want to import the following tab-separated file into table oldemp:

```
1       Paul Stallman       18000    USD
2       Steven Neundorf      4000    DM
3       Josef Russell       20000    USD
4       Alan Torvalds       22000    USD
```

Here is the required COPY command:

```
COPY oldemp FROM '/tmp/people.data' USING DELIMITERS '\t';
```

You import the file people.data in /tmp into the table called oldemp. You use tabs (\t) as delimiters; but let's try to import the file again:

```
name=# COPY oldemp FROM '/tmp/people.data' USING DELIMITERS '\t';
ERROR:  copy: line 1, Cannot insert a duplicate key into unique index emp_id_key
```

It can't be done again because primary keys have to be unique. Importing the data a second time leads to double entries.

In this example, we manually inserted data into a column that uses a serial as its primary key. What happened to the sequence the serial uses to generate the row ids? You use a SELECT statement to retrieve the value (you learn about SELECT in Chapter 4):

```
name=# SELECT sequence_name, last_value FROM emp_id_seq;
 sequence_name | last_value
---------------+------------
 emp_id_seq    |          1
(1 row)
```

You can see that the value of the sequence is still 1, although we have already inserted four values into the table. This can lead to real difficulties when you start to insert values into the database using INSERT statements:

```
INSERT INTO oldemp (empname, salary, currency)
       VALUES ('John Blundell',19000,'USD');
ERROR:  Cannot insert a duplicate key into unique index emp_id_key
```

Because we want the serial to generate the primary key, we don't add the name and the value of the field id to the INSERT statement. During the INSERT, the current value of the emp_id_seq sequence is selected and the value of the sequence is incremented by 1 if the insert succeeds. Accidentally, the sequence's value is still 1, and 1 is already used in the table. Because primary keys have to be unique, the INSERT fails. Temporary tables can be used to solve the problem. If you want to use sequences for your primary key, create a temporary table and import the data to that table. Then perform a SELECT INTO operation to copy the data to the final table. An advantage of that algorithm is that you don't have to remove trash when the import fails. Removing trash from tables can be tricky in production environments.

Pipes are a powerful feature on UNIX systems and can be used to redirect the standard output of a process directly to a PostgreSQL server. Using them is simple:

yourprocess.pl | psql yourdatabase

The output of yourprocess.pl must be formatted properly so that psql can use it as standard input. A good choice of a properly formatted standard output is an SQL statement.

> **Note**
> The standard error of the yourprocess.pl process is being omitted, because only standard output is redirected.

If you have processes that run for hours or produce a lot of standard output or standard errors, you might want to store the result of the process in a file. In this case, the UNIX command nohup might be useful. If you start a background process with the help of nohup, you can log out while the process is working. This is not possible when starting a command with & only. Here is an example of a nohup command:

```
nohup ./myprocess.pl &
```

`myprocess.pl` might be a Perl script that performs complex PostgreSQL commands. If you have logged in to a remote machine using your favorite terminal software and if your network is not a reliable one, `nohup` can save you a lot a time (imagine a process getting killed after 26 hours because of a network interruption).

Retrieving Data

Let's look at a sample database called shop. The database is a prototype of a bookshop, and we will use this database in most parts of this chapter. It might look a bit confusing at first, but we'll work though every detail of the SQL code and the database structure. The following is the output of pg_dump, an interface for dumping databases into ASCII files:

```
CREATE SEQUENCE "products_id_seq" start 5 increment
        1 maxvalue 2147483647 minvalue 1  cache 1 ;
SELECT nextval ('"products_id_seq"');
CREATE SEQUENCE "prodtext_id_seq" start 8 increment
        1 maxvalue 2147483647 minvalue 1  cache 1 ;
SELECT nextval ('"prodtext_id_seq"');
CREATE SEQUENCE "prodcat_id_seq" start 9 increment
        1 maxvalue 2147483647 minvalue 1  cache 1 ;
SELECT nextval ('"prodcat_id_seq"');
CREATE SEQUENCE "customer_id_seq" start 3 increment
        1 maxvalue 2147483647 minvalue 1  cache 1 ;
SELECT nextval ('"customer_id_seq"');
CREATE SEQUENCE "sales_id_seq" start 4 increment
        1 maxvalue 2147483647 minvalue 1  cache 1 ;
SELECT nextval ('"sales_id_seq"');

CREATE TABLE "products" (
        "id" int4 DEFAULT
                nextval('products_id_seq'::text) NOT NULL,
        "prodid" int8 NOT NULL,
        "price" numeric(9,2) NOT NULL,
        "stored" numeric(9,2) DEFAULT 0,
        PRIMARY KEY ("prodid")
);
```

```
CREATE TABLE "prodtext" (
        "id" int4 DEFAULT
                nextval('prodtext_id_seq'::text) NOT NULL,
        "prodid" int8,
        "lang" text,
        "proddesc" text
);

CREATE TABLE "prodcat" (
        "id" int4 DEFAULT
                nextval('prodcat_id_seq'::text) NOT NULL,
        "prodid" int8 NOT NULL,
        "prodcat" character varying(50) NOT NULL,
        PRIMARY KEY ("id")
);

CREATE TABLE "customer" (
        "id" int4 DEFAULT
                nextval('customer_id_seq'::text) NOT NULL,
        "name" character varying(50) NOT NULL,
        "email" character varying(50),
        "state" character varying(50) NOT NULL,
        PRIMARY KEY ("name")
);

CREATE TABLE "sales" (
        "id" int4 DEFAULT
                nextval('sales_id_seq'::text) NOT NULL,
        "salestime" timestamp,
        "prodid" int8,
        "prodprice" numeric(9,2),
        "amount" int4,
        "name" character varying(50),
        "email" character varying(50),
        "state" character varying(50),
        PRIMARY KEY ("id")
);

COPY "products" FROM stdin;
1       385343  44.99   20.00
2       385342  49.99   64.00
3       394568  39.99   18.00
```

```
4        106666  39.99  120.00
5        765354  29.99  98.00
\.


COPY "prodtext" FROM stdin;
1        385343  english Python Developer's Handbook
2        385343  german  Python Entwickler Handbuch
3        385342  english Linux Socket Programming
4        394568  english Linux Hardware Handbook
5        394568  german  Das Linux Hardware Buch
6        106666  english Linux: Networking for your Office
7        106666  german  Linuxnetzwerke fürs Büro
8        765354  english Palm Programming
\.


COPY "prodcat" FROM stdin;
1        385343  Python
2        385343  Developer
3        385343  Handbook
4        385342  Linux
5        394568  Linux
6        394568  Handbook
7        106666  Networking
8        106666  Linux
9        765354  Palm
\.


COPY "customer" FROM stdin;
1        John    john@no.any     Florida
2        Robert  rober@no.any    Georgia
3        Peter   peter@no.any    Alaska
\.


COPY "sales" FROM stdin;
1        2001-04-03 15:01:27+02 106666 39.99    1       John    john@no.any
Florida
2        2001-05-12 16:22:09+02 394568 39.99    1       John    john@no.any
Florida
3        2001-05-12 17:19:04+02 385343 49.99    2       Robert  robert@no.any
Florida
4        2001-06-12 17:19:04+02 385343 44.99    1       Robert  robert@no.any
Florida
\.
```

```
CREATE INDEX "products_id_key" on "products"
        using btree ( "id" "int4_ops" );

CREATE INDEX "prodtext_id_key" on "prodtext"
        using btree ( "id" "int4_ops" );

CREATE INDEX "prodcat_id_key" on "prodcat"
        using btree ( "id" "int4_ops" );

CREATE INDEX "customer_id_key" on "customer"
        using btree("id" "int4_ops" );

CREATE INDEX "customer_email_key" on "customer"
        using btree ( "email" "varchar_ops" );

CREATE INDEX "sales_email_key" on "sales"
        using btree ( "email" "varchar_ops" );

CREATE CONSTRAINT TRIGGER "<unnamed>" AFTER DELETE
        ON "products" NOT DEFERRABLE INITIALLY IMMEDIATE
        FOR EACH ROW EXECUTE PROCEDURE
        "RI_FKey_noaction_del" ('<unnamed>', 'prodtext',
        'products', 'UNSPECIFIED', 'prodid', 'prodid');

CREATE CONSTRAINT TRIGGER "<unnamed>" AFTER UPDATE
        ON "products" NOT DEFERRABLE INITIALLY
        IMMEDIATE FOR EACH ROW EXECUTE PROCEDURE
        "RI_FKey_noaction_upd" ('<unnamed>', 'prodtext',
        'products', 'UNSPECIFIED', 'prodid', 'prodid');

CREATE CONSTRAINT TRIGGER "<unnamed>" AFTER
        INSERT OR UPDATE ON "prodtext"
        NOT DEFERRABLE INITIALLY IMMEDIATE FOR EACH ROW
        EXECUTE PROCEDURE "RI_FKey_check_ins" ('<unnamed>',
        'prodtext', 'products', 'UNSPECIFIED',
        'prodid', 'prodid');
```

Let's take a closer look at this code. First, sequences are created. Every table has a column called id, and the sequences assign a unique id to every row in the database. Then we create a table called products to store all information about the products in the shop. The column called prodid will be a unique product id. prodid is also the primary key of the table. price will contain the current price of the product, and stored will contain the number of available units of the product.

prodcat contains the product categories. One book might have multiple entries. The table is referred to by the product id. prodtext stores the title of a book in multiple languages. The customer table stores information about all registered users, and the sales table stores all information about sales, such as the number of books a user purchased or the price of a product.

The COPY commands are used to read data directly from the input file. Then, indices are created on the id column of all tables. At this point, it is useful to add additional indices for certain columns to speed up queries. It depends on the type of queries the user wants to perform on which columns to define indices.

> **Note**
> Creating indices is not always good, because sometimes disk space is wasted. Reduced storage is not the only drawback. Sometimes indices can slow the database down, especially when performing INSERT statements. This happens because the database must update the index *and* the data, which is actually slower than just doing the updates *for* the data.

Finally, triggers are added to guarantee the integrity of the database. It is not useful to have a product in table prodtext that doesn't exist in table products anymore—the triggers help the user to do some data cleaning.

If you want to create a database with the data shown previously, create an empty database (use createdb shop) and write a simple text file containing the SQL code. Then type

```
psql shop < yourtextfile.sql
```

As soon as the import is ready, you can connect to your database with psql.

Simple Queries

Retrieving data is probably the most important activity when dealing with databases. Storing data is useful only if you can find the right piece of information any time it is needed. In case of relational databases, you use the SELECT command to retrieve data from a database. SELECT statements can be very simple but also very tricky. This section should give you a short overview of how to use SELECT for simple queries. Let's start with an example. We want to retrieve where the product id is 385343:

```
SELECT * FROM products WHERE prodid='385343';
```

The database executes the query and if everything is configured correctly, displays this result:

```
 id | prodid | price | stored
----+--------+-------+--------
  1 | 385343 | 44.99 |  20.00
(1 row)
```

The database has returned all requested records and all columns of the table. If you want to have only the last three columns of the table and only products with a `prodid` that is higher than 385343, you use the following query:

```
SELECT prodid,price,stored FROM products WHERE prodid > '385343';
```

The result is

```
 prodid | price | stored
--------+-------+--------
 394568 | 39.99 |  18.00
 765354 | 29.99 |  98.00
(2 rows)
```

Sometimes it is necessary to build more complex `WHERE` clauses. Imagine a query where we want to retrieve all records where the product id is higher than 385343 and the price is lower than 35$. The query looks like this:

```
SELECT * FROM products WHERE prodid > '385343' AND price < 35;
```

The result contains only one value, because the price of product number 394568 is higher than 35$. The `AND` token tells the database to return only values where both conditions are fulfilled.

Very often `AND` and `OR` tokens have to be combined to find the right result. The following query retrieves all records in table `products` where the product id is 385343 if the price is lower than 35%. Additionally, all records are displayed where the price is exactly 44.99$. With the help of the `OR` token, the database returns all records where the left expression (`prodid > '385343' AND price < 35`) or the right expression (`price='44.99'`) returns true:

```
SELECT * FROM products WHERE (prodid > '385343'
        AND price < 35) OR price='44.99';
```

Here is the result for this query:

```
 id | prodid | price | stored
----+--------+-------+--------
  1 | 385343 | 44.99 |  20.00
  5 | 765354 | 29.99 |  98.00
```

The product with id of 385343 is returned because the price matches the right expression exactly. The product with number 765354 is returned because the product is higher than 385343 and the price is lower than 29.99$.

You can see in these first few examples that SQL offers an easy syntax to perform simple queries quickly and without writing huge amounts of code.

Let's look at another example, finding all categories in table prodcat. Because some categories might be listed twice, you can use the DISTINCT operator to make sure that each word appears only once in the result:

SELECT DISTINCT prodcat FROM prodcat;

The result is

```
  prodcat
-----------
Developer
Handbook
Linux
Networking
Palm
Python
(6 rows)
```

Only 6 rows are returned, although 9 rows are in the database, because the words Handbook and Linux appear more than once in the table. Use the following if you want the database to return only the first 3 rows in alphabetical order:

**SELECT DISTINCT prodcat FROM prodcat
        ORDER BY prodcat ASC LIMIT 3;**

The result is

```
  prodcat
-----------
Developer
Handbook
Linux
(3 rows)
```

You use the ORDER BY clause to sort the result. ASC means that the result has to be sorted in ascending order. If you want the database to return the result in descending order, you use the DESC token. The LIMIT command saves time when performing

SELECT * operations on extremely huge tables. You also can display all but the first three records. With the help of OFFSET, you can skip the first *n* records returned.

You can use OFFSET and LIMIT together. If you want to get only the fourth record returned by the query, you use the following:

```
SELECT DISTINCT prodcat FROM prodcat
        ORDER BY prodcat ASC LIMIT 1 OFFSET 3;
```

This query returns Networking. The explanation for the result is simple: OFFSET 3 makes the database skip the first 3 rows. LIMIT 1 takes the first line and omits the rest.

Performing Simple Calculations

In many cases, it is useful to perform simple calculations directly within an SQL statement. Assume a query where you want to calculate the total amount of money a user has to pay:

```
SELECT prodid, prodprice, amount, prodprice*amount, name
        FROM sales;
```

You take the price of one unit of the product and multiply it with the amount of units the user bought. The result is

```
prodid | prodprice | amount | ?column? | name
--------+-----------+--------+----------+--------
106666 |     39.99 |      1 |    39.99 | John
394568 |     39.99 |      1 |    39.99 | John
385343 |     49.99 |      2 |    99.98 | Robert
385343 |     44.99 |      1 |    44.99 | Robert
```

You also can write more complex queries. In all cases, SQL uses the "infix" syntax.

Joining Tables

Joining tables is an extremely important issue when talking about relational and object relational databases. Joins are used to select and combine information from multiple columns. The tables you want to join must have at least one column in common.

Suppose you want to create a list with all product descriptions, their price, and the amount of books stored. The amount of books stored and the price can be found in the products table. The description of the products can be found in the prodtext table. Both tables have a column for the product id, so you can join the tables with the help of the product id:

```
SELECT prodtext.lang, prodtext.proddesc,
       products.price, products.stored
       FROM products, prodtext
       WHERE products.prodid=prodtext.prodid;
```

The result is the following list of eight records containing the German and English titles of the books:

```
   lang    |              proddesc              | price | stored

----------+-----------------------------------+-------+--------
 english  | Linux: Networking for your Office | 39.99 | 120.00
 german   | Linuxnetzwerke fürs Büro          | 39.99 | 120.00
 english  | Linux Socket Programming          | 49.99 |  64.00
 english  | Python Developer's Handbook       | 44.99 |  20.00
 german   | Python Entwickler Handbuch        | 44.99 |  20.00
 english  | Linux Hardware Handbook           | 39.99 |  18.00
 german   | Das Linux Hardware Buch           | 39.99 |  18.00
 english  | Palm Programming                  | 29.99 |  98.00
```

If you now want to retrieve all books (English title only) where more than 80 books are stored, you use the following query:

```
SELECT prodtext.lang, prodtext.proddesc,
       products.price, products.stored
       FROM products, prodtext
       WHERE products.prodid=prodtext.prodid
             AND prodtext.lang='english'
             AND products.stored>80;
```

The result is

```
   lang    |              proddesc              | price | stored

----------+-----------------------------------+-------+--------
 english  | Linux: Networking for your Office | 39.99 | 120.00
 english  | Palm Programming                  | 29.99 |  98.00
```

Only two books are left. In the example, you can see that combining data using AND tokens is extremely easy. Remember the most important point when joining tables: The tables must have at least one column in common. This example contains the column called prodid. Don't forget to perform the actual join (products.prodid=prodtext.prodid) in your query. If you do forget, you will get the

Cartesian product of the two tables as the result. The Cartesian product is a join without a WHERE clause. Try the following:

```
SELECT * FROM products, prodtext;
```

to find out about the outcome. The result will be 40 lines long, and most of the lines won't have anything in common.

In the next example, we want to generate a complete list of all sales including the product description:

```
SELECT sales.salestime, prodtext.proddesc, sales.amount
       FROM sales, prodtext
       WHERE prodtext.prodid=sales.prodid
             AND prodtext.lang='english';
```

This joins the table prodtext and the table sales via the product id:

```
       salestime          |          proddesc           | amount

-------------------------+-----------------------------+--------
 2001-05-12 17:19:04+02  | Python Developer's Handbook  |    2
 2001-06-12 17:19:04+02  | Python Developer's Handbook  |    1
 2001-05-12 16:22:09+02  | Linux Hardware Handbook      |    1
 2001-04-03 15:01:27+02  | Linux: Networking for your Office|    1
```

Self-Joins and Aliases

This section gives you insight into aliasing and self-joins. Aliases can be used to assign an additional name to a column. On the one hand, it is possible to write shorter and easier-to-read queries (aliasing can speed up writing a query significantly, especially when the query string is more complex). On the other hand, aliases can be used to perform self-joins. With a *self-join*, a table performs a join with itself. You will see an example of this later. First let's look at a simple example using aliases:

```
SELECT * FROM products AS a where a.stored=20;
```

This query selects all records from table products where the amount of books stored is exactly 20. In this case, a is an alias for products. The query can also be written the following way:

```
SELECT * FROM products a where a.stored=20;
```

It is not necessary to use the AS token, but AS can sometimes make the query easier to read.

Let's look at a shop where each product can be assigned to multiple product categories. Because the number of categories of a product should not be limited, we won't define a separate column for every category. It would be nice to have a table with just one table for the product category. The following table is called `prodcat` in the sample database (use "`SELECT`

```
* FROM prodcat;"):
 id | prodid |  prodcat
----+--------+------------
  1 | 385343 | Python
  2 | 385343 | Developer
  3 | 385343 | Handbook
  4 | 385342 | Linux
  5 | 394568 | Linux
  6 | 394568 | Handbook
  7 | 106666 | Networking
  8 | 106666 | Linux
  9 | 765354 | Palm
```

First you write a query to find all products that are assigned to the category `Handbook`:

```
SELECT * FROM prodcat WHERE prodcat='Handbook';
```

Two records are returned:

```
 id | prodid | prodcat
----+--------+----------
  3 | 385343 | Handbook
  6 | 394568 | Handbook
```

Then we want to find all products that are listed in categories `Handbook` and `Developer`. We use a self-join:

```
SELECT *
      FROM prodcat AS a, prodcat AS b
      WHERE a.prodcat='Handbook'
            AND b.prodcat='Developer'
            AND a.prodid=b.prodid;
```

The result is

```
 id | prodid | prodcat  | id | prodid |  prodcat
----+--------+----------+----+--------+------------
  3 | 385343 | Handbook |  2 | 385343 | Developer
```

The database performs the join as if we had two identical tables. The result is only one record because only this record matches both categories. It is also possible to look for all records that match three categories.

> **Note**
> When working with multiple tables, you should use the * operator with care, because
> * displays all columns from all tables listed in the FROM clause.

In the next example, we look for all records that are assigned to Handbook, Developer, and Python:

```
SELECT *
      FROM prodcat AS a, prodcat AS b, prodcat AS c
      WHERE a.prodcat='Handbook'
            AND b.prodcat='Developer'
            AND c.prodcat='Python'
            AND a.prodid=b.prodid
            AND a.prodid=c.prodid
            AND b.prodid=c.prodid;
```

The result is again one record:

```
id  | prodid | prodcat   | id | prodid | prodcat   | id | prodid | prodcat
----+--------+-----------+----+--------+-----------+----+--------+--------
  3 | 385343 | Handbook  |  2 | 385343 | Developer |  1 | 385343 | Python
```

You can see in these examples that self-joins can be done rather easily. The only crucial point is that you must not forget the actual joins to get the right result. If you try your queries on small testing tables, make sure that you have every possible difficulty in them. If the result of a query seems to be right, try to go through the code again and check whether you have all necessary join operations in it. If you don't test thoroughly, you might have bad luck when performing the query on large tables.

The output of the previous query is not a beautiful one. Try the following query to make the result easier to understand:

```
SELECT a.id AS rowid, a.prodid AS "product id"
      FROM prodcat AS a, prodcat AS b, prodcat AS c
      WHERE a.prodcat='Handbook'
            AND b.prodcat='Developer'
            AND c.prodcat='Python'
            AND a.prodid=b.prodid
            AND a.prodid=c.prodid
          AND b.prodid=c.prodid;
```

The result is much nicer than the previous one:

```
rowid | product id
------+-----------
    3 |     385343
```

In this example, you see how you can change the description of a table with the help of aliases. If the new heading contains whitespace characters, such as blanks, the new heading has to be quoted in the SQL query—if not, it can be written without quotes. The table can now be read easier.

Aggregation Functions

Aggregates are a powerful feature of relational databases. They can be used to perform operations with multiple lines involved. Let's look at an example where we want to count the lines in a table with the help of the count() function:

```
SELECT COUNT(*) FROM products;
```

The result is

```
count
-------
    5
(1 row)
```

The count() function can also be combined with a WHERE clause. The following example shows you how to count all records where the amount of stored books is equal to or higher than 64:

```
SELECT COUNT(*) FROM products WHERE stored >= 64;
```

The result of the query is 3. As you might have noticed in the previous example, we queried and displayed only one column; now we also want the product id to be displayed:

```
SELECT prodid, COUNT(*) FROM products;
```

This query leads to an error:

```
ERROR:  Attribute products.prodid must be GROUPed or used in an aggregate
function
```

The count() function doesn't know what to count any more and the database won't perform the query. The problem can be solved by adding an aggregate function to the query:

```
SELECT prodid, COUNT(*) FROM products GROUP BY prodid;
```

The result is a list with all product ids and the frequency they appear in the table:

```
prodid | count
-------+-------
106666 |     1
385342 |     1
385343 |     1
394568 |     1
765354 |     1
(5 rows)
```

In the example, you can see that every product id appears only once in the table.

Now we want to write a more complex query. We want to get a list with the sum of all sales of a certain book, including the product description. We have to perform a join of table `sales` and table `prodtext`. We want only the English titles to be displayed. Here is the query:

```
SELECT a.proddesc, SUM(b.amount)
        FROM prodtext AS a, sales AS b
        WHERE a.prodid=b.prodid
                AND a.lang='english'
        GROUP BY b.prodid, a.proddesc;
```

The result is

```
            proddesc              | sum
----------------------------------+-----
 Linux: Networking for your Office |   1
 Python Developer's Handbook       |   3
 Linux Hardware Handbook           |   1
(3 rows)
```

We use the `sum()` function to get the sum of all sales. In the example, we use the `GROUP BY` token two times. This is necessary because one product id can have many titles. We have also used aliasing to make the actual code of the query shorter. Don't forget the actual join operation in the query; in this example, the join is performed by the `a.prodid=b.prodid` expression.

In some cases, it can be useful to get only a small piece of the result of a query using aggregate functions. Imagine an example where we want to get all products that have been sold more than once:

```
SELECT prodid, SUM(amount) AS "total sum"
        FROM sales
        GROUP BY prodid
        HAVING SUM(amount) > 1;
```

The result is very short:

```
 prodid | total sum
--------+-----------
 385343 |         3
(1 row)
```

Only product number 385343 is available in the list, where more than one unit has
been sold. The query contains a HAVING clause. HAVING is used to perform condition
tests on aggregate functions. In our case, we check whether the result of the GROUP BY
is higher than 1. A query can also have AND or OR tokens in the HAVING clause. The
following example adds an AND token to the query we used earlier:

```
SELECT prodid, SUM(amount) AS "total sum"
        FROM sales
        GROUP BY prodid
        HAVING SUM(amount) > 1
                AND SUM(amount) < 10;
```

The result is the same as the result of the query used before, because no product was
sold more often than nine times.

Now we want to calculate the average price of the products in table products:

```
SELECT AVG(price) FROM products;
```

The database performs the calculation and returns the following:

```
      avg
---------------
 40.9900000000
(1 row)
```

The value returned is precise, but in many cases not suitable. We want the result to be
displayed like a currency, which means only two numbers after the comma. For that
purpose, we use the round() function, which needs two arguments. The first argument
is the actual value that has to be processed, and the second argument is used to define
the precision. In our case, the query looks like this:

```
SELECT ROUND(AVG(price),2) FROM products;
```

The result is

```
 round
-------
 40.99
(1 row)
```

This result is what we expected. Now we want the result to be displayed in full dollars without a comma:

```
SELECT ROUND(AVG(price),0) FROM products;
```

The result of the query is now 41, because 41 is the closest integer value. The second parameter of the function can also be negative:

```
SELECT ROUND(AVG(price),-2) FROM products;
```

As you might have thought, the result is 0. You can see in these examples that PostgreSQL supports nested functions.

The next example shows how to calculate the minimum or the maximum of a column:

```
SELECT MIN(price) FROM products;
```

The result is

```
  min
-------
 29.99
(1 row)
```

> **Note**
> Check out the docs of your PostgreSQL database to determine whether your version
> can also perform MAX() and MIN() with the help of indices. Otherwise, your query
> can be very slow on large tables.

Subqueries

Subqueries are used to calculate values that are needed within the query that is executed. To make it clearer, here is an example: Imagine you want to find all persons in a table whose income is higher than the average income of the persons stored in the table. You need the average income to find the persons with a higher income. One possibility to solve the problem is to perform two separate statements, but what do you do when half of the persons stored in the tables are removed by another user while processing the two SELECT statements? The only way to solve the problem properly is to use subqueries. A *subquery* is actually a query within a query.

Here is an example where we select all products with a higher price than the average price:

```
SELECT *
        FROM products
        WHERE price >
                (SELECT AVG(price) FROM products);
```

First, the result of the subquery is calculated. After that, the result is used to perform the main query. Let's try it:

```
SELECT *
        FROM products
        WHERE price >
                (SELECT * FROM products);
```

The database displays the following error:

```
ERROR:  Subselect must have only one field
```

It is obvious that the database can't perform the query because a price is only one value. When performing subqueries, you have to make sure that the subquery returns exactly one field.

One query can contain many subselects. The following is a query with two subselects for selecting all products that are more expensive than the average price, but less expensive than the average price plus 5$:

```
SELECT *
        FROM products
        WHERE price >
                (SELECT AVG(price) FROM products)
        AND   price <
                (SELECT AVG(price)+5 FROM products);
```

There will be only one record left in the result:

```
 id | prodid | price | stored
----+--------+-------+--------
  1 | 385343 | 44.99 |  20.00
(1 row)
```

Not only a query can contain many subselects, subselects can also contain subselects. This feature is powerful and useful—especially when working with complex queries and data. Just insert a subquery in your SQL code where you need a special value that has to be calculated at runtime.

Using SELECT and INSERT

INSERT statements can easily be combined with SELECT statements. These are usually done when a large amount of data has to be copied from one table into another or when the results of complex queries are stored in temporary tables to achieve better performance. In the following example, we create a temporary table and insert some values into it. Here is the CREATE TABLE command:

```
CREATE TEMPORARY TABLE temptable
        (id integer, prodid int8, price numeric(9,2));
```

> **Note**
> The temporary table won't be listed by a \d command, but the table can be treated like a nontemporary table.

Now we insert some data from table products into table temptable:

```
INSERT INTO temptable(prodid, price) (SELECT prodid, price FROM products);
```

Let's see whether the operations have been performed correctly:

```
SELECT * FROM temptable;
```

The test result is

```
 id | prodid | price
----+--------+-------
    | 385343 | 44.99
    | 385342 | 49.99
    | 394568 | 39.99
    | 106666 | 39.99
    | 765354 | 29.99
(5 rows)
```

You can see that the database has done all INSERT operations properly.

Pattern Matching and Regular Expressions in SQL

A *regular expression* is a formula for matching strings that follow some pattern. Many people are afraid to use regular expressions, but when you get used to them, you can't live without them. Perl hackers especially seem to be addicted to regular expressions, because they are a fast and precise way of performing substring searching.

Regular expressions are implemented in all major databases and can therefore also be used in PostgreSQL. Although the syntax of regular expressions differs slightly from the syntax programming languages such as Perl, it is easy to learn.

Regular expressions consist of characters and metacharacters. *Metacharacters* are used to tell the database that a pattern has to occur more than once or something like that. In the simplest case, a regular expression can be a search string. Let's start with an example: We want to retrieve all people in table customer whose name is John:

```
SELECT * FROM customer WHERE name LIKE 'John';
```

The result is

```
 id | name |    email    |  state
----+------+-------------+---------
  1 | John | john@no.any | Florida
(1 row)
```

> **Note**
> The database performs a substring search for John.

The LIKE token can be used to perform the pattern matching, but it is also possible to use the ~ operator instead.

Let's write a query where all names starting with R are displayed:

```
SELECT * FROM customer WHERE name ~ '^R';
```

The ^ operator is used to match the beginning of a string. The R must be the first character after the beginning.

```
 id |  name  |    email     |  state
----+--------+--------------+---------
  2 | Robert | rober@no.any | Georgia
(1 row)
```

What happens if the name starts with r instead of R? The ~ operator performs case-sensitive searching. We can use the ~* operator to perform case-insensitive queries:

```
SELECT * FROM customer WHERE name ~* '^r';
```

The result is the same as the previous one. Now let's query all names that do not start with r:

```
SELECT * FROM customer WHERE name !~ '^R';
```

The result contains the remaining records:

```
id | name  |    email     |  state
---+-------+--------------+---------
 1 | John  | john@no.any  | Florida
 3 | Peter | peter@no.any | Alaska
(2 rows)
```

The case-insensitive version of the query is

```
SELECT * FROM customer WHERE name !~* '^r';
```

In some cases, it is necessary to search for a sequence of characters in a string. Here is an example where we search for all names that have er somewhere in them:

```
SELECT * FROM customer WHERE name ~* 'er';
```

The query returns the records of Robert and Peter. It is also possible to see whether certain characters appear in a string:

```
SELECT * FROM customer WHERE name ~ '[A-P]';
```

This query returns all names that contain one of the letters from A to P. If you don't want to have the records from A to P, but do want all others, write [^A-P] instead. The same kind of query can be done with numbers.

Suppose we want to look for all records that do not have the numbers 2 or 3 in the id and contain the letters from A to P:

```
SELECT * FROM customer WHERE id ~ '[^23]' AND name ~ '[A-P]';
```

The result is

```
id | name |    email    |  state
---+------+-------------+---------
 1 | John | john@no.any | Florida
(1 row)
```

The $ operator symbolizes the end of a string. If we want to query all records that end with an n, we can use the following SQL command:

```
SELECT * FROM customer WHERE name ~ 'n$';
```

The only name ending with an n is John, so that is the only record returned. What happens if we want to query records containing a $ or any other metacharacter? To show the solution for such a problem, let's create a temporary table and insert one record:

```
CREATE TEMPORARY TABLE demo(demo text);
INSERT INTO demo VALUES ('demo$');
```

Now we want to write a query that retrieves the records:

```
SELECT * FROM demo WHERE demo ~ '\$';
```

The character has to be masqueraded using a backslash (\). The result of the query is

```
 demo
-------
 demo$
(1 row)
```

In this example, you can see how powerful regular expressions are, but the real power of regular expressions can be seen when you have to perform complex queries. Assume a situation where someone tells you that he has bought a book on "the third." You don't know the month but you know that it must have been in the year 2001. You can write a query that selects all possible records from table sales:

```
SELECT id, salestime
       FROM sales
       WHERE salestime ~ '2001-.{2}-03';
```

The query selects all records whose salestime contains 2001, a - and exactly 2 characters before -03. The two undefined characters are the month when the sale took place. A period (.) matches any character exactly once. Parentheses can be used to tell the database how many undefined characters must be found before the rest. If you don't know whether the month is stored with one or two numbers, you can use the following:

```
SELECT id, salestime
       FROM sales
       WHERE salestime ~ '2001-.{1,2}-03';
```

The result of the query contains the requested record:

```
id |        salestime
----+------------------------
  1 | 2001-04-03 15:01:27+02
(1 row)
```

Assume that you knew that the sale took place in March or April; you can use this query:

```
SELECT id, salestime
       FROM sales
       WHERE salestime ~ '2001-.3?4?-03';
```

A question mark (?) symbolizes that a certain character may occur zero times or once. In this example, we look for March (3) or April (4). If one of the characters is found, the right result will be displayed.

Two additional operators are the + and the *. + means that the previous character must match at least once. * means that the previous character must match at least zero times. Imagine a query where you are looking for a certain product id. The only thing you know is that it started with 106 and continued with 6, but you don't know how many times the 6 is in the product id. Here is the solution for your problem:

```
SELECT * FROM products WHERE prodid ~ '106*';
```

In this example, 6 has to occur after 10 at least zero times; the result will contain the requested product id:

```
id | prodid | price | stored
----+--------+-------+--------
  4 | 106666 | 39.99 | 120.00
(1 row)
```

Tables 3.1 and 3.2 present an overview of the most important operators and metacharacters, respectively, of regular expressions.

Table 3.1   *Operators of Regular Expressions*

Operator	Description
~	Case-sensitive matching
~*	Case-insensitive matching
!~	Does not match, case-sensitive
!~*	Does not match, case-insensitive

Table 3.2   *Metacharacters of Regular Expressions*

Special Metacharacter	Description
^	Matches the beginning of a string.
$	Matches the end of a string.
.	Matches any character exactly once.
+	Matches previous character once or more often.
*	Matches previous character zero times or more often.
?	Matches previuous character zero times or more often.
[abc]	Matches one of the characters in the list.
[^abc]	Doesn't match one of the characters in the list.
[a-c]	Matches all characters from *a* to *c*.
[^a-c]	Doesn't match the characters from *a* to *c*.
{x}	The previous character must occur exactly *x* times.
{x,y}	The previous character must occur *x* to *y* times.
( )	Parentheses are used to group expressions.

Groups occur as one character for the expression after the parentheses (for example, the * operator after the parentheses means that the whole expression in parentheses has to match zero times or more often).

The examples of regular expressions might seem a bit strange. You might wonder who is looking for persons or for products with a stupid sequence of characters in it. Don't be surprised, but most of the examples are taken from real-world situations. Sometimes a customer wants to know something, but he can't say precisely what. He might say, "It must be something like that." In these cases, you can use regular expressions. Regular expressions can save you a lot of time and lots of code. You can solve complex problems within a few seconds and with only a few characters or lines of code.

Those people who are already addicted to regular expressions—like me—know what I am talking about.

Using SELECT INTO Statements

You use SELECT INTO to redirect the result of a query into a table. This is sometimes useful when debugging code; or you can use it to write two simple, rather than one complex, SQL statement:

```
SELECT prodid, price
        INTO TABLE sel
        FROM products;
```

The SELECT INTO statement creates a new table called sel. Let's look at whether the table has been created and filled correctly:

```
shop=# SELECT * FROM sel;
 prodid | price
--------+-------
 385343 | 44.99
 385342 | 49.99
 394568 | 39.99
 106666 | 39.99
 765354 | 29.99
(5 rows)
```

sel has two columns called prodid and price, and contains the complete result of the SELECT statement. sel is not a temporary table, so it cannot be seen only by the user who created it. If you want sel to be a temporary table, try the following command:

```
DROP TABLE sel;
SELECT prodid, price
        INTO TEMPORARY TABLE sel
        FROM products;
```

The data you want to insert into a table created by SELECT INTO can be the result of a very complex SQL query.

> **Note**
> If you want to add data to a table without creating a new table, use INSERT in combination with SELECT statements.

Formatting the Output and Casting

When performing SELECT statements, psql creates a header for the tables. This header might not be, in many cases, the result you want to see. Let's see how you can make the output look right. We start with a simple SELECT statement:

```
SELECT AVG(price) FROM products;
```

The result of the query does *not* look right:

```
      avg
---------------
 40.9900000000
(1 row)
```

We want to change the header to average price, which can be done with the following query:

```
shop=# SELECT AVG(price) AS "average price" FROM products;
 average price
---------------
 40.9900000000
(1 row)
```

Now we want to display the price and cast it to integer:

```
SELECT CAST(AVG(price) AS int4) AS "average price"
        FROM products;
```

The result of the query looks like this:

```
 average price
---------------
            41
(1 row)
```

In this example, we perform an explicit cast. First the average price is calculated, and then the cast to integer is done. We can use the CAST() function to perform the operation. Casts can also be done without the help of the CAST() function. Simply add a colon and the datatype you want to receive to the column:

```
SELECT AVG(price)::int4 AS "average price"
        FROM products;
```

Finally we want the price to be displayed with a $ at the end of the number, so we use the following code:

```
SELECT '$' || CAST(AVG(price) AS int4)  AS "average price"
    FROM products;
```

The || operator concatenates values in SQL. In our case, we add the $ symbol to the result:

```
 average price
---------------
 $41
(1 row)
```

> **Note**
>
> Not all types of casts can be performed by the database. PostgreSQL 7.0.3, for instance, does not support casts from numeric to text; we had to use integer in the example , but to_char()is also possible.

Now we want to write a query where multiple columns are treated as one:

```
SELECT name || ' bought ' || amount || ' units' AS "result"
       FROM sales;
```

We select and concatenate multiple columns and assign the name `result` to the column. The table is now displayed as one column:

```
        result
- - - - - - - - - - - - - - - - - - - - -
 John bought 1 unit
 John bought 1 unit
 Robert bought 2 units
 Robert bought 1 unit
(4 rows)
```

In the next example, we add a `WHERE` clause to the query that selects only those records that contain `John`:

```
SELECT name || ' bought ' || amount || ' units' AS result
       FROM sales
       WHERE name || ' bought ' || amount || ' units'
             ~ 'John';
```

The result contains two records:

```
       result
- - - - - - - - - - - - - - - - - - - -
 John bought 1 unit
 John bought 1 unit
(2 rows)
```

We can't use the alias of the column in the `WHERE` clause because this would lead to an error in PostgreSQL 7.0.3. We have to use the full name of the column as it is shown in the previous example:

```
shop=# SELECT name || ' bought ' || amount || ' units'
       AS result
       FROM sales
       WHERE result ~ 'John';
ERROR:  Attribute 'result' not found
```

Generating HTML

HTML is the most important language when dealing with Web applications. psql offers a flag that tells the database to generate HTML code instead of ordinary ASCII text. Unfortunately, this feature is supported only by psql and not by other interfaces of PostgreSQL. Because most Web interfaces won't use psql in combination with pipes, the flag is not used very often.

Use psql with the -H flag to enable HTML output. From now on, all results will be returned as HTML code. The most common way of performing a query that returns HTML code is to use your favorite UNIX shell.

Here is an example where we select all products that are more expensive than 40 dollars:

```
echo "SELECT * FROM products WHERE price > 40;" | psql -H shop
```

The result will be a table including all HTML tags:

```
<table border=1>
  <tr>
    <th align=center>id</th>
    <th align=center>prodid</th>
    <th align=center>price</th>
    <th align=center>stored</th>
  </tr>
  <tr valign=top>
    <td align=right>1</td>
    <td align=right>385343</td>
    <td align=right>44.99</td>
    <td align=right>20.00</td>
  </tr>
  <tr valign=top>
    <td align=right>2</td>
    <td align=right>385342</td>
    <td align=right>49.99</td>
    <td align=right>64.00</td>
  </tr>
</table>
(2 rows)<br>
```

Updating and Deleting Data

Data cannot only be inserted and selected from a table. UPDATE and DELETE are two essential commands for modifying and removing data from a table. The syntax of

UPDATE and DELETE is similar to that of SELECT statements. In this section, you will learn to use those two commands efficiently.

Writing UPDATE **Queries**

SQL supports UPDATE queries. Updating means that the database searches for records that fulfill certain conditions and changes the values of some fields of those records. The syntax of UPDATE queries is simple:

```
Command:    UPDATE
Description: Replaces values of columns in a table
Syntax:
UPDATE table SET col = expression [, ...]
    [ FROM fromlist ]
    [ WHERE condition ]
```

First you define the table. After the SET token, you specify a list of columns that have to be updated. With the help of the FROM clause, a table can be updated by taking data from other tables into consideration. The WHERE clause can be used like the WHERE clause of SELECT statements; the syntax is the same.

Let's look at some examples. We will write a query that updates the sales table by changing the amount of books bought by John from 2 to 3:

```
UPDATE sales SET amount=3 WHERE id=3;
```

You see, the query is indeed very simple. Use the following to determine whether the query has been performed correctly:

```
SELECT id, amount FROM sales WHERE id=3;
```

If no error has been displayed, the result is

```
 id | amount
----+--------
  3 |      3
(1 row)
```

The update has been completed successfully. Now we want to lower the price of all books in the database by 1$. This example also shows that an UPDATE statement does not always need a WHERE clause:

```
UPDATE products SET price=price-1;
```

The query assigns the price of the product minus 1 dollar to the products. UPDATE queries can also use subqueries to calculate the result of a value that has to be updated. Here is an example of assigning the price from table sales to the price in table products:

```
UPDATE products
      SET price=
              (SELECT MAX(prodprice)
                      FROM sales
                      WHERE prodid='385343')
      WHERE prodid='385343';
```

The update has been done for exactly one record, which is correct. The next example uses UPDATE queries with multiple columns. We will update the prices in table products with the value from table sales:

```
UPDATE products
      SET price=sales.prodprice
      FROM sales
      WHERE products.prodid=sales.prodid;
```

Update queries can also contain self-joins. The next example changes all entries from Linux to UNIX for all books that are assigned to the categories Handbook and Linux:

```
UPDATE prodcat
      SET prodcat='UNIX'
      FROM prodcat AS a
      WHERE prodcat.prodid=a.prodid
              AND prodcat.prodcat='Linux'
              AND a.prodcat='Handbook';
```

The database performs an update for product number 394568 and now has the following entries:

```
shop=# SELECT * FROM prodcat WHERE prodid='394568';
 id | prodid | prodcat
----+--------+----------
  6 | 394568 | Handbook
  5 | 394568 | UNIX
(2 rows)
```

Using DELETE

The DELETE command is used to remove records that match certain criteria from a table. Here is an overview of the DELETE command's syntax:

```
Command:     DELETE
Description: Removes rows from a table
Syntax:
DELETE FROM table [ WHERE condition ]
```

We create a table called `temp` and insert some values into it:

SELECT prodid, price, stored INTO temp FROM products;

The table now contains the following:

```
 prodid | price | stored
--------+-------+--------
 385342 | 48.99 |  64.00
 765354 | 28.99 |  98.00
 106666 | 39.99 | 120.00
 385343 | 44.99 |  20.00
 394568 | 39.99 |  18.00
(5 rows)
```

The next query deletes all books that are more expensive than 40 dollars:

DELETE FROM temp WHERE price > 40;

The database deletes two records. If you want to delete all records from the table, you write the following:

DELETE FROM temp;

The table is now empty. The DELETE command is simple. The only mistake people make is to write DELETE * FROM table instead of DELETE FROM table. This mistake leads to a syntax error, and the DELETE can't do its job because DELETE removes a record completely. It is not possible to remove half of a dataset; you would have to update a column to NULL instead of deleting it.

Writing Advanced SQL Code

For performing complex operations, PostgreSQL supports a pool of features that can make the life of a database developer much easier. Features such as arrays and datatypes for storing network information are often essential for building sophisticated database applications.

Another important topic is masquerading. In the next section, you take a closer look at the idea behind masquerading, and you will learn in which situations characters have to be masqueraded.

Masquerading

Masquerading characters is extremely important and can save you a lot of time.

The purpose of character masquerading can be explained in a few words. Imagine a situation where you have to insert a string into a field that contains special characters. In SQL, characters such as single quotes (') have to be masqueraded because the database must distinguish between characters that will be inserted in a field and characters that are syntax components.

Assume that we want to add a French title to table prodtext. The title of the book in our example is Qu'est-ce que Python, which includes a single quote in the title. We try the following SQL command:

```
shop=# INSERT INTO prodtext(prodid, lang, proddesc) VALUES
(385343,'french','Qu'est-ce que Python');
shop'#
```

The database did not perform the query and is still prompting for some input. If you look closer at the value in the column called proddesc, you can see that the database has problems distinguishing between the single quotes used for the SQL command and the single quote in the text that has to be added. There are two possibilities to solve the problem: You can use a backslash or use a second single quote to make the INSERT command work properly; here is the code for the two methods:

```
shop=# INSERT INTO prodtext(prodid, lang, proddesc) VALUES
(385343,'french','Qu''est-ce que Python');
INSERT 51554 1
```

```
shop=# INSERT INTO prodtext(prodid, lang, proddesc) VALUES
(385343,'french','Qu\'est-ce que Python');
INSERT 51555 1
```

Both methods work the same way. The following shows how the values are stored in the database:

```
shop=# SELECT * FROM prodtext WHERE prodid='385343' AND lang='french';
 id | prodid | lang  |       proddesc
----+--------+-------+---------------------
 11 | 385343 | french | Qu'est-ce que Python
 12 | 385343 | french | Qu'est-ce que Python
(2 rows)
```

The same result can be reached with the following query. We look for all records that contain a single quote. Because we have inserted only two records, the result will be the same as before:

```
SELECT * FROM prodtext
        WHERE lang='french' AND proddesc ~ '\'';
```

Not only single quotes have to be treated in a special way when dealing with regular expressions. Other characters—such as $ and ^, for instance—have to be masqueraded. This also can be done with the help of a backslash.

Deciding which characters to masquerade is easy: Do it for all characters that have a special meaning in regular expressions and try it with a backslash.

Working with Arrays

Arrays are data structures that enable the user to store multiple values of a certain datatype in one data structure in one field. Arrays are so called *non-atomic values*, which means that they consist of components. The size of an array can be limited or unlimited depending on the users' needs.

The next example creates a table that contains a one-dimensional array for storing comments. The array is of undefined size, which means unlimited:

```
CREATE TABLE comments (id serial, prodid int8, comment text[]);
```

We will now insert a dataset into the table:

```
INSERT INTO comments(prodid, comment)
        VALUES ('385343',
                '{"language","programming","Python"}');
```

The array is used to store three values in one column. The syntax of the INSERT command is not too difficult. The values are actually passed to the database in single quotes. The brackets within the two single quotes contain the three values of the array—all in double quotes.

Let's see how the values are returned when selecting the record from the table:

```
 id | prodid |             comment
----+--------+------------------------------------------
  1 | 385343 | {"language","programming","Python"}
(1 row)
```

If you want to retrieve values from the array, you use a SELECT statement. The WHERE clause has to be modified slightly by adding the index of the array to the name of the column. You can see in the next example that it is not enough to use the name of the column only:

```
shop=# SELECT * FROM comments WHERE comment='programming';
ERROR:  array_in: Need to specify dimension
```

Here is the correct version of the query:

```
shop=# SELECT * FROM comments WHERE comment[1]='programming';
 id | prodid | comment
----+--------+---------
(0 rows)

shop=# SELECT * FROM comments WHERE comment[2]='programming';
 id | prodid |                  comment
----+--------+---------------------------------------
  1 | 385343 | {"language","programming","Python"}
(1 row)
```

The examples show that a record can be retrieved from an array only when the correct index of the array is specified in the query. This can sometimes be very tricky; because every array might have a different size, the user might not know about the required records.

Arrays also can be defined with a maximum size, by adding the size between the parentheses in the CREATE TABLE statement:

```
CREATE TABLE comments (id serial, prodid int8, comment text[5]);
```

The example creates a table with an array with a maximum of 5 entries.

Arrays are not limited to one dimension. In many cases, you can use multidimensional data structures. Here is an example where we create a table with a two-dimensional data structure:

```
CREATE TABLE comments (id serial, comments text[][]);
```

The table is used to store comments. We use the array to store the category and the text of the comment. Now let's insert some data into the table:

```
INSERT INTO comments(comments)
        VALUES ('{{"language"}, {"Python"}}');
```

The table contains one record now. The category is set to language; the text of the category is Python. We can easily retrieve the data from the table:

```
shop=# SELECT * FROM comments WHERE comments[1][1] ~ '.';
 id |          comments
----+--------------------------
  2 | {{"language"},{"Python"}}
(1 row)

shop=# SELECT * FROM comments WHERE comments[1][2] ~ '.';
 id | comments
----+----------
(0 rows)
```

In this example, the columns of the array have to be indexed correctly to receive a result from the database. A two-dimensional array can be compared with a system of coordinates. Every point in the system can be assigned to a value. Multidimensional arrays can be useful for scientific databases. Assume a query where you want to know all employees in a certain area, their income, their profession, and their gender. The output of that query can be a three-dimensional array. The number of employees is assigned to every combination of income, profession, and gender. The required result (for example, income = 2000$, gender = female, profession = lawyer) can be found by indexing the array containing all results. The algorithm just described is used in a real-world situation because this is (possibly) the only way of keeping the load of the database low even when generating a lot of data.

Arrays and the COPY Command

Inserting data cannot always be done with INSERT commands, because this would be too slow when treating huge amounts of data. The next example shows how simple it is to use the COPY command to insert data into an array. The database uses nearly the same syntax for the array as the INSERT command:

```
COPY "comments" FROM stdin;
2       {{"language"},{"Python"}}
\.
```

Working with BLOBs

Many advanced databases, including PostgreSQL, support treatment of a binary large object (BLOB). Storing a BLOB means storing a file. It does not matter what's in that file; it can be binary data, ASCII, EBCDIC, and so forth. BLOBs have to be treated differently than "ordinary" data, because it would be complicated to use a plain 500MB file within an INSERT command like ordinary text. BLOBs have to be loaded into the database.

> **Note**
> BLOBs don't store the position of the file in the file system. BLOBs are stored directly in the database.

The file upload can be done with the `lo_import()` function. If you want to export the file, the `lo_export()` function can be used to export the data in the database to a file in the file system.

Let's create a table where we want to store the product id and the image of a product directly within the database:

```
CREATE TABLE prodimages (id serial, prodid int8, image OID);
```

Recall that OID is the acronym for *object identifier*. In Chapter 7, "Backup and Recovery," you will see what that means when you want to back up your complete database.

For now, let's insert a picture in the database:

```
shop=# INSERT INTO prodimages(prodid, image) VALUES ('385343',
lo_import('/tmp/385343.jpg'));
INSERT 51759 1
```

The database generates a unique object id for the file and loads it into the database where it is stored. The unique id of our file in the example is 51745:

```
shop=# SELECT * FROM prodimages;
 id | prodid | image
----+--------+-------
  1 | 385343 | 51745
(1 row)
```

You can see in the example that a SELECT statement returns only the object id of the file we have just uploaded. Internally, PostgreSQL creates separate files for every file uploaded:

```
bash-2.04$ ls -l *51745*
-rw-------    1 postgres postgres     8192 Apr  7 15:18 xinv51745
-rw-------    1 postgres postgres    16384 Apr  7 15:18 xinx51745
```

Now we want to export the file stored in the record to a file. This can be done with the help of the `lo_export()` function. The syntax is similar to the syntax of the `lo_import()` function:

```
SELECT lo_export(prodimages.image,'/tmp/export.jpg')
       FROM prodimages
       WHERE prodid='385343';
```

The database exports the image to the file /tmp/export.jpg. If the files in the database become very big, this might take some time—so watch out when writing Web applications. If a user wants to upload large files into the database, this can lead to trouble. Make sure that the maximum size of the file is limited to a certain size.

Now we want to delete and reinsert the records. You must keep one issue in mind when deleting BLOBs. Never perform DELETE commands on tables containing BLOBs before you have deleted the actual image in the database. If you delete the records, the files in the database containing the image won't be deleted—the database deletes only the object id—but the data will become something like a zombie. So make sure that you use the lo_unlink() function to drop the image first:

```
SELECT lo_unlink(prodimages.image) FROM prodimages;
```

The file has now been deleted from the database; let's see whether the files are still there:

```
bash-2.04$ ls -l *51745* 2> /dev/null | wc -l
      0
```

The files has been found zero times; everything is okay so far, but what about the record in the table?

```
shop=# SELECT * FROM prodimages;
 id | prodid | image
----+--------+-------
  1 | 385343 | 51745
(1 row)
```

You can see that the record is still in the table. You can perform a DELETE operation now to safely eliminate the entry.

If you are working on high-availability systems, make sure that no one can access a record whose file has already been deleted. Implement some kind of locking mechanism, such as a locking flag for the datasets.

Using Network-Specific Datatypes

PostgreSQL has special datatypes for storing IP and MAC addresses. These datatypes offer input checking and some special functions and operators. IPs and MAC addresses can also be stored in ASCII text fields, but we strongly recommend using PostgreSQL's functions for network datatypes. Table 3.3 lists PostgreSQL network datatypes (for version 7.0.3).

Table 3.3   *PostgreSQL Network Datatypes*

Name	Storage	Range
cidr	12 bytes	Stores valid IPv4 network addresses
inet	12 bytes	Stores IPv4 hosts or network addresses
macaddr	6 bytes	Stores MAC addresses (Ethernet card hardware addresses)

The next example creates a table to store logging information in our shop database and shows you how to treat network addresses in PostgreSQL:

```
CREATE TABLE shoplog(id serial, fieldone cidr,
        fieldtwo inet, mac macaddr);
```

The table contains one field of each datatype. Let's see how we can insert valid data into it:

```
INSERT INTO shoplog(fieldone, fieldtwo, mac)
        VALUES ('192.168.1.0/24', '192.168.1.1/25',
                '00:50:FC:1E:7C:26');
```

The most important difference between `cidr` and `inet` is that `cidr` does not support data with nonzero bits to the right of the netmask. As you can see in the previous example, the netmask has to be written as one number instead of something like `255.255.255.0`; otherwise, the system will report a parse error:

```
shop=# INSERT INTO shoplog(fieldone, fieldtwo, mac)
        VALUES ('192.168.1.0/255.255.255.0', '192.168.1.1/25',
                '00:50:FC:1E:7C:26');
ERROR:  could not parse "192.168.1.0/255.255.255.0"
```

If we now select all data from the table, we get this result:

```
shop=# SELECT * FROM shoplog;
 id |   fieldone   |    fieldtwo    |        mac
----+--------------+----------------+-------------------
  2 | 192.168.1/24 | 192.168.1.1/25 | 00:50:fc:1e:7c:26
(1 row)
```

Every column has a valid IP address. In `fieldone`, the zeros on the right edge of the IP address are omitted because this is redundant information (the database has the netmask of the IP). If we insert an IP address without explicitly adding the netmask, the database takes a default netmask of 32 for the `cidr` datatype; the `inet` datatype won't have a netmask:

```
INSERT INTO shoplog(fieldone, fieldtwo, mac)
        VALUES ('192.168.1.0', '192.168.1.1/25', '00:50:FC:1E:7C:26');
INSERT INTO shoplog(fieldone, fieldtwo, mac)
        VALUES ('192.168.1.1', '192.168.1.1/25', '00:50:FC:1E:7C:26');
INSERT INTO shoplog(fieldone, fieldtwo, mac) VALUES
('0.0.0.0','0.0.0.0','00:50:FC:1E:7C:26');
shop=# SELECT * FROM shoplog;
 id |    fieldone     |    fieldtwo     |        mac
----+-----------------+-----------------+-------------------
  2 | 192.168.1/24    | 192.168.1.1/25  | 00:50:fc:1e:7c:26
  3 | 192.168.1.0/32  | 192.168.1.1/25  | 00:50:fc:1e:7c:26
  4 | 192.168.1.1/32  | 192.168.1.1/25  | 00:50:fc:1e:7c:26
  5 | 0.0.0.0/32      | 0.0.0.0         | 00:50:fc:1e:7c:26
(4 rows)
```

In the last three lines of the result, you see what happens when performing the three INSERT statements.

PostgreSQL supports a number of input formats for the MAC address. Here is a complete list of the most important ways (for PostgreSQL 7.0.3):

- 00-50-FC-1E-7C-26

- 0050FC:1E7C26

- 0050FC-1E7C26

- 0050.FC1E.7C26

Working with Geo-Data

PostgreSQL offers datatypes for geometric operations. PostgreSQL can therefore be used to build powerful solutions to fit scientific demands that can hardly be done with commercial mainstream databases. This section gives a brief insight into the wonderful world of modeling geographic data with PostgreSQL.

Geometric objects can be stored with the help of the datatypes described in the following sections.

point

A point is, in a way, the fundamental data structure when dealing with geometric objects point and can be handled easily and efficiently by the user. A point consists of two values: The first value is the *x-axis coordinate*, the second value is the *y-axis coordinate*. Both values are internally stored as floating-point numbers.

The syntax of a point is (x, y).

A point needs 16 bytes of storage:

```
CREATE TABLE temppoint(fieldname point);
INSERT INTO temppoint(fieldname) VALUES ('1,2');
INSERT INTO temppoint(fieldname) VALUES ('(1,3)');
```

We have created a table called temppoint with one column, and we have inserted two records into the table. One very important detail when dealing with a point is that a it has to be written within single quotes. Otherwise, a syntax error will be displayed:

```
shop=# INSERT INTO temppoint(fieldname) VALUES (1,2);
ERROR:  Attribute 'fieldname' is of type 'point' but expression is of type
'int4'
        You will need to rewrite or cast the expression
```

Let's see how the two points are returned by a query:

```
shop=# SELECT * FROM temppoint;
 fieldname
-----------
 (1,2)
 (1,3)
(2 rows)
```

line

A line is a pair of two points. One point matches the beginning of a line; the other point matches the end of the line. A line can be defined as two points: (x1, y1), (x2, y2) or to make the whole thing a little clearer ((x1, y1), (x2, y2)).

A line can also be specified by using x1, y1, x2, y2, but we strongly recommend using one of the versions with parentheses to make the code clearer and easier to understand.

A line needs 32 bytes of storage (twice the storage of a point). lseg (line seqment) is an alternative datatype to line.

Let's create a table using line:

```
CREATE TABLE templine(fieldname line);
```

The table can already be created, but PostgreSQL 7.0.3 doesn't support INSERT statements yet:

```
shop=# INSERT INTO templine(fieldname) VALUES ('(1,3), (4,12)');
ERROR:  line not yet implemented
```

At the time this book is written, full support of `line` is not available. You can use `path` instead of `line`.

box

A `box` is used to store a rectangle. A rectangle is defined by two `points` that are situated opposite each other on the rectangle. The syntax is therefore the same as the syntax of lines. When entering a `box` into the database, the lower-left corner is determined from the input and stored in the database first. You need not define the lower-left of the rectangle first; this is done by the database internally, and the user does not need to care about the order of the input (not implemented in PostgreSQL 7.0.3 yet).

A `box` needs 32 bytes of storage.

Here is some code:

```
CREATE TABLE tempbox(fieldname box);
INSERT INTO tempbox(fieldname) VALUES ('(8,9), (1,3)');
INSERT INTO tempbox(fieldname) VALUES ('(1,3), (4,12)');

shop=# SELECT * FROM tempbox;
  fieldname
---------------
 (8,9),(1,3)
 (4,12),(1,3)
(2 rows)
```

path

A `path` is a sequence of `points` and can either be open or closed. Closed means that the last `point` of the `path` "returns" to the beginning. The length of a `path` is dynamic. PostgreSQL offers special functions to make sure that a `path` is either open or closed. `popen()` and `pclose()` can be used to force a path to be open or closed. In queries, `isopen()` and `isclosed()` can be used to check whether the path is open or closed.

A path needs 4 bytes plus 32 bytes for every node to be stored.

Here are some examples of how you can create a table and insert some values. You can see that a `path` does not have a fixed number of `points`.

```
CREATE TABLE temppath(fieldname path);
INSERT INTO temppath(fieldname) VALUES ('(1,3), (4,12)');
INSERT INTO temppath(fieldname) VALUES ('(3,1), (2,8), (10,4)');
```

```
shop=# SELECT fieldname FROM temppath;
      fieldname
---------------------
 ((1,3),(4,12))
 ((3,1),(2,8),(10,4))
(2 rows)
```

polygon

A polygon is actually a closed path, but is stored differently and therefore has its own function.

A polygon needs 4 bytes plus 32 bytes for every node to be stored.

Here is some sample code to create a table and to insert some data:

```
CREATE TABLE temppoly(fieldname polygon);
INSERT INTO temppoly(fieldname) VALUES ('(1,3), (4,12), (2,4)');
INSERT INTO temppoly(fieldname) VALUES ('(2,0), (-5,12), (2,0)');

shop=# SELECT * FROM temppoly;
      fieldname
---------------------
 ((1,3),(4,12),(2,4))
 ((2,0),(-5,12),(2,0))
(2 rows)
```

circle

A circle consists of a point and the radius, and needs 24 bytes of storage.

The following creates a table and inserts two values:

```
shop=#  CREATE TABLE tempcircle(fieldname circle);
CREATE
shop=# INSERT INTO tempcircle(fieldname) VALUES ('10, 4, 10');
INSERT 51916 1
shop=# INSERT INTO tempcircle(fieldname) VALUES ('10, 4, -10');
ERROR:  Bad circle external representation '10, 4, -10'
shop=# INSERT INTO tempcircle(fieldname) VALUES ('10.3 , 2, 4');
INSERT 51917 1
```

You can see in the second INSERT statement that the radius of a circle must not be negative and that the database makes sure that no trash is inserted into the table.

Retrieving Geo-Data and Operators

Retrieving data from fields that contain geographic data is a little more complex than retrieving "ordinary" data.

Remember that the ~= operator has to be used instead of the = operator. In the following example, we select a specific point from a table:

```
SELECT fieldname  FROM temppoint WHERE fieldname ~= '(1,2)';
```

PostgreSQL's geographic datatypes offer much more than just retrieving. The next piece of code calculates the distance of two points:

```
SELECT '(1,1)'::point <-> '(2,2)'::point;
```

```
The result is
    ?column?
- - - - - - - - - - - - - - - -
 1.4142135623731
(1 row)
```

which is exactly the square root of 2 (for further information see "Pythagoras' Theorem" at http://www.geocities.com/researchtriangle/system/8956/problems/pyth.htm or http://www.cut-the-knot.com/pythagoras/index.html). In the previous example, the <-> operator is used to calculate the distance.

You also can add a point by using the + operator, as you do for simple addition:

```
shop=# SELECT '(1,1)'::point + '2,2'::point;
 ?column?
- - - - - - - - - -
 (3,3)
(1 row)
```

The operators -, * and / are also supported for performing an operation with a point:

```
shop=# SELECT '(1,1)'::point - '2,2'::point;
 ?column?
- - - - - - - - - -
 (-1,-1)
(1 row)
```

```
shop=# SELECT '(1,1)'::point * '2,2'::point;
 ?column?
- - - - - - - - - -
```

```
 (0,4)
(1 row)

shop=# SELECT '(1,1)'::point / '2,2'::point;
 ?column?
----------
 (0.5,0)
(1 row)
```

The ?- operator is used to see whether two points are horizontal; the ?-| operator checks whether two objects are perpendicular:

```
shop=# SELECT '(0,0)'::point ?- '-1,0'::point;
 ?column?
----------
 t
(1 row)
```

PostgreSQL offers four operators to check the position of a point relative to a position. The << operator checks whether a point is located left of another point, <^ checks whether the point is below another point, >> checks whether the point is on the right side, and >^ checks whether the point is above another point. In the next example, you can see how such a check can be performed:

```
shop=# SELECT '(0,0)'::point << '-1,0'::point;
 ?column?
----------
 f
(1 row)
```

PostgreSQL is also able to calculate intersections. The following example calculates the intersection of two line segments:

```
shop=# SELECT '((0,0),(10,0))'::lseg # '((0,0),(0,10))'::lseg;
 ?column?
----------
 (0,0)
(1 row)
```

PostgreSQL does not return only true or false; it also returns the right value. This is done when evaluating the point of closest proximity:

```
shop=# SELECT '(99,99)'::point ## '((3,2),(12,4))'::lseg;
 ?column?
----------
```

```
(12,4)
(1 row)
```

In the example, (12, 4) is nearer to (99, 99) than any other point on the line segment.

You can see in these examples that PostgreSQL offers powerful operators you can use to build complex and sophisticated applications. In addition to the operators we have already discussed in this section, the following operators are also available in PostgreSQL:

- && (A overlaps B or not)

- &< (overlaps to left)

- &> (overlaps to right)

- ?# (intersects or overlaps)

- @-@ (length or circumference)

- ?| (is vertical)

- ?|| (is parallel)

- @ (contained or on)

- @@ (center of)

If you want to get a complete list of all operators in PostgreSQL—or if you simply want to know which datatypes the operator you need is defined for—check out the online help of PostgreSQL by typing \do in your psql-shell.

Combining Queries

One problem encountered when writing SQL statements is that queries might have to be combined because the result of one SQL query might not lead to the final result you want to achieve. Combining queries means that more than one SELECT statement is used in a query. The result of the SELECT statements is put together by using one of the following keywords: UNION, INTERSECT, or EXCEPT.

UNION is used to add the results of SELECT statements, INTERSECT returns only the data the SELECT statements have in common, and EXCEPT returns all records that are not included in the second SELECT statement. For some real-world scenarios, let's go back to the shop database.

Think of a query where we want to retrieve all persons from table `employees` that are not in table `sales`. We try the following query:

```
SELECT * FROM customer EXCEPT SELECT * FROM sales;
```

Let's see what the data structure of those two tables looks like (use \d to display the data structures):

```
shop=# \d customer
                       Table "customer"
 Attribute |    Type     |                    Modifier
-----------+-------------+------------------------------------------------
 id        | integer     | not null default nextval('customer_id_seq'::text)
 name      | varchar(50) | not null
 email     | varchar(50) |
 state     | varchar(50) | not null
Indices: customer_email_key,
         customer_id_key,
         customer_pkey
```

```
shop=# \d sales
                        Table "sales"
 Attribute |    Type      |                   Modifier
-----------+--------------+------------------------------------------------
 id        | integer      | not null default nextval('sales_id_seq'::text)
 salestime | timestamp    |
 prodid    | bigint       |
 prodprice | numeric(9,2) |
 amount    | integer      |
 name      | varchar(50)  |
 email     | varchar(50)  |
 state     | varchar(50)  |
Indices: sales_email_key,
         sales_pkey
```

You can see that those two tables have just a few columns in common. Try to imagine how the database can perform the EXCEPT operation. You will run into trouble when you come to a column that is contained by only one of the two tables

```
ERROR:  Each UNION | EXCEPT | INTERSECT query must
        have the same number of columns.
```

An operation must have the same number of columns. If we perform the query like this:

```
SELECT name
        FROM customer
EXCEPT SELECT name
        FROM sales;
```

we receive a correct result:

```
 name
- - - - - - -
 Peter
(1 row)
```

Peter is the only person registered as customer who has never bought products. We use the following to retrieve all persons that are in table sales and table customer:

```
shop=# SELECT name
                FROM customer
        INTERSECT SELECT name
                FROM sales;
  name
- - - - - - - -
 John
 John
 Robert
 Robert
(4 rows)
```

> **Note**
> This can also be done with a join.

In the result, the database returns four records. If we want to get only one entry for every name, we can use DISTINCT:

```
SELECT DISTINCT name
        FROM customer
INTERSECT SELECT DISTINCT name
        FROM sales;
```

In the example, we have to use DISTINCT in both SELECT statements; otherwise, an error is displayed:

```
shop=# SELECT DISTINCT name
                FROM customer
        INTERSECT SELECT name
                FROM sales;
```

```
ERROR: get_sortgroupclause_tle: ORDER/GROUP BY
       expression not found in targetlist
```

Now we create a temporary table and insert values into it:

```
CREATE TEMPORARY TABLE person(name varchar(50),
       email varchar(50));
INSERT INTO person(name, email) VALUES ('Theodore Ts\'o',
       'no@none.any');
```

If we want to write a query that returns a list containing all names in table sales and table person, we can use UNION:

```
shop=# SELECT name FROM person UNION SELECT name FROM sales;
     name
---------------
 John
 Robert
 Theodore Ts'o
(3 rows)
```

Not only can you combine the two SELECT statements. Here is an example where we combine the tables:

```
shop=# SELECT name
       FROM person UNION
             (SELECT name FROM customer
              EXCEPT SELECT name FROM sales);
```

The result contains two records:

```
     name
---------------
 Peter
 Theodore Ts'o
(2 rows)
```

Building Complex Data Structures and Modeling Techniques

Choosing the right data structure is essential for building sophisticated applications, because the way data is organized in a database is the basis of success for the entire application. In this section, you learn how complex data structures can be built efficiently with PostgreSQL.

Creating and Dropping Views

It has been said that eyes are the window to the soul. This might be true. Definitely true is that views can be used to build more complex applications, and they can help you obtain a broader perspective of your data and the data structure. A view can be seen as a virtual table that is a kind of preprocessor for your data. In reality, a *view* is the result of a SELECT statement that looks like a table.

Views are also used in the system tables; one example of a view in system tables is the pg_indexes view. The following is the definition of that view:

```
shop=# \d pg_indexes
      View "pg_indexes"
 Attribute | Type | Modifier
-----------+------+----------
 tablename | name |
 indexname | name |
 indexdef  | text |
View definition: SELECT c.relname AS tablename, i.relname AS indexname,
pg_get_indexdef(x.indexrelid) AS indexdef FROM pg_index x, pg_class c, pg_class
i WHERE ((c.oid = x.indrelid) AND (i.oid = x.indexrelid));
```

The definition of the view contains only a SELECT statement.

Recall the data structure of the sales table:

```
                       Table "sales"
 Attribute |      Type     |                 Modifier
-----------+---------------+-------------------------------------------------
 id        | integer       | not null default nextval('sales_id_seq'::text)
 salestime | timestamp     |
 prodid    | bigint        |
 prodprice | numeric(9,2)  |
 amount    | integer       |
 name      | varchar(50)   |
 email     | varchar(50)   |
 state     | varchar(50)   |
Indices: sales_email_key,
         sales_pkey
```

Let's create a view that contains only the total price a user has to pay. You calculate this price by multiplying prodprice and amount. Because this operation is a fundamental one, you can use a view to avoid bugs and make your SQL statements shorter and easier to understand:

```
CREATE VIEW sales_price_view AS
        SELECT id, salestime, prodid,
                prodprice*amount AS totalprice,
                name, email, state
        FROM sales;
```

The view is now listed as a relation in the database. It is labeled as view, but it can be used like any other table:

```
shop=# \d
            List of relations
        Name     |   Type   |  Owner
-----------------+----------+---------
 customer        | table    | postgres
 customer_id_seq | sequence | postgres
 prodcat         | table    | postgres
 prodcat_id_seq  | sequence | postgres
 prodtext        | table    | postgres
 prodtext_id_seq | sequence | postgres
 products        | table    | postgres
 products_id_seq | sequence | postgres
 sales           | table    | postgres
 sales_id_seq    | sequence | postgres
 sales_price_view| view     | postgres
(11 rows)
```

We will now perform a SELECT statement. The result contains all records we store in table sales. The view calculates the required results for the prices implicitly:

```
shop=# SELECT id, totalprice FROM sales_price_view;
 id | totalprice
----+------------
  1 |      39.99
  2 |      39.99
  4 |      44.99
  3 |     149.97
(4 rows)
```

Views can also be created on top of other views. The following example shows the creation of a view consisting of components from table prodtext and view sales_price_view. We will use it to add the title of the book to the result:

```
CREATE VIEW sales_prodtext AS
        SELECT prodtext.proddesc, sales_price_view.prodid,
               sales_price_view.totalprice
        FROM prodtext, sales_price_view
        WHERE sales_price_view.prodid=prodtext.prodid
               AND prodtext.lang='english';
```

If we perform a full table scan on the view, we receive the following result:

```
shop=# SELECT * FROM sales_prodtext;
              proddesc          | prodid | totalprice
--------------------------------+--------+-----------
 Python Developer's Handbook    | 385343 |      44.99
 Python Developer's Handbook    | 385343 |     149.97
 Linux Hardware Handbook        | 394568 |      39.99
 Linux: Networking for your Office | 106666 |   39.99
(4 rows)
```

Like any other table in the system, a view can also be joined easily with other tables. If your hierarchy of views gets complicated, you have to take care of system performance. If a view contains a slow query, all views on top of that view will also become slow. If you are working on a high-availability system with a lot of data and complex queries, you can run into trouble easily. Make sure that you have tested your data structure under real-world load.

Data Integrity with Constraints

Data integrity can be a very tricky thing. But what does integrity mean? Imagine two tables that store information about a product. One product stores the product id and the price of a product, the second table stores some more details about the product. The second table has multiple entries for one product. Picture a situation where a product id is changed in table one. This leads you into trouble when performing joins because the product id in table two stays unchanged. It can be a problem taking care of issues like these in production environments and to change multiple keys in countless tables by hand. In this case, foreign keys are defined to make sure that data integrity is guaranteed. Here is an example where foreign keys would be useful:

```
shop=# SELECT DISTINCT name, email from sales WHERE name='Robert';
  name  |     email
--------+--------------
 Robert | robert@no.any
(1 row)
```

```
shop=# SELECT name, email from customer WHERE name='Robert';
  name  |    email
--------+-------------
 Robert | rober@no.any
(1 row)
```

If you compare the results of the two queries, you might recognize that the email address of Robert seems to be wrong in table customer (a *t* is missing). This is a tricky bug because it isn't likely to be found on first sight. It would be useful to have something that checks the data when the INSERT statement is performed. Foreign keys are usually used to perform the job.

Let's re-create the tables we have used in the sample database (at least a short version of the tables) and add some foreign keys to it (don't forget to drop the old tables before using the CREATE TABLE command):

```
CREATE TABLE "customer" (
        "id" serial NOT NULL,
        "name" character varying(50) NOT NULL,
        "email" character varying(50),
        "state" character varying(50) NOT NULL,
        PRIMARY KEY ("name", "email")
);

CREATE TABLE "sales" (
        "id" serial NOT NULL,
        "prodid" int8,
        "prodprice" numeric(9,2),
        "amount" int4,
        "name" character varying(50),
        "email" character varying(50),
        PRIMARY KEY ("id"),
        FOREIGN KEY (name, email) REFERENCES customer
);

COPY "customer" FROM stdin;
1       John    john@no.any     Florida
2       Robert  rober@no.any    Georgia
3       Peter   peter@no.any    Alaska
\.
```

First we create the customer table. Note that we have defined a multicolumn primary key to ensure that a combination of name and email address has to be unique.

Furthermore the primary key will be referred by the `sales` table. We have created table `sales` and added the foreign key. Because we have a multicolumn primary key, we have to use the `FOREIGN KEY` constraint.

Let's try to insert some values into the database:

```
INSERT INTO sales(prodid, prodprice, amount, name, email)
      VALUES ('385343','20','3','John','john@no.any');
```

Inserting this record works perfectly well because the name `John` and the correct email address can be found in the master table. What happens if we want to perform the operation with a slightly different email address:

```
shop=# INSERT INTO sales(prodid, prodprice, amount, name, email) VALUES
('385343','20','3','John','johnathan@no.any');
ERROR:  <unnamed> referential integrity violation - key referenced from sales
not found in customer
```

You can see that the `INSERT` failed because the required email address is not found in table `customer`. If we want to update the name of the record we have already inserted into table `sales`, we also receive an error, because this leads to a violation of the referential integrity:

```
shop=# UPDATE sales SET name='Alex';
ERROR:  <unnamed> referential integrity violation - key referenced from sales
not found in customer
```

What if we are planning to change the values of the keys we have in our tables? The next example defines the integrity rules of a column precisely.

```
CREATE TABLE "customer" (
        "id" serial NOT NULL,
        "name" character varying(50) NOT NULL,
        "email" character varying(50),
        "state" character varying(50) NOT NULL,
        PRIMARY KEY ("name")
);

CREATE TABLE "sales" (
        "id" serial NOT NULL,
        "prodid" int8,
        "prodprice" numeric(9,2),
        "amount" int4,
        "name" character varying(50)
                REFERENCES customer
```

```
                    ON UPDATE CASCADE,
        "email" character varying(50),
        PRIMARY KEY ("id")
);
COPY "customer" FROM stdin;
1       John    john@no.any     Florida
2       Robert  rober@no.any    Georgia
3       Peter   peter@no.any    Alaska
\.
```

We have modified the data structure slightly. The primary key for table customer has only one column now. In table sales, we have defined a foreign key on column name. This key references, as in the earlier example, to the customer tables. The difference is that we use ON UPDATE, which defines the action that has to happen when the primary key of the master table is updated. In the earlier example, we combined the ON UPDATE with the CASCADE command. Using CASCADE means that an update on the primary key of the master table leads to the update of all foreign key columns that refer to it.

Other commands are supported by PostgreSQL. We can also define certain database activities with the help of ON DELETE, which is always used when an entry in the master table is deleted. The following is a short overview of all commands that can be combined with ON UPDATE and ON DELETE:

Command	Action
NO ACTION	This is the default value; UPDATES and DELETES won't be performed to protect referential integrity.
CASCADE	All foreign keys will be updated when the primary key changes (with ON UPDATE). All foreign key records will be deleted when the primary key record is deleted (ON DELETE).
SET NULL	The foreign key is set to NULL when the primary key is updated or deleted.
SET DEFAULT	The foreign key is set to the default value of the column when the primary key is deleted or updated.

Here is an example of how ON UPDATE CASCADE works:

```
INSERT INTO sales(prodid, prodprice, amount, name, email)
        VALUES ('385343','20','3','John','john@no.any');
```

The INSERT command works because John is a valid name in table customer. Let's update the name to Paul:

```
UPDATE customer SET name='Paul' WHERE name='John';
```

The update has been performed without any trouble; the following shows what
happened inside the two tables:

```
shop=# SELECT * FROM sales;
 id | prodid | prodprice | amount | name |    email
----+--------+-----------+--------+------+-------------
  1 | 385343 |     20.00 |      3 | Paul | john@no.any
(1 row)
```

```
shop=# SELECT * FROM customer WHERE name='Paul';
 id | name |    email    |  state
----+------+-------------+---------
  1 | Paul | john@no.any | Florida
(1 row)
```

You can see that both tables have been updated to Paul as we expected it to be.

> **Note**
>
> ON UPDATE and ON DELETE can both be defined for one column; you need not decide
> whether ON UPDATE or ON DELETE is more important to you—simply use both for one
> column.

The CHECK Constraint

Some applications demand some sort of input restriction. This can be done with the
CHECK constraint, which checks whether a list of conditions is fulfilled before an INSERT
command is processed. In the next example, we want to except only orders where the
total price is higher than 100 dollars; otherwise, the INSERT command should fail:

```
CREATE TABLE "sales" (
        "id" serial NOT NULL,
        "prodid" int8,
        "prodprice" numeric(9,2),
        "amount" int4,
        "name" character varying(50),
        "email" character varying(50),
        PRIMARY KEY ("id"),
        CHECK (amount*prodprice > 100)
);
```

We try to insert an order:

```
shop=# INSERT INTO sales(prodid, prodprice, amount, name, email)
VALUES('385343', '39.99', '1', 'John', 'john@no.any');
ERROR:  ExecAppend: rejected due to CHECK constraint $1
```

This fails because one book costs only 39.99 dollars. The minimum is much higher, so the database displays an error. Now we try to order three books that cost 39.99 each. The total price is higher than 100 dollars, so the INSERT statement will be processed successfully:

```
shop=# INSERT INTO sales(prodid, prodprice, amount, name, email)
VALUES('385343', '39.99', '3', 'John', 'john@no.any');
INSERT 53120 1
```

In many cases, one condition might not be enough for an application. PostgreSQL's CHECK constraint can be used with multiple conditions, as in the next example. We simply have to connect the conditions with the help of AND or OR tokens:

```
CREATE TABLE "sales" (
        "id" serial NOT NULL,
        "prodid" int8,
        "prodprice" numeric(9,2),
        "amount" int4,
        "name" character varying(50),
        "email" character varying(50),
        PRIMARY KEY ("id"),
        CHECK (amount*prodprice > 100
                AND amount*prodprice < 1000)
);
```

Now we can insert only values that are higher than 100 but lower than 1000; all other attempts to insert data will fail:

```
shop=# INSERT INTO sales(prodid, prodprice,
                amount, name, email)
        VALUES('385343', '39.99', '300',
                'John', 'john@no.any');
NOTICE:  sales_id_seq.nextval: sequence was re-created
ERROR:  ExecAppend: rejected due to CHECK constraint $1
```

Using Inheritance

Inheritance is one of the key features of object-relational databases. Objects have certain properties that can be inherited by other classes; in PostgreSQL, tables can inherit from other tables.

Tables can be in a parent-child relationship, which means that all information a parent has is also available in the child (see Figure 3.4).

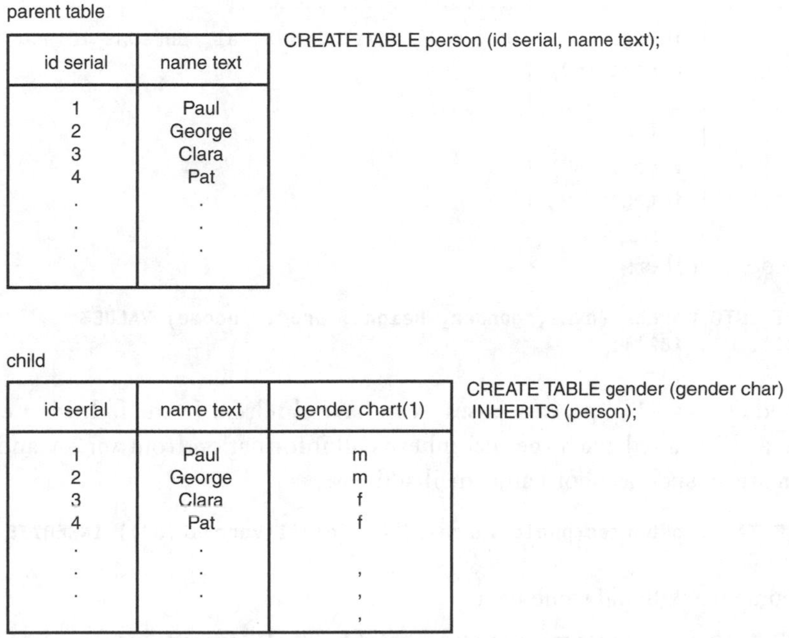

parent table

id serial	name text
1	Paul
2	George
3	Clara
4	Pat
.	.
.	.
.	.

CREATE TABLE person (id serial, name text);

child

id serial	name text	gender chart(1)
1	Paul	m
2	George	m
3	Clara	f
4	Pat	f
.	.	,
.	.	,
.	.	,

CREATE TABLE gender (gender char)
INHERITS (person);

Figure 3.4
A simple parent-child example.

Imagine a class person that stores all information persons normally have (height, gender, and so on).

```
CREATE TABLE persons(id serial, name varchar(50), gender char(1), height int4);
INSERT INTO persons(name, gender, height) VALUES ('George','m','178');
```

Now we create a class of persons where we have some additional information about this group of persons, such as profession and income.

```
CREATE TABLE worker(prof varchar(50), income int4) INHERITS (persons);
```

We have additional information about workers, which means that we also have all information about "ordinary" persons. The following is the data structure of table worker:

```
persons=# \d worker
                         Table "worker"
 Attribute |     Type     |               Modifier
-----------+--------------+-------------------------------------------------
 id        | integer      | not null default nextval('persons_id_seq'::text)
 name      | varchar(50)  |
 gender    | char(1)      |
 height    | integer      |
 prof      | varchar(50)  |
 income    | integer      |
```

Let's add a worker:

```
INSERT INTO worker (name, gender, height, prof, income) VALUES
('Carl','m','182');
```

Derived classes—like parent classes—can have children. In the following example, we create a class called cybertec that inherits all information from worker and adds more information, such as photo and email address:

```
CREATE TABLE cybertec(photo varchar(50), email varchar(50)) INHERITS (worker);
```

Of course we will add some data:

```
INSERT INTO cybertec(name, gender, height, prof, income, photo, email)
        VALUES ('Ewald Geschwinde','m','182', 'technical director', '1',
                'www.cybertec.at/epi/ps2.jpg','eg@cybertec.at');
INSERT INTO cybertec(name, gender, height, prof, income, photo, email)
        VALUES ('Hans-Juergen Schoenig','m','178', 'director of marketing', '1',
                'www.cybertec.at/hans/1.jpg','hs@cybertec.at');
```

If we want to write a query to retrieve all persons from table persons, this can easily be done:

```
persons=# SELECT * FROM persons;
 id |  name  | gender | height
----+--------+--------+--------
  1 | George | m      |    178
(1 row)
```

One record has been returned by the database, but let's modify the SQL command slightly:

```
persons=# SELECT * FROM persons*;
 id |          name           | gender | height
----+-------------------------+--------+--------
  1 | George                  | m      |    178
  2 | Carl                    | m      |    182
  3 | Ewald Geschwinde        | m      |    182
  4 | Hans-Juergen Schoenig   | m      |    178
(4 rows)
```

We have added an asterisk (*) to the name of the table, but now the database returns all values from table persons, including all tables derived from persons.

> **Note**
> Only the columns that are available in persons are displayed.

If we try the same thing with one of the other tables, we will receive more columns.

The next example shows how you can query all records from table cybertec and table worker. First we select all records available and exclude those that are in table persons:

```
persons=# SELECT name FROM persons* EXCEPT SELECT name FROM persons;
        name
---------------------
 Carl
 Ewald Geschwinde
 Hans-Juergen Schoenig
(3 rows)
```

A new table cannot only inherit from one table; it also is possible to define multiple parents for one table. The next example shows how the son inherits from mother and father:

```
CREATE TABLE father(name text);
CREATE TABLE mother(address text);
CREATE TABLE son(gender char(1)) INHERITS (father, mother);
```

The table data structure of son now looks like this:

```
persons=# \d son
         Table "son"
 Attribute |  Type   | Modifier
-----------+---------+----------
 name      | text    |
 address   | text    |
 gender    | char(1) |
```

After we have successfully created the tables, we try to delete one of them:

```
persons=# DROP TABLE father;
ERROR:  Relation '53451' inherits 'father'
```

As you might have thought, no table can be dropped that is the parent of another table. If you want to delete tables in a hierarchy, you have to do it "bottom up," which means children first:

```
persons=# DROP TABLE son;
DROP
persons=# DROP TABLE father, mother;
DROP
```

The previous examples work for PostgreSQL database releases earlier than 7.1. In 7.1 and later, inherited tables will be accessed automatically, and therefore an asterisk is not needed. If you want to access noninherited tables, you can use ONLY as a keyword.

Modeling Techniques

This section is dedicated to those who want a brief insight into modeling techniques. You learn how to build entity relationship models and explore the normalization rules for databases.

The Entity Relationship Model

In almost any application, a database is used to build a model of reality. Our reality consists of objects that have certain properties and certain relations with other objects. We will call these objects *entities*.

The *entity relationship model* is designed to represent real-world objects and processes to build data structures. For every entity, the relation to other entities is shown. Three types of relations are recognized:

- Two entities can be in a *1:1 relationship*, which means that one entity might have exactly one entity related to it.

- A *1:m relationship* means that one entity can have multiple entities related to it. An example of this is a product that has multiple categories assigned to it (one product <-> many categories).

- Entities can also be in an *m:n relationship*, which means that *m* entities are related with *n* entities.

An entity relationship model tries to model these issues in a graphical way. Every entity is represented as a box, and the relation between the boxes is shown as arrows or lines.

Entity relationship models are often used in real-world scenarios, because it is easier to understand a graphical overview of complex data structures than a huge amount of code.

Normalization

When designing a database from scratch, you normally end with a set of large tables with everything packed into it. This can soon lead to confusing data structures and a lot of redundancy in the tables. Redundancy means that values are stored more often than necessary. To get rid of the problems, a normalization can be performed. With *normalization*, the data model's anomalies, redundancies, and inconsistencies are reduced in every step of the process.

Normalization is a fundamental issue in database theory, and many modeling techniques are based on E.F. Codd's rules for normalization. In this section, you explore normalization through a short and easy-to-understand example.

The following is a table that has not been normalized:

Name	Address	Training Course
John Gore	Sesamestreet 1; 1010 Vienna	German, Chemistry, Sports
Lisa Bush	John Street 33; 1150 Vienna	Maths, Computer Science, English

In this example, if a teacher had more than three courses, we would soon run into trouble because there is no space left in the field (let's assume that it has a fixed length).

According to Codd's theories, a table is in first normal form when every value is stored separately and when one value does not consist of further values. Here is the same table, but now in *first norm form (1 NF)*:

pid	first name	surname	street	town	cid	training course
15	John	Gore	Sesame Street 1	1010 Vienna	44	German
15	John	Gore	Sesame Street 1	1010 Vienna	45	Chemistry
15	John	Gore	Sesame Street 1	1010 Vienna	46	Sports
6	Lisa	Bush	John Street 33	1150 Vienna	47	Maths
6	Lisa	Bush	John Street 33	1150 Vienna	48	Computer Science
6	Lisa	Bush	John Street 33	1150 Vienna	49	English

We have added an id in order to distinguish the records (`pid` for persons and `cid` for the id of the training course). One problem with the first normal form is that if one teacher changes address, we have to change that in three records. Another problem is that a new teacher can be added only when assigned to a training course. To put it in another way, we would have to remove teachers when they have no more training courses. This might not fit reality; for that reason, we should change our first normal form to a *second normal form*.

All components that have a separate key are now treated as separate tables. In our case, we create two tables—one for the teachers and one for the training courses.

Here is the table for the teachers:

pid	firstname	surname	street	town
15	John	Gore	Sesame Street 1	1010 Vienna
6	Lisa	Bush	John Street 33	1150 Vienna

Here is the table for the courses:

pid	cid	training course
15	44	German
15	45	Chemistry
15	46	Sports
6	47	Maths
6	48	Computer Science
6	49	English

We can now connect those two tables without storing the name of the teacher in a redundant way. According to Codd's theories, this must not happen because this could lead to anomalies we could have when using the first normal form.

In the mid-seventies, Codd discovered that the second normal form can also lead to anomalies. Assume that we add a column `category` to the table where we store the courses. Because many courses might belong to the same category, we would still have redundancies in the table and would have to update many rows when one value changes. In this case, we would have to introduce a third table to store the categories. This would be a data model using the *third normal form*.

In most cases, a data model in third normal form is also called a *Boyce-Codd normal form*.

In the following cases, a third normal form is *not* a Boyce-Codd normal form:

- Candidate keys in the relation are composite keys, which means that they are not single attributes.

- There is more than one candidate key in the relation.

- The keys are not *disjoint*, which means that some attributes in the key are common.

When designing data models, keep Codd's theories about normalization in mind, because you will build more flexible data structures when taking the most important points of the theory into consideration.

It is a good idea to create a highly flexible data model. If your data structure is not flexible enough, you will soon run into trouble and extending your application can become truly painful.

The Waterfall Model

A guide to database design says: "Using waterfall model, maybe is for cowards. Using no model is for kamikazes only!" (quoted from `http://www.cdt.luth.se/~jmb/presents/19990903/index.htm`) Many situations have proven that the author of this sentence knows what he is talking about.

The waterfall model is one of the most widespread models available. Academics seem to be especially enthusiastic about it; every student who has to deal with databases and modeling techniques will face the waterfall model at least once.

The waterfall model is a systematic, step-by-step approach to software development, in which the next phase of the project is entered as soon as one phase is completed. According to the basic waterfall model, the whole process is straightforward only.

Nowadays, many slightly different and more sophisticated versions of the waterfall model exist, but the most widespread version still seems to be the original model.

A process described by the waterfall model consists of seven steps (see Figure 3.5):

1. **Feasibility study.** Determine whether a project can be done.

2. **Requirement analysis and specification.** If the project can be done, find out what the basic requirements are. Requirements are not only hardware; human resources are, in most cases, more important than hardware. Define the key features of the product.

3. **Design and specification.** Define every detail of the final product precisely. The waterfall model is like a one-way street—you can't revise the specification for the rest of the project. Everything has to be clear; the better the specification, the better the final product. In software design, four parts have to be defined: data structure, software architecture, procedural detail, and the user interface, or human computer interface (HCI).

4. **Coding and module testing.** While programming the code, extensively test the modules to ensure high quality of the final product. If the specification is good, coding is a small part of the process.

5. **Integration and system testing.** Integrate and connect code with other components. Test the system under real-world circumstances (using people who have not participated in the project to this point) to find all bugs.

6. **Delivery.** Deliver the product to the customer(s) and implement it on site.

7. **Maintenance.** Make ongoing changes to correct errors and meet new demands. Reapply every step during changes.

Remember, in the original waterfall model, when you finish one step of the process, there is no way back. If you keep this in mind when designing and implementing an IT system, you will ensure a product of good quality.

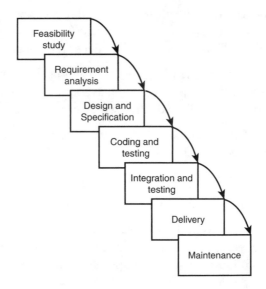

Figure 3.5

An original waterfall model.

As mentioned before, many versions of waterfall models exist. In some versions, you can go one step back in the process if something turns out to be wrong (see Figure 3.6).

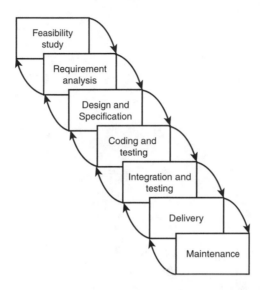

Figure 3.6
A waterfall model in which you can go back to a previous state in the process.

Many people and project leaders are using a "let's see later" strategy. This can lead to real disaster. If you start coding immediately, you will most likely find out that you have forgotten some crucial points and features. In this case, you have to rewrite a lot of code, which leads to bugs or hard-to-understand software. You have to know perfectly well what you are doing when writing the first line of code.

CHAPTER 4

Understanding Transactions

Transactions are an interesting and useful feature of PostgreSQL. All sophisticated database systems offer some kind of transaction code these days.

When modifying data in a transaction-enabled database, the database uses some kind of "everything or nothing" algorithm. Imagine a DELETE statement that has to delete several thousand rows. If someone presses the reset button while the operation is running, you might run into trouble because only half of the table might have been deleted. You also might face integrity problems. To avoid such nasty occurrences, a highly sophisticated transaction-based system has been implemented in PostgreSQL.

Imagine a user starting a DELETE statement that affects millions of rows. If someone presses the reset button, the database will jump back to the state it had before the DELETE statement. If the DELETE statement quits successfully, however, the changes will be visible to all users. An operation has to be completed successfully or the changes made by it will silently be discarded. This can be very useful. Imagine a query that updates the amount of products stored in your bookshop. If the query terminates after half of the records, it would be difficult to find out which records have already been processed. Doing all changes again is, in most cases, easier and safer.

Transactions are also very important for Multi-Version Concurrency Control (MVCC). MVCC is an extremely sophisticated method of providing all users a consistent snapshot of the database when performing a query. MVCC is also a technique that significantly speeds up the database's performance in multiuser environments. It is important for you to understand what is meant by "consistent snapshot of the database." Imagine a situation where one user performs a full-table scan on a huge table while a second user performs INSERT, UPDATE, and DELETE statements on the same table. Assume that the changes of user two affect the data user one is currently reading. If user one is performing join operations, his or her query might look for data that user two has already deleted or updated. The result of user one's query would be trash if the data used by a query changes while performing the query.

Many databases use a simple way of solving the problem by performing a table lock. If a query locks a table, all other queries would have to wait until the lock is released. This makes sure that nothing evil can happen to the table meanwhile. Imagine a high-availability system where huge queries that take hours to be processed are executed—the system would actually be down for hours if table locking were done. PostgreSQL offers the MVCC system instead.

In PostgreSQL environments, every query sees a consistent snapshot of the data (internally, processing is done using *Lehman-Yao high-concurrency btrees*, which is a very efficient data structure for that purpose). PostgreSQL uses a multiversion model for that purpose. No table locking has to be done because PostgreSQL uses an advanced row-locking system (table-locking is used as seldom as possible).

One important issue is transaction isolation. According to the ANSI/ISO SQL standard, four levels of transaction isolation are defined. Three events have to be prevented from happening:

- **Dirty reads**. Data from unfinished sessions are read by a query. This leads to inconsistent input data.

- **Nonrepeatable reads**. A transaction must be able to read data more often than once. All reads must lead to the same result. Therefore, no other transaction might change the data used by a transaction; otherwise, the database will run into trouble.

- **Phantom read**. A transaction executes a query again, but the result differs from the first query because the input data has changed. The database can't perform the transaction correctly in this case.

PostgreSQL does not support *nested transactions*, which are transactions started and committed inside another transaction. This won't have a significant restriction for most applications, but you should consider it when using PostgreSQL's transaction code for your applications.

How the Transaction Code Affects Daily Work

In most cases, you won't recognize what transactions are going on inside your database, but it is sometimes useful to start and end transactions manually—especially when performing critical operations where you want to return to a previous state of the database. You can start transactions explicitly by using the BEGIN command. Let's have a look at what the database tells us about BEGIN:

```
persons=# \h BEGIN
Command:     BEGIN
Description: Begins a transaction in chained mode
Syntax:
BEGIN [ WORK | TRANSACTION ]
```

To end a transaction explicitly, you can use the COMMIT command:

```
persons=# \h COMMIT
Command:     COMMIT
Description: Commits the current transaction
Syntax:
COMMIT [ WORK | TRANSACTION ]
```

BEGIN and COMMIT are usually done implicitly. Here is a piece of code that shows how starting and ending transactions look like in SQL:

```
persons=# BEGIN TRANSACTION;
BEGIN
persons=# CREATE TABLE person(name VARCHAR(50), gender CHAR(1), height INTEGER);
CREATE
persons=# END TRANSACTION;
COMMIT
```

Up to now, you haven't seen any difference; you can see in the following code that the table has been created successfully:

```
persons=# \d
      List of relations
  Name  | Type  |  Owner
--------+-------+----------
 person | table | postgres
(1 row)
```

Rollbacks

Recall that transactions can be used when performing critical operations where you might want to return to a previous state. PostgreSQL supports the ROLLBACK command, which is a kind of undo function. Here is an example of how ROLLBACK works:

```
persons=# BEGIN TRANSACTION;
BEGIN
persons=# CREATE TABLE person(name VARCHAR(50), gender CHAR(1), height INTEGER);
CREATE
persons=# \d
      List of relations
  Name  | Type  |  Owner
--------+-------+----------
 person | table | postgres
(1 row)

persons=# ROLLBACK;
ROLLBACK
persons=# \d
No relations found.
```

Suppose that you start a transaction and create the table the same way you did in the previous example, but now you recognize in the middle of the transaction that you have created the wrong table and that the name of the table should be different. You can perform a ROLLBACK. All commands performed in the current transaction will be obsolete, and you will have the same database you had at the beginning. Let's have a look at what PostgreSQL tells us about ROLLBACK:

```
persons=# \h ROLLBACK
Command:     ROLLBACK
Description: Aborts the current transaction
Syntax:
ROLLBACK [ WORK | TRANSACTION ]
```

You can see that ROLLBACK stops the current transaction; therefore, you do not need to use COMMIT manually.

Concurrent Transactions

Always remember that other users can see only the result of transactions that have already been finished. A user won't read the result of an unfinished transaction, because this would be a dirty read (refer to the description earlier in this chapter). Table 4.1 summarizes an example with multiple users working on a table simultaneously.

Table 4.1   *Example of Multiple Users on the Same Table*

User One	User Two	Result
CREATE TABLE children(name VARCHAR(50), gender CHAR(1), height INTEGER);	\d	Table "children" can be seen by user two.
BEGIN WORK;	\d	No relations found.
DROP TABLE children;	\d	Table "children" can be seen by user two.
COMMIT;	\d	No relations found.

User two can still see a table that user one has already dropped. One issue when dealing with transactions and DROP TABLE is shown in this code:

```
NOTICE:  Caution: DROP TABLE cannot be rolled back, so don't  abort now
```

No ROLLBACK can be performed after a DROP TABLE in PostgreSQL database version 7.1.

Now we want to start multiple transactions at once:

```
persons=# BEGIN TRANSACTION;
BEGIN
persons=# BEGIN TRANSACTION;
NOTICE:  BEGIN: already a transaction in progress
BEGIN
persons=# END TRANSACTION;
COMMIT
persons=# END TRANSACTION;
NOTICE:  COMMIT: no transaction in progress
COMMIT
```

Recall that PostgreSQL can run only one transaction per login at once.

Currently, PostgreSQL does not support savepoints in transactions—the way that Oracle does, for instance. Savepoints are especially useful in long transactions where the user doesn't want to scrap all changes because of a small error. Let's hope we see this feature in future versions of PostgreSQL.

Transaction Isolation

Another important command that affects your daily life when working with transaction is the SET command. SET is used to define the level of transaction isolation. Here is what the database tells us about SET:

```
persons=# \h set
Command:     SET
Description: Set run-time parameters for session
Syntax:
SET variable { TO | = } { value | 'value' | DEFAULT }
SET CONSTRAINTS {ALL | constraintlist} mode
SET TIME ZONE { 'timezone' | LOCAL | DEFAULT }
SET TRANSACTION ISOLATION LEVEL { READ COMMITTED | SERIALIZABLE }
```

SET let's you see what you can do with SET TRANSACTON ISOLATION LEVEL. As described earlier, three major events should be prevented: dirty reads, nonrepeatable reads, and phantom reads. According to the ANSI/ISO SQL standard, four levels of transaction isolation levels are defined:

- Read uncommitted

- Read committed

- Repeatable read

- Serializable

PostgreSQL supports read committed and serializable as its transaction levels. Serializable transaction levels makes sure that each transaction sees an absolutely consistent view of the database. Neither dirty reads, nonrepeatable reads, nor phantom reads may happen. With read committed, nonrepeatable reads and "phantom reads" may happen.

PostgreSQL uses read committed as the default isolation level. This book won't go further into detail, because PostgreSQL internals won't affect practical work significantly. The most important issue is that a query will read only data that has already been committed by another transaction.

Serialization seems to work as if all transactions would run one after the other (it actually does some kind of emulation of serial transactions) and therefore provides the highest level of transaction isolation.

In most cases, the default level of transaction isolation will satisfy your demands, and it's not necessary to use a different setting than the default one.

Locking

Locking is an interesting and important feature. In most cases, the user doesn't have to care about it because the database manages the whole locking stuff by itself. There are a few cases, however, where the user has to care about locking on the application level.

Assume an example where you perform a full-table scan in a multiuser environment. You select all rows from a table and process the rows one after the after with the help of a program. The program decides whether a row has to be deleted or updated. Thanks to transactions, you get a consistent snapshot of the data returned by the database, but what if a row has already been deleted by another transaction when you want to perform an update? If a query returns rows, it is not sure that the record returned still exists, because other users might already have deleted it. This can happen especially when certain queries are very big and transferring the data to the user takes a long time. To avoid the problem, a user can lock a table.

PostgreSQL offers a variety of locking commands. The most important ones are SELECT FOR UPDATE and LOCK. As you can see in the following code, LOCK offers many possibilities for locking:

```
persons=# \h LOCK
Command:     LOCK
Description: Explicitly lock a table inside a transaction
Syntax:
LOCK [ TABLE ] name
LOCK [ TABLE ] name IN [ ROW | ACCESS ] { SHARE | EXCLUSIVE } MODE
LOCK [ TABLE ] name IN SHARE ROW EXCLUSIVE MODE
```

Table 4.2 summarizes a locking example.

Table 4.2   *Locking Example with Multiple Users*

User One	User Two	Comment
CREATE TABLE children(name VARCHAR(50), gender CHAR(1), height INTEGER);		User one creates a table.

Table 4.2   *(continued)*

User One	User Two	Comment
INSERT INTO children(name, gender, height) VALUES ('Oliver','m','110');		User one inserts a value.
INSERT INTO children(name, gender, height) VALUES ('Jenny','f','117');		User two inserts a value.
BEGIN WORK;		User one starts a transaction.
LOCK children;		User two locks the table.
INSERT INTO children(name, gender, height) VALUES ('Etschi','f','103');		User one inserts a value.
INSERT INTO children(name, gender, height) VALUES ('David','m','105');		The database waits.
COMMIT;		The database performs the INSERT of user two as soon as user one ends the transaction.

User two can insert David as soon as user one quits the transaction. You would not run into trouble when performing INSERT statements, but if user one performed an UPDATE query on all records (let's say changing all genders to NULL), David's record would also be affected. If user one wanted only to update the record he or she inserted into the database, it would have gone wrong.

You can see in this simple example how useful locking can be, and it can save you a lot of headaches if you use locking correctly. One event you must take care of when working with explicit locks is a deadlock. A *deadlock* is a situation where one process is waiting for another process to perform an action that never happens. The second process is waiting for the first process. Both processes are waiting for each other, but nothing happens.

The following ways of table locking are supported:

- AccessShareLock is an internal locking mechanism.

- RowShareLock is used by SELECT FOR UPDATE and LOCK TABLE in IN ROW SHARE MODE statements.

- RowExclusiveLock is used by UPDATE, INSERT, DELETE, and LOCK TABLE in ROW EXCLUSIVE MODE.

- ShareLock is used by CREATE INDEX and LOCK TABLE with IN SHARE MODE statements.

- `ShareRowExclusiveLock` is used by `LOCK TABLE` with `IN SHARE ROW EXCLUSIVE MODE` statements.

- `ExclusiveLock` is used by `LOCK TABLE` with `IN EXCLUSIVE MODE` statements.

- `AccessExclusiveLock` is used by `ALTER TABLE`, `DROP TABLE`, `VACUUM`, and `LOCK TABLE`.

Row-level locking is used when certain fields of a record are updated by the user.

You need not know every method your PostgreSQL server uses to lock something; just be aware of how important locking is when building applications and how you can perform locking and unlocking.

CHAPTER 5

PL/PGSQL

PostgreSQL provides a special programming language for developing functions within SQL code. This programming language (that's the reason why it is called *PL*/pgSQL) offers the programmer far more execution potential than simple SELECT, INSERT, or UPDATE commands. The power of PL/pgSQL can be used to solve problems that cannot be solved with pure SQL statements. The package was initially written by Jan Wieck. Let's take a look at the main ideas and basic concepts of PL/pgSQL.

PL/pgSQL is a procedural language and is similar to Oracle's PL/SQL (see the section titled "Why Use PL/pgSQL," later in this chapter). Like PL/SQL, PL/pgSQL is a block-oriented language that supports variable declaration, loops, logical constructs, and advanced error handling.

Why Use PL/pgSQL?

PL/pgSQL is a powerful extension for SQL. Not all common problems can be solved with plain SQL code. PL/pgSQL was designed to be a programming language that can be used within the database, and for this reason PL/pgSQL is always a good choice to build enhancements and new features for a PostgreSQL database.

One advantage of PL/pgSQL is *platform independence*, which means that there is no reason for the programmer to care whether the function runs on an x86-CPU, an Alpha machine, or any other platform supported by PostgreSQL. All machine matters are solely a problem of PL/pgSQL's internals (who wants to care about byte order and so on?), and that is why PL/pgSQL functions do not need to be ported to other platforms. PL/pgSQL is a part of the database, and this is possibly the most significant advantage over any other way of building functions in PostgreSQL environments.

However, debugging PL/pgSQL code can be real pain. Inserting the function into the database does not guarantee that the function can be called.

Up to now, there is no debugger available, and PostgreSQL often does not offer precise error messages that help the user find an error quickly. Functions containing many lines of source code can hardly be debugged. We strongly recommend that you not write a number of functions at once; it is often better to start with something like "Hello World" and improve the function step by step. This guarantees—in a way—that the programmer can locate the lines where a syntax error might have occurred.

Enabling a Database with PL/pgSQL

When you create a new database, you have to enable PL/pgSQL manually. Type the following lines in your UNIX shell:

```
[hs@athlon hs]$ createdb yourdb
CREATE DATABASE
[hs@athlon hs]$ createlang plpgsql yourdb
```

On some UNIX systems, (for example, RedHat 7.0), the environment variables PGDATA and PGLIB have to be set to make createlang work properly (set PGLIB to the directory containing the file called plpgsql.o and PGDATA to the directory containing the PostgreSQL databases). If the two commands finished without errors, your database now supports PL/pgSQL.

The Structure of PL/pgSQL

As mentioned, PL/pgSQL is a block-oriented language. A block can be defined using DECLARE, BEGIN, and END. All variables have to be declared within the DECLARE section and are initialized with NULL every time a block is entered.

PostgreSQL supports database transactions (see Chapter 5, "Understanding Transactions"). Functions and triggers (*triggers* are a feature used to start a certain task after a predefined event) can be embedded only in a transaction started by an external query—they don't start separate transactions, because PostgreSQL doesn't support nested transactions.

Understanding transactions is an extremely important issue; don't confuse BEGIN/END for transaction control with BEGIN/END in PL/pgSQL functions.

Writing Functions

Writing user-defined functions is one of the core features of a sophisticated relational database system. PostgreSQL makes writing, inserting, and deleting a function very easy, as you will learn in this section.

Inserting PL/pgSQL Functions into a Database

Functions can directly be written in the psql shell. Because functions are usually many lines long, you should use your favorite text editor— vi, for example. The text file containing the source code can then easily be inserted into the database using a command like the following:

```
psql yourdb < yourcode.sql
```

If the command quits successfully, the function can be used in the database. The output of this command varies, depending on the SQL code you want to insert into the database.

> **Note**
> Don't forget to enable PL/pgSQL for your database.

A Simple Example

Let's get to some practical stuff. Here is a simple function that calculates the length of a string passed to it:

```
CREATE FUNCTION calclength (text) RETURNS int4 AS
'
        DECLARE
                intext ALIAS FOR $1;
                result int4;
```

```
      BEGIN
              result := (SELECT LENGTH(intext));
              RETURN result;
      END;
' LANGUAGE 'plpgsql';
```

The code starts with the CREATE FUNCTION and a name of the function is given. The datatypes of the parameters passed to the function are given in brackets. In this example, a single parameter of type text is passed to the function, but it could be any other datatype supported by SQL. All datatypes that can be used in plain SQL code can also be used by PL/pgSQL The next step is to specify the datatype of the return value—in this case, the function should return a 4-byte integer, which is the length of the string.

The body of the function has to be passed to the database as *one* string (Yyou can see that the first and the last line start with a single quote). After the string, the programming language used to execute the string is defined by using the LANGUAGE command. In this case, we use plpgsql (PL/pgSQL) for executing the code. PostgreSQL not only supports PL/pgSQL; you can also use PL/Perl or C code to write functions. It is important to know that the definition of the programming language is not part of the PL/pgSQL code. The LANGUAGE command is used only to tell PostreSQL what kind of source code is passed to the database engine.

Let's take a closer look at the DECLARE section. First, the variable intext is being declared as an alias for $1. $1 is the first parameter passed to the function (Bourne Shell uses the same notation). A second parameter would be called $2, and so on. In the next line, a 4-byte integer variable has to be declared. This variable will be used as the return value of the function. You can see that the variable result is being assigned the same datatype as the return value of calclength(text); compare RETURNS int4

AS.

The BEGIN/END section contains the actual code of the function. The length of intext is assigned to result.

> **Note**
> You have to use := instead of = for assigning a value to a variable.

Within a BEGIN/END section, SQL code can be used as it is within the psql shell. After inserting the function into the database, the function can be called the following way:

```
SELECT calclength('abc');
```

The result of the function call is 3:

```
 calclength
------------
          3
(1 row)
```

To remove the function from the database, you can use the DROP FUNCTION command:

```
yourdb=# DROP FUNCTION calclength(text);
```

Using Typecast Operations

Typecasting is very important for database programming. Typecasting means that a variable with a certain datatype is converted into a different type. Let's see how typecasting can be used in combination with PL/pgSQL functions.

PostgreSQL converts the variables to the right datatype implicitly. When I wrote that text there was no PostgreSQL 7.1 available yet. I have changed the entire section and added some additonal information.

We have already seen in the previous example that PostgreSQL assumes that the string **abc** is a text variable. If we do not call calclength with a string value, PostgreSQL will try to convert the value to a suitable datatype:

```
yourdb=# SELECT calclength(3);
 calclength
------------
          1
(1 row)
```

The integer value **3** can be cast to integer, so the function can be executed successfully.

Casting a value to the appropriate datatype is not always possible:

```
yourdb=# SELECT calclength('2,0'::point);
ERROR:  Function 'calclength(point)' does not exist
        Unable to identify a function that satisfies the given argument types
```

You can see in the listing that PostgreSQL cannot find the right function, because point cannot be converted to text. You can see an explicit cast in the next example:

```
yourdb=# SELECT calclength('2,0'::point::text);
ERROR:  Cannot cast type 'point' to 'text'
```

point cannot be cast to text, so the function call fails.

Casting cannot only be performed by using the :: operator. PostgreSQL supports a variety of functions to perform cast operations.

`text('abc')` casts `'abc'` to text. Let's try another cast:

```
SELECT int4('3');
```

This returns 3.

As you have seen before not every variable can be cast to every datatype:

```
SELECT int4('a');
```

This returns the following error:

```
ERROR: pg_atoi: error in "a": can't parse "a"
```

This error message means that PostgreSQL cannot perform an ASCII-to-integer conversion when using the string "a" (atoi = ASCII to integer).

Simple Flow of Control Structures

Programs and functions are not usually executed from the beginning to the end without interruption. In most cases, functions contain control structures that are used to influence the behavior of a program depending on the data that is processed. Like all programming languages PL/pgSQL supports a pool of control structures:

Using IF/ELSE

Now we want to write a function that calculates the length of two strings and returns the length of the longer one:

```
CREATE FUNCTION calclonger(text,text) RETURNS int4 AS
'
        DECLARE
                in_one  ALIAS FOR $1;
                in_two  ALIAS FOR $2;
                len_one int4;
                len_two int4;
                result  int4;
        BEGIN
                len_one := (SELECT LENGTH(in_one));
                len_two := (SELECT LENGTH(in_two));

                IF      len_one > len_two THEN
                        RETURN len_one;
```

```
            ELSE
                    RETURN len_two;
            END IF;
    END;
' LANGUAGE 'plpgsql';
```

PL/pgSQL supports, like most other languages, IF/ELSE statements. Our example is indeed very simple. We calculate the length of both strings and return the higher value. Because PL/pgSQL is block-oriented, we do not need brackets inside the IF.

If more than one condition has to be fullfilled, IF can be used with AND or OR statements:

```
IF      len_one > 20 AND len_one < 40 THEN
        RETURN len_one;
ELSE
        RETURN len_two;
END IF;
```

In this case, len_one is returned when len_one is higher than 20 but lower than 40. We would recommend using brackets to make the code clearer:

```
IF      (len_one > 20) AND (len_one < 40) THEN ...
```

Using LOOP/EXIT, WHILE, and FOR Loops

Loops can be used to execute a piece of source code several times. Now we want to write a function that counts the frequency of a certain character in a string:

```
CREATE FUNCTION countc (text, text) RETURNS int4 AS '
    DECLARE
            intext ALIAS FOR $1;
            inchar ALIAS FOR $2;
            len     int4;
            result  int4;
            i       int4;
            tmp     char;
    BEGIN
            len     := length(intext);
            i       := 1;
            result  := 0;
            WHILE   i<= len LOOP
                    tmp := substr(intext, i, 1);
                    IF      tmp = inchar THEN
                            result := result + 1;
```

```
                    END IF;
                    i:= i+1;
            END LOOP;
            RETURN result;
       END;
' LANGUAGE 'plpgsql';
```

The first parameter passed to the function is the string that has to be scanned by the
function. The second parameter contains the character the function is looking for.
First, the length of the first parameter is assigned to the variable len, and then i and
result are initialized. Then the string is scanned from the first character to the last,
and for every character scanned, the code within the WHILE/END LOOP statements is
executed. If the scanned character matches the second parameter, which has been
passed to the function, the value of result is incremented by 1. Finally, the result is
returned by the function.

PL/pgSQL also supports FOR *loops:*

```
CREATE FUNCTION countc(text, text, int4, int4) RETURNS int4 AS '
       DECLARE
                intext          ALIAS FOR $1;
                inchar          ALIAS FOR $2;
                startspos       ALIAS FOR $3;
                eendpos         ALIAS FOR $4;
                tmp             text;
                i               int4;
                len             int4;
                result          int4;
       BEGIN
                result = 0;
                len := LENGTH(intext);
                FOR i IN startpos..endpos LOOP
                        tmp := substr(intext, i, 1);
                        IF      tmp = inchar THEN
                                result := result + 1;
                        END IF;
                END LOOP;
                RETURN result;
       END;
' LANGUAGE 'plpgsql';
```

The syntax of FOR loops in PL/pgSQL is simple. This example can be used to search a character in a string from position number startpos to position number endpos. The FOR loop assigns a value to i whenever the loop is processed. **startpos..endpos** means that processing is started at startpos, and i is incremented by 1 until endpos is reached.

The function can also be implemented differently. This time we want to write a function without using a FOR loop. With the help of LOOP/EXIT, this can be done easily:

```
CREATE FUNCTION countc(text, text, int4, int4) RETURNS int4 AS '
        DECLARE
                intext      ALIAS FOR $1;
                inchar      ALIAS FOR $2;
                startpos    ALIAS FOR $3;
                endpos      ALIAS FOR $4;
                i           int4;
                tmp         text;
                len         int4;
                result      int4;
        BEGIN
                result = 0;
                i := startpos;
                len := LENGTH(intext);
                LOOP
                        IF      i <= endpos AND i <= len THEN
                                tmp := substr(intext, i, 1);
                                IF      tmp = inchar THEN
                                        result := result + 1;
                                END IF;
                                i := i + 1;
                        ELSE
                                EXIT;
                        END IF;
                END LOOP;
                RETURN result;
        END;
' LANGUAGE 'plpgsql';
```

FOR loops are not used here, so the function is more complex than its counterpart, which you saw before. LOOP/EXIT must perform a check, which tells the interpreter whether to leave the block. Otherwise, the loop won't stop.

Using Functions in PL/pgSQL

Functions are the heart of most programming languages. In PostgreSQL, functions are stored directly in the database and are called by the backend. When you insert a PL/pgSQL function into the database, the source code is converted into bytecode that can be executed efficiently by the PL/pgSQL bytecode interpreter. Each function is assigned an object ID.

Function Overloading

A very powerful feature of PL/pgSQL is *function overloading*, which means that a certain name for a function can be used to represent various versions of a function. Let's assume a function called `calc_middle()` that calculates the average of two integer values. Because it also might be useful to have a function that calculates the average of two dates, the programmer might use the same name for the two functions: `calc_middle(int4, int4)` for calculating the average of two integer values, and `calc_middle(timestamp, timestamp)` for calculating the average of two timestamps.

Functions that have the same name need not have the same number of parameters passed to it. You can also create a function named `calc_middle(int4, int4, int4)`, which is used to calculate the average of three integer values.

SELECT Statements and PL/pgSQL Functions

Imagine a table containing the name of an employee, the number of the room the employee works in, and the salary of the employee:

```
CREATE TABLE employees(id serial, name varchar(50), room int4, salary int4);
INSERT INTO employees (name, room, salary) VALUES ('Paul', 1, 3000);
INSERT INTO employees (name, room, salary) VALUES ('Josef', 1, 2945);
INSERT INTO employees (name, room, salary) VALUES ('Linda', 2, 3276);
INSERT INTO employees (name, room, salary) VALUES ('Carla', 1, 1200);
INSERT INTO employees (name, room, salary) VALUES ('Hillary', 2, 4210);
INSERT INTO employees (name, room, salary) VALUES ('Alice', 3, 1982);
INSERT INTO employees (name, room, salary) VALUES ('Hugo', 4, 1982);
```

Our target is to write a function that checks whether a user is in the table and performs an INSERT or an UPDATE operation:

```
CREATE FUNCTION insertupdate(text, int4) RETURNS bool AS '
        DECLARE
                intext  ALIAS FOR $1;
                newsal  ALIAS FOR $2;
                checkit record;
```

```
        BEGIN
                SELECT INTO checkit * FROM employees
                        WHERE name=intext;
                IF NOT FOUND THEN
                        INSERT INTO employees(name, room, salary)
                        VALUES(intext,''1'',newsal);
                        RETURN ''t'';
                ELSE
                        UPDATE employees SET
                                salary=newsal, room=checkit.room
                        WHERE name=intext;
                        RETURN ''f'';
                END IF;
                RETURN ''t'';
        END;
' LANGUAGE 'plpgsql';
```

In the DECLARE section, a variable called checkit is defined as type record. In PostgreSQL, the datatype record is used to store entire rows. The SELECT statement assigns the entire row returned by it to checkit. If no rows match the SELECT statements, PL/pgSQL performs an INSERT statement and inserts the value of intext, 1, and the value of newsal into the database.

If a row is found, an UPDATE query is performed.

> **Note**
> If a SELECT statement returns more than one row, all rows but the first will silently be omitted by the database in case of a SELECT INTO recordname statement.

Let's take a closer look at the INSERT statement.

In PL/pgSQL, variables such as intext have to be used without using quotes; otherwise, the name of the variable would be interpreted as a string. Values, however, have to be used quoted (with single quotes).

PL/pgSQL functions are passed to the server as one string with single quotes. Single quotes within that string have to be escaped.

This can easily be done by writing '' instead of ' (two single quotes instead of one single quote). An example for escaping a character is RETURN ''t'' instead of RETURN 't', as it would be in the psql shell.

In the example database, the function insertupdate(text, int4) can be called with the name and the salary of the person that should be inserted or updated:

```
yourdb=# SELECT insertupdate('Alf',700);
 insertupdate
--------------
 t
(1 row)
```

The database now contains a person named `Alf` who has a salary of `700`. This can easily be found out by using this command:

```
SELECT * FROM employees WHERE name='Alf';
```

Here is the result:

```
 id | name | room | salary
----+------+------+--------
  8 | Alf  |    1 |    700
(1 row)
```

Let's call the function `insertupdate(text, int4)` again:

```
yourdb=# SELECT insertupdate('Alf',1250);

 insertupdate

--------------

 f

(1 row)
```

And the result:

```
SELECT * FROM employees WHERE name='Alf';


 id | name | room | salary
----+------+------+--------
  8 | Alf  |    1 |   1250
(1 row)
```

An important issue can be found in the UPDATE query:

The salary is set to its new value, and `room` is set to `checkit.room`.

Setting room to checkit.room is redundant, because room already has the value of checkit.room. We included this into the statement to show you how a variable of type record can be accessed in PL/pgSQL. The syntax is simple:

Just add a dot and the name of the column to the variable's name.

Working with SELECT and Loops

Sometimes SELECT statements return multiple rows. In case of SELECT INTO, everything but the first row is silently omitted by PL/pgSQL. In this section, you explore an example where a SELECT that returns multiple rows is processed using a simple FOR loop without losing data:

```
CREATE FUNCTION countsel(text) RETURNS int4 AS '
        DECLARE
                inchar  ALIAS FOR $1;
                colval  record;
                tmp     text;
                result  int4;
        BEGIN
                result = 0;
                FOR colval IN SELECT name FROM employees LOOP
                        tmp := substr(colval.name, 1, 1);
                        IF      tmp = inchar THEN
                                result := result + 1;
                        END IF;
                END LOOP;
        RETURN result;
        END;
' LANGUAGE 'plpgsql';
```

The function can be used to find out how many records start with a certain character in column employees.name.

The parameter inchar is used to pass the letter to look for to the function. Then a variable called colval is defined as record.

In the FOR loop, all records returned by the SELECT statement are assigned to colval, one each time the loop is processed.

Exception Handling

PostgreSQL has an exception handling model that is far from perfect.

It is extremely difficult to find out where the real error occurred and what to do about it.

Exception handling is an extremely important matter in all programming languages. Sometimes functions can't go on calculating the result of a function call, and an error has to be displayed. The following example shows you how the sum of integer values reaching from a lower limit to a higher limit can be found by using Carl Friedrich Gauss's formula for finding the sum of an arithmetic progression.

> **Note**
> The sum of integer values from 1 to n can easily be found with the formula
> $(n+1)*n/2$.

```
CREATE FUNCTION calcsum(int4, int4) RETURNS int4 AS '
     DECLARE
               lower   ALIAS FOR $1;
               higher  ALIAS FOR $2;
               lowres  int4;
               lowtmp  int4;
               highres int4;
               result  int4;
     BEGIN
               IF (lower < 1) OR (higher < 1) THEN
               RAISE EXCEPTION ''both param. have to be > 0'';
               ELSE
                         IF      (lower <= higher) THEN
                                 lowtmp  := lower - 1;
                                 lowres  := (lowtmp+1)*lowtmp/2;
                                 highres := (higher+1)*higher/2;
                                 result  := highres-lowres;
                         ELSE
                                 RAISE EXCEPTION ''The first value (%) has to be
higher than the second value (%)'', higher, lower;

                         END IF;
               END IF;
               RETURN result;
     END;
' LANGUAGE 'plpgsql';
```

If the lower value or the higher value is smaller than 1, we want the function to raise an exception and to abort calculation. Displaying exceptions can easily be done with the RAISE EXCEPTION command. The error message the function will display has to be written between single quotes (two single quotes are necessary because the single quotes have to be escaped).

We also want to display an error when the lower value is higher than the higher value passed to the function. In this case, we want our error message to contain the two values. The symbol % can be used to put variables into the error message—in this example, the first % is substituted by higher, the second % by lower.

Making Functions More Independent from Datatypes

Sometimes a datatype for a column is not suitable any more. Imagine a text field for storing names that is currently a char(20) field. Someone decides to enlarge the field to char(30)—dumping the database, changing the attributes of the field, and reinsertings the data into the table. And what about our dozens of functions? In this case, it is useful to have functions that are as independent from datatypes as possible.

PostgreSQL offers some powerful but easy methods for obtaining this goal. Let's take a look at the following example:

```
CREATE FUNCTION checksal(text) RETURNS int4 AS '
        DECLARE
                inname  ALIAS FOR $1;
                sal     employees%ROWTYPE;
                myval   employees.salary%TYPE;

        BEGIN
                SELECT INTO myval salary
                        FROM employees WHERE name=inname;
                RETURN myval;
        END;
' LANGUAGE 'plpgsql';
```

Let's run the code:

```
SELECT checksal('Paul');
```

The result contains one record:

```
 checksal
----------
     3000
(1 row)
```

This function can be used to retrieve the salary of a person from the table employees. In the database we used before, the field salary is a 4-byte integer. But who would like to rewrite the function if salary becomes numeric?

The solution of the problem lies in the capability of PostgreSQL of assigning a datatype of a certain field or a row to a variable. In this case, we assign the datatype of the column `salary` in table `employees` to `myval`. We have added an additional line in the `DECLARE` section to show you how the type of a row can be assigned to a variable.

`ROWTYPE` and `TYPE` can sometimes be very tricky and should be used carefully. Imagine a function that simply divides one value by another. If both values and the result are integer values, everything will be okay; but what if the result is not an integer value? Problems like that can easily occur when changing datatypes (let's say for example, from numeric to integer). Remember that when you change datatypes, the result of a function can suddenly be wrong and the function won't display an error.

The following example should point out the problem more clearly:

```
mydb=# select 5/2;
 ?column?
----------
 2
(1 row)
```

The result of 5 divided by 2 is 2.5, but PostgreSQL silently casts to `integer`. Here is an even more interesting one:

```
mydb=# select timestamp(5000000/2);
       timestamp
-----------------------
 1970-01-29 23:26:40+01
(1 row)
```

PostgreSQL adds 2,500,000 microseconds to January 1, 1970 (UNIX starting time).

Writing Triggers

Triggers are used to call predefined functions after certain events. Let's assume a real-world example. We use a database to store all sales of a shop. Whenever a product is bought, the price, the number of products sold, and the name of the products have to be inserted into a table. Because we want to know the exact time we sold the products, we create a trigger that inserts the current time into a certain column automatically.

Our table looks like this:

```
shop=# \d shop
          Table "shop"
```

```
Attribute |   Type    | Modifier
----------+-----------+----------
prodname  | text      |
price     | integer   |
amount    | integer   |
sold      | timestamp |
```

Before an example of a trigger is presented, look at the online help available about triggers:

```
yourdb=# \h CREATE TRIGGER
Command:     CREATE TRIGGER
Description: Creates a new trigger
Syntax:
CREATE TRIGGER name { BEFORE | AFTER } { event [OR ...] }
    ON table FOR EACH { ROW | STATEMENT }
    EXECUTE PROCEDURE func ( arguments )
```

Triggers define the kind of action that has be performed after or before events such as INSERT or UPDATE operations. Usually a function is executed by the trigger.

Here are the code of the function and the code of the trigger:

```
CREATE FUNCTION timetrigger() RETURNS opaque AS '
        BEGIN
                UPDATE shop SET sold=''now'' WHERE sold IS NULL;
                RETURN NEW;
        END;
' LANGUAGE 'plpgsql';


CREATE TRIGGER inserttime AFTER INSERT
        ON shop FOR EACH ROW EXECUTE
PROCEDURE timetrigger();
```

First, the function used by the trigger has to be implemented. After that, the trigger for a certain event can be created. In this case, the trigger is fired after an INSERT operation on shop. We use the now function to get the current time.

Let's see what happens when inserting data into the table:

```
INSERT INTO shop (prodname,price,amount)
        VALUES('Knuth''s Biography',39,1);
```

Here is the result:

```
 SELECT * FROM shop ;
```

```
    prodname     | price | amount |        sold
-----------------+-------+--------+-----------------------
 Knuth's Biography |   39 |      1 | 2001-03-05 01:49:03+01
(1 row)
```

You can see that a correct timestamp can be found in shop.sold.

> **Note**
> Trigger procedures are created as functions with no arguments and a return type of
> opaque. opaque is a datatype that is used only in combination with triggers. It can be
> compared to void (C datatype).

Automatically Created Variables

Triggers create special variables when being executed. This section gives you a short overview of these variables. It is taken from the official PostgreSQL manual and has been adopted slightly.:

- NEW holds the new database row on INSERT/UPDATE statements on row-level triggers. The datatype of NEW is record.

- OLD contains the old database row on UPDATE/DELETE operations on row-level triggers. The datatype is record.

- TG_NAME contains the name of the trigger that is actually fired (datatype name).

- TG_WHEN contains either AFTER or BEFORE (see the syntax overview of triggers shown earlier).

- TG_LEVEL tells whether the trigger is a ROW or a STATEMENT trigger (datatype text).

- TG_OP tells which operation the current trigger has been fired for (INSERT, UPDATE, or DELETE; datatype text).

- TG_RELID contains the object ID (datatype oid), and TG_RELNAME (datatype name) contains the name of the table the trigger is fired for.

- TG_RELNAME contains the name of the table that caused the trigger invocation. The datatype of the return value is name.

- TG_ARGV[] contains the arguments from the CREATE TRIGGER statement in an array of text.

- TG_NARGS is used to store the number of arguments passed to the trigger in the CREATE TRIGGER statement. The arguments themselves are stored in an array called TG_ARGV[] (datatype array of text). TG_ARGV[] is indexed starting with 0.

Some of these variables are helpful for debugging trigger functions. `TG_OP`, for example, can be used to find out why a trigger has been executed and what event caused the trigger to be fired.

Oracle's PL/SQL and PL/pgSQL—Comparing Two Worlds

This section is mainly dedicated to those who want to port their PL/SQL functions from Oracle to PostgreSQL, but we also want to point out some major differences between the two languages to ensure that people make their decision of whether to use Oracle or PostgreSQL objectively.

PL/pgSQL and PL/pgSQL are similar in many respects. Not only are both languages block-oriented and directly executed by the database, PL/SQL and PL/pgSQL have many more things in common.

The Main Differences

Although PostgreSQL's PL/pgSQL does not have as many features as Oracle's PL/SQL, PL/pgSQL can be used to build functions with tremendous functionality. But there are major differences between the two.

Quoting

The most apparent difference is that the programmer needs to be careful with single quotes. This circumstance can lead to quite interesting pieces of code. Imagine a situation where two single quotes are used in the result:

```
CREATE FUNCTION testfunc() RETURNS text AS '
      DECLARE
              a text;
      BEGIN
              a := ''many quotes: \'\'\'\' '';
              RETURN a;
      END;
' LANGUAGE 'plpgsql';
```

Every quote in the output has to be masked using a backslash. Single quotes that are part of the function code have to be masked using two single quotes:

```
CREATE FUNCTION testfunc() RETURNS text AS '
      BEGIN
              RETURN ''t'';
      END;
' LANGUAGE 'plpgsql';
```

To use one single quote in the PL/pgSQL function, we have to send two single quotes to the function in order to escape one single quote.

Function Overloading

PostgreSQL supports function overloading, which can be used as a workaround for the lack of default parameters. Function overloading is a powerful feature that fits well into PostgreSQL's object-oriented concepts. Keep in mind that DROP FUNCTION has to be called with the correct parameters; otherwise, the wrong function gets dropped.

PostgreSQL and Database Cursors

Oracle's PL/SQL has sophisticated and highly developed concepts for cursors, which is quite an advantage over PL/pgSQL. In PostgreSQL, the lack of Oracle-like cursors can be worked around by using queries in combination with FOR loops. To refresh your memory, review the example of this in the section titled "Using LOOP/EXIT, WHILE, and FOR Loops," earlier in this chapter.

Creating and Replacing Functions

In Oracle, functions can easily be created and replaced by using CREATE OR REPLACE FUNCTION." In PostgreSQL, functions have to be dropped and created explicitly with DROP FUNCTION functionname(datatype, ...) and CREATE FUNCTION.

Making Life Easier with instr

Oracle datatbases provide a function called instr, which is used to obtain the corresponding position of a pattern match in a given FILE or LOB. PL/pgSQL does not, unlike Oracle, offer an instr() function. This does not make life easier for PostgreSQL users, so some people have written various versions of instr() functions that can be found on the Internet.

Locking Tables

PostgreSQL supports sophisticated locking mechanisms. When a PL/pgSQL function locks a table, as in the following command, the lock is released when the PL/pgSQL function resumes:

```
LOCK TABLE employees IN EXCLUSIVE MODE;
```

Functions and Transactions

You can't have transactions in PL/pgSQL functions. Every function is executed in one transaction, and an implicit ROLLBACK is performed if something goes wrong inside the function. This protects both the database and the programmer if something dangerous happens inside a transaction.

CHAPTER 6

Database Administration

How to Configure PostgreSQL

This chapter is dedicated to all database administrators and to those who want to become PostgreSQL administrators. Database administration can be either a simple or a difficult task, depending on the demands your database has to face and the level of security you have to provide.

PostgreSQL is indeed a database system that can easily be administered as long as the database administrator (DBA) understands the basic concepts of databases, backup strategies, and security issues. Security demands are always increasing and it is necessary to have a high standard for security, even if your database is only used in a protected environment. But let's get to some practical stuff.

Configuring the Postmaster

The heart of every PostgreSQL database server is the so called *"postmaster*, the supervisor daemon of your database. The postmaster has a lot of parameters that can be configured to make your database run better and faster.

By using

```
postmaster --help
```

we can get a little help about working with the postmaster.

On Unix systems, the postmaster is usually started when the default runlevel starts its processes, but it can also be started manually. No matter how the postmaster is started, you can use the flags just shown. Let's take a closer look at some flags.

- -B   Defines the number of shared memory buffers PostgreSQL uses for the backend processes. One shared memory buffer is usually 8KB, but the size can be redefined in `src/include/config.h` (see `BLCKSZ`).

- -D   Specifies the directory PostgreSQL will use for the data. `-D` defines the root directory of a cluster of databases. If the database directories are not defined via the shell, PostgreSQL will use the environment variable `$PGDATA` instead. If you want to set this variable, check out your Unix manual and look for the `export` command (Bourne Shell).

- -N   Sets the maximum number of backend processes that are allowed to run on the machine. The default value is set to 32 but can also be changed in `src/include/config.h`.

- -S   Starts the postmaster in silent mode, which means that all messages the postmaster normally produces—no matter whether on standard output or standard error—are redirected to `/dev/null`. This is extremely bad for troubleshooting because you will loose important information.

- -d   Defines the debugging level your PostgreSQL server will use. The debugging level can be set from 1 to 5. The higher the debugging level is, the more information will be displayed. In most cases, it is useful to redirect the output to a file because this is the only way to get a complete history of what is going on with your PostgreSQL server.

- -i   Allows remote users to connect to your PostgreSQL server. Without `-i` set, only local Unix domain socket connections can be established.

- -l   Provides secure connections in combination with the `-i` flag. This works only when SSL has been enabled at compile time.

- -o   Passes options to the backend processes. This can be very useful when tuning or debugging your server. Many users consider `-o` more comfortable than editing files.

- -p   Defines the port your server will use. If no port is defined, PostgreSQL will use the value of the environment variable `$PGPORT`. Normally, PostgreSQL uses 5432 as the default port (the value that is usually compiled into the binaries).

> **Note**
> All changes that are done in `src/include/config.h` require a recompile of
> PostgreSQL.

If you want to start PostgreSQL using an `init` script, the parameters passed to the
postmaster have to be added to the `init` scripts in `/etc/rc.d/init.d` for users of
RedHat Linux or `/etc/init.d` for users of Debian Linux. Just go through the shell
script and add the desired flags to the section where `pg_ctl` is started. `init` scripts are
very hardware dependent, so there is more than just one way of how things can be
done.

PostgreSQL 7.1—The `pg_options` **File**

PostgreSQL databases version 7.1 use a file called `pg_options` to configure runtime
parameters. The `pg_options` file is used to configure a variety of parameters. It can
usually be found in `$PGDATA/data`. All values defined in `pg_options` can be changed at
runtime. You don't have to restart PostgreSQL because the parameters in `pg_options`
are re-read when a new backend starts, becase everytime the backend is started a
connection to the PostgreSQL database is established.

This feature is extremely useful because it avoids unpleasant downtimes.

> **Note**
> Queries that are already running are not affected by the changes.

The syntax of the `pg_options` file is extremely simple, a shown in the following:

```
verbose=2
query=2
syslog=0
```

First `verbose` is set to two which makes PostgreSQL display some runtime
information on the screen. The seond line tells PostgreSQL to print information
about queries. Syslog is turned off so that all information is sent to `stdout` and `stderr`.
Adding an option can easily be done by adding it to the file. The following is a
complete list of all currently supported options:

- `all`   `all` is the global trace flag. It can be set to `0` (trace messages enabled
  individually), `1` (enable all trace messages), or `-1` (disable all trace messages).
  Tracing means that the internals of the database can be monitored.

- `verbose`   The `verbose` flag is used to define the amount of message the database
  provides. `0` means that no messages are displayed. `1` provides more messages, and
  `2` displays as many messages as possible.

- `query`   This flag is used to define the way queries are traced. `0` means that no query is displayed, `1` writes one line per query, and `4` prints the full query.

- `plan`   Prints the query plan.

- `parse`   Prints the output of the parser.

- `rewritten`   Prints rewritten queries.

- `pretty_plan`   Pretty-print query plan.

- `pretty_parse`   Prints pretty-print parser output.

- `pretty_rewritten`   Prints pretty-print rewritten queries.

- `parsestats`   Prints the statistics of the parser.

- `plannerstats`   Prints the statistics of the planner.

- `executorstats`   Prints the statistics of the executor.

- `locks`   Used to trace locking.

- `userlocks`   Used to trace user locks.

- `spinlocks`   Used to trace spin locks.

- `notify`   Used to trace notify functions.

- `lock_debug_oidmin`   Minimum relation `oid` traced by locks.

- `lock_debug_relid`   `oid`, if not zero, of relation traced by locks.

- `deadlock_timeout`   Deadlock check timer.

- `syslog`   Defines the behavior of `syslog`. `0` prints all messages to standard output or standard error, `1` prints all messages to standard output, standard error, and `syslog`. `2` sends the messages to `syslog` only.

- `hostlookup`   Enables hostname lookups in `ps_status`.

- `showportnumber`   Shows port numbers in `ps_status`.

- `nofsync`   Disables `fsync` on a per-backend basis.

The `nofsync` flag may be especially interesting for you, and it is worth going into a little more into detail. `int fsync(int fd)` can be found in the `unistd.h` C library and is used to flush all data to disk. This is useful because it protects your data from being lost when the machine crashes. But `fsync` can also cost a lot of performance when dealing with huge amounts of data. We will focus on the performance aspect of `fsync` in Chapter 8, called "Performance Tuning."

PostgreSQL 7.1—postgreSQL.conf

Since PostgreSQL 7.1, all runtime parameters can be found in postgresql.conf. Like its predecessor, the file can be found in $PGDATA/data. Let's take a look at the default config file:

```
#
# PostgreSQL configuration file
# ---------------------------
#
# This file consists of lines of the form
#
#    name = value
#
# (The `=' is optional.) White space is collapsed, comments are
# introduced by `#' anywhere on a line. The complete list of option
# names and allowed values can be found in the PostgreSQL
# documentation. Examples are:

#log_connections = on
#fsync = off
#max_connections = 64

# Any option can also be given as a command line switch to the
# postmaster, e.g., 'postmaster -c log_connections=on'. Some options
# can be set at run-time with the 'SET' SQL command.


#=========================================================================


#
#     Connection Parameters
#
#tcpip_socket = false
#ssl = false

#max_connections = 32 # 1-1024

#port = 5432
#hostname_lookup = false
#show_source_port = false
```

```
#unix_socket_directory = ''
#unix_socket_group = ''
#unix_socket_permissions = 0777

#virtual_host = ''

#krb_server_keyfile = ''

#
#     Performance
#
#sort_mem = 512
#shared_buffers = 2*max_connections # min 16
#fsync = true

#
#     Optimizer Parameters
#
#enable_seqscan = true
#enable_indexscan = true
#enable_tidscan = true
#enable_sort = true
#enable_nestloop = true
#enable_mergejoin = true
#enable_hashjoin = true

#ksqo = false
#geqo = true

#effective_cache_size = 1000   # default in 8k pages
#random_page_cost = 4
#cpu_tuple_cost = 0.01
#cpu_index_tuple_cost = 0.001
#cpu_operator_cost = 0.0025
#geqo_selection_bias = 2.0 # range 1.5-2.0

#
#     GEQO Optimizer Parameters
#
#geqo_threshold = 11
#geqo_pool_size = 0   #default based in tables, range 128-1024
#geqo_effort = 1
```

```
#geqo_generations = 0
#geqo_random_seed = -1 # auto-compute seed


#
#     Inheritance
#
#sql_inheritance = true


#
#     Deadlock
#
#deadlock_timeout = 1000


#
#     Expression Depth Limitation
#
#max_expr_depth = 10000 # min 10


#
#     Write-ahead log (WAL)
#
#wal_buffers = 8 # min 4
#wal_files = 0 # range 0-64
#wal_sync_method = fsync # fsync or fdatasync or open_sync or open_datasync
# Note: default wal_sync_method varies across platforms
#wal_debug = 0 # range 0-16
#commit_delay = 0 # range 0-100000
#commit_siblings = 5 # range 1-1000
#checkpoint_segments = 3 # in logfile segments (16MB each), min 1
#checkpoint_timeout = 300 # in seconds, range 30-3600


#
#     Debug display
#
#silent_mode = false

#log_connections = false
#log_timestamp = false
#log_pid = false

#debug_level = 0 # range 0-16
```

```
#debug_print_query = false
#debug_print_parse = false
#debug_print_rewritten = false
#debug_print_plan = false
#debug_pretty_print = false

#ifdef USE_ASSERT_CHECKING
#debug_assertions = true
#endif

#
#     Syslog
#
#ifdef ENABLE_SYSLOG
#syslog = 0 # range 0-2
#syslog_facility = 'LOCAL0'
#syslog_ident = 'postgres'
#endif

#
#     Statistics
#
#show_parser_stats = false
#show_planner_stats = false
#show_executor_stats = false
#show_query_stats = false
#ifdef BTREE_BUILD_STATS
#show_btree_build_stats = false
#endif

#
#     Lock Tracing
#
#trace_notify = false
#ifdef LOCK_DEBUG
#trace_locks = false
#trace_userlocks = false
#trace_spinlocks = false
#debug_deadlocks = false
#trace_lock_oidmin = 16384
#trace_lock_table = 0
#endif
```

We will take a look at the most important parameters that affect your daily work with PostgreSQL.

- `log_connections`   Prints one line for every connection established to the server.

- `fsync`   Tells the database whether to turn `fsync()` on or off. If `fsync()` is on, the database makes sure that the data is physically written to disk.

- `max_connections`   By default, PostgreSQL allows 32 simultaneous connections. This value can be changed by setting `max_connections` to the desired value. By default, there is a compile limit of 1024 connections, which can only be changed by recompiling the server.

- `tcpip_socket`   If this flag is turned on, PostgreSQL accepts TCP/IP connections and not only Unix domain socket connections.

- `ssl`   Enables secure connections via SSL.

- `port`   Defines the TCP-port to which the server is listening. This value can only be set when the server starts; you can't change it for individual backend processes.

- `hostname_lookup`   If you want hostnames instead of IP addresses to be logged, `hostname_lookup` has to be turned on. Don't forget that DNS lookups can take some time.

- `show_source_port`   With this flag enabled, the database shows the outgoing port of the host connecting to PostgreSQL.

- `unix_socket_directory`   Defines the directory of the Unix domain socket the postmaster is listening to for connections from client applications. The default value is usually set to `/tmp`.

- `unix_socket_group`   Defines the group owner of the Unix domain socket. By default, it is an empty string, which means that the default group of the current user is taken.

- `unix_socket_permissions`   The value must be defined by using the default Unix syntax for setting file system permissions. For example, `0777` means that everybody can connect.

- `virtual_host`   Works pretty much the same like Apache's `virtual_host` directly. By default, PostgreSQL listens to all hostnames assigned to the machine.

- `krb_server_keyfile`   Defines the location of the Kerberos key file.

- `sort_mem`   If PostgreSQL has to sort data, it is usually done in memory as long as the size of the sort buffer is not exceeded. If that happens, the database uses temporary files for sorting. Compared to sorting in memory, this is ghastly slow, but if the amount of data that has to be processed is extremely huge, it cannot be done in any other way. Keep in mind that if many concurrent sorts are running, the amount of memory defined by `sort_mem` is used multiple times. The size of the sort buffer is defined in kilobytes.

- `shared_buffers`   Sets the shared memory buffers the database will use. A buffer is usually 8KB; the default value is set to 32.

- `enable_seqscan`   If you want to avoid the planner using sequential scans, you can unset the `enable_seqscan` flag. It is not possible to turn sequential scans off completely, but their use can be reduced to the minimum.

- `enable_indexscan`   Defines whether the database use indexscans.

- `enable_tidscan`   Defines whether the planner uses TID scan plan types.

- `enable_sort`   If you want to influence the number of sort operations, you can unset the `enable_sort` flag. Sorting can be turned off completely because the planner cannot always find a workaround.

- `enable_nestloop`   Enables the use of nested loops.

- `enable_mergejoin`   Enables the use of merge joins.

- `enable_hashjoins`   Enables the use of has joins.

- `ksqo`   The Key Set Query Optimizer (KSQO) makes the planner convert queries with many ANDs and ORs in the WHERE clause to queries using UNION. This is usually done when working with Microsoft Access.

- `geqo`   Defines whether generic query optimization is used. Generic query optimization means that query planning is done without exhaustive searching. The database uses on by default.

- `effective_cache_size`   Defines the value the optimizer assumes for the size of the disk cache.

- `random_page_cost`   In many cases, PostgreSQL cannot do sequential reading. Jumping from block to block takes longer than sequential reading. `random_page_cost` can be used to tell the query optimizer how much longer random reading takes (for example, 4 times). This is a floating point value and allows very fine tuning.

- `cpu_tuple_cost`   Defines the value the optimizer will assume to process a tuple. It is measured as a fraction of the cost of a sequential page fetch.

- `cpu_index_tuple_cost`   Similar to `cpu_tuple_cost` but sets the time for processing a tuple using an index.

- `cpu_operator_cost`   Sets the time to process an operator in a `WHERE` clause. It is also measured as a fraction of the cost of a sequential scan.

- `sql_inheritance`   Defines the behavior of the database when dealing with inheritance. As described in the section called "Inheritance" in Chapter 8), PostgreSQL treats inherited tables slightly different. If you find the old way better, set this value to `off`.

- `deadlock_timeout`   In a few cases, the database has to face a deadlock. `deadlock_timeout` defines the time to wait when waiting for a lock before checking whether the conditions for a deadlock are fulfilled. The time is measured in milliseconds.

- `max_expr_depth`   Tells the database how many expressions can be nested within each other. If this is set to a very high value, the backend can crash because of buffer overflows.

- `wal_buffers`   Defines the number of disk page buffers stored in shared memory for WAL log. WAL is short for Write Ahead Log.

- `wal_files`   PostgreSQL creates log files in advance. `wal_files` defines how many of these files are created.

- `silent_mode`   This has actually the same effect as the `-S` flag of the postmaster. No standard error and no standard output is produced.

- `log_timestamp`   Adds a timestamp to each entry in the logfile. The default value is set to `off`, but we strongly recommend that you turn it on, because it allows you to find out what kind of action was performed by the database.

- `log_pid`   The process ID can be added to every entry in the logfile by using the `log_pid` flag.

- `debug_level`   The higher this value is, the more debugging information will be displayed. The default value is set to `0`. During development, it is useful to turn the debug level up and then down again for production.

- `syslog`   `syslog` is a powerful logging tool supported by all current Linux distributions. If this value is set to `0`, `syslog` is turned off completely. `1` means that messages are written to standard output and `syslog`. If you use `2`, `syslog` only is used.

`postgresql.conf` is simply a wonderful thing. All major configuration tasks can be done within just one file, and this makes PostgreSQL administration even more simple.

Adding Users and Managing User Rights

Managing user rights in PostgreSQL is an important thing. However, PostgreSQL's system for managing user rights is not that sophisticated as yet. In this section, you will learn the basics of PostgreSQL's way of managing users.

A General Overview

One of the primary tasks of a database administrator is user management. Managing users is an extremely important issue, not only in multiuser environments. Restrictions for certain users do not only protect your database from being accessed by someone who is not allowed to modify the data, it also helps you to protect yourself from accidental operations.

PostgreSQL offers a Unix-like system for managing users. Users can be assigned to groups and therefore have certain rights for modifying certain tables. All user information, as you might expect, is stored in tables. This is done by almost all advanced databases.

The supervisor user is called `postgres`. The `postgres` user has all rights and is allowed to perform all modifications.

Adding and Deleting Users

Let's come to some practical stuff and create some users. PostgreSQL offers two methods for creating new users. One is to use a simple SQL command, and the other one is to use a simple program called `createuser`. Let's take a look at the `createuser` program first because this will give you a good overview of the options we have when creating users. To find out more about `createuser` use

`createuser --help`

in your favorite Unix shell.

```
createuser creates a new PostgreSQL user.

Usage:
  createuser [options] [username]
```

```
Options:
  -d, --createdb              User can create new databases
  -D, --no-createdb           User cannot create databases
  -a, --adduser               User can add new users
  -A, --no-adduser            User cannot add new users
  -i, --sysid=SYSID           Select sysid for new user
  -P, --pwprompt              Assign a password to new user
  -h, --host=HOSTNAME         Database server host
  -p, --port=PORT             Database server port
  -U, --username=USERNAME     Username to connect as (not the one to create)
  -W, --password              Prompt for password to connect
  -e, --echo                  Show the query being sent to the backend
  -q, --quiet                 Don't write any messages

Report bugs to <pgsql-bugs@postgresql.org>.
```

You can see that there are quite a few options when creating a new user. In the following example, we create a user called epi who will not be allowed to create new databases but will be allowed to create new users. The user will have the password anypasswd. To show you what happens inside the database, we have enabled the -e (echo) flag:

```
bash-2.04$ createuser -D -a -P -e epi
Enter password for user "epi":
Enter it again:
CREATE USER "epi" WITH  PASSWORD 'anypasswd' NOCREATEDB CREATEUSER
CREATE USER
```

PostgreSQL performs a simple SQL command to create the new user. We could have used the same SQL command with psql to achieve the result.

The CREATE USER command has a variety of options:

```
persons=# \h CREATE USER
Command:     CREATE USER
Description: Creates a new database user
Syntax:
CREATE USER username
    [ WITH
    [ SYSID uid ]
    [ PASSWORD 'password' ] ]
    [ CREATEDB   | NOCREATEDB ] [ CREATEUSER | NOCREATEUSER ]
    [ IN GROUP    groupname [, ...] ]
    [ VALID UNTIL  'abstime' ]
```

You may have noticed that the flags of the createuser program are very similar to the options of the CREATE USER command because createuser produces SQL. That is not surprising.

The following is another example of a CREATE USER command:

```
CREATE USER hans WITH PASSWORD 'anypasswd';
```

Now we want to connect to the database as user hans. We have to use an additional flag when starting psql. -U defines the user we want to use to connect to the database:

```
psql -U hans shop
```

If the user has successfully been created, the command above should work. We can now work with the database and do all modifications we are allowed to do.

As we have mentioned before, user information is stored in tables. In the case of PostgreSQL, we can use the view called pg_user to check for user information:

```
persons=# \d pg_user
          View "pg_user"
  Attribute   |  Type    | Modifier
--------------+----------+-----------
 usename      | name     |
 usesysid     | integer  |
 usecreatedb  | boolean  |
 usetrace     | boolean  |
 usesuper     | boolean  |
 usecatupd    | boolean  |
 passwd       | text     |
 valuntil     | abstime  |
View definition: SELECT pg_shadow.usename, pg_shadow.usesysid,
pg_shadow.usecreatedb, pg_shadow.usetrace, pg_shadow.usesuper, pg_shadow.
usecatupd, '********'::text
AS passwd, pg_shadow.valuntil FROM pg_shadow;
```

pg_user combines a lot of information. Let's see what is already in pg_user:

```
persons=# SELECT * FROM pg_user;
 usename | usesysid | usecreatedb | usetrace | usesuper | usecatupd |  passwd
|
valuntil
----------+----------+-------------+----------+----------+-----------+----------
+----------
 postgres |       26 | t           | t        | t        | t         | ********
```

```
|
 hans        |         27 | f             | f          | f          | f           | ********
|
 epi         |         28 | f             | f          | t          | t           | ********
|
(3 rows)
```

The users postgres, hans, and epi are already in the table. Every user has been assigned a unique user ID, and we can see in the various columns which of the most important rights a user has. We have created the user epi with the -D flag. As you can see in the previous table, the column called usercreatedb is false for user epi.

The password is not listed in plain text because this would be indeed very insecure—everybody could read it. We can see in the definition of the view that the column containing the password is in pg_shadow. Let's try to query pg_shadow as user epi:

```
shop=> SELECT * FROM pg_shadow;
ERROR:  pg_shadow: Permission denied.
```

User epi doesn't have the right to do that. Let's try as user postgres:

```
persons=# SELECT usename, passwd FROM pg_shadow;
 usename  |  passwd
----------+-----------
 postgres |
 hans     | anypasswd
 epi      | anypasswd
(3 rows)
```

Voilá, it works for user postgres because he is the super user. We can also see the passwords now.

For creating groups, PostgreSQL does not offer a command-line tool yet. The CREATE GROUP command creates a new group account using the values specified on the command line and the default values from the system. The syntax of CREATE GROUP is as simple as the syntax of the CREATE USER command:

```
persons=# \h CREATE GROUP
Command:     CREATE GROUP
Description: Creates a new group
Syntax:
CREATE GROUP name
    [ WITH
```

```
    [ SYSID gid ]
    [ USER  username [, ...] ] ]
```

We will create a group called cybertec that contains the users epi and hans:

```
CREATE GROUP cybertec WITH USER epi, hans;
```

There is only one line of SQL. We have to define the name of the new group and a list of all users that should be in that group.

The definition of a group is stored in the pg_group table. Look at the data structure:

```
persons=# \d pg_group
          Table "pg_group"
 Attribute |   Type    | Modifier
-----------+-----------+----------
 groname   | name      |
 grosysid  | integer   |
 grolist   | integer[] |
Indices: pg_group_name_index,
         pg_group_sysid_index
```

The first column stores the name of the group. The second is used to store the group ID, and the array in the first column contains a list of all group members. In our case, the table contains the definition of exactly one group:

```
persons=# SELECT * FROM pg_group;
 groname  | grosysid | grolist
----------+----------+---------
 cybertec |        1 | {28,27}
(1 row)
```

The third column of pg_group contains the IDs of the users and not the names. The values are stored in an array of integers.

One very important thing when creating new users is that the CREATE USER command is rather badly mislabeled. CREATE USER grants super user status to new users. This can lead to extremely critical security holes in your PostgreSQL system. For example, if user postgres creates a new user, let's say the name is paul, who is allowed to create new users but nothing else, paul is allowed to create new users who have more rights than he has. This is very critical because paul could grant himself additional rights with the help of a new user.

Keep this in mind when working with user rights. Most database systems, such as Oracle, treat user rights differently and are, in this case, safer than PostgreSQL. When working with PostgreSQL, avoid creating users that have the right to create new users.

If we want to get rid of a user or a group, we can use the DROP command. Imagine a situation where we want to remove the user called testuser from our database. This can be done with the following SQL statement:

```
DROP USER testuser;
```

If we want to remove the group called testuser, we can use the following command:

```
DROP GROUP testuser;
```

Changing User and Group Attributes

Creating users and groups is not enough. After your configuration is up and running, it can easily happen that changes have to be made. Almost all basic administration tasks can be done with the ALTER command.

Before we come to the sample code and some more details, the following is an overview of the syntax of ALTER USER and ALTER GROUP:

```
persons=# \h alter user
Command:     ALTER USER
Description: Modifies user account information
Syntax:
ALTER USER username
    [ WITH PASSWORD 'password' ]
    [ CREATEDB | NOCREATEDB ] [ CREATEUSER | NOCREATEUSER ]
    [ VALID UNTIL 'abstime' ]

persons=# \h alter group
Command:     ALTER GROUP
Description: Add users to a group, remove users from a group
Syntax:
ALTER GROUP name ADD USER username [, ... ]
ALTER GROUP name DROP USER username [, ... ]
```

One very important thing that sometimes has to be done is changing the password of a user. The following example will show how the password of user epi can be changed to anyagain:

```
ALTER USER epi WITH PASSWORD 'anyagain';
```

ALTER USER can also be used to grant or revoke rights from a user. The next example shows how we make user kertal a little more powerful:

```
ALTER USER kertal WITH PASSWORD 'anyagain'
        CREATEDB CREATEUSER VALID UNTIL '2005-04-12 14:22:35+02';
```

kertal has now the rights to create new users and databases. The only restriction is that his account is only valid until a certain date (defined by the VALID UNTIL command).

ALTER GROUP is used to add or remove users from a group. In the next example, we will remove user kertal from cybertec:

```
ALTER GROUP cybertec DROP USER kertal;
```

Let's check whether kertal is still in the group:

```
persons=# SELECT * FROM pg_group;
 groname  | grosysid | grolist
----------+----------+---------
 cybertec |        1 | {27,28}
(1 row)
```

kertal has been removed successfully. Because we want to re-employ kertal here at Cybertec, we will use the following command to add kertal to the group called cybertec again:

```
ALTER GROUP cybertec ADD USER kertal;
```

You can see that managing and maintaining the key attributes of users and groups are extremely easy tasks, and the whole process is as simple as maintaining user rights on a Unix system.

Using GRANT and REVOKE

This section of the book is dedicated to those who care about user rights and data security on their PostgreSQL servers. The privilege system of PostgreSQL allows the database administrator to define the abilities and rights of all users. The two most important commands when dealing with user rights are GRANT and REVOKE. GRANT is used to give a user certain rights, while REVOKE is used to take rights away from a user. GRANT and REVOKE can be used to modify the user rights of individual users, groups, and the so-called public. Public means that everybody gets or looses the right to perform a certain action.

Before we go into more detail and get to some practical examples; the following is what the database tells us about GRANT and REVOKE:

```
persons=# \h GRANT
Command:    GRANT
Description: Grants access privilege to a user, a group or all users
Syntax:
GRANT privilege [, ...] ON object [, ...]
    TO { PUBLIC | GROUP group | username }

persons=# \h REVOKE
Command:    REVOKE
Description: Revokes access privilege from a user, a group or all users.
Syntax:
REVOKE privilege [, ...]
    ON object [, ...]
    FROM { PUBLIC | GROUP groupname | username }
```

As you can see, GRANT and REVOKE need privileges and objects. Privileges are certain rights to perform certain operations.

We have compiled a complete list of all types of privileges provided by PostgreSQL:

- SELECT   Allows a user to access all columns of a table or a view.

- INSERT   Allows a user to perform INSERT operations on a certain table.

- UPDATE   Allows a user to update data in a table.

- DELETE   Allows a user to delete data in a table.

- RULE   Defines rules on a table or view.

- ALL   all is used to grant or revoke all these privileges at once.

Privileges are defined for objects. Objects can be tables, views, or sequences.

Before we get to some examples, we will show you how you can find what permissions are set for your objects. We will create a new table and check the permissions for that table by using the \z command:

```
persons=# CREATE TABLE hackers(name varchar(50), location varchar(50));
CREATE
persons=# \z
Access permissions for database "persons"
 Relation | Access permissions
```

```
----------+-------------------
 hackers  |
(1 row)
```

We have created the table as user `postgres`. If we want to insert data as user `epi`, we have the required permissions to do it:

```
persons=# INSERT INTO hackers VALUES ('Donald Becker',NULL);
INSERT 53792 1
```

If we don't want `epi` to insert data into that table anymore, we can revoke the permissions. In the following example, we revoke all rights on `hackers` from `epi`:

```
REVOKE ALL ON hackers FROM epi;
```

Now we connect to the database as `epi`:

```
[hs@duron hs]$ psql -U epi persons;
```

And now we will try to insert some data into the table:

```
persons=> INSERT INTO hackers VALUES ('Alexandre Julliard',NULL);
ERROR:  hackers: Permission denied.
```

Because `epi` does not have the permission to perform the operation, the `INSERT` fails.

The result of the `\z` command looks a little different now:

```
persons=# \z
Access permissions for database "persons"
 Relation | Access permissions
----------+-------------------
 hackers  | {"="}
(1 row)
```

If `epi` should have the permissions to perform `INSERT` and `UPDATE` operations, we can grant them to him. This operation has to be done as user `postgres`, because a user can't grant rights to himself.

> **Note**
> You can grant or revoke multiple privileges with just one SQL statement. For example,
> ```
> GRANT INSERT, UPDATE ON hackers TO epi;
> ```

\z shows us that `epi` has the required permissions now:

```
persons=# \z
Access permissions for database "persons"
 Relation | Access permissions
----------+--------------------
 hackers  | {"=","epi=aw"}
(1 row)
```

`epi` is now allowed to do a and w, but what does that mean? PostgreSQL uses shortcuts for displaying permissions. We have compiled a complete list of all shortcuts:

- r   SELECT

- w   UPDATE and DELETE

- a   INSERT

- R   rule

- arwR   Means that the user has all rights on a certain object.

User `epi` tries to perform the `INSERT` operation again:

```
persons=> INSERT INTO hackers VALUES ('Alexandre Julliard',NULL);
INSERT 37632 1
```

You can see that it works now.

Granting and revoking can be done for entire groups or for the public. This is very similar to the privilege system of Unix. Groups can be defined to save a lot of time when granting rights to many users.

If you want to know if you are allowed to grant or revoke rights from a table, you can use the \d command to see to whom a table belongs:

```
persons=> \d
        List of relations
    Name      | Type  | Owner
--------------+-------+----------
 hackers      | table | postgres
 kertalstable | table | kertal
(2 rows)
```

We recommend that you define a very restrictive set of permissions for your database because this can truly save you a lot of headache. The more rights users have, the more that can happen to your data. Not all problems are caused by "evil" persons. Many things can happen unexpectedly, and user rights can protect you from errors.

Many people might find user rights to be something really annoying, which can actually be true in many cases. But being annoyed, in most cases, is more comfortable than facing trouble when you can't recover your database.

Modifying Databases

After a data structure has been created, you may have to change it because of new demands or things you have not considered when developing the structure of the tables. In this case, modifications have to be performed. This section shows how that can be done.

A General Overview

Building advanced and modular data structures does not always completely protect you from modifying your data structure.

Renaming tables, dropping columns, or changing data types has always been something unpleasant when working with relational databases. Many databases support only fundamental features for changing existing databases or data structures.

This section is dedicated to all database administrators and developers who have to modify their PostgreSQL database. We will try to cover all crucial things concerning operations, such as changing the name of a table or modifying constraints.

Using ALTER

ALTER is an essential command when modifying objects, such as tables and users. In this section, you will learn to use ALTER efficiently.

A Short Overview

ALTER TABLE is an extremely useful command. We cannot only use it to add columns to a table (as we have seen), we can also use it to perform important changes.

Before we get to some real-world examples where we will use the ALTER TABLE command, let's take a look at the syntax overview:

```
Command:    ALTER TABLE
Description: Modifies table properties
Syntax:
ALTER TABLE table [ * ]
```

```
    ADD [ COLUMN ] column type
ALTER TABLE table [ * ]
    ALTER [ COLUMN ] column { SET DEFAULT value | DROP DEFAULT }
ALTER TABLE table [ * ]
    RENAME [ COLUMN ] column TO newcolumn
ALTER TABLE table
    RENAME TO newtable
ALTER TABLE table
    ADD table constraint definition
```

Now we'll present some examples that show you how you can effectively use the ALTER TABLE command.

Changing Names

In the previous section, we created a table called hackers, and we now want to rename it programmers.

ALTER TABLE hackers RENAME TO programmers;

If we have the permission to change the name, we have now successfully changed the name of the table:

```
persons=# \d programmers
        Table "programmers"
 Attribute |    Type     | Modifier
-----------+-------------+----------
 name      | varchar(50) |
 location  | varchar(50) |
```

Changing the name of a table is sometimes not enough. We will now rename a column in programmers table:

ALTER TABLE programmers RENAME location TO project;

Changing the name of a column is as easy as changing the name of a table. You can see in the example that the only thing we have to define is the name of the table we want to change, the old name of the column, and the new name for the column.

These changes are very easy, but how do these changes create an effect on tables or views related to that column?

How Changes Affect Objects Related to other Objects

In the following example, we will create a view that accesses the table we want to change and we will see what happens:

```
CREATE VIEW withname_view AS
        SELECT 'name: ' || name, project FROM programmers;
```

The view we have just defined does nothing more than add name: to the first column:

```
persons=# SELECT * FROM withname_view ;
        ?column?            | project
---------------------------+---------
 name: Donald Becker       |
 name: Alexandre Julliard  |
(2 rows)
```

The view is defined as:

```
persons=# \d withname_view
        View "withname_view"
 Attribute |    Type     | Modifier
-----------+-------------+---------
 ?column?  | varchar()   |
 project   | varchar(50) |
View definition: SELECT ('name: '::"varchar" || programmers.name),
programmers.project FROM programmers;
```

But what happens when we change the name of a column the view accesses? Let's perform the change:

```
persons=# ALTER TABLE programmers RENAME project TO softwareproject;
ALTER
persons=# SELECT * FROM withname_view;
        ?column?            | project
---------------------------+---------
 name: Donald Becker       |
 name: Alexandre Julliard  |
(2 rows)
```

We can see that the view still returns the right result for the query.

```
persons=# \d withname_view
        View "withname_view"
 Attribute |    Type     | Modifier
-----------+-------------+---------
 ?column?  | varchar()   |
 project   | varchar(50) |
View definition: SELECT ('name: '::"varchar" || programmers.name),
programmers.softwareproject AS project FROM programmers;
```

When looking at the definition of the view, we recognize that project has been changed to softwareproject automatically. This is indeed very comfortable and takes away a lot of troubles when working with PostgreSQL. Imagine a situation where you have to deal with dozens of tables or views that are all related to each other. It would be a nightmare to have to make all changes in all those views manually. PostgreSQL does the job for you.

Dropping Columns

Sometimes, sweeping your database might be a very useful task. The "cut off your toe" approach to database alteration can bring back some simplicity and clarity to your data structure and save a lot of disk space. But how can we remove columns from a table?

As with most other ANSI SQL supporting databases, PostgreSQL offers no command to remove columns from a table. In a way, this is not very convenient for the user, but it also has some important advantages. Databases are mostly used in combination with complex applications. Imagine a database administrator who recognizes that a column is no longer needed. If he simply drops the column, what happens to the applications that works on the database? Some SQL statements using that column will not work anymore. This error may be very obvious, but the following example written in Perl will show you a problem that is much more difficult to solve. Things can be a little tricky, especially when such things happen in complex applications that are not programmed properly. We have included this example here to make clear that a DROP COLUMN command can be a dangerous feature:

```
$getabhol="SELECT * FROM house WHERE prodid='1234' ";
$stha=$dbhlocal->prepare("$getabhol") or
        &makelog("cannot proceed\n",1);
$stha->execute() or
        &makelog("cannot proceed\n",1);
@prod = $stha->fetchrow_array;
$id=@prod[0];
$prodname=@prod[1];
$prodcat=@prod[2];
```

The example has been taken from a real-world system; we have just added some nasty "features" to show you which hazards you might have to face.

In the first line, we compile an SQL command that is executed. Then the first line of the result is assigned to the array called @prod. The first field of the array @prod[0] is assigned to $id. The next two fields of the first line of the result are also assigned to variables. Assume that the house table has ten columns of data type text. We use the first three columns of those ten columns and assign them to variables. Now imagine that the second column of the house table is removed by the database administrator. The previous code would still work without any trouble. The only problem is that $prodname and $prodcat will get the wrong values. The problem is indeed very obvious as long as the code is very small, but in complex applications, a wrong result could appear anywhere and in any output the application produces. If the error is not discovered immediately, this can lead to enormous problems in production environments. The main problem in the previous code is that we use SELECT * and not something like SELECT id, prodname, prodcat (this would lead to an error as soon as prodname is not available anymore) instead.

In most cases, adding columns will not lead to problems; removing columns can indeed be very dangerous for your system, as you can see in the previous example.

In the next example, we will show a method that can be used as a workaround for the missing DROP COLUMN command. You can use it if you want to drop columns, if you know exactly what you are doing, and if you don't damage an application that uses your database. This workaround is a little more difficult than a DROP COLUMN command.

Assume that we want to drop the column called softwareproject from the following table.

```
persons=# \d programmers
          Table "programmers"
    Attribute    |    Type     | Modifier
-----------------+-------------+----------
 name            | varchar(50) |
 softwareproject | varchar(50) |
```

We need the following commands:

```
CREATE TABLE newtable AS SELECT name FROM programmers;
DROP TABLE programmers;
ALTER TABLE newtable RENAME TO programmers;
```

Let's see whether all data has successfully been inserted into the new table:

```
persons=# SELECT * FROM programmers;
        name
--------------------
 Donald Becker
 Alexandre Julliard
(2 rows)
```

The table has only one column now because we haven't included the second column of the previous table into the AS SELECT statement. In this sample code, you can see that we have created a new table with all the columns we need in the new table first. This is done with a CREATE TABLE command. Then we drop the old table and rename the temporary table to the name of the old column.

System Tables

This section will give you a short overview about PostgreSQL's system tables. As with most advanced database systems, PostgreSQL stores a major part of information concerning the database itself in system tables. This makes it very easy to access this data for analyzing, debugging, or any other purpose. This is very comfortable because the user can hardly mix up his own tables with PostgreSQL's system tables.

The following is an overview of the system tables. We can get the following list by typing "\d pg_ and clicking the Tab button in the psql's command line:

```
persons=# \d pg_
pg_aggregate    pg_class        pg_inheritproc   pg_operator    pg_statistic
pg_am           pg_database     pg_inherits      pg_proc        pg_tables
pg_amop         pg_description  pg_ipl           pg_relcheck    pg_trigger
pg_amproc       pg_group        pg_language      pg_rewrite     pg_type
pg_attrdef      pg_index        pg_listener      pg_rules       pg_user
pg_attribute    pg_indexes      pg_opclass       pg_shadow      pg_views
```

We have already dealt with some of the tables listed here, but let's go into detail now. In the next few sections, we will give you an overview of the most important system tables (this is NOT a complete reference). This will make you understand many things about PostgreSQL's behavior in a better way.

pg_aggregatepg_aggregate is used to store all information about PostgreSQL's aggregate functions. The following is the definition of the table:

```
persons=# \d pg_aggregate
        Table "pg_aggregate"
   Attribute   |  Type   | Modifier
---------------+---------+----------
 aggname       | name    |
 aggowner      | integer |
 aggtransfn1   | regproc |
 aggtransfn2   | regproc |
 aggfinalfn    | regproc |
```

```
aggbasetype   | oid    |
aggtranstype1 | oid    |
aggtranstype2 | oid    |
aggfinaltype  | oid    |
agginitval1   | text   |
agginitval2   | text   |
Index: pg_aggregate_name_type_index
```

You can see in the definition of the table that every aggregate function has a name and an owner. This is especially important when working in multiuser environments. The default value of all predefined aggregate functions is the user ID of user postgres.

By default, PostgreSQL offers five aggregate functions. You can see that those functions can be found in pg_aggregate:

```
persons=# SELECT DISTINCT aggname FROM pg_aggregate;
 aggname
---------
 avg
 count
 max
 min
 sum
(5 rows)
```

Users can define their own aggregate functions. If a user does, his functions will be listed in pg_aggregate too.

pg_attribute

All columns stored in the database are listed in this table. If a user wants to have precise information about a specific column, he can query the pg_attribute table to find out more than with a simple \d tablename command. If you take a closer look at the data structure, you can see which attributes of a column are stored in this table:

```
persons=# \d pg_attribute
        Table "pg_attribute"
   Attribute   |   Type   | Modifier
---------------+----------+----------
 attrelid      | oid      |
 attname       | name     |
 atttypid      | oid      |
 attdisbursion | float4   |
 attlen        | smallint |
```

```
attnum          | smallint |
attnelems       | integer  |
attcacheoff     | integer  |
atttypmod       | integer  |
attbyval        | boolean  |
attstorage      | char     |
attisset        | boolean  |
attalign        | char     |
attnotnull      | boolean  |
atthasdef       | boolean  |
Indices: pg_attribute_relid_attnam_index,
         pg_attribute_relid_attnum_index
```

Many important attributes are stored in this table. For example, `attnotnull` defines whether a table can contain NULL values.

`pg_classpg_class` contains all classes defined in a database. In PostgreSQL, tables are classes, and information about tables is stored in `pg_class`.

`pg_class` contains a lot of attributes of a class:

```
persons=# \d pg_class
         Table "pg_class"
  Attribute    |   Type     | Modifier
---------------+------------+----------
 relname       | name       |
 reltype       | oid        |
 relowner      | integer    |
 relam         | oid        |
 relpages      | integer    |
 reltuples     | integer    |
 rellongrelid  | oid        |
 relhasindex   | boolean    |
 relisshared   | boolean    |
 relkind       | char       |
 relnatts      | smallint   |
 relchecks     | smallint   |
 reltriggers   | smallint   |
 relukeys      | smallint   |
 relfkeys      | smallint   |
 relrefs       | smallint   |
 relhaspkey    | boolean    |
 relhasrules   | boolean    |
 relacl        | aclitem[]  |
```

```
Indices: pg_class_oid_index,
         pg_class_relname_index
```

To give you an impression of how data is stored in this system table, we have selected some information from `pg_class` about the `programmers` table we have used before:

```
persons=# SELECT relname, relowner, relpages, reltriggers
       FROM pg_class WHERE relname='programmers';
   relname   | relowner | relpages | reltriggers
-------------+----------+----------+-------------
 programmers |       26 |       10 |           0
(1 row)
```

You can see that PostgreSQL stores some very important attributes, such as the name of the class, the ID of the owner (in the previous example, the table belongs to user `postgres`), the number of pages the classes need to be stored (a table is usually 8KB in PostgreSQL), and the number of triggers defined on a table.

In the data structure, you can see that a class belongs to a certain type of classes. This flag is very useful because it offers developers great flexibility.

`pg_database`pg_database contains a list of all databases that can be accessed by the postmaster. Every postmaster running must have a separate data directory. We can see a list of all databases that are in the data directory we are currently accessing using a postmaster process.

The data structure of `pg_database` is indeed an easy one. It contains only the name of the database, the ID of the database administrator (in our case, `postgres`), information about encoding, and the path to the actual data within the base directory of the current data directory:

```
persons=# \d pg_database
      Table "pg_database"
 Attribute |  Type   | Modifier
-----------+---------+----------
 datname   | name    |
 datdba    | integer |
 encoding  | integer |
 datpath   | text    |
```

To make this description a little clearer, we have included a simple SELECT statement that shows all the databases we currently have on our system:

```
persons=# SELECT * FROM pg_database ;
  datname  | datdba | encoding |  datpath
-----------+--------+----------+-----------
 template1 |    26  |        0 | template1
 persons   |    26  |        0 | persons
(2 rows)
```

pg_description

In PostgreSQL, objects can have a description. The use of descriptions is especially useful when database administrators and developers want to know how things work when they have to deal with data structures and code they have written a while ago. In general, documentation is very often seen as burden, but it isn't. Documentation can save you a lot of time and is extremely necessary, especially when multiple developers are working on one project.

PostgreSQL, compared to other systems, is a very well documented piece of software. PostgreSQL's source code is structured clearly and contains a lot of documentation. One of Vienna's best C hackers (Erich Frühstück —a true friend) said once that studying PostgreSQL server code is the best method to learn writing C code properly. I think he is right. If your data structures and your code is as clear as it should be, using and extending your code should be a rather easy task. But let's get back to pg_descritpption. The structure of the table is also very easy:

```
persons=# \d pg_description
     Table "pg_description"
  Attribute  | Type | Modifier
-------------+------+----------
 objoid      | oid  |
 description | text |
Index: pg_description_objoid_index
```

Every object can have a description. Objects are accessed via a unique ID and, because PostgreSQL is an object-relational database system, the list of objects stored in this table is truly a long one. For example, we can find the description of PostgreSQL's data types. The following is a short extract from the list:

```
600 | geometric point '(x, y)'
601 | geometric line segment '(pt1,pt2)'
602 | geometric path '(pt1,...)'
603 | geometric box '(lower left,upper right)'
604 | geometric polygon '(pt1,...)'
```

You can see that this extract contains the same text we can find in the list of PostgreSQL's data types (try `\dT`) we have included earlier in the book.

For example, if we add a description of a column to a table, the text would also appear in table `pg_description`.

pg_group

`pg_groups` is used to manage the user groups of a database. Multiple users can be assigned to a group.

```
persons=# \d pg_group
          Table "pg_group"
 Attribute |    Type   | Modifier
-----------+-----------+----------
 groname   | name      |
 grosysid  | integer   |
 grolist   | integer[] |
Indices: pg_group_name_index,
         pg_group_sysid_index
```

pg_index **and** pg_indexes

The attributes of the indexes you are using in your database are stored in the `pg_index` table. `pg_indexes` offers a view that allows access to columns from `pg_index` and `pg_class`. In the following, we have compiled the data structure of `pg_index` and the definition of `pg_indexes`:

```
persons=# \d pg_index
            Table "pg_index"
    Attribute    |    Type    | Modifier
-----------------+------------+----------
 indexrelid      | oid        |
 indrelid        | oid        |
 indproc         | oid        |
 indkey          | int2vector |
 indclass        | oidvector  |
 indisclustered  | boolean    |
 indislossy      | boolean    |
 indhaskeytype   | boolean    |
 indisunique     | boolean    |
 indisprimary    | boolean    |
 indreference    | oid        |
 indpred         | text       |
```

```
Index: pg_index_indexrelid_index

persons=# \d pg_indexes
      View "pg_indexes"
 Attribute | Type | Modifier
-----------+------+----------
 tablename | name |
 indexname | name |
 indexdef  | text |
View definition: SELECT c.relname AS tablename, i.relname AS indexname,
pg_get_indexdef(x.indexrelid) AS indexdef FROM pg_index x, pg_class c,
pg_class i
WHERE ((c.oid = x.indrelid) AND (i.oid = x.indexrelid));
```

As you can see, all important parameters of the CREATE INDEX command are nothing more and nothing less than the columns in the pg_index table.

The view pg_indexes is used to perform a join of table pg_index and pg_class.

pg_inherits, pg_inheritprocpg_inherits and pg_inheritoproc are used to store information about inheritance. pg_inherits stores the IDs of an object and the ID of the parent. If an object has multiple parents, it has multiple entries that are consecutively numbered in column inhseqno.

The data structure of pg_inherits consists of only three columns:

```
persons=# \d pg_inherits
      Table "pg_inherits"
 Attribute |  Type   | Modifier
-----------+---------+----------
 inhrelid  | oid     |
 inhparent | oid     |
 inhseqno  | integer |
Index: pg_inherits_relid_seqno_index
```

pg_inheritproc stores information about inheritance concerning functions. We have included the definition of the table:

```
persons=# \d pg_inheritproc
    Table "pg_inheritproc"
 Attribute  | Type | Modifier
------------+------+----------
 inhproname | name |
 inhargrelid | oid |
```

```
inhdefrelid | oid |
inhproc     | oid |
```

pg_languagepg_language stores information about the languages a database supports. The following is an example of a PL/pgSQL-enabled database:

```
persons=# SELECT * FROM pg_language;
 lanname  | lanispl | lanpltrusted | lanplcallfoid | lancompiler
----------+---------+--------------+---------------+------------
 internal | f       | f            |             0 | n/a
 C        | f       | f            |             0 | /bin/cc
 sql      | f       | f            |             0 | postgres
 plpgsql  | t       | t            |         37856 | PL/pgSQL
(4 rows)
```

This example contains one record for PL/pgSQL; all other lines are default values.

pg_operatorpg_operator is an extremely important table in a PostgreSQL system. It stores information about operators, as you can see in the following listing of the data structure:

```
persons=# \d pg_operator
      Table "pg_operator"
 Attribute  |   Type   | Modifier
------------+----------+----------
 oprname    | name     |
 oprowner   | integer  |
 oprprec    | smallint |
 oprkind    | char     |
 oprisleft  | boolean  |
 oprcanhash | boolean  |
 oprleft    | oid      |
 oprright   | oid      |
 oprresult  | oid      |
 oprcom     | oid      |
 oprnegate  | oid      |
 oprlsortop | oid      |
 oprrsortop | oid      |
 oprcode    | regproc  |
 oprrest    | regproc  |
 oprjoin    | regproc  |
Indices: pg_operator_oid_index,
         pg_operator_oprname_l_r_k_index
```

We won't go too deeply into detail because `pg_operator` contains a lot of information about operators that would lead too far.

We only want to point out how big the table is. This shows the power of PostgreSQL and how many operators are defined for nearly all demands a modern database system may have to face.

The default installation of PostgreSQL (7.0.3) has 559 predefined records in `pg_operator`. 59 of these are used for the = operator. You can see that = is defined for a lot of different data types.

`pg_proc``pg_proc` contains the list of functions supported by your database. A function can have multiple overloadings. The data structure of the `pg_proc` table looks as follows:

```
persons=# \d pg_proc
            Table "pg_proc"
   Attribute     |    Type    | Modifier
-----------------+------------+----------
 proname         | name       |
 proowner        | integer    |
 prolang         | oid        |
 proisinh        | boolean    |
 proistrusted    | boolean    |
 proiscachable   | boolean    |
 pronargs        | smallint   |
 proretset       | boolean    |
 prorettype      | oid        |
 proargtypes     | oidvector  |
 probyte_pct     | integer    |
 properbyte_cpu  | integer    |
 propercall_cpu  | integer    |
 prooutin_ratio  | integer    |
 prosrc          | text       |
 probin          | bytea      |
Indices: pg_proc_oid_index,
         pg_proc_proname_narg_type_index
```

`pg_shadow``pg_shadow` is the most important table when dealing with user accounts. In most cases, `pg_shadow` is referenced via `pg_user`, a view that contains the most important information. `pg_shadow` contains the following fields:

```
persons=# \d pg_shadow
        Table "pg_shadow"
```

```
Attribute   |  Type    | Modifier
------------+--------+----------
usename     | name     |
usesysid    | integer  |
usecreatedb | boolean  |
usetrace    | boolean  |
usesuper    | boolean  |
usecatupd   | boolean  |
passwd      | text     |
valuntil    | abstime  |
```

You can see that these fields contain all information usually required when adding a new user using the CREATE USER command.

pg_statisticspg_statistics is an extremely important table for PostgreSQL's optimizer. With the help of this table, PostgreSQL tries to find the best way of executing a query. It is not necessary to understand every detail of pg_statistics, but it is important to see what data PostgreSQL uses to find its way through an SQL-query:

```
persons=# \d pg_statistic
        Table "pg_statistic"
   Attribute    |   Type    | Modifier
----------------+-----------+----------
 starelid       | oid       |
 staattnum      | smallint  |
 staop          | oid       |
 stanullfrac    | float4    |
 stacommonfrac  | float4    |
 stacommonval   | text      |
 staloval       | text      |
 stahival       | text      |
Index: pg_statistic_relid_att_index
```

pg_tables

As you can see in the following definition, pg_tables is a view that allows comfortable access to data related to tables.

```
persons=# \d pg_tables
         View "pg_tables"
   Attribute   |  Type    | Modifier
------------+--------+----------
```

```
tablename    | name    |
tableowner   | name    |
hasindexes   | boolean |
hasrules     | boolean |
hastriggers  | boolean |
View definition: SELECT c.relname AS tablename, pg_get_userbyid(c.relowner)
AS tableowner, c.relhasindex AS hasindexes, c.relhasrules AS hasrules,
(c.reltriggers
> 0) AS hastriggers FROM pg_class c WHERE (((c.relkind = 'r'::"char") OR
(c.relkind = 's'::"char")) AND (NOT (EXISTS (SELECT pg_rewrite.rulename FROM
pg_rewrite WHERE ((pg_rewrite.ev_class = c.oid) AND (pg_rewrite.ev_type
= '1'::"char"))))));
```

pg_trigger

Information about triggers can be found in `pg_trigger`. The following is an overview of the data structure.

```
persons=# \d  pg_trigger
          Table "pg_trigger"
   Attribute    |   Type    | Modifier
----------------+-----------+----------
 tgrelid        | oid       |
 tgname         | name      |
 tgfoid         | oid       |
 tgtype         | smallint  |
 tgenabled      | boolean   |
 tgisconstraint | boolean   |
 tgconstrname   | name      |
 tgconstrrelid  | oid       |
 tgdeferrable   | boolean   |
 tginitdeferred | boolean   |
 tgnargs        | smallint  |
 tgattr         | int2vector |
 tgargs         | bytea     |
Indices: pg_trigger_tgconstrname_index,
         pg_trigger_tgconstrrelid_index,
         pg_trigger_tgrelid_index
```

Security and Access Restrictions

PostgreSQL's security systems can be divided into two components. One part is access restriction for certain users and certain objects. These settings are valid for objects inside a database.

The second part has to do with global access restriction and user authentification.

With the help of the operating system, it is possible to achieve even higher levels of security by using commonly known network security methods, such as Netfilter or SSH.

In this section, we try to give you an overview of what can be done with PostgreSQL's security features, and how you can make your database as secure as possible.

User Authentification

When working with more than just one user, authentification is an essential component of every application. PostgreSQL provides lots of methods for dealing with users efficiently. This section will guide you through the basics of user authentification.

Overview

When a user tries to connect to a database, PostgreSQL checks whether the user is allowed to connect and which objects he or she is allowed to access. This process is called *authentification*.

PostgreSQL offers two types of client authentification. Authentification can be done by client or by database. Both methods can be used in combination with various authentification methods.

Authentification by client means that the database checks the host that wants to establish the connection. This is done with the help of the IP address.

Authentification by database means that the database checks whether a user has the right to access a certain database.

To configure the client authentification system, we have to use a file called `pg_hba.conf` that can be found in the `$PGDATA` directory on your machine.

`pg_hba.confpg_hba.conf` contains the information about what hosts can connect to which databases. Every time a user tries to connect to the database, the `pg_hba.conf` is read. This is very convenient because you don't have to restart your PostgreSQL server when making simple changes in your configuration. This is also very important on high-availability systems.

Three types of lines can be found in `pg_hba.conf`:

- *Comments*—Comments are lines that start with #.

- *Empty*—Empty lines are ignored.

- *Record*—Contains "real" configuration data.

Records consist of fields that can be separated by tabs or spaces. All spaces at the beginning or the end of a line are ignored. One record can only be one line; there is no way to continue records across multiple lines.

PostgreSQL supports three types of records:

- `host` A `host` record defines a list of hosts that are allowed to connect to the database. This works only when the server is started with the `-i` flag enabled; otherwise, the database won't accept connections via a TCP/IP network.

- `hostssl` This works if you have compiled your server with SSL enabled. You also have to enable SSL when starting the server. This can be done with the `-1` option. `hostssl` is also used to define a list of hosts allowed to connect to your database.

- `local` These records tell the server which configuration to use when connecting to a local database.

The following two lines of code should give you an impression of how `pg_hba.conf` records look.

```
host/hostssl DBNAME IP_ADDRESS ADDRESS_MASK AUTHTYPE [AUTH_ARGUMENT]
local DBNAME AUTHTYPE [AUTH_ARGUMENT]
```

Before we get to a sample configuration, let's take a look at PostgreSQL's authentification methods:

- `trust` PostgreSQL establishes a connection, no matter who wants to connect to the server.

- `reject` `reject` is the opposite of `trust`. In the case of `reject`, nobody is allowed to connect to the database. In many cases, `reject` can be a good method for debugging purposes when you want to reject connections during your work.

- `password` Every user who wants to connect to the database has to use his or her password. This is no secure way of connecting to your server because using `password` does not make the database transfer the password in an encrypted way.

This is especially dangerous over Internet connections because hackers can discover the passwords easily by using a packet sniffer.

- `crypt`   This method transfers the password in an encrypted way over the network. The password is encrypted by using a simple challenge/response protocol.

- `krb4`   Kerberos V4 is another method for user authentification and is only available over TCP/IP connections. To use Kerberos with PostgreSQL, you have to enable it at compile time. This can be done with `./configure --with-krb4 --with-krb5`.

- `krb5`   Kerberos V5 is the successor of Kerberos V4 and is also only available over TCP/IP connections.

- `ident`   ident is a very useful feature of PostgreSQL. The database server asks the client system who wants to connect to the server. PostgreSQL decides whether the user is allowed to establish a connection. `ident` authentification can only be done over TCP/IP networks. `ident` authentification is based on the "Identification Protocol" (RFC 1413). On Unix systems, an `ident` server is usually listening on TCP port 113. Because it is fairly easy for a hacker to fake the behavior of an `ident` server, we recommend that you use it only in highly-protected LAN networks. In a public network, a hacker could pretend to be any user. In RFC 1413, it says, "The identification Protocol is not intended as an authorization or access control protocol." Please keep that in mind when working with public PostgreSQL systems.

To help you better you understand what we have just described theoretically, we have included a `pg_hba.conf` file that contains some examples of typical entries:

```
# TYPE    DATABASE     IP_ADDRESS     MASK                   AUTHTYPE   MAP
host      template1    192.168.1.0    255.255.255.0          ident      sameuser
host      template1    192.168.12.10  255.255.255.255        crypt
host      all          192.168.2.1    255.255.255.255        reject
host      all          0.0.0.0        0.0.0.0                trust
```

The first line allows every user that connects from network 192.168.1.x because the user was identified by the `ident` server. The access is restricted to the database called `template1`.

The second line allows users on machine 192.168.12.10 to connect to the PostgreSQL server by using their passwords. The password is transmitted over the network in an encrypted way.

The third line rejects all users from host 192.168.2.1. The restriction is defined for all databases. Users from that machine won't have access to the database server at all.

The fourth line allows anyone from any machine to connect to the database, no matter who the user is. 0.0.0.0 means that any IP address is considered to be valid.

Summary

PostgreSQL provides a very flexible and powerful system for restricting access over the network. It allows you to define which hosts can access what database with the help of which kind of authentification. This makes PostgreSQL a great solution for network databases. However, PostgreSQL has a far from perfect user and group system that can hardly be used for building really secure applications.

CHAPTER 7

Backup and Recovery

Every database administrator has to take care of backups. In case of disaster, backups are essential for restoring data. But not only hard- and software errors demand backup strategies. Sometimes a user deletes files accidentally, and it is the administrator's task to restore these files.

In this chapter, you learn to back up PostgreSQL databases and see how data can be restored+.

Common Errors

Mastering backups and recovery is perhaps one of the most important areas of database administration. However, the maintenance of restorable copies can, in many cases, be very difficult—especially on systems that have to do a lot of INSERT and UPDATE operations.

In general, you can make four mistakes when working with a database server:

- **You have no backup at all.** We don't have to mention that this can lead to some real trouble.

- **You create a backup but you have never tested the recovery process.** This is maybe one of the worst errors you can make when working with backups. You create backups and feel secure that nothing can happen to you because you have copies of your data. If something goes wrong, you might be in deep trouble if you don't know how recovery works. If you have never tried it, you feel insecure during the recovery process, and this can take a lot of time and lead to errors. Make sure that you know perfectly well how to restore a backup. This is an extremely important point that most people forget about.

- **You create a backup but nobody but you knows about it**. Machines are generally more reliable than humans. You should take this into consideration when designing database systems and thinking of backup strategies. In many companies we dealt with in the past few years, we saw something extremely dangerous: The person who was responsible for the backup or the entire IT system knew everything, but was the only one who did. What happens if that person is on holiday or decides to leave the company? Many companies could be in deep trouble when facing such a situation. No matter how redundant and reliable your IT system is, if no one knows how it works and what has to be done in case of failure, you will be in deep trouble. Redundant knowledge among people working with a system is as least as important redundant hardware. Documentation of all crucial processes in an IT system has to be available, and more than just one person must know how things work. Many companies try to save money by neglecting documentation—recovery processes are, in most cases, more expensive and more dangerous than writing a short piece of documentation. Finally, don't forget that documentation must also be maintained.

- **You create a backup on the same volume as the original data.** In the last few years, we have also seen some other horror scenarios. We have found backup systems where the backup was actually on the same volume as the original data. Assume a situation where your hard disk has stopped working. If you can still read the backup, you are very lucky. In most cases this won't be possible. You have to use separate volumes for your backup and the original data or you will face trouble when you try to recover.

- **The backup and the original data are in the same room.** In case of fire, it is essential to have one version of the data stored in an another location; otherwise, the data and backup might be destroyed. In that case, the data is lost and there is no way to restore it.

- **You have only the most recent backup.** If you have only the most recent backup available, you might have a problem. In most cases, you don't know that something has gone wrong on the system, so the most recent backup will also contain errors and recovery will be difficult.

Full Backup Versus Incremental Backup

Many companies rely on redundant storage systems; they are a good choice for protecting your data, but they are not enough. Backup does not mean buying a lot of additional and expensive hardware. Real backup starts in the brain of every person involved in the process of data processing and backup. Everybody has to take care of data security and documentation to guarantee a fully working IT environment.

Most backup systems available on the net support two types of backups:

- **Full backup**. *Full backup* means that all the data is saved at once. This is the most comfortable way to provide backups that can easily be recovered. Depending on the amount of data, however, full backups can sometimes be a problem. When dealing with a lot of data, a full backup might not fit on a backup medium or copying all data might take too long.

- **Incremental backup**. Incremental backup is usually used in combination with full backup. In an *incremental backup*, only data that is newer than the last backup is saved. The advantage of this method is that significantly less data has to be saved. The problem is that the recovery process can be complicated and annoying (depending on the backup software you use). On systems where full backups are not possible because the amount of data is too large, some sort of incremental backup has to be used. Many people use full backups periodically and run incremental backups more frequently. Withdatabases, incremental backups are difficult because backing up is not done on the row level.

Starting Backups Using cron

On Unix systems, backups are usually started by cron, a daemon used to execute scheduled commands. cron is flexible and easy-to-configure software. Also called "Vixie Cron" because the most important implementation of the cron daemon is provided by Paul Vixie, this implementation is currently used by all major Linux distributors.

If you want to add a job to your cron, you can do this by typing `crontab -e` in your favorite Unix shell. cron starts the default editor of your system, which in many cases, is ed. ed is a line-oriented text editor some of you might know from ancient Unix times. On some systems, the default editor is vi, and one of the most powerful and widespread editors on Unix systems. If you don't want to use ed or vi to configure cron, you set the environment variables $EDITOR or $VISUAL to your favorite editors. This can be done with the following command (for Bourne Shell users):

```
export EDITOR=vim
export VISUAL=vim
```

vim is a text editor that is upward-compatible to vi. On Linux systems, vi is usually an alias for vim. vim has some nice advantages over vi, such as syntax highlighting.

You can use cron to define all times when you want to start a backup. Check out your man pages for a complete reference on cron and `crontab`.

Here is an example of an entry in crontab:

```
0 3 * * *       /full_path_to_script/myscript.pl
```

`myscript.pl` is started at 3 o'clock every day. Every entry in crontab consists of six fields. The first five fields are used to define the times the program in field six has to be started by cron.

The first field defines the minute to start the programm, field two defines the hour, field three is responsible for the day of the month, field four defines the month, and field five can be used to restrict the day of the week the process has to be started. A field might contain an ordinary value or an asterisk (*), which indicates that the process is always started. You can see in the example that the script is started every day at three o'clock—this means every day of the month, every month, and every day of the week, but only at three o'clock and zero minutes.

Backup Hardware

A lot of backup hardware is available. Whether you need to back up a few files or an entire mainframe, the hardware industry provides nearly everything you can imagine to back up your data.

The dinosaurs in the backup business are tapes. Some of you might already have dealt with DDSx tapes or IBM tapes, such as 3480 or 3490. Most people feel a insecure when working with streamers, because tapes have to be accessed differently than CDs, for instance. Unix systems offer a powerful set of commands to handle tapes, but for many users, it's difficult to get used to these tools.

Some companies offer *jukeboxes*, which are cartridges that contain multiple tapes (for example, 6 tapes). You don't have to change tapes every day, and can use cron to make this happen automatically. If you have to use multiple tapes to back up your data, you can also use robots. Some very powerful solutions are currently available to manage dozens of backup tapes automatically. Robots are commonly used mainframe environments to avoid changing tapes manually.

Backup servers are, in many cases, the most comfortable way to back up data. Backup servers are sometimes also cheaper than expensive streamer hardware. A backup server is nothing else than a machine used to receive copied data. Recovery from a backup server is usually easy because you merely copy the data over the network back to the machine that has crashed—this can usually be done quickly.

Backup Strategies and Tools for PostgreSQL

There are several backup strategies that can be used in combination with PostgreSQL. Let's take a look at some of them.

pg_dump **and** pg_dumplo

The most important tool when you have to back up your PostgreSQL server is pg_dump. If you want to get a description of pg_dump, you can use pg_dump --help:

```
bash-2.04$ pg_dump --help
pg_dump dumps a database as a text file.

Usage:
  pg_dump [options] dbname

Options:
  -a, --data-only          dump out only the data, not the schema
  -c, --clean              clean (drop) schema prior to create
  -d, --inserts            dump data as INSERT, rather than COPY, commands
  -D, --attribute-inserts  dump data as INSERT commands with attribute names
  -h, --host <hostname>    server host name
  -i, --ignore-version     proceed when database version != pg_dump version
  -n, --no-quotes          suppress most quotes around identifiers
  -N, --quotes             enable most quotes around identifiers
  -o, --oids               dump object ids (oids)
  -p, --port <port>        server port number
  -s, --schema-only        dump out only the schema, no data
  -t, --table <table>      dump for this table only
  -u, --password           use password authentication
  -v, --verbose            verbose
  -x, --no-acl             do not dump ACL's (grant/revoke)

If no database name is not supplied, then the PGDATABASE environment
variable value is used.
```

```
Report bugs to <pgsql-bugs@postgresql.org>.
```

As you can see in the description, pg_dump is a powerful tool. Remember that pg_dump writes data to standard output. You have to take this into consideration when backing up data. Here is an example of how you can use pg_dump

pg_dump person > backupfile.sql

We have dumped the database called person and redirected the output to backupfile.sql. Let's have a look at what backfile.sql contains:

```
\connect - postgres
CREATE TABLE "programmers" (
        "name" character varying(50)
);
CREATE FUNCTION "plpgsql_call_handler" ( ) RETURNS opaque AS
'/usr/local/postgres-7.0.3/lib//plpgsql.so' LANGUAGE 'C';
CREATE TRUSTED PROCEDURAL LANGUAGE 'plpgsql' HANDLER "plpgsql_call_handler"
LANCOMPILER 'PL/pgSQL';
COPY "programmers" FROM stdin;
Donald Becker
Alexandre Julliard
\.
```

The first line tells the database that the following operations will be done as user postgres. Then a table is created. The next two lines tell us that the database supports PL/pgSQL; the database creates a call handler function. After the data structure and the call handlers have been created, the actual data is listed in the COPY command.

Recovering a dumped database is an easy task. Assume that we want to insert the data and the data structure in file backupfile.sql into a database called people:

```
bash-2.04$ createdb people
CREATE DATABASE
bash-2.04$ psql people < backupfile.sql
You are now connected as new user postgres.
CREATE
CREATE
CREATE
```

First we use the createdb command to create the database. Then we start psql in batch mode and insert the file into the database. The < operator of the shell is used to transfer the data in backupfile.sql to psql. We can also achieve the same result with the help of the cat command and a pipe (|):

```
cat backupfile.sql | psql people
```

Some Unix gurus say that the cat command is absolutely useless. It is certainly true that a Unix shell without the cat command provides the same power as a system featuring cat. You decide how you want to insert data.

pg_dump is sometimes used to dump the data structure only, which is useful when you want to set up multiple databases with the same tables, sequences, views, and other components. You can dump the structure of a database without data to a file. This can easily be done with the -s flag:

```
pg_dump -s people > /tmp/structure.sql
```

structure.sql contains data now:

```
\connect - postgres
CREATE TABLE "programmers" (
        "name" character varying(50)
);
CREATE FUNCTION "plpgsql_call_handler" ( ) RETURNS opaque AS
'/usr/local/postgres-7.0.3/lib//plpgsql.so' LANGUAGE 'C';
CREATE TRUSTED PROCEDURAL LANGUAGE 'plpgsql' HANDLER "plpgsql_call_handler"
LANCOMPILER 'PL/pgSQL';
```

If you dump large databases, the output of pg_dump will be a very large file. On Unix systems, backups are very often stored as compressed tar archives. A tar archive is a comfortable way of storing data and can easily be compressed with tools such as gzip or compress.

People use tar archives around the world, so it is easy to exchange files. When surfing through software archives on an FTP server, you might have noticed that nearly all Unix programs available for download have the extension .tar.gz.

The problem with tar archives is that you cannot easily dump a database directly into a tar archive without dumping the data to a file first, which takes a lot of space. The best thing to get around the problem is to use gzip without tar:

```
pg_dump people | gzip -cv > people.gz
```

-c makes gzip write the compressed output to standard output. -v is not necessary, but gives you a little information about the compression process. The whole result (standard output) is now redirected to a file.

If you want to check whether people.gz has been written correctly, you can use zcat:

```
bash-2.04$ zcat people.gz
\connect - postgres
CREATE TABLE "programmers" (
        "name" character varying(50)
);
CREATE FUNCTION "plpgsql_call_handler" ( ) RETURNS opaque AS
'/usr/local/postgres-7.0.3/lib//plpgsql.so' LANGUAGE 'C';
CREATE TRUSTED PROCEDURAL LANGUAGE 'plpgsql' HANDLER "plpgsql_call_handler"
LANCOMPILER 'PL/pgSQL';
COPY "programmers" FROM stdin;
Donald Becker
Alexandre Julliard
\.
```

zcat uncompresses the file on-the-fly and writes the output to standard output. You can also use gunzip"":

```
zcat people.gz | psql people
gunzip -c people.gz | psql people
```

Many PostgreSQL environments consist of many databases stored on more than just one server. In such environments, you can manage the backup strategy of all servers on one machine by using pg_dump network functions. Simply define the host you want to connect to (-h) and the port the remote server is listening to (-p) in your pg_dump command. If you decide to back up your server remotely this way, keep in mind that all data you want to back up has to be transferred over the network. The use of network connections is most likely slower than dumping data to a hard disk on the machine that is backed up.

pg_dump is useful and easy to use, although some important features are still missing. Many commercial database developers should consider implementing a similar tool. The output of pg_dump is, by default, SQL, and can therefore be converted easily into every other data format.

Dumping binary data is not possible with pg_dump. This is a weak spot of pg_dump, because it is impossible to back up binary data comfortably.

Thanks to Karel Zak (Czech Republic), a powerful tool can be found in the contributed directory of PostgreSQL's source code. The tool is called pg_dumplo and can be used to back up binary data. The following is an overview of pg_dumplo:

```
[hs@duron pg_dumplo]$ ./pg_dumplo --help
pg_dumplo 7.1.0 - PostgreSQL large objects dump
pg_dumplo [option]
```

```
-h --help                   this help
-u --user=<username>        username for connection to server
-p --password=<password>    password for connection to server
-d --db=<database>          database name
-t --host=<hostname>        server hostname
-s --space=<dir>            directory with dump tree (for export/import)
-i --import                 import large obj dump tree to DB
-e --export                 export (dump) large obj to dump tree
-l <table.attr ...>         dump attribute (columns) with LO to dump tree
-a --all                    dump all LO in DB (default)
-r --remove                 if is set '-i' try remove old LO
-q --quiet                  run quietly
-w --show                   not dump, but show all LO in DB

Example (dump):   pg_dumplo -d my_db -s /my_dump/dir -l t1.a t1.b t2.a
                  pg_dumplo -a -d my_db -s /my_dump/dir
Example (import): pg_dumplo -i -d my_db -s /my_dump/dir
Example (show):   pg_dumplo -w -d my_db

Note:  * option '-l' must be last option!
       * option '-i' without option '-r' make new large obj in DB
         not rewrite old, the '-i' UPDATE oid numbers in table.attr only!
       * if is not set option -s, the pg_dumplo use $PWD
```

You can see that this tool is easy to use. If you want to find out more about this software, check out the **readme** file in **contrib/pg_dumplo**.

For backing up an entire database cluster, PostgreSQL offers a program called pg_dumpall. Using pg_dumpall is easier than backing up individual databases, because everything can be backed up in one file. Because pg_dumpall produces ASCII files, the data is portable. Let's look at the syntax overview of pg_dumpall:

```
[hs@duron pg_dumplo]$ pg_dumpall --help
pg_dumpall extracts a PostgreSQL database cluster into an SQL script file.

Usage:
  pg_dumpall [ options... ]

Options:
  -c, --clean           Clean (drop) schema prior to create
  -g, --globals-only    Only dump global objects, no databases
  -h, --host=HOSTNAME   Server host name
  -p, --port=PORT       Server port number
```

```
   -U, --username=NAME     Connect as specified database user
   -W, --password          Force password prompts (should happen automatically)
Any extra options will be passed to pg_dump.  The dump will be written
to the standard output.

Report bugs to <pgsql-bugs@postgresql.org>.
```

The list of options provided by pg_dumpall is not as long as the list of options provided by pg_dump, because it pg_dump_all cannot dump individual tables. pg_dump all is used only for dumping entire database clusters.

Backup Server

One way of storing your backup files is to use a backup server. Backup servers are easy to handle, especially when dealing with large amounts of data. The backup server and the production server can be connected using a network file system—such as NFS, SMB, or Coda—but FTP or SCP can also be used. In the case of a file system (NFS, SMB, or Coda), dump your database to a file that is physically stored on the remote machine. Make sure that the remote file system is mounted correctly.

If you back up your database, we recommend that the name of the backup files contains a timestamp. This can be achieved with a shell script like the following:

```
#!/bin/sh

TIMESTAMP=`date +%Y%m%d"_"%H%M`
pg_dump people | gzip > backup${TIMESTAMP}.sql.gz
```

The dump of the database will be compressed using gzip, and the name of the backup file will contain the word backup plus the date in ISO format (*YYYYMMDD*). The ISO format is, in this case, the best one because sorting by date can easily be done with a sort command. Europeans sometimes write dates in this format: *DD.MM.YYYY*. If you have multiple files using that format, it is rather difficult to find the most recent or the oldest file. If you write the date in the ISO format, the result of a simple sort command (Unix shell) is a result that is sorted by date (old to new). Here is an example of a filename using ISO date format:

```
backup20010417_1915.sql.gz
```

As you can see, the file was created on April 17, 2001. Some of you might think that storing the date within the filename is redundant since the file system already stores the date. This is true, but what if someone destroys the system timestamp by performing operations on the file? It is more secure to have the date in the filename— it can save you a lot of time.

In many network environments, the machines are not connected via a network file system. If you have to back up your machine over the Internet it is useful to encrypt the data before you transfer it. Secure network transfers can be achieved in many ways. You can copy your data using an SSH tunnel or you can use the secure copy command (scp).

scp copies files between hosts on a network. Normally scp asks for a password before transmitting the data. Because backups should work automatically, inserting the password is not a suitable solution.

Check out the man pages of ssh, ssh-agent, and ssh-add to learn how you can get around typing the password every time (www.openssh.org).

Network file systems, such as NFS, are another way of connecting your backup server to the production server. Remote file systems can easily be mounted and used like local disc space. Check out the documentation about the network file system you want to use to find out more.

Jukeboxes and Basic Tape Operations

As mentioned earlier, jukeboxes are a useful hardware component. In general, jukeboxes consist of an array of tapes (usually 6 or more) that can be loaded and unloaded with the help of software. The advantage of a jukebox is that changing the tapes can be done by the jukebox itself and therefore no user is needed.

In this section, you explore basic tape operations on Unix systems and a backup solution using tapes and PostgreSQL. We will also share a brief insight of how tapes can be handled on a Unix system, using some powerful Unix commands.

In the early days, tapes were the most important medium for storing data and performing backups. Although times have changed, tapes still play an important role. People still rely on streamers, especially in mainframe environments. PostgreSQL is no mainframe database, but if the amount of data that has to be saved increases, the importance of tapes also grows because it is a rather cheap and portable method to back up huge amounts of data.

Jukeboxes are not common on Windows machines, although some programs, such as Backup Exec, are capable of handling tapes.

In general, tapes don't need a file system on Unix systems. They are simply treated as a "special" file. A tape drive appears as a *list of devices*. We will explain this in detail a little later.

The most important Unix commands to work with these devices are

- `tar` (tape archiver) was initially written to manage tape.

- `dd` (disk dump) is an important tool to convert data for use with various media. `dd` is a low-level command and can convert data while copying it. Especially when working with mainframe data, `dd` does an essential job because it supports EBCDIC (used mainly on mainframe machines), to ASCII conversion and vice versa, and much more.

- `mt` (control magnetic tape drive operation) is used for all basic tape operations. If you want to go to a specific position on the tape or if you simply want to rewind, you can use `mt`. `mt` is an essential command if you want to store multiple archives on one tape.

- `mtx` (control SCSI media changer devices) enables you to load and unload tapes in your jukebox. Jukeboxes are media change devices.

On AIX 3 systems, the device is called "/dev/rmt0". The device can be accessed like a file. If you want to create a `tar`- archive on the tape containing a dumped PostgreSQL database you can simply use the following:

```
tar cvfz /dev/st0 datadump*
```

The system creates a `tar` archive that contains all files starting with `datadump`. If the tape seems to work slowly, you can set the block size to 1024 using the `mt` command:

```
mt -f /dev/st0 setblk 1024
```

This should significantly speed up the process.

In the example, we wrote the `tar` archive to `/dev/st0`. Because devices are treated like files, the system starts to write at the beginning of the tape. This seems very obvious, because `tar` also starts to write at the beginning of the file that has to be created. If you want to write a second file on the tape, you will face the following situation: After you have written the first `tar` archive on the tape, the tape is rewound automatically so that the next call of `tar` can start at the beginning of the file (in this case at the beginning of the tape). The first `tar` archive would be destroyed immediately by the second `tar` command. This is a very common error and hardly anyone would think of the problem the first time using tapes. Remember that you have to check whether your backup has been created successfully—if you do, you will find an error before facing a critical situation.

If you want to add a second archive to the data on the tape, you have to use the `mt` command to find the correct position on the tape to start writing. In the following example, we use the second face of /dev/st0 called /dev/nst0. /dev/nst0 is the same as /dev/st0 but does not rewind (/dev/rmt0.1 on AIX). The correct position to start writing on the table is immediately after the first file:

```
mt -f /dev/nst0 fsf 1
```

fsf (forward space count files) brings us to file number two. The tape is now positioned on the first block of the next file and we can start writing using a tar command, for instance:

```
tar cvfz /dev/nst0 backup*
```

Restoring data from a tape works nearly the same way as writing. Go to the directory where you want the data to be restored, find the correct position on the tape (use mt), and use the following:

```
tar xvfz /dev/st0
```

> **Note**
> The z flag in every tar command we use in this section is used to perform compression and decompression using gzip. The z flag is mostly used on Linux systems. If you are using a version of Unix that does not support gzip in combination with tar, you can either install the required GNU tools or simply use a workaround with the help of pipes. Systems using the GNU version of tar support the **z** flag.

Let's look at a backup system that creates backups with the help of a jukebox. Assume that the amount of data you have to store is small enough to fit on one tape. Here is a short shell script you can use to save your data:

```
#!/bin/sh

# Load the next tape
mtx -f /dev/st0 next

# Dump data, compress it and write it to /dev/st0
pg_dump yourdb | gzip > /dev/st0
```

Simply start the script with the help of cron.

First we unload the drive and load the next tape in sequence. If the drive is empty, we load the first tape into the drive (this is done by the next command). Finally, we dump the data and compress it with gzip before writing it to the tape.

Saving Large Amounts of Data on Multiple Tapes

The backup strategy described in the last section works pretty well with data that fits on one tape. If the amount of data increases, you have to find a different solution for the problem if you still want to perform full backups. One way is to use more than one tape drive. The most important point when performing full backups is to find a way to perform just *one* dump. If you perform multiple (smaller) dumps (for example, one table after the other) to save a database, you might find yourself in deep trouble.

What happens if you use foreign keys and people change the data during the dumps? This might lead to problems with data integrity. A foreign key used in one table might already be deleted in another table. Combining your dumps to one correct database might become extremely difficult if not impractical. A dump of your database must therefore be done at once—but how can we store the data? One easy solution would be to dump the database to disk and use a simple split command to create many smaller files that can easily be stored on a tape:

```
pg_dump person | split -l 3 - prefix_
```

This creates a set of files:

```
bash-2.04$ ls -l
insgesamt 16
-rw-rw-r--    1 postgres postgres         79 Apr 18 21:50 prefix_aa
-rw-rw-r--    1 postgres postgres        222 Apr 18 21:50 prefix_ab
-rw-rw-r--    1 postgres postgres         64 Apr 18 21:50 prefix_ac
-rw-rw-r--    1 postgres postgres          3 Apr 18 21:50 prefix_ad
```

This command stores three lines per file and uses prefix_ as the prefix for the files created by split. Lines might not be a good choice for splitting a file because lines can have variable length. Bytes can, in some cases, be better (see man split for further information).

Usually, split is not used for splitting a file by lines. For backup, it is more useful to tell split to start a new file after a predefined number of bytes. This makes sure that all backup files have the same size. Defining the size in bytes can be done by using the -b flag.

We can save the files to tape by using a simple tar command now, but how can we restore the files? We can write a one-line shell script that restores the data and inserts the values into the database called person:

```
for i in `ls | sort`; do cat $i; done | psql person
```

We process every file returned by the `ls` command (the `sort` command is redundant; it is just for better understanding) in ascending order.

> **Note**
> Mind the order of the files.

We perform a `cat` on each of the files and pipe the whole result to psql, which inserts the data into the database. We simply stick the files together into one stream of data again.

In many cases, you won't have the disk space to perform an operation like that. How can you use all tapes, one after the other, to back up the data? If you take a closer look at the filenames created by the `split` command, you can see that the files are consecutively numbered using letters. If you have multiple tape drives available, the devices assigned to the driver are also consecutively numbered—but not the same way. SCSI tapes usually start with st0 and continue with st1, st2, st3, and so on. `split` starts with aa and continues with `ab`, `ac`, and so on (if the number of files is higher, `split` uses more than two letters). It would be nice to have devices and files numbered the same way.

Well, that's easy. Simply create hard links for your devices that have the required name. Here is an example:

```
ln /dev/st0 /dev/st0aa
```

st0aa is now an alias for st0. You can create a link for every tape drive now. Saving for data on the array of tape drives is easy:

```
pg_dump person | split -l 3 - /dev/st0
```

Dump the data, split it, and use the devices as the files for the result.

> **Note**
> The - specifies that we want to take input from standard input. If we omitted the -,
> the next parameter we provide (`/dev/st0`) would be used for input.

Many of you might find the algorithm just described is not an everyday solution. It is not supposed to be. This example is taken from a real-world scenario, the solution we implemented to back up the PostgreSQL server in our company (see `http://postgres.cybertec.at`). It works well for us and recovery does also. We have tested this several times, of course. Thanks to PostgreSQL, Debian, and RedHat, we have never had to recover the database because of problems with the operating system or the database.

Journaling

Journaling and logging are two useful steps when dealing with any kind of system or application. An application can be fully debugged only when you know perfectly well what is going on inside the software. Logging is not only useful for debugging purposes; it can be very handy for analyzing and backup.

Assume a situation where PostgreSQL is used as the database for an online shop. The shopping cart of a user is stored in the database and updated by the application every time the customer adds or removes a product or leaves the shop. It might be interesting for you to find out which products are added or removed from the shopping cart while the user is shopping. A logging table can offer significant advantage over log files because data in a database can be processed much easier.

Logging can also be used for backup purposes. A backup application built on logging will be something like incremental backup, and that's the way you can use it:

```
snapshot + journal = current status
```

Create a database on a separate machine that is used for journaling only, and create an entry for every transaction that has been completed on the production system and assign a unique id to it. Every time you dump the production database, you have to make sure that you save the id of the last transaction completed on the server for recovery purposes.

When designing a solution such as we have described, you have to keep PostgreSQL's transaction code in mind. This might be tricky because a few changes in the database might be forgotten "near" the pg_dump. This is a very crucial point.

If the application that uses the database is designed and implemented properly, a journaling server can provide you a lot of information about the processes happening on your system. You can perform any kind of data mining that will be of use to your company.

Another advantage of journaling over other backup methods is that you always have the most recent backup of your database—at least you can restore the most recent snapshot of the data.

In database environments where journaling is used, applications have to be designed to satisfy the demands of the backup system. On the other hand, the backup system is designed to satisfy the demands of your application.

Summary

PostgreSQL databases can easily be backed up, because the standard file format used by PostgreSQL is ASCII. This makes PostgreSQL backups portable and easy to modify.

In combination with Unix systems, powerful backup solutions can be built to increase the availability and security of your database.

CHAPTER 8

Performance Tuning

Measuring Performance

Tuning a PostgreSQL database is done for many reasons and can be done in many ways. On the one hand, users and developers want to see their applications run faster; on the other hand, performance is a good argument for selling a product to a customer. One way to achieve higher performance is to invest in the latest hardware, such as faster processors, more memory, or faster I/O systems. This is a good solution, but higher performance can also be reached by tuning and focusing on the intelligent design of your application. It is up to you to decide which way to go if you need higher performance. We will describe some ways to tune your PostgreSQL database and see how much performance we can gain.

Tuning can be done in many ways, and the number of parameters affecting the speed of your application is nearly endless. The most important components on the hardware side are the power of your CPU, memory, and the speed of your I/O system. The I/O system has an especially great influence on the behavior of your system. In most cases, a database system has to perform a lot of I/O operations, but only a few calculations. Retrieving data means reading data, and reading data needs a lot of I/O performance, but very little CPU time. You should keep this in mind when planning database environments and deciding which hardware to use.

If you want to tune your database, it is necessary to do some kind of performance measuring. Tuning can only be done by comparing data and testing various settings.

One very important parameter for tuning is the average CPU load of the system. On Unix systems, the uptime command gives us some information about the CPU load:

```
[hs@bachata hs]$ uptime
 3:03pm  up 68 days,  1 user,  load average: 0.20, 0.16, 0.07
```

uptime tells us how long the machine has been up and running. In the previous example, we can see that the machine has been running for 68 days. One user is currently logged in.

We get three values that show us the average load of the system:

- The first value tells us that during the past minute we had a 20 percent average load.

- The second number means that during the past 5 minutes we had a 16 percent average load of; over the past 15 minutes we had an 7 percent average load of.

It is important to mention that the system load can also be higher than 100 percent. If this happens, you can feel that the speed of the system is decreasing and that processes take longer to finish.

The higher the three values are, the worse for your system. It is important to keep the CPU time under 100 percent; otherwise, you should consider an upgrade of your hardware or further tuning.

I/O performance cannot be as easily evaluated as CPU time. Some benchmark suites exist for various operating systems, but in most cases, it depends on the kind of database you want to build as to which settings and which hardware will be suitable.

If you want to find out which hardware components are available, we recommend that you check out the hardware guide by Tom Pabst (the guy who found latency errors in Intel's 1.13Ghz CPU that caused Intel to recall the chip) that can be found at www.tomshardware.com. www.anandtech.com, by Anand Shimpi, is also a good choice for objective hardware reviewing.

One of the most important hardware parameters in database business is the amount of memory of your system. Memory is not only needed to perform sort operations faster. Memory is also used for caching queries and data. The amount of shared memory PostgreSQL uses can be defined when starting the postmaster.

When tuning your database, it is very important to know how much memory is consumed by your system and how memory is used by the database. On Linux systems, you can use a command called `free` to find some basic information about memory use of the operating system. `free` will inform you about the peak amount of memory used by the system. That information will help you to get an idea of what is going on on your system:

```
[hs@duron hs]$ free
             total      used      free    shared   buffers    cached
Mem:        257532    254060      3472    135556      5280     99412
-/+ buffers/cache:    149368    108164
Swap:       265032     15488    249544
```

The information provided by `free` is directly read from the kernel. If you want to see which processes use how much memory, we recommend to use a tool called `top`. `top` provides an ongoing look at processor activity in real time. You can even sort the processes by memory (Shift+M) or CPU usage (Shift+P).

We won't discuss memory management of all those operating systems out there in detail because this information is very hardware-dependent and may change from one version to the other. As far as Windows and Linux are concerned, some powerful tools with nice GUIs to monitor memory management are available.

In the next sections of the book, we will discuss database performance with the help of some scripts. Most of the results will be very hardware and platform-dependent, but the scripts can help you to tune your database efficiently.

Indexes and Performance

Indexes are a very important method to achieve higher performance. In most cases, when working with indexes, we are not talking about performance gains of 1 or 2 percent; it is possible to gain millions of percentage of performance when the amount of data stored in a table is huge. As a rule of thumb, we can say that the higher the amount of data in a table, the more we will gain by using an index. Indexes are very efficient when many different values are stored in a column. We won't gain performance with an index when working with Boolean fields because a Boolean field can only have up to three values (`true`, `false`, and `NULL`).

We have discussed how indexes work and what types of indexes are available in PostgreSQL in the section about components of relational databases. To show you how an index can speed up your query, we will create a table and write a script that generates 10 million records. We will use the output of the script as a sample database in the following section.

Let's create a table first:

```
CREATE TABLE perftest (id int, astring text, anumber int);
```

We have created an empty table with no index. The following script called gendata and can be used to generate random records we will insert into the database called performance:

```perl
#!/usr/bin/perl

$maxrecords = 10000000;          # 10 million

if      (1 eq 1)
{
        open(PIPE,"| psql -U postgres performance") or
                die "can't open pipe: $!\n";
}
else
{
        open(PIPE,"> /dev/null") or
                die "can't open pipe: $!\n";
}

$command='COPY "perftest" FROM stdin;';
@chars=("A" .. "Z", "a" .. "z", 0 .. 9 );
@figure=( 0 .. 9 );

print PIPE "$command\n";
for($i=1; $i<=$maxrecords; $i++)
{
        $astring=join("", @chars[ map { rand @chars } (1 .. 8 ) ]);
        $numbers=join("", @figure[ map { rand @figure } (1 .. 8 ) ]);
        $check = $numbers;
        if      ($check < 1)
        {
                # do nothing
        }
        else
        {
```

```
            print PIPE "$i\t$astring\t$numbers\n";
      }
}
print PIPE "\\.\n";
close(PIPE);
```

Let's see how the script works. $maxrecords contains the number of records we want to create. Then we open a pipe to psql for inserting data into database performance. We can connect to the database as user postgres. In the else branch, we open a pipe for writing the data to /dev/null. /dev/null is the trashcan of the system. We have included this here to find out how long the program needs to create the data (will be done with the help of the time command); we need this value to calculate the time PostgreSQL needs to insert the data.

The data will be inserted into the data with the help of the COPY command; in $command, we can find the header of the command. Then the loop is processed. Inside the loop we create two random values. $astring is a 8-byte–ong random string. $numbers is a random integer value.

The ID of the records and the two random fields are then written into the pipe. Finally, the pipe is closed. We have included five random sample datasets next so you can see how the random table might look:

```
1       QqMwNEjR        90972712
2       Eqprz14z        74727204
3       0eRwFecC        16321694
4       DxVbTxhv        97166380
5       XgIuvPtl        37298281
```

This script will generate 10 million records, such as the ones shown previously. Let's execute the script.

```
[hs@duron code]$ time ./gendata.pl

real    17m51.043s
user    11m15.240s
sys     0m5.510s
```

We have started the script with the help of time. time is a Unix command that measures the time for executing a script. You can see that it took 17 minutes and 51 seconds to execute the Perl script.

Now we want to select a value from the table. We did not define an index for the column yet:

```
bash-2.04$ time echo "SELECT * FROM perftest WHERE id=5000000" | psql
performance
   id    | astring  | anumber
---------+----------+----------
 5000000 | 1wfi0e57 | 45326076
(1 row)


real    3m36.231s
user    0m0.010s
sys     0m0.020s
```

We simply pipe the result of the echo command to psql. We use the Unix shell instead of the psql shell, so we can measure the time the command takes to complete. Indeed, the query takes a lot of time. Because we haven't created an index, the database performs a so-called "full table scan." This means that the database reads the table from the beginning to the end and checks every record whether is fulfills the required conditions or not.

We create an index called idx_id_perftest on column id now:

```
bash-2.04$ time echo "CREATE INDEX idx_id_perftest ON perftest(id)" |
psql performance
CREATE


real    8m52.278s
user    0m0.020s
sys     0m0.000s
```

As you can see, it takes nearly nine minutes. We perform the query a second time:

```
bash-2.04$ time echo "SELECT * FROM perftest WHERE id=5000000" | psql
performance
   id    | astring  | anumber
---------+----------+----------
 5000000 | 1wfi0e57 | 45326076
(1 row)


real    3m53.837s
user    0m0.030s
sys     0m0.010s
```

The database still seems to perform a full table scan. This happens because the information in the system tables read by the optimizer, the part of the database which is responsible to find the right way through a query, have not been updated yet. We will discuss things like that in the "Using EXPLAIN and Understanding the Optimizer" section later in this chapter. To solve the problem concerning the index, we can use the VACUUM command, as shown in the following example:

```
bash-2.04$ time echo "VACUUM VERBOSE ANALYZE perftest" | psql performance
NOTICE:  --Relation perftest--
NOTICE:  Pages 68494: Changed 0, reaped 0, Empty 0, New 0; Tup 10000000:
Vac 0, Keep/VTL 0/0, Crash 0, UnUsed 0, MinLen 52, MaxLen 52; Re-using:
Free/Avail. Space 0/0; EndEmpty/Avail. Pages 0/0. CPU 23.63s/66.78u sec.
NOTICE:  Index idx_id_perftest: Pages 19688; Tuples 10000000.
CPU 5.81s/13.38u sec.
VACUUM


real    5m38.913s
user    0m0.020s
sys     0m0.030s
```

After running "VACUUM" the query will run significantly faster:

```
bash-2.04$ time echo "SELECT * FROM perftest WHERE id=5000000" | psql
performance
   id    | astring  | anumber
---------+----------+----------
 5000000 | 1wfi0e57 | 45326076
(1 row)


real    0m0.085s
user    0m0.010s
sys     0m0.000s
```

It takes only 0.085 seconds to process the query, which means that the query is about 2,750 times faster than before, only because of the index.

When measuring performance, we recommend that you use more than just one SQL statement because the result may vary when executing it several times. Good input for a performance test would be a logfile. If you write all SQL statements done by your application into a logfile, you can take the SELECT statements out of that file to test your database. This would be a good method to do performance tests under real-world circumstances.

> **Note**
> The more SQL statements you use for testing, the more representative the result of the performance test.

By default, PostgreSQL creates B-tree indexes, but we can also use hashing or R-trees instead (depending on the data type of the column we want to index).

Indexes can not only be defined for one column. One index can also be used to index two columns at once. Indexing more columns with one index will significantly speed up your query when you want to retrieve values from exactly those columns covered by the index. We will drop the index we have created before and create a new index that covers id and astring:

```
DROP INDEX idx_id_perftest;
CREATE INDEX idx_id_perftest ON perftest (id, astring);
```

We will perform two queries now. You can see that the second query is much faster than the first one. The second query uses the index very efficiently and is, therefore, very fast:

```
bash-2.04$ time echo "SELECT * FROM perftest WHERE id=6000001" | psql
performance
    id    |  astring  | anumber
----------+-----------+----------
 6000001  | FnHdo3RL  | 53523975
(1 row)


real    0m0.419s
user    0m0.000s
sys     0m0.020s
bash-2.04$ time echo "SELECT * FROM perftest WHERE id=6000001 AND
astring='FnHdo3RL'" | psql performance
    id    |  astring  | anumber
----------+-----------+----------
 6000001  | FnHdo3RL  | 53523975
(1 row)


real    0m0.054s
user    0m0.020s
sys     0m0.000s
```

But indexes are not only used to speed up queries. Unique indexes can be used to ensure that a value can only occur once in a table. Primary keys are also unique indexes. If we use unique values on multiple columns, PostgreSQL ensures that no combination of values exist more than once. Additionally, unique indexes are faster than indexes that can contain multiple entries of one value.

Whenever a relationship between data occurs, a join can be performed. Joining means that the database has to find the corresponding data for certain values in another table. To find the right value quickly, it is extremely useful to create indexes on all columns involved in the join operation to speed up the operation significantly.

Using EXPLAIN and Understanding the Optimizer

Understanding the internals of the database is important when tuning a system. Knowing what is going on inside the database will allow you to detect bottlenecks and inefficient sequences of code. This section will guide you through the world of PostgreSQL's internals, and you will see what PostgreSQL does internally to find a way through a query.

Understanding Execution Plans

PostgreSQL users can use EXPLAIN to determine how the optimizer will execute a query. Simply submit a query to the database by using EXPLAIN to the database, and the database will provide a list of all necessary steps to process a query. The following is an overview of the EXPLAIN command:

```
performance=# \h EXPLAIN
Command:     EXPLAIN
Description: Shows statement execution plan
Syntax:
EXPLAIN [ VERBOSE ] query
```

Simply add the query you want to analyze to EXPLAIN, and the database will show the execution plan:

```
performance=# EXPLAIN SELECT * FROM perftest WHERE anumber=68374313;
NOTICE:  QUERY PLAN:

Seq Scan on perftest  (cost=0.00..193494.00 rows=1 width=20)

EXPLAIN
```

Because we have not created an index on anumber, the database can only perform a sequential scan on perftest to find the right value. Sequential scan means that the database has to read the entire table to find the result. In many books about databases, sequential scans are also called *full table scans*.

In the previous example, we can see that the database estimates the cost of executing the query. The cost is measured in units of disk page fetches, and PostgreSQL counts only these disk page fetches that are important for the query planner. Everything that is not affecting the query plan will silently be omitted.

The database also estimates how many rows will be returned by the query and tells us how many bytes per row are used (this value is also estimated by the database).

In the previous example, we have shown the short version of the execution plan. For those who want to go deeper into detail, we have included a short and a long version of the execution plan of 1 + 1. You will see in the long version how complicated simple operations can be and the huge amount of information the PostgreSQL tells the user.

The following is the short version:

```
performance=# EXPLAIN SELECT 1 + 1;
NOTICE:  QUERY PLAN:

Result  (cost=0.00..0.00 rows=0 width=0)

EXPLAIN
```

As you might have expected, the short version looks very simple, but let's come to the long version now. We have to use EXPLAIN with VERBOSE enabled:

```
performance=# EXPLAIN VERBOSE SELECT 1 + 1;
NOTICE:  QUERY DUMP:

{ RESULT :startup_cost 0.00 :total_cost 0.00 :rows 0 :width 0 :state <>
:qptargetlist ({ TARGETENTRY :resdom { RESDOM :resno 1 :restype 23
:restypmod -1 :resname ?column? :reskey 0 :reskeyop 0 :ressortgroupref 0
:resjunk false } :expr { CONST :consttype 23 :constlen 4 :constisnull false
:constvalue  4 [ 2 0 0 0 ]  :constbyval
true }}) :qpqual <> :lefttree <> :righttree <> :extprm () :locprm () :initplan
<>
:nprm 0  :resconstantqual <>}
NOTICE:  QUERY PLAN:

Result  (cost=0.00..0.00 rows=0 width=0)
```

The whole thing looks a little more difficult now, but if you take a closer look at the query, plan you will see that it is not as difficult as it seems at first sight. In line two, for example, you can see the name of the column displayed in the result (`?column?`) but also most other columns can be understood when dealing with PostgreSQL more extensively. We want to go further into detail at this point, because this would lead too far and won't help you when tuning your database. We have just included this here to show you that building a database server is truly a little more complicated than writing `Hello World` applications. As you can see, `verbose` makes PostgreSQL display a lot of information that is used only internally, such as the data types involved in the query (see `restype 23` or `resname ?column?`) that tells us the name of a column in the result of the query.

After this small insight into PostgreSQL's internals, we will go through some queries including the optimizer information now.

The following example shows a very simple query using an index. The query retrieves a certain ID from the table.

```
performance=# EXPLAIN SELECT * FROM perftest WHERE id=1;
NOTICE:  QUERY PLAN:

Index Scan using idx_id_perftest on perftest  (cost=0.00..4.98 rows=1 width=20)
```

`id` is indexed and the database uses that index to perform the query quickly. You can see that the database tells us which index is used and which is the table for which the index was defined. If you take a closer look at the cost, you will recognize that the database needs only `4.98` units instead of `193494.00` units, as we had before.

The next query is a little more complex. We want to count how often an ID appears in the table.

```
performance=# EXPLAIN SELECT id, COUNT(*) FROM perftest GROUP BY id;
NOTICE:  QUERY PLAN:

Aggregate  (cost=0.00..1551879.15 rows=1000000 width=4)
  -> Group  (cost=0.00..1526879.15 rows=10000000 width=4)
       -> Index Scan using idx_id_perftest on perftest  (cost=0.00..1501879.15
rows=10000000 width=4)

cx
EXPLAIN
```

As you can see, the database has to perform three different types of operations: Aggregation, grouping, and scanning the index.

The result of the previous query is 10 million rows long. For debugging purposes, it is sometimes useful to display only the first few values of the result. We can use the LIMIT command to skip records. Now we want to compare the query plan of the following query by using LIMIT with the previous query that does not use LIMIT.

```
performance=# EXPLAIN SELECT id, COUNT(*) FROM perftest GROUP BY id LIMIT 5;
NOTICE:  QUERY PLAN:

Aggregate  (cost=0.00..1551879.15 rows=1000000 width=4)
  -> Group  (cost=0.00..1526879.15 rows=10000000 width=4)
       -> Index Scan using idx_id_perftest on perftest  (cost=0.00..1501879.15
rows=10000000 width=4)

EXPLAIN
```

You can see that the query plan is exactly the same. The query that does not use LIMIT takes much longer to complete because the database starts to display the result when the query is ready and a query that returns 10 millions of records will take longer to complete.

This shows that LIMIT can have a significant advantage, but it also shows that the way the database processes a query internally won't differ.

The next example performs the same query but returns only records where the result of the COUNT operation is higher than one.

```
performance=# EXPLAIN SELECT id, COUNT(*) FROM perftest GROUP BY id
HAVING COUNT(*) > 1;
NOTICE:  QUERY PLAN:

Aggregate  (cost=0.00..1576879.15 rows=1000000 width=4)
  -> Group  (cost=0.00..1526879.15 rows=10000000 width=4)
       -> Index Scan using idx_id_perftest on perftest  (cost=0.00..1501879.15
rows=10000000 width=4)

EXPLAIN
```

The query plan is the same again because the HAVING clause is not more than an additional condition that won't affect the way the data is read. Grouping, sorting, and aggregation usually take longer than testing conditions, so there is no reason for the optimizer to change the query plan.

The whole thing looks a little different when we try to find values that occur more than once in a column that is not indexed.

```
performance=# EXPLAIN SELECT astring, COUNT(*) FROM perftest GROUP BY astring
HAVING COUNT(*) > 1 LIMIT 10;
NOTICE:  QUERY PLAN:

Aggregate  (cost=2104428.83..2179428.83 rows=1000000 width=12)
  -> Group  (cost=2104428.83..2129428.83 rows=10000000 width=12)
      -> Sort  (cost=2104428.83..2104428.83 rows=10000000 width=12)
            -> Seq Scan on perftest  (cost=0.00..168494.00 rows=10000000
width=12)

EXPLAIN
```

The database has to sort the data now and can't use an index because no index has
been defined. In reality, an index is no more than a sorted list; if you take this into
consideration, it seems obvious that the database has to sort all records if no index is
defined. In general, sorting takes a lot of time, and in most cases it is very bad for the
performance of your system.

Analyzing queries is extremely interesting when dealing with joins. As you can see in
the following, we create a table called jointab and insert three values into it. Keep in
mind that the values we are going to insert are taken from pertest table and have
been generated stochastically. To test the example, select values from your table and
use them instead of the stochastic values used here:

```
CREATE TABLE jointab(id int4, bstring text, bnumber integer, [ic::ccc]PRIMARY
KEY (id));
INSERT INTO jointab VALUES(183,'ggzrsFgz',59457349);
INSERT INTO jointab VALUES(207,'Aht5d1wa',59457349);
INSERT INTO jointab VALUES(56841,'loghwtfc',45671023);
```

We write a query that returns all IDs existing in the perftest and jointab tables. This
is a very simple join operation that can be performed quickly by PostgreSQL:

```
performance=# EXPLAIN SELECT a.id AS perftest, b.id AS jointab FROM perftest
AS a, jointab AS b WHERE a.id=b.id;
NOTICE:  QUERY PLAN:

Nested Loop  (cost=0.00..16.02 rows=3 width=8)
  -> Seq Scan on jointab b  (cost=0.00..1.03 rows=3 width=4)
  -> Index Scan using idx_id_perftest on perftest a
(cost=0.00..4.98 rows=1 width=4)

EXPLAIN
```

perfest is processed by scanning the index. A sequential scan is used to retrieve data from jointab. Nested loops are something very dangerous because whole loops have to be processed for all records. Depending on how long the loop takes to be processed, the query can be rather fast or extremely slow. When you find a nested loop in your execution plan, you have to be very careful with the query.

Let's see what the database does when we create an index on id in the jointab table. To create an index, CREATE INDEX can be used. Before we create the index, we will have a look at the syntax overview of CREATE INDEX:

```
performance=# \h CREATE INDEX
Command:     CREATE INDEX
Description: Constructs a secondary index
Syntax:
CREATE [ UNIQUE ] INDEX index_name ON table
    [ USING acc_name ] ( column [ ops_name ] [, ...] )
CREATE [ UNIQUE ] INDEX index_name ON table
    [ USING acc_name ] ( func_name( column [, ... ]) [ ops_name ] )
```

With the help of the syntax overview, creating the index will be simple:

```
CREATE INDEX idx_id_jointab ON jointab (id);
```

After vacuuming the table, we look at the execution plan again:

```
performance=# EXPLAIN SELECT a.id AS perftest, b.id AS jointab FROM perftest AS
a, jointab AS b WHERE a.id=b.id;
NOTICE:  QUERY PLAN:

Nested Loop  (cost=0.00..16.02 rows=3 width=8)
  ->  Seq Scan on jointab b  (cost=0.00..1.03 rows=3 width=4)
  ->  Index Scan using idx_id_perftest on perftest a
(cost=0.00..4.98 rows=1 width=4)


EXPLAIN
```

Things haven't changed. The execution plan is exactly the same as previously shown. This shows that it is not always useful for the database to use an index if an index exists for a column. In the previous query, it seems faster for the execution planner to use a sequential scan instead of an index scan. Indexes are very fast for huge amounts of data, but when the amount of data stored in a table is very small, the overhead of processing the index is much higher than performing a sequential scan.

In the next example, we will show one way the database processes aggregation and join operations:

```
performance=# EXPLAIN SELECT COUNT(*) FROM perftest AS a, jointab AS b
WHERE a.id=b.id AND astring=bstring;
NOTICE:  QUERY PLAN:

Aggregate  (cost=16.04..16.04 rows=1 width=32)
  -> Nested Loop  (cost=0.00..16.04 rows=1 width=32)
       -> Seq Scan on jointab b  (cost=0.00..1.03 rows=3 width=16)
       -> Index Scan using idx_id_perftest on perftest a
(cost=0.00..4.99 rows=1 width=16)

EXPLAIN
```

The query is processed nearly the same way as the previous example. The only thing that had to be added was the aggregation.

Subqueries are used to determine unknown criteria for using the information in the main query. In the following example, we will run a subquery to find the average value of all records in anumber. The result of the subquery is used to select all records from the jointab table that are higher than the result of the subquery.

```
performance=# EXPLAIN SELECT jointab.bnumber FROM perftest, jointab
WHERE jointab.bnumber > (SELECT AVG(perftest.anumber) FROM perftest);
NOTICE:  QUERY PLAN:

Nested Loop  (cost=0.00..268495.04 rows=10000000 width=8)
  InitPlan
    -> Aggregate  (cost=193494.00..193494.00 rows=1 width=4)
      -> Seq Scan on perftest  (cost=0.00..168494.00 rows=10000000 width=4)
  -> Seq Scan on jointab  (cost=0.00..1.04 rows=1 width=4)
  -> Seq Scan on perftest  (cost=0.00..168494.00 rows=10000000 width=4)

EXPLAIN
```

The database uses a sequential scan to retrieve all data from the perftest table. No index is used because no selection has to be done for the records in the perftest table. A sequential scan is also used for scanning table jointab.

Views are virtual tables that can be defined on top of views or tables. What happens when PostgreSQL has to perform SELECT statements with views involved, and what will the execution plan look like? We will try to answer the question with the help of an example. We create a view first:

```
CREATE VIEW view_perftest AS SELECT anumber/id AS first, astring FROM perftest;
```

Let's take look at the execution plan of a simple full table scan.

```
performance=# EXPLAIN SELECT * FROM view_perftest;
NOTICE:  QUERY PLAN:

Seq Scan on perftest  (cost=0.00..168494.00 rows=10000000 width=20)

EXPLAIN
```

The database performs a sequential scan on the perftest table. This seems obvious because perftest is the only table used by the view. The execution plan won't tell us anything about the view we use. The most important information for the optimizer is which tables have to be scanned. Views are virtual tables and are based on "real" tables.

The way PostgreSQL presents the execution plan is truly a useful and easy to understand one. To tune your PostgreSQL database, reading execution plans can be recommended because this will make you understand the database in a better way, and you can write faster SQL statements when you know what can go wrong inside the database. We have also tried to show that defining an endless number of indexes is not the fastest way to achieve a result in all cases. Tuning is sometimes nothing more than trial and error; you should keep this in mind. Try to define an index on a column and see how much performance you will gain or loose.

Another important point when working with indexes is indexing and function. In some cases, functions and indexes can be a problem. Like most databases, PostgreSQL can't use an index when a function is involved in the query. Look at the following example. Executing the query will take a very long time, so you can interrupt the query using Ctrl+C:

```
performance=# SELECT id FROM perftest WHERE id*2=4;
Cancel request sent
ERROR:  Query was cancelled.
performance=# EXPLAIN SELECT id FROM perftest WHERE id*2=4;
NOTICE:  QUERY PLAN:

Seq Scan on perftest  (cost=0.00..218966.00 rows=100000 width=4)

EXPLAIN
```

We want to find all values in the perftest table where id multiplied by 2 is exactly 4. We have an index on the id column, and this index is used when performing a simple search for a value without a multiplication in the WHERE clause. However, if a function such as a multiplication is performed with a column, PostgreSQL won't be able to use an index anymore. Keep this in mind when working with functions because this knowledge will make you write faster SQL statements, and you don't need to wonder anymore why a query performs ghastly slow.

VACUUM

The VACUUM command removes expired rows from the files in which the table of a database is stored. PostgreSQL creates new records in a file when performing updates and marks the old records as expired; updated records are not overwritten immediately. This may seem strange, but is very important for the database. Expired rows can be useful for users who are still in a transaction and have to see the expired data for completing the transaction.

VACUUM removes the expired records from a row and speeds up the database. Let's take a look at what the system tells us about VACUUM:

```
performance=# \h VACUUM
Command:     VACUUM
Description: Clean and analyze a Postgres database
Syntax:
VACUUM [ VERBOSE ] [ ANALYZE ] [ table ]
VACUUM [ VERBOSE ] ANALYZE [ table [ (column [, ...] ) ] ]
```

As you can see, VACUUM can be used for tables and columns. If VACUUM is called without arguments, PostgreSQL vacuums all tables in the database. We recommend that you VACUUM all tables periodically when the load of the system is low. VACUUMing will speed up your system significantly, especially on systems that have to perform a lot of SQL statements that are used to change data.

> **Note**
> PostgreSQL databases version 6.5 have to lock a table completely while performing VACUUM.

With the help of the verbose flag, we can find out a little bit more about what is done by VACUUM:

```
performance=# VACUUM VERBOSE perftest;
NOTICE:  --Relation perftest--
NOTICE:  Pages 68494: Changed 0, reaped 0, Empty 0, New 0; Tup 10000000:
```

```
Vac 0, Keep/VTL 0/0, Crash 0, UnUsed 0, MinLen 52, MaxLen 52; Re-using:
Free/Avail. Space 0/0; EndEmpty/Avail. Pages 0/0. CPU 33.99s/12.25u sec.
NOTICE:  Index idx_id_perftest: Pages 34604; Tuples 10000000.
CPU 16.05s/15.29u sec.
VACUUM
```

We can see in the previous listing that the database displays quite a lot of information about the table, such as the number of pages used to store the database (a page is a block of data that is read at once by the database to achieve better performance).

One of the most important commands for tuning a database is VACUUM ANALYZE This command is similar to VACUUM but collects important information when the optimizer needs to find the best way through a query, such as the number of duplicated values and so on. The information collected by VACUUM ANALYZE is stored in pg_statistics.

We have used VACUUM ANALYZE in a previous section to make the query use an index. Before using VACUUM ANALYZE, the optimizer has no suitable statistical information about the table so it did a sequential scan. Every time the data in a table changes significantly, we recommend using VACUUM ANALYZE. Loading a table, as we did in the previous section, is a significant change because we were loading 10 million records into an empty table.

Next, we have added an example of how VACUUM ANALYZE can be used to process one column of a certain table.

```
performance=# VACUUM VERBOSE ANALYZE perftest(id);
NOTICE:  --Relation perftest--
NOTICE:  Pages 68494: Changed 0, reaped 0, Empty 0, New 0; Tup 10000000:
Vac 0, Keep/VTL 0/0, Crash 0, UnUsed 0, MinLen 52, MaxLen 52; Re-using:
Free/Avail. Space 0/0; EndEmpty/Avail. Pages 0/0. CPU 21.10s/28.76u sec.
NOTICE:  Index idx_id_perftest: Pages 34604; Tuples 10000000.
CPU 10.28s/18.38u sec.
VACUUM
```

There are plans for PostgreSQL supporting a separate command called ANALYZE instead of using VACUUM ANALYZE in future versions.

Tuning SQL

The first things people do when writing applications is to write code that does the desired job. However, the first solution might not always be the best one. In many cases, the next step is to tune an application to reach higher performance. In this section, you will learn to tune SQL statements efficiently.

Rewriting Queries

Tuning is not only concerned with indexing. Especially complex queries can be made faster by choosing the right SQL code. Most problems can be solved in many ways with SQL.

Imagine a query where we want to find all records that are higher than a certain value or lower than a certain value. The problem can be solved with two different queries:

```
SELECT COUNT(*)
        FROM perftest
        WHERE anumber > 90000000
UNION
SELECT COUNT(*)
        FROM perftest
        WHERE anumber<10000000;
```

or

```
SELECT COUNT(*)
        FROM perftest
        WHERE anumber > 90000000
                OR anumber < 10000000;
```

The first query calculates the result with the help of two queries that are combined using UNION. The second query simply uses OR and processes the whole operation with only one SELECT statement. Take a look at the execution plans of the two queries. Query number one has a rather complicated execution plan because the result of the two SELECT statements have to be merged. This will be ghastly slow, and it is not a good choice to write an SQL statement like the following:

```
performance=# EXPLAIN SELECT COUNT(*) FROM perftest WHERE anumber > 90000000
UNION SELECT COUNT(*) FROM perftest WHERE anumber<10000000;
NOTICE:  QUERY PLAN:

Unique  (cost=391988.01..391988.01 rows=0 width=4)
  -> Sort  (cost=391988.01..391988.01 rows=2 width=4)
        -> Append  (cost=195994.00..391988.00 rows=2 width=4)
              -> Aggregate  (cost=195994.00..195994.00 rows=1 width=4)
                    -> Seq Scan on perftest  (cost=0.00..193494.00
rows=999998 width=4)
```

```
              -> Aggregate  (cost=195994.00..195994.00 rows=1 width=4)
                   -> Seq Scan on perftest  (cost=0.00..193494.00
rows=1000000 width=4)
```

EXPLAIN

The second query works more efficiently because the full table scan has only to be performed once:

```
performance=# EXPLAIN SELECT COUNT(*) FROM perftest WHERE anumber > 90000000
OR anumber < 10000000;
NOTICE:  QUERY PLAN:

Aggregate  (cost=223244.00..223244.00 rows=1 width=4)
  -> Seq Scan on perftest  (cost=0.00..218494.00 rows=1899998 width=4)
```

EXPLAIN

The previous example shows that a lot of performance can be gained with very little effort.

Influencing the Optimizer

If you have to deal with extremely complex queries with a dozen of very big tables involved, it may occur that the planner of the database won't find the fastest way through the query. In many cases, even VACUUM ANALYZE may not help the optimizer.

No matter which database you will use, you will always face critical situations where the database's optimizer does not find the fastest way through a query. This is not a problem only affecting PostgreSQL. All databases can do something wrong in special situations, including Oracle, DB2, and Informix databases. It is hard to say which database actually has the optimizer that makes at least mistakes.

But what are the main reasons that prevent a planner from finding the fastest way of executing a query? One explanation for the problem can be very simple. If the number of tables involved in a query increases, the number of possible join orders increases exponentially. If the number of table reaches a certain limit, it is no longer useful for the database.

But what do to if the optimizer of PostgreSQL fails? Since 7.1, it is possible to influence the order PostgreSQL joins the tables. This is an extremely convenient feature because it offers a lot of tuning potential, especially for very complex queries. Before we get to an example, let's take a look at view_perftest:

```
performance=# \d view_perftest
      View "view_perftest"
 Attribute |  Type   | Modifier
-----------+---------+----------
 first     | integer |
 astring   | text    |
View definition: SELECT (perftest.anumber / perftest.id), perftest.astring FROM
perftest;
```

To make the code we are going to write a little easier, we rename the name of the column:

```
ALTER TABLE view_perftest RENAME COLUMN "?column?" TO first;
```

We want to write a query that retrieves all values where the first column of view_perftest is equal to id in the perftest table and id in the jointab table. The SQL-statement is rather easy but has some tuning potential:

```
SELECT perftest.id
        FROM view_perftest, perftest, jointab
        WHERE view_perftest.first=perftest.id
              AND jointab.id=perftest.id;
```

Let's take a look at the execution plan of the query:

```
performance=# EXPLAIN SELECT perftest.id FROM view_perftest, perftest,
jointab WHERE view_perftest.first=perftest.id AND jointab.id=perftest.id;
NOTICE:  QUERY PLAN:

Nested Loop  (cost=0.00..956914.02 rows=3 width=16)
  -> Nested Loop  (cost=0.00..16.02 rows=3 width=8)
        -> Seq Scan on jointab  (cost=0.00..1.03 rows=3 width=4)
        -> Index Scan using idx_id_perftest on perftest
(cost=0.00..4.98 rows=1
width=4)
  -> Seq Scan on perftest  (cost=0.00..168966.00 rows=10000000 width=8)

EXPLAIN
```

Wow, that looks awful! The database has to process nested loops and a sequential scan on the biggest table. Luckily, the other tables are very small and the nested loops won't take too long. Because the first column in view_perftest contains values that have to be calculated, the database can't use an index to query the view efficiently.

As we promised, it is possible to tell the planner in which order the tables have to be joined. A planner is responsible for generating the execution plan of a query so that the database knows how to execute a query best. The following query is equivalent to the query shown previously:

```
SELECT perftest.id
        FROM view_perftest CROSS JOIN perftest CROSS JOIN jointab
        WHERE view_perftest.first=perftest.id
                AND jointab.id=perftest.id;
```

Although the query will produce the same result, the execution plan looks different:

```
performance=# EXPLAIN SELECT perftest.id FROM view_perftest CROSS JOIN perftest
CROSS JOIN jointab WHERE view_perftest.first=perftest.id AND
jointab.id=perftest.id;
NOTICE:  QUERY PLAN:

Hash Join  (cost=1.04..50588969.10 rows=3 width=16)
   -> Nested Loop  (cost=0.00..50188968.03 rows=10000000 width=12)
         -> Seq Scan on perftest  (cost=0.00..168966.00 rows=10000000 width=8)
         -> Index Scan using idx_id_perftest on perftest
(cost=0.00..4.99 rows=1
width=4)
   -> Hash  (cost=1.03..1.03 rows=3 width=4)
         -> Seq Scan on jointab  (cost=0.00..1.03 rows=3 width=4)


EXPLAIN
```

The execution plan may, at first sight, not look very different but when we try to execute the queries we will see that there is a significant difference in speed.

When executing the first query on the test system we will get theis result:

```
real    12m50.877s
user    0m0.030s
sys     0m0.030s
```

The query takes nearly 14 minutes on the test system to be processed but what about the second query:

```
real    10m13.528s
user    0m0.010s
sys     0m0.060s
```

The second query is about 20 percent faster—a significant performance gain.

If you want to gain performance by influencing the way your planner works, you have to do a lot of testing. Testing not only means that you have to see which query is the fastest, you have also to make sure that the query will return the same result. This is very important because the whole process is about achieving higher performance and not about producing bugs.

For checking whether the first and the second query are equal, we can use an SQL statement. We take all records returned by query one, except those returned by query two:

```
SELECT count(perftest.id)
        FROM view_perftest, perftest, jointab
        WHERE view_perftest.first=perftest.id
              AND jointab.id=perftest.id
EXCEPT SELECT count(perftest.id)
        FROM view_perftest CROSS JOIN perftest CROSS JOIN jointab
        WHERE view_perftest.first=perftest.id
              AND jointab.id=perftest.id;
```

It can sometimes be useful to tell the planner to use indexes instead of sequential scans. As we have discussed before, indexes can sometimes decrease the performance of your system because the overhead of processing the index can take longer than a sequential scan. In general, the database will find the right decision for you, but if you know for sure that an index scan is more efficient than a sequential scan, PostgreSQL offers possibilities to influence the result of the planner by setting special variables to the desired value. Take a look at the following example:

```
performance=# EXPLAIN SELECT * FROM jointab WHERE id=207;
NOTICE:  QUERY PLAN:

Seq Scan on jointab  (cost=0.00..1.04 rows=1 width=20)

EXPLAIN
```

Because the table contains only a few values, the database decides to use a sequential scan to find the result. Now we want to force the database to use an index. We have to turn sequential scans off:

```
SET ENABLE_SEQSCAN TO OFF;
```

As you can see in the following code, the database now performs an index scan instead of a sequential scan:

```
performance=# EXPLAIN SELECT * FROM jointab WHERE id=207;
NOTICE:  QUERY PLAN:

Index Scan using idx_id_jointab on jointab  (cost=0.00..2.01 rows=1 width=20)

EXPLAIN
```

Now we want to set ENABLE_SEQSCAN back to the original value:

```
SET ENABLE_SEQSCAN TO DEFAULT;
```

You can influence more than the way indexes are processed. Since PostgreSQL 7.1, a list of parameters concerning the optimizer can be compiled in postgresql.conf. The following is an overview:

```
#       Optimizer Parameters
#
#enable_seqscan = true
#enable_indexscan = true
#enable_tidscan = true
#enable_sort = true
#enable_nestloop = true
#enable_mergejoin = true
#enable_hashjoin = true

#ksqo = false
#geqo = true

#effective_cache_size = 1000  # default in 8k pages
#random_page_cost = 4
#cpu_tuple_cost = 0.01
#cpu_index_tuple_cost = 0.001
#cpu_operator_cost = 0.0025
#geqo_selection_bias = 2.0 # range 1.5-2.0

#       GEQO Optimizer Parameters
#
#geqo_threshold = 11
#geqo_pool_size = 0  #default based in tables, range 128-1024
#geqo_effort = 1
#geqo_generations = 0
#geqo_random_seed = -1 # auto-compute seed
```

In this list, you can see a lot of optimizer parameters. Feel free to modify these parameters to your needs and try to figure out which effect a change of these parameters has on the performance and the behavior of your system. If you want to find out more about `postgresql.conf`, check out Chapter 6, "Database Administration."

Caching the Result of Functions

In many applications, programmers use self-defined functions to perform special operations. Imagine a situation where a function is used to perform deterministic operations such as calculating the geometric mean of two values. The same values passed to the function will always lead to the same result. If a function is called with the same values several times, it may be useful to cache the result instead of repeatedly calculating it. PostgreSQL is able to cache the result of a function. You only have to tell the database that the result of a function has to be changed when creating it.

We have included a PL/pgSQL function next that supports caching:

```
CREATE FUNCTION geomean_c(int4, int4) RETURNS numeric(10,3) AS
'
        BEGIN
                RETURN numeric_sqrt($1*$1 + $2*$2);
        END;
' LANGUAGE 'plpgsql' WITH (iscachable);
```

Before using this function, the PL/pgSQL has to be added to the database:

```
[hs@athlon postgres]$ createlang plpgsql performance
```

Let's see how it works:

```
performance=# SELECT geomean(94,57);
    geomean
----------------
 109.9317970380
(1 row)
```

Simply add `WITH (iscachable)` to the definition of the function, and the results will be cached. If the function is very simple, such as the one shown previously, the performance gain won't be very high because parsing the SQL statement, displaying the result, and so on is more complex than performing the calculation. For complex functions, caching is a good idea to speed up your applications.

System Performance

Tuning a system is one of the most important tasks a system administrator has to face. In this section, you will learn how to speed up your system and how to improve performance.

The Impact of I/O on System Performance and CPUs

On the hardware side, I/O and CPU power are the most important factors. Of course, hardware is not the only thing affecting the performance of your system, but it is a major component. Let's take a look at what can be done to tweak your hardware.

CLUSTER

Without a doubt, the performance of the I/O subsystem of a server is one of the most important things when working with databases. Tuning the I/O system plays a major part if you want to speed up your application.

Tuning can be done in many ways. On the one hand, the database provides some very useful tools to speed up I/O. On the other hand, performance gains can be achieved by tuning the file system.

Let's start with PostgreSQL's onboard tools first. The most important command when tuning I/O is CLUSTER. PostgreSQL stores indexes in separate files. When many INSERT, UPDATE, or DELETE statements are performed, the values of an index are not stored sequentially in the file. This does not mean that the index is somehow broken or that the result of queries will be wrong. It simply means that the overhead of reading the file increases because the database has to jump around inside the file to read the right piece of data. When the CLUSTER command is called, the database creates a temporary file where the values are stored in the same order as in the index. The temporary file will be used as the new index file as soon as the operation is ready. This will lead to a significant gain of performance, especially when many duplicate values are stored in the index.

Look at the syntax of the CLUSTER command:

```
performance=# \h CLUSTER
Command:     CLUSTER
Description: Gives storage clustering advice to the server
Syntax:
CLUSTER indexname ON tablename
```

As you can see, the syntax is really easy. The only two things you have to define are the name of the index and the table for which it is defined.

We recommend that you run CLUSTER when the load on your system is low.

Tuning the File System

The file system is a very crucial point of the operation system. Today, a file system is more than just an indexed container for the files on your operating system.

Advanced file systems provide quite a lot of tuning parameters that may affect speed in many ways. Tuning a file system is somewhat trial and error. Simply try some settings and find out which one is the fastest for your system. But speed is not the only thing; tuning has always something to do with security. It is of no use to gain speed when the security of the data on your system decreases significantly. Security is very often much more important than speed, especially on high-availability systems. CPU clockspeeds are constantly increasing, and so do new challenges concerning security.

We will try to give you an overview of how tuning can be done. We will use the ext2 (second extended file system) for this purpose.

The ext2 file system is one of the most reliable file systems available. It is the standard file system on Linux platforms. ext2 has no journaling features, but developers (open-source people and companies such as SGI) around the globe are working hard to provide journaling for Linux too.

The most important commands when tuning ext2 file systems are mke2fs and tune2fs, which are used to adjust tunable file system parameters such as maximum-mount-count and so on.

mke2fs is used to create an ext2 file system and supports a huge number of parameters that can be defined. Most of these parameters won't affect the speed of your system, but let's get to the parameters that do.

One of these parameters is the block size of the file system. A file system usually reads an entire block of a predefined size and not single bytes, because this is much faster and works much more efficiently. The size of the blocks affects the speed of your system. On a system with lots of small files, a smaller blocksize may be more useful because the overhead for small files can be reduced. When usually working with large files, the situation may be different. Depending on the application you want to build, the right block size may vary. Currently, ext2 supports three different possible block sizes—1024, 2048, and 4096 bytes.

Another important flag is the `-R` flag that is used to pass options for RAID systems to the file system. To find out which options are currently supported by your version of the file system, check the documentation.

Another important parameter when tuning file systems is the size of a file system. The smaller a file system, the faster data can be accessed by the system. When building databases, you should think a moment about the amount of data that has to be stored. If only a few records have to be stored, it is useful to use a smaller partition for storing the data. This can lead to performance gains, especially for I/O-dependent queries.

The impact of tuning the file system on the performance of the system may be rather small, but after you have found the right setting for your system, it can be a simple way to get a little more power of your system.

fsync

The `fsync` flag has tremendous impact on the overall performance of your system. It can be useful to set the `fsync` flag to `off` temporarily, especially when building up huge databases. We don't recommend that you turn `fsync` off completely because the security of your data may suffer.

We would like to explain in a few words what `fsync` is and what it is good for. On Unix systems, data is not necessarily written to disk when an application writes data into the file. The data is cached by the operating system to achieve higher performance by reducing the number of disk accesses.

`fsync` is a system call that flushes the data to disk. This costs performance but provides higher security in case of a failure because the data in the file is always recent.

On PostgreSQL systems version 7.1, `fsync` can be turned on and off in `pg_options`. Since 7.1, most configuration parameters can be found in `postgresql.conf`. Another way to turn `fsync` off is to use the `-F` flag when starting the postmaster.

PostgreSQL on SMP Machines

It sometimes happens that one CPU is simply not enough for your PostgreSQL server. In this case, you can use machines with multiple CPUs. When running PostgreSQL on an SMP machines, the performance of the system will raise significantly when you are running many queries at once—you won't gain speed (at least no significant gain) on an SMP machines when running only one query at a time.

If your database is very huge (5GB perhaps), we recommend that you use 64-bit CPUs for your PostgreSQL box, such as Digital Alpha, Sun Ultra Sparc 64, IBM 64bit CPUs, SGI 64 bit CPUs, HPUX machines, or 64-bit machines by AMD or Intel.

Simply recompile your PostgreSQL server and you will see that the performance for huge databases increase.

The Impact of Memory on System Performance and Restricted Access to System Resources

In general, databases are very memory consuming applications. Depending on the type of application and the type of queries you want to run on your PostgreSQL server, the amount of needed memory may vary. As a rule of thumb, it can be said that the more memory a system has, the better for the performance of your system.

PostgreSQL's memory management can be configured by the user. This is very useful because you can try set the parameters of the system to your needs; this can lead to a significant increase in performance.

One of the most memory consuming tasks is sorting. Some components of SQL, such as ORDER BY, require internal sorting. Consequently, PostgreSQL uses a so-called sort buffer. The size of the sort buffer can be configured in postgresql.conf. If the amount of memory used for sorting is higher than the size of the sort buffer, PostgreSQL will use temporary files to perform the sort operation. Check the following example to see how temporary files are used by the database. Therefore, you can enter the directory where the database cluster your postmaster is working on is located:

```
bash-2.04$ ls -l *sort*
-rw-------     1 postgres postgres 131211264 Apr 25 19:27 pg_sorttemp12516.0
```

To change the size of the default sort buffer, set sort_mem in postgresql.conf to the desired value that is measured in kilobytes.

We recommend that you use sort buffers that are not too small because temporary files are much slower than internal sorting.

In general, it can be said that it is more efficient to let the database instead of the operating system manage the system resources.

But how can you find out how much memory is used by a query? Simply use top, as, and sort the list by memory use (Shift+M). If you want to find the memory consumption of the entire system, you can use free.

If you have many applications running with different user IDs on your system, it might be useful to restrict resources for certain purposes. Imagine a situation where PostgreSQL is one of two database servers running on the system. In this case, you can define the maximum amount of memory or CPU time that can be used by the user (for example, user `postgres`). Things like these can be defined on most Unix systems with the help of the `ulimit` command. The syntax of the command is very easy:

```
ulimit: usage: ulimit [-SHacdflmnpstuv] [limit]
```

Unfortunately, man pages are only available for the C-function (`long ulimit(int cmd, long newlimit)`) and not for the shell command. For that reason, we have included a full overview of `ulimit` on Linux systems:

```
-S Change and report the soft limit associated with a resource.
-H Change and report the hard limit associated with a resource.
-a All current limits are reported.
-c The maximum size of core files created.
-d The maximum size of a process's data segment.
-f The maximum size of files created by the shell.
-l The maximum size that may be locked into memory.
-m The maximum resident set size.
-n The maximum number of open file descriptors.
-p The pipe buffer size.
-s The maximum stack size.
-t The maximum amount of cpu time in seconds.
-u The maximum number of processes available to a single user.
-v The maximum amount of virtual memory available to the process.
```

Restricting access to resources by using `ulimit` is also a very comfortable way to raise the level of security on your system. "Evil" people can easily make DOS (Denial of Service) attacks by allocating all the memory available on the server if you don't set `ulimits` to restrict the memory a user is allowed to use.

If you want to learn more about the current setting of your system, simply use `ulimit` in your Bash Shell.

Working with Large Amounts of Data

When you want to build a database containing huge amounts of data, it can be very convenient to speed up the process a little. Consequently, it is interesting to know whether to create indexes on certain columns before or after inserting the data.

In general, it is faster to create the index after inserting the data, because the index has to build only once instead of being changed after every record inserted into the database.

Another important issue when working with large amounts of data is the comparison of COPY and INSERT. In general, we can say that inserting data with the help of COPY is much faster than with INSERT commands because of parsing and transaction overhead.

PostgreSQL is capable of handling even enormous amounts of data and is perfectly stable under high load. The test database we use in this chapter consists of 10 million records, but most operations can still be done quickly when using indexes. You will most likely not face any problems with PostgreSQL, even if the database has to face dozens of gigabytes of data. Linux kernels version 2.4 don't support files that are bigger than 2GB. PostgreSQL uses many separate files to get around the problem, and the user does not have to care about operating system or file system specifics.

Regular Expressions and Performance

Regular expression have a significant impact on system performance. The regular expression itself can be processed quickly, but what about indexes and how do regular expressions influence the optimizer?

Let's take a look at a simple query where we want to retrieve 100 from the perftest table:

```
performance=# EXPLAIN SELECT * FROM perftest WHERE id=100;
NOTICE:  QUERY PLAN:

Index Scan using idx_id_perftest on perftest  (cost=0.00..4.98 rows=1 width=20)

EXPLAIN
```

The database performs as you might expect—an index scan and quickly returning the result. Now we try to retrieve the same value with the help of a regular expression:

```
performance=# EXPLAIN SELECT * FROM perftest WHERE id ~ '^100$';
NOTICE:  QUERY PLAN:

Seq Scan on perftest  (cost=100000000.00..100218966.00 rows=100000 width=20)

EXPLAIN
```

The database does a sequential scan now and our query has suddenly become ghastly slow. We can do nothing about it but try to reduce the amount of data that has to be processed by the regular expression.

Reducing the amount of data can be achieved by using temporary tables. Of course, this can only be done with SQL statements containing expressions that significantly reduce the amount of data.

Regular expressions are very powerful, but you can see in the previous example that you have to use them very carefully when you want to write fast applications. If you have only small tables, the impact on performance may not be huge; but when tables grow and many joins with many regular expressions are involved, it may happen that the query cannot be processed anymore.

Summary

There are many ways to improve the performance of a database system. On the one hand, you can improve the design of your database to avoid unnecessary joins and inefficient ways of storing data. On the other hand, a lot of performance can be gained by tweaking your hardware and the operating system.

CHAPTER 9

Programming Interfaces

Connecting PostgreSQL to other software packages is an important issue. When building applications, it is necessary to have interfaces for talking to the server. Because PostgreSQL is a flexible and sophisticated piece of software, it provides a lot of programming interfaces for many different languages. This chapter will guide you through the world of PostgreSQL's programming interfaces and you will learn to build powerful applications based on PostgreSQL.

C/C++

Today, C and C++ are very widespread. A lot of software has been written in C or C++, especially for Unix. PostgreSQL is written in C as well, so it seems obvious that PostgreSQL provides a powerful C/C++ interface. In this section, you will take a closer look at this interface.

An Overview of C/C++

Before we get to the C programming interface for PostgreSQL, we will have a closer look at the history and the development of C. C was developed at Bell Laboratories by Dennis Ritchie in 1972 and is today's most widespread programming language. C compilers are available on almost any platform, so C code is very portable as long as developers stick closely to the ANSI C standard.

When Dennis Ritchie developed C, he took many of the principles and ideas from the earlier language, B, and B's earlier ancestors BCPL and CPL. Combined Programming Language (CPL) was a language that was designed to be a high-level programming language that also allows the programmer to influence the behavior of the hardware itself. Platform independency has also always played a major part in C development. One major disadvantage of CPL was that it was too large for use in many applications at that time. In 1967, Basic CPL (BCPL) was created as a scaled-down version of CPL while still retaining the basic features of CPL.

In 1970, Ken Thompson (Bell Labs) developed B—a scaled-down language of BCPL that was especially optimized for system programming. In 1972, Dennis Richie brought back some generality to the programming language and the result is now known as the C programming language.

Up to that time, the UNIX operating system was still mostly written in Assembler. When the advantages of C became apparent, the major parts of the operating system were rewritten in C. From that time on, the C programming language has always been strongly related to UNIX, and C is still the language of UNIX hackers.

Soon, C was used by many organizations all around the globe. In 1983, an ANSI standard was created to make C applications compatible because many slightly different accents of the language already existed.

C is a procedural language. People soon recognized that some sort of object-orientation would be useful for the language. In October 1970, a first version of "C with classes" was used. In December 1983, "C with classes" finally became known as C++. Along with C, C++ was rapidly developed and became very widespread around the globe. Many compilers, libraries, and documentation were written for C/C++ to make it the language it is today.

Despite the development of many other languages, C/C++ is still the number one and loved by many people. One of the main advantages of the language is its speed. C programs perform extremely well but are, in contrast to Assembler, still readable and, which is very important, portable.

Like most of the software packages used on a UNIX system, PostgreSQL is written in C. Therefore, the C/C++ interface is highly developed and used as the base for building future programming interfaces.

In the next few sections, we will take a closer look at the C/C++ interface of PostgreSQL and how this interface can be used efficiently in some examples. Major parts of the sample code shown in this section have been provided and developed by Erich Fruehstueck, our long time UNIX teacher and C guru. Erich Fruehstueck is the developer and maintainer of the EFEU (EFEU is short for **E**rich **F**ruehstueck **E**ntwicklungs**u**mgebung) package; a package containing a very powerful C/C++-like UNIX interpreter that can easily be used for working with multidimensional data structures.

Connecting

The first thing we will deal with in this section is connecting to the database.

The C programming interface to PostgreSQL is called libpq. libpq is the base for other programming interfaces, such as libpq++ (C++), libpgtcl (Tcl), Perl, ECPG, and many others.

The most important function when establishing a connection is PQconnectdb that returns a PGconn object representing one open connection. In general, PQconnectdb and PQsetdbLogin return no null pointer as long as there is enough memory available on the system to create the PGconn object. To check whether a connection has successfully been established, the PQstatus function has to be used. We will have a closer look at that function later in this section.

To expound how a connection can be established using the libpq interface, we have included two examples. The main target is to write a program that establishes a connection to the database and supports some command-line parameters, as is shown in the following code line. We will also have a look at exception handling.

conn1 db user=hs host=localhost port=5432

The file containing the main function will be called main.c and contains the code as follows:

```
// main1.c
#include <stdlib.h>
#include "example.h"

#define       ARGS         "db [host=name] [port=num] [user=name]
[password=auth]"

int main (int argc, char **argv)
{
```

```
char *cinfo;
PGconn *conn;
int i;

/*     Build connection info string from command args.
*/
if        (argc < 2)
{
        fprintf(stderr, "usage: %s %s\n", argv[0], ARGS);
        exit(EXIT_FAILURE);
}

cinfo = paste("dbname", "=", argv[1]);

for (i = 2; i < argc; i++)
{
        char *save = cinfo;
        cinfo = paste(save, " ", argv[i]);
        free(save);
}

/*     Make a new connection to the database server
*/
conn = PQconnectdb(cinfo);

if        (conn == NULL)
{
        fputs("not enough memory to create PGconn data.\n", stderr);
        exit(EXIT_FAILURE);
}

/*     Check the status of the connection
*/
if        (PQstatus(conn) == CONNECTION_BAD)
{
        char *msg = PQerrorMessage(conn);
        fputs(msg ? msg : "PQconnectdb() failed.\n", stderr);
        info(stderr, conn);
        PQfinish(conn);
        exit(EXIT_FAILURE);
}
```

```
/*      Frontend commands
*/
      info(stdout, conn);

/*      Finish connection
*/
      PQfinish(conn);
      free(cinfo);
      exit(EXIT_SUCCESS);
}
```

First, we include the required C libraries in the program and add a preprocessor command to set the variable ARGS that contains the definition of the command-line parameters accepted by the program.

In main.c, we include only stdlib.h and example.h—the library we need for interacting with the database is included in example.h:

```
/*      header for connection examples - example.h
*/

#ifndef      _example_h
#define      _example_h      1

#include <pgsql/libpq-fe.h>

extern char *paste (const char *s1, const char *delim, const char *s2);
extern void info (FILE *file, PGconn *conn);

#endif /* example.h */
```

As you can see, example.h includes libpq-fe.h, which is the library for interacting with PostgreSQL. Depending on your system, the location of this library may vary. Users of Debian (the program has been tested on Debian 2.2r2) can simply use #include <libpq-fe.h> instead of #include <pgsql/libpq-fe.h>, as has to be done on RedHat 7.1 for example (if you use the standard RPM packages of PostgreSQL). To find out where the required library can be found on the system, simply use the following:

```
find /usr/ -name libpq*h -print 2> /dev/null
```

example.h also contains the header information we use for the self-defined function we will use in the main.c file.

In the `main` function, we define three variables we will use later in the program:

`*paste (const char *s1, const char *delim, const char *s2)` will be used to make one string out of the command line flags. `info(FILE *file, PGconn *conn)` will be used to retrieve information about the authentification process.

Let's get back to main.c.

After defining the variables, we start building the connect string we need to establish the connection to the database. The first parameter passed to the function is the name of the database; if it is not defined, an error will be displayed and `fprintf` is used to display the error:

```
fprintf(stderr, "usage: %s %s\n", argv[0], ARGS);
```

The error message itself is defined in the preprocessor command in line 4 in the `main.c` file. Let's see what happens when we execute the script without parameters:

```
[erich@duron ex1]$ ./conn1
usage: ./conn1 db [host=name] [port=num] [user=name] [password=auth]
```

In the next step, the connect string is compiled using `paste`—the complete connect string is assigned `cinfo`:

```
for (i = 2; i < argc; i++)
{
        char *save = cinfo;
        cinfo = paste(save, " ", argv[i]);
        free(save);
}
```

The paste function used here is defined in `paste.c`:

```
// paste.c
#include <stdlib.h>
#include "example.h"


/*        paste strings
*/


char *paste (const char *s1, const char *delim, const char *s2)
{
        size_t n1, nx, n2;
        char *s;
```

```
        n1 =strlen(s1);
        nx = strlen(delim);
        n2 = strlen(s2);

        s = malloc(n1 + nx + n2 + 1);

        if        (s == NULL)
        {
                fprintf(stderr, "malloc(%d) failed.\n", n1 + nx + n2);
                exit(EXIT_FAILURE);
        }

        strcpy(s, s1);
        strcpy(s + n1, delim);
        strcpy(s + n1 + nx, s2);
        return s;
}
```

After we have computed the connect string, we can easily establish the connection to the database by using:

```
conn = PQconnectdb(cinfo);
```

If PQconnectdb returns a NULL pointer, the connect process has failed due to a lack of memory. Checking the NULL pointer is the first thing that should be done when establishing the connection. The second thing is to check the result of the PQstatus function. PQstatus has to be called with the result of the PQconnectdb function. If PQstatus returns CONNECTION_BAD, the connection has not been established successfully. We extract the error using PQerrorMessage and display it by using the following:

```
fputs(msg ? msg : "PQconnectdb() failed.\n", stderr);
info(stderr, conn);
```

info is a function defined in info.c:

```
// info.c
/*      Connection Info
*/

#include <stdlib.h>
#include "example.h"
```

```
static void pval (FILE *file, const char *name, const char *val)
{
        if      (val)
        {
                fprintf(file, "\t%s = \"%s\"\n", name, val);
        }
        else    fprintf(file, "\t%s = NULL\n", name);
}

void info (FILE *file, PGconn *conn)
{
        fprintf(file, "PGconn = {\n");
        pval(file, "status", (PQstatus(conn) == CONNECTION_OK) ? "ok" : "bad");
        pval(file, "dbname", PQdb(conn));
        pval(file, "user", PQuser(conn));
        pval(file, "pass", PQpass(conn));
        pval(file, "host", PQhost(conn));
        pval(file, "port", PQport(conn));
        pval(file, "tty", PQtty(conn));
        pval(file, "options", PQoptions(conn));
        fprintf(file, "}\n");
}
```

After compiling the program, we can easily execute it by using a command such as follows:

```
[erich@duron ex1]$ conn1 db user=bad_user
```

Some people do not like this kind of syntax. To show you that options can be extracted from the command line differently, we have included a version of the program that uses getopt instead of paste and PQsetdbLogin instead of PQconnectdb to establish the connection to the database. Both versions of the program perform exactly the same task but use different functions for connecting to the database:

```
// main2.c
#include <stdlib.h>
#include <unistd.h>
#include "example.h"

#define         OPTIONS         "?h:p:u:a:"
#define         ARGS            "[-h host] [-p port] [-u user] [-a auth] db"
```

```
/*        main program
*/

int main (int argc, char **argv)
{
        char *pghost, *pgport, *login, *passwd, *dbname;
        PGconn *conn;
        int opt;

/*      Parse command line options
*/
        pghost = NULL;
        pgport = NULL;
        login = NULL;
        passwd = NULL;
        dbname = NULL;

        while ((opt = getopt(argc, argv, OPTIONS)) != -1)
        {
                switch (opt)
                {
                case '?':
                        fprintf(stderr, "usage: %s %s\n", argv[0], ARGS);
                        exit(EXIT_SUCCESS);
                case 'h':
                        pghost = optarg;
                        break;
                case 'p':
                        pgport = optarg;
                        break;
                case 'u':
                        login = optarg;
                        break;
                case 'a':
                        passwd = optarg;
                        break;
                default:
                        exit(EXIT_FAILURE);
                }
        }
```

```
        if      (optind == argc - 1)
        {
                dbname = argv[optind];
        }
        else
        {
                fprintf(stderr, "usage: %s %s\n", argv[0], ARGS);
                exit(EXIT_FAILURE);
        }

/*      Make a new connection to the database server
*/

        conn = PQsetdbLogin(pghost, pgport, NULL, NULL, dbname, login, passwd);

        if      (conn == NULL)
        {
                fputs("not enough memory to create PGconn data.\n", stderr);
                exit(EXIT_FAILURE);
        }

/*      Check the status of the connection
*/
        if      (PQstatus(conn) == CONNECTION_BAD)
        {
                char *msg = PQerrorMessage(conn);
                fputs(msg ? msg : "PQsetdbLogin() failed.\n", stderr);
                info(stderr, conn);
                PQfinish(conn);
                exit(EXIT_FAILURE);
        }

/*      Frontend commands
*/

        info(stdout, conn);

/*      Finish connection
*/

        PQfinish(conn);
        exit(EXIT_SUCCESS);
}
```

The program accepts the same parameters as our first example. This time, the syntax is different:

```
[erich@duron ex1]$ ./conn2 -?
usage: ./conn2 [-h host] [-p port] [-u user] [-a auth] db
```

The name of the database does not have to be the first parameter anymore because all flags are extracted using getopt.

After we have presented and explained all components of our two examples, we can write a Makefile to compile the programs. Using Makefiles (or software that generates Makefiles) for compiling your software is very useful because it saves a lot of time when compiling huge applications. If the Makefile has been written properly, it is even possible to install and remove a compiled application correctly.

We have included a Makefile that compiles the previous code. We have tried to write a "beautiful" Makefile so that C newbies and Windows hackers can see how a Makefile should look. In general, we have tried to show you short Makefiles in the book that do the basic job. I guess this section about C is a good place to show a "full" Makefile containing a little bit more than just the plain compiler commands.

```
#        Makefile for running example

#        Configuration parameters

DB=        db                 # Name of database
PSQL=        psql -q                 # PostgreSQL - frontend

PQINC=        -I/usr/include/postgresql
PQLIB=        -lpq

#        Compiling rules

CC=        gcc
CPPFLAGS= $(PQINC)
CFLAGS= -O2
LDFLAGS= $(PQLIB)

#        Show usage of make for current example

usage::
        @echo "usage: make setup | run | clean"
```

```
#         Rules for commands

main1.o: example.h main1.c
         $(CC) $(CFLAGS) $(CPPFLAGS) -c main1.c -o $@

main2.o: example.h main2.c
         $(CC) $(CFLAGS) $(CPPFLAGS) -c main2.c -o $@

paste.o: example.h paste.c
         $(CC) $(CFLAGS) $(CPPFLAGS) -c paste.c -o $@

info.o: example.h info.c
         $(CC) $(CFLAGS) $(CPPFLAGS) -c info.c -o $@

clean::
         rm -f main1.o main2.o paste.o info.o

setup:: conn1

clean::
         rm -f conn1

conn1: main1.o paste.o info.o
         $(CC) $(CFLAGS) main1.o paste.o info.o -o $@ $(LDFLAGS)

setup:: conn2

clean::
         rm -f conn2

conn2: main2.o info.o
         $(CC) $(CFLAGS) main2.o info.o -o $@ $(LDFLAGS)

#         Rules for example database

setup::        stamp_db

clean::
         -dropdb $(DB)
         rm -f stamp_db

stamp_db:
         if test -f $@; then dropdb $(DB); fi
```

```
        createdb $(DB)
        touch $@

#       Run the example

run:: setup conn1 conn2
        @echo "Running example"
        -conn1 $(DB)
        -conn1 $(DB) user=postgres
        -conn1 $(DB) user=bad_user
        -conn1 bad_database
        -conn2 $(DB)
        -conn2 -u postgres $(DB)
        -conn2 -u bad_user $(DB)
        -conn2 bad_database
```

Let's test the Makefile:

```
[erich@duron ex1]$ make
usage: make setup | run | clean
```

make tells us that three major targets are defined in the Makefile. We have not set up a database yet, because generating and removing the database is also included in the Makefile.

Let's have a look at what has to be done when setting up the database and compiling the code:

```
[erich@duron ex1]$ make setup -n
gcc -O2  -I/usr/include/postgresql -c main1.c -o main1.o
gcc -O2  -I/usr/include/postgresql -c paste.c -o paste.o
gcc -O2  -I/usr/include/postgresql -c info.c -o info.o
gcc -O2  main1.o paste.o info.o -o conn1 -lpq
gcc -O2  -I/usr/include/postgresql -c main2.c -o main2.o
gcc -O2  main2.o info.o -o conn2 -lpq
if test -f stamp_db; then dropdb db            ; fi
createdb db
touch stamp_db
```

First, we compile our source files with the help of Richard M. Stallman's (in my opinion one of the greatest hackers in history and the father of free software and the GPL) C compiler (GNU C compiler). If make setup has been used before, a file called stamp_db exists. If this file does not exist, the database has to be recreated.

`make run` is used to execute the software. We can use `make run` without running `make setup` first. Our Makefile runs `make setup` implicitly if the sources have not been compiled and if the database has not been initialized yet.

`make run` executes the sample code with various settings. Some of these settings will not work.

```
[erich@duron ex1]$ make run -n
echo "Running example"
conn1 db
conn1 db                    user=postgres
conn1 db                    user=bad_user
conn1 bad_database
conn2 db
conn2 -u postgres db
conn2 -u bad_user db
conn2 bad_database
```

Our sample program tells us which connect string is used to establish the connection to the database and whether the connection has been established successfully. Look at what happens when we execute the software:

> **Note**
> We execute the programs as user erich. You have to make sure that this user has
> enough rights to run the batch job.

```
[erich@duron ex1]$ make run
Running example
conn1 db
PGconn = {
        status = "ok"
        dbname = "db"
        user = "erich"
        pass = ""
        host = NULL
        port = "5432"
        tty = ""
        options = ""
}
conn1 db                    user=postgres
FATAL 1:  user "postgres" does not exist
PGconn = {
        status = "bad"
        dbname = "db"
```

```
            user = "postgres"
            pass = ""
            host = NULL
            port = "5432"
            tty = ""
            options = ""
}
make: [run] Error code 1 (ignored)
conn1 db                    user=bad_user
FATAL 1:  SetUserId: user 'bad_user' is not in 'pg_shadow'


PGconn = {
            status = "bad"
            dbname = "db"
            user = "bad_user"
            pass = ""
            host = NULL
            port = "5432"
            tty = ""
            options = ""
}
make: [run] Error code 1 (ignored)
conn1 bad_database
FATAL 1:  Database "bad_database" does not exist in the system catalog.
PGconn = {
            status = "bad"
            dbname = "bad_database"
            user = "erich"
            pass = ""
            host = NULL
            port = "5432"
            tty = ""
            options = ""
}
make: [run] Error code 1 (ignored)
conn2 db
PGconn = {
            status = "ok"
            dbname = "db"
            user = "erich"
            pass = ""
            host = NULL
```

```
        port = "5432"
        tty = ""
        options = ""
}
conn2 -u postgres db
FATAL 1:  user "postgres" does not exist
PGconn = {
        status = "bad"
        dbname = "db"
        user = "postgres"
        pass = ""
        host = NULL
        port = "5432"
        tty = ""
        options = ""
}
make: [run] Error code 1 (ignored)
conn2 -u bad_user db
FATAL 1:  user "bad_user" does not exist
PGconn = {
        status = "bad"
        dbname = "db"
        user = "bad_user"
        pass = ""
        host = NULL
        port = "5432"
        tty = ""
        options = ""
}
make: [run] Error code 1 (ignored)
conn2 bad_database
FATAL 1:  Database "bad_database" does not exist in the system catalog.
PGconn = {
        status = "bad"
        dbname = "bad_database"
        user = "erich"
        pass = ""
        host = NULL
        port = "5432"
        tty = ""
        options = ""
}
make: [run] Error code 1 (ignored)
```

Our Makefile not only produces binaries and creates a database, it also makes sure that the stuff created can be removed from the system safely. Therefore, we have included make clean. In the following code, you can see what make clean is good for:

```
[erich@duron ex1]$ make clean -n
rm -f main1.o main2.o paste.o info.o
rm -f conn1
rm -f conn2
dropdb db
rm -f stamp_db
```

Finally, it can be said that connecting and disconnecting with the help of the libpq library is an easy task. In the next section, we will see how other things, such as selecting data, can be done.

Simple Selects—An Example

After dealing with the authentification process and database connections, we will see how data can be retrieved from the database by using simple SELECT statements.

We have compiled a small sample database that we will use in this section to show you how things work:

```
-- Seting up example tables
--

CREATE TABLE "persons" (
        "name" text,
        "birth" date,
        "gender" character(1)
);

CREATE UNIQUE INDEX persons_name_key on persons ("name");

CREATE TABLE "income" (
        "name" text,
        "year" integer,
        "income" integer
);

CREATE INDEX income_name_key on income ("name");

COPY "persons"  FROM stdin;
Albert          1970-01-01          m
```

```
John              1973-04-04        m
Carla             1963-10-21        f
Jenny             1982-09-21        f
Hans              1978-08-09        m
Epi               1976-06-12        m
Etschi            1960-02-20        f
Bill              1980-07-12        m
\.

COPY "income"  FROM stdin;
Albert         1997         32000
Albert         1998         28000
Albert         1999         30000
Albert         2000         35000
Jon            1998         20000
Jon            1999         40000
Jon            2000         50000
Carla          1998         30000
Carla          1999         32000
Jenny          1999         45000
Jenny          2000         45000
Hans           1999         47000
Hans           2000         59000
Epi            1999         25000
Epi            2000         21000
Etschi         1999         30000
Etschi         2000         34000
Bill           1999         41000
Bill           2000         43000
\.

CREATE VIEW pincome
        AS SELECT p.name, p.gender, i.year, i.income
        FROM persons p, income i
        WHERE p.name = i.name;
```

The following example shows how data can be retrieved from a table. Like our first example, the program supports some command-line parameters:

```
// main1.c
#include <stdlib.h>
#include "example.h"
```

```
#define        ARGS          "db [host=name] [port=num] [user=name]
[password=auth]"

int main (int argc, char **argv)
{
        char *cinfo;
        PGconn *conn;
        int i;

/*      Build connection info string from command args.
*/
        if      (argc < 2)
        {
                fprintf(stderr, "usage: %s %s\n", argv[0], ARGS);
                exit(EXIT_FAILURE);
        }

        cinfo = paste("dbname", "=", argv[1]);

        for (i = 2; i < argc; i++)
        {
                char *save = cinfo;
                cinfo = paste(save, " ", argv[i]);
                free(save);
        }

/*      Make a new connection to the database server
*/
        conn = PQconnectdb(cinfo);

        if      (conn == NULL)
        {
                fputs("not enough memory to create PGconn data.\n", stderr);
                exit(EXIT_FAILURE);
        }

/*      Check the status of the connection
*/
        if      (PQstatus(conn) == CONNECTION_BAD)
        {
                char *msg = PQerrorMessage(conn);
                fputs(msg ? msg : "PQconnectdb() failed.\n", stderr);
```

```
            info(stderr, conn);
            PQfinish(conn);
            exit(EXIT_FAILURE);
    }

/*      Frontend commands
*/
    example_select(conn);

/*      Finish connection
*/
    PQfinish(conn);
    free(cinfo);
    exit(EXIT_SUCCESS);
}
```

The first thing that has to be done is to include the header files, such as `example.h`:

```
// example.h
/*      header for connection examples
*/

#ifndef _example_h
#define _example_h      1

#include <pgsql/libpq-fe.h>

extern char *paste (const char *s1, const char *delim, const char *s2);
extern void info (FILE *file, PGconn *conn);
extern PGresult *query (PGconn *conn, const char *cmd);
extern void example_select (PGconn *conn);

#endif /* example.h */
```

As in previous examples, we connect to the database and display an error if the connect process fails. To execute the query, use

```
example_select(conn);
```

The function is defined in `select.h`. We simply have to pass the database handle to the function.

The code of `select.c` is as follows:

```
// select.c
/*        Selection example
*/

#include <stdlib.h>
#include "example.h"

#define        QUERY "SELECT * FROM pincome ORDER BY name, year"

void example_select (PGconn *conn)
{
        PGresult *res;
        int i, j, n, k;

        printf("query: %s\n", QUERY);
        res = query(conn, QUERY);

        if        (PQresultStatus(res) != PGRES_TUPLES_OK)
        {
                fprintf(stderr, "Command didn't return tuples properly\n");
                PQclear(res);
                return;
        }

        n = PQntuples(res);
        k = PQnfields(res);

        for (j = 0; j < k; j++)
        {
                if        (j)        printf(" | ");

                printf("%10s", PQfname(res, j));
        }

        printf("\n");

        for (i = 0; i < n; i++)
        {
                for (j = 0; j < k; j++)
                {
                        if        (j)        printf(" | ");
```

```
                        printf("%10s", PQgetvalue(res, i, j));
                }

                printf("\n");
        }

        PQclear(res);
}
```

After including all required header files, we define the query string using a preprocessor command.

In `example_select`, we define several variables: `res` is a pointer to the result of the query. The integer values defined next are used in the loops that display the header and the result of the query.

To execute the query, call the query function defined in `query.c`:

```
// query.c
/*          Connection Info
*/

#include <stdlib.h>
#include "example.h"

PGresult *query (PGconn *conn, const char *cmd)
{
        PGresult *result;
        char *msg;

        result = PQexec(conn, cmd);

        if      (result == NULL)
        {
                fputs("not enough memory to create PGresult data.\n", stderr);
                PQfinish(conn);
                exit(EXIT_FAILURE);
        }

        switch (PQresultStatus(result))
        {
        case PGRES_BAD_RESPONSE:
        case PGRES_NONFATAL_ERROR:
```

```
case PGRES_FATAL_ERROR:
        msg = PQresultErrorMessage(result);
        fputs(msg ? msg : "PQexec() failed.\n", stderr);
        PQclear(result);
        PQfinish(conn);
        exit(EXIT_FAILURE);
default:
        break;
}

        return result;
}
```

In query.c, we call PQexec to select data from the table. If the function returns NULL, the system has run out of memory and we terminate the program. Otherwise, we use PQresultStatus to check the return value of the query. Depending on the return value, we decide whether we have to quit the application. If no error has occurred, we return a pointer to the result to the calling function that is, in our case, example_select. Back in example_select, we use the PQresultStatus function to check for errors again and compute the number of tuples and fields. We will need this information to display the result correctly.

The first thing we have to display is the header of the result. Consequently, we use the PQfname function to find out which label is assigned to a certain column. After displaying the header, we extract and display the data. PQgetvalue extracts one field from the result, and we can display the result by using a simple printf command. In the previous example, we want the result to be displayed as a string that is 10 bytes long.

Finally, we clear the result of the query.

To compile the sources, we use a Makefile again. The following is the code of a very simple Makefile:

```
setup   :       main1.c paste.c info.c query.c select.c example.h
        gcc -g  -I/usr/include/postgresql -c main1.c -o main1.o
        gcc -g  -I/usr/include/postgresql -c paste.c -o paste.o
        gcc -g  -I/usr/include/postgresql -c info.c -o info.o
        gcc -g  -I/usr/include/postgresql -c query.c -o query.o
        gcc -g  -I/usr/include/postgresql -c select.c -o select.o
        gcc -g  main1.o paste.o info.o query.o select.o -o sel1 -lpq
        if test -f stamp_db; then dropdb db           ; fi
        createdb db
        touch stamp_db
```

```
        psql -q db < setup.sql

clean   :
        rm -f main1.o paste.o info.o query.o select.o
        rm -f sel1
        dropdb db
        rm -f stamp_db

run     :
        ./sel1 db
```

To set up the database and compile the sources, we use make again:

```
[erich@duron ex2]$ make setup
gcc -g  -I/usr/include/postgresql -c main1.c -o main1.o
gcc -g  -I/usr/include/postgresql -c paste.c -o paste.o
gcc -g  -I/usr/include/postgresql -c info.c -o info.o
gcc -g  -I/usr/include/postgresql -c query.c -o query.o
gcc -g  -I/usr/include/postgresql -c select.c -o select.o
gcc -g  main1.o paste.o info.o query.o select.o -o sel1 -lpq
if test -f stamp_db; then dropdb db            ; fi
createdb db
CREATE DATABASE
touch stamp_db
psql -q          db           < setup.sql
```

The paste.c and info.c files are the same as in the previous examples, so we have not included the code again.

To execute the program, we use make run:

```
[erich@duron ex2]$ make run
Running example
sel1 db
query: SELECT * FROM pincome ORDER BY name, year
      name |   gender |   year |    income
    Albert |        m |   1997 |    32000
    Albert |        m |   1998 |    28000
    Albert |        m |   1999 |    30000
    Albert |        m |   2000 |    35000
      Bill |        m |   1999 |    41000
      Bill |        m |   2000 |    43000
     Carla |        f |   1998 |    30000
     Carla |        f |   1999 |    32000
```

```
     Epi |         m |      1999 |      25000
     Epi |         m |      2000 |      21000
  Etschi |         f |      1999 |      30000
  Etschi |         f |      2000 |      34000
    Hans |         m |      1999 |      47000
    Hans |         m |      2000 |      59000
   Jenny |         f |      1999 |      45000
   Jenny |         f |      2000 |      45000
```

All records in `pincome` are returned and displayed onscreen.

Of course, we have also defined `make clean` to safely remove the binaries and the database created by `make setup`:

```
[erich@duron ex2]$ make clean -n
rm -f main1.o paste.o info.o query.o select.o
rm -f sel1
dropdb db
rm -f stamp_db
```

Binary Cursors and COPY

In this section, we will see how data can be sent to PostgreSQL using some sort of COPY and how data can be retrieved with the help of binary cursors. In some cases, binary cursors have a significant advantage over "ordinary" cursors because many C programs work with binary data internally. If the database has to convert the binary data to ASCII, the application has to convert the result back to a binary format. If the data is retrieved in binary format, the whole transformation process can be skipped, and your applications will run faster.

The program we will present next is already quite long, and we recommend that you spend some time to understand every line completely:

```
// main.c
#include <stdlib.h>
#include <unistd.h>
#include "example.h"

#define        OPTIONS          "?h:p:u:a:dcn:"
#define        ARGS             "[-h host] [-p port] [-u user] [-a auth] \
[-d] [-c] [-n anz] db tab"

/*      main program
*/
```

```
int main (int argc, char **argv)
{
        char *pghost, *pgport, *login, *passwd;
        char *dbname, *tabname;
        int debug, create, ngrp;
        PGconn *conn;
        int opt;

/*      Parse command line options
*/
        pghost = NULL;
        pgport = NULL;
        login = NULL;
        passwd = NULL;
        dbname = NULL;
        tabname = NULL;
        debug = 0;
        create = 0;
        ngrp = 2;

        while ((opt = getopt(argc, argv, OPTIONS)) != -1)
        {
                switch (opt)
                {
                case '?':
                        fprintf(stderr, "usage: %s %s\n", argv[0], ARGS);
                        exit(EXIT_SUCCESS);
                case 'h':
                        pghost = optarg;
                        break;
                case 'p':
                        pgport = optarg;
                        break;
                case 'u':
                        login = optarg;
                        break;
                case 'a':
                        passwd = optarg;
                        break;
                case 'd':
                        debug = 1;
                        break;
```

```
                case 'c':
                        create = 1;
                        break;
                case 'n':
                        ngrp = strtol(optarg, NULL, 0);
                        break;
                default:
                        exit(EXIT_FAILURE);
                }
        }

        if      (optind == argc - 2)
        {
                dbname = argv[optind];
                tabname = argv[optind + 1];
        }
        else
        {
                fprintf(stderr, "usage: %s %s\n", argv[0], ARGS);
                exit(EXIT_FAILURE);
        }

/*      Make a new connection to the database server
*/
        conn = PQsetdbLogin(pghost, pgport, NULL, NULL, dbname, login, passwd);

        if      (conn == NULL)
        {
                fputs("not enough memory to create PGconn data.\n", stderr);
                exit(EXIT_FAILURE);
        }

/*      Check the status of the connection
*/
        if      (PQstatus(conn) == CONNECTION_BAD)
        {
                char *msg = PQerrorMessage(conn);
                fputs(msg ? msg : "PQsetdbLogin() failed.\n", stderr);
                info(stderr, conn);
                PQfinish(conn);
                exit(EXIT_FAILURE);
```

```
        }

        if          (debug)
                PQtrace(conn, stderr);

/*      Frontend commands
*/
        if          (create)
                sample_data(conn, tabname, ngrp);
        else        cursor_example(conn, tabname, ngrp);

/*      Finish connection
*/

        PQfinish(conn);

        exit(EXIT_SUCCESS);
}
```

First, we include the required libraries and define some variables. In the next step, some variables are initialized. One of these values is debug. If debug is set to a value different than zero, the application will display debugging information during the execution of the program. This can be very useful if you are looking for tricky bugs. We use PQtrace for generating the debugging information. PQtrace enables the frontend and backend messages.

> **Note**
> Using PQtrace is only useful if you know the basics of PostgreSQL's internal protocols.

To turn off tracing, PQuntrace has to be used.

Because we want the program to understand command-line options, we use getopt to extract the flags from the input.

If you want to import a huge amount of data into the database, it is not recommended to use a set of INSERT statements because of speed. INSERT statements are ghastly slow compared to COPY, so the performance of your application will suffer when the amount of data increases. In this example, we will show how COPY can be used. Let's have a closer look at sample.c:

```
//sample.c
*       Selection example
*/
```

```
#include <stdlib.h>
#include "example.h"

#define        SQL_CREATE         "CREATE TABLE %s (idx int4, val real)"
#define        SQL_COPY        "COPY %s from stdin"

void sample_data (PGconn *conn, const char *name, int rows)
{
        PGresult *res;
        char buf[256];
        int i;

        vquery(conn, sql(SQL_CREATE, name), PGRES_COMMAND_OK);
        res = xquery(conn, sql(SQL_COPY, name), PGRES_COPY_IN);
        srand48(0);

        for (i = 1; i <= rows; i++)
        {
                sprintf(buf, "%d\t%.5f\n", i, drand48());

                if        (PQputline(conn, buf) != 0)
                        fprintf(stderr, "PQputline() failed\n");
        }

        if      (PQputline(conn, "\\.\n") != 0)
                fprintf(stderr, "PQputline() failed\n");
                if        (PQendcopy(conn) != 0)
                fprintf(stderr, "PQendcopy() failed\n");

        PQclear(res);
}
```

The function generates random records and stores them in a table. sample_data needs two additional files. Let's have a look at sql.c first:

```
// sql.c
/*      Function to insert parameters in a sql-command:
        In real applications there should be checks to avoid
        buffer overflow. Using a fixed size buffer is not a good idea.
*/

#include <stdlib.h>
#include <stdarg.h>
```

```
#include "example.h"

static char sql_buf[1024];

char *sql (const char *fmt, ...)
{
        va_list args;

        va_start(args, fmt);
        vsprintf(sql_buf, fmt, args);
        va_end(args);
        return sql_buf;
}
```

The second file needed is query.c:

```
// query.c
/*          Connection Info
*/

#include <stdlib.h>
#include "example.h"

PGresult *query (PGconn *conn, const char *cmd)
{
        PGresult *result;
        const char *msg;

        result = PQexec(conn, cmd);

        if      (result == NULL)
        {
                fputs("not enough memory to create PGresult data.\n", stderr);
                PQfinish(conn);
                exit(EXIT_FAILURE);
        }

        switch (PQresultStatus(result))
        {
        case PGRES_BAD_RESPONSE:
        case PGRES_NONFATAL_ERROR:
        case PGRES_FATAL_ERROR:
```

```
                fprintf(stderr, "PQexec() failed.\n");
                fprintf(stderr, "Command was: %s.\n", cmd);

                if      ((msg = PQresultErrorMessage(result)) != NULL)
                        fputs(msg, stderr);

                PQclear(result);
                PQfinish(conn);
                exit(EXIT_FAILURE);
        default:
                break;
        }
                return result;
}

PGresult *xquery (PGconn *conn, const char *cmd, ExecStatusType type)
{
        PGresult *result = query(conn, cmd);
        int stat = PQresultStatus(result);

        if      (stat != type)
        {
                fprintf(stderr, "PQexec() returns %s where %s is expected.\n",
                        PQresStatus(stat), PQresStatus(type));
                fprintf(stderr, "Command was: %s.\n", cmd);
                PQclear(result);
                PQfinish(conn);
                exit(EXIT_FAILURE);
        }

        return result;
}

void vquery (PGconn *conn, const char *cmd, ExecStatusType type)
{
        PQclear(xquery(conn, cmd, type));
}
```

The code for working with the database cursor is included in cursor.c:

```
// cursor.c
/*      Selection example
```

```c
*/

#include <stdlib.h>
#include <stdarg.h>
#include "example.h"
#include "pgsql/postgres.h"

/*      SQL-Commands are defined as Macro
*/

#define       SQL_BEGIN        "BEGIN"
#define       SQL_DECL         "DECLARE tmpcursor BINARY CURSOR FOR select *
from %s"
#define       SQL_FETCH        "FETCH %d in tmpcursor"
#define       SQL_CLOSE        "CLOSE tmpcursor"
#define       SQL_COMMIT        "COMMIT"


/*      Function to get index of column with diagnostic-messages
*/

static int getidx (PGresult *res, const char *name)
{
        int i = PQfnumber(res, name);

        if      (i < 0)
                fprintf(stderr, "Column %s not defined.\n", name);

        return i;
}

/*      Binary cursor example
*/

void cursor_example (PGconn *conn, const char *name, int rows)
{
        PGresult *res;
        int i, n, k;
        int i_idx, i_val;
        int *p_idx;
        double *p_val;
```

```
/*      start a transaction block
*/
        vquery(conn, SQL_BEGIN, PGRES_COMMAND_OK);
        vquery(conn, sql(SQL_DECL, name), PGRES_COMMAND_OK);


/*      get the column index after first request.
*/
        res = xquery(conn, sql(SQL_FETCH, rows), PGRES_TUPLES_OK);
        n = PQntuples(res);
        i_idx = getidx(res, "idx");
        i_val = getidx(res, "val");


/*      if i_idx or i_val ist not defined, set n to 0 to
        omit data evaluation.
*/
        if        (i_idx < 0 || i_val < 0)        n = 0;


/*      get data as long as FETCH returns tuples
*/
        for (k = 1; n > 0; k++)
        {
                printf("# group %d: %d rows\n", k, n);

                for (i = 0; i < n; i++)
                {
                        p_idx = (int *) PQgetvalue(res, i, 0);
                        p_val = (double *) PQgetvalue(res, i, 1);
                        printf("%d\t%g\n", *p_idx, *p_val);
                }

                PQclear(res);
                res = xquery(conn, sql(SQL_FETCH, rows), PGRES_TUPLES_OK);
                n = PQntuples(res);
        }

        PQclear(res);

/*      close transaction
*/
        vquery(conn, SQL_CLOSE, PGRES_COMMAND_OK);
        vquery(conn, SQL_COMMIT, PGRES_COMMAND_OK);
}
```

First, we include the header files and declare some preprocessor variables. `getidx` is used to get the index of a column. `cursor_example` shows how binary cursors can be used.

To compile the sources and generate binaries out of it, we use a Makefile:

```
[erich@duron ex3]$ make setup
gcc -g -O2 -I/usr/include/postgresql -c main.c -o main.o
gcc -g -O2 -I/usr/include/postgresql -c paste.c -o paste.o
gcc -g -O2 -I/usr/include/postgresql -c info.c -o info.o
gcc -g -O2 -I/usr/include/postgresql -c query.c -o query.o
gcc -g -O2 -I/usr/include/postgresql -c sql.c -o sql.o
gcc -g -O2 -I/usr/include/postgresql -c cursor.c -o cursor.o
gcc -g -O2 -I/usr/include/postgresql -c sample.c -o sample.o
gcc -g -O2 main.o paste.o info.o query.o sql.o cursor.o sample.o -o tprog -lpq
if test -f stamp_db; then dropdb db          ; fi
createdb db
CREATE DATABASE
touch stamp_db
```

Now we want to execute the program. We can use `make run` to start `tprog`:

```
[erich@duron ex3]$ make run
Running example
tprog -c -n 8 db                 data
tprog -n 5 db              data
# group 1: 5 rows
1       5.00302e-270
2       5.24281e-315
3       5.12022e-315
4       5.25281e-315
5       5.22851e-315
# group 2: 3 rows
6       5.00302e-270
7       5.23803e-315
8       5.20034e-315
echo "DROP TABLE data;" | psql -q db
```

We execute the script twice. First we create eight random records. The second time the script is executed, we want the result to be displayed.

Environment Variables

Like many other programming interfaces, libpq can access environment variables. For example, PQconnectdb or PQsetdbLogin can access the following variables. Usually, the value of the environment variables is taken. If required, the value is not defined by the user:

- PGHOST   Sets the default server name.

- PGPORT   Sets the TCP port to which PostgreSQL is listening.

- PGDATABASE   This sets the default database used by PostgreSQL.

- PGUSER   Sets the default username we use to connect to the database.

- PGPASSWORD   If password authentification is required, the password can be defined in PGPASSWORD.

- PGREALM   This variable is used in combination with Kerberos authentification and defines the Kerberos realm used with PostgreSQL.

- PGOPTIONS   Additional runtime parameters for the backend can be defined using PGOPTIONS.

- PGTTY   Sets the file or tty on which debugging information from the backend processes is displayed.

- PGDATESTYLE   Use this variable to set the default style for displaying dates and time.

- PGTZ   Is used to set the default time zone.

- PGCLIEBTENCODING   If MULTIBYTE support was enabled at compile time, this variable can be used to set the default client encoding used by PostgreSQL.

- PGGEQO   Sets the default mode for the generic optimizer.

Because libpq is the base for many other programming interfaces, the environment variables just listed are also supported by most other programming interfaces.

A Reference of the C Interface

After showing you some examples of how libpq can be used and after dealing with environment variables, we have included a complete reference of libpq.

Database Connection Functions

PostgreSQL provides some functions that are essential for connecting to a database. In this section, you will see how these functions can be used efficiently.

- `PGconn *PQconnectdb(const char *conninfo)`   Makes a new connection to the database server. `conninfo` is a string containing the parameters accepted by the function. The following parameters are valid: `host`, `hostaddr`, `port`, `dbname`, `user`, `password`, `options`, `tty`, and `requiressl`. An example of a valid connect string would be `user=hs dbname=db port=5432 host=localhost`. If an error occurs, `CONNECTION_BAD` is returned.

- `PGconn *PQsetdbLogin(const char *pghost, const char *pgport, const char *pgoptions, const char *pgtty, const char *dbName, const char *login, const char *pwd)`   Can also be used to establish a connection to the database. In contrast to `*PQconnectdb`, `*PQsetdbLogin` uses a fixed number of parameters but offers the same functionalities as `*PQconnectdb`. If an error occurs, `CONNECTION_BAD` is returned.

- `PGconn *PQsetdb(char *pghost, char *pgport, char *pgoptions, char *pgtty, char *dbName)`   This macro is used to call `*PQsetdbLogin`. The parameters for `login` and `password` are set to `NULL`. If an error occurs, `CONNECTION_BAD` is returned.

- `PGconn *PQconnectStart(const char *conninfo)` and `PostgresPollingStatusType PQconnectPoll(PGconn *conn)`   These are used to connect to the database server. This is done in a way that the application's thread of execution is not blocked on remote I/O while doing so. The format of the connect string is the same as in the previously described functions described. If an error occurs, `CONNECTION_BAD` is returned.

- `PQconninfoOption *PQconndefaults(void)`   Returns the default connection parameters in the following struct:

```
struct PQconninfoOption
    {
        char    *keyword;
                /* The keyword of the option */
        char    *envvar;
                /* Fallback environment variable name */
        char    *compiled;
                /* Fallback compiled in default value */
        char    *val;
                /* Option's current value, or NULL */
```

```
        char    *label;
                /* Label for field in connect dialog */
        char    *dispchar;
                /* Character to display for this field
                   in a connect dialog. Values are:
                   ""        Display entered value as is
                   "*"       Password field - hide value
                   "D"       Debug option - don't show by default */
        int     dispsize;
                /* Field size in characters for dialog */

    }
```

- `void PQfinish(PGconn *conn)`   Terminates a connection to the database server. If the connect process fails, it is recommended to call `PQfinish` to free the allocated memory. The pointer to the connection should not be used after closing it.

- `void PQreset(PGconn *conn)`   Resets the connection, which means that the current connection is closed and reestablished using the same parameters. This function may be essential for you, especially when connections get lost or when an error occurs.

- `int PQresetStart(PGconn *conn)` and `PostgresPollingStatusType PQresetPoll(PGconn *conn)`   Resets the connection in a non-blocked manner.

- `char *PQdb(const PGconn *conn)`   Returns the name of the database to which we are currently connected. The content of the `PGconn` object used to compute the result stays the same while the connection is established. This affects the `*PQdb` and the functions used to retrieve information about that object.

- `char *PQuser(const PGconn *conn)`   Extracts the user from the `PGconn` object.

- `char *PQpass(const PGconn *conn)`   Returns the password used when establishing the current connection.

- `char *PQhost(const PGconn *conn)`   Returns the name of the database host to which we are currently connected.

- `char *PQport(const PGconn *conn)`   Used to retrieve the port the connection is using.

- `char *PQtty(const PGconn *conn)`   Returns the `tty` used for debugging purposes.

- `char *PQoptions(const PGconn *conn)`   Returns the options passed to the backend when the connection was established.

- `ConnStatusType PQstatus(const PGconn *conn)`   Returns the status of the connection. This function is normally used to check whether a connection has been established successfully. Valid connections return `CONNECTION_OK`, while invalid connection return `CONNECTION_BAD`.

- `char *PQerrorMessage(const PGconn* conn)`   Used to extract the most recent error messages that are occurring during the work with the connection handle.

- `int PQbackendPID(const PGconn *conn)`   Returns the `PID` (process id) of the backend process related to the connection.

- `SSL *PQgetssl(const PGconn *conn)`   Returns `NULL` if SSL is not used. In case of an SSL connection, the SSL structure used will be the result. `USE_SSL` must be defined to get the prototype for this function.

Query Execution Functions

Now that you have seen how you can connect to the database, you will take a closer look at the functions needed for executing queries.

- `PGresult *PQexec(PGconn *conn, const char *query)`   Passes a query defined by a string to the PostgreSQL server. If the query cannot be executed successfully, a `NULL` pointer is returned; otherwise, a pointer to a `PGresult` structure is generated. If an error occurs, the `PQerrorMessage` message will be used to find out more about the error. `PGresult` contains the data passed to the application by the backend. To access the data, use one of the functions to retrieve data provided by PostgreSQL:

- `ExecStatusType PQresultStatus(const PGresult *res)`   Can return the status of a result. The following is a list of all possible values:

    - `PGRES_EMPTY_QUERY`   An empty string was sent to the backend.

    - `PGRES_COMMAND_OK`   The result is empty, but the query has been executed successfully.

    - `PGRES_TUPLES_OK`   The query was successfully executed.

    - `PGRES_COPY_OUT`   Copy Out (from server) data transfer started.

    - `PGRES_COPY_IN`   Copy In (to server) data transfer started).

    - `PGRES_BAD_RESPONSE`   The response of the server cannot be understood.

- • `PGRES_NONFATAL_ERROR`   A non-fatal error occurred.

  • `PGRES_FATAL_ERROR`   The query could not be executed, and a fatal error occurred.

- SQL commands, such as `INSERT` and `UPDATE`, do not return tuples, so the status of the query is `PGRES_COMMAND_OK`. If `PGresult` contains tuples and the query can be executed, the result will be `PGRES_TUPLES_OK`.

- `char *PQresultErrorMessage(const PGresult *res)`   Returns the most recent error.

- `int PQntuples(const PGresult *res)`   Used to find the number of tuples in the result.

- `int PQnfields(const PGresult *res)`   Returns the number of fields in every tuple.

- `int PQbinaryTuples(const PGresult *res)`   Returns binary data. Currently, this function can only be used in combination with a binary cursor.

- `char *PQfname(const PGresult *res, int field_index)`   Used to extract the label of a certain field in the result.

- `int PQfnumber(const PGresult *res, const char *field_name)`   Helps to find the correct index of a field for a given name.

- `Oid PQftype(const PGresult *res, int field_index)`   Returns the type of a field as an integer value. To find the name of the data type, simply query `pg_type`.

- `int PQfsize(const PGresult *res, int field_index)`   Finds how many bytes are used for a specific field.

- `int PQfmod(const PGresult *res, int field_index)`   Returns the type-specific modification data of a field.

- `char* PQgetvalue(const PGresult *res, int tup_num, int field_num)`   Returns the value of exactly one field as a `NULL` terminated ASCII string. If `PQbinaryTuples()` is set to 1, the value returned by `PQgetvalue` is in binary format (PostgreSQL's internal data structure is used).

- `int PQgetlength(const PGresult *res, int tup_num, int field_num)`   Returns the length of a field. You have to keep in mind that the binary size may have nothing to do with the size of the field represented as ASCII characters. Use `PQfsize` to find the binary size of the field.

- `int PQgetisnull(const PGresult *res, int tup_num, int field_num)` Checks whether a given field contains a NULL value. In case of a NULL value, the function returns 1.

- `char * PQcmdStatus(const PGresult *res)` Returns the command status string of the PGresult object.

- `char * PQcmdTuples(const PGresult *res)` Returns the number of rows affected by an SQL command. This command is extremely useful when working with DELETE, UPDATE, and INSERT. If PQcmdTuples is used with a different command, an empty string is returned.

- `Oid PQoidValue(const PGresult *res)` Extracts the object ID of the tuples inserted. If the command is not used in combination with INSERT, InvalidOid is returned.

- `char * PQoidStatus(const PGresult *res)` Does the same as PQoidValue, but it is not thread safe.

- `void PQprint(FILE* fout, const PGresult *res, const PQprintOpt *po)` Prints all tuples and, optionally, the attribute names to the specified output stream. In the past, this function was used by psql but is currently no longer supported.

- `void PQclear(PQresult *res)` Has to be used to get rid of a PGresult object. Using PQclear is the only way to do the job, because closing a connection does not free the memory allocated by a PGresult structure.

- `PGresult* PQmakeEmptyPGresult(PGconn *conn, ExecStatusType status)` Creates an empty PGresult object that has a certain status. In general, this function is used by the library internally. The function is exported because it might be useful in some applications.

Asynchronous Query Processing

Queries sent to the server using PQexec have some significant restrictions. In general, the application has to wait until the query has been processed successfully. In the meantime, the application could have done something useful, such as refreshing the user interface. Another problem is that the entire program is controlled by Pqexec, and there is no way to quit an ongoing query.

To solve some of these restrictions, PostgreSQL supports some additional functions:

- `int PQsetnonblocking(PGconn *conn, int arg)` Sets the nonblocking status of a connection. `TRUE` means that the status is set to non-blocking; FALSE means blocking. In case of non-blocking, calling `PQputline`, `PQputnbytes`, `PQsendQuery`, and `PQendcopy` will return an error if they have to be called again. `PQexec` automatically sets the state to blocking during execution.

- `int PQisnonblocking(const PGconn *conn)` Can be used to find the current blocking status. If `TRUE` is returned, the connection is set to non-blocking mode; `FALSE` means blocking.

- `int PQsendQuery(PGconn *conn, const char *query)` Sends a query to the server, but does not wait for the result. If the query has been stated successfully, `TRUE` is returned; otherwise, an error has occurred. The error can be checked by using `PQerrorMessage`. To find the result of a query we have started with the help of `PqsendQuery`, we have to call the `PQgetResult` function. `PQsendQuery` cannot be called again until `PQgetResult` has returned `NULL`. `NULL` tells us that the query has been processed successfully.

- `PGresult *PQgetResult(PGconn *conn)` Has to be called until `NULL` is returned to get the result of a query started with `PQsendQuery`.

- `int PQconsumeInput(PGconn *conn)` Uses input from the backend. If the result of the function is 1, no error has occurred; otherwise, something has gone wrong.

- `int PQisBusy(PGconn *conn)` Returns 1 if a query is currently busy. 0 indicates that `PQgetResult` can be called with assurance of not blocking. `PQconsumeInput` must be called before `PQisBusy`, or the system will stay in busy state because `PQisBusy` does not read data from the backend.

- `int PQflush(PGconn *conn)` Tries to flush all data queued to the backend. In case of an error, `EOF`" is returned. If the function terminates successfully, the result will be 0. `PQflush` has to be called in combination with a non-blocking connection before finding out whether a response has arrived.

- `int PQsocket(const PGconn *conn)` Can be used to extract the file descriptor number for the backend connection socket. If the result of the function is zero or higher than zero, the descriptor is valid; otherwise, no connections are open. The function should be used before using `SELECT`. If the result of `SELECTselect` tells us that data can be read from the backend, `PQconsumeInput` can be called to read the data. After that, `PQisBusy`, `PQgetResult`, and `PQnotifies` can be used to process the response.

- `int PQrequestCancel(PGconn *conn)`   Tells the database to quit the current query. In case of 1 being returned, the query has been cancelled successfully.

Fastpath

The "fast path" interface is the gateway to PostgreSQL's internals and can be used to communicate directly with the backend. In many cases, the features won't be used for security reasons. The following is an overview of the fastpath function:

`PGresult* PQfn(PGconn* conn, int fnid, int *result_buf, int *result_len, int result_is_int, const PQArgBlock *args, int nargs)` tells the backend to execute a backend function using the fastpath interface. The `PQArgBlock` is defined as follows:

```
typedef struct {
        int len;
        int isint;
        union {
            int *ptr;
            int integer;
        } u;
    } PQArgBlock
```

`fnid` defined the object identifier of the function that has to be executed. `result_buf` will contain the result, and `result_len` will contain its length. `result_is_int` has to be set to 1 if a 4-byte integer is expected; otherwise, it should be set to 0. Every time the `PQfn` is returned, a valid `PGresult` is returned. Simply check the object before using the result.

Asynchronous Notification

PostgreSQL supports asynchronous notification and provides special `LISTEN` and `NOTIFY` commands. In general, `LISTEN` and `UNLISTEN` commands are sent to the database as ordinary SQL queries. `PQnotifies()` checks whether `NOTIFY` messages have arrived. It does not read data from the backend, but it compiles messages that have been absorbed by another `libpq` function. The best way to use `PQnotifies` is the following sequence of commands.

After sending the query to the server, use `PQconsumeInput()` first and the check `PQnotifies()`. In the next step, use a `SELECT` function to retrieve the data.

The following is a syntax overview of the `PQnotifies` function.`PGnotify* PQnotifies(PGconn *conn")` returns a structure containing the following components:

```
typedef struct pgNotify {
        char relname[NAMEDATALEN];          /* name of relation
                                             * containing data */
        int  be_pid;                        /* process id of backend */
} PGnotify
```

Functions Related to the COPY Command

The COPY command is used to read or write huge amounts of data. To provide a powerful interface to the command, several functions can be used:

- int PQgetline(PGconn *conn, char *string, int length)   Reads length bytes of data into a buffer. 0 is returned if the string has been read successfully; if not, EOF is returned. When the transmission of the data is over, the application has to send a string indicating that no more data will be sent. This string has to be \.

  Note
  Only use this function when receiving a PGRES_COPY_OUT or a PGRES_COPY_IN result object.

- int PQgetlineAsync(PGconn *conn, char *buffer, int bufsize)   Reads length bytes of data into a buffer without blocking. The function is very similar to PQgetline, but it has to be used by a function that has to read the data without blocking. After having issued the COPY command and if PGRES_COPY_OUT was returned, the application should call PQconsumeInput and PQgetlineAsync until the end-of-data signal is detected. In contrast to PQgetline, the function takes care of detecting the end-of-data signal.

- int PQputline(PGconn *conn, const char *string)   Transmits a string to the backend. The applications must explicitly send \. to tell the backend that the transmission has ended.

- int PQputnbytes(PGconn *conn, const char *buffer, int nbytes)   Sends a NULL-terminated string to the backend. The difference between PQputline and PQputnbytes is that the string does not have to be NULL-terminated if PQputnbytes is used, because the number of bytes is defined in the function call.

- int PQendcopy(PGconn *conn)   Synchronizes with the backend, which means that it waits until the backend has finished the COPY process. The function must be used when the last line has been sent or received from the backend; otherwise, the backend and the frontend may be "out of sync." After using PQendcopy, the backend can accept the next query.

Tracing Functions

For monitoring the communication between backend and frontend, PostgreSQL supports so-called tracing functions. In this section, we will take a closer look at these functions:

- `void PQtrace(PGconn *conn,  FILE *debug_port)`   Enables tracing and sends the data to a debugging file stream.

- `void PQuntrace(PGconn *conn)`   Stops tracing.

Control Functions

`NOTICE` messages are normally written to standard error. Standard error should always be used for messages from the system because the output is, in contrast to standard output, displayed unbuffered. The behavior of PostgreSQL when dealing with messages can be changed by implementing a callback function that treats the messages differently. `PQsetNoticeProcessor` is used to control reporting of notice and warning messages generated by `libpq`. The following is an overview of the command's syntax:

```
typedef void (*PQnoticeProcessor) (void *arg, const char *message);
PQnoticeProcessor PQsetNoticeProcessor(PGconn *conn,

PQnoticeProcessor proc, void *arg);
```

To use your own function to process messages, simple call `PQsetNoticeProcessor` after establishing a connection to the database.

Working with Large Objects

PostgreSQL allows you to import complete files into a database. Imagine a situation where workgroups communicate via a network. Files have to be stored in combination with information about those files. One software solution would be to load all files into the database and to store all data, including the required files, in the database. PostgreSQL offers a powerful interface. Whether you have to deal with ASCII files or binary files, PostgreSQL can manage those files efficiently.

In Postgres 4.2, PostgreSQL supported three standard implementations for dealing with large objects:

- Files external to Postgres

- External files managed by Postgres

- Data stored within the database

In a way, the system was confusing, so it was decided to support only large objects that are stored within the database. This is slower, but it provides a higher level of data integrity and does not lead to much confusion.

In this section, we will take a look at the C interface provided for dealing with large objects. You will see that Large Objects (LOBs) and Binary Large Objects (BLOBs) are great tools and that they can easily be handled.

Look at the following program. We want to import a file into the database and display the object ID of the new file with the help of a simple C program:

```c
#include <stdio.h>
#include <stdlib.h>
#include <pgsql/libpq-fe.h>
#include <pgsql/libpq/libpq-fs.h>

#define         FILE            "textfile.txt"

int main(int argc, char **argv)
{
        PGconn          *conn;
        PGresult        *res;
        Oid                 objid;
                // Connecting
        conn = PQconnectdb("dbname=db host=localhost user=hs");
        if      (PQstatus(conn) == CONNECTION_BAD)
        {
                char *msg = PQerrorMessage(conn);
                fputs(msg ? msg : "PQconnectdb() failed.\n", stderr);
                PQfinish(conn);
                exit(EXIT_FAILURE);
        }

        // Starting transaction
        res = PQexec(conn, "BEGIN");
        PQclear(res);

        // Inserting a BLOB into the database
        objid = lo_import(conn, FILE);
        printf("Object ID: %i\n", objid);

        // End transaction and quit
        res = PQexec(conn, "COMMIT");
```

```
        PQclear(res);
        PQfinish(conn);

        return 0;
}
```

With just 38 lines of C code, including documentation, we have managed to import the file. First, we connect to the database and check for an error. We explicitly start a transaction and import the file. lo_import returns an object ID that we will display onscreen. Finally, we commit the transaction, free the memory allocated, close the connection, and exit the program.

We use a very simple Makefile to compile the sources. This time, we have just written a very small Makefile:

```
compile :        main.c Makefile
         gcc -O3 -Wall main.c -o prog  -I/usr/include/postgresql -lpq


run      :       prog
         ./prog
```

The file we want to import is called textfile.txt. We will need this file in the next examples to show you how BLOBs can be changed with the help of a C program and PostgreSQL:

```
[hs@duron c]$ cat textfile.txt
This is indeed a very simple but very useful text.
We have included this to show you how to work with C and BLOBs efficiently.
I hope you like this little text.
```

We use make run to start the program:

```
[hs@duron c]$ make run
./prog
Object ID: 29988
```

The object ID is displayed onscreen.

To see whether the file has really been loaded into the database, we start a psql and try to export the file, so we need to know the object ID of the file:

```
db=# SELECT lo_export(29988, '/tmp/outfile.txt');
 lo_export
-----------
         1
(1 row)
```

The file has been exported to /tmp/outfile.txt:

```
[hs@duron c]$ cat /tmp/outfile.txt
This is indeed a very simple but very useful text.
We have included this to show you how to work with C and BLOBs efficiently.
I hope you like this little text.
```

To remove the object from the database, we can use lo_unlink. We will also use the following function as a C function later in the section:

```
db=# SELECT lo_unlink(29988);
 lo_unlink
-----------
         1
(1 row)
```

> **Note**
> Large objects can be created by using the Oid lo_creat(PGconn *conn, int
> mode) function. mode defined the bitmask for the new objects. All symbolic bitmask
> can be found in $PGROOT/src/backend/libpq/libpq-fs.h.

In the next example, we will perform some basic operations, such as modifying and export BLOBs to a file:

```
#include <stdio.h>
#include <stdlib.h>
#include <pgsql/libpq-fe.h>
#include <pgsql/libpq/libpq-fs.h>

#define      FILE        "textfile.txt"
#define EXFILE          "/tmp/outfile.txt"

int main(int argc, char **argv)
{
        PGconn              *conn;
        PGresult        *res;
        Oid             objid;
        int             ostatus=0;
        int             fd=0;
        Oid              delvar;
            // Connecting
        conn = PQconnectdb("dbname=db host=localhost user=hs");
        if      (PQstatus(conn) == CONNECTION_BAD)
        {
```

```
            char *msg = PQerrorMessage(conn);
            fputs(msg ? msg : "PQconnectdb() failed.\n", stderr);
            PQfinish(conn);
            exit(EXIT_FAILURE);
     }

     // Starting transaction
     res = PQexec(conn, "BEGIN");
     PQclear(res);

     // Inserting a BLOB into the database
     objid = lo_import(conn, FILE);
     printf("importing object: %i\n", objid);

     // Opening and modifying object
     fd = lo_open(conn, objid, INV_WRITE);
     if       (ostatus < 0)
     {
            fprintf(stderr, "ERROR: %s\n", PQerrorMessage(conn));
            exit(EXIT_FAILURE);
     }

     ostatus = lo_write(conn, fd, "Hello world", 10);
     printf("Writing to %i --- status: %i\n", objid, ostatus);
            // Exporting object to a file
     ostatus = lo_export(conn, objid, EXFILE);
     printf("exporting %i to %s --- status: %i\n", objid, EXFILE, ostatus);
            // Deleting BLOB
     delvar = lo_unlink(conn, objid);
     printf("deleted object %i --- status: %i\n", objid, delvar);
                   // End transaction and quit
     res = PQexec(conn, "COMMIT");
     PQclear(res);
     PQfinish(conn);

     return 0;
}
```

To compile the sources, we can use a Makefile like the ones we have already shown. This time, it has to contain the following command to compile the sources:

```
gcc -lpq main.c -o prog
```

Let's see what the program we have just compiled does internally. First, we connect to the database and import a file, just as we did in the previous example. To modify the object we have just inserted into the database, we open the object. After opening the file, the pointer is set to the first character in the file. We modify the BLOB by writing Hello world into the BLOB. Modifying means that the first 10 bytes of the file are overwritten.

To see whether the content of the file has changed, we export the object to a file. Because we don't want the object to remain in the database, we delete it using lo_unlink.

Now, run the program:

```
[hs@duron c]$ make run
./prog
importing object: 30006
Writing to 30006 --- status: 10
exporting 30006 to /tmp/outfile.txt --- status: 1
deleted object 30006 --- status: 1
```

In outfile.txt, we can see that the changes have successfully been executed.

```
[hs@duron hs]$ cat /tmp/outfile.txt
Hello worldeed a very simple but very useful text.
We have included this to show you how to work with C and BLOBs efficiently.
I hope you like this little text.
```

It is sometimes necessary to go to the right position inside a file and read data. The following example shows how this can be done:

```
#include <stdio.h>
#include <stdlib.h>
#include <unistd.h>
#include <pgsql/libpq-fe.h>
#include <pgsql/libpq/libpq-fs.h>


#define FILE            "textfile.txt"
#define EXFILE          "/tmp/outfile.txt"
#define BUFSIZE         10

int main(int argc, char **argv)
{
        PGconn                  *conn;
        PGresult        *res;
```

```
Oid                objid;
int                ostatus=0;
int                fd=0;
Oid                 delvar;
char                    mybuf[BUFSIZE];
        // Connecting
conn = PQconnectdb("dbname=db host=localhost user=hs");
if      (PQstatus(conn) == CONNECTION_BAD)
{
        char *msg = PQerrorMessage(conn);
        fputs(msg ? msg : "PQconnectdb() failed.\n", stderr);
        PQfinish(conn);
        exit(EXIT_FAILURE);
}

// Starting transaction
res = PQexec(conn, "BEGIN");
PQclear(res);

// Inserting a BLOB into the database
objid = lo_import(conn, FILE);
printf("importing object: %i\n", objid);

// Opening and modifying object
fd = lo_open(conn, objid, INV_READ);
if       (ostatus < 0)
{
        fprintf(stderr, "ERROR: %s\n", PQerrorMessage(conn));
        exit(EXIT_FAILURE);
}

// Checking the current position
ostatus = lo_tell(conn, fd);
printf("Checking %i --- current position: %i\n", objid, ostatus);
        // Reading from file
ostatus = lo_read(conn, fd, mybuf, BUFSIZE);
        // Changing the current position
ostatus = lo_lseek(conn, fd, 10, SEEK_SET);
printf("Changing %i --- setting to: %i\n", objid, ostatus);
        // Checking the current position
ostatus = lo_tell(conn, fd);
printf("Checking %i --- current position: %i\n", objid, ostatus);
```

```
        // Deleting BLOB
        delvar = lo_unlink(conn, objid);
        printf("deleted object %i --- status: %i\n", objid, delvar);
                        // End transaction and quit
        res = PQexec(conn, "COMMIT");
        PQclear(res);
        PQfinish(conn);

        return 0;
}
```

We create a BLOB, open it, and jump inside the file. After reading 10 bytes from the current position, we check the current position again and delete the file.

Now execute the script:

```
[hs@duron c]$ make run
./prog
importing object: 30058
Checking 30058 --- current position: 0
Changing 30058 --- setting to: 10
Checking 30058 --- current position: 10
deleted object 30058 --- status: 1
```

A Reference of the C++ Interface

As you might expect, the C++ (libpq++) interface to PostgreSQL is very similar to the libpq interface. libpq++ is a set of classes designed for manipulating and retrieving data from your PostgreSQL database. In this section, we will take a closer look at this powerful interface. To understand the text, we recommend that you go through the description of the standard C interface quickly.

The PgConnection Object

The PgConnection object is responsible for establishing a connection to a database server and is inherited by all classes accessing the database:

- PgConnection::PgConnection(const char *conninfo)   Used to establish a connection to the database. The connection parameters are passed to the function as a string, such as we have seen it in the "Connecting" section in this chapter. libpq++ also supports the same set of environment variables for non-defined parameters, such as libpq.

- int PgConnection::ConnectionBad()   Checks whether a connection is valid. If FALSE is returned, the connection to the server should work.

- ConnStatusType PgConnection::Status()   Tells us the status of a connection. A connection can either be CONNECTION_OK or CONNECTION_BAD.

- const char *PgConnection::DBName()   Returns the name of the current database.

- PGnotify* PgConnection::Notifies()   Returns the next notification from a list of unhandled notification messages returned by the backend.

- ExecStatusType PgConnection::Exec(const char* query)   Sends a query to the backend. The values returned are equal to those returned by the PQresultStatus function.

- int PgConnection::ExecTuplesOk(const char *query)   Sends a query to the server and returns TRUE if the command was executed successfully.

- const char *PgConnection::ErrorMessage()   Returns the error message that has occurred.

The PgDatabase Object

Let's get to the next object needed for interacting with the database and see what functions are provided by PostgreSQL:

- PgDatabase(const char *conninfo)   Establishes a connection to the database.

- int PgDatabase::Tuples()   Returns the number of tuples the result of a query contains.

- int PgDatabase::CmdTuples()   Can be used to compute the number of rows affected by a query.

- int PgDatabase::Fields()   Retrieves the number of fields in the query result.

- const char *PgDatabase::FieldName(int field_num)   Returns the name of a field related to the given index.

- int PgDatabase::FieldNum(const char* field_name)   Returns the index of a field related to a given name.

- Oid PgDatabase::FieldType(int field_num)   Returns the data type of a certain field. The value returned matches the data type's internal representation of PostgreSQL.

- `Oid PgDatabase::FieldType(const char* field_name)`   Returns the same data as `PgDatabase::FieldType(int field_num)`, but the function is called by using the name and not the index of the column.

- `short PgDatabase::FieldSize(int field_num)`   Returns the size of a field in bytes (the binary size of PostgreSQL's internal representation).

- `short PgDatabase::FieldSize(const char *field_name)`   Does the same as `PgDatabase::FieldSize(int field_num)`, but is called by using the name of the field.

- `const char *PgDatabase::GetValue(int tup_num, int field_num)`   Can be used to extract one field in the `PGresult` object. The value returned can either be binary or a `NULL`-terminated ASCII string.

- `const char *PgDatabase::GetValue(int tup_num, const char *field_name)`   Has the same functionality as the `const char *PgDatabase::GetValue(int tup_num, int field_num)` function, but is called by using the name of the field instead of the index.

- `int PgDatabase::GetLength(int tup_num, int field_num)`   Computes the length of a field. In general, the size of ASCII-represented values has nothing to do with the binary size returned by `PQfsize`.

- `int PgDatabase::GetLength(int tup_num, const char* field_name)`   Does the same as `PgDatabase::GetLength(int tup_num, int field_num)`, but is called by using the name instead of the index of the field.

- `void PgDatabase::DisplayTuples(FILE *out = 0, int fillAlign = 1, const char* fieldSep = "|",int printHeader = 1, int quiet = 0)`   Prints all tuples and, if required, the attribute names to an output stream.

- `void PgDatabase::PrintTuples(FILE *out = 0, int printAttName = 1, int terseOutput = 0, int width = 0)`   Prints all tuples to a output stream.

- `int PgDatabase::GetLine(char* string, int length)`   Reads a newline-terminated line of characters into a buffer string of size `length`.

- `void PgDatabase::PutLine(const char* string)`   Sends a string to the backend process.

- `const char *PgDatabase::OidStatus()`   Checks a status.

- `int PgDatabase::EndCopy()`   Defines the end of a `COPY` sequence.

Asynchronous Notification

A `libpq++`-enabled application has to check whether the backend has some queued notification information.

`PgDatabase::Notifies()` has to be used to poll the backend:

- `PGnotify* PgDatabase::Notifies()`   Retrieves notifications from the server

Embedded SQL C Preprocessor (ECPG)

Just like Oracle, PostgreSQL provides a powerful preprocessor C. The idea is to have an easy and efficient interface for generating optimized C code. In this section, you will learn to use this interface efficiently.

The Basic Concepts of ECPG

One of the most powerful and comfortable programming interfaces is Embedded SQL C Preprocessor (ECPG). ECPG is a preprocessor that does nothing else but generate C code. Files containing ECPG code are converted to C code and can be compiled and linked like any other C program. The advantage of writing ECPG code over writing normal C code is that it is much easier to write ECPG code than to write a C program.

All those hardcore C hackers among you will think that this is not correct, but I guess simplicity was the reason why ECPG was introduced.

The package was initially written by Linus Tolke, who also maintained the package up to version 0.2. Currently, Michael Meskes develops and maintains ECPG. The software can be copied and distributed under the same terms as the rest of PostgreSQL.

Many database systems support embedded SQL, and there is also a description of an ANSI standard available. As you might have guessed, the developers of ECPG try to make ECPG as close to the standard as possible.

The advantage of taking the standard into consideration is that an application using embedded SQL can easily be ported from one database system to the other.

A First Example

In general, examples are much easier to understand than any theoretical description of a topic. We have included a very simple example that does nothing but compute the result of one plus one. The result is not displayed. In the first step, we just want to show you how you can connect to the database and execute a simple command. We create a file called first.pgc:

```
#include <stdio.h>

EXEC SQL BEGIN DECLARE SECTION;
int result;
EXEC SQL END DECLARE SECTION;

int main()
{
        EXEC SQL CONNECT TO myecpg;
        EXEC SQL SELECT (1+1) INTO :result;

        return 0;
}
```

You can see that ECPG code is a mixture of SQL and C. From my point of view, the code is easy to read and much easier to understand than a native C program.

Let's go through the code.

First, we include stdio.h (stdio.h is the standard library for I/O operations). In the next step, we tell the preprocessor that the section for defining variables starts. In this section, we define an integer variable called result. The section for defining the variables ends, and we start with the main function, just as we would do in a "normal" C program. In the next step, we connect to the database called myecpg and execute the SQL command. The result is assigned to the result, the variable we have defined as integer before. Finally, the program returns 0 and quits.

Now we have to run the preprocessor and convert the source code to C code. The output of the preprocessor is as follows:

```
/* Processed by ecpg (2.8.0) */
/* These three include files are added by the preprocessor */
#include <ecpgtype.h>
#include <ecpglib.h>
#include <ecpgerrno.h>
#line 1 "first.pgc"
/* exec sql begin declare section */


#line 1 "first.pgc"
```

```
   int  result   ;
/* exec sql end declare section */
#line 2 "first.pgc"


{ ECPGdo(__LINE__, NULL, "select  1 + 1      ", ECPGt_EOIT,
      ECPGt_int,&(result),1L,1L,sizeof(int),
      ECPGt_NO_INDICATOR, NULL , 0L, 0L, 0L, ECPGt_EORT);}
#line 4 "first.pgc"

int main()
{
      return 0;
}
```

We could have written the code ourselves, using the preprocessor is much easier than coding real C code. We use a Makefile to compile the program:

```
INC=    /usr/include/pgsql
LIB=    /usr/share/pgsql
FILE=   first.pgc
TEMP=   file.c

x       :       $(FILE) Makefile
        ecpg -o $(TEMP) $(FILE)


        gcc -g -I $(INC) -o prog $(TEMP) -L $(LIB) -lecpg -lpq
```

In the first four lines of the Makefile, we define the variables we will use next.

$FILE contains the input file. $TEMP contains the name of the C file you want to generate by using the preprocessor.

$INC and $LIB contain the directory the linker will use to look for the files that are needed for linking.

If we execute the script now, nothing will be displayed. Let's write the result of the query to standard output:

```
#include <stdio.h>

EXEC SQL BEGIN DECLARE SECTION;
int result;
```

```
EXEC SQL END DECLARE SECTION;

int main()
{
        EXEC SQL CONNECT TO myecpg;
        EXEC SQL SELECT (1+1) INTO :result;

        printf("result: %i\n", result);
        return 0;
}
```

We simply add `printf` that displays the result as an integer value to the program; we use normal C code for printing the output. We compile the code using `make` and execute the program again:

```
[hs@duron ecpg]$ ./prog
result: 2
```

2 is the result most of us have expected.

Error Handling

Error handling is one of the most important things when writing a program. Imagine when we change the name of the database we want to connect to from `myecpg` to `nodb`. The database `nodb` does not exist on the system. If we execute the script, the result will be 0 instead of 2, and no error will be displayed. The script behaves the same way as it would if we had a working database called `nodb`. This is very dangerous indeed, and some sort of error and exception handling has to be implemented. If you want to include error and exception handling in your application, you have to add the line

```
EXEC SQL INCLUDE sqlca;
```

to the application. The line makes sure that a struct and a variable called `sqlca` will be defined. We will look at the data structure of the `sqlca` struct later in this section.

Now we try to connect to a database that does not exist on the system:

```
#include <stdio.h>

EXEC SQL INCLUDE sqlca;

EXEC SQL BEGIN DECLARE SECTION;
int result;
EXEC SQL END DECLARE SECTION;
```

```
int main()
{
        EXEC SQL CONNECT TO ondb;
        if      (sqlca.sqlcode)
        {
                printf("Error connecting to database server.\n");
                printf("%i\n", sqlca.sqlcode);
                exit(0);
        }
        EXEC SQL SELECT (1+1) INTO :result;

        printf("result: %i\n", result);
        return 0;
}
```

If an error occurs, `sqlca.sqlcode` will contain a non-zero value. In this case, we want the application to quit and print an error message onscreen. If we can connect to the database successfully, the program will work just like the one we saw in the previous section.

We have included the C code of the previous program here because it is a good chance to take a look at the definition of the `sqlca` struct:

```
/* Processed by ecpg (2.8.0) */
/* These three include files are added by the preprocessor */
#include <ecpgtype.h>
#include <ecpglib.h>
#include <ecpgerrno.h>
#line 1 "first.pgc"
#include <stdio.h>

#line 1 "/usr/include/pgsql/sqlca.h"
#ifndef POSTGRES_SQLCA_H
#define POSTGRES_SQLCA_H

#define SQLERRMC_LEN            70

#ifdef __cplusplus
extern                  "C"
{
#endif

        struct sqlca
```

```
        {
                char            sqlcaid[8];
                long            sqlabc;
                long            sqlcode;
                struct
                {
                        int                     sqlerrml;
                        char            sqlerrmc[SQLERRMC_LEN];
                }                       sqlerrm;
                char            sqlerrp[8];
                long            sqlerrd[6];
                /* Element 0: empty
*/

                /* 1: OID of processed tuple if applicable
*/

                /* 2: number of rows processed                          */
                /* after an INSERT, UPDATE or                           */
                /* DELETE statement                                     */
                /* 3: empty                                             */
                /* 4: empty                                             */
                /* 5: empty                                             */
                char            sqlwarn[8];
                /* Element 0: set to 'W' if at least one other is 'W'       */
                /* 1: if 'W' at least one character string          */
                /* value was truncated when it was                  */
                /* stored into a host variable.
*/

                /*
                 * 2: if 'W' a (hopefully) non-fatal notice occurred
                 *//* 3: empty */
                /* 4: empty                                             */
                /* 5: empty                                             */
                /* 6: empty                                             */
                /* 7: empty                                             */

                char            sqlext[8];
        };

        extern struct sqlca sqlca;
```

```
#ifdef __cplusplus
}

#endif

#endif

#line 2 "first.pgc"


/* exec sql begin declare section */


#line 5 "first.pgc"
   int   result   ;
/* exec sql end declare section */
#line 6 "first.pgc"


int main()
{
        { ECPGconnect(__LINE__, "ondb" , NULL,NULL , NULL, 0); }
#line 10 "first.pgc"

        if        (sqlca.sqlcode)
        {
                printf("Error connecting to database server.\n");
                printf("%i\n", sqlca.sqlcode);
                exit(0);
        }
        { ECPGdo(__LINE__, NULL, "select  ( 1 + 1 )      ", ECPGt_EOIT,
        ECPGt_int,&(result),1L,1L,sizeof(int),
        ECPGt_NO_INDICATOR, NULL , 0L, 0L, 0L, ECPGt_EORT);}
#line 17 "first.pgc"


        printf("result: %i\n", result);
        return 0;
}
```

You can see that the C code we have written is not affected by the preprocessor; only embedded SQL is processed and converted to C code. Although the ECPG code is still very brief, the C code is already quite long. But let's look at sqlca now.

One of the most important fields in the structure is `sqlca.errm.sqlerrmc`. It contains the error message as a string and not as a number. We recommend that your applications display both the ID and the description of error, because your applications can debugged more easily.

After running the preprocessor and compiling the C code, we can execute the software and, what a surprise, an error will be displayed:

```
[hs@duron ecpg]$ ./prog
Error connecting to database server.
-402
```

`-402` means that the application was not able to open the database. A huge number of different error messages are provided by PostgreSQL. We have compiled a complete list of all error messages available in the Table 9.1.

Table 9.1   *Error messages and Error Codes*

Error Code and Error String	Comment
`-12`, Out of memory in line %d.	If that error occurs, all memory available on the system has been allocated.
`-200`, Unsupported type %s on line %d.	The preprocessor has most likely created something that does not work with the library used by the application. Check whether the versions of preprocessor and software are compatible or not.
`-201`, Too many arguments line %d.	The database returns more values than your application can handle. Check if you have defined enough host variables.
`-202`, Too few arguments line %d.	This error is the opposite of error "`-201`." PostgreSQL does not return enough values for your application.
`-203`, Too many matches line %d.	The query returned too many rows. Maybe you want to SELECselecTt many rows into one variable that is not an array.

Table 9.1   *(continued)*

Error Code and Error String	Comment
-204, Not correctly formatted int type: %s line %d.	The field returned by PostgreSQL is not an integer and cannot be converted to integer.
-205, Not correctly formatted unsigned type: %s line %d.	The variable returned cannot be used as unsigned value. The type of variable returned by PostgreSQL does not match the type you use in the application.
-206, Not correctly formatted floating point type: %s line %d.	The field returned cannot be interpreted as float.
-207, Unable to convert %s to bool on line %d.	The field in your PostgreSQL does not contain "t" or "f", so it and can therefore not be converted to a bool.
-208, Empty query line %d.	PGRES_EMPTY_QUERY was returned.
-220, No such connection %s in line %d.	Your application tries to access a connection that does not exist anymore.
-221, Not connected in line %d.	Your application tries to access an existing connection that is closed.
-230, Invalid statement name %s in line %d.	The statement your application tries to execute has not been prepared.
-400, Postgres error: %s line %d.	This is an error message from the backend.
-401, Error in transaction processing line %d.	PostgreSQL tells us that we cannot start, commit, or rollback a transaction.
-402, connect: could not open database %s.	Connecting to your database does not work.
100, Data not found line %d.	It tells you that what you are querying cannot be found or that you have gone through the cursor.

All types of errors listed in Table 9.1 can be accessed with the help of the sqlca struct.

Connecting

Connecting to a PostgreSQL database by using ECPG can be done in more than just one way. You may wonder why we have not included this part at the beginning of this section, but some basics about error handling is essential for dealing with connections.

In the previous examples, we connected to the database simply by using a command such as:

```
EXEC SQL CONNECT TO myecpg;
```

If the database is on a remote host or if the port the database is listening to is not the default one, it is necessary to use a different CONNECT string.

Two possibilities are provided to connect to the database:

```
dbname[@server][:port]
```

or

```
<tcp|unix>:postgresql://server[:port][/dbname][?options]
```

In this section, we will present some practical examples that show how to connect to the database.

In the following example, we connect to the database called myecpg on localhost port number 5432:

```
#include <stdio.h>

EXEC SQL INCLUDE sqlca;

int main()
{
        EXEC SQL CONNECT TO myecpg@localhost:5432;
        if      (sqlca.sqlcode) {
                printf("%s\n", sqlca.sqlerrm.sqlerrmc);
                exit(0); }
        return 0;
}
```

The example works perfectly well if the postmaster has been started with the -i flag enabled. Otherwise, the connection can't be established because PostgreSQL is not allowed to listen to remote hosts. Every host that is defined explicitly in the code is considered to be a remote host.

The port does not have to be explicitly defined; it also works if we use the default settings for the port.

Depending on whether we want to connect via TCP or UNIX domain sockets, we can use two different methods for connecting. We have included full examples that can be directly compiled.

For connecting via TCP, use the following:

```
#include <stdio.h>

EXEC SQL INCLUDE sqlca;

int main()
{
        EXEC SQL CONNECT TO tcp:postgresql://localhost:5432/myecpg;
        if      (sqlca.sqlcode) {
                printf("%s\n", sqlca.sqlerrm.sqlerrmc);
                exit(0); }
        return 0;
}
```

If you want to use UNIX domain sockets instead, you can use the following:

```
#include <stdio.h>

EXEC SQL INCLUDE sqlca;

int main()
{
        EXEC SQL CONNECT TO unix:postgresql://localhost:5432/myecpg";
        if      (sqlca.sqlcode) {
                printf("%s\n", sqlca.sqlerrm.sqlerrmc);
                exit(0); }
        return 0;
}
```

Up to now, we have connected to the database as the default user. In most cases, this is not what you want to do. Defining a certain user and a password is a very important thing. In the following example, you can see how you can add the username to the CONNECT string. Let's try to connect to the database as user hs:

```
#include <stdio.h>

EXEC SQL INCLUDE sqlca;
```

```
int main()
{
        EXEC SQL CONNECT TO myecpg user hs;
        if      (sqlca.sqlcode) {
                printf("%s\n", sqlca.sqlerrm.sqlerrmc);
                exit(0); }
        return 0;
}
```

The password can be defined as follows:

```
#include <stdio.h>

EXEC SQL INCLUDE sqlca;

int main()
{
        EXEC SQL CONNECT TO myecpg@localhost USER hs/apassword;
        if      (sqlca.sqlcode) {
                printf("%s\n", sqlca.sqlerrm.sqlerrmc);
                exit(0); }
        return 0;
}
```

Make sure that the user who wants to connect to the database is existing and that he or she has enough rights.

Simple Queries and Retrieving Data

Now we want to write some small applications that retrieve data from the following table:

```
CREATE TABLE os(id int4, name text);

COPY "os"  FROM stdin;
1       Open Bsd
2       RedHat Linux
3       Windows ME
4       Solaris
5       QNX
\.
```

The first application shows how you can retrieve all data and display it onscreen:

```
#include <stdio.h>

EXEC SQL INCLUDE sqlca;

EXEC SQL BEGIN DECLARE SECTION;
int id;
char name[20];
EXEC SQL END DECLARE SECTION;

int main()
{
        EXEC SQL CONNECT TO myecpg;
        if        (sqlca.sqlcode)
        {
                printf("%s\n", sqlca.sqlerrm.sqlerrmc);
                exit(0);
        }

        EXEC SQL PREPARE mystat FROM "SELECT id, name FROM os";
        EXEC SQL DECLARE mycurs CURSOR FOR mystat;

        EXEC SQL OPEN mycurs;
        EXEC SQL WHENEVER NOT FOUND DO BREAK;

        while        (1)
        {
                EXEC SQL FETCH IN mycurs INTO :id, :name;
                printf("%i - %s\n", id, name);
        }

        EXEC SQL CLOSE mycurs;                    EXEC SQL DISCONNECT;

        return 0;
}
```

Actually the code looks more difficult than it is. In the DECLARE section, we define two variables we use to store the result of the query. id will contain the first column, while name will be used for the second column of the result. In the next step, we establish a connection to the database and check whether the connection has been established successfully. If an error has occurred, the application quits. Then we prepare a statement called mystat that contains the query we want to execute. Because we expect the result of the query to have more than just one line, we have to declare a so-called cursor. Cursors are used to move inside the result of a query. In general, you go from the first line to the last line of the result step-by-step. In this case, the cursor can be processed using a simple WHILE loop.

If no result is found the application stops.

EXEC SQL FETCH IN mycurs INTO :id, :name; fetches one row of data. The first column of the result is assigned to id, the second column to name. We have to add a colon before the variables to tell the preprocessor that the C variables have to be used to assign the values. We display the values with a simple printf command. The first column is displayed as an integer, while the second column has to be displayed as a string. After executing the WHILE loop, we close the cursor and disconnect from the database. After running the preprocessor and compiling the C code, we try to execute the program:

```
[hs@duron ecpg]$ ./prog
1 - Open Bsd
2 - RedHat Linux
3 - Windows ME
4 - Solaris
5 - QNX
```

All values have been displayed correctly.

Some data types supported by PostgreSQL are not native data types of the C programming language. In this case, it is necessary to perform simple cast operations. We do not want to go too deep into detail, but we want to include a short example that shows how a numeric value can be converted to double:

```
#include <stdio.h>
#include <stdlib.h>

EXEC SQL INCLUDE sqlca;

EXEC SQL BEGIN DECLARE SECTION;
char id[20];
char * pEnd;
double result;
EXEC SQL END DECLARE SECTION;

int main()
{
        EXEC SQL CONNECT TO myecpg;
        if      (sqlca.sqlcode)
        {
```

```
                printf("%s\n", sqlca.sqlerrm.sqlerrmc);
                exit(0);
        }
        EXEC SQL SELECT '1.22'::numeric(6,2) INTO :id;
        printf("numeric as string: %s\n", id);
        result = strtod (id ,&pEnd);
        printf ("numeric as double: %lf\n",result);

        return 0;
}
```

We simply include stdlib.h and perform the cast by converting the text returned by the database to double. This works fine for values that are in the range of a valid double. If the numeric values stored in the database exceed the range of double, the whole thing will become a little bit more difficult.

If we execute the script, we can see that the conversion works without any problems:

```
[hs@duron ecpg]$ ./prog
numeric as string: 1.22
numeric as double: 1.220000
```

In the previous example, we can simply use SELECT INTO to assign the result of the query to id because the query returns only one row. If we had a query returning more than just one row, we would have to define a cursor and process the result line-by-line.

A Final Example

Let's get back to the table containing the list of operating systems. To avoid some unnecessary page turning, we have included the data in the table again:

```
CREATE TABLE os(id int4, name text);
COPY "os"  FROM stdin;
1       Open Bsd
2       RedHat Linux
3       Windows ME
4       Solaris
5       QNX
\.
```

We want to write a simple application where the user can select a record from the table. If the record does not exist, the user is asked to insert the record:

```
#include <stdio.h>

EXEC SQL INCLUDE sqlca;

EXEC SQL BEGIN DECLARE SECTION;
int id;
char name[256];
char intext[10];                        // will contain the id of the
                                        //  line we are looking for
char inos[256];                              // name of the new OS
char myquery[256];                      // will contain the query for
searching
char insql[256];                        // used to insert new OS
int  flag=0;                                 // if records found ...
EXEC SQL END DECLARE SECTION;

EXEC SQL WHENEVER SQLERROR sqlprint;

int main()
{
        // connecting ...
        EXEC SQL CONNECT TO myecpg;
        if      (sqlca.sqlcode)
        {
                printf("%s\n", sqlca.sqlerrm.sqlerrmc);
                exit(0);
        }

        // reading input data ...
        printf("Insert an id: ");                   scanf("%2s", intext);
        sprintf(myquery, "SELECT id, name FROM os WHERE id='%s' ", intext);
        printf("%s\n\n", myquery);

        EXEC SQL PREPARE mystatement FROM :myquery;
        if      (sqlca.sqlcode)
        {
                printf("%s\n", sqlca.sqlerrm.sqlerrmc);
                exit(0);
        }

        EXEC SQL DECLARE mycursor CURSOR FOR mystatement;
        EXEC SQL OPEN mycursor;
```

```
EXEC SQL WHENEVER NOT FOUND DO BREAK;
while        (1)
{
        EXEC SQL FETCH IN mycursor INTO :id, :name;
        flag=1;
        printf("records found: %i, %s\n\n", id, name);
}
EXEC SQL CLOSE mycursor;

EXEC SQL WHENEVER NOT FOUND CONTINUE;

if        (flag == 0)
{
        printf("Insert the name of the OS: ");
scanf("%256s", inos);
        EXEC SQL INSERT INTO os (id, name) VALUES ( :intext, :inos);
        EXEC SQL COMMIT;
        if        (sqlca.sqlcode)
        {
                printf("%s\n", sqlca.sqlerrm.sqlerrmc);
                exit(0);
        }
        else
        {
                printf("Record successfully imported\n");
        }
}

EXEC SQL DISCONNECT;
return 0;
}
```

We first declare all the variables we will need in the script. After connecting to the database, the program prompts for an ID. scanf inserts the value inserted by the user into the variable called intext. We declare a cursor and perform a SELECT statement to retrieve all records containing the ID the user has just entered. If records are found, flag is set to 1 so that the script does not ask for the name of the operating system anymore because the record already exists. The records are displayed, and the cursor is closed.

If no records are found, the program prompts for input again. This time, we have to insert the name of the new operating system.

The new record is inserted into the database, and the application quits.

> **Note**
> After inserting the record into the table, it is necessary to perform a COMMIT;
> otherwise, the record will never be inserted into the database.

Finally, we disconnect from the database, and 0 is returned by the application.

To compile the program, we can write a simple Makefile:

```
INC=    /usr/include/pgsql
LIB=    /usr/share/pgsql
FILE=   retrieve.pgc
TEMP=   file.c


x        :       $(FILE) Makefile
         ecpg $(FILE) -o $(TEMP)
         gcc -g -I $(INC) -o prog $(TEMP) -L $(LIB) -lecpg -lpq
```

If we want to find what has to be done by make, we can use make -n:

```
[hs@duron ecpg]$ make -n
ecpg retrieve.pgc -o file.c
gcc -g -I /usr/include/pgsql -o prog file.c -L /usr/share/pgsql -lecpg -lpq
```

You can see that some additional compiler flags for linking are required. Keep this in mind when writing your own ECPG applications.

Let's execute the program:

```
[hs@duron ecpg]$ ./prog
Insert an id: 3
SELECT id, name FROM os WHERE id='3'

records found: 3, Windows ME
```

The ID 3 can already be found in the database, so the result is displayed.

```
[hs@duron ecpg]$ ./prog
Insert an id: 93
SELECT id, name FROM os WHERE id='93'

Insert the name of the OS: myOS
Record successfully imported
```

98 cannot be found in the database, so the software prompts for some input, and the new record is inserted in the database:

```
myecpg=# SELECT * FROM os WHERE id=93;
 id | name
----+------
 93 | myOS
(1 row)
```

Perl

Today, Perl is one of the most widespread programming languages, and millions of people all around the globe rely on this powerful programming language. This section is dedicated to all Perl freaks among you who want to connect your applications to PostgreSQL.

Overview

"It's the Magic that counts," Larry Wall on Perl's apparent ugliness. Well, I guess Larry, the father of Practical Extraction and Report Language (Perl), knows what he is talking about. It's the magic that counts, but I guess that's the same for every available programming language. In some cases, it is simply a matter of personal philosophy which language is best, but that's not all. Speed, stability, portability, and availability can be weighty arguments. Perl is a scripting language, so it's a little slower than native C code in most cases; it has to be because Perl's internals are actually C code. People say that there are some situations where Perl can even outperform a native C program. Personally, I must say that I can hardly imagine anything faster than a highly-optimized C program—anything but hand-coded Assembler, of course. One thing can be said for sure, Perl is one of the fastest and most flexible scripting languages available. Some people are still discussing whether Perl is a "real" interpreter language. We want to answer this question with a quote taken from a Perl tutorial, "Perl is a compiler that thinks he is an interpreter."

Perl is one of the most powerful and widespread languages available. Perl is used by man people, especially for parsing purposes, Web applications, and network programming. The number of available modules seems to be endless, and their number is constantly increasing. Before we get to some programming stuff concerning PostgreSQL, we want to tell you something about the history of Perl. Perl was posted to the Usenet group comp.sources on October 18, 1987.

In 1988, Perl 2.0 was released and offered a lot of additional features. Larry Wall has stated,

"Randal can write one-liners again.

Everyone is happy,

and peace spreads over the whole Earth."

I think this sentence shows exactly what Perl hacking was all about. In 1988, Randal invented the very famous "Just another Perl hacker" signature that is often included in emails today.

Perl 3 was released in 1989, and Perl 4 followed on March 21, 1991. Perl 5 was born in 1994, and Tim Bunce introduced DBI, an abstract Perl interface to databases and a DBI driver for Oracle. Today, DBI is the most widespread Perl module for dealing with databases.

Since 1987, many improvements and modules have been implemented, and Perl has become one of the most flexible, fastest, and powerful language available.

In the summer of 1995, Andreas König started the Perl module repository. Later, König's archive turned into Comprehensive Perl Archive Network (CPAN), which is the standard archive for Perl modules.

Developers all around the globe are working hard to make Perl even more powerful. Currently, Perl works on nearly all hardware platforms and operating systems, because the core of the Perl language is entirely written in ANSI C so it's very portable. In a documentation about PostgreSQL by Alavoor Vasudevan, in the section about Perl it says, "Perl will be in use for thousands of years in the future!" Well, we will see whether Alavoor is right.

Currently, two major Perl interfaces for PostgreSQL are available. The Pg module is distributed with PostgreSQL and provides access to all functions in the `libpq` interface for PostgreSQL. The target of the module is to provide an interface that is as close as possible to the `libpq` interface. The Pg module is said to be a little faster than the second important interface—the so-called DBI interface. We will take a close look at both interfaces in the following sections. It is up to you to decide which module you prefer and what is best for your application.

The Pg Module

The DBI module is not the only Perl module for PostgreSQL. The Pg module is PostgreSQL's onboard library and is the Perl version of the `libpg` interface. This section will guide you through the Pg module.

Overview

The Pg module is not related to the DBI interface in any way. The Pg module is an independent piece of software and, in addition to PostgreSQL and Perl, does not need additional Perl modules to work correctly.

Two different styles are supported by the Pg module.

The new style has some advantages over the old style. Destructures are automatically called when the last reference to an object has gone away. This is some sort of internal garbage collection that is very comfortable because the programmer does not have to take care about deleting connections and result structures. When a new object is created, the appropriate `libpq` function is used as a virtual method.

Connecting

We will start with a simple example in which we want to connect to a database called `performance` as user `postgres`. In the following example, user `postgres` has no password:

```perl
#!/usr/bin/perl

use Pg;

$conn = Pg::connectdb("dbname=performance user=postgres") or
        die "can't open: $!";
print $conn->status."\n";
```

To establish the connection, we use a function called `connectdb` that can be found in the Pg module. We have to pass a list of arguments to the function that define all necessary values. If not all parameters the functions accepts are provided by the programmer, the database uses the default value. We compiled a list of all available parameters and their default value in Table 9.2.

Table 9.2   *Environment Variables*

Parameter	Environment	Default Value
Hosthost	PGHOST	localhost
pPort	PGPORT	5432
oOptions	PGOPTIONS	" "
Ttty	PGTTY	" "
dDbname	PGDATABASE	current userid
uUser	PGUSER	current userid
pPassword	PGPASSWD	" "

In the previous example, we have not defined the host storing the database, so localhost will be used by default.

After establishing the connection, we use a function called status to find whether the connection has successfully been created. If 0 is returned, the connection has successfully been established; otherwise, an error occurred.

> **Note**
> In the previous example, we have included die to end the program when the connection cannot be established. This does not work with the Pg module. If we define the wrong database, the program won't stop. We can only determine an error when checking the result of the status function.

If we want to see the error message when no connection can be established, we can use a function called errorMessage:

```
#!/usr/bin/perl

use Pg;

$conn = Pg::connectdb("dbname=xy user=postgres");
print $conn->errorMessage."\n";
```

We have no database called xy on the system, so an error will be displayed:

```
[hs@duron code]$ ./pg.pl
FATAL 1:  Database "xy" does not exist in the system catalog.
```

The structure returned by the CONNECT function is called PGconn and consists of various parameters that can easily be accessed:

```
#!/usr/bin/perl

use Pg;

$conn = Pg::connectdb("dbname=performance user=postgres") or
        die "can't open: $!";
print $conn->port."\n";
print $conn->user."\n";
```

If we try to execute the program, we will see the following results printed onscreen:

```
[hs@duron code]$ ./pg.pl
5432
postgres
```

318

The names of the fields are slightly different than the parameters that have to be passed to the `connectdb` function. They are listed in Table 9.3.

Table 9.3   *Field Names*

Field	Key
Name of the database	Db
Name of the user	User
Password of the user	Pass
Host where the database is stored	Host
Port to which the database is listening to	Port
Options passed to the database	Options

Another option for establishing a connection to a PostgreSQL server is to use `Pg::setdb`. The syntax is easy:

```
$conn = Pg::setdb($pghost, $pgport, $pgoptions, $pgtty, $dbname);
```

The `setdb` method should be used when establishing a connection where a username and password are not needed.

If you want to find out about all possible options of the `connectdb` function, you can use `Pg::conndefaults`. The following is a short script that shows how this functions works:

```
#!/usr/bin/perl

use Pg;

$Option_ref = Pg::conndefaults();
while(($key, $value) = each %$Option_ref)
{
        print "$key: $value\n";
}
```

If we execute the script, we will get the following result:

```
[hs@duron code]$ ./pg.pl
service:
port: 5432
hostaddr:
host:
password:
options:
```

```
user: hs
authtype:
tty:
dbname: hs
```

The values shown in the previous listing are the current default values.

You may sometimes want to reset the connection to your database and reconnect. The Pg module offers a simple function called reset to perform the operation. In the following code, we show a simple example where we reconnect to the database after establishing a connection:

```perl
#!/usr/bin/perl

use Pg;

$conn = Pg::connectdb("dbname=performance user=postgres");
if      ($conn->status eq 0) { print "Connection established ...\n"; }
$conn->reset;
if      ($conn->status eq 0) { print "Connection re-established ...\n"; }
```

If both connections are being created successfully, the script should produce two lines of output such as the following:

```
[hs@duron code]$ ./pg.pl
Connection established ...
Connection re-established ...
```

Disconnects will not be used in any of the scripts in this section. As mentioned before, this is done automatically. Up to now, we have already connected to the database several times, but there are no "old" backends running. We can check that with a simple grep command:

```
[hs@duron code]$ ps ax | grep post
 1872 ?        S      0:00 /usr/bin/postmaster -D /var/lib/pgsql/data
 2710 pts/1    S      0:00 grep post
```

Only the supervisor daemon is running; no backend processes are in memory because the processes have been deleted by Perl automatically.

Collecting Information about the Backend

Sometimes it is useful to collect information about the backend process related to a certain query. The Pg module offers some very comfortable functions to get information about the backend. If we want to know the descriptor number of the backend connection socket, we can use a function called socket:

```perl
#!/usr/bin/perl

use Pg;

$conn = Pg::connectdb("dbname=performance user=postgres");
print $conn->socket."\n";
```

If we execute this script, we will see one number printed onscreen (in our case, it is 3). If no backend process is open, -1 will be returned.

Every process on a system is assigned to a unique process ID when being started, just like backend processes. To find out which PID has been assigned to the current backend process, the backendPID function can be used:

```perl
#!/usr/bin/perl

use Pg;

$conn = Pg::connectdb("dbname=performance user=postgres");
print $conn->backendPID."\n";
```

We received the following result when executing the previous sample code shown:

```
[hs@duron code]$ ./pg.pl
15533
```

For debugging purposes, or simply because of curiosity, the messages exchanged between the backend and frontend can be sent to a debugging port. In most cases, you won't need this in your applications, but it can be a very interesting information for PostgreSQL developers. Turning messaging on can be done with trace; turning messaging off can be done with untrace:

```perl
$conn->trace(debug_port);
$conn->untrace;
```

Running Queries

The Pg module is not only used to establish connections. The most important thing when working with databases is retrieving data with the help of queries. The following example shows how we can perform a very simple query with the help of the Pg module:

```perl
#!/usr/bin/perl

use Pg;
```

```
$conn = Pg::connectdb("dbname=performance user=postgres");
if      ($conn->status eq 0)
{
        $query="SELECT 1+1";
        $result=$conn->exec($query);
        if        ($result->resultStatus eq PGRES_TUPLES_OK)
        {
                print "ok ...\n";
        }
        else
        {
                print "error ...\n";
        }
}
```

First, we connect to the database and check whether the connection has been
established successfully. If status returns 0, the connection works and we can execute
the query. With the help of a function called exec, we perform a simple SELECT
statement. Before we can safely use $result, we have to check whether the database
encountered any problems with the SQL-statement, so we use resultStatus.
resultStatus can return values from 0 to 7 but, as you can see in the previous sample
code, it is possible to check more than the number being returned by status. Table 9.4
provides an overview which strings are related to which numbers.

Table 9.4   *Overview of Query Status*

Value	String
0	PGRES_EMPTY_QUERY
1	PGRES_COMMAND_OK
2	PGRES_TUPLES_OK
3	PGRES_COPY_OUT
4	PGRES_COPY_IN
5	PGRES_BAD_RESPONSE
6	PGRES_NONFATAL_ERROR
7	PGRES_FATAL_ERROR

We do not just want to execute queries, we also want to use the result of a query. In
the following example, we perform the SELECT statement shown previously and print
the result onscreen:

```
#!/usr/bin/perl

use Pg;
```

```
$conn = Pg::connectdb("dbname=performance user=postgres");
if      ($conn->status eq 0)
{
        $query="SELECT 1+1";
        $result=$conn->exec($query);
        $value=$result->fetchrow;
        print "value: $value\n";
}
```

We can get the result of the query by calling the `fetchrow` function. To display the result onscreen, we use a simple print command.

The `SELECT` query just shown only returns one field and one row, but how can multiple rows with multiple columns be processed? The solution is very easy. If one row has many columns, the database returns an array. To get the complete result, we simply go through all rows of the result using a `WHILE` loop:

```
#!/usr/bin/perl

use Pg;

$conn = Pg::connectdb("dbname=performance user=postgres");
if      ($conn->status eq 0)
{
        $query="SELECT id, id*2 AS double FROM perftest WHERE id=4 or id=9";
        $result=$conn->exec($query);
        while   (@value=$result->fetchrow)
        {
                print "@value\n";
        }
}
```

When executing the program, we will get two lines with two columns each:

```
[hs@duron code]$ ./pg.pl
4 8
9 18
```

Extracting the result is sometimes not enough, so the Pg module offers additional features to provide a little more information about the query and the result of the query for the user.

Retrieving Information about the Result

In the following example, we will retrieve some important information about the query:

```perl
#!/usr/bin/perl

use Pg;

$conn = Pg::connectdb("dbname=performance user=postgres");
if      ($conn->status eq 0)
{
        $query="SELECT id, id*2 AS double FROM perftest WHERE id<4";
        $result=$conn->exec($query);
        print "tuples: ".$result->ntuples."\n";
        print "fields: ".$result->nfields."\n";
        print "fieldname: ".$result->fnumber(id)."\n";

}
```

ntuples returns the number of tuples in the query result. nfields returns the number of fields in the result, and fnumber tells us where in the array a certain column is stored. When executing the script, we will get the following result:

```
[hs@duron code]$ ./pg.pl
tuples: 3
fields: 2
fieldname: 0
```

You can see that the column called id can be found in position number 0, which is actually the first column.

Some programmers prefer binary data instead of ASCII. The advantage of binary data is that it can be processed faster, because the database stores the data in a binary format. The binaryTuples function can be used to see whether the result is binary. In the following code, you can see how the function has to be used:

```perl
#!/usr/bin/perl

use Pg;

$conn = Pg::connectdb("dbname=performance user=postgres");
if      ($conn->status eq 0)
{
```

```
    $query="SELECT id, id*2 AS double FROM perftest WHERE id<4";
    $result=$conn->exec($query);
    print "tuples: ".$result->binaryTuples."\n";
}
```

The function returns 1 if the data returned is binary; othwerwise, 0 will be returned.

In many cases ,fields have a fixed length. If you need the size of a field to define a data structure, you can use fmod. fmod returns the size of the field or a -1 if the field has no fixed length.

```
#!/usr/bin/perl

use Pg;

$conn = Pg::connectdb("dbname=performance user=postgres");
if      ($conn->status eq 0)
{
        $query="SELECT id FROM perftest WHERE id<4";
        $result=$conn->exec($query);
        print "length: ".$result->fmod("id")."\n";
        print "length: ".$result->fmod(0)."\n";
}
```

Let's execute the script:

```
[hs@duron code]$ ./pg.pl
length: -1
length: -1
```

You can see that Perl supports two ways of using commands such as fmod. On the one hand, you can see that we use the name of the column in the result to access the data. On the other hand, we can use the ID. In general, we recommend the use of the name to make sure that you get the right column.

In most cases, a result of -1 looks as if something has gone wrong during the process. Everything worked just fine in the previous example, but we recommend to that you test every statement handle before using it to make 100 percent sure that really everything has been working.

We may want to know more than the length of a field. In the next example, we will show how the data type of a field can be found:

```
#!/usr/bin/perl
```

```
use Pg;

$conn = Pg::connectdb("dbname=performance user=postgres");
if      ($conn->status eq 0)
{
        $query="SELECT id FROM perftest WHERE id<4";
        $result=$conn->exec($query);
        print "type: ".$result->ftype("id")."\n";
}
```

If we execute the previous script, we see that 23 is returned. Now the problem is, what is meant by 23? The problem can be solved with the help of PostgreSQL's system tables. If we query pg_type by using

```
SELECT * FROM pg_description WHERE objoid=23;
```

The result of the query is not surprising:

```
 objoid |                     description
--------+-------------------------------------------------
     23 | -2 billion to 2 billion integer, 4-byte storage
(1 row)
```

The column is an integer value. PostgreSQL always returns the ID instead of the description of an object, because the object is also used in the system tables. It is much shorter and not confusing at all. The behavior of objects, operators, or aggregates supported by PostgreSQL can be changed by the superuser. For that reason, names can also be slightly confusing. You simply have to get used to that.

Imagine a situation where you want to find the status of the query used in the previous example. cmdStatus can be applied to do the job for you:

```
#!/usr/bin/perl

use Pg;

$conn = Pg::connectdb("dbname=performance user=postgres");
if      ($conn->status eq 0)
{
        $query="SELECT id FROM perftest WHERE id<4";
        $result=$conn->exec($query);
        print "status: ".$result->cmdStatus."\n";
```

```
$query="SEL id FROM perftest WHERE id<4";
$result=$conn->exec($query);
print "status: ".$result->cmdStatus."\n";
}
```

You may have noticed that the second SELECT statement has a syntax error; the first
SQL statements works perfectly well. If we execute the script, we will receive the
following result shown:

```
[hs@duron code]$ ./pg.pl
status: SELECT
status:
```

The first SQL statement produces a useful status, while the second one produces an
empty string.

Working with BLOBs

Working with BLOBs by just using a command-line tool, such as psql, might not fit
your demands. Sometimes, it is more comfortable to use a Perl script to get the job
done. Because the Pg module is the Perl version of libpq, it also offers functions to
work with BLOBs. The following is a Perl script that creates a table to store the names
of songs and the binary file containing the songs:

```perl
#!/usr/bin/perl

use Pg;

$conn = Pg::connectdb("dbname=performance user=postgres");
if      ($conn->status eq 0)
{
        $create="CREATE TABLE songs(name text, mp3file OID)";
        $result=$conn->exec($create);
        print $conn->errorMessage."\n";

        $path="/tmp/data/";
        $upload="Falco-Rock_me_Amadeus.mp3";
        $sql="INSERT INTO songs VALUES('Falco - Rock me Amadeus',
                lo_import('$path$upload')) ";

        $ret=$conn->exec($sql);
        print $conn->errorMessage."\n";
}
```

We loaded one of the highlights of Austrian music into the database. We have done this with the help of a simple SQL command. The Pg module supports a function called `lo_import`, but we think that it is a lot easier to use the SQL version.

Although the Pg module offers a number of functions for treating BLOBs, many people still have some troubles with it. We recommend that you use simple SQL commands, such as we have shown in the "Working with BLOBs" section in Chapter 3, "An Introduction to SQL." In the case of BLOBs, using Pg can easily become a little bit painful.

Final Word

Pg is a very powerful programming interface for your PostgreSQL database. You should keep in mind that the interface is designed to be a 100 percent counterpart of the `libpg` module (C). Some real Perl hackers among you will recognize that the Pg module is not a real Perl-ish interface. If you want a little more Perl feeling try the DBI module.

The DBI Interface and DBD for PostgreSQL

Let's get to the DBI interface for PostgreSQL. As you have already seen, two Perl modules for working with PostgreSQL are available. In this section, you will learn how to use the standard DBI module and the DBD driver for PostgreSQL.

Overview

Initially, the DBI interface was written by Tim Bunce, who also started writing the Oracle driver for DBI. The DBI interface is the most widespread database interface available for Perl today, and a lot of people around the globe build database applications relying on the tremendous flexibility of this module. DBI provides a huge set of functions that you can use to make your applications support databases.

When dealing with DBI, the most important thing to mention is that the DBI module has nothing to do with PostgreSQL. DBI is only a layer between the driver and the application, used to access the database, and your application.

In the case of PostgreSQL, `DBD::Pg` does the job. If an application wants to communicate with a database (it can even be a simple ASCII file), the DBI interface passes the data to the DBD driver of the database. Then the DBD driver does all the communication with the database engine, so DBI can be seen as the glue between the database driver and your applications.

Currently, a huge number of drivers is available for nearly all databases. If you want to find a list of all official modules available, simply check out CPAN at `http://search.cpan.org`.

At the time of writing, current version of DBI was 1.15, released on March 30, 2001. We strongly recommend that you use the most recent version of DBI because the specification of DBI is evolving constantly.

Installation

At the moment, the DBI module and the DBD driver for PostgreSQL are not included in PostgreSQL's source distribution, so the modules must be installed on your system. In general, installing Perl modules is a very easy task, just like DBI and DBD.

The first module you have to install on your system is DBI. Get the module from a local FTP site and unpack the archive:

tar xvfz DBI-1.15.tar.gz

If the process terminates without displaying any error messages, you can switch to the directory containing the sources of your DBI module. The content of the directory will look something like the following:

```
[root@duron DBI-1.15]# ls
blib          DBI.o         dbish        Driver.xst   Perl.c        README
Changes       DBI.pm        dbish.PL     lib          Perl.o        t
dbd_xsh.h     dbipport.h    dbi_sql.h    Makefile     Perl.xs       test.pl
DBI.bs        dbiproxy      DBI.xs       Makefile.PL  Perl.xsi      ToDo
DBI.c         dbiproxy.PL   DBIXS.h      MANIFEST     pm_to_blib
```

After reading the README file, you can call perl Makefile.PL to generate a new Makefile that you'll need to continue installing the module:

```
[root@duron DBI-1.15]# perl Makefile.PL
*** Note:
    The optional PlRPC-modules (RPC::PlServer etc) are not installed.
    If you want to use the DBD::Proxy driver and DBI::ProxyServer
    modules, then you'll need to install the RPC::PlServer, RPC::PlClient,
    Storable and Net::Daemon modules. The CPAN Bundle::DBI may help you.
    You can install them any time after installing the DBI.
    You do *not* need these modules for typical DBI usage.

Optional modules are available from any CPAN mirror, in particular
    http://www.perl.com/CPAN/modules/by-module
    http://www.perl.org/CPAN/modules/by-module
    ftp://ftp.funet.fi/pub/languages/perl/CPAN/modules/by-module

Writing Makefile for DBI
```

Remember to actually *read* the README file!
Use 'make' to build the software (dmake or nmake on Windows).
Then 'make test' to execute self tests.
Then 'make install' to install the DBI and then delete this working
directory before unpacking and building any DBD::* drivers.

As you can see, Perl displays some information about the installation process and tells us how to continue. Let's try Perl's suggestions and use make. Perl now compiles the sources and we can test the module using make test:

```
[root@duron DBI-1.15]# make test
PERL_DL_NONLAZY=1 /usr/bin/perl -Iblib/arch -Iblib/lib -
I/usr/lib/perl5/5.6.0/i386-linux -I/usr/lib/perl5/5.6.0 -e 'use Test::Harness
qw(&runtests $verbose); $verbose=0; runtests @ARGV;' t/*.t
t/basics...........ok
t/dbidrv...........ok
t/examp............ok
t/meta.............ok
t/proxy............skipped test on this platform
t/shell............ok
t/subclass.........ok
All tests successful, 1 test skipped.
Files=7, Tests=183,  4 wallclock secs ( 1.32 cusr +  0.25 csys =  1.57 CPU)
PERL_DL_NONLAZY=1 /usr/bin/perl -Iblib/arch -Iblib/lib
-I/usr/lib/perl5/5.6.0/i386-linux -I/usr/lib/perl5/5.6.0 test.pl
test.pl
DBI test application $Revision: 10.5 $
Using /mnt/data/perl/DBI-1.15/blib
Switch: DBI 1.15 by Tim Bunce, 1.15
Available Drivers: ADO, ExampleP, Multiplex, Pg, Proxy, mysql
dbi:ExampleP:: testing 5 sets of 20 connections:
Connecting... 1 2 3 4 5 6 7 8 9 10 11 12 13 14 15 16 17 18 19 20
Disconnecting...
Connecting... 1 2 3 4 5 6 7 8 9 10 11 12 13 14 15 16 17 18 19 20
Disconnecting...
Connecting... 1 2 3 4 5 6 7 8 9 10 11 12 13 14 15 16 17 18 19 20
Disconnecting...
Connecting... 1 2 3 4 5 6 7 8 9 10 11 12 13 14 15 16 17 18 19 20
Disconnecting...
Connecting... 1 2 3 4 5 6 7 8 9 10 11 12 13 14 15 16 17 18 19 20
Disconnecting...
Made 100 connections in  0 wallclock secs ( 0.06 usr +  0.00 sys =  0.06 CPU)
```

```
Testing handle creation speed...
5000 NullP statement handles cycled in 0.7 cpu+sys seconds (6756 per sec)

test.pl done
```

It seems that the test has been completed successfully and we can finish the installation process. This can be done with the help of `make install`. If `make install` terminates successfully, the module has been installed correctly on the system.

Because the DBI module is ready, we can add the DBD driver for PostgreSQL to the system. First, we have to unpack the sources:

`tar xvfz DBD-Pg-0.98.tar.gz`

We have to use `perl Makefile.PL`, as we did for the DBI module, to generate the Makefile we need for the rest of the installation process:

```
[root@duron DBD-Pg-0.98]# perl Makefile.PL
Configuring Pg
Remember to actually read the README file !
please set environment variables POSTGRES_INCLUDE and POSTGRES_LIB !
```

Oh dear, what happened? Some of you might think that something has gone wrong, but keep calm—everything is still on track.

The installation process can't find PostgreSQL, and we have to define the right location for the software with the help of two environment variables. In the case of RedHat 7.1, this can easily be done with the following two commands:

```
[root@duron DBD-Pg-0.98]# export POSTGRES_INCLUDE=/usr/include/pgsql/
[root@duron DBD-Pg-0.98]# export POSTGRES_LIB=/usr/lib/pgsql/
```

If we have set the two variables correctly, we can try `perl Makefile.PL` again:

```
[root@duron DBD-Pg-0.98]# perl Makefile.PL
Configuring Pg
Remember to actually read the README file !
OS: linux
Using DBI 1.15 installed in /usr/lib/perl5/site_perl/5.6.0/i386-linux/auto/DBI
Writing Makefile for DBD::Pg
```

You can see that it works now. To complete the installation process, use `make` and `make install` now. If no errors are displayed, you have successfully installed the module.

Connecting

We now try to establish a connection to the PostgreSQL server. Connecting means that we create a connection handle:

```perl
#!/usr/bin/perl

use DBI;

$user="hs";
$password="anypasswd";
$dbname="performance";

$dsn="dbi:Pg:dbname=$dbname;port=5432";
$dbh=DBI->connect("$dsn", "$user", "$password") or
        die "can't connect: $!\n";
```

In this example, we establish a connection to the PostgreSQL server running at `localhost` listening to port 5432. The database we want to connect to is called `performance`. We try to establish the connection as user `hs` whose password is `anypasswd`. In the source code, you can see that the first thing happening is including the DBI module. We do not have to explicitly include the DBD module for PostgreSQl because this is done automatically by the DBI module.

When establishing a connection, PostgreSQL checks if a value is defined in the connect string. If a certain value is not defined, PostgreSQL checks whether environment variables are set. If a value still can't be found, the database uses the hard-coded default values.

Table 9.5 shows all parameters supported by PostgreSQL.

Table 9.5   *Environment variables*

Parameter	Environment	Default Value
host	PGHOST	localhost
port	PGPORT	5432
options	PGOPTIONS	" "
tty	PGTTY	" "
dbname	PGDATABASE	current userid
user	PGUSER	current userid
password	PGPASSWD	" "

After we have seen how establishing a connection works, we will present a very simple, but sometimes very useful, command to count the number of databases available:

```
#!/usr/bin/perl

use DBI;

print DBI->data_sources("Pg")."\n";
```

When executing the script on my PostgreSQL server, the result will be 5, because I have 5 PostgreSQL databases on my system.

If you want to check whether the database connection you are working on is still in business, the ping method would be a good choice for testing.

```
#!/usr/bin/perl

use DBI;

$dbh=DBI->connect("dbi:Pg:dbname=performance; port=5432",
        "hs", "anypasswd") or
                die "can't connect: $!\n";
$rc=$dbh->ping or
        die "can't ping database\n";
print "rc: $rc\n";
```

This program does nothing else but ping the database to which we are connected. A ping's return value is critical. Check the module you are using to connect to your PostgreSQL server to find which values are returned in case of which scenarios.

The DBI specification supports some additional features that can be quite useful. Currently, the following function is not supported completely by PostgreSQL's DBD driver, but it works fine and it can be used to enhance the speed of your application when porting it to other databases:

```
#!/usr/bin/perl

use DBI;

$one=DBI->connect("dbi:Pg:dbname=performance; port=5432", "hs", "anypasswd") or
        die "can't connect: $!\n";
$two=DBI->connect_cached("dbi:Pg:dbname=performance; port=5432",
        "hs", "anypasswd") or die "can't connect: $!\n";
```

The connect_cached can be used to save authentification overhead, especially in performance critical environments. connect_cached is like connect but returns a cached database handle if it is still valid. If you have to connect to the database very often, this can speed up the connection process significantly.

Working with DBI

Working with the DBI module is extremely comfortable because DBI really feels like something very Perl-ish, and it is very easy for a programmer to understand the basic concept and handling of a system using DBI. Because DBI is the standard Perl interface for database programming, applications written for the DBI interface can be easily ported to other databases. If the SQL code used inside the application is 100 percent ANSI SQL 92-compliant and the application is written properly, the only thing that has to be modified is the connect string, which should be a rather easy task.

Let's start with a very simple program that does nothing but display the result of a simple SELECT statement:

```
#!/usr/bin/perl

use DBI;

$dbh=DBI->connect("dbi:Pg:dbname=performance; port=5432", "hs", "anypasswd") or
        die "can't connect: $!\n";

$sql="SELECT 1+1";

$sth=$dbh->prepare($sql) or
        die "can't prepare: $sql\n";
$sth->execute or
        die "can't execute: $sql\n";
while    (@row=$sth->fetchrow_array)
{
        print "row: @row\n";
}
```

This may look a little bit confusing, but let's go through it line by line.

After connecting to the database, as shown in the previous section, we define a simple SQL statement ($sql). After that, we prepare the execution of the statement. Many databases support some information after preparing the statement. PostgreSQL does not support a concept like that, so prepare does nothing but store the statement after checking for placeholders.

> **Note**
> The DBI specification also defines prepare_cached, but PostgreSQL supports no
> interaction with the statement.

If prepare fails, we want to display an error and quit. In the previous example, this is done by using a simple Perl command for exception handling called die. When the application terminates because of an error, $! will contain some information about the origin of the error.

After preparing the statement, we want to execute it by using the execute command. Again, if an error occurs, we want the application to quit and raise an error.

Finally, we read the result of the query and write it to standard output. With the help of @row=$sth->fetchrow_array, we can read one line of data and assign the result to an array called @row. All lines are displayed onscreen with the help of a simple print command. print is repeated as long as WHILE extracts data from the query.

In many cases, it is interesting to find out how many lines are returned by the database. This can very easily be done by checking the return value of the execute statement. In the following example, we select the first 100 lines of table perftest (from the database we have used in Chapter 8, "Performance Tuning"):

```perl
#!/usr/bin/perl

use DBI;

$dbh=DBI->connect("dbi:Pg:dbname=performance; port=5432", "hs", "anypasswd") or
        die "can't connect: $!\n";

$sql="SELECT * FROM perftest LIMIT 100";

$sth=$dbh->prepare($sql) or
        die "can't prepare: $sql\n";
$ret=$sth->execute or
        die "can't execute: $sql\n";
print "lines: $ret\n";
```

$ret contains the number of lines returned by the statement. If we execute the script, we will get a result such as the following:

```
[hs@duron code]$ ./dbi1.pl
lines: 100
```

The query used in this program shown returns exactly 100 rows; I guess that is what we expected.

In most cases, we want to use the result created by one query in another query. In the next example, we select the first 100 records and add one to the last column by using an UPDATE query:

```
#!/usr/bin/perl

use DBI;

$dbh=DBI->connect("dbi:Pg:dbname=performance; port=5432", "hs", "anypasswd") or
        die "can't connect: $!\n";

$sql="SELECT * FROM perftest WHERE id < 101";

$sth=$dbh->prepare($sql) or
        die "can't prepare: $sql\n";
$ret=$sth->execute or
        die "can't execute: $sql\n";
while   (@row=$sth->fetchrow_array)
{
        $rv=$dbh->do("UPDATE perftest SET anumber=anumber+1 WHERE id=@row[0]")
or
                die "can't update: $id\n";
}
```

After connecting and retrieving the desired records in the database, we go through the result line-by-line. For every line, we perform an UPDATE operation by using the do command provided by the DBI module and its DBD driver.

do is prepare and execute combined in a single statement. You might wonder why we have included prepare and execute here if all wonderful things can simply be done with do. Well, some things, such as retrieving data, cannot be done with do, because do only returns the number of lines affected by an SQL statement and not the statement handle that we need to extract the data from the result. Usually, do is used for non SELECT statements that are used only once or cannot be prepared because of driver restrictions.

Sometimes you want to execute the same SQL statements more than once using different sets of parameters. In this scenario, you don't have to prepare the SQL statement every time you want to execute it:

```
#!/usr/bin/perl

use DBI;

$dbh=DBI->connect("dbi:Pg:dbname=performance; port=5432",
        "hs", "anypasswd") or
                die "can't connect: $!\n";
```

```
$sql="SELECT * FROM perftest WHERE id < 2";

$stha=$dbh->prepare($sql) or die "can't prepare: $sql\n";
$ret=$stha->execute or die "can't execute: $sql\n";

$sthb=$dbh->prepare("UPDATE perftest SET anumber=anumber+? WHERE id=?") or
        die "can't prepare\n";
while    (@row=$stha->fetchrow_array)
{
        $sthb->execute(@row[0], @row[0]) or
                die "can't update: $id\n";
}
```

We prepare and execute a SELECT statement. Before processing the WHILE loop, we prepare a second statement. Note, that we have included two question marks instead of real values in the statement. In the WHILE loop, we execute the statement and pass two parameters to it. Every parameter will be used to substitute one question mark so the statement can be executed correctly. Substitution is done with the help of so-called bind variables.

If you use bind variables and execute statements more often, your application will speed up significantly, because preparing the statement has to be done only once.

Many queries are very small and are designed to return only one line. To make the code easier to understand, the DBI interface offers some very useful commands. Look at the following sample code:

```
#!/usr/bin/perl

use DBI;

$dbh=DBI->connect("dbi:Pg:dbname=performance; port=5432",
        "hs", "anypasswd") or
                die "can't connect: $!\n";

$sql="SELECT * FROM perftest WHERE id < 4 LIMIT 1";

@row=$dbh->selectrow_array($sql);
print "row: @row\n";
```

We perform a query that returns only one line of data. In this case, it would be much too long to use prepare, execute, and a WHILE loop to extract the data. Real Perl hackers want to write entire operating systems with just one line of code (that nobody understands if the line is written by a real Perl hacker), so the DBI interface has to offer a command for those people, too.

To prepare and execute the statement and for extracting the first line of data from the result, we can use the selectrow_array function. Don't confuse this with the fetchrow_array function we have used in the previous examples.

The DBI supports some more functions for retrieving data from a query, but covering them all is beyond the scope of in this book. If you want complete information about all functions, check out the man pages of the DBI interface.

Working with Arrays

You may sometimes want to use arrays in your SQL statements. In this section, we will show you how you can access data in arrays that are returned by your PostgreSQL database server. Let's create a table and insert some data first:

```
CREATE TABLE children (
    name        text,
    children    text
);

INSERT INTO children
    VALUES ('Paul',
    '{Josef, Pat, Amy}');

INSERT INTO children
    VALUES ('Carol',
    '{Epi, Gerwin}');
```

A table called children contains two records now. We will retrieve and display both records using the following short Perl script:

```
#!/usr/bin/perl

use DBI;

$dbh=DBI->connect("dbi:Pg:dbname=performance; port=5432", "hs", "anypasswd",
        {PrintError => 0, RaiseError => 1} ) or
        die "can't connect: $!\n";

$sql="SELECT * FROM children";
$sth=$dbh->prepare($sql);
$ret=$sth->execute;
while    (@row=$sth->fetchrow_array)
```

```
{
        print "row: @row[0] - @row[1]\n";
}
```

If we execute the program, we will get the following result:

```
[hs@duron code]$ ./db3.pl
row: Paul - {Josef, Pat, Amy}
row: Carol - {Epi, Gerwin}
```

You can see that the values of the array are returned by the database as one string. Depending on the way you want to work with the data, you can convert the string to any data structure you want.

Transactions

When building complex applications, it can be useful to influence the way PostgreSQL treats transactions. To build a robust system, many atomic database operations can be combined into one unit to avoid errors. The DBI interface offers a flag to influence the way transactions are treated. By default, AutoCommit is set and every operation is treated as a separate transaction.

In the following example, we perform two simple operations in one transaction.

```
#!/usr/bin/perl

use DBI;

$dbh=DBI->connect("dbi:Pg:dbname=performance; port=5432",
        "hs", "anypasswd") or
                die "can't connect: $!\n";

$dbh->{AutoCommit} = 0;          # enable transactions
eval
{
        $rv=$dbh->do("UPDATE perftest SET anumber=anumber+1 WHERE id < 10");
        $rv=$dbh->do("DELETE FROM perftest WHERE id < 5");
        $dbh->commit;
};
if      ($@)
{
        warn "An error occurred: $@\n";
        $dbh->rollback;
}
```

We first enable the transaction by turning `AutoCommit` off. Then we perform all operations with the help of the `eval` command. If `eval` fails, an error is displayed and the rollback function is called.

Errors and Exception Handling

No programming language can live without some sort of error and exception handling. Because the DBI module interacts closely with the database, some additional functions for exception handling have been implemented in Perl. We have already used some Perl functions to display warnings or to quit applications. Now let's look at the functions provided by the DBI interface now:

```
#!/usr/bin/perl

use DBI;

$dbh=DBI->connect("dbi:Pg:dbname=performance; port=5432",
        "hs", "anypasswd") or
                die "can't connect: $!\n";

$sql=" * FROM perftest WHERE id < 10 LIMIT 1";

@row=$dbh->selectrow_array($sql);
print "error: ".$dbh->err."\n";

print "row: @row\n";
```

A function called `err` is defined for every handle and can be used to display errors. In the code, we have included an SQL statement where we simply omitted `SELECT` from the query string. This leads to a syntax error. We will execute the script now and see what happens:

```
[hs@duron code]$ ./db2.pl
DBD::Pg::db selectrow_array failed: ERROR:  parser: parse error
at or near at ./db2.pl line 10.
error: 7
row:
```

An error is displayed, and that's what we expected Perl to do. The first error displayed comes directly from the `selectrow_array` function because the statement cannot be executed. After that, `err` returns 7 as error code. You will see how to receive more comfortable output in the next example.

Finally, we try to display the result of the query, but the array that should contain the result is empty.

The next example actually does actually the same thing, but the code looks a little more beautiful. We use the `errstr` function instead of `err` to get an error message that can be more easily understood.

```perl
#!/usr/bin/perl

use DBI;

$dbh=DBI->connect("dbi:Pg:dbname=performance; port=5432",
        "hs", "anypasswd") or
                die "can't connect: $!\n";

$sql=" * FROM perftest WHERE id < 10 LIMIT 1";

@row=$dbh->selectrow_array($sql) or
        warn "error: ".$dbh->errstr."\n";

if      (@row[0])
{
        print "row: @row\n";
}
```

We only want the result of the function to be displayed when the query terminated successfully.

```
[hs@duron code]$ ./db2.pl
DBD::Pg::db selectrow_array failed: ERROR:  parser: parse error
at or near at ./db2.pl line 10.
error: ERROR:  parser: parse error at or near
```

You can see that a real error message is being displayed now.

Debugging and Monitoring
After a connection has been established and a few lines of code have been written, you will soon find yourself doing some debugging work. The most important thing when debugging is to find out what is going on in the program. The Perl debugger or some simple `print` statements can satisfy your demands in some but not all cases. The DBI interface supports a method to trace the things going on inside the database. Look at the following example:

```perl
#!/usr/bin/perl
```

```
use DBI;

$dbh=DBI->connect("dbi:Pg:dbname=performance; port=5432",
        "hs", "anypasswd") or
                die "can't connect: $!\n";

DBI->trace(2, '/tmp/pg_trace.txt');

$sql="SELECT * FROM perftest WHERE id < 2";

$sth=$dbh->prepare($sql) or
        die "can't prepare: $sql\n";
$ret=$sth->execute or
        die "can't execute: $sql\n";
while   (@row=$sth->fetchrow_array)
{
        $rv=$dbh->do("UPDATE perftest SET anumber=anumber+1 ".
                "WHERE id=@row[0]") or
                        die "can't update: $id\n";
}
```

We have slightly modified one of the previous examples to show you how trace can be used. Six levels of messaging are defined in Table 9.6.

Table 9.6   *Status Codes*

Value	Action
0	No tracing
1	Traces DBI method calls with results and errors
2	Traces method entries with parameters and results
3	Adds some additional internal information about DBI
4	Displays more detailed information from the driver and displays DBI mutex information the in case of multithreaded Perl

trace can be called with up to two parameters. The first parameter defines the trace level as described in Table 9.6. The second parameter can be used to define a file to which to redirect the output. This is not only useful for debugging purposes, but it also gives you a good insight into what is happening inside your applications. We have included the output of the trace function that we used in the previous program to show you how debugging information produced by trace may look.

```
    DBI 1.15-nothread dispatch trace level set to 2
    Note: perl is running without the recommended perl -w option
    -> prepare for DBD::Pg::db (DBI::db=HASH(0x81de338)~0x81de2fc
'SELECT * FROM perftest WHERE id < 2')
dbd_st_prepare: statement = >SELECT * FROM perftest WHERE id < 2<
dbd_st_preparse: statement = >SELECT * FROM perftest WHERE id < 2<
    <- prepare= DBI::st=HASH(0x81de440) at dbi1.pl line 12.
    -> execute for DBD::Pg::st (DBI::st=HASH(0x81de440)~0x8102d78)
dbd_st_execute
dbd_st_execute: statement = >SELECT * FROM perftest WHERE id < 2<
    <- execute= 1 at dbi1.pl line 14.
    -> fetchrow_array for DBD::Pg::st (DBI::st=HASH(0x81de440)~0x8102d78)
dbd_st_fetch
    <- fetchrow_array= ( '1' 'WV3SGAmq' '34800423' ) [3 items] at dbi1.pl line
16.
    -> do in DBD::_::db for DBD::Pg::db (DBI::db=HASH(0x81de338)~0x81de2fc
'UPDATE perftest SET anumber=anumber+1 WHERE id=1')
2   -> prepare for DBD::Pg::db (DBI::db=HASH(0x81de2fc)~INNER 'UPDATE perftest
SET anumber=anumber+1 WHERE id=1' undef)
dbd_st_prepare: statement = >UPDATE perftest SET anumber=anumber+1 WHERE id=1<
dbd_st_preparse: statement = >UPDATE perftest SET anumber=anumber+1 WHERE id=1<
2   <- prepare= DBI::st=HASH(0x81de4d0) at DBI.pm line 939.
    -> execute for DBD::Pg::st (DBI::st=HASH(0x81de4d0)~0x8174320)
dbd_st_execute
dbd_st_execute: statement = >UPDATE perftest SET anumber=anumber+1 WHERE id=1<
    <- execute= 1 at DBI.pm line 940.
    -> rows for DBD::Pg::st (DBI::st=HASH(0x81de4d0)~0x8174320)
dbd_st_rows
    <- rows= 1 at DBI.pm line 941.
    <- do= 1 at dbi1.pl line 18.
    -> DESTROY for DBD::Pg::st (DBI::st=HASH(0x8174320)~INNER)
dbd_st_destroy
    <- DESTROY= undef at dbi1.pl line 18.
    -> fetchrow_array for DBD::Pg::st (DBI::st=HASH(0x81de440)~0x8102d78)
dbd_st_fetch
    <- fetchrow_array= ( ) [0 items] at dbi1.pl line 16.
    -- DBI::END
    -> disconnect_all for DBD::Pg::dr (DBI::dr=HASH(0x8170fc0)~0x81de380)
dbd_discon_all
    <- disconnect_all= '' at DBI.pm line 454.
    -> DESTROY for DBD::Pg::st (DBI::st=HASH(0x8102d78)~INNER)
dbd_st_finish
dbd_st_destroy
```

```
    <- DESTROY= undef during global destruction.
    -> DESTROY for DBD::Pg::db (DBI::db=HASH(0x81de2fc)~INNER)
dbd_db_disconnect
dbd_db_destroy
    <- DESTROY= undef during global destruction.
    -> DESTROY in DBD::_::common for DBD::Pg::dr (
DBI::dr=HASH(0x81de380)~INNER)
    <- DESTROY= undef during global destruction.
```

You can see that the output is already quite long, although we have not used level two yet.

If we don't want to rely on the messages provided by the system, we can add our own messages to the logfile. This can be done by using the trace_msg function:

```
#!/usr/bin/perl

use DBI;

$dbh=DBI->connect("dbi:Pg:dbname=performance; port=5432",
        "hs", "anypasswd") or
                die "can't connect: $!\n";

DBI->trace(1, '/tmp/pg_trace.txt');

$sql="SELECT * FROM perftest WHERE id < 9 LIMIT 1";

$sth=$dbh->prepare($sql) or die "can't prepare: $sql\n";
$ret=$sth->execute or die "can't execute: $sql\n";
while    (@row=$sth->fetchrow_array)
{
        DBI->trace_msg("Using @row[0]\n",1);
        $rv=$dbh->do("UPDATE perftest SET anumber=anumber+1 ".
                "WHERE id=@row[0]") or
                        die "can't update: $id\n";
}
```

pg_trace in /tmp contains one additional line for every time the WHILE loop is processed. It is also possible to define the trace level of an individual statement. If a second parameter is defined, the message is printed, but only if the trace level is equal to or greater than that level. The default value is 1.

Although we have already set the trace level to 1 and only two SQL commands have to be processed, the logfile is still very long:

```
    DBI 1.15-nothread dispatch trace level set to 1
    Note: perl is running without the recommended perl -w option
dbd_st_prepare: statement = >SELECT * FROM perftest WHERE id < 9 LIMIT 1<
dbd_st_preparse: statement = >SELECT * FROM perftest WHERE id < 9 LIMIT 1<
    <- prepare('SELECT * FROM perftest WHERE id < 9 LIMIT 1' CODE)=
DBI::st=HASH(0x81de858) at dbi1.pl line 12.
dbd_st_execute
    <- execute(CODE)= 1 at dbi1.pl line 13.
dbd_st_fetch
    <- fetchrow_array= ( '5' 'Kq6NJr5Z' '34864453' ) [3 items] at dbi1.pl line
14.
Using 5
dbd_st_prepare: statement = >UPDATE perftest SET anumber=anumber+1 WHERE id=5<
dbd_st_preparse: statement = >UPDATE perftest SET anumber=anumber+1 WHERE id=5<
2    <- prepare('UPDATE perftest SET anumber=anumber+1 WHERE id=5' undef ...)=
DBI::st=HASH(0x81de8d0) at DBI.pm line 939.
dbd_st_execute
    <- execute(CODE)= 1 at DBI.pm line 940.
dbd_st_rows
    <- rows= 1 at DBI.pm line 941.
    <- do('UPDATE perftest SET anumber=anumber+1 WHERE id=5' CODE)= 1 at dbi1.pl
line 17.
dbd_st_destroy
    <- DESTROY= undef at dbi1.pl line 17.
dbd_st_fetch
    <- fetchrow_array= ( ) [0 items] at dbi1.pl line 14.
dbd_discon_all
    <- disconnect_all= '' at DBI.pm line 454.
dbd_db_disconnect
dbd_db_destroy
    <- DESTROY= undef during global destruction.
    <- DESTROY= undef during global destruction.
dbd_st_finish
dbd_st_destroy
    <- DESTROY= undef during global destruction.
```

Another powerful flag for debugging is PrintError. By default, DBI->connect turns on PrintError and warnings are displayed in the case of an error. PrintError is a simple attribute that is common to all handles and can easily be turned off.

In the next example, we will turn `PrintError` off and `RaiseError` on:

```
#!/usr/bin/perl

use DBI;

$dbh=DBI->connect("dbi:Pg:dbname=performance; port=5432", "hs", "anypasswd",
        {PrintError => 0, RaiseError => 1} ) or
        die "can't connect: $!\n";

print $dbh->{PrintError}."\n";
print $dbh->{RaiseError}."\n";
```

We just have to add brackets to the `connect` string and add all variables we want to redefine. A complete list of all parameters can be found in the man pages of your DBI module and the DBD driver for your PostgreSQL database (try **"man DBD::Pg"**).

```
[hs@duron code]$ ./db2.pl


1
```

`PrintError` is not defined now, and `RaiseError` is set to 1. `RaiseError` is a rather strict parameter. It is turned off by default, but turning it on can change the behavior of your software significantly. Normally, simple error codes are returned. With `RaiseError` turned on, real exceptions will be raised and DBI will do a `die("$class $method failed: $DBI::errstr")`. What we want to point out is that this parameter should be used very carefully. Only use it when your are 100 percent sure of what you're doing.

Notation and Conventions

In some cases the DBI module can be slightly confusing, especially for beginners. We included this section here to give you a little overview of some conventions usually used by DBI programmers. We don't want to make it into a dogma, but we strongly recommend that you use the conventions shown in Table 9.7 to make your software easier to read and easier to understand.

Table 9.7   *Conventions for Variable Names*

Notation	Meaning
$dbh	Database handle object
$sth	Statement handle object
$drh	Driver handle object
$h	Any handle

Table 9.7   *(continued)*

Notation	Meaning
$rc	General return code
$rv	General return value
@ary	List of values returned from the database
$rows	Number of rows processed
$fh	Filehandle
undef	NULL values

DBI is one of the most powerful modules available for PostgreSQL and Perl. Many people today are using DBI, and the number of programmers is constantly increasing. Recently, the use of DBI in Web applications has decreased a little because PHP has turned out to be a suitable solution for building Web applications. DBI is the most important force for building database enabled Perl solutions.

DBI Proxies

Accessing a database without any specific driver over the Internet or accessing an MS Access database from a Linux host may sound a little bit strange, but Perl offers a solution for all these purposes. This section is dedicated to those who have to deal with hybrid database environments.

Proxy servers today are used in almost all Web environments to provide and restrict access to certain resources and to speed up the way data is processed over the network. In addition to access restriction and speed, security plays a major part in today's proxy server business.

Like other proxy servers, the DBI proxy is a piece of software that operates between the client and the server application. On the surface, this overhead seems unnecessary, but it has some very big advantages:

- You can define any restriction you want for your database.

- You can access databases that were not designed for use in network environments.

- Sometimes commercial software, such as Oracle databases, need special interfaces that have to be available on every client.

The DBI::ProxyServer module helps you to manage all those things in a very comfortable way. Luckily, PostgreSQL supports all standard interfaces for databases, such as ODBC or JDBC, so accessing a PostgreSQL database is very easy.

Initially, the DBI proxy was developed for security reasons. In many real-world situations, an intranet database has to be accessed by a Web server. To protect the intranet database, the Web application connects to the DBI proxy running on the firewall. The DBI proxy can be used to access any kind of database used in the intranet, even modules, for accessing simple CSV files (simple ASCII files) are available. In intranet/Internet environments, the DBI proxy can also be used to save a lot of network traffic. Databases, such as MS Access, are not capable of running in real network environments because the query is always processed on the client, so all data has to be transmitted over the network.

Surprisingly, the architecture of the DBI proxy itself is not very complicated. The reason is that Jochen Wiedmann, the father of the DBI proxy, extensively used Perl components that are already available on the Internet. The advantage of that strategy is that the code of the DBI proxy itself is rather brief and easy to understand.

Currently, the `DBI::ProxyServer` module is distributed with the DBI module by Tim Bunce and, for that reason, it is free software that can be distributed under the same terms as Perl.

We have not included a full example of a DBI proxy in this section because that would go beyond the scope of its content. We just want to encourage you to use the DBI proxy because it is a very comfortable and reliable way to build powerful Perl applications.

PHP

The the past few years, PHP has become more and more popular. The number of users is constantly increasing, and the group responsible for developing PHP is gaining members. This section is dedicated to all those people out there who want to build PostgreSQL-enabled PHP applications.

A Short History of PHP

PHP shows quite well what can result when people try to build simple Perl-based "Personal Home Page Tools." I don't think that anybody back in 1994 could have imagined that a short Perl CGI program would be the start of something really big. Today, PHP is one of the most widespread languages for Web programming available and supports more databases than many of us might be able to enumerate.

Back in the early days, "Personal Home Page Tools" supported only a few macros and a parsing engine. The parser was written in 1995 and called PHP/FI version 2. The FI actually came from a second package to work with data forms that Rasmus Lerdorf wrote. PHP/FI became popular, and people started contributing code to it.

In the middle of 1997, the way PHP was developed changed significantly. PHP was not the pet project of Rasmus anymore, and a real team was formed. The parser was completely rewritten by Zeev Suraski and Andi Gutmans. The new code became the base of PHP 3. A lot of code was ported to PHP 3 or was completely rewritten.

At the time of writing, PHP 4 is the most recent version. The engine was entirely replaced by the so-called Zend scripting engine, and the development of PHP goes on even faster. A huge number of modules and libraries have been implemented for PHP, and the number of people building PHP Web sites is constantly increasing. At the moment, several millions of PHP-enabled Web sites are set up around the globe, and their number is growing and growing.

PHP has become a very reliable platform for building complex Web sites. One of the most important and most powerful components of PHP is its ability to interact with databases. The number of databases supported by PHP is large, and the flexibility, as well as the number of functions provided by the database interfaces, could not be better. No matter what kind of database you want to use, PHP will provide the right interface.

PostgreSQL is also supported by PHP, and we will try to provide you insight into building PHP- and PostgreSQL-enabled databases.

Connecting

Before we can start working with PostgreSQL and PHP, we have to establish a connection to the server. Connecting to a database with the help of PHP is an extremely easy task because everything is done by a function called pg_connect. The following is a brief syntax overview of the pg_connect command:

```
int pg_connect (string host, string port, string dbname)
int pg_connect (string host, string port, string options, string dbname)
int pg_connect (string host, string port, string options,
        string tty, string dbname)
int pg_connect (string conn_string)
```

The pg_connect function returns a so-called "connection index" that you have to use to work with other functions.

We create a small PHP script called connect.php and copy it to the html or cgi-bin directory of our Web server. We strongly recommend that you use the cgi-bin directory of your Web server because this is the more secure way. Imagine yourself in a situation where something goes wrong with your PHP file, the full source code of your program will be displayed if you have the files in the html directory. People would be able to steal your source code, which is bad itself, but the most dangerous thing is that people can see the passwords you may have hardcoded in your software. This can lead to some real trouble. Before we get to a little workaround for this problem, the following is a small piece of software that shows how you can connect to your server:

```
<?
        $user="hs";
        $dbname="performance";

        echo ("trying to connect ...<br>\n");
        $db=pg_connect("user=$user dbname=$dbname");
        if      ($db)
        {
                echo ('connection ok<br>');
        }
        else
        {
                echo ('no connection<br>');
        }
?>
```

We connect to the database using pg_connect. $db will now contain the database handle. If the connection process fails, we want no connection to be displayed. With the help of a simple if statement, we try to find out whether $db is defined.

If you are building big Web sites, connecting to the database may be necessary several times. We recommend that you place the data required to establish the connection in a separate file. Now connect.php looks as follows:

```
<?
        include("globals.php");

        echo ("trying to connect ...<br>\n");
        $db=pg_connect("user=$user dbname=$dbname");
        if      ($db)
        {
                echo ('connection ok<br>');
```

```
        }
        else
        {
                echo ('no connection<br>');
        }
?>
```

`globals.php` contains the data to establish the connection. The file looks very simple indeed:

```
<?
        $user="hs";
        $dbname="performance";
?>
```

PHP uses the variables in the included file as if they were defined in `connect.php`. This is indeed very comfortable because changing passwords, users, or any other variable used in the authentification process can be changed by editing just one file. For those among you who are afraid of `vi`, this is a significant advantage.

Connections can be closed explicitly with the help of the `pg_close` command. Closing connections is not necessary because non-persistent open links are automatically closed at the end of the script's execution. We will look at persistent database connections with PHP later in Chapter 18, "Persistent Database Connections with PHP." Working with persistent connections is rather easy". Although connections are closed automatically, we recommend that you close all open connections explicitly, especially when a huge number of connections are open on the server; this can save you some troubles.

If you want to know which database you are currently connected to, the `pg_dbname` function can be used:

```
<?
        include("globals.php");

        $conn=pg_connect("user=$user dbname=$dbname");
        if      (!$conn)
        {
                echo ('cannot establish connection<br>');
                exit;
        }
        $dbname=pg_dbname($conn);
        echo ("name of the current database: $dbname<br>\n");
?>
```

This example just displays the name of the database we are currently using.

PHP offers also a way to display the name of the host to which we are currently connected. `pg_host` can be used to resolve the name of the computer on which the database is running. If you want to find the port PostgreSQL is listening to, use `pg_port`.

Working with PHP

Let's get to some real SQL action now. Because we want to do a little more than simply connecting to the database, we will present some additional functions in this section.

We start with a PHP script that creates a table and inserts some data:

```php
<?
        include("globals.php");

        $conn=pg_connect("user=$user dbname=$dbname");
        if      (!$conn)
        {
                echo ('cannot establish connection<br>');
                exit;
        }
        echo ('creating table ...<br>');
        $create="CREATE TABLE messageb(name text, message text)";
        $result=pg_exec($conn, $create);
        if      (!$result)
        {
                echo ("could not execute: $create<br>");
                exit;
        }
        else
        {
                $sql="INSERT INTO messageb VALUES('Tom', 'Hello World')";
                $result=pg_exec($conn, $sql);
                echo ("Result: $result<br>");
        }
?>
```

We first establish a connection to the database by using the variables defined in `globals.php`. Then we create the table with the help of the `pg_exec` command.

The syntax of pg_exec is very simple:

```
int pg_exec (int connection, string query)
```

Use the database handle as the first parameter and the SQL code you want to execute as the second parameter, and everything will work just fine. To determine whether everything really worked out, we check whether $result contains an error. After creating the table, we insert one record into the database using pg_exec again.

Most SQL statements you execute with pg_exec affect certain rows in the database. To determine how many rows are affected by a statement, the programmer can use a function called pg_cmdtuples that returns the desired value. The following piece of code shows you how pg_cmdtuples can be used:

```
<?
        include("globals.php");

        $conn=pg_connect("user=$user dbname=$dbname");
        if      (!$conn)
        {
                echo ('cannot establish connection<br>');
                exit;
        }
        $sql="INSERT INTO messageb VALUES('Tom', 'Hello World')";
        $result=pg_exec($conn, $sql);
        $cmdtuples = pg_cmdtuples ($result);
        echo ("Result: $cmdtuples<br>");
?>
```

The function returns an integer value that can easily be displayed with the help of PHP's echo command. In the previous example, 1 will be displayed because an INSERT statement affects only one row of data.

But not only the rows of data affected by a query might be interesting for the user. Sometimes, even the result of a query might be interesting:

```
<?
        include("globals.php");

        $conn=pg_connect("user=$user dbname=$dbname");
        if      (!$conn)
        {
                echo ('cannot establish connection<br>');
                exit;
```

```
        }
        $sql="SELECT * FROM messageb";
        $result=pg_exec($conn, $sql);
        $rows = pg_numrows($result);

        echo ("Rows returned: $rows<br>\n");
        for($i=0; $i < $rows; $i++)
        {
                $myarray = pg_fetch_row($result,$i);
                echo ("Array: $myarray[0] - $myarray[1]<br>\n");
        }
?>
```

We first check the number of rows returned by the query. This is done by using pg_rows. Then we process the data line-by-line and print the result onscreen. The whole process is very simple and easy to understand. Thanks to PostgreSQL's transaction code, we do not have to worry if a piece of data is still in the database while reading it. Every query done by PHP returns a consistent snapshot of data. If you want a little more information about the topic, check out Chapter 5, "Understanding Transactions."

Sometimes the name of a column is easier to use than an index created by the interpreter. You can use pg_fetch_array instead of pg_fetch_row. In addition to storing the data in the numeric indexes of the result array, pg_fetch_array also stores the data in associative indexes, using the field names as keys. This is very comfortable and helps the programmer avoid a lot of errors. Errors very often occur when the data structure changes. In case of a change, the indexes change as well, and this will lead to trouble. In the next example, we will show how pg_fetch_array can be used. We have not included the command directly in the echo command so the code is a little bit easier for you to understand:

```
<?
        include("globals.php");

        $conn=pg_connect("user=$user dbname=$dbname");
        if      (!$conn)
        {
                echo ('cannot establish connection<br>');
                exit;
        }
        $sql="SELECT * FROM messageb";
```

```
        $result=pg_exec($conn, $sql);
        $rows = pg_numrows($result);

        echo ("Rows returned: $rows<br>\n");
        for($i=0; $i < $rows; $i++)
        {
                $myarray = pg_fetch_array($result,$i);
                $one=$myarray["name"];
                $two=$myarray["message"];
                echo ("Array: $one - $two<br>\n");
        }
?>
```

According to the PHP docs, pg_fetch_array is not significantly slower than
pg_fetch_row, and it adds some very powerful features. pg_fetch_row and
pg_fetch_array are not the only tools you can use to retrieve data from a query. If you
want the result of a query to be returned as an object, PHP supports a function called
pg_fetch_object:

```
<?
        include("globals.php");

        $conn=pg_connect("user=$user dbname=$dbname");
        if      (!$conn)
        {
                echo ('cannot establish connection<br>');
                exit;
        }
        $sql="SELECT * FROM messageb";
        $result=pg_exec($conn, $sql);
        $rows = pg_numrows($result);

        echo ("Rows returned: $rows<br>\n");
        for($i=0; $i < $rows; $i++)
        {
                $myarray = pg_fetch_object($result,$i);
                $one=$myarray->name;
                $two=$myarray->message;
                echo ("Array: $one - $two<br>\n");
        }
?>
```

Now the values in $myarray can be accessed like those of any other object. Many programmers prefer working with objects rather than arrays. PHP supports both methods, objects, and arrays.

For those of you who have decided not to use PHP's object-oriented capabilities, PHP offers some other nice functions for you, such as pg_fieldname:

```
<?
        include("globals.php");

        $conn=pg_connect("user=$user dbname=$dbname");
        if      (!$conn)
        {
                echo ('cannot establish connection<br>');
                exit;
        }
        $sql="SELECT * FROM messageb";
        $result=pg_exec($conn, $sql);

        echo ('Fieldname: '.pg_fieldname($result, 1).'<br>');
?>
```

In this example, we print the name of a certain field onscreen with the help of pg_fieldname. 1 means that the second field is displayed because PHP starts counting with 0, as is done by almost all other programming languages. If we want to know the field number of a certain field, we can use pg_fieldnum instead of pg_fieldname:

```
echo ('Fieldnumber: '.pg_fieldnum($result, "name").'<br>');
```

Sometimes we want to find out a little bit more about the result of a query or about special fields. Imagine a situation where we need the data type and the length of a certain field. For that, PHP offers some easy-to-use functions:

```
<?
        include("globals.php");

        $conn=pg_connect("user=$user dbname=$dbname");
        if      (!$conn)
        {
                echo ('cannot establish connection<br>');
                exit;
        }
        $sql-"SELECT * FROM messageb";
        $result=pg_exec($conn, $sql);
```

```
        echo ("field type: ".pg_fieldtype($result, 0)."<br>\n");
        echo ("field size: ".pg_fieldsize($result, 0)."<br>\n");
?>
```

If we execute the script with the help of our favorite Web server, we will see two lines printed onscreen:

```
field type: text
field size: -1
```

The first column in the database is text.

> **Note**
> PHP displays the name of the data type, not the ID of the data type. Many programming languages do this differently.

pg_fieldsize returns -1. -1 is usually displayed when the length of the field is variable. Because we are using text, the length is not defined exactly.

Like most other high-level scripting languages, PHP does all memory management itself. Usually, all memory allocated during the execution process is freed when the script terminates. This is indeed very comfortable for the programmer. He or she does not have to be concerned about memory management because everything is done by PHP in a reliable way. A little control of PHP's and PostgreSQL's memory management can be very useful, especially on high-performance and high-availability systems. If many people perform memory consuming operations simultaneously, it may be good for system performance to free the memory allocated by a query as soon as the result is not used any more. To do this, PHP provides a function called pg_freeresult. The following example shows how the function can be used:

```
<?
        include("globals.php");

        $conn=pg_connect("user=$user dbname=$dbname");
        if      (!$conn)
        {
                echo ('cannot establish connection<br>');
                exit;
        }
        $sql="SELECT name FROM messageb";
        $result=pg_exec($conn, $sql);
        $rows=pg_numrows($result);
```

```
        $array=pg_fetch_object($result, 0);
        echo ("The first field: ".$array->name."<br>\n");

        $status=pg_freeresult($result);
        echo ("Status: $status<br>\n");
?>
```

We have seen that huge amounts of data can easily be inserted into the database with the help of a COPY command. Usually, COPY commands are not sent to the server as one string; it is much handier to send the data line-by-line. Consequently, three commands are necessary. Let's look at the following script we use to insert two values into a table:

```
<?
        include("globals.php");

        $conn=pg_connect("user=$user dbname=$dbname");
        if      (!$conn)
        {
                echo ('cannot establish connection<br>');
                exit;
        }

        pg_exec($conn, "COPY messageb FROM STDIN");
        pg_put_line($conn, "Etschi\tSomebody to love\n");
        pg_put_line($conn, "Hans\tGive me something to believe in\n");
        pg_put_line($conn, "\\.\n");
        pg_end_copy($conn);
?>
```

After connecting to the database server, we need pg_exec to send the COPY command to the database. PostgreSQL is now waiting for some data to come. The data is passed to the server line-by-line using pg_put_line. \t (tab) tells the database that the next column is about to come. After sending two lines of data to the server, we send \. and a linefeed to the backend. All components used by the COPY command have now been sent to the server, and we can finish the operation with pg_end_copy.

Note
The whole COPY command is processed as one transaction.

Large amounts of data can be transferred that way.

Errors and Exception Handling

Up to now, we have not dealt with errors and exceptions. Because exception handling is a very important issue, we will show some ways of dealing with errors. In many cases, errors and exceptions are caused by the programmer, but sometimes an error simply occurs if something has gone wrong. When working with databases, PHP usually displays an error if something unexpected happens during the communication process. If you want to get rid of those awful warnings and errors displayed when something goes wrong with your SQL statements, you can use PHPs wonderful abilities of handling exceptions.

The following script tries to execute a simple SQL statement, but somehow, something goes wrong:

```
<?
        include("globals.php");

        $conn=pg_connect("user=$user dbname=$dbname");
        if      (!$conn)
        {
                echo ('cannot establish connection<br>');
                exit;
        }

        $sql="SELECT * FROM notthere";
        $result=pg_exec($sql);
?>
```

The query fails and PHP displays an error. The table called notthere does not seem to be in the database. The following error will be displayed:

```
Warning: PostgreSQL query failed: ERROR: Relation 'notthere' does not exist in
/var/www/html/action.php on line 12
```

The error is very useful for debugging purposes, but it may not look too good on a business Web site.

PHP offers a nice onboard tool to suppress errors, simply use a @ before the command you expect will produce the error:

```
<?
        include("globals.php");

        $conn=pg_connect("user=$user dbname=$dbname");
        if      (!$conn)
```

```
        {
                echo ('cannot establish connection<br>');
                exit;
        }

        $sql="SELECT * FROM notthere";
        $result=@pg_exec($sql);
        if      (!$result)
        {
                echo ("This is a much more beautiful error ...<br>\n");
        }
        else
        {
                echo ("Everything works just fine ...<br>\n");
        }
?>
```

@ does a good job, so only the error we want to be displayed can be seen onscreen:

```
This is a much more beautiful error ...
```

But PHP also offers a function to display errors for PostgreSQL:

```
<?
        include("globals.php");

        $conn=pg_connect("user=$user dbname=$dbname");
        if      (!$conn)
        {
                echo ('cannot establish connection<br>');
                exit;
        }

        echo ("Trying SELECT ... <br>\n");
        $sql="SELECT * FROM notthere";
        $result=@pg_exec($sql);
        if      (!$result)
        {
                echo (pg_errormessage($conn)."<br>\n");
        }
?>
```

Simply use `pg_errormessage` to display the previous error message associated with a connection. The error displayed is actually generated by the backend process and can easily be compared with the errors displayed by other programming languages. If we execute the previous script, we will receive two lines of output:

```
Trying SELECT ...
ERROR: Relation 'notthere' does not exist
```

But errors are not only displayed onscreen. If you want PHP to send error messages somewhere else, a function called `error_log` can be used. In general, `error_log` offers four possibilities of logging:

- 0   Send the message to a file or the operating system's logging mechanism, depending on what the `error_log` configuration directive is set.

- 1   Message is sent by email to the address in the third parameter. This is the only message type where the fourth parameter `extra_headers` is used.

- 2   The message is sent through the PHP debugging connection. If remote debugging has been enabled, the message will be sent to the host defined in the third parameter.

- 3   PHP appends the message to the file defined by the third parameter.

Notation	Meaning
0	Depending on what the error_log configuration directive is set to, PHP sends the message to a file or the operating system's logging mechanism.

Before we get to a simple example, the following is an overview of `error_log`'s syntax:

```
int error_log (string message, int message_type [, string destination
        [, string extra_headers]])
```

In the next example, you can see how an error message can be written to a file:

```
<?
        include("globals.php");

        $conn=pg_connect("user=$user dbname=$dbname");
        if      (!$conn)
        {
```

```
                echo ('cannot establish connection<br>');
                exit;
        }

        echo ("Trying SELECT ... <br>\n");
        $sql="SELECT * FROM notthere";
        $result=@pg_exec($sql);
        if      (!$result)
        {
                echo ("Error ...<br>\n");
                error_log ("Cannot execute $sql\n", 3, "/tmp/my-errors.log");
        }
?>
```

Note

Don't forget the \n at the end of the error message because PHP does not use a linefeed by itself.

Working with BLOBs and File Uploads

In Web applications, BLOBs are very often used in combination with file uploads. Today, file uploads are used for many purposes. Imagine a simple Web-based mailing system where people add their attachments to email using a file upload.

Before we start working with BLOBs, we will present a simple example of how a file can be uploaded using a simple HTML form.

The following is a short example of a HTML form:

```
<FORM ENCTYPE="multipart/form-data" ACTION="action.php" METHOD=POST>
        <INPUT TYPE="hidden" name="MAX_FILE_SIZE" value="1000000">
        Send this file: <INPUT NAME="userfile" TYPE="file">
        <INPUT TYPE="submit" VALUE="Send File">
</FORM>
```

Figure 9.1 shows how this simple form looks.

Simply select a file and click the Send File button. As soon as you click the button, action.php will be called:

```
<?
        include("globals.php");
        echo ("Userfile: $userfile<br>\n");
?>
```

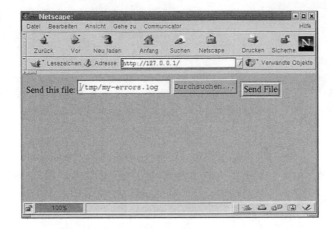

Figure 9.1
A simple form for file uploads.

PHP accepts file uploads from all RFC-1867–compliant browsers. There are no restrictions on what type of file is being uploaded. It doesn't matter if the file contains ASCII or binary data, the file upload will be processed the same way. The most important thing that has to be defined in the HTML code is the maximum size of the file being uploaded. The maximum size has to be defined in bytes.

Click the Send File button and see what happens:

```
Userfile: /tmp/phpDFtNrW
```

PHP now creates a temporary file we can use for further operations. Nothing has been uploaded yet; this is just a temporary filename.

Since PHP 4.02, it is a very easy task, because everything is done by a function called `move_uploaded_file`.

In the next example, we will try to insert the uploaded file into the database. First we create a table called `upload`:

```
CREATE TABLE upload(id serial, file oid);
```

The following script copies the uploaded file to a temporary directory, imports it into the database, displays the contents of the database, and removes the garbage produced by the upload process:

```
<?
        include("globals.php");

        # Connecting to the database
        $conn=pg_connect("user=$user dbname=$dbname");
        if      (!$conn)
        {
                echo ('cannot establish connection<br>');
                exit;
        }

        # Creating a unique temporary filename
        $tmpfname = tempnam ("/tmp", "upl_");

        # Copy uploaded file
        if       (is_uploaded_file($userfile))
        {
                move_uploaded_file($userfile, "$tmpfname");
        }
        else
        {
                echo ('no file uploaded<br>');
                exit;
        }

        # Starting transaction
        pg_exec ($conn,  "BEGIN");

        # Writing BLOB and OID
        $oid=pg_loimport ($tmpfname,  $conn);
        pg_exec ($conn, "INSERT INTO upload (file) VALUES ('$oid') ");

        # Stopping transaction
        pg_exec ($conn,  "COMMIT");
        echo ("File $tmpfname has been inserted into the database<br><br>\n");
        echo ("Data already stored in table:<br>\n");

        # Selecting data
        $result = pg_exec ($conn, "SELECT * FROM upload");
        if (!$result)
        {
```

```
                echo "An error occurred.\n";
                exit;
        }
        $num = pg_numrows($result);
        for ($i=0; $i<$num; $i++)
        {
                $r = pg_fetch_row($result, $i);
                for ($j=0; $j<count($r); $j++)
                {
                        echo "$r[$j]  ";
                }
                echo "<br>";
        }

        # Removing temporary file and disconnecting
        unlink($tmpfname);
        pg_close ($conn);
?>
```

After connecting to the database, we create a unique temporary filename. We will use this filename to store the uploaded file. I would consider using a temporary filename instead of the real filename because in multi-user environments or on systems with many people accessing the system simultaneously, two files may have the same name, and people would start hampering each other. That is not what we want.

With the help of move_uploaded_file, we copy the uploaded file to the temporary location.

File uploads have to be processed in one transaction, so we start a transaction explicitly. After importing the file into the database, we insert the object ID of the file into the table we use to store uploaded files. This is necessary because the files would be "lost" in the database otherwise. The data has now successfully been inserted into the database, and we can now commit the transaction now.

Finally, we display all records stored in the table and remove the temporary file so that not too much trash has to be stored in the directory for temporary files on the system.

Figure 9.2 shows how the output of the PHP file looks when uploading a file.

We have not stored the original name of the file on the user's system in the database to keep the example simple. If you need additional information, check out Table 9.8.

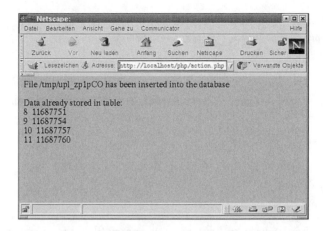

Figure 9.2
Some files have already been uploaded successfully.

Table 9.8   *Variables Containing Additional Information*

Variable	Content
$userfile	Contains the temporary filename of the uploaded file.
$userfile_name	Contains the name of the file on the user's system
$userfile_size	Contains the size of the uploaded file in bytes
$userfile_type	Contains the mime type of the file if the browser provided this information

Exporting a file from the database is as easy as importing a file into the database. Simply generate a temporary filename and export the file from the database using pg_loexport, as in the following:

```
<?
        include("globals.php");

        # Connecting to the database
        $conn=pg_connect("user=$user dbname=$dbname");
        if      (!$conn)
        {
                echo ('cannot establish connection<br>');
                exit;
        }
```

```
$tmpfname = tempnam ("/tmp", "exp_");
$var=pg_loexport('', '$tmpfname', $conn);

if      ($var == 't')
{
        echo ("Export of file '$tmpfname' successful <br>\n");
}
else
{
        echo ("Export of file '$tmpfname' failed <br>\n");
}
?>
```

We connect to the database and create a temporary filename, just as we did in the previous example. In the next step, we export the file with the object ID 11687766 to the temporary file (see Figure 9.3).

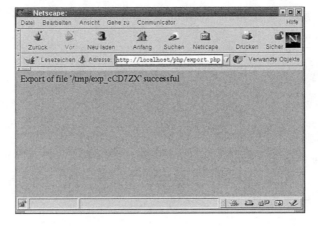

Figure 9.3
The file has been successfully exported.

Debugging

So far we have discussed a lot of PHP commands, but we haven't covered debugging sufficiently yet. Debugging a database-enabled PHP application is not that different from debugging any other application, but PHP, in combination with PostgreSQL, offers some very powerful and easy-to-use methods for making your applications work better.

trace (also available in Perl) allows the programmer to trace the communication between the backend process and the frontend. The information provided by pg_trace is redirected to a file and can be used very easily for debugging purposes.

We have included a very simple example to show you how tracing can be enabled and how a logfile created by pg_trace looks:

```
<?
        include("globals.php");

        # Connecting to the database
        $conn=pg_connect("user=$user dbname=$dbname");
        if      (!$conn)
        {
                echo ('cannot establish connection<br>');
                exit;
        }

        $res=pg_trace("/tmp/trace_log.log", w, $conn);

        $res=pg_exec($conn, "SELECT 1+1");
        echo ('nothing ...');
        pg_close($conn);
?>
```

The script does nothing other than connect to the database and compute the result of 1+1. Although the operation is very simple, the output looks quite complex:

```
[hs@duron php]# cat /tmp/trace_log.log
To backend> Q
To backend> SELECT 1+1
From backend> P
From backend> "blank"
From backend> T
From backend (#2)> 1
From backend> "?column?"
From backend (#4)> 23
From backend (#2)> 4
From backend (#4)> -1
From backend> D
From backend (1)> _
From backend (#4)> 5
From backend (1)> 2
From backend> C
```

```
From backend> "SELECT"
From backend> Z
From backend> Z
To backend> X
```

Tracing can be turned off again by using pg_untrace.

In most cases, analyzing the output of pg_trace is only useful when you understand the basics of PostgreSQL's internal protocol. A more efficient way to debug your applications is to use a simple function, such as the following:

```
<?
        debug("Starting script ...");
        include("globals.php");

        # Connecting to the database
        $conn=pg_connect("user=$user dbname=$dbname");
        if      (!$conn)
        {
                debug("cannot establish connection");
                echo ('cannot establish connection<br>');
                exit;
        }
        debug("connection successfully established");
        echo ('connection successfully established<br>');

        debug("terminating script");

function debug($var)
{
        setlocale("LC_TIME","de_DE");
        $datum=strftime("[%d/%b/%Y:%T %Z]");
        $log_str="$datum -- $var\n";
        $fp=fopen("/tmp/debug.log","a+");
        if ($fp)
        {
                fwrite($fp,$log_str);
                fclose($fp);
        }
}
?>
```

The logfile produced by the function may look like the following:

```
[hs@duron php]$ cat /tmp/debug.log
[29/Mai/2001:22:38:32 CEST] -- Starting script ...
[29/Mai/2001:22:38:32 CEST] -- connection successfully established
[29/Mai/2001:22:38:32 CEST] -- terminating script
```

At first glace, the output of the function might not seem very useful. So why should someone use that function?

The code of the debug function is taken from a real-world application implemented by us (see http://postgres.cybertec.at). If your applications use logging extensively, it is very easy to locate errors inside an application. It is necessary to know exactly what is going on inside your application, especially when dealing with complex and very business-critical software. In many situations, it may happen that the user of a system does something wrong and blames the software for the problems occurring. With the help of good logging information, it is an easy task to protect yourself against unjustifiable impeachment.

Another comfortable side effect of logging is that the logging information can be used for monitoring the demands and the behavior of your system under heavy load. Monitoring is an extremely important task, specially in database environments, because "slow" queries can easily impair the way your system works. Logfiles will help you to find the real problems of your system very quickly.

Of course, PHP also has some onboard debugging tools. Because PHP is permanently being improved, we have not included a full overview of PostgreSQL's debugging tools.

A Final Example

After all the theory about PostgreSQL and PHP, we have decided to include a small example to show you how easy it is to build applications using PostgreSQL.

Figure 9.4 shows a small prototype for a messageboard.

Messages can be put on the board, and all messages are automatically displayed when a user enters the forum. The data structure we use for the demo application is rather trivial:

```
performance=# \d messageb
     Table "messageb"
 Attribute | Type | Modifier
-----------+------+---------
 name      | text |
 message   | text |
```

Figure 9.4
A simple messageboard.

We only use two columns to store the data. The first column is used to store the name of the person who made the posting, and the second column is used to store the message.

Let's get to the source code of the application:

```php
<?
        include("globals.php");
                // Connecting to the database
        $conn=pg_connect("user=$user dbname=$dbname");
        if      (!$conn)
        {
                echo ("Cannot connect to the database<br>\n");
                exit;
        }


        // Displaying welcome message and some HTML                  echo
("<b>Welcome to the messageboard</b><br>\n");

        // Checking whether data has to inserted into the database
        if      (($username) && ($message))
        {
```

```
            // both messages provided
            $insert="INSERT INTO messageb VALUES('$username', '$message')";
            $result=pg_exec($conn, $insert);
            if        ($result)
            {
                    echo ('insert successful ...<br>');
            }
            else
            {
                    echo ('insert failed ...<br>');
            }                    }
    else
    {
            echo ('<font size=-1>now new messages to be inserted into
                    the database<br><font size=+0>');
    }
            // Executing SQL statement
    $sql="SELECT * FROM messageb";
    $result=pg_exec($conn, $sql);
    $rows=pg_numrows($result);

    // Displaying messages that are already in the database
    echo ("<hr><br>Messages: <br>\n");
    echo ("<table BORDER COLS=2 WIDTH=\"100%\" NOSAVE > \n");

    for($i=0; $i<$rows; $i++)
    {
            $array=pg_fetch_object($result, $i);
            echo ("<tr><td>$array->name</td><td>$array-
>message</td></tr>\n");
    }
    echo ("</table>\n");
    echo ("<br><hr>Insert new messages:<br>\n");

    // Displaying input form
    echo ('<FORM ENCTYPE="multipart/form-data" ACTION="board.php"
            METHOD=POST> ');
    echo ('name: <INPUT name="username"> <br>
            message: <INPUT name="message"> <br>
            <INPUT TYPE="submit" VALUE="Submit Message"> ');
    echo ('</FORM> ');
```

```
            // Closing connection
            pg_close($conn);
    ?>
```

As you can see, the code is brief. First, we connect to the database and display a message. If the database cannot be accessed, we quit the program. Then we check whether someone has got data. If username and message are defined, the script tries to insert the data into the database. Depending on whether the operation works, a message or a failure is displayed.

In the next step, we select all data from the database and display it in a table. After that, we display a form to insert the data again.

In the messageboard example, you can see how easy programming PHP is and that you can build simple applications with little effort. If applications become more complex than this one, we recommend that you keep the source code object-orientated. PHP offers wonderful object-oriented capabilities, and this will make your applications more extensible and easier to understand.

Java

Since the invention of Java, the programming language has gained more and more fans all around the globe. More than just the fact that Java provides the possibility to write platform independent code has made it so successful. Like all major database systems, PostgreSQL provides a Java interface that you will have a closer look at in this section.

A short history of Java

Before starting to work with a new programming language, it is useful to have a slight idea about the history of the programming language to be able to understand various components in a better way and see the language from a broader perspective.

"As if you were God," that is what Scott McNealy, CEO of Sun Microsystems, told Patrick Naughton. Naughton was to make a list of his complaints and suggest a solution for the problems Sun was facing. The main problem was that developers were fed up from supporting hundreds of software components used by the company.

A team was formed, and the only target of the work was to "make something cool."

One of the first things the team recognized was the problem that all manufactures of computers or any other electronic devices were using different hardware. Most of the components delivered by the various companies were not compatible with each other, and it was very painful in most cases to connect devices with each other.

The idea was to build a platform-independent, object-orientated programming language. The developers called the language Oak; the reason for the name Oak was chosen was that an oak tree was growing outside the window of James Gosling, the originator of Java.

Oak was suitable for performing complex remote control. The key feature of Oak, however, was it's hardware independency. Every piece of hardware that was suitable to run the virtual machine was capable of running applications written in Oak.

During the development, it turned out that a programming language called Oak already existed, and the language was finally renamed to Java.

The Internet became more widespread and Sun recognized that the market for a language like Java was the Web, because the Internet is a pool of different machines with different hardware. The idea was to have a programming language that could run on top of these machines. The most important thing is that the source code of an application can be the same on any platform; there are no hardware-dependent components in Java code.

Java was announced in May 1995 and the Java Development Kit (JDK) was made available on the Internet for free. The JDK consisted of a command-line compiler and a run-time environment. The integration of applets made Java the widespread language it is today.

In addition to Java's platform independency, Java offers more features. Things like pointers and multiple inheritance have been removed from the programming language, because pointers are the biggest source of trouble C and C++ programmers have to face. The language was designed to be as close to C++ as possible, so it was easy for C and C++ programmers to switch to Java.

Java code is executed in a virtual machine. In general, it can be said that Java is an interpreted rather than a compiled language. Interpreted languages are slower than compiled languages, so Java code will be significantly slower in most cases than C and C++ code. It is nearly a religious question whether it is useful to sacrifice performance for gaining platform independencies. Real C/C++ hackers say that C code is also platform-independent as long as the GNU tools, such as `automake` and `autoconf`, are used and an ANSI C compatible compiler is available on the desired platform. It's up to you to decide whether you want to use Java.

JDBC

JDBC is the database interface of Java. In this section, you will learn how to use this interface efficiently.

What is JDBC?

Like almost all advanced database systems, PostgreSQL provides a powerful Java interface. In this section, we will have a closer look at PostgreSQL's Java Database Connectivity Application Programming Interface (JDBC API) and show you how JDBC can be used efficiently.

Before we get to the details concerning PostgreSQL, we will have a look at JDBC in general. JDBC has been defined to be a core part of Java by JavaSoft, Inc. Like any other programming language, Java should have an interface to work with databases. JDBC plays a key part in Java development and is for sure one of the reasons why Java has become so popular in the past few years.

JDBC is designed to be database independent. There is absolutely no difference if you want to connect to Oracle, PostgreSQL, or any other database. The standard language for accessing a database is SQL. SQL provides an excellent way for an application to interact with a database server.

Another important point when dealing with JDBC is that the interface does not depend on the network environment the application is working in because it is suitable for intranet and Internet solutions.

From the description of all the features, it may seem to you that we have copied it directly from an Open Database Interconnectivity (ODBC) tutorial because JDBC and ODBC have a lot of things in common.

JDBC uses a traditional client/server model for the communication process. The client sends the request to a server and receives the result of the request. The client and server can either be on the same machine or not; it makes absolutely no difference.

Components of a JDBC-Enabled System

In general, a JDBC-enabled system consists of four components:

- *The application*—The application contains calls of JDBC methods and sends SQL requests to the database. The results of the queries are computed and can be processed by the application, if necessary. Things like exception and error handling are also done at the application level.

- *The driver manager*—The driver manager receives the calls of JDBC methods and sends the requests to the data source. The driver manager is also responsible for establishing a connection to the database, formatting error to JDBC standard errors, returning the data to the application, cursor managing, and transaction management. It can also happen that the driver manager translates and optimizes the requests so that they can be processed by the underlying database system.

The driver manager is responsible for interaction with the driver.

- *The driver*—The driver is the layer that is talking to the database. The driver manager has to use the right driver to communicate with the database.

- *The data source*—Up to now, we have only dealt with "overhead." Because we want to retrieve and generate data, we need a database system to which we can connect. The database itself is the component that does the real work for you, such as executing the SQL commands and returning the result to the next layer (to the driver).

The initial concept behind JDBC is very similar to the concept of ODBC. The main idea is to keep the system as independent from the database as possible. The only component in the whole system that is not platform-independent is the driver for the database.

A Few Words about Java, SQL, and JDBC Driver

Unlike Java, SQL is not a full programming language because it can only be used inside a database. According to the ANSI 1989 standard, three programming interfaces are defined:

- *Modules*—Procedures can be defined in separate modules and then called by a "real" programming language.

- *Embedded SQL*—This interface allows the definition of static SQL commands inside an application.

- *Calling SQL directly*—The database is depending on the implementation and differs on the various platforms.

In most cases, you will write applications that use either static or dynamically-generated SQL commands that will be sent to the server. As we have mentioned before, this is done by the driver manager. In general, three types of drivers can be distinguished:

- *Native drivers*—Native drivers can be distinguished in drivers that are entirely in Java and drivers that are only partly written in Java. Those drivers that are not entirely written in Java usually pass the function calls to libraries written in C. Drivers that are entirely written in Java use only Java onboard tools, so they are very portable but in general slower than the counterparts using C code.

- *Bridges*—Sometimes drivers are used as bridges to map JDBC function calls to other interfaces, such as ODBC. In most cases, these bridges are entirely written in Java. The most important bridge available is the JDBC-ODBC interface.

- *Database -independent drivers*—In many cases, databases use proprietary protocols for communication. Database-independent drivers use public network protocols and are entirely written in Java.

When building database applications, you will often not care about the software architecture of your drivers. But if you are planning to use your software on many platforms, it might be useful to have a closer look at the driver you are planning to use. Java is designed to be platform-independent, but who can say for sure that there are no "evil" guys around who want to build something proprietary that you cannot use for your applications.

Installing JDBC under Linux RedHat

The first thing that has to be done when you want to use Java in combination with your PostgreSQL server is to install the JDBC. We have already dealt with installing a PostgreSQL server in this book, but in the case of Java, it is necessary to have a closer look at the installation processes. This is because we have seen in the past that many people have real trouble with it.

The first thing to do is to unpack PostgreSQL's source code and run `configure`. The following is a typical configuration for your PostgreSQL server:

```
./configure --prefix=/usr/local/postgres --datadir=/data/postgres
--enable-debug --with-tcl --with-perl --with-python --enable-odbc
--with odbcinst=/usr/local/postgres/odbc --with-CXX --with-java
```

You can see that we have enabled a lot of programming interfaces, such as Python, Tcl, and Java.

If `configure` terminates successfully, you can start building the binaries by typing `"make`.

On some systems, the compilation process may fail if you have Java enabled. We have tried to build PostgreSQL on RedHat Linux 7.1 and had some minor troubles with ant. ant is part of the Apache Jakarta project and is designed to be the successor of GNU. According to ant's developers, ant has some significant advantages over `make` because the configuration files of ant are XML based.

If the compilation problem fails because of an error related to ant, we recommend that you update ant to the latest version available on the Internet. We don't think that this is the only solution for the problems you may face, but it is a comfortable way to build binaries as fast as possible.

During the compilation process, a file called `postgresql.jar` is generated that contains the JDBC driver for PostgreSQL.

Note
Don't extract the JAR file; the JDBC package may not work if the package is extracted.

`postgresql.jar` will not be installed in a directory where it can be found by Java. Consequently, the file has to be made available to Java. This can be done in several ways:

- Place `postgresql.jar` in your `$CLASSPATH` by setting the environment variable to the right path.

- Use the command-line parameter `-cp` to tell the virtual machine where to find the file.

- Copy the file to the virtual machines `lib/ext` directory.

We strongly recommend that you copy the file, because we think that it is any easy way for beginners to get the system up-and-running as soon as possible. We have already seen systems in the past where people had serious problems connecting to the database because the virtual machine could not find the driver because of slight errors in the settings for the path. In our opinion, copying the file is the best way to come to a solution quickly:

```
cp /data/data/java/postgresql.jar /usr/local/j2re1.3/lib/ext/
```

To connect to the database, make sure that the postmaster is started with the `-i` flag enabled.

Connecting

After installing JDBC on your system, we can try to establish a connection to the database. We have included a deluxe version of the world's most useful application, `Hello World`:

```java
import java.sql.*;

class oconnect
{
        static void main (String[] args)
        {
                try
                {
                        System.out.println("Hello World ...\n");
                        Connection connection;
```

```
                    String url ="jdbc:postgresql:myjava";
                    Class.forName("org.postgresql.Driver");
                    connection = DriverManager.getConnection(url,
                            "eg", "anypasswd");
            }
            catch (java.lang.Exception ex)
            {
                    System.out.println("Error ...\n" + ex);
            };

        }
}
```

Let's take a closer look at this code. In the first line, we import the required classes for dealing with SQL code. In the third line, we define the class called oconnect we will use in this section. The main function now tries to establish a connection to the server. The first thing to do is to create a variable of type Connection. In the next line, we define the URL of the database; we want to connect to the database called myjava using the PostgreSQL driver for JDBC. To establish the connection, we call the getConnection method of the DriverManager object with the URL, the name of the user we want to connect as, and the password.

If an error inside the try block occurs, the exception will be caught and an error will be displayed.

To compile the code, we write a simple Makefile that calls the compiler and executes the program:

```
JAVAC=  /usr/local/j2sdk1.3/bin/javac
JAVA=   /usr/local/j2re1.3/bin/java


x       :       oconnect.java
        $(JAVAC) oconnect.java
        $(JAVA) oconnect
```

If we execute the program, Hello World will be displayed.

```
[hs@duron java]# /usr/local/j2re1.3/bin/java oconnect
Hello World ...
```

Because no error is displayed, the connection to the database has been established successfully.

Simple Queries and Retrieving Data

Let's get to a simple example that does a little bit more than just connecting to the database. We want to write a simple application that executes a simple query and displays the result onscreen. As we did in most of the sections in this chapter, we start with 1+1 because this is the easiest case:

```java
import java.sql.*;

class oconnect
{
        static void main (String[] args)
        {
                try {
                        // Connection
                    String url = "jdbc:postgresql:myjava";
                    Class.forName("org.postgresql.Driver");
                    Connection connection = DriverManager.getConnection(url,
                            "eg", "anypasswd");
                                        // Executing SQL-command
String sqlcommand = "SELECT 1+1";
                    Statement statement = connection.createStatement();
                    ResultSet res = statement.executeQuery(sqlcommand);

                    // Displaying the output
                    int outp;
                    while        (res.next())
                    {
                            outp = res.getInt(1);
                            System.out.println("Result: " + outp + "\n");
                    }
                    connection.close();
                }                               // Catching the exception
                catch (java.lang.Exception ex) {
                        System.out.println("Connect and execute query: " + ex);
}
        }
}
```

After connecting to the database, we create a new object called sqlcommand that contains the SQL code we want to execute. The next object that has to be created is using data type Statement. This object is strongly related to the Connection object because a statement can only be used in combination with an open connection.

In the next step, we create an instance of `ResultSet` that should contain the result of the query we execute in this line. The `executeQuery` method is called for the `Statement` object. The query is sent to the server and executed. It might be interesting for you to see how the SQL command is transformed to the database's needs. A method called `nativeSQL` can be used to compute the output of the `preprocessor`. The code you can use to get the native SQL code is as follows:

```
String nat = connection.nativeSQL(sqlcommand);
System.out.println("native: " + nat + "\n");
```

The output of the query can be processed by using a simple loop. In this example, the output will only be one line, but we have included a loop so that you can see how things work. The `WHILE` loop is executed as long as the result of `res.next()` is defined. `next()` sets the cursor to the next line in the array containing the results. Within the array, we can now easily extract the various fields of the result by accessing the array using special functions.

Depending on the data type you want to extract, you have to use different functions for accessing the various fields. In the previous example, we try to extract an integer value because we expect 1+1 to be an integer value.

If we change the SQL command to

SELECT 1+1.2

the result is not an integer value anymore, and the program will display an error:

```
Connect and execute query: Bad Integer 2.2
```

It is important to use the right function to extract the data; otherwise, errors will occur.

In the following example, we will show how various data types can be accessed. First we create a table called products:

```
myjava=# \d products
              Table "products"
  Attribute  |          Type          | Modifier
-------------+------------------------+----------
 id          | bigint                 |
 prodname    | text                   |
 price       | numeric(7,2)           |
 validuntil  | timestamp with time zone |
```

We insert four records into the table:

```
myjava=# SELECT * FROM products;
 id |   prodname   | price |        validuntil
----+--------------+-------+--------------------------
  1 | bread        |  1.29 | 2001-05-31 16:21:16+02
  2 | hamburger    |  1.39 | 2001-05-31 16:22:46+02
  3 | orange juice |  0.89 | 2002-01-12 00:00:00+01
  4 | lemon juice  |  0.89 | 2002-03-04 00:00:00+01
(4 rows)
```

We use the same Java program we have used before, but we change the lines where we extract the data from the lines returned by the database:

```java
import java.sql.*;

class oconnect
{
        static void main (String[] args)
        {
                try {

                        String url = "jdbc:postgresql:myjava";
                        Class.forName("org.postgresql.Driver");
                        Connection connection = DriverManager.getConnection(url,
                                "eg", "anypasswd");
                                        // Executing SQL-command
String sqlcommand = "SELECT * FROM products";
                        Statement statement = connection.createStatement();
                        ResultSet res = statement.executeQuery(sqlcommand);

                        // Displaying the output
                        long id;
                        String name;
                        double price;
                        java.sql.Timestamp dbtime;

                        while       (res.next())
                        {
                                id = res.getLong(1);
                                name = res.getString(2);
                                price = res.getDouble(3);
                                dbtime = res.getTimestamp(4);
                                System.out.println("Result: " + id + " - " +
```

```
                                        name + " - " + price + " - " + dbtime);
                    }
                    connection.close();
            }                              // Catching the exception
            catch (java.lang.Exception ex) {
                    System.out.println("Connect and execute query: " + ex); }
        }
}
```

You can see that processing the input data is a very easy task indeed. If we execute the script, we will get the required result:

```
/usr/local/j2re1.3/bin/java oconnect
Result: 1 - bread - 1.29 - 2001-05-31 16:21:16.0
Result: 2 - hamburger - 1.39 - 2001-05-31 16:22:46.0
Result: 3 - orange juice - 0.89 - 2002-01-12 00:00:00.0
Result: 4 - lemon juice - 0.89 - 2002-03-04 00:00:00.0
```

Up to now, we have indexed the fields in the array returned, using the number of the field. In many cases, this might not fit your demands because indexing with numbers can easily lead to troubles when the data structure changes. When tables have many columns, it may also be a little bit annoying to find the index of a column every time it is needed. The easiest and most secure way of accessing a field is to use its name. Indexing with names has many advantages. On the one hand, your applications can be debugged much easier when the data structure of your database changes because the error can be seen at first sight. On the other hand, your applications are easier to read and easier to understand, which can save you a lot of money.

In the previous example, indexing the columns by using the name would lead to code similar to the following:

```
id = res.getLong("id");
name = res.getString("prodname");
price = res.getDouble("price");
dbtime = res.getTimestamp("validuntil");
```

In many cases, SELECT statements will return more than just one row, and the result has to be processed using a loop. Other operations, such as INSERT, UPDATE, or DELETE, return just one number that tells us how many rows have been effected by the SQL command. If we delete all records from a table, for example, the value returned tells us how many records were stored in the table before the DELETE statement. Java offers a very simple method for retrieving the integer value returned by a non-SELECT statement:

```
import java.sql.*;

class oconnect
{
        static void main (String[] args)
        {
                try {

                        String url = "jdbc:postgresql:myjava";
                        Class.forName("org.postgresql.Driver");
                          Connection connection = DriverManager.getConnection(url,
                                "eg", "anypasswd");
                                        // Executing SQL-command
                        String sqlcommand = "UPDATE products SET[ic:ccc] price='0.99'
WHERE price='0.89' ";
                        Statement statement = connection.createStatement();
                        int res = statement.executeUpdate(sqlcommand);
                        System.out.println("rows affected: " + res);
                        connection.close();
                }                       // Catching the exception
                catch (java.lang.Exception ex) {
                        System.out.println("Connect and execute query: " + ex); }
        }
}
```

In this example, we update all records where the price is exactly 0.89. The update query affects two records, and that is what executeUpdate returns:

```
[hs@duron java]$ /usr/local/j2re1.3/bin/java oconnect
rows affected: 2
```

It will sometimes be necessary to find how many columns are returned by a query and which names those columns have at runtime. We have included a simple program that performs a full table scan on products, computes the number of columns returned, and displays the name of those columns:

```
import java.sql.*;

class oconnect
{
        static void main (String[] args)
        {
                try {
```

```
                    String url = "jdbc:postgresql:myjava";
                    Class.forName("org.postgresql.Driver");
                    Connection connection = DriverManager.getConnection(url,
                            "eg", "anypasswd");
                                            // Executing SQL-command
      String sqlcommand = "SELECT * FROM products ";
                    Statement statement = connection.createStatement();
                    ResultSet res = statement.executeQuery(sqlcommand);

                    // Retrieving information about result
                    ResultSetMetaData metad = res.getMetaData();
                    int cols = metad.getColumnCount();
                    System.out.println("total amount of columns: " + cols);

                    for        (int i = 1; i <= cols; i++)
                    {
                            System.out.println("column " + i + " " +
                                    metad.getColumnLabel(i) );
                        }

                    connection.close();
              }                             // Catching the exception
           catch (java.lang.Exception ex) {
                    System.out.println("Connect and execute query: " + ex); }
        }
}
```

Before we can start extracting the desired information, we have to execute the query we want to analyze. In the next step, we create an instance of the `ResultSetMetaData` object. This object will be needed for all further operations.

With the help of the `getColumnCount`, we find out how many columns are returned. The result is displayed onscreen. Because we want all names of the various columns to be displayed, we write a loop. Let's execute the script:

```
[hs@duron java]$ /usr/local/j2re1.3/bin/java oconnect
total amount of columns: 4
column 1 id
column 2 prodname
column 3 price
column 4 validuntil
```

An Overview of the JDBC-API

The two main components of JDBC are the JDBC API and the JDBC driver-API. The JDBC API is a programming interface for developing applications. The JDBC driver-API is usually used by developers of drivers because it is the low-level part of JDBC.

If you are a developer of applications using JDBC, you can use the following interfaces and classes. This section is meant to be an overview. We have already dealt with some of the listed objects.

- `java.sql.DriverManager` This class provides methods for loading the required driver and methods for establishing connections to a database.

- `java.sql.Connection` The `Connection` object is needed for dealing with database connections.

- `java.sql.Statement` This class has to be used in combination with a connection. At runtime, queries are sent to the database server using the `Statement` object.

- `java.sql.CallableStatement` This object has the same purpose as the `Statement` object but is used in combination with stored procedures.

- `java.sql.PreparedStatement` `PreparedStatement` is used for dealing with precompiled statements.

- `java.sql.ResultSet` `ResultSet` allows the user to access the result of a query easily.

- `java.sql.ResultSetMetaData` This object provides access to information about the result of a query, such as the number of columns returned.

- `java.sql.DatabaseMetaData` In contrast to the `ResultSetMetaData` object, `DatabaseMetaData` provides information about the database itself.

In the previous section, you saw how data can be extracted from the result of a query. We have used functions such as `getLong("id")`. In this section, we will show you a complete overview of all methods provided by Java:

```
String getString(int columnIndex);
boolean getBoolean(int columnIndex);
byte getByte(int columnIndex);
short getShort(int columnIndex);
int getInt(int columnIndex);
```

```
long getLong(int columnIndex);
float getFloat(int columnIndex);
double getDouble(int columnIndex);
java.math.BigDecimal getBigDecimal(int columnIndex, int scale);
byte[] getBytes(int columnIndex);
java.sql.Date getDate(int columnIndex);
java.sql.Time getTime(int columnIndex);
java.sql.Timestamp getTimestamp(int columnIndex);
java.io.Inputstream getAsciiStream(int columnIndex);
java.io.Inputstream getUnicodeStream(int columnIndex);
java.io.InputStream getBinaryStream(int columnIndex);
Object getObject(int columnIndex);
```

> **Note**
> All functions can also be used with the name of the column you want to index
> instead of the number of the column.

You can see that JDBC provides a lot of functions for almost all data types. The
following is an example where we want to extract a point from the result of the query:

```
...
String sqlcommand = "SELECT '(1,1)'::point";
Statement statement = connection.createStatement();
ResultSet res = statement.executeQuery(sqlcommand);

// Displaying the output
String outp;
while   (res.next())
{
        outp = res.getString(1);
        System.out.println("Result: " + outp + "\n");
}
...
```

If you have to retrieve data types for which Java does not provide a suitable function,
simply use the result as `String` as just shown. The output of the previous code would
look like the following:

```
Result: (1,1)
```

If you want to use the data, simply write a class for the required data type or look for
an already existing object. Many objects you may need can be found in PostgreSQL's
extensions to JDBC.

The JDBC interface provides many methods to make the interaction between your application and the database very simple. We have not included a full reference of JDBC here. If you need a full reference of JDBC and Java in general, check out the Web site at `http://java.sun.com/products/jdk/1.1/docs/api/Package-java.sql.html`.

JDBC and Transactions

Transactions are an essential feature of all sophisticated database systems. We have already dealt with transactions in this book extensively. In this section, we will have a closer look at how transactions can be influenced and treated with the help of JDBC.

By default, JDBC opens a connection in `AutoCommit` mode, which means that every command sent to the database is treated as a transaction. `AutoCommit` is very comfortable because the programmer does not have to commit transactions manually.

Sometimes, however, it is necessary to influence the way transactions are treated, especially if you are working with entire blocks of SQL commands. If something goes wrong inside a block, the ability to perform a single `ROLLBACK` may save you a lot of headaches in combination with exception and error handling.

Look at a simple example:

```
import java.sql.*;

class oconnect
{
        static void main (String[] args)
        {
                try {
                        // Connection
                        String url = "jdbc:postgresql:myjava";
                        Class.forName("org.postgresql.Driver");
                        Connection connection = DriverManager.getConnection(url,
                                "eg", "anypasswd");
                                        // Insert with Rollback
connection.setAutoCommit(false);
                        String sqlcommand = "INSERT INTO products VALUES(5, " +
                                "'cheeseburger', '1.49', now()+'1 year'::reltime)";
                        Statement statement = connection.createStatement();
                        int rows = statement.executeUpdate(sqlcommand);
                        connection.rollback();

                        // Insert with Commit
connection.setAutoCommit(false);
```

```
                    sqlcommand = "INSERT INTO products VALUES(6, " +
                            "'french fries', '1.64', now()+'1 year'::reltime)";
                    statement = connection.createStatement();
                    rows = statement.executeUpdate(sqlcommand);
                    connection.commit();

                    // Displaying the output
                    sqlcommand="SELECT * FROM products";
    Statement st = connection.createStatement();
                    ResultSet res = st.executeQuery(sqlcommand);

                    int outid;
                    String outstring;
                    while        (res.next())
                    {
                            outid = res.getInt(1);
                            outstring = res.getString(2);
                            System.out.println("Result: " + outid + " - " +
                                    outstring);
                    }
                    connection.close();
            }                       // Catching the exception
            catch (java.lang.Exception ex) {
                    System.out.println("Connect and execute query: " + ex);
    }
        }
    }
```

Before we compile and execute this script shown, the products table contains the
following values:

```
myjava=# SELECT * FROM products;
 id |   prodname   | price |        validuntil
----+--------------+-------+------------------------
  1 | bread        |  1.29 | 2001-05-31 16:21:16+02
  2 | hamburger    |  1.39 | 2001-05-31 16:22:46+02
  3 | orange juice |  0.89 | 2002-01-12 00:00:00+01
  4 | lemon juice  |  0.89 | 2002-03-04 00:00:00+01
(4 rows)
```

Four records are in the table. The previous script executes two transactions. The first
transaction is implicitly started by setting AutoCommit to false. This is done by calling
setAutoCommit for an instance of the Connection object. We try to insert cheeseburger

into the table. The INSERT statement terminates successfully, but in the next step we perform a ROLLBACK. Consequently, the record will not be saved in the database. commit closes a transaction and starts the next transaction by setting AutoCommit to false again.

This time, we insert french fries into the database. We commit the transaction and query the table to see which records have been inserted into products table.

Let's execute the program:

```
[hs@duron java]$ /usr/local/j2re1.3/bin/java oconnect
Result: 1 - bread
Result: 2 - hamburger
Result: 3 - orange juice
Result: 4 - lemon juice
Result: 6 - french fries
```

You can see that no cheeseburgers can be found in the database because we performed a ROLLBACK operation.

Everything worked just as we expected, but what happens if someone forgets to commit the transaction if AutoCommit is set to false? The database commits the transaction automatically and the script terminates successfully. If a connection is committed twice, the database won't display an error. Although the whole system is very permissive, we recommend that you explicitly commit every transaction you have opened. This will help you avoid errors, especially if you have to deal with exception handling and errors. If a script crashed and you have not committed your transaction explicitly, you may find yourself in deep trouble, because you may not know whether certain SQL commands have been committed to the database successfully.

Another important point when dealing with transactions is transaction isolation. We have already described transaction isolation in Chapter 5. JDBC offers simple a interface to influence the level of transaction isolation on application level. Look at the following example:

```
import java.sql.*;

class oconnect
{
        static void main (String[] args)
        {
                try {
                        // Connection
                        String url = "jdbc:postgresql:myjava";
```

```
                    Class.forName("org.postgresql.Driver");
                    Connection connection = DriverManager.getConnection(url,
                            "eg", "anypasswd");

                    // the current transaction level ...
    int level = connection.getTransactionIsolation();
                    System.out.println("default level (read committed): "
                            + level);

                    String sql="SET SESSION CHARACTERISTICS AS " +
                            "TRANSACTION ISOLATION LEVEL SERIALIZABLE";
                    Statement statement = connection.createStatement();
                    int rows = statement.executeUpdate(sql);
                    level = connection.getTransactionIsolation();
                    System.out.println("serializable (by SQL):  " + level);

                    // setting the transaction level to serializable
                    connection.setTransactionIsolation(8);
                    level = connection.getTransactionIsolation();
                    System.out.println("serializable (by JDBC):  " + level);

                    connection.close();
            }                               // Catching the exception
        catch (java.lang.Exception ex) {
                System.out.println("Connect and execute query: " + ex);
    }
        }
    }
```

The Connection object supports a function called getTransactionIsolation() to find the current transaction isolation level. According to the JDBC docs, five levels of transaction isolation levels are supported:

- TRANSACTION_READ_UNCOMMITTED

- TRANSACTION_READ_COMMITTED

- TRANSACTION_REPEATABLE_READ

- TRANSACTION_SERIALIZABLE

- TRANSACTION_NONE

The first four levels of transaction isolation are also defined in the ANSI standard. PostgreSQL supports TRANSACTION_READ_COMMITTED and TRANSACTION_SERIALIZABLE.

In the previous example, we try to modify the transaction isolation level in two ways. Before performing the modification, we try to find the default value. The first way is to use a simple SQL command as we would do it using `psql`. To set the value to `SERIALIZABLE`, we can use

```
myjava=# SET SESSION CHARACTERISTICS AS TRANSACTION ISOLATION LEVEL
SERIALIZABLE;
SET VARIABLE
```

To see whether the command has successfully changed the required variable, we use `SHOW`:

```
myjava=# SHOW TRANSACTION ISOLATION LEVEL;
NOTICE:  TRANSACTION ISOLATION LEVEL is SERIALIZABLE
SHOW VARIABLE
```

The second way to modify the transaction isolation level is to use JDBC's onboard tools. In the previous example, we set the value to 8. If `setTransactionIsolation` returns 0, no transactions are supported by the database.

Let's execute the program:

```
[hs@duron java]$ /usr/local/j2re1.3/bin/java oconnect
default level (read committed): 2
serializable (by SQL):  8
serializable (by JDBC):  8
```

You can see that the default transaction isolation level in PostgreSQL is 2, which means `TRANSACTION_READ_COMMITTED`.

We recommend that you keep the default transaction isolation level if you don't know exactly what is going on inside the database.

Exception Handling with `java.sql.SQLWarning`

Exception handling is one of the most important things when dealing with databases. If a program does not check whether something has gone wrong, things can become dangerous. JDBC offers two very simple classes called `java.sql.SQLWarning` and `java.sql.SQLException` that perform all necessary operations related to exception handling.

Let's look at the following program that demonstrates how error handling can be done:

```
import java.sql.*;

class oconnect
```

```
{
        static void main (String[] args)
        {
                try {
                        // Connection
                        String url = "jdbc:postgresql:nodb";
                        Class.forName("org.postgresql.Driver");
                        Connection connection = DriverManager.getConnection(url,
                                "eg", "anypasswd");
                                        checkWarn(connection.getWarnings()
);                      connection.close();
                }                       catch(ClassNotFoundException
classException) {
                        System.out.println("Class not found exception\n");
                }
                catch(SQLException sqlException) {
                        System.out.println("SQLException occurred, printing " +
                                "chained Exceptions:");
                        do {
                                System.out.println(sqlException.getMessage());
                        }
                        while( (sqlException = sqlException.getNextException()) !=
null);
                }
        }

        private static void checkWarn (SQLWarning mywarn) throws SQLException
        {
                while           (mywarn != null)
                {
                        System.out.println("checkwarn: " + mywarn);
                        mywarn=mywarn.getNextWarning();
                }
        }
}
```

In this example, we try to catch some errors. Connecting to the database will fail, because the nodb database does not exist on the system. When executing the script, you can see which error messages are displayed by the system:

```
SQLException occurred, printing chained Exceptions:
Something unusual has occurred to cause the driver to fail. Please report this
exception: Exception: java.sql.SQLException: FATAL 1:  Database "nodb" does
not exist in the system catalog.
```

```
Stack Trace:

java.sql.SQLException: FATAL 1:  Database "nodb" does not exist in the
system catalog.

        at org.postgresql.Connection.openConnection(Connection.java:241)
        at org.postgresql.Driver.connect(Driver.java:122)
        at java.sql.DriverManager.getConnection(DriverManager.java:517)
        at java.sql.DriverManager.getConnection(DriverManager.java:177)
        at oconnect.main(oconnect.java:11)
End of Stack Trace
```

The listing of the error is already quite long. Keep in mind that the only error in the script is the name of the database.

In the previous example, you can see that catching errors is truly an easy task in Java. With just a few lines of code, it is possible to check for almost all errors that can occur during a simple connect.

Prepared Commands

Up to now, we have executed SQL commands directly by using just one command. If many SQL commands have to be processed where only the values of the fields differ but the "body" of the query itself stays the same, it may be useful to use prepared commands. We have already described this concept when dealing with other programming languages, such as Perl (DBI and Pg module). The advantage of prepared SQL commands is that your application will be faster. If commands are executed without being prepared explicitly, the entire query is sent to the database every time the SQL command has to be executed. If we prepare the command first, the only things that have to be passed to the database are the parameters of the SQL command. To make the process more clear, we have included a simple example:

Imagine a situation where you want to insert values into a column using a command such as

```
INSERT INTO products VALUES (6, 'french fries', 1.64, '2002-06-04 13:52:29+02');
```

Let's say that the INSERT statement is executed twice. If the command is executed using just one command, the whole query is transmitted twice. If we prepare the query first, the whole query is only transferred the first time. The second time we execute the SQL statement, only the parameters of the INSERT statement have to be sent to the database, which in our case is 6, 'french fries', 1.64 and '2002-06-04 13:52:29+02'. On the basis of this example, you can see that the data that has to be transmitted is much shorter. The main advantage of preparing a query before executing it is that a lot of parsing work can be avoided. But let's get to some code now:

```java
import java.sql.*;

class oconnect
{
    static void main (String[] args)
    {
        try {
            // Connection
            String url = "jdbc:postgresql:myjava";
            Class.forName("org.postgresql.Driver");
            Connection connection = DriverManager.getConnection(url,
                    "eg", "anypasswd");
                            // Executing SQL-command
            ResultSet res;
            PreparedStatement statement = connection.prepareStatement
                    "SELECT * FROM products WHERE id=? ");
            for(int i=1; i<=3; i++)
              {
                  // 1: first parameter; i contains value
                    statement.setInt(1, i);
                    res = statement.executeQuery();
                    displayResult(res);
              }

            connection.close();
        }                               // Catching the exception
        catch (java.lang.Exception ex) {
            System.out.println("ERROR: " + ex); }
    }

    static void displayResult(ResultSet myres)
    {
        int outid;
        String outstring;
        try
        {
            while         (myres.next())
              {
                    outid = myres.getInt(1);
                    outstring = myres.getString(2);
```

```
                    System.out.println(outid + " - " + outstring);
            }
       }
       catch (java.sql.SQLException ex)
       {                                 System.out.println("ERROR: " +
ex);
       }
     }
}
```

The example does nothing but search for all IDs from one to three. Before processing the loop, we create a `PreparedStatement` object that will contain the prepared query. Every time the loop is processed, we pass a parameter to the statement and execute it. The result is assigned to `res`, and we display it by calling the `displayResult` function.

After executing the script, the result will look as follows:

```
[hs@duron java]$ /usr/local/j2re1.3/bin/java oconnect
1 - bread
2 - hamburger
3 - orange juice
```

All records from one to three are displayed.

Assigning values to the prepared statement is the only crucial point in the whole process. In the previous example, we have used `setInt` to assign an integer value. Because other data types have to be processed too, JDBC offers a variety of functions. We have compiled a complete list of all functions available:

```
void setNull(int parameterIndex, int sqlType)
void setByte(int parameterIndex, byte x)
void setShort(int parameterIndex, short x)
void setInt(int parameterIndex, int x)
void setLong(int parameterIndex, long x)
void setFloat(int parameterIndex, float x)
void setDouble(int parameterIndex, double x)
void setBigDecimal(int parameterIndex, java.math.BigDecimal x)
void setString(int parameterIndex, String x)
void setBytes(int parameterIndex, byte x[])
void setDate(int parameterIndex, java.sql.Date x)
void setTime(int parameterIndex, java.sql.Time x)
void setTimestamp(int parameterIndex, java.sql.Timestamp x)
void setAsciiStream(int parameterIndex, java.io.InputStream x, int length)
void setUnicodeStream(int parameterIndex, java.io.InputStream x, int length)
```

```
void setBinaryStream(int parameterIndex, java.io.InputStream x, int length)
void setObject(int parameterIndex, Object x)
void setObject(int parameterIndex, Object x, int targetSqlType)
void setObject(int parameterIndex, Object x, int targetSqlType, int scale)
void clearParameters();
```

As you can see, JDBC offers functions for nearly all available data types. Many databases offer special data types (for example, PostgreSQL offers geometric data types) for which JDBC does not offer functions. In this case, you can use `setObject(int parameterIndex, Object x, int targetSqlType)`, which allows you to pass the target data type to the driver so that everything can be converted to the correct format.

Stored Procedures

JDBC supports stored procedures. In some cases, stored procedures can help the programmer achieve his goal more quickly.

At time of writing, (latest version of PostgreSQL is 7.1.2) stored procedures were not supported.

According to Peter Mount (information taken from a newsgroup posting), the developer of PostgreSQL's JDBC interface, there are plans to include stored procedures in the near future.

PostgreSQL Extensions to the JDBC API

PostgreSQL provides some extensions to the JDBC standard. Most of these extensions are related to geometric data types and other PostgreSQL specifics. This section will give you a brief overview of PostgreSQL's JDBC extensions.

A Few Words about JDBC Extensions

PostgreSQL is one of the most flexible and extensible database systems available. Many features of PostgreSQL are nearly unique in the database world, and many people rely on these features. JDBC is a standard database interface, so the standard specs of JDBC do not support PostgreSQL specific features. Many things can be achieved by building simple workarounds, but some targets can only be reached easily by using the PostgreSQL extensions for JDBC. In this section, we will take a closer look at these extensions and try to provide an overview of the most important methods and objects available. Keep in mind that using these functions will decrease the portability, because all functions are specific to PostgreSQL.

fastpath

The `fastpath` object is not part of JDBC and can be used to access functions on the PostgreSQL backend. Accessing PostgreSQL's backend is a very powerful feature and is often essential.

In many cases, `fastpath` is used to deal with large objects.

The following is an example of how an instance of the `fastpath` object can be created:

```
import java.sql.*;
import org.postgresql.fastpath.*;

class oconnect
{
        static void main (String[] args)
        {
                try {
                        // Connection
                        String url = "jdbc:postgresql:myjava";
                        Class.forName("org.postgresql.Driver");
                        Connection connection = DriverManager.getConnection(url,
                                "eg", "anypasswd");
                        Fastpath fp =
((org.postgresql.Connection)connection).getFastpathAPI();
                        connection.close();
                }                               // Catching the exception
                catch (java.lang.Exception ex) {
                        System.out.println("ERROR: " + ex); }
        }
}
```

Geometric Objects

The PostgreSQL extensions for the JDBC interface provide some objects for dealing with geometric objects. We have not included an example here because the documentation for these objects was extremely bad or nonexistent at the time of writing.

If you have to use these objects, check the developers' Web site and ask the newsgroup for help.

Large Objects

As with geometric objects, the extensions for the JDBC interface provide some classes for working with LOBs. The documentation on these objects is also not good, and we have decided not to include examples because no reliable information is available.

I hope that we will be able to include useful information in future releases of this book.

Object Serialization

With the release of Java 1.1, some powerful features were introduced. One of these features was object serialization. PostgreSQL's JDBC extensions also support this feature. Before we get to a simple example, we want to explain what is meant with object serialization.

Object serialization provides a program the ability to read or write a whole object to and from a raw byte stream. It allows Java objects to be encoded into a byte stream suitable for streaming to some type of network, to a file-system, or, more generally, to a transmission medium or storage facility.

This explanation may sound a little complicated; in other words, object serialization is a way to write (or read) objects to an interface.

Look at a simple example:

In PostgreSQL, it is possible to have one table that refers to a row in an other table:

```
myjava=# CREATE TABLE users(firstname text, lastname text);
CREATE
myjava=# CREATE TABLE server(servername text, admin users);
CREATE
myjava=# INSERT INTO users VALUES('Ewald', 'Geschwinde');
INSERT 27273 1
myjava=# SELECT * FROM server;
 servername | admin
------------+-------
(0 rows)

myjava=# SELECT * FROM users;
 firstname |  lastname
-----------+------------
 Ewald     | Geschwinde
(1 row)

myjava=# INSERT INTO server VALUES('bachata', 27273::users);
INSERT 27274 1
myjava=# SELECT * FROM server;
 servername | admin
------------+-------
 bachata    | 27273
(1 row)
```

What does this example have to do with Java? In Java, object serialization can be used to save an object to a stream, so complex objects can be inserted into the database. `org.postgresql.util.Serialize` provides methods of storing an object as a table. The advantage of that is that you don't have to use large objects, which means that you can search for values more efficiently.

A Final Example

In this example, we try to write a simple interactive tool for sending SQL commands to the database server:

```java
import java.sql.*;
import java.io.*;
import java.util.*;

public class oconnect
{
        static Connection connection;

        // main program
        public static void main(String argv[])
        {
                // connecting to the database
                try
                {
                        String url ="jdbc:postgresql:myjava";
                        Class.forName("org.postgresql.Driver");
                        connection = DriverManager.getConnection(url,
                                "eg", "anypasswd");
                }
                catch (java.lang.Exception ex)
                {
                        System.out.println("ERROR: " + ex);
                };

                // loop for retrieving user data
                boolean proceed = true;
                String inputline;
                while       (proceed == true)
                {
                        // calling function for reading user input
                        inputline = oconnect.getinputline();
                        System.out.println(inputline);
```

```
                                    // if no input was passed to the
program, quit loop
                if      (inputline.length() < 1)
                {
                        proceed = false;
                }
                // otherwise process the input
                else
                {
                        oconnect.querydb(inputline);
                }
        }

        System.out.println("Terminating application");
}


// Retrieving user input ...
public static String getinputline()
{
        BufferedReader myinput = new BufferedReader(
                new InputStreamReader(System.in));
        String inputline="";
        try
        {
                // reading from the keyboard
                System.out.print("Enter an SQL-statement: ");
                inputline=myinput.readLine();
        }
        catch (java.lang.Exception ex)
        {
                System.out.println("ERROR: " + ex);
        };
        return inputline;
}


// sending query to the server
public static void querydb(String query)
{
        try
        {
                // executing query
                Statement statement = connection.createStatement();
                ResultSet res = statement.executeQuery(query);
```

```
            // extracting meta information
            ResultSetMetaData metad = res.getMetaData();
            int colnumber = metad.getColumnCount();

            Object obj;
            String coltype;
            String colname;

            int i;

            // header
            for(i=1; i<=colnumber; i++)
            {
                    coltype = metad.getColumnTypeName(i);
                    colname = metad.getColumnLabel(i);
                    System.out.print(colname+" ("+coltype+") | ");
            }
            System.out.println();

            // data
            while       (res.next())
            {
                    // processing every single column
                    for(i=1; i<=colnumber; i++)
                    {
                            obj = res.getObject(i);
                            System.out.print(obj + " | ");
                    }
                    System.out.println();

            }
        }
        catch (java.lang.Exception ex)
        {
                System.out.println("ERROR: " + ex);
        };
    }
}
```

The code of the application is quite long, but it is still very simple and easy to understand—at least we tried to keep it as simple as possible.

The first thing that has to be done in the main function is to connect to the database. If establishing the connection fails, an error is displayed. In the next step, we declare two variables we will need in the WHILE loop. This loop is executed as long as the user inserts data. By default, proceed is set to true, but if the length of the line inserted by the user is 0, the value of the variable is changed to false and this causes the loop to terminate. The data from the keyboard is caught by the getinputline function, which is defined later in the program. The function does nothing but display a prompt (Enter an SQL-statement:), read the data from the keyboard, and raise an error in case of failure. If the string returned by getinputline is long enough, the string is passed to querydb—the function that performs the query and displays the result.

After executing the input string, we extract some metadata from the result that we will need to compile the header and display the correct number of columns.

The first for loop processed displays the header of the table. The header contains the name of the columns as returned by the database and the data types of the various columns. The second for loop displays the data on the string. Because we do not know the data types of the returned column (not at compile time, at least), we use getObject to extract the fields. No further processing, but displaying the data has to be done, so we do not have to take care of the data types of the column. JDBC provides an output function for Object, so we can easily display the result of the query.

Let's execute the program and perform some simple queries with it:

```
[hs@duron java]$ /usr/local/j2re1.3/bin/java oconnect
Enter an SQL-statement: SELECT * FROM products
SELECT * FROM products
id (int8) | prodname (text) | price (numeric) | validuntil (timestamp) |
1 | bread | 1.29 | 2001-05-31 16:21:16.0 |
2 | hamburger | 1.39 | 2001-05-31 16:22:46.0 |
3 | orange juice | 0.89 | 2002-01-12 00:00:00.0 |
4 | lemon juice | 0.89 | 2002-03-04 00:00:00.0 |
6 | french fries | 1.64 | 2002-06-04 13:52:29.0 |
Enter an SQL-statement: SELECT cos(id) FROM products
SELECT cos(id) FROM products
cos (float8) |
0.54030230586814 |
-0.416146836547142 |
-0.989992496600445 |
-0.653643620863612 |
0.960170286650366 |
Enter an SQL-statement: SELECT now()::time
SELECT now()::time
?column? (time) |
```

```
23:34:40 |
Enter an SQL-statement:

Terminating application
```

You can see that building interactive database applications with Java is an easy task, indeed.

In general, it can be said that JDBC is a good choice when you want to build database-enabled applications. A negative aspect that should be taken into consideration is that other languages might execute programs faster than Java. Depending on the type of application you want to build, this may influence your work in one way or the other.

In many cases, using Java or not is simply a religious question. Hardcore Python hackers can usually be persuaded to write a Java program only if someone holds a pistol to their heads. It's up to you to decide which religion you want to choose and whether you want to use Java.

Python

Python is another language that can easily be combined with PostgreSQL. Python's interface to PostgreSQL can easily be handled. In this section, you will learn how powerful applications can be built with the help of PostgreSQL.

A Short Overview of Python

In the past few years, Python has become a very widespread language. In this section, we'll try to explain the basic concepts of Python and take a brief look at this powerful, open-source programming language.

Python was born in December 1989. Guido van Rossum, the father of Python, was looking for a hobby to work on during the week around Christmas. Guido decided to write an interpreter that would be similar to ABC but would be more suitable for a UNIX/C hacker. The name Python was chosen because Guido is a real fan of *Monty Python's Flying Circus*. I guess back in 1989, nobody expected Python to become the programming language it is today.

The idea behind Python was to create a language that was not bound to UNIX and had some significant improvements over ABC. Some of ABC's features were aimed at novice programmers but were not suitable for the intended audience of experienced UNIX programmers. One point was also that the integrated editor of ABC was not liked by many people. Python, however, would rely on the infrastructure and conventions provided by a UNIX system. This made Python more accepted by advanced programmers.

But when designing Python, Guido was not only influenced by ABC. Some components were taken from C and Modula 3, an elegant programming language that many of you might have seen back in the early days.

Python uses indentation for statement grouping. This feature is inherited from ABC and is today one of the most contentious features of Python because not many other languages use indentation. In general, it is a religious question whether it is a good feature. According to Guido, indentation for statement grouping has two important advantages:

- It reduces visual clutter and makes programs shorter because no lines are wasted for brackets. There is also no discussion about which is the best way to use brackets in the source code as there is for languages like C/C++.

- Programmers have less freedom when formatting the code. At first glance, this sounds like a disadvantage, but it makes the code of various programmers look the same way. This makes programs easier to read and easier to understand.

It's up to you to decide whether you like "Python-style" programs. Guido von Rossum once said, "Rich syntax is more of a burden than a help." There should be only one simple way to achieve a target. Many programming languages, such as C, C++, and Perl (I guess Perl is in this case even "worse"), offer many ways to solve a problem. Depending on the knowledge of the programmer who has to read the code, some of these ways can be very hard to understand. The target of Python is to provide a programming platform that focuses on the reusability of code and the production of easier to understand programs. The first point is an especially important issue.

Python is an object-orientated programming language, so all components are clustered in objects. Object-orientation is one of the core features of Python because it is the best way to allow programmers to share their code. The way objects are accessed in the code does not differ from other programming languages, because the syntax used by other languages should be familiar to almost all programmers, and switching to Python should be an easy task.

Compared to most compiled languages, Python is a rather slow language. The Python community tries to improve the speed, but the main focus is not on increasing the speed of the language itself but decreasing the time it takes a programmer to write a program. Today, the main costs for establishing and running a program rise with the time it takes to write the program. The speed of hardware is constantly increasing, so programming time gains more and more importance. You will soon recognize that Python is a perfect language for prototyping and developing applications very fast.

Currently, you can choose between the pg module and the newer pgdb interface that is compliant with the DB-API 2.0 specification.

Now let's look at Python's interface to PostgreSQL.

Connecting

We will first look closer at how a connection can be established to the database, and how we can check whether the authentification process has failed.

In the following example, you can see how easy a connection to the database can be opened using Python:

```
#!/usr/bin/python

# importing the PostgreSQL module
import pg

# connecting to the database
try:
        conn = pg.connect(dbname='mypython', host='localhost', user='hs')
        print "The connection has successfully been established"
except:
        print "Connection to the database could not be established"
```

We first import the Python module for PostgreSQL. In the next step, we try to connect to the database. The various connection parameters are passed to the function in brackets. You can see that the names of the parameters are directly derived from the C interface of PostgreSQL.

If an error occurs, a message is displayed. Let's execute the script:

```
[hs@duron python]$ make
python script.py
The connection has successfully been established
```

The connection has successfully been established. Python offers a second way to connect to PostgreSQL:

```
#!/usr/bin/python

# importing the PostgreSQL module
import pg
```

```
# connecting to the database
try:
        conn = pg.connect('mypython', 'localhost', 5432, None,
                None, 'hs', None)
        print "The connection has successfully been established"
except:
cx
        print "Connection to the database could not be established"
```

In the first example, we passed the name and the value of a parameter to the function. In this example, we use a fixed parameter list to connect. You can see which parameter has to be in which position in the following:

```
connect([dbname], [host], [port], [opt], [tty], [user], [passwd])
```

If a parameter has to keep the default setting, we simply use None in the parameter list of the connect function.

To overwrite the default parameters, Python offers some very simple functions. In the next example, you an see how easy it is to set a default value of a variable:

```
#!/usr/bin/python

# importing the PostgreSQL module
import pg

pg.set_defbase('mypython')
pg.set_defhost('localhost')
pg.set_defport(5432)
pg.set_defopt('-i')
pg.set_deftty('tty3')

try:
        conn = pg.connect(user='hs')
        print "The connection has successfully been established"
except:
        print "Connection to the database could not be established"
```

When running the script, the connection can easily be established, although the connect string only contains the username:

```
[hs@duron python]$ make
python script.py
The connection has successfully been established
```

In addition to setting default values, it is also possible to retrieve the value of the variables. Python offers functions that have names similar to those we used for setting the values (simply change the set in the name of the functions to get). The following script sets the default variables to a certain value, connects to the database, and tells us the default values:

```python
#!/usr/bin/python

# importing the PostgreSQL module
import pg

pg.set_defbase('mypython')
pg.set_defhost('localhost')
pg.set_defport(5432)
pg.set_defopt('-i')
pg.set_deftty('tty3')

try:
        conn = pg.connect(user='hs')
        print "The connection has successfully been established"
        print "default database: ", pg.get_defbase()
        print "default host: ", pg.get_defhost()
        print "default port: ", pg.get_defport()
        print "default options: ", pg.get_defopt()
        print "default tty: ", pg.get_deftty()
except:
        print "Connection to the database could not be established"
```

Let's execute the script:

```
[hs@duron python]$ make
python script.py
The connection has successfully been established
default database:  mypython
default host:  localhost
default port:  5432L
default options:  -i
default tty:  tty3
```

> **Note**
> The functions just shown do not check environment variables; the values have to be set using the Python functions to be retrieved.

To close a connection explicitly, use the `close()` method.

`pgobject` and `pgqueryobjectpgobject` handles a connection to the database. The object contains several important variables we may need in our scripts:

```
#!/usr/bin/python

# importing the PostgreSQL module
import pg

try:
        conn = pg.connect(dbname='mypython', host='localhost', user='hs')
        print "The connection has successfully been established"
        print "current database: ", conn.db
        print "current host: ", conn.host
        print "current port: ", conn.port
        print "current options: ", conn.options
        print "current tty: ", conn.tty
        print "current user: ", conn.user
        print "status: ", conn.status
        print "errors: ", conn.error
except:
        print "Connection to the database could not be established"
```

As you can see in the source code, `pgobject` allows us to access the parameters of the connection:

```
[hs@duron python]$ make
python script.py
The connection has successfully been established
current database:  mypython
current host:  localhost
current port:  5432
current options:
current tty:
current user:  Deprecated facility
status:  1
errors:
```

The only variable that can't be accessed in the previous example is the username on the database system. The status of the connection is 1, which means that everything is up and running. No errors have occurred.

After establishing a connection to the database, we will perform some simple SQL commands. First, we insert some sample data into the database:

```
CREATE TABLE "persons" (
        "name" text,
        "birth" date,
        "gender" character(1), PRIMARY KEY(name)
);

CREATE TABLE "income" (
        "name" text,
        "year" integer,
        "income" integer
);

COPY "persons"  FROM stdin;
Albert          1970-01-01          m
John         1973-04-04          m
Carla        1963-10-21          f
\.

COPY "income"  FROM stdin;
Albert          1998          28000
Albert          1999          30000
Jon      1998      20000
Jon      1999      40000
Carla       1998          30000
Carla       1999          32000
\.

CREATE   INDEX "income_name_key" on "income" using btree ( "name" "text_ops" );
```

When using Python, interacting with a PostgreSQL database is truly an easy task. In the next example, we will select all records in the income table and display them onscreen:

```
#!/usr/bin/python

# importing the PostgreSQL module
import pg

try:
```

```
        conn = pg.connect(dbname='mypython', host='localhost', user='hs')
        print "The connection has successfully been established"

        res = conn.query("SELECT name, year, income FROM income")
        print res
except:
        print "An error with the database has occurred."
```

We send a query to the server with the help of the query method, which is defined for connections. If we want to display the complete result onscreen, we use a simple `print` command to do the job:

```
[hs@duron python]$ make
python script.py
The connection has successfully been established
name   |year|income
------+----+------
Albert|1998| 28000
Albert|1999| 30000
Jon   |1998| 20000
Jon   |1999| 40000
Carla |1998| 30000
Carla |1999| 32000
(6 rows)
```

You can see that we do not even have to define a cursor or a loop to display the result; everything is done internally by Python. I would say that this is a very comfortable feature and makes writing small applications very easy indeed.

In many cases, displaying the entire result without processing the data returned, won't be enough. The more comfortable way is to process the query line-by-line. Every line returned should be a dictionary consisting of the fields selected by the SQL command:

```
#!/usr/bin/python

# importing the PostgreSQL module
import pg

try:
        conn = pg.connect(dbname='mypython', host='localhost', user='hs')
        print "The connection has successfully been established"

        rowindex = 0
        sqlcommand = "SELECT * FROM income WHERE year=1998"
```

```
        for res in  conn.query(sqlcommand).dictresult():
                rowindex = rowindex + 1
                print rowindex, res
except:
        print "An error with the database has occurred."
```

This time, we process the data using a simple loop. With the help of the `dictresult` method, we make the database return the data in a dictionary—a very efficient data structure provided by Python. If we execute the script now, we will see what a dictionary looks like if it is displayed without being indexed:

```
[hs@duron python]$ make
python script.py
The connection has successfully been established
1 {'year': 1998, 'income': 28000, 'name': 'Albert'}
2 {'year': 1998, 'income': 20000, 'name': 'Jon'}
3 {'year': 1998, 'income': 30000, 'name': 'Carla'}
```

In the previous listing, you can see that the names of the columns retrieved from the query are used as keys. Because we want the output to look more beautiful, we will now display the output using fixed fields with fixed length. This can be done by using print:

```
#!/usr/bin/python

import pg

try:
        conn = pg.connect(dbname='mypython', host='localhost', user='hs')
        print "The connection has successfully been established"

        rowindex = 0
        sqlcommand = "SELECT * FROM income WHERE year=1998"
        for res in  conn.query(sqlcommand).dictresult():
                rowindex = rowindex + 1
                print '%(name)15s %(year)15s %(income)15d' % res
except:
        print "An error with the database has occurred."
```

Every field except the last one is displayed as a 15 character string; the last field will be displayed as decimal value:

```
[hs@duron python]$ make
python script.py
```

```
The connection has successfully been established
        Albert          1998            28000
           Jon          1998            20000
         Carla          1998            30000
```

But the result does not have to be returned as a dictionary. Sometimes it is easier to process a list instead of a dictionary. In this case, getresult() has to be used. In the next listing, you can see how this can be done:

```python
#!/usr/bin/python

import pg

try:
        conn = pg.connect(dbname='mypython', host='localhost', user='hs')
        print "The connection has successfully been established"

        rowindex = 0
        sqlcommand = "SELECT * FROM income WHERE year=1998"
        for res in  conn.query(sqlcommand).getresult():
                rowindex = rowindex + 1
                print res
                print res[0], res[1], res[2], "\n"
except:
        print "An error with the database has occurred."
```

We want the result to be printed line-by-line, we first display the whole list onscreen. Then we want the various elements of the list to be displayed:

```
 [hs@duron python]$ make
python script.py
The connection has successfully been established
('Albert', 1998, 28000)
Albert 1998 28000

('Jon', 1998, 20000)
Jon 1998 20000

('Carla', 1998, 30000)
Carla 1998 30000
```

Sometimes it is necessary to find out which fields are returned by the database. It might be useful for you to retrieve a list of all columns, especially if you are working with SELECT * statements. Python offers the listfields() method to do the job:

```
#!/usr/bin/python

import pg

try:
        conn = pg.connect(dbname='mypython', host='localhost', user='hs')
        print "The connection has successfully been established"

        sqlcommand = "SELECT * FROM income WHERE year=1998"
        res = conn.query(sqlcommand)
        print "fields: ", res.listfields()
except:
        print "An error with the database has occurred."
```

The method returns the names of the three columns returned as a list:

```
[hs@duron python]$ make
python script.py
The connection has successfully been established
fields:  ('name', 'year', 'income')
```

Of course, finding the names is not the only thing that can be done. In the next example, we present two additional examples you can use in your scripts:

```
#!/usr/bin/python

import pg

try:
        conn = pg.connect(dbname='mypython', host='localhost', user='hs')
        print "The connection has successfully been established"

        sqlcommand = "SELECT * FROM income WHERE year=1998"
        res = conn.query(sqlcommand)
        for x in res.listfields():
                print res.fieldnum(x), " - ", x

        print "\nfield #2: ", res.fieldname(2), "\n"
        print res.dictresult()
except:
        print "An error with the database has occurred."
```

The first new function used in this script is called `fieldnum()` and returns the position of a field in the result. But the operation can also be done the other way around—`fieldname()` returns the name of a field related to a given index.

Both functions can be used before extracting the result of the query. The output of the script is as follows:

```
[hs@duron python]$ make
python script.py
The connection has successfully been established
0  -  name
1  -  year
2  -  income

field #2:  income

 [{'year': 1998, 'income': 28000, 'name': 'Albert'}, {'year': 1998,
'income': 20000, 'name': 'Jon'}, {'year': 1998, 'income': 30000,
'name': 'Carla'}]
```

The most interesting part of the output is the last line. We extract the whole result of the query with just one command, and we receive a data structure that contains all lines returned as a dictionary. Use Python's onboard functions to process the object returned.

Some scripts have to find the number of tuples returned by the query. The Python interface provides the ntuples function we will need in the next script:

```
#!/usr/bin/python

import pg

try:
        conn = pg.connect(dbname='mypython', host='localhost', user='hs')
        print "The connection has successfully been established"

        sqlcommand = "SELECT * FROM income WHERE year=1998"
        res = conn.query(sqlcommand)
        print "tuples: ", res.ntuples()
except:
        print "An error with the database has occurred."
```

Our query returns three tuples; that is what we have the ntuples function expected to return:

```
[hs@duron python]$ make
python script.py
```

```
The connection has successfully been established
tuples:  3
```

Sometimes you may find it useful to reset the connection to your database. Resetting means that the current connection is closed and opened with the same parameters as before:

```python
#!/usr/bin/python

import pg

try:
        conn = pg.connect(dbname='mypython', host='localhost', user='hs')
        print "The connection has successfully been established"
        conn.reset();
        print "reset ..."
except:
        print "An error with the database has occurred."
```

We simply apply the reset() method on the connection handle to reset the connection and run the application again:

```
[hs@duron python]$ make
python script.py
The connection has successfully been established
reset ...
```

Retrieving notifications from the backend is as easy as performing a reset:

```python
#!/usr/bin/python

import pg

try:
        conn = pg.connect(dbname='mypython', host='localhost', user='hs')
        print "The connection has successfully been established"
        notif = conn.getnotify()
        print "notification: ", notif
except:
        print "An error with the database has occurred."
```

Because nothing happened, no notifications are returned by the backend:

```
[hs@duron python]$ make
python script.py
```

```
The connection has successfully been established
notification:  None
```

The Database Wrapper Class DB

The DB class is a very powerful part of the pg module and contains many extremely useful functions. We will take a closer look at these functions in this section.

The first example shows you how we can retrieve a list of all databases installed on the system:

```
#!/usr/bin/python

import pg

try:
        conn = pg.DB(dbname='mypython', host='localhost', user='hs')
        print "The connection has successfully been established"
        print conn.get_databases()
except:
        print "An error with the database has occurred."
```

Python returns the names of the databases in a list that can easily be used for further processing. get_databases() is an extremely useful function, especially for administration purposes. Imagine a situation where you have to work with dynamically created databases. With the help of simple Python scripts, checking these databases should be an easy task (in many cases, it is much easier than using a shell script).

```
[hs@duron python]$ make
python script.py
The connection has successfully been established
['myodbc', 'template1', 'template0', 'myjava', 'mypython', 'lebenslauf', 'db']
```

You can see that we have seven databases up and running on the test system.

Another useful method is pkey(). It is used to retrieve the name of the primary key defined on a table. If no primary key is defined or if the table does not exist in the database, an exception is caused.

The following script checks two tables to see whether a primary key is defined:

```
#!/usr/bin/python

import pg
```

```
try:
        conn = pg.DB(dbname='mypython', host='localhost', user='hs')
        print "The connection has successfully been established"

        try:
                print "primary key (persons): ", conn.pkey('persons')
        except:
                print "no primary key on table persons defined"

        try:
                print "primary key (income): ", conn.pkey('income')
        except:
                print "no primary key on table persons defined"

except:
        print "An error with the database has occurred."
```

name is the column used as primary key for the first table. The second table has no primary key, so the exception is caught and a message is displayed:

```
[hs@duron python]$ make
python script.py
The connection has successfully been established
primary key (persons):  name
primary key (income):  no primary key on table persons defined
```

Before looking for the primary key of a table, it might be useful to find out which tables can be found in a database. We can use the get_tables() method to do this:

```
#!/usr/bin/python

import pg

try:
        conn = pg.DB(dbname='mypython', host='localhost', user='hs')
        print "The connection has successfully been established"

        try:
                print "tables: ", conn.get_tables()
        except:
                print "an error has occurred ..."
except:
        print "An error with the database has occurred."
```

Two tables can be found in the database to which we are currently connected:

```
[hs@duron python]$ make
python script.py
The connection has successfully been established
tables:  ['persons', 'income']
```

The next function we want to present in this section is called `get_attnames()` and is used to find the attribute names of a table. The result is returned as a list. Look at the source code of the sample script:

```
#!/usr/bin/python

import pg

try:
        conn = pg.DB(dbname='mypython', host='localhost', user='hs')
        print conn.get_attnames('income')
except:
        print "An error with the database has occurred."
```

The list generated by the function contains four fields. The table has only three columns, but four columns are returned. The mysterious fourth column we cannot see in the description of the table is the object ID of the rows of the table. The data type of this column is `Oid`:

```
[hs@duron python]$ make
python script.py
{'income': 'int', 'name': 'text', 'oid': 'int', 'year': 'int'}
```

`get()` is a function you can use to get a tuple from a database table. In the following example, you can see how things work:

```
#!/usr/bin/python

import pg

conn = pg.DB(dbname='mypython', host='localhost', user='hs')
x = conn.get('income', '1998', 'year')
print x
```

One record is retrieved from the table:

```
[hs@duron python]$ make
python script.py
```

```
{'income': 28000, 'name': 'Albert', 'oid': 28963, 'year': 1998,
'oid_income': 28963}
```

The module also offers a very easy method to insert data into a table. Imagine that we want to insert the salary of Hans into the database. One way to insert the data is to send a simple SQL statement to the server. Another way (and I would consider this the more elegant way) is to use the insert() function:

```
#!/usr/bin/python

import pg

try:
        conn = pg.DB(dbname='mypython', host='localhost', user='hs')
        ret=conn.insert('income', {'income': 88000, 'name': 'Hans', 'year':
2002})

        res=conn.query("SELECT * FROM income WHERE name='Hans'").dictresult()
        print "result: ", res
except:
        print "an error has occurred ..."
```

We pass a dictionary to the function and Python does the rest for us. To see if the data has been inserted successfully, we retrieve the new record from the table.

Let's see what is displayed by the script:

```
[hs@duron python]$ make
python script.py
result:  [{'year': 2002, 'income': 88000, 'name': 'Hans'}, {'year': 2002,
[ic:ccc]'income': 88000, 'name': 'Hans'}]
```

Updating works pretty much the same way as selecting data. The parameters passed to the function are the name of the table that has to be updated and an object. The object should contain the object ID so that the value can be found in the database.

In the next example, we select the affected data from the table first and display it onscreen. Then we add 1000 to the income of Hans, perform the update operation, and query the table again to see if the variables have changed to the correct values:

```
#!/usr/bin/python

import pg

try:
```

```
        conn = pg.DB(dbname='mypython', host='localhost', user='hs')
        res = conn.query("SELECT * FROM income WHERE name='Hans'").dictresult()
        print "result before: ", res
                val = conn.get('income', '2002', 'year')
        print "\nval: ", val, "\n"
        val["income"] = val["income"] + 1000
        oid = conn.update('income', val);

        res = conn.query("SELECT * FROM income WHERE name='Hans'").dictresult()
        print "result after: ", res
except:
        print "an error has occurred ..."
```

We execute the script to see what has happened:

```
[hs@duron python]$ make
python script.py
result before:  [{'year': 2002, 'income': 88000, 'name': 'Hans'}]

val:  {'income': 88000, 'name': 'Hans', 'oid': 28974, 'year': 2002,
'oid_income': 28974}

result after:  [{'year': 2002, 'income': 89000, 'name': 'Hans'}]
```

The income of Hans is now 1000 units higher than before.

Other important functions supported by the DB class are

clear(table, [a]) ([a] is a dictionary of values) is used to clear a database table, and delete(table, [a]) ([a] is a dictionary of values) is used to delete the row from a table.

TcL/TK

Tcl/TK is another language providing a powerful interface to PostgreSQL. Tcl/TK is widely used, especially for implementing graphical user interfaces. In this section, you will learn to build simple PostgreSQL enabled Tcl/TK applications.

The History of TcL

Tcl was invented by John Ousterhout in the 1980s at the University of California at Berkeley. The project grew out of his work on design tools for integrated circuits. Ousterhout and his students had some interactive tools for IC design, such as Magic and Crystal. Not much time was invested in the programming languages for the tools and finally every tool had its own programming language. As a result, the languages were in general very weak and not suitable for all demands.

During a sabbatical at DEC's Western Research Laboratory in the fall of 1987, the idea of an interpreted, embeddable command language was born. The idea was to build a language that could be used as library package in many applications. Tcl (Tool Command Language) should provide basic components of a programming language, such as control structures, variables, and procedures, while the application in which Tcl has to be included should provide additional features.

Embeddability is the most important aspect when dealing with Tcl and is strongly related with the three major goals of the language:

- The language must easily be extensible, and new features have to fit into the concept as if they were part of the language from the beginning.

- The language must be easy so that interaction with applications is easy. The language must not restrict the features an application provides.

- Tcl is designed to glue the extensions of an application together and must have good facilities for integration.

The work on Tcl started in early 1988 and was more for academic purpose than for anything else. Ousterhout had already stopped working on IC design tools at that time, and he didn't think that anybody other than him was interested in an embeddable language. Well, he was wrong.

During that time, GUIs become more and more popular, and Ousterhout feared that it would become impossible for small teams to develop interactive applications if essential parts of an application were not parts of reusable components. Components for building GUIs would play an especially important part for small groups of developers.

He started to create a set of GUI components for Tcl. Tcl could be used to compile the GUI components to a graphical interface. This set of components became very widespread and is now known as Tk. Because Tk was only a part-time project, it took about two years until Tk became "useful."

In 1989, Ousterhout gave copies of Tcl away because people and companies were interested in an embeddable language. In January 1999, a paper about Tcl was presented at the USENIX Conference. Hundreds of people attended Ousterhout's talk, and many people started asking for Tcl. The Tcl source code become freely available on Berkeley's FTP site. Tcl spread over the Internet. Don Libes of the National Institute of Standards and Technology was one of the people at the USENIX Conference. When he heard of Tcl, he started hacking on a software called `expect`. The software was freely available after presenting a paper in the Summer of 1990. `expect` became widespread among system administrators and was the first Tcl application that was widely used. In late 1990, a version of Tk was also available, and the popularity of Tcl started to grow.

The number of people using Tcl grew quickly because Tcl/Tk was the easiest way to write graphical user interfaces on UNIX systems. Other toolkits, such as Motif, were much more complicated and could not be used without writing C code. It became obvious that writing Tcl/Tk code was five to ten times faster than writing a C program using Motif.

Over the years, the Tcl community grew rapidly. A huge community was formed and people exchanged their ideas and thoughts in mailing lists and newsgroups. In 1993, a workshop took place at Berkley. The Tcl community contributed many features, and a lot of code was even included in the core distribution of Tcl.

During that period, new releases were made every 6 to 12 months. Most new features were suggested by the community, and Ousterhout even introduced some sort of ranking of which features have to be included first. At the Tcl conference, this voting became famous as the so called *"Ouster-votes.* These votes were heavily discussed, and some people say that the vote was not always totally objective.

After a 14-year academic career, Ousterhout left Berkley in 1994 and started to build up a Tcl developers team at Sun Microsystems. He felt that Tcl needed some sort of commercial background to grow even more rapidly. Up to that time, every line of Tcl and Tk code was entirely written by himself. At Sun Microsystems, dozens of members worked together to develop Tcl. Tcl and Tk were ported to Windows and to the Macintosh. Over time, a lot of code was handed over to Sun developers, and Tcl became a wonderful cross-platform development environment. In spite of Sun being involved in the development, Tcl stayed free software. The number of users was still increasing, and several hundred thousand people were developing software by 1997 with the help of Tcl.

In late 1997, Ousterhout left Sun Microsystem and founded Scriptics (now Tcl)—a company focused entirely on the development of Tcl. A lot of former Sun programmers joined Scriptics, and the first product shipped in September 1998. Tcl is still free software, and it is still going to be free software in the future.

Connecting

The first thing to do when working with a database is establishing a connection. In this section, we will see how this can be done with the help of Tcl.

We create a database called `mytcl` that will be used in this section:

```
[hs@duron tcl]$ createdb mytcl
CREATE DATABASE
```

We will use `pgtclsh` as the Tcl shell client. `pgtclsh` is a Tcl interface that includes the functions used for PostgreSQL. Connecting to the server is a simple task:

```
#!/usr/bin/pgtclsh

set conn [pg_connect -conninfo "dbname=mytcl"]
puts "Connection successfully established";
pg_disconnect $conn;
```

In this example, we connect to `mytcl`, write a message on the screen, and disconnect again.

Let's execute the script:

```
[hs@duron tcl]$ ./connect.tcl
Connection successfully established
```

Before we get into further details concerning connecting to a PostgreSQL database, the following is a short overview of `pg_connect`'s syntax:

```
pg_connect -conninfo connectOptions
pg_connect dbName [-host hostName]
  [-port portNumber] [-tty pqtty]
  [-options optionalBackendArgs]
```

Look at the next example:

```
#!/usr/bin/pgtclsh

set conn [pg_connect mytcl -host 195.34.143.8 -port 5432]
puts "Connection successfully established";
pg_disconnect $conn;
```

We have now defined the IP address of the host and the port to which the database is listening. If we execute the script, the connection can be established successfully:

```
[hs@duron tcl]$ ./connect.tcl
Connection successfully established
```

If you want to define options directly for the backend, you can use the `-options` flag. All flags specified in the `-option` flag are directly passed to the backend processes.

It might sometimes be useful to find out a little bit more about the default connection parameters. The next example shows how this information can be obtained and displayed onscreen:

```
#!/usr/bin/pgtclsh

set conn [pg_connect -conninfo "dbname=mytcl host=195.34.147.7 port=5432"]

puts "Connection successfully established";
puts [ pg_conndefaults];

pg_disconnect $conn;
```

If we execute the script, we can see the default parameters:

```
[hs@duron tcl]$ ./connect.tcl
Connection successfully established
{authtype Database-Authtype D 20 {}} {service Database-Service {} 20 {}}
{user Database-User {} 20 hs} {password Database-Password * 20 {}} {dbname
Database-Name {} 20 hs} {host Database-Host {} 40 {}} {hostaddr Database-Host-
IPv4-Address {} 15 {}}
{port Database-Port {} 6 5432} {tty Backend-Debug-TTY D 40 {}} {options
Backend-Debug-Options D 40 {}}
```

The result is returned as a list of all possible connection options in a sublist and the default value of these options. The information can actually be obtained by using `pg_connect -conninfo`.

The parameters in the sublists returned have a special format:

```
{optname label dispchar dispsize value}
```

Simple Examples

In the first example, we show you how you can retrieve values from a table. We have included a table storing the information that can typically be found in a menu:

```
CREATE TABLE "menu" (
        "name" text,
        "price" numeric(6,2)
);
```

```
COPY "menu"  FROM stdin;
Pork Chop Suey  5.19
Fish Chop Suey  6.49
Hamburger       1.39
Cheeseburger    1.49
French Fries    0.99
\.
```

What follows is a simple script that selects and displays the values in the first column:

```
#!/usr/bin/pgtclsh

set conn [pg_connect -conninfo "dbname=mytcl"]

set res [pg_exec $conn "SELECT name FROM menu "]
set ntups [pg_result $res -numTuples]

for {set i 0} {$i < $ntups} {incr i} {
        puts stdout [lindex [pg_result $res -getTuple $i] 0]
}

pg_disconnect $conn;
```

First we connect to the database. If the connection can be established, the script continues and executes the SQL command using the pg_exec command. pg_result finds the number of tuples returned by the query. We go through the result line-by-line and display the result onscreen. The output of the script is as follows:

```
[hs@duron tcl]$ ./simple.tcl
Pork Chop Suey
Fish Chop Suey
Hamburger
Cheeseburger
French Fries
```

If we want both columns of the query to be displayed, we can use a script such as follows:

```
#!/usr/bin/pgtclsh

set conn [pg_connect -conninfo "dbname=mytcl"]

set res [pg_exec $conn "SELECT * FROM menu "]
set ntups [pg_result $res -numTuples]
```

```
for {set i 0} {$i < $ntups} {incr i} {
        puts stdout "[lindex [pg_result $res -getTuple $i] 0], \
                [lindex [pg_result $res -getTuple $i] 1] ";
}

pg_disconnect $conn;
```

When we execute the script, we will receive a result such as follows:

```
[hs@duron tcl]$ ./simple.tcl
Pork Chop Suey,  5.19
Fish Chop Suey,  6.49
Hamburger,  1.39
Cheeseburger,  1.49
French Fries,  0.99
```

Up to now, we have not checked whether a query has been executed successfully. Tcl offers a very easy method to check whether PostgreSQL returned an error. Look at the following example:

```
#!/usr/bin/pgtclsh

set conn [pg_connect -conninfo "dbname=mytcl"]

set res [pg_exec $conn "SELECT * FROM nothere "]
set ntups [pg_result $res -numTuples]
set error [pg_result $res -error]

puts stdout "ntups: $ntups";
puts stdout "error: $error";

pg_disconnect $conn;
```

The table called nothere is not in the database, so the query can not be executed:

```
[hs@duron tcl]$ ./simple.tcl
ntups: 0
error: ERROR:  Relation 'nothere' does not exist
```

error contains the description of the error. You can also see that the number of rows returned is 0.

You do not have to check the error string to find whether an error has occurred, because you can simply check the status of the query:

```
#!/usr/bin/pgtclsh

set conn [pg_connect -conninfo "dbname=mytcl"]
set res [pg_exec $conn "SELECT * FROM nothere "]

set status [pg_result $res -status]
puts stdout "status: $status";

pg_disconnect $conn;
```

The query returns a fatal error because the table does not exist in the database:

```
[hs@duron tcl]$ ./simple.tcl
status: PGRES_FATAL_ERROR
```

Sometimes, it can be useful to find how many attributes are returned by a query:

```
#!/usr/bin/pgtclsh

set conn [pg_connect -conninfo "dbname=mytcl"]
set res [pg_exec $conn "SELECT name, price FROM menu "]

set attrs [pg_result $res -numAttrs]
puts stdout "attrs: $attrs";

pg_disconnect $conn;
```

We select two columns from the table, so the number of attributes is 2. -numAttrs is used to find the number of attributes.

```
[hs@duron tcl]$ ./simple.tcl
attrs: 2
```

As we expected, the script returns 2.

It can also be useful to clear the result of a query. For that purpose, pg_result offers the appropriate functionality:

```
#!/usr/bin/pgtclsh

set conn [pg_connect -conninfo "dbname=mytcl"]

set res [pg_exec $conn "SELECT name FROM menu "]
set code [pg_result $res -clear]
```

```
set ntups [pg_result $res -numTuples]
puts stdout "ntups: $ntups";

pg_disconnect $conn;
```

In this example, we try to access the result of a query that has already been reset. This will lead to an error:

```
[hs@duron tcl]$ ./simple.tcl
Invalid result handlepgsql3.0 is not a valid query result
    while executing
"pg_result $res -numTuples"
    invoked from within
"set ntups [pg_result $res -numTuples]"
    (file "./simple.tcl" line 8)
```

We do not have a valid query result anymore, and the script fails.

Using PL/Tcl

Tcl is designed to be an embedded language. PostgreSQL provides an embedded version of Tcl as well, and you will take a closer look at it in this section.

An Overview of PL/Tcl

As we have already mentioned, PostgreSQL does not only offer one embedded language. Many people don't want to use PL/pgSQl for their function; they use PL/Tcl instead. PL/Tcl provides Tcl functionalities for PostgreSQL. Because Tcl is designed to be an embedded language, it is also suitable for PostgreSQL.

PL/Tcl code is executed in a safe Tcl interpreter. The user can perform almost all operations possible with C code. The only restriction is that only a few command are available to access the database via the SPI interface. There is also no way to access internal information about the backend process.

One of the most important restrictions of PL/Tcl is that no I/O functions can be created for new databases. In a way, this is a little bit uncomfortable because Tcl would be comfortable language for a purpose like that.

As we have mentioned before, PL/Tcl code is usually executed by a safe Tcl interpreter, which means that PL/Tcl can do nothing that harms the rest of the system (such as killing files or things such as that). If you want to build applications that use "unsafe" features, you can use PL/TclU (U for stands for untrusted). PL/TclU has to be installed as an untrusted language and functions can only be created by the superuser. The problem with untrusted functions is that a certain function may be used to damage a system. You have to keep in mind that a user can do the same things from inside the database that he or she can do with a shell program. This can lead to severe security holes.

Simple Examples

Let's get to some practical stuff. If we want to use PL/Tcl functions in our applications, we have to enable Tcl in the database:

```
[hs@duron tcl]$ createlang pltcl mytcl
```

This can simply be done using the createlang command. If the command has been executed successfully, the work can begin. Let's start with a simple example:

```
CREATE FUNCTION mysum(int4, int4) RETURNS int4 AS
'
        return [expr $1 + $2]
' LANGUAGE 'pltcl';
```

This function can be used to add two integer values. You can see that the head of the function looks exactly the same as the header of a PL/pgSQL function. The actual code of the function has to be passed to the database with single quotes.

After inserting the function into the database using a simple Makefile, we can try the function:

```
mytcl=# SELECT mysum(10, 30);
 mysum
-------
    40
(1 row)
```

Function Overloading

Functions in PostgreSQL can have the same name if the number of input parameters or the type of these parameter differs. This is a very convenient feature because it allows you to build applications that are much easier to understand.

Function overloading is not supported by Tcl itself. To enable function overloading for PL/Tcl, the internal procedure names contain the object ID of the procedures pg_proc row. With the help of this little trick, the name of the function is unique and can be used by Tcl.

To make the process clear, we have included an example:

```
CREATE FUNCTION mysum(int4, int4) RETURNS int4 AS
'
```

```
        return [expr $1 + $2]
' LANGUAGE 'pltcl';

CREATE FUNCTION mysum(float, float) RETURNS float AS
    '
        return [expr $1 + $2]
' LANGUAGE 'pltcl';
```

Both functions have the same name, and the only difference between the two functions is that the first function accepts integer values, while the second function can be used for floats only:

```
mytcl=# SELECT mysum(10.1, 30.1);
 mysum
-------
  40.2
(1 row)
```

In this example, the second function is used because the function is called with two floats.

If we take a closer look at pg_proc, we can see that the only difference between the two functions is the parameter list:

```
mytcl=# SELECT proname, prolang, proargtypes FROM pg_proc WHERE proname='mysum';
 proname | prolang  | proargtypes
---------+----------+------------
 mysum   | 11687448 |    23 23
 mysum   | 11687448 |   701 701
(2 rows)
```

Accessing a Database with PL/Tcl

PL/Tcl offers a lot of commands to access the database from inside a PL/Tcl function. One of the most important commands when accessing the database is spi_exec. The prefix spi in the name of the function does not occur perchance. Tcl uses the PostgreSQL SPI interface to interact with the database. We have included a very simple example:

```
CREATE FUNCTION priceupdate(text, numeric) RETURNS bool AS
    '
        spi_exec -array C "UPDATE menu SET price=$2 WHERE name=''$1''"

        return "t";
' LANGUAGE 'pltcl';
```

priceupdate sets the price of the product defined by the first parameter to the price passed to the function in the second parameter.

> **Note**
> ''$1'' has to appear with two single-quotes because it is a string that has to be quoted in SQL. Using only one single-quote would lead to a syntax error.

The function can easily be called. The only thing we need to be sure of is that the parameters passed to the function are cast to the right data type:

```
mytcl=# SELECT priceupdate('Hamburger'::text, '1.59'::numeric(4,2));
 priceupdate
-------------
 t
(1 row)
```

If we look at the record for Hamburger, we can see that the price has changed.

```
mytcl=# SELECT * FROM menu WHERE name='Hamburger';
   name    | price | red_price
-----------+-------+-----------
 Hamburger |  1.59 |
(1 row)
```

UPDATE operations are an easy task because no result has to be extracted from the query. If you want to perform SELECT statements, this is different because you will need the result for further calculations.

We have included a simple example to show you how the result can be accessed by using a simple array:

```
CREATE FUNCTION priceupdate(text) RETURNS text AS
'
        spi_exec -array C "SELECT * FROM menu WHERE name=''$1'' LIMIT 1"

        return "$C(name) - $C(price)";
' LANGUAGE 'pltcl';
```

The result of the SQL statement is selected into an array called C. We can easily access it by indexing the array with the names of the columns we want to extract. If we want to find the price of a Hamburger, we can simply use the following SQL statement:

```
mytcl=# SELECT priceupdate('Hamburger'::text);
   priceupdate
------------------
 Hamburger - 1.59
(1 row)
```

A similar result can also be achieved differently. In the next example, we prepare the query explicitly and execute the query plan in the next step:

```
CREATE FUNCTION prodtext(text) RETURNS text AS
'
        set GD(plan) [ spi_prepare \\
                "SELECT * FROM menu WHERE name=''$1'' LIMIT 1" text ]
        spi_execp -array C $GD(plan) $1

        return "$C(name)";
' LANGUAGE 'pltcl';
```

The result of this query is selected into the array called C again. The only difference in the output is that we don't display the price of the product:

```
mytcl=# SELECT prodtext('Hamburger'::text);
 prodtext
-----------
 Hamburger
(1 row)
```

In some cases, it may be very useful to write small PL/Tcl functions that either add some logging information to the logfile or insert data into a separate logging table, especially for logging. However, the easiest way is to print some output into PostgreSQL's standard logfile. Tcl provides a function called elog:

```
CREATE FUNCTION makelog(text, text) RETURNS text AS
'
        elog $1 $2
        return "t"
' LANGUAGE 'pltcl';
```

The first parameter defines the logging level. The levels supported by PostgreSQL are NOTICE, ERROR, FATAL, DEBUG, and NOIND.

> **Note**
> These levels are the same for the C function called elog.

If we execute the function, the message will be displayed onscreen and written into the logfile:

```
mytcl=# SELECT makelog('NOTICE', 'Function executed successfully');
NOTICE:  Function executed successfully
 makelog
----------
```

```
t
(1 row)
```

Depending on how PostgreSQL is configured, the entry in the logfile may look different. The following is the entry declared by the test system:

```
2001-05-28 16:54:45 [20309]  NOTICE:  Function executed successfully
```

Writing Triggers with PL/Tcl

You sometimes have to write a trigger to make special events happen automatically. PL/Tcl is a good language for writing triggers, and we will take a closer look at how this can be done in this section.

Triggers can be defined on functions that return opaque. The return value of a trigger can be OK, which means that the trigger has been executed successfully, SKIP if the trigger manager has to suppress the operation, or a list as returned by the Tcl command array get.

Some important information is given to the function by the trigger manager. We have compiled an overview of all variables available in the PL/Tcl function:

- $TG_name   Contains the name of the trigger fired.

- $TG_relid   Contains the object ID of the table in which the trigger has been fired.

- $TG_relatts $TG_relatts is a list with an empty element in first position that contains all entries in the pg_attribute system table. The position of an element in the list is the same as in pg_attribute.

- $TG_when   Contains either BEFORE or AFTER, depending on the configuration of the trigger.

- $TG_level   Contains ROW or STATEMENT, depending on the event for which the trigger is fired.

- $TG_op   Contains INSERT, UPDATE, or DELETE, depending on the event for which the trigger is fired.

- $NEW   In case of INSERT and UPDATE operations, $NEW contains the values of the new table row. In case of DELETE, the variable is empty.

- $OLD   In case of UPDATE and DELETE, $OLD contains the old values of the row that has to be updated. In case of an INSERT operation, the field is empty.

- $GD $GD is the global data status array.

- $args   Contains a list of arguments passed to the function as defined in the CREATE TRIGGER statement.

To show you how a simple trigger works, we add a column called red_price to the menu table.

```
ALTER TABLE menu ADD COLUMN red_price int4;
```

This column will contain the reduced price of a product. To keep the function simple, the price is always set to 1:

```
mytcl=# \d menu
            Table "menu"
 Attribute |     Type     | Modifier
-----------+--------------+----------
 name      | text         |
 price     | numeric(6,2) |
 red_price | integer      |
```

The code of the function is very easy indeed:

```
CREATE FUNCTION trigfunc_addprice() RETURNS OPAQUE AS
'
        set NEW($2) 1;
        return [array get NEW];
' LANGUAGE 'pltcl';

CREATE TRIGGER trigger_addprice BEFORE INSERT ON menu
        FOR EACH ROW EXECUTE PROCEDURE trigfunc_
addprice('price', 'red_price');
```

We first create a function called trigfunc_addprice that sets the value of the second argument to 1. $NEW is returned by the function to tell PostgreSQL which values have to inserted into the database. After creating the function, we create the trigger on the menu table. The trigger has to be fired before inserting a value into the table. If we used the same function after the INSERT, nothing would happen because no value would be changed. Two parameters are passed to the function. In the previous example, these two parameters match the names of the column. We have included this here so that you can see how $NEW can be accessed.

Let's insert a value:

```
INSERT INTO menu VALUES('Schnitzel', 10);
```

menu has three columns, but we call INSERT with just two values; the third value will automatically be added by the trigger.

After the INSERT operation, the table will look as follows:

```
mytcl=# SELECT * FROM menu;
      name       | price | red_price
-----------------+-------+-----------
 Pork Chop Suey  |  5.19 |
 Fish Chop Suey  |  6.49 |
 Hamburger       |  1.39 |
 Cheeseburger    |  1.49 |
 French Fries    |  0.99 |
 Schnitzel       | 10.00 |         1
(6 rows)
```

We have added Schnitzel to the table and red_price has been set to 1.

Removing a trigger from a table is very easy. You can see how the function and the trigger can be removed in the following:

```
DROP TRIGGER trigger_addprice ON menu;
DROP FUNCTION trigfunc_addprice();
```

Building a Simple Tcl/Tk Frontend for PostgreSQL

In this section, we will show you how you can build a simple user interface for Tcl/Tk. The shell used to build Tk applications in combination with Tcl is called wish. wish is used by a lot of scripts, such as the graphical configuration tool of the Linux kernel (try make xconfig).

For our purposes, we cannot use wish because we need the PostgreSQL interface for Tcl. Instead of using pgtclsh as we did before, we have to use pgtksh. pgtksh is a Tcl shell with Tk and PostgreSQL functions. In reality, it is nothing more than wish with libpgtcl loaded.

In this section, we will present a simple example of a tool for querying a PostgreSQL database. We have tried to make the script as simple as possible:

```
#!/bin/sh
# the next line restarts using wish \
exec pgtksh "$0" "$@"
```

```
wm title . ExecLog

# creates a frame
frame .top -borderwidth 10
pack .top -side top -fill x

# generate a command buttons
button .top.quit -text Quit -command exit
set but [button .top.run -text "Run it" -command Run]
pack .top.quit .top.run -side right

# label and entry field for the command
label .top.l -text Command: -padx 0
entry .top.cmd -width 20 -relief sunken \
        -textvariable command
pack .top.l -side left
pack .top.cmd -side left -fill x -expand true

# binding functions to the buttons
bind .top.cmd <Return> Run
bind .top.cmd <Control-c> Stop
focus .top.cmd

# generting text widget for logging the output
frame .t
set log [text .t.log -width 70 -height 30 \
        -borderwidth 2 -relief raised -setgrid true \
        -yscrollcommand {.t.scroll set}]
scrollbar .t.scroll -command {.t.log yview}
pack .t.scroll -side right -fill y
pack .t.log -side left -fill both -expand true
pack .t -side top -fill both -expand true

# connecting to the database and displaying the output on the screen
proc Run {} {
        global command input log but
        puts stdout "$command"

        set conn [pg_connect -conninfo "dbname=mytcl"]

        set res [pg_exec $conn "$command "]
        set ntups [pg_result $res -numTuples]
```

```
        set attrs [pg_result $res -numAttrs]

        for {set i 0} {$i < $ntups} {incr i} {
                for { set j 0} {$j <= $attrs} {incr j} {
                        $log insert end "[lindex [pg_result $res -getTuple $i]
$j] "

                        $log see end
                }
                $log insert end "\n"
                $log see end
        }
        $log insert end "\n"
        $log see end
}


# stop
proc Stop {} {
        $but config -text "Run it" -command Run
}
```

Take a good look at the first three lines of the script. Depending on how you have
installed your system, the location of pgtksh may differ. This can be a little bit
uncomfortable, especially if you want to run your software on multiple systems. Good
old Bourne Shell offers a little trick to get around the problem:

```
#!/bin/sh
# the next line restarts using wish \
exec pgtksh "$0" "$@"
```

The first line must contain the full path to the shell. The second line contains a
comment. In the third line, we call exec, replace the current shell (Bourne Shell), and
pass all arguments passed to the Bourne Shell to the new shell. The only thing we
have to take be sure is that the path to pgtksh is included in $PATH. It may be a real
advantage if you don't have to take care where the shell can be found, specially if you
have a lot of scripts, but let's have a look at the rest of the previous code.We first set
the title of the main widget. In the second step, we create a frame and generate two
command buttons. The first button is labeled "Run it," and the second button is
labeled "Quit." Buttons are only useful if you bind certain operations to them. In our
case, we bind the functions Run and Stop to the two buttons. Every time somebody
clicks Run It, Run will be executed.

To display the output, we create widget frame for the text.

Run establishes a connection to the database and executes the command the user enters into the command line. The result is displayed in the field we created for the logging in the widget. After every query, a newline is displayed so the results of various queries can easily be distinguished.

Let's execute the script:

```
[hs@duron tcl]$ ./tk.sh
```

A widget will be displayed, as shown in Figure 9.5:

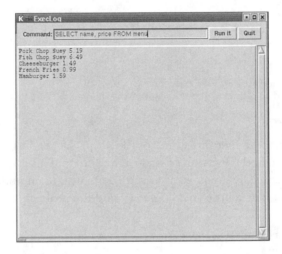

Figure 9.5
A tool for executing SQL commands.

With only 64 lines of code (including empty lines), we have written a quite comfortable user interface. I guess that this really shows how easy user interfaces can be built with the help of Tcl and Tk.

ODBC

ODBC is widely used in Microsoft and office environments. A powerful ODBC interface is provided by PostgreSQL. The most important facts about ODBC will be covered in this section.

An Overview of ODBC

In the traditional database, an application is a piece of software that performs a specific database task for a specific database system. Such applications are usually using embedded SQL. This is very efficient and, in many cases, is very portable across different platforms and database systems. The problem is that the code has to be recompiled for each new environment. Embedded SQL is not the best solution for analyzing data stored in databases such as DB2 and Oracle. For example, if you want to integrate your data in office applications, things have to be done differently. If many data sources have to be integrated in one application, it is useful to have a standard interface. Imagine having 10 different database systems with each system having its own proprietary interface. This would lead to very complicated and bad software, if not to disaster.

Open Database Connectivity (ODBC) offers a new approach. A separate program is used to extract the data, while the application simply has to import the data. There will always be different database systems with different features, but ODBC offers a standard interface for accessing all databases supporting ODBC.

If you want your Windows application to connect to a database server, the application should be able connect to any database providing an ODBC driver. As long as the data in two databases is the same, there should be no difference between connecting to an Oracle database and connecting to a PostgreSQL server.

Using ODBC with PostgreSQL

The idea behind ODBC is very simple, but let's look at how PostgreSQL can be used in combination with ODBC.

Making your PostgreSQL database support ODBC should be a rather easy task. If you are working on a Linux machine, simply install the binaries you can find on any PostgreSQL mirror. If you are a user of Linux Debian, simply convert the RPMs to Debian archives by using `alien`. After installing the binaries, your database will support ODBC.

If you want to use the sources instead of compiling the server, you have to use `--with-odbcinst` at compile time. In addition to that, you should add the commands in the file `odbc.sql` in your database. `odbc.sql` is distributed with the source distribution of your PostgreSQL server and contains some extensions mandated by the ODBC standard that are not included in PostgreSQL by default. The file has to be inserted into `template1` so that all databases created after inserting the file can use the additional functions.

You will need a driver to access your database. The driver manager for UNIX can be downloaded from `www.iodbc.org`. Simply compile the sources and you can use the driver. If you want to use the ODBC driver for Perl's DBI module, a driver manager will also be necessary.

To access your PostgreSQL server from a Windows platform, you have to download the appropriate ODBC driver for PostgreSQl from `ftp://download.sourceforge.net/pub/mirrors/postgresql/odbc/versions`. On the FTP site (a PostgreSQL mirror site), you can find zip-archives containing the necessary software.

ODBC and Security

Security demands are constantly increasing. Security is one of the most important topics, especially when dealing with database environments.

We have to admit that every computer system around the globe can be hacked or at least severely be impaired. In spite of that issue, it is important to take care of security to make sure that hackers have a hard job.

Applications using NT security do not pass user IDs and passwords across an ODBC connection. This is a very important issue because a transmission can, in many cases, be sniffed. This would lead to security problems. IBM's DB2, Microsoft's SQL server, and all BackOffice products can be configured to use `integrated` NT security.

Some applications have a security system implemented on top of ODBC, and passwords are encrypted before they are transmitted over the network. If someone scans the data transmitted via ODBC, he or she can only find encrypted passwords.

Make sure that applications prevent tracking of sensitive commands. On Windows 95 and Windows NT systems, simply delete the file called `odbctrac.dll`. This will make sure that tracing is really disabled on your system.

The Microsoft Knowledge Base offers a lot of additional information concerning ODBC and security. If you want to build business-critical applications based on ODBC, we strongly recommend to check these sources.

CHAPTER 10

Extended PostgreSQL—
Software for PostgreSQL

Contributed Software

Some programmers have developed tools, modules, and examples that have not been included in the core distribution of PostgreSQL, but can be found in the contributed section, which is included in the tar-ball containing the source code of PostgreSQL.

These tools are not maintained by the PostgreSQL core development team, because some of them are addressed to only a small audience or are not high-quality software, like the core of PostgreSQL.

Although contributed software is not a core part of PostgreSQL, it is worth having a closer look at some of the tools. This section presents an overview of the most useful tools included in the contributed section of the PostgreSQL distribution.

cube—A Self-Defined Datatype

Some specific applications have to store information about multidimensional cubes in a database. Cubes need not always be three-dimensional. In some cases, they are even five- or six-dimensional. In addition to storing the data, a huge set of operators and GiST support methods are available. Gene

Selkov, Jr. (a computational scientist at the Mathematics and Computer Science Division atof the Argonne National Laboratory) has implemented this datatype, and we will have you take a closer look at it in this section.

Installing cube

To compile and install this extension, go to the contrib/cube directory in your PostgreSQL source distribution and install the code by using make and `make install`. This will work fine if you have installed PostgreSQL from source.

In the next step, you insert the datatype into the template1 database so that it can be inherited by all databases you will create in the future; it does not affect databases that already exist. You use the following command:

```
[hs@athlon cube]$
psql template1 < cube.sql
```

> **Note**
> If you don't want cube to be inherited by all databases, insert cube.sql into only those databases that you want to support the datatype.

Now that the datatype has successfully been inserted into a database, we can test the datatype by performing a small regression test:

```
[hs@athlon cube]$ make installcheck
make -C ../../src/test/regress pg_regress
make[1]: Entering directory `/usr/src/redhat/SOURCES/postgresql-
7.1.2/src/test/regress'
make[1]: `pg_regress' is up to date.
make[1]: Leaving directory `/usr/src/redhat/SOURCES/postgresql-
7.1.2/src/test/regress'
../../src/test/regress/pg_regress cube
(using postmaster on Unix socket, default port)
============== dropping database "regression"         ==============
ERROR:  DROP DATABASE: database "regression" does not exist
dropdb: database removal failed
============== creating database "regression"         ==============
CREATE DATABASE
============== installing PL/pgSQL                     ==============
============== running regression test queries        ==============
test cube                 ... ok


=====================
 All 1 tests passed.
=====================
```

As you can see, the test has been passed successfully, and therefore it is safe to use `cube` now.

Working with cubes

This section introduces some simple examples of how you can work with cubes efficiently.

Cubes can be one- or multi-dimensional. There are no restrictions on the number of axes a cube might contain. Before starting, we create a database called `contributed`:

```
[hs@athlon cube]$ createdb contributed
CREATE DATABASE
```

The following example shows the easiest way to define a cube:

```
contributed=# SELECT '4'::cube AS cube;
 cube
-------
 (4)
(1 row)
```

You can see that a one-dimensional cube can be defined by casting a `float` value to `cube`. This cube is actually a point, which is the same as a one-dimensional cube.

Let's look at a slightly more complex example, which shows a point in space:

```
contributed=# SELECT '4, 5, 6'::cube AS cube;
   cube
-----------
 (4, 5, 6)
(1 row)
```

We simply have to pass the various values to PostgreSQL by defining a simple list. The list is cast to `cube` in order to tell PostgreSQL, how to treat the input.

The following is an n-dimensional box represented by a pair of opposite corners:

```
contributed=# SELECT '(0,0,0,0),(1,-2,3,-4)'::cube AS cube;
            cube
------------------------------
 (0, 0, 0, 0),(1, -2, 3, -4)
(1 row)
```

This cube starts at (0, 0, 0, 0) and ends at (1, -2, 3, -4). Those two points passed to PostgreSQL define two opposite corners of the cube. When defining the cube, PostgreSQL makes sure that the lower-left is stored first (internally).

If you define cubes, make sure that the points defining the cube have the same dimensionality. If the first element in the cube is represented by a point in four-dimensional space, the second component must also be a four-dimensional point. If it is not, the following error is displayed:

```
contributed=# SELECT '(1,-2,3,-4),(0,0,0)'::cube;
ERROR:   (3) bad cube representation; different point dimensions in (1,-2,3,-4)
and (0,0,0)
```

Sometimes it is necessary to compute the intersection of two cubes. Therefore, cube offers a function called cube_inter. The following shows how it can be used:

```
contributed=# SELECT cube_inter('(1,2,3,4),(0,0,0,0)','(0,0,0,0),(-1,-2,-3,-
4)');
  cube_inter
- - - - - - - - - - - - - -
 (0, 0, 0, 0)
(1 row)
```

The result is (0, 0, 0, 0), because this is the only point the two cubes have in common.

It is not only possible to compute the intersection of two cubes; you also can combine two cubes:

```
contributed=# SELECT cube_union('(1,2,3,4),(0,0,0,0)','(0,0,0,0),(-1,-2,-3,-
4)');
            cube_union
- - - - - - - - - - - - - - - - - - - - - - - - - - - - - -
 (-1, -2, -3, -4),(1, 2, 3, 4)
(1 row)
```

(-1, -2, -3, -4),(1, 2, 3, 4) contains all points that the two cubes passed to the function contain. If you want to combine more than two cubes in one, you combine the list of cubes recursively, as shown in the following example:

```
contributed=# SELECT cube_union(cube_union('(1,2,3,4),(0,0,0,0)','(0,0,0,0),(-
1,-2,-3,-4)'), '(0,0,0,0),(9,-10,11,-12)');
              cube_union
- - - - - - - - - - - - - - - - - - - - - - - - - - - - - - - -
 (-1, -10, -3, -12),(9, 2, 11, 4)
(1 row)
```

To find out whether a cube contains a certain point, cube provides a function called cube_contains. We have to pass a valid cube and a valid point to the function:

```
contributed=# SELECT cube_contains('(1,-2,3,-4),(0,0,0,0)','(0,-1,1,-2)');
 cube_contains
---------------
 t
(1 row)
```

t (true) is returned, which means that the point '0,-1,1,-2' is a part of the cube.

Let's look at the operators. As with all datatypes, = and != operators are provided to check whether two cubes are equal. = and != are essential for the datatype; otherwise, it would be impossible to perform join operations (when performing a join, two values have to be compared, so a = is necessary).

The operators < and > are also defined for cubes:

```
contributed=# SELECT '(0,0,0,0),(1,2,3,4)'::cube < '(0,0,0,0),(2,2,3,4)'::cube;
 ?column?
----------
 t
(1 row)
```

< and > are normally used for sorting (ORDER BY). In most cases, they do not have a practical reason. To show you why these two operators are suitable only for sorting, let's look at how they work.

The first element of each cube is compared, and if the two elements differ, the smaller/higher value has been found. If both values are equal, PostgreSQL checks the second element, and so on.

> **Note**
> < (less than) and > (greater than) have nothing to do with the volume of the two cubes.

cube is based on GiST, which allows the PostgreSQL implementation of R-tree, an index structure for indexing geometric data types, to be used with any data type. GiST supports a set of operators that can be used in combination with a self-defined datatype.

The operator << finds out whether a cube is left of another cube:

```
contributed=# SELECT '(-2,-3),(-1,-2)'::cube << '(0,0),(2,2)'::cube;
 ?column?
----------
 t
(1 row)
```

'(-2,-3),(-1,-2)' is left of '(0,0),(2,2)', so true is returned. The counterpart of the << operator is the >> operator used to find out whether a cube is on the right side of the second cube defined.

Some other operators are also defined for cubes. The following table lists the most important operators defined for cubes:

Operator	Meaning
<<	Left of
>>	Right of
&<	Left over
&>	Right over
&&	Overlaps
=	Equal
!=	Not equal
@	Contains
~	Contained in

cube and Indices

When working with large amounts of data, it is necessary to define indices in order to speed up queries. To show you how to define an index on a column, we create a table called mycubes:

```
contributed=# CREATE TABLE mycubes(a cube DEFAULT '0,0'::cube);
CREATE
```

We define an index of type gist. PostgreSQL supports a number of different types of indexing a column. gist is the appropriate type in this case:

```
contributed=# CREATE INDEX cube_idx ON mycubes USING gist (a);
CREATE
```

To find out more about indexing, refer to Chapter 3, "An Introduction to SQL." Now that we have defined the table and the index, we can have a look at the overview of the table:

```
contributed=# \d mycubes
            Table "mycubes"
 Attribute | Type |        Modifier
-----------+------+------------------------
 a         | cube | default '(0, 0)'::cube
Index: cube_idx
```

Working with `fulltext` Indices

The more data you have to process, the longer queries will take if no indices are used. Indices are efficient data structures, which enable the database to access single rows or groups of rows much faster. If no indices are used, the database has to perform a so called *sequential scan* (or *full table scan*), which means that a table has to be read from the beginning to the end. On large tables, this can take a lot of time, and the overall performance of your database system will slow down significantly.

The Problem with Indices and Substring Searching

Not all problems can be solved by defining an index. The next example shows a common problem in combining indices and PostgreSQL:

We define a table, which contains one text column. We also define an index for that column in order to access the column fast:

```
fulltext=# \d mytexts
        Table "mytexts"
 Attribute | Type | Modifier
-----------+------+----------
 a         | text |
Index: mytext_idx
```

We insert four records into the table:

```
fulltext=# SELECT * FROM mytexts;
    a
---------
 Charles
 Paul
 Etschi
 Epi
(4 rows)
```

To make sure that the database does not perform a sequential scan, if it is not absolutely necessary to complete the query, we set `enable_seqscan` to `off`:

```
fulltext=# SET enable_seqscan TO off;
SET VARIABLE
```

In the next step, we perform a query to look for `Etschi`:

```
fulltext=# SELECT * FROM mytexts WHERE a='Etschi';
    a
--------
```

```
Etschi
(1 row)
```

As we have expected, one record has been found in the table. Let's look at the execution plan of the query:

```
fulltext=# EXPLAIN SELECT * FROM mytexts WHERE a='Etschi';
NOTICE:  QUERY PLAN:

Index Scan using mytext_idx on mytexts  (cost=0.00..2.01 rows=1 width=12)

EXPLAIN
```

The database performs an index scan to find the result as fast as possible.

> **Note**
> If enable_seqscan is not turned off, PostgreSQL still performs a sequential scan, because the table is too small to justify the overhead of using an index. The gist of the example is that an index scan can be used by the database.

The ituation will be different if we use ~ (case-sensitive regular expression) instead of =:

```
fulltext=# SELECT * FROM mytexts WHERE a ~ 'Etschi';
    a
--------
 Etschi
(1 row)
```

The result is still the same because we look for the full record, but the execution plan has changed:

```
fulltext=# EXPLAIN SELECT * FROM mytexts WHERE a ~ 'Etschi';
NOTICE:  QUERY PLAN:

Seq Scan on mytexts  (cost=100000000.00..100000001.15 rows=1 width=12)

EXPLAIN
```

The database has to perform a sequential scan, although enable_seqscan has been turned off. Unfortunately, that substring searching cannot be done with indices in PostgreSQL. To get rid of the problem, we can use the fulltextindex package in the contributed directory of the PostgreSQL source code.

The package is not an extremely sophisticated solution, but it will solve most of the problems people normally have in combination with substring searching.

Working with the `fulltextindex` Package

Installing the package on your PostgreSQL server is an easy task. Go to the contrib/fulltextindex directory in your PostgreSQL source tree and use `make` and `make install`.

The target of the next example is to have the opportunity to perform substring searching on table `mytexts`. Therefore, we write an SQL script:

```
-- creating a function needed for fulltext searching
CREATE FUNCTION fti() RETURNS opaque AS
        '/usr/local/postgresql/lib/contrib/fti.so' LANGUAGE 'C';

-- creating a table to store the substrings
CREATE TABLE mytexts_fti (string varchar(25), id oid);

-- creating the table that will contain the "real" data
CREATE TABLE mytexts(a text);

-- creating indices
CREATE INDEX mytexts_fti_idx ON mytexts_fti (string);
CREATE INDEX mytexts_idx ON mytexts (a);

-- creating a trigger that causes the substrings to be created
CREATE TRIGGER mytexts_fti_trigger AFTER update OR insert OR delete ON mytexts
FOR EACH ROW EXECUTE PROCEDURE fti(mytexts_fti, a);

-- inserting data into the "real" table
COPY mytexts FROM stdin;
Charles
Paul
Etschi
Epi
\.

-- vacuuming db
VACUUM VERBOSE ANALYZE;
```

The idea behind the whole package is to define a trigger, which splits up all data inserted into a column and stores a list of substrings in a separate table that can easily be indexed. First we create a function called `fti`, which will be needed by the trigger processing every record inserted into `mytexts`.

> **Note**
> The path to the shared object might differ on your system and depends on the
> location where you have installed PostgreSQL.

In the next step we define a table labeled `mytexts_fti` that will contain all substrings
and `mytexts` (the table containing the original values). After that, we index all columns
involved in the process; we define three indices.

Now that all indices and tables are ready, we can define the trigger. In the previous
source code, it is executed on every insert, update, or delete operation. This is
necessary to keep the table containing the substrings maintained. Depending on the
event the trigger is fired for, the action performed by the `fti` function differs. This is
possible, because the function can access special variables containing the reason that
has caused the trigger to be fired (see Chapter 4, "PL/PGSQL").

The most crucial part, when defining the trigger, is the list of parameters the `fti`
function has to be called with. The first parameter defines the relation in which to
store the substrings. The second trigger tells the function which field to extract
substrings from. The table we want the substrings to be added to has to look like the
one in the next example:

```
fulltext=# \d mytexts_fti
           Table "mytexts_fti"
 Attribute |          Type          | Modifier
-----------+------------------------+----------
 string    | character varying(25)  |
 id        | oid                    |
```

The first column has to contain the text, and the second column must contain the
object id of the row containing the full string. If the data structure differs, the trigger
cannot be executed successfully.

After adding the script we have just discussed to the database, here is the content of
the two tables involved in the process now:

```
fulltext=# SELECT * FROM mytexts;
    a
---------
 Charles
 Paul
 Etschi
 Epi
(4 rows)
```

The `mytexts` table contains the records, as we saw before. `mytexts_fti` contains a list of substrings and an object id:

```
fulltext=# SELECT * FROM mytexts_fti;
 string  |    id
---------+----------
 es      | 20272538
 les     | 20272538
 rles    | 20272538
 arles   | 20272538
 harles  | 20272538
 charles | 20272538
 ul      | 20272539
 aul     | 20272539
 paul    | 20272539
 hi      | 20272540
 chi     | 20272540
 schi    | 20272540
 tschi   | 20272540
 etschi  | 20272540
 pi      | 20272541
 epi     | 20272541
(16 rows)
```

The list of the substrings is several times longer than the original list, and an additional column is needed to refer to the original list. When working with huge amounts of data, this costs a lot of storage.

Here's how we can perform the substring search now:

```
SELECT p.*
       FROM mytexts p, mytexts_fti f1
       WHERE f1.string='schi'
             AND p.oid=f1.id;
```

To compute the same result we achieved with the help of the ~ operator, we have to perform a join operation now. At first sight this seems more complicated—especially for more complex queries. To get rid of the additional complexity, a view can be defined. Here is the result of the previous query:

```
   a
--------
 Etschi
(1 row)
```

Let's look at the execution plan of the query now. To avoid sequential scans, we set enable_seqscan to off again (this has to be done for every session, respectively, for every new backend):

```
fulltext=# SET enable_seqscan TO off;
SET VARIABLE
fulltext=# EXPLAIN SELECT p.* FROM mytexts p, mytexts_fti f1 WHERE
f1.string='schi' AND p.oid=f1.id;
NOTICE:  QUERY PLAN:

Nested Loop  (cost=100000000.00..100000003.10 rows=1 width=20)
  -> Index Scan using mytexts_fti_idx1 on mytexts_fti f1  (cost=0.00..2.01
rows=1 width=4)
  -> Seq Scan on mytexts p  (cost=100000000.00..100000001.04 rows=4 width=16)

EXPLAIN
```

The database still performs a sequential scan on oid. We have not defined an index on that column yet, because we want to say a few more words about that index. Every object in PostgreSQL has a unique object identifier. In case of rows, these object identifiers do not appear in the table when using \d, but it can be indexed like any other column. Let's index the column:

```
fulltext=# CREATE INDEX mytexts_fti_idx3 ON mytexts(oid);
CREATE
```

Now that all columns needed for the join operation are indexed, let's look at the execution plan again:

```
fulltext=# EXPLAIN SELECT p.* FROM mytexts p, mytexts_fti f1 WHERE
f1.string='schi' AND p.oid=f1.id;
NOTICE:  QUERY PLAN:

Nested Loop  (cost=0.00..4.04 rows=1 width=20)
  -> Index Scan using mytexts_fti_idx1 on mytexts_fti f1  (cost=0.00..2.01
rows=1 width=4)
  -> Index Scan using mytexts_fti_idx3 on mytexts p  (cost=0.00..2.01 rows=1
width=16)

EXPLAIN
```

PostgreSQL uses two indices now. When the amount of data grows, the query won't slow down significantly (at least not as much).

Working with ISBN and ISSN

At the Third International Conference on Book Market Research and Rationalization in the Book Trade, held in November 1966 in Berlin, an international numbering system for books was first discussed. Some publishers were already thinking of a computer-based system to make identification and numbering easier.

The International Standard Book Number (ISBN) system was developed out of the book numbering system introduced in the United Kingdom in 1967 by J. Whitaker & Sons, Ltd., and in the United States in 1968 by R. R. Bowker.

The International Organization for Standardization (ISO) Technical Committee 46 on Information and Documentation finally investigated whether it was possible to use the English standard as the worldwide standard for book identification. Finally, ISBN was approved as ISO standard 2108 in 1970.

Now ISBN is an international standard used by publishers all over the world, and every new book is assigned to a unique ISBN number.

In this section, you explore the ISBN module, which was contributed to PostgreSQL by Garrett A. Wollman in 1998.

To show you how you can work with ISBN as a datatype, we create a table containing two columns:

```
isbnissn=# CREATE TABLE myisbn(name text, number isbn);
CREATE
```

Let's insert a record into the table:

```
isbnissn=# INSERT INTO myisbn VALUES('Apache Administration', '3-8266-0554-3');
INSERT 20273569 1
```

As you can see, the record has been inserted successfully, because the number we passed to the INSERT statement is a valid ISBN number. If we query the table, we can see that the value is stored in the table:

```
isbnissn=# SELECT * FROM myisbn;
         name          |    number
-----------------------+---------------
 Apache Administration | 3-8266-0554-3
(1 row)
```

Let's try it with an invalid ISBN number:

```
isbnissn=# INSERT INTO myisbn VALUES('no book', '324324324324234');
ERROR:  isbn_in: invalid ISBN "324324324324234"
```

The ISBN module makes sure that no invalid ISBN numbers can be inserted into a field. But why do we have to use a self-defined datatype, if we can also use something like char(16)? The reason for that is simple. Imagine a user interface where someone can insert data into a table. If we used char(16), it would hardly be possible to check whether the input was okay or to work with operators such as < and >. These two operators cannot hardly be defined for character types.

Let's look at the next example. We try to figure out whether the ISBN of the book *Barbarians Led by Bill Gates* is smaller than the ISBN of the book about Apache:

```
isbnissn=# SELECT * FROM myisbn WHERE number>'3-8266-0506-3'::isbn;
        name          |     number
----------------------+---------------
 Apache Administration | 3-8266-0554-3
(1 row)
```

The book about Bill Gates is newer than the book about Apache, so it is still displayed in the list. This example shows why to use such datatypes.

The module also supports ISSN. The International Standard Serial Number (ISSN) is a code used on catalogs, databases, and commercial transactions each time serial publications are involved. It is also universally used.

PostgreSQL Large Object Dumper

You have already learned that binary large objects cannot be dumped as easily as other datatypes. The PostgreSQL large object dumper (pg_dumplo) by Karel Zak provides an easy way to do the job and is easy to use.

Backup

To install the package, we go to the contrib/pg_dumplo directory in the PostgreSQL source tree and use make and make install. With these commands, the software is compiled and installed on the system.

Let's get to some examples and see how pg_dumplo can be used. First we create a table where we will store the object handle:

```
lodumper=# CREATE TABLE lo (id oid);
CREATE
```

Then we import a simple ASCII file into the table. To show you how that can be done, we use the /etc/passwd file.

```
lodumper=# \lo_import /etc/passwd
lo_import 20273581
```

The table is still empty because we have imported only the file into the database; this does not mean that the object id is automatically inserted into the table:

```
lodumper=# SELECT * FROM lo;
 id
----
(0 rows)
```

To insert the object handle into the table, we perform a simple INSERT statement:

```
lodumper=# INSERT INTO lo VALUES (20273581);
INSERT 20273583 1
```

> **Note**
> The id passed to the INSERT statement has to be the id returned by the import function.

As you can see, the table contains one record now:

```
lodumper=# SELECT * FROM lo;
    id
----------
 20273581
(1 row)
```

Now that we have added a large object to the database, we can show you how to back up a table containing binary objects only. For backup purposes, we use pg_dumplo. Here is a syntax overview of the program:

```
[hs@athlon pg_dumplo]$ pg_dumplo --help

pg_dumplo 7.1.0 - PostgreSQL large objects dump
pg_dumplo [option]

-h --help                  this help
-u --user=<username>       username for connection to server
-p --password=<password>   password for connection to server
-d --db=<database>         database name
-t --host=<hostname>       server hostname
-s --space=<dir>           directory with dump tree (for export/import)
-i --import                import large obj dump tree to DB
-e --export                export (dump) large obj to dump tree
-l <table.attr ...>        dump attribute (columns) with LO to dump tree
-a --all                   dump all LO in DB (default)
-r --remove                if is set '-i' try remove old LO
```

```
-q --quiet              run quietly
-w --show               not dump, but show all LO in DB

Example (dump):    pg_dumplo -d my_db -s /my_dump/dir -l t1.a t1.b t2.a
                   pg_dumplo -a -d my_db -s /my_dump/dir
Example (import):  pg_dumplo -i -d my_db -s /my_dump/dir
Example (show):    pg_dumplo -w -d my_db

Note:   * option '-l' must be last option!
        * option '-i' without option '-r' make new large obj in DB
          not rewrite old, the '-i' UPDATE oid numbers in table.attr only!
        * if is not set option -s, the pg_dumplo use $PWD
```

To back up the table, we can use a command like this one:

```
[hs@athlon test]$ pg_dumplo -s . -d lodumper -l lo.id
dump lo.id (1 large obj)

Exported 1 large objects.
```

You can see that one object has been saved to disk successfully. The `-s` flag defines the directory where the result of the dump has to be stored. In this example, we want the output to be saved in the current directory. The `-d` flag defines the database we want to dump, and `-l` tells `pg_dumplo` which columns have to be dumped.

After executing the shell command, here is the output:

```
[hs@athlon test]$ tree *
lodumper
|-- lo
|   `-- id
|       `-- 20273581
`-- lo_dump.index

2 directories, 2 files
```

`pg_dumplo` organizes the output in subfolders. The object ids of the various files are taken as filenames so that the objects can easily be identified. The file `lo_dump.index` contains a list of the dumped objects:

```
#
# This is the PostgreSQL large object dump index
#
#       Date:    Sun Jul 22 17:24:27 2001
```

```
#       Host:     localhost
#       Database: lodumper
#       User:     hs
#
# oid   table   attribut        infile
#
20273581        lo      id      lodumper/lo/id/20273581
```

This file is needed for restoring the backup.

Recovery

Now that we have dumped the BLOBs in our database, we want to have a look at the recovery process, because dumping the files without knowing how to perform the recovery process is not useful.

The file we created before is not enough for recovering a database completely, because only information about BLOBs is stored. Therefore we have to perform an ordinary pg_dump:

```
[hs@athlon lodumper]$ pg_dump lodumper > lo.sql
```

Let's look at the recovery process. First we create the database where the data will be inserted during the recovery process. In the next step, we insert the dump of the database into the database we just created:

```
[hs@athlon lodumper]$ createdb lodumper
CREATE DATABASE
[hs@athlon lodumper]$ psql lodumper < lo.sql
```

All data but the binary objects have been inserted into our database; next we deal with the BLOBs:

```
[hs@athlon lodumper]$ pg_dumplo -s /tmp/test -i -d lodumper
20273581        lo      id      lodumper/lo/id/20273581

Imported 1 large objects.
```

The recovery process works just like the backup process. We use the -i flag to tell pg_dumplo that an import has to be performed instead of an export.

pg_dump and pg_dumplo are two reliable programs for saving databases. However, there is one problem you have to be aware of when working with the two programs: When dumping a database with pg_dump, the database makes sure that a consistent snapshot of the database is saved to disk. pg_dumplo also makes sure that no inconsistent data is saved, but if the two scripts are executed one after the other, it cannot be guaranteed that both scripts will see the same snapshot of the database. Consider this in production environments; otherwise, you might have problems during the recovery process.

Benchmarking with pgbench

To perform simple benchmarks, you can use a program called pgbench, which can be found in contrib/pgbench in your PostgreSQL sources. Compiling and installing the program works just like the installation process for the software, we have already presented (use make and make install).

The program pgbench provides many command-line flags. Here is an overview of all options provided by the program:

```
[hs@athlon pgbench]$ ./pgbench --help
./pgbench: invalid option -- -
usage: pgbench [-h hostname][-p port][-c nclients][-t ntransactions][-s
scaling_factor][-n][-v][-S][-d][dbname]
(initialize mode): pgbench -i [-h hostname][-p port][-s scaling_factor][-
d][dbname]
```

As you can see, we have quite a lot of options to define the way the benchmark has to be processed. Beside the flags needed to define the host and the database we want to benchmark, we can use the -c flag to tell pgbench the number of clients simulated by the benchmarking software. The -s flag defines the scaling factor, which influences the size of the test database (if it is set to 100, 10 million records will be used for testing). -t sets the size of a transaction.

Before we can start the benchmark, we have to initialize the database, which can be done by using the -i flag:

```
[hs@athlon pgbench]$ ./pgbench -i pgbench
NOTICE:  CREATE TABLE/PRIMARY KEY will create implicit index 'branches_pkey' for
table 'branches'
NOTICE:  CREATE TABLE/PRIMARY KEY will create implicit index 'tellers_pkey' for
table 'tellers'
NOTICE:  CREATE TABLE/PRIMARY KEY will create implicit index 'accounts_pkey' for
table 'accounts'
creating tables...
10000 tuples done.
20000 tuples done.
30000 tuples done.
40000 tuples done.
```

```
50000 tuples done.
60000 tuples done.
70000 tuples done.
80000 tuples done.
90000 tuples done.
100000 tuples done.
vacuum...done.
```

The test is performed with 100,000 records. If -s is set, the number of records is changed.

Let's perform a test:

```
[hs@athlon pgbench]$ ./pgbench pgbench -c 20 -t 100
starting vacuum...end.
transaction type: TPC-B (sort of)
scaling factor: 1
number of clients: 20
number of transactions per client: 100
number of transactions actually processed: 2000/2000
tps = 76.807278(including connections establishing)
tps = 78.277629(excluding connections establishing)
```

Our test system can perform around 77 transactions per second (tps). Depending on the type of benchmark we run (size of transaction, and so forth), this value changes significantly.

The seg module

Often, scientific results contain intervals of floating-point numbers. Although it is possible to model an interval with the help of two columns, it is, in most cases, not the most elegant way to solve the problem. In view of these problems, a datatype called seg has been developed to perform all important operations in combination with intervals on PostgreSQL.

The seg package has been developed by Gene Selkov, Jr. and can be found in the contrib/seg directory of the PostgreSQL source tree. In this section, you take a closer look at this module and see how it can be used efficiently.

After compiling the module using make and make install, we insert the SQL code for adding the seg module to our database with the following command:

```
[hs@athlon seg]$ psql myseg < seg.sql
```

If the SQL script can be added without any problems, seg is available in the database called myseg now. To make sure that everything is working correctly, we perform a small regression test:

```
[hs@athlon seg]$ make installcheck
make -C ../../src/test/regress pg_regress
make[1]: Entering directory `/data/postgresql-7.1.3/src/test/regress'
make[1]: `pg_regress' is up to date.
make[1]: Leaving directory `/data/postgresql-7.1.3/src/test/regress'
../../src/test/regress/pg_regress seg
(using postmaster on Unix socket, default port)
============== dropping database "regression"        ==============
ERROR:  DROP DATABASE: database "regression" does not exist
dropdb: database removal failed
============== creating database "regression"        ==============
CREATE DATABASE
============== installing PL/pgSQL                    ==============
============== running regression test queries       ==============
test seg              ... ok


=====================
 All 1 tests passed.
=====================
```

The test has been passed successfully, so we can start to work with the module safely. First we create a table consisting of one column:

```
myseg=# CREATE TABLE myseg (a seg);
CREATE
```

The next examples show how data can be added to the table:

```
myseg=# INSERT INTO myseg VALUES ('1');
INSERT 24800338 1
myseg=# INSERT INTO myseg VALUES ('2.0');
INSERT 24800339 1
myseg=# INSERT INTO myseg VALUES ('3.00');
INSERT 24800340 1
myseg=# INSERT INTO myseg VALUES ('~ 4.00');
INSERT 24800341 1
myseg=# INSERT INTO myseg VALUES ('< 5.00');
INSERT 24800342 1
myseg=# INSERT INTO myseg VALUES ('> 6.00');
INSERT 24800343 1
```

Now that we have added six records to the table, we check whether the records have been inserted successfully:

```
myseg=# SELECT * FROM myseg;
   a
- - - - - - -
 1
 2.0
 3.00
 ~4.00
 <5.00
 >6.00
(6 rows)
```

All six records are stored in the table. Let's take a closer look at the INSERT statements now. You might wonder why the first three values have been defined with different precision and why the database seems to distinguish the amount of digits on the right side of the comma. The reason lies in the way scientists report results. In scientific environments, it makes a difference whether the value is 1.0 or 1.00. Every digit in the number is a reliable one. 1.00 means that both digits right of the comma are reliable; therefore, 1.0 is not as precise as 1.00. The seg datatype takes care of things such as that. In record four, ~ means *approximately* and tells the user that the value is not defined in full precision. ~, < and > have no influence over how the record is treated, but they help the user interpret the meaning of a value correctly.

In many cases, the seg datatype is used to define an interval of values:

```
myseg=# INSERT INTO myseg VALUES ('7(+-)0.3');
INSERT 24800344 1
```

This example shows how an interval can be defined. In the next example, we define an interval ranging from 6.7 to 7.3:

```
myseg=# INSERT INTO myseg VALUES ('6.7 .. 7.3');
INSERT 24800345 1
```

Intervals do not need to have an upper or a lower border. If you want an interval to contain all values that are equal or higher than 8, we define it like the following:

```
myseg=# INSERT INTO myseg VALUES ('8 ..');
INSERT 24800346 1
```

After inserting various records, we want to retrieve values from the table. In contrast to other datatypes, there are a few things, that have to be considered.

As you have seen before, we inserted the interval `'7(+-)0.3'` into the database twice. Let's look for a value that is exactly 7:

```
myseg=# SELECT * FROM myseg WHERE a='7'::seg;
 a
---
(0 rows)
```

No records are retrieved, because no records are exactly 7. Let's find all values that are higher than 7:

```
myseg=# SELECT * FROM myseg WHERE a>'7'::seg;
  a
------
 8 ..
(1 row)
```

One record is found—the only record that is entirely higher than 7. The interval `'7(+-)0.3'` is not found, because a part of the interval is smaller than 7.

If we want our result to contain the entire interval, we need a query like this one:

```
myseg=# SELECT * FROM myseg WHERE a>'6.6'::seg;
     a
-----------
 6.7 .. 7.3
 6.7 .. 7.3
 8 ..
(3 rows)
```

seg has been built on the GiST interface, which is a generalized interface to R-trees (the ones used for spatial searching). When using this interface, some operators are always defined. The next example shows how we can find all records containing 7:

```
myseg=# SELECT * FROM myseg WHERE a @ '7'::seg;
     a
-----------
 6.7 .. 7.3
 6.7 .. 7.3
(2 rows)
```

As we expect, two records are returned.

The following table lists operators supported by the datatype:

Operator	Meaning
<<	Left of
>>	Right of
&<	Left over
&>	Right over
&&	Overlaps
=	Equal
!=	Not equal
@	Contains
~	Contained in

The soundex Code

This section introduces the soundex module, which implements the soundex code as a PostgreSQL user-defined function.

The Soundex system is a method of matching similar- sounding names (or any words) to the same code. In 1880, 1900, and 1910, the code was used by the United States Census Bureau. The idea behind the system is to retrieve similar-sounding values.

To install the module, we go to the soundex directory in the contributed section of our PostgreSQL sources and run make and make install. Then we add the required function to a database (in our example, the database is called soundex):

```
[hs@athlon soundex]$ psql soundex < soundex.sql
CREATE
CREATE
```

We define a table called mysoundex:

```
soundex=# \d mysoundex
      Table "mysoundex"
 Attribute | Type | Modifier
-----------+------+----------
 a         | text |
```

In the next step we insert two records into that table:

```
soundex=# INSERT INTO mysoundex VALUES('John');
INSERT 24800378 1
soundex=# INSERT INTO mysoundex VALUES('Joan');
INSERT 24800379 1
```

Before we try to retrieve the value from the database, we try to find out what the text_soundex function does:

```
soundex=# SELECT text_soundex('john');
 text_soundex
--------------
 J500
(1 row)
```

A code is generated that is based on the value that has to be encoded. The records sound similar, and the target is to retrieve both records from the table:

```
soundex=# SELECT * FROM mysoundex WHERE text_soundex(a) = text_soundex('john');
   a
------
 John
 Joan
(2 rows)
```

With the help of the text_soundex function, we compute the soundex code of john and compare it with the soundex code of the values in the table. If the soundex code of john and the soundex code of the value in the table match, the row is retrieved.

> **Note**
> The database has to perform a sequential scan; if we use a query such as the next one, PostgreSQL cannot use indices.

Let's search for josef and see what we can find:

```
soundex=# SELECT * FROM mysoundex WHERE text_soundex(a) = text_soundex('josef');
 a
---
(0 rows)
```

No values are retrieved, because josef has a different soundex code, as we can see in the next example:

```
soundex=# SELECT text_soundex('josef');
 text_soundex
--------------
 J210
(1 row)
```

Removing Lost Binary Objects from a Database

When inserting a binary large object into a database, an object id is generated and the new object can be accessed using this object id. If the object id is not inserted into a table immediately, the object id might get lost and the object will become an *orphan*. A tool called vacuumlo has been implemented to remove orphaned large objects from a PostgreSQL database.

To install the tool, we go to the contrib/vacuumlo directory in the source tree of PostgreSQL and run make and make install. After installing the software, we have a look at the syntax overview of the command:

```
[hs@athlon vacuumlo]$ ./vacuumlo
Usage: ./vacuumlo [-v] database_name [db2 ... dbn]
```

The -v flag (verbose) tells the program to tell the user something about the output. If it's not defined, vacuumlo performs the job silently. Let's run the program:

```
[hs@athlon vacuumlo]$ ./vacuumlo -v lodumper
Connected to lodumper
Checking id in lo
Removed 3 large objects from lodumper.
```

Three objects have been removed from the database. vacuumlo is a reliable and useful tool for all database administrators that have to do some database cleaning. If applications accessing a database have not been implemented properly, BLOBs might get lost. In this case, database administrators have to deal with trash and growing databases. vacuumlo can solve all these problems once and forever, if you start it from time to time using cron.

pg_controldata

You might be annoyed if you have to collect information about your database. That was exactly the problem Oliver Elphick had to face when he implemented pg_controldata, which collects information about the database quickly and reliably.

To run the program, we have to set the environment variable $PGDATA first:

```
[root@athlon pg_controldata]# export PGDATA=/var/lib/pgsql/data/
```

Then we can run the program:

```
[root@athlon pg_controldata]# pg_controldata
pg_control version number:            71
Catalog version number:               200101061
```

```
Database state:                        IN_PRODUCTION
pg_control last modified:              Tue Jul 24 14:32:08 2001
Current log file id:                   0
Next log file segment:                 164
Latest checkpoint location:            0/A31CD444
Prior checkpoint location:             0/A31CD404
Latest checkpoint's REDO location:     0/A31CD444
Latest checkpoint's UNDO location:     0/0
Latest checkpoint's StartUpID:         96
Latest checkpoint's NextXID:           41410
Latest checkpoint's NextOID:           24800380
Time of latest checkpoint:             Mon Jul 23 18:31:01 2001
Database block size:                   8192
Blocks per segment of large relation:  131072
LC_COLLATE:                            C
LC_CTYPE:                              C
```

Several values are collected and printed on the screen. Some of these messages might be useful for you, others are not. No matter which information you want to retrieve, pg_controldata offers an easy and reliable way to do the job.

Administration Tools

Some graphical interfacing with PostgreSQL is already available. In this section, you learn to use phpPgAdmin.

phpPgAdmin

One of the most widespread administration tools in the world of PostgreSQL is phpPgAdmin. The tool has been implemented in PHP and therefore can easily be modified. phpPgAdmin is easy to use and provides a lot of useful functions in a reliable way. Because the application is written in PHP, the tool has to be accessed via a Web browser. We recommend running it in a protected directory of your Web server, to make sure that no unauthorized people can access phpPgAdmin on your system.

```
phpPgAdmin is available under the terms of the GNU General Public License and
can be downloaded from the following URL:
http://freshmeat.net/projects/phppgadmin/
```

Installing phpPgAdmin

After downloading the software, you install it on your system. First, unpack the `tar` archive that you downloaded with the following shell command:

```
[hs@athlon /tmp]$ tar xvfz phpPgAdmin_2-3.tar.gz
```

You have to unpack the code in a directory, which can be accessed by your Web server, in order to run phpPgAdmin. If the source code has been installed properly, you configure the software by editing the file config.inc.php, which can be found in the directory containing the sources of phpPgAdmin.

We go to line 56 (in our version of phpPgAdmin) and create a new user who can access all databases. Here is an example:

```
$cfgServers[1]['local']      = true;
$cfgServers[1]['host']       = 'localhost';
$cfgServers[1]['port']       = '5432';
$cfgServers[1]['adv_auth']   = true;
$cfgServers[1]['stduser']    = 'hs';
$cfgServers[1]['stdpass']    = 'apassword';
$cfgServers[1]['user']       = 'hs';
$cfgServers[1]['password']   = 'apassword';
$cfgServers[1]['only_db']    = '';   // if set to a db-name, only this db is
accessible
```

User hs is allowed to log into phpPgAdmin in order to administer and modify the database now.

You can see in the config file that a lot of other things can be configured as well. Every parameter that can be modified in that file is documented, and it should be an easy task to set up a configuration for your PostgreSQL server.

Working with phpPgAdmin

When you have successfully configured the server, you log into the administration tool by using the Web interface (index.php). You have to use the user and the password that you have just defined. If the authentification succeeds, weyou can start working with PostgreSQL now. Figure 10.1 shows the user interface.

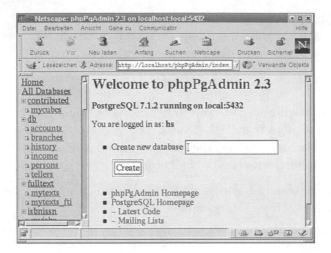

Figure 10.1
The phpPgAdmin user interface.

On the left side of the screen is a list of all databases on the system, including the list of tables that each database contains. It can be accessed by clicking the item that you want to see more information about, in the right frame of the site.

A lot of functions are provided. You can create or drop tables, browse the data, or perform tasks such as defining an index. Nearly all things can be done with the help of a simple mouse click, because the tool is intuitional and easy to use.

PART II

Practical PostgreSQL Solutions

CHAPTER

CHAPTER **11**

Importing Data and Working with Binary Data

When setting up a PostgreSQL server, migrating data to PostgreSQL is one of the first hurdles you have to clear. Although importing data is not difficult, it is important to know the fundamentals. In addition to that, it can also be useful to know how other formats can be treated. This is extremely important in hybrid environments. In this chapter, you will learn to import data into PostgreSQL and deal with EBCDIC data.

Importing ASCII and Binary Data Using COPY

Although it is only covered in a few pages in most books, importing data in various formats into your database is an extremely difficult task for a database administrator, because the data in a database doesn't usually come from nowhere. The way data has to be inserted into your PostgreSQL server can differ, depending on the type and the amount of data you have to process.

The easiest case is to have a file that contains the output of a pg_dump command. Importing will be an easy task, because you only have to create a database and insert the data with a simple shell command:

```
psql yourdatabase < pg_dump-file.sql
```

Unfortunately, not everybody uses PostgreSQL's data format to exchange data. If large amounts of data have to be imported, it is usually done with the help of ASCII files. These files can either have record or variable record lengths.

Fixed record length means that one line of data has a fixed and predefined length and consists of fields that also have a fixed size. This format is a very comfortable one, because the fields of a row can very easily be extracted using simple substring operations.

Another possibility is to use variable record length in combination with a delimiter. The beginning of a field is not defined by a fixed position but is symbolized by a delimiter field. Every time the delimiter is found in a row, that system knows the next column has begun.

To show you, how a simple ASCII file with variable record length can be imported, we create a table called homes we use to store a row ID, the name of a person, and the city and the country from which a person comes:

```
CREATE TABLE homes(id int4, name text, city text, country text);
```

The most important command when importing files is the COPY command. The following is a short overview of the command's syntax:

```
import=# \h COPY
Command:    COPY
Description: Copies data between files and tables
Syntax:
COPY [ BINARY ] table [ WITH OIDS ]
    FROM { 'filename' | stdin }
    [ [USING] DELIMITERS 'delimiter' ]
    [ WITH NULL AS 'null string' ]
COPY [ BINARY ] table [ WITH OIDS ]
    TO { 'filename' | stdout }
    [ [USING] DELIMITERS 'delimiter' ]
    [ WITH NULL AS 'null string' ]
```

You can see that the COPY command can even import binary data and read from standard input. To show you how COPY works, we will import data in the following file:

```
1;Julia;London;England
2;Paul;Vienna;Austria
3;Linda;Miami;USA
```

```
4;Etschi;Tokyo;Japan
5;Chris;Berlin;Germany
```

The file consists of four columns separated by a semicolon. Importing the file is an easy task. We have to define the table where we want to add the data, the file we want to import, and the delimiter:

```
import=# COPY homes FROM '/mnt/data/code/import.txt' USING DELIMITERS ';';
COPY
```

If no error is displayed, the data has successfully been inserted into the table:

```
import=# SELECT * FROM homes;
 id |  name  |  city  | country
----+--------+--------+---------
  1 | Julia  | London | England
  2 | Paul   | Vienna | Austria
  3 | Linda  | Miami  | USA
  4 | Etschi | Tokyo  | Japan
  5 | Chris  | Berlin | Germany
(5 rows)
```

During the input process, it might happen that the database displays an error, such as the one shown next. Errors like that occur if the columns defined in the input file do not match the number of columns in your table. If your table is too "small," PostgreSQL will simply omit columns in the input file, but the import does not fail.

```
NOTICE:  copy: line 1, CopyReadNewline: extra fields ignored
NOTICE:  copy: line 2, CopyReadNewline: extra fields ignored
NOTICE:  copy: line 3, CopyReadNewline: extra fields ignored
NOTICE:  copy: line 4, CopyReadNewline: extra fields ignored
NOTICE:  copy: line 5, CopyReadNewline: extra fields ignored
```

Before importing data, you also have to make sure that every cell in the file can be converted to the required data type by the database; otherwise, the import fails.

Let's see, what happens if we change the content of the first column:

```
x;Julia;London;England
x;Paul;Vienna;Austria
x;Linda;Miami;USA
x;Etschi;Tokyo;Japan
x;Chris;Berlin;Germany
```

If we set the value in the first field to x, the database cannot cast the data to `integer`.

```
import=# COPY homes FROM '/mnt/data/code/import.txt' USING DELIMITERS ';';
ERROR:  copy: line 1, pg_atoi: error in "x": can't parse "x"
```

PostgreSQL displays a `pg_atoi` error and aborts the process.

Another important issue is that the import is executed by the database as one transaction. Let's change the values of the first column in the first two lines to a valid number:

```
8;Julia;London;England
9;Paul;Vienna;Austria
x;Linda;Miami;USA
x;Etschi;Tokyo;Japan
x;Chris;Berlin;Germany
```

Importing this data will fail because the first column in the third line cannot be converted into `integer`. Most of us might have expected that these two records would be imported by PostgreSQL, but this won't happen. If we take a look at the content of the table after the import, we can see that the table still contains the same data as before:

```
import=# SELECT * FROM homes ;
 id |  name  |  city  | country
----+--------+--------+---------
  1 | Julia  | London | England
  2 | Paul   | Vienna | Austria
  3 | Linda  | Miami  | USA
  4 | Etschi | Tokyo  | Japan
  5 | Chris  | Berlin | Germany
(5 rows)
```

In this case, PostgreSQL's transaction code is very comfortable, because importing very huge amounts of data will mostly lead to trouble. It is rather unlikely that a file with millions of rows does not contain a single error if the file has been created by someone who is not used to working with PostgreSQL.

Exporting a table is just as simple as importing a file:

```
COPY homes TO '/tmp/file.txt';
```

This command creates a file called `file.txt` located in `/tmp`. By default, PostgreSQL uses tabs for separating the columns:

```
1       Julia   London  England
2       Paul    Vienna  Austria
3       Linda   Miami   USA
4       Etschi  Tokyo   Japan
5       Chris   Berlin  Germany
```

The data can also be exported using a binary format. This can have some advantages, but it is generally easier to use ASCII text instead.

```
COPY BINARY homes TO '/tmp/file.bin';
```

We won't include the binary code here, because it would not be of any use in this context.

A comfortable way to read binary files is to use a hex editor. We have included the output of `hexdump`—a tool used to display a file as hexadecimal values:

```
[hs@duron /tmp]$ hexdump file.bin
0000000 4750 4342 504f 0a59 0dff 000a 0304 0102
0000010 0000 0000 0000 0000 0004 0004 0001 0000
0000020 ffff 0009 0000 754a 696c ff61 0aff 0000
0000030 4c00 6e6f 6f64 ff6e 0bff 0000 4500 676e
0000040 616c 646e 0004 0004 0002 0000 ffff 0008
0000050 0000 6150 6c75 ffff 000a 0000 6956 6e65
0000060 616e ffff 000b 0000 7541 7473 6972 0461
0000070 0400 0300 0000 ff00 09ff 0000 4c00 6e69
0000080 6164 ffff 0009 0000 694d 6d61 ff69 07ff
0000090 0000 5500 4153 0004 0004 0004 0000 ffff
00000a0 000a 0000 7445 6373 6968 ffff 0009 0000
00000b0 6f54 796b ff6f 09ff 0000 4a00 7061 6e61
00000c0 0004 0004 0005 0000 ffff 0009 0000 6843
00000d0 6972 ff73 0aff 0000 4200 7265 696c ff6e
00000e0 0bff 0000 4700 7265 616d 796e ffff
00000ee
```

I guess that all crackers among you have already dealt with hexadecimal data and hex editors. We will come back to hexadecimal values later in this chapter in section "Taking Care of Byte Order" when dealing with byte order.

Importing a binary file into a table can also be done with the help of the `COPY` command:

```
import=# COPY BINARY homes FROM '/tmp/file.bin';
COPY
```

```
import=# SELECT * FROM homes;
 id |  name  |  city  | country
----+--------+--------+---------
  1 | Julia  | London | England
  2 | Paul   | Vienna | Austria
  3 | Linda  | Miami  | USA
  4 | Etschi | Tokyo  | Japan
  5 | Chris  | Berlin | Germany
(5 rows)
```

As you can see in the previous code, no data was lost during the process, and all data has successfully been reimported.

If you use the binary format to export the data, DELIMITERS and WITH NULL cannot be used.

Working with ASCII and EBCDIC

In hybrid IT environments, ASCII might not be the only format with which you will have to deal. In this section, you will learn to work with EBCDIC, a character set defined by IBM.

An Overview and a Short History of EBCDIC

ASCII is not the only character set available. Mainframe environments, especially IBM, use Extended Binary Coded Decimal.

Interchange Code (EBCDIC) is the default character set. EBCDIC is actually a family of 8-bit character sets and not a single character set. In books, people often refer to EBCDIC as one character set, but it isn't. Let's look at a short history of EBCDIC.

Around the year 1965, IBM announced a new computer series that is known as System 360. A new character set, which was based on Hollerith punched card conventions, was introduced. It turned out that the development was totally different from ASCII. IBM had invested far too much to be able to change the design. EBCDIC was a further development of BCDIC, BCD, and back to Hollerith. It was designed as 8-bit code and used in combination with 32-bit machine words. EBCDIC even got national versions. As a consequence, EBCDIC is no longer a single code table. We will not cover the various versions of EBCDIC in this section because that is beyond the scope of this book.

The characters included in EBCDIC conform to those included in the ASCII code, but some characters differ, which makes converting EBCDIC to ASCII and vice-versa a task for experts.

Up to the 70s, EBCDIC was the most widespread code. However, personal computers are based on ASCII and, with the ascent of PCs, ASCII became the most widespread code available. Today, EBCDIC is mostly used on IBM zSeries machines (formally known as S/390) and IBM AS/400 machines. In PC environments, EBCDIC is only used when data has to be imported from EBCDIC machines. We will take a closer look at how data can be converted to EBCDIC or from EBCDIC to ASCII. Knowing this will be important for building data converters that you will need in combination with your PostgreSQL server.

An Overview and a Short History of ASCII

Today, ASCII is the most widespread character code available. In contrast to EBCDIC, ASCII is a single-byte character set. The standard version of ASCII uses 7 bits, but older versions of ASCII (before June 1961) used even fewer.

In 1963, the American Standards Association (ASA) announced the American Standard Code for Information Interchange (ASCII), which originally seems to have been named the American National Standard Code for Information Interchange (ANSCII).

> **Note**
> ASA was later changed to "American National Standards Institute [ANSI].

However, ASCII, as it was announced in 1963, left many positions, such as those for the lowercase Latin letters, unallocated. It was not until 1968 that a character set of 128 characters (7 bits with no spare positions) was defined. This 7-bit code consisted of 32 control characters and 96 printing characters. Later, ASCII was extended to 8 bits and the number of printed characters increased to 190.

ASCII was adopted by all computer manufacturers except IBM. ASCII finally became the de-facto standard for exchanging data. Some minor adoptions have to be done, of course, especially for the languages of Western Europe. In 1967, the International Organization for Standardization (ISO) in Geneva, Switzerland issued the ISO Recommendation 646 that called for a ASCII code with 10 positions reserved for language-specific characters. ASCII code was also used as the basis for creating 7-bit character codes for languages that did not employ the Latin alphabet, such as Arabic and Greek. In 1969, it was also included in the JIS character code of Japan.

Understanding BCD Coding

Binary Coded Decimal (BCD) is a very widespread technique for coding numeric values. BCD is very often used in mainframe environments, but BCD can also be used in PC environments because it is a comfortable and easy way of storing data (numbers).

BCD arithmetic has fallen out of favor among modern hardware designers, and it is poorly supported in most modern programming languages. However, it is still used in some cases.

Let's take a closer look at how numbers can be represented using BCD coding.

BCD numbers can be coded in many ways. The most obvious and, I guess, the most widespread way is to use *"packed BCD."* One byte consists of eight bits, but only 4 bits are used to store a single number. Up to 16 values can be stored in 4 bits (2^4), but only 10 possibilities are necessary to represent a number. It would be a waste of 4 bits if you store a single number in one byte. Using packed BCD makes it possible to store 2 numbers in one byte. This system allows 4 digits to be packed into a 16-bit word (=2 bytes) or 8 digits into a 32-bit word. You can see that data can be stored very efficiently using BCD code. Figure 11.1 shows how an 8-digit long number is stored in an array of 32 bits.

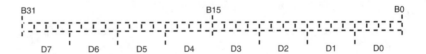

Figure 11.1
ASCII 32-bit BCD-coded value.

Coding a digit as a 4-bit BCD code is an easy task. Table 11.1 shows how a digit has to be treated.

Table 11.1   *An Overview of BCD and Decimal Codes*

BCD	Decimal
0000	
0001	
0010	
0011	
0100	

Table 11.1   *(continued)*

BCD	Decimal
0101	
0110	
0111	
1000	8
1001	9

You can see that it is really simple.

Back in the early days, packed BCD was not the only system used. Many old computer systems were using 6-bit BCD codes. Today, hardly anybody uses 6-bit BCD coding, but it may happen that you find yourself in a situation where you have to convert data coming from such a system. In this case, it can be a real advantage to have an idea how things work. The reason for choosing 6-bit for coding is that it was compatible with the 36-, 48-, and 60-bit words used by many computers in the 1950s and 1960s. On many machines, the format was used without special hardware support.

Taking Care of Byte Order

A very important point when dealing with binary data is the byte order of a system. We have included this section in the book because we think that it is important for database administrators and developers to know how data is stored on various systems. You normally don't have to worry about byte order, because the database and the operating system take care of these things. If you have to import binary data that has been generated on other systems, it is important to know what byte order is and that you have to take care of it.

Before we go into detail, we will try to explain what byte order is in a few words.

A computer is said to be big-endian or little-endian, depending on whether the least significant bit is in the lowest or highest addressed byte. For example, SPARC CPUs are big-endian systems because the bytes are ordered from left to right. The least significant bit is in the highest byte, which is on the right side.

Alpha systems use the so-called little-endian architecture, which means that the most significant bit is on the right side and the least significant bit is on the left side.

The different byte order does not affect the order of the bits inside a byte; it is just a different way of storing multibyte quantities. To make the difference between big-endian and little endian clear, we have included an example of a hex constant.

Imagine the hex constant 0x11AABBCC. No matter on which machine you use the hex constant, it will always be equal to 296.401.868. After the previous explanation, this may seem a little strange, but you will see what is meant. The constant we use is coded the same way in a C program, so the programmer does not have to be concerned about that. The only difference is the way the numbers are stored (see Table 11.2).

Table 11.2   *Big-Endian Versus Little-Endian*

Byte address	0x1000	0x1001	0x1002	0x1003
Little-endian	0xCC	0xBB	0xAA	0x11
Big-endian	0x11	0xAA	0xBB	0xCC

You have to keep in mind that only the order of a byte is changed; the order of bits inside a byte is not affected. To make this clearer, we have included a second example.

Let's have a look the hex value 0x12345678 in Table 11.3.

Table 11.3   *Big-Endian vs. Little-Endian*

Byte address	0x1000	0x1001	0x1002	0x1003
Little-endian	0x78	0x56	0x34	0x12
Big-endian	0x12	0x34	0x56	0x78

You can see, that 12 is always 12, no matter which byte order is used because two digits represent one byte in hex code.

Depending on the machine you use, the data will be written to disk differently. Consequently, it must be read differently. If you want to read binary data written to a file by a machine using big-endian on a machine using little-endian, *"byte-swapping"* has to be performed.

If you are using low-level data converters, you have to make sure that the applications contain routines to perform byte-swapping if necessary; otherwise, your data will look different on various systems. If you are dealing with ASCII files only, the byte order of a system has no influence on the way data has to be processed, because ASCII characters are single-byte characters so they cannot be in a "wrong" order.

On the database level, you don't have to be concerned about byte order as well because everything related to byte order is done by PostgreSQL automatically. Database systems, such as PostgreSQL, are designed to run on many hardware platforms and data can, in most cases, be exchanged safely.

As a rule of thumb, we can say that ASCII is always the most secure way to exchange data, because it is commonly used and characters are atomic, single-byte values.

It is interesting to mention that the terms big-endian and little-endian are derived from the Lilliputians of Gulliver's Travels, who see a major political issue whether soft-boiled eggs should be opened on the big side or the little side. In the case of computing, the discussion about using big- or little-endian is pretty much the same. According to a chip designer working at the Technical University of Vienna, it makes absolutely no difference in performance whether a chip is using big-endian. The thing that has an impact on the performance of the system is the type of application you want to run. If you have to deal with huge amounts of little-endian–coded data on a big-endian machine, the performance will decrease. To give you a better overview of the topic, we have included some pros and cons of using big-endian.

Let's get to the pros first:

- Reading the arithmetic sign bit of the wrong word size, integer size, or floating point number size will always return the right result, because the most significant bit can be found on the left side.

- Most network header codes and bitmapped graphics are using big-endian. When dealing with graphics, little-endian machines will be slower than big-endian machines (this is one of Apple's advantage over Intel when dealing with graphics) because byte swapping has to be performed.

- Hex dumps can be read much easier, because the bytes are in the "right" order, which means that the order of the digits is internally the same as it is displayed onscreen.

- When decoding variable length bit codes, such as Huffman codes (Huffman coding is the most effective compression algorithm available), the code word can be used as an index in a lookup table.

But big-endian does not only have pros. Let's have a look at the cons:

- When reading a value of the wrong word size, an incorrect value will be the result. On machines using little-endian, the result can be correct.

- Non-Intel architectures do not allow words written on odd addresses (alignment traps). On Intel machines, odd addresses can be used for writing and reading, which is a real advantage for computer programmers.

In many cases, the discussion whether to use big-endian is a philosophical question. None of the two systems will normally have a significant advantage if the machine is not used for a special purpose only. The Internet committee has chosen big-endian for use in network packets, but I guess we would not see a real difference if it was little-endian.

We have compiled all important hardware platforms and the "endian" they are using.

Big-endian:

- Motorola CPUs (used in Macintosh systems)

- SGI Irix machines

- SPARC CPUs

- IBM pSeries (formally known as RS/6000)

Little-endian:

- x86-CPUs (Intel, AMD, ...)

- Alpha CPUs

- VAX

We have already mentioned that it is sometimes necessary to convert one format into the other. Because it is not convenient to write your own functions, we have included a small piece of software written in ANSI C that performs simple conversions:

```c
#include <stdio.h>
#include <netinet/in.h>

int main(int argc, char **argv)
{
        int network;
        int host=0x12345678;

        network=htonl(host);
        printf("Host to network %x\n", network);

        host=ntohl(network);
        printf("Network back to host %x\n", host);

        return 0;
}
```

First, we include a header file called in.h. On BSD systems, sys/types.h has to be included first; this won't be necessary on Linux systems. This has to be done to include the functions we need for converting the data. In the next step, we define two variables. host is converted to network byte order (big-endian) and then assigned to network. After displaying the result, we convert the variable back to little-endian and display the result using printf. We want the result to be displayed as hexadecimal value, so we have to use %x. If you want to find out more about the printf function, check out the man pages by typing:

```
man 3 printf
```

To compile the code, we write a simple Makefile:

```
prog    :       main.c Makefile
        gcc -O3 -Wall -ansi main.c -o prog
```

The Makefile is very simple. We only have to compile one file called main.c. -Wall displays all compiler warnings, and -ansi makes the compiler assume that the code is ANSI C compliant. prog will be the executable:

```
[hs@duron c]$ make
gcc -O3 -Wall -ansi main.c -o prog
```

We can now execute the program:

```
[hs@duron c]$ ./prog
Host to network 78563412
Network back to host 12345678
```

The description of the library we have used in main.c can be found in the man pages about byte order (use "man byteorder).

Knowing about byte order is extremely important if you have to convert binary data, which has to be done very often when working with database systems like PostgreSQL.

The ASCII—EBCDIC Table

Table 11.4 contains the ASCII and EBCDIC character set. It includes the decimal and the hex values of the various characters.

The following is a list of the abbreviations used in Table 11.4:

- (1) Introducer
- (2) String Delimiter

- (CC) Communication Control
- (FE) Format effector
- (IS) Information Separator

Table 11.4 *An ASCII - EBCDIC Table*

Dec	Hex	ASCII	EBCDIC		
0	00	NUL	Null	NUL	Null
1	01	SOH	Start of Heading (CC)	SOH	Start of Heading
2	02	STX	Start of Text (CC)	STX	Start of Text
3	03	ETX	End of Text (CC)	ETX	End of Text
4	04	EOT	End of Transmission (CC)	PF	Punch Off
5	05	ENQ	Enquiry (CC)	HT	Horizontal Tab
6	06	ACK	Acknowledge (CC)	LC	Lower Case
7	07	BEL	Bell	DEL	Delete
8	08	BS	Backspace (FE)		
9	09	HT	Horizontal Tabulation (FE)		
10	0A	LF	Line Feed (FE)	SMM	Start of Manual Message
11	0B	VT	Vertical Tabulation (FE)	VT	Vertical Tab
12	0C	FF	Form Feed (FE)	FF	Form Feed
13	0D	CR	Carriage Return (FE)	CR	Carriage Return
14	0E	SO	Shift Out	SO	Shift Out
15	0F	SI	Shift In	SI	Shift In
16	10	DLE	Data Link Escape (CC)	DLE	Data Link Escape
17	11	DC1	Device Control 1	DC1	Device Control 1
18	12	DC2	Device Control 2	DC2	Device Control 2
19	13	DC3	Device Control 3	TM	Tape Mark
20	14	DC4	Device Control 4	RES	Restore
21	15	NAK	Negative Acknowledge (CC)	NL	New Line
22	16	SYN	Synchronous Idle (CC)	BS	Backspace
23	17	ETB	End of Transmission Block (CC)	IL	Idle
24	18	CAN	Cancel	CAN	Cancel

Table 11.4   *(continued)*

Dec	Hex	ASCII	EBCDIC		
25	19	EM	End of Medium	EM	End of Medium
26	1A	SUB	Substitute	CC	Cursor Control
27	1B	ESC	Escape	CU1	Customer Use 1
28	1C	FS	File Separator (IS)	IFS	Interchange File Separator
29	1D	GS	Group Separator (IS)	IGS	Interchange Group Separator
30	1E	RS	Record Separator (IS)	IRS	Interchange Record Separator
31	1F	US	Unit Separator (IS)	IUS	Interchange Unit Separator
32	20	SP	Space	DS	Digit Select
33	21	!	Exclamation Point	SOS	Start of Significance
34	22	"	Quotation Mark	FS	Field Separator
35	23	#	Number Sign, Octothorp, "pound"		
36	24	$	Dollar Sign	BYP	Bypass
37	25	%	Percent	LF	Line Feed
38	26	&	Ampersand	ETB	End of Transmission Block
39	27	'	Apostrophe, Prime	ESC	Escape
40	28	(	Left Parenthesis		
41	29	)	Right Parenthesis		
42	2A	*	Asterisk, "star"	SM	Set Mode
43	2B	+	Plus Sign	CU2	Customer Use 2
44	2C	,	Comma		
45	2D	-	Hyphen, Minus Sign	ENQ	Enquiry
46	2E	.	Period, Decimal Point, "dot"	ACK	Acknowledge
47	2F	/	Slash, Virgule	BEL	Bell
48	30	0	0		
49	31	1	1		
50	32	2	2	SYN	Synchronous Idle

Table 11.4   *(continued)*

Dec	Hex	ASCII	EBCDIC		
51	33	3	3		
52	34	4	4	PN	Punch On
53	35	5	5	RS	Reader Stop
54	36	6	6	UC	Upper Case
55	37	7	7	EOT	End of Transmission
56	38	8	8		
57	39	9	9		
58	3A	:	Colon		
59	3B	;	Semicolon	CU3	Customer Use 3
60	3C	<	Less-than Sign	DC4	Device Control 4
61	3D	=	Equal Sign	NAK	Negative Acknowledge
62	3E	>	Greater-than Sign		
63	3F	?	Question Mark	SUB	Substitute
64	40	@	At Sign	SP	Space
65	41	A	A		
66	42	B	B		
67	43	C	C		
68	44	D	D		
69	45	E	E		
70	46	F	F		
71	47	G	G		
72	48	H	H		
73	49	I	I		
74	4A	J	J	¢	Cent Sign
75	4B	K	K	.	Period, Decimal Point, "dot"
76	4C	L	L	<	Less-than Sign
77	4D	M	M	(	Left Parenthesis
78	4E	N	N	+	Plus Sign
79	4F	O	O	|	Logical OR
80	50	P	P	&	Ampersand

Table 11.4   *(continued)*

Dec	Hex	ASCII	EBCDIC		
81	51	Q	Q		
82	52	R	R		
83	53	S	S		
84	54	T	T		
85	55	U	U		
86	56	V	V		
87	57	W	W		
88	58	X	X		
89	59	Y	Y		
90	5A	Z	Z	!	Exclamation Point
91	5B	[	Opening Bracket	$	Dollar Sign
92	5C	\	Reverse Slant	*	Asterisk, "star"
93	5D	]	Closing Bracket	)	Right Parenthesis
94	5E	^	Circumflex, Caret	;	Semicolon
95	5F	_	Underline, Underscore	¬	Logical NOT
96	60	`	Grave Accent	-	Hyphen, Minus Sign
97	61	a	a	/	Slash, Virgule
98	62	b	b		
99	63	c	c		
100	64	d	d		
101	65	e	e		
102	66	f	f		
103	67	g	g		
104	68	h	h		
105	69	i	i		
106	6A	j	j		
107	6B	k	k	,	Comma
108	6C	l	l	%	Percent
109	6D	m	m	_	Underline, Underscore

Table 11.4 *(continued)*

Dec	Hex	ASCII	EBCDIC		
110	6E	n	n	>	Greater-than Sign
111	6F	o	o	?	Question Mark
112	70	p	p		
113	71	q	q		
114	72	r	r		
115	73	s	s		
116	74	t	t		
117	75	u	u		
118	76	v	v		
119	77	w	w		
120	78	x	x		
121	79	y	y		
122	7A	z	z	:	Colon
123	7B	{	Opening Brace	#	Number Sign, Octothorp, "pound"
124	7C	|	Vertical Line	@	At Sign
125	7D	}	Closing Brace	'	Apostrophe, Prime
126	7E	~	Tilde	=	Equal Sign
127	7F	DEL	Delete	"	Quotation Mark
128	80		Reserved		
129	81		Reserved	a	a
130	82		Reserved	b	b
131	83		Reserved	c	c
132	84	IND	Index (FE)	d	d
133	85	NEL	Next Line (FE)	e	e
134	86	SSA	Start of Selected Area	f	f
135	87	ESA	End of Selected Area	g	g
136	88	HTS	Horizontal Tabulation Set (FE)	h	h
137	89	HTJ	Horizontal Tabulation with Justification (FE)	i	i

Table 11.4   *(continued)*

Dec	Hex	ASCII	EBCDIC		
138	8A	VTS	Vertical Tabulation Set (FE)		
139	8B	PLD	Partial Line Down (FE)		
140	8C	PLU	Partial Line Up (FE)		
141	8D	RI	Reverse Index (FE)		
142	8E	SS2	Single Shift Two (1)		
143	8F	SS3	Single Shift Three (1)		
144	90	DCS	Device Control String (2)		
145	91	PU1	Private Use One	j	j
146	92	PU2	Private Use Two	k	k
147	93	STS	Set Transmit State	l	l
148	94	CCH	Cancel Character	m	m
149	95	MW	Message Waiting	n	n
150	96	SPA	Start of Protected Area	o	o
151	97	EPA	End of Protected Area	p	p
152	98		Reserved	q	q
153	99		Reserved	r	r
154	9A		Reserved		
155	9B	CSI	Control Sequence Introducer (1)		
156	9C	ST	String Terminator (2)		
157	9D	OSC	Operating System Command (2)		
158	9E	PM	Privacy Message (2)		
159	9F	APC	Application Program Command (2)		
160	A0				
161	A1				
162	A2			s	s
163	A3			t	t
164	A4			u	u
165	A5			v	v
166	A6			w	w
167	A7			x	x
168	A8			y	y

Table 11.4   *(continued)*

Dec	Hex	ASCII	EBCDIC		
169	A9			z	z
170	AA				
171	AB				
172	AC				
173	AD				
174	AE				
175	AF				
176	B0				
177	B1				
178	B2				
179	B3				
180	B4				
181	B5				
182	B6				
183	B7				
184	B8				
185	B9			`	Grave Accent
186	BA				
187	BB				
188	BC				
189	BD				
190	BE				
191	BF				
192	C0				
193	C1			A	A
194	C2			B	B
195	C3			C	C
196	C4			D	D
197	C5			E	E
198	C6			F	F
199	C7			G	G
200	C8			H	H

Table 11.4   *(continued)*

Dec	Hex	ASCII	EBCDIC		
201	C9			I	I
202	CA				
203	CB				
204	CC				
205	CD				
206	CE				
207	CF				
208	D0				
209	D1			J	J
210	D2			K	K
211	D3			L	L
212	D4			M	M
213	D5			N	N
214	D6			O	O
215	D7			P	P
216	D8			Q	Q
217	D9			R	R
218	DA				
219	DB				
220	DC				
221	DD				
222	DE				
223	DF				
224	E0				
225	E1				
226	E2			S	S
227	E3			T	T
228	E4			U	U
229	E5			V	V
230	E6			W	W
231	E7			X	X
232	E8			Y	Y

Table 11.4   *(continued)*

Dec	Hex	ASCII	EBCDIC		
233	E9			Z	Z
234	EA				
235	EB				
236	EC				
237	ED				
238	EE				
239	EF				
240	F0			0	0
241	F1			1	1
242	F2			2	2
243	F3			3	3
244	F4			4	4
245	F5			5	5
246	F6			6	6
247	F7			7	7
248	F8			8	8
249	F9			9	9
250	FA				
251	FB				
252	FC				
253	FD				
254	FE				
255	FF				

Performing Simple EBCDIC—ASCII Conversions

If you have to import data from IBM mainframe machines, you may have to convert the data from EBCDIC to ASCII. In the previous section, you can find a table with the two character sets. Using software available on the Internet is more comfortable than writing your own converter.

The easiest way to perform EBCDIC to ASCII conversions on Unix systems is to use good old dd. dd is one of the most reliable and best pieces of software available on the

Internet. It has been written to convert data. dd is often used to convert data stored on tapes. In this section, we will use dd to convert a file from ASCII to EBCDIC and back to ASCII.

We first create a file called ascii.file:

```
[hs@duron /tmp]$ cat ascii.file
This file contains wonderful data.
```

Converting to EBCDIC is an easy task:

```
[hs@duron /tmp]$ dd conv=ebcdic if=ascii.file of=ebcdic.file
0+1 Records ein
0+1 Records aus
```

The conversion has been successful because no error has been displayed. With the help of the conv flag, we tell dd to convert the data to EBCDIC. if defines the input file and of defines the file for the output. If you want to convert the data to IBM special EBCDIC, use ibm instead of ebcdic with the conv flag.

Converting from EBCDIC to ASCII works nearly the same way:

```
[hs@duron /tmp]$ dd conv=ascii if=ebcdic.file of=ascii.file
0+1 Records ein
0+1 Records aus
```

If we have a look at the ascii.file, we can see that nothing evil has happened to the contents of the file:

```
[hs@duron /tmp]$ cat ascii.file
This file contains wonderful data.
```

After the data is converted to ASCII, it will be an easy task to import it into your PostgreSQL database. How complex the converter you may have to write will be depends on the data structure of the raw data.

If you want to perform the ASCII-to-EBCDIC conversions on the application level, you can use one of the numerous modules and libraries available on the Internet. An example for such a module can be found on CPAN and is called Convert-IBM390. The module is very powerful and can be installed easily. Download the code of the module on your machine and extract the tar archive using tar xvfz Convert-IBM390-x.xx.tar.gz. Enter the directory created by tar and type "perl Makefile.PL, "make, and "make install to install the module on your system. All information you need to use the module can be found in the man pages of the module (use "man Convert::IBM390).

We have included a small Perl program to show how easy it is to build a simple converter. It will be easy to enlarge the program with some PostgreSQL interaction:

```perl
#!/usr/bin/perl

use Convert::IBM390 qw(:all);

$input="please convert me";

$ebc=asc2eb($input);
$asc=eb2asc($ebc);

print "$asc\n";
```

This program does nothing but convert the text stored in $input to EBCDIC and back to ASCII. If we execute the script, we will receive the original text defined in $input:

```
[hs@duron code]$ ./asc_and_ebc.pl
please convert me
```

In most cases, performing conversions between ASCII and EBCDIC is no problem (as long a no special characters are involved). The more interesting task is to pack or unpack data in an EBCDIC record.

Convert::IBM390 offers two functions called packeb and unpackeb to do the job. Covering these two functions in beyond the scope of this book. Simply check out the man pages of the module to find out more.

Summary

PostgreSQL offers simple interfaces to import, export, or exchange data. These interfaces can easily be handled and provide an intuitive solution. Although ACSCII is the standard format for exchanging data in most cases, it is important to know how to treat EBCDIC data. This knowledge will be essential for you, especially when dealing with IBM mainframe machines.

CHAPTER 12

Generating Multidimensional Results

This chapter is dedicated to those PostgreSQL users who have to deal with reporting and data mining. Multidimensional results are used for many reasons, especially in scientific environments. Imagine a huge database with dozens of millions of records. If similar questions are posed to the database, it might take too long to compute the results one after the other. Therefore, it might be useful to generate the results in one step to save CPU time and extract the components of the result afterward.

In general, there are two ways of dealing with multidimensional data structures. One way is to generate the results on the database level. Another way is to calculate the result on the application level.

Generating Multidimensional Results on the Database Level

In this section, you learn how multidimensional data can be generated on the application level and how to build complex queries step by step, using views and temporary tables. Let's start with an example.

Imagine a report with dozens of tables about a certain topic (a labor market, for example). The tables contain the number of employees belonging to a certain gender (every column contains a certain gender). The rows contain the states where people are employed (for example, Alaska or Florida). Every table shows the number of people employed in a certain part of the economy (for example, agriculture or finance).

If we want to find out how many people in Kansas were employed in companies belonging to the financial sector in 2002, we just have to check out the right cell in the appropriate table.

In general, a single table is a two-dimensional data structure; one dimension is the x-axis, the second dimension is the y-axis of the table. If you have many tables that look the same but contain different data, the whole thing can be seen as a three-dimensional data structure. In the example, the first dimension contains the gender, the second dimension is used to store the state, and the third dimension stores the various sectors of the economy. Every cell in the table has a certain, unique meaning and is equal to a point in the three-dimensional cube.

This model can be used for building highly sophisticated applications managing extremely huge amounts of data. Imagine that you have to build reports containing dozens of tables about a certain topic. It would be nearly impossible to query the database for every cell in the tables. If the amount of data is extremely huge, the number of queries that have to be processed by the database has to be minimal; otherwise, the database will not perform well. Therefore, you should try to build one query for all tables, which produces a multidimensional array. You can use that array to insert the data into the table. Keep in mind that a huge query demands some tuning in order to execute efficiently.

If certain reports have to be created often, you can write an application that creates LaTex code. LaTex is the most reliable piece of software available. It also is the most important piece of software, because no errors have been found in Tex in the past few years. Donald E. Knuth, the father of Tex, pays money for every error found in the software. No errors have been found in the past few years, because the software is so stable.

LaTex is used to produce wonderful documents (the output is a DVI file that can easily be converted to Postscript or PDF). The biggest advantage of LaTex over nearly all other systems for word processing is that the software creates the documents out of simple ASCII files that can be created by easy-to-write programs.

To show you how multidimensional data can be created, we will create a table containing data about persons:

```
CREATE TABLE "persons" ( "id" serial, "name" text, "state" text, "start" date,
        "finish" date, "income" int4, "sector" text, "gender" char(1));
```

After creating the table and inserting data, let's look at the records in the table:

```
SELECT * FROM persons;
```

The table contains six records:

```
id |  name   |  state  |   start    |   finish   | income |   sector    | gender
---+---------+---------+------------+------------+--------+-------------+-------
 1 | Frank   | Alabama | 2001-01-01 | 2001-08-09 | 32000  | agriculture | m
 2 | Paula   | Florida | 1999-11-21 | 2003-02-01 | 29000  | finances    | f
 3 | Gigi    | Alaska  | 1976-04-23 | 2000-01-21 | 17000  | mining      | f
 4 | Etschi  | Florida | 1998-07-16 | 2001-09-10 | 34000  | finances    | f
 5 | Sue     | Alabama | 1999-10-12 | 2001-01-02 | 20000  | agriculture | f
 6 | Joe     | Florida | 1970-01-01 | 2002-05-12 | 35000  | finances    | m
(6 rows)
```

Multidimensional results can be generated in two ways: by using PostgreSQL's onboard tools, or by performing calculations on the application level. You will look at both methods in this section, but let's start with the possibilities provided by PostgreSQL. The following creates a three-dimensional result:

```
SELECT state, sector, gender, COUNT(*)
       FROM persons
       GROUP BY state, sector, gender;
```

This query counts the number of persons for every combination of state, sector, and gender:

```
 state   |   sector    | gender | count
---------+-------------+--------+------
 Alabama | agriculture | f      |   1
 Alabama | agriculture | m      |   1
 Alaska  | mining      | f      |   1
 Florida | finances    | f      |   2
 Florida | finances    | m      |   1
(5 rows)
```

The result shows that two persons from Florida are female and work in companies situated in the financial sector.

Imagine that we want to generate two tables out of this result, one table per gender. The easiest and most effective way is to use a temporary table:

```
SELECT state, sector, gender, COUNT(*) INTO TEMP tmp_tab1
    FROM persons
    GROUP BY state, sector, gender;
```

We can easily select the data for the two tables from the temporary table now. The advantage of this algorithm is that persons has to be scanned only once. In the example, this is no advantage. If the amount of data is large, this enables a significant increase in speed if we perform two queries on a very small table instead of two queries on a huge table by using a WHERE clause. In the previous example, we would use the following:

```
WHERE gender = 'm'
```

or

```
WHERE gender = 'f'
```

The SQL code for querying the temporary table is easy:

```
SELECT * FROM tmp_tab1 WHERE gender='f';
SELECT * FROM tmp_tab1 WHERE gender='m';
```

We receive the following tables:

```
 state  |    sector    | gender | count
--------+--------------+--------+-------
 Alabama | agriculture | f      |   1
 Alaska  | mining      | f      |   1
 Florida | finances    | f      |   2
(3 rows)


 state  |    sector    | gender | count
--------+--------------+--------+-------
 Alabama | agriculture | m      |   1
 Florida | finances    | m      |   1
(2 rows)
```

The only step left to take is output formatting so that the data can be used directly by the application the table is generated for. Formatting the output should be an easy task.

Sometimes not all data in a multidimensional array will be interesting for you. To minimize the size of the result, the amount of data can be reduced by using a HAVING clause when generating the multidimensional array. In the next example, we want only values in the result that are higher than 1:

```
SELECT state, sector, gender, COUNT(*)
       FROM persons
       GROUP BY state, sector, gender
               HAVING COUNT(*)>1;
```

The result of the query consists of one record, because only one combination of values is higher than 1:

```
 state  |  sector  | gender | count
--------+----------+--------+-------
 Florida | finances | f      |   2
(1 row)
```

All queries used to generate multidimensional results contain components, such as COUNT, GROUP BY, or HAVING. Usually queries such as these are rather slow, because the database has to perform internal sorts and aggregations. Let's look at the execution plan of the previous query:

```
NOTICE:  QUERY PLAN:

Aggregate  (cost=1.14..1.21 rows=1 width=36)
   -> Group  (cost=1.14..1.18 rows=6 width=36)
        -> Sort  (cost=1.14..1.14 rows=6 width=36)
             -> Seq Scan on persons  (cost=0.00..1.06 rows=6 width=36)
```

Sorting huge amounts of data slows down your query significantly. If you perform huge queries, you have to analyze the execution plan for your query carefully to make sure that the time needed to execute the query will not exceed the time you have. If you want to analyze extremely huge log files, you have to make sure that a process quits before the same process is started by cron again. If this happens on your system, you will find yourself in deep trouble.

To avoid these problems, it can sometimes be faster to perform calculations on the application level instead of letting the database do the work.

Creating Multidimensional Arrays on the Application Level

In this section, you learn how multidimensional arrays can be generated on the application level. Depending on the programming language you choose, the processes might differ, but there are basic algorithms and ways of processing huge amounts of data.

Processing data on the application level usually starts with reading data from the database. During this step, the amount of data has to be reduced and a suitable data format has to be chosen. The second step is to create an array or to allocate some space in memory where the result of the process will be stored. The memory allocated must contain a field for all combinations of data that can occur in the result. You will find it useful to know which values can occur in the output so that the right amount of memory can be allocated and you know where to insert the data at runtime. If you don't know which values the output contains, the process is much more complicated.

In the next step, the allocated memory is initialized with 0, and the data returned by the database is processed line by line.

In this section we will show you sample code written in Perl. You will see that the way data can be processed differs significantly depending on the language you use.

To show you how it works, we use the database about the labor market that we used in the previous section. We want to write a Perl script that counts all combinations of values in the database. This can easily be done on the database level, but sometimes complex calculations have to be performed that can hardly be done on the database level. In our example we won't use complex algorithms. We just want to give an insight into how it can be done in general:

```perl
#!/usr/bin/perl

use DBI;

# connecting
$dbh=DBI->connect("dbi:Pg:dbname=labormarket; port=5432", "hs", "anypasswd") or
        die "can't connect: $!\n";

# executing SELECT-statement
$sql="SELECT state, sector, gender FROM persons";
$sth=$dbh->prepare("$sql") or
        die "Cannot prepare $sql\n";
$sth->execute() or
        die "Cannot prepare $sql\n";

# Retrieving data
while   (@row = $sth->fetchrow_array)
{
        @result{"@row[0] @row[1]"}++;
}

print "Financial Sector in Florida: ".@result{'Florida finances'}."\n";
```

We select the data we need from the database and add 1 to the array for every combination of state and sector. Finally, we display the result for the financial sector in Florida. In the example, we used a one-dimensional array to store the data. We could have used a two-dimensional data structure, because we want to calculate how often every combination of state and sector occurs. In real-world scenarios, one-dimensional data structures for storing the result are, in some cases, the better way, because they are more flexible. If you know how many elements the axis of your data structure has, it is an easy task to find out the appropriate position of an element in a one-dimensional data structure.

The next example shows how a two-dimensional data structure can be stored in a one-dimensional array:

```perl
#!/usr/bin/perl

use DBI;

# connecting
$dbh=DBI->connect("dbi:Pg:dbname=labormarket; port=5432", "hs", "anypasswd") or
        die "can't connect: $!\n";

# executing SELECT-statement
$sql="SELECT state, sector, gender FROM persons";
$sth=$dbh->prepare("$sql") or
        die "Cannot prepare $sql\n";
$sth->execute() or
        die "Cannot prepare $sql\n";

# Retrieving all values in a certain column
($sta_size, @states)=&getvalues("state");
($gen_size, @gender)=&getvalues("gender");

print "\nstates: @states \n";
print "gender: @gender\n";

# Calculating and displaying the size of the required array
$size=$sta_size*$gen_size;
print "number of elements: $size\n\n";
for($temp=1; $temp<=$size; $temp++)
{
    @result[$temp]=0;
}
```

```perl
# Processing the input data row by row
while(@line = $sth->fetchrow_array)
{
    $final_pos=((&getpos(@line[0], @states)-1)*$gen_size)+
            &getpos(@line[2], @gender);
    print "elements: $final_pos - @line[0] - @line[2]\n";
    @result[$final_pos]++;
}
print "\n";

# Displaying the result of the query
for($i=1; $i<=$size; $i++)
{
    print "$i: @result[$i]\n";
}
print "\n";


# Reading all possible values ...
sub getvalues
{
    local @row=(), $x=0, @result=();

    $sql="SELECT DISTINCT $_[0] FROM persons";
    $sthx=$main::dbh->prepare("$sql") or
            die "Cannot prepare $sql\n";
    $sthx->execute() or
            die "Cannot prepare $sql\n";

    # Retrieving data
    while   (@row = $sthx->fetchrow_array)
    {
            @result[$x]=@row[0];
            $x++;
    }
    return $x, @result;
}

# Find the position of an element in an array
sub getpos
{
    local $index=0, $i;
    foreach $i (@_)
```

```
        {
                $index++;
                if      ($i eq $_[0] and $index>1)
                {
                        return($index-1);
                }
        }
}
```

At first sight, this Perl script seems terribly complicated. Let's analyze it. First, we execute a query that retrieves all persons. The main target of the program is to generate a two-dimensional data structure that contains all combinations of gender and state. Therefore, we retrieve a list of all possible values of gender and state that we have in the database. This is done with the help of a function called getvalues, which returns the list of values and the amount of values returned. We need this information for the gender and the state where a person is employed.

The size of the array required to store the result can be computed by multiplying the amount of fields every dimension should have. In our case, the result is 6, because we found three states and two genders in the database.

In the next step, we initialize the array that we need for the result with 0. This has to be done to remove the trash that can be in the array. Then we process every record, line-by-line, using a WHILE loop. We have to calculate the position in the array containing the result next. Therefore, we need a function called getpos that returns the index of a certain element in the array containing all valid values. Florida, for instance, can be found on position number three in @states. Finding the right position in the array is rather easy, even if the number of axes used is high. To keep the example as simple as possible, we have implemented the calculation for the position for only a two-dimensional data structure.

Then we increment the value of the appropriate cell by 1.

Finally, we display the result. If we execute the script, the result looks like this:

```
[hs@duron code]$ ./count.pl

states: Alabama Alaska Florida
gender: f m
number of elements: 6

elements: 2 - Alabama - m
elements: 5 - Florida - f
elements: 3 - Alaska - f
```

```
elements: 5 - Florida - f
elements: 1 - Alabama - f
elements: 6 - Florida - m

1: 1
2: 1
3: 1
4: 0
5: 2
6: 1
```

In the example, we extracted the list of values occurring in a certain column out of the database. Sometimes this is not the best version, because, in many cases, a lot of CPU time is needed to do the job. In real-world applications, it might be clear which values might occur in a certain column, and it is not necessary to extract the list every time the script is processed.

When processing data on the application level, one of the biggest advantages is that the output can easily be transformed to any format you need. If you treat your multidimensional data structures as one-dimensional, you are free to create any output you want, and it is extremely easy to transpose the output, for instance. You can create a table that contains the various states in the x-axis, or you can create a table that uses the gender as the x-axis of the table. It depends on the way you process the array. Transposing the result of a query can sometimes be a difficult process when you want to do it with a database, because it is not supported by SQL. You can use temporary tables and some PL/pgSQL code of course, but it is not as easy as performing the operation on the application level. The EFEU package (which can be downloaded from http://efeu.cybertec.at) can easily be used to perform any transformations on the application level.

The previous script is nothing else than a prototype. If you have to build such applications, you have to make sure that the applications are far more flexible than this one. We kept it as simple as possible to show the concept of the process.

Until now, you have explored how multidimensional data can be created. Writing software to output multidimensional data structures is an easy task. Simply compute the position of a certain element of the array and write it to standard output. In most cases, it will be useful to implement the ability to transpose the result, but this depends on the type of application you have to write.

Summary

Multidimensional results can be generated and processed on the application or database level. Depending on the type of application, it might be useful to perform the major part of all operations on the database level.

The decision of where to perform which operation also depends on the level of platform independence of your software.

Chapter 13

Classification of Data— Real-World Examples

Selecting data is not the only purpose for relational databases. For reporting, it is essential to perform some sort of aggregation and classification. You have already learned about aggregation functions in this book. A lot of software can be used to deal with classification and aggregation. In this chapter, you learn to work with SQL and the EFEU package. These two ways of working with data are good examples for different concepts.

Working with SQL

In this section, you take a close look at how data can be classified with the help of joins and tables.

In general, classification means that certain values are combined in one group, which is assigned to a new name. How can you tell the database which values have to be combined? The problem can be solved in several ways. The following table shows you how classification and aggregation can be done with PostgreSQL:

```
persons=# SELECT * FROM persons;
 id |  name  |   birth    | gender | income
----+--------+------------+--------+--------
  1 | Albert | 1970-01-01 | m      |  35000
  2 | John   | 1973-04-04 | m      |  50000
  3 | Carla  | 1963-10-21 | f      |  32000
  4 | Jenny  | 1982-09-21 | f      |  45000
  5 | Hans   | 1978-08-09 | m      |  59000
  6 | Epi    | 1976-06-12 | m      |  21000
  7 | Etschi | 1960-02-20 | f      |  34000
  8 | Bill   | 1980-07-12 | m      |  43000
(8 rows)
```

This table contains the id, name, day of birth, gender, and income of each person. In most situations, the income of the people in the table will vary, and many different values can be found. You will never find income reports where each income stored in the table is listed in a report. In all scientific studies about income, the data is divided into groups. Each group is assigned to a certain interval of incomes so that the statistics can be displayed comfortably. How can you do this with the help of SQL? This chapter presents some solutions for the problem.

Here is a table that contains the classification:

```
persons=# SELECT * FROM income_class;
 id | label | lower |  upper
----+-------+-------+----------
  1 | 10k   |     0 |     9999
  2 | 20k   |  9999 |    19999
  3 | 30k   | 19999 |    29999
  4 | 40k   | 29999 |    39999
  5 | 50k   | 39999 |    49999
  6 | more  | 49999 | 10000000
(6 rows)
```

The first column contains a simple serial number. The second column contains the label that we use for a group of values. The third column contains the lower border of a classification. The value found in the column is not included in the classification. The last column contains the upper value. This value is unlike the lower part of the interval.

Let's look at a simple example:

```
SELECT b.label, a.income
       FROM persons AS a, income_class AS b
       WHERE a.income>b.lower
              AND a.income<=b.upper;
```

This query looks for the appropriate label for the group where the income of a person belongs.

```
label | income
------+--------
40k   | 35000
more  | 50000
40k   | 32000
50k   | 45000
more  | 59000
30k   | 21000
40k   | 34000
50k   | 43000
(8 rows)
```

The income of 35000 is lower, and therefore belongs to the group labeled 40k.

In the example, the values are displayed in the same order that they appear in the database. If we want the records to be returned sorted, we have to add an ORDER BY statement to the query:

```
SELECT b.label, a.income
       FROM persons AS a, income_class AS b
       WHERE a.income>b.lower
              AND a.income<=b.upper
       ORDER BY b.label;
```

The records are returned the way we want them to be returned now:

```
label | income
------+--------
30k   | 21000
40k   | 35000
40k   | 32000
40k   | 34000
50k   | 45000
50k   | 43000
more  | 50000
more  | 59000
(8 rows)
```

Performing the join and sorting the output is an easy task, but what happens inside the database? To find out what PostgreSQL has to do to complete the query, we use EXPLAIN and have a look at the execution plan:

```
persons=# EXPLAIN SELECT b.label, a.income  FROM persons AS a, income_class AS b
WHERE a.income>b.lower AND a.income<=b.upper;
NOTICE:   QUERY PLAN:

Nested Loop  (cost=0.00..281.08 rows=889 width=24)
  -> Seq Scan on persons a  (cost=0.00..1.08 rows=8 width=4)
  -> Seq Scan on income_class b  (cost=0.00..20.00 rows=1000 width=20)

EXPLAIN
```

The first query performs a sequential scan on both tables involved in the query. The join is done by using a nested loop. Because the amount of data is very small, this is no problem. If the amount of data grows, we recommend using an index so that the database can perform the join easier. Here is the execution plan of the second query:

```
persons=# EXPLAIN SELECT b.label, a.income  FROM persons AS a, income_class AS b
WHERE a.income>b.lower AND a.income<=b.upper ORDER BY b.label;
NOTICE:   QUERY PLAN:

Sort  (cost=324.62..324.62 rows=889 width=24)
  -> Nested Loop  (cost=0.00..281.08 rows=889 width=24)
        -> Seq Scan on persons a  (cost=0.00..1.08 rows=8 width=4)
        -> Seq Scan on income_class b  (cost=0.00..20.00 rows=1000 width=20)

EXPLAIN
```

The database has to perform an additional sort operation to compute the result. If the amount of data involved in the process is very large, the sort operation slows down the query significantly.

Statisticians are usually interested in how many people belong to a certain group. A count has to be performed:

```
SELECT b.label, a.income, COUNT(*)
       FROM persons AS a, income_class AS b
       WHERE a.income>b.lower
            AND a.income<=b.upper
       GROUP BY b.label
       ORDER BY b.label;
ERROR:  Attribute a.income must be GROUPed or used in an aggregate function
```

This SQL statement contains an error that is commonly made when dealing with the COUNT function. The database can display only the columns you include in the GROUP BY clause. The following query is correct:

```
SELECT b.label, COUNT(*)
       FROM persons AS a, income_class AS b
       WHERE a.income>b.lower
             AND a.income<=b.upper
       GROUP BY b.label
       ORDER BY b.label;
```

The database displays the correct result:

```
label | count
------+------
30k   |   1
40k   |   3
50k   |   2
more  |   2
(4 rows)
```

The result is ordered by the first column. That is, what we want it to be, because we included an ORDER BY clause in the query. In this case, the ORDER BY is redundant, because the GROUP BY already performs an internal sort. The following query returns the same result as the previous query:

```
SELECT b.label, COUNT(*)
       FROM persons AS a, income_class AS b
       WHERE a.income>b.lower
             AND a.income<=b.upper
       GROUP BY b.label;
```

If you look at the execution plans of the two SQL commands, you will see why both statements return the same result:

```
persons=# EXPLAIN SELECT b.label, COUNT(*)  FROM persons AS a, income_class AS b
WHERE a.income>b.lower AND a.income<=b.upper GROUP BY b.label;
NOTICE:   QUERY PLAN:

Aggregate  (cost=324.62..329.06 rows=89 width=24)
  -> Group  (cost=324.62..326.84 rows=889 width=24)
       -> Sort  (cost=324.62..324.62 rows=889 width=24)
            -> Nested Loop  (cost=0.00..281.08 rows=889 width=24)
                 -> Seq Scan on persons a  (cost=0.00..1.08 rows=8 width=4)
```

```
                          -> Seq Scan on income_class b  (cost=0.00..20.00 rows=1000
width=20)


EXPLAIN
persons=# EXPLAIN SELECT b.label, COUNT(*)  FROM persons AS a, income_class AS b
WHERE a.income>b.lower AND a.income<=b.upper GROUP BY b.label ORDER BY b.label;
NOTICE:  QUERY PLAN:

Aggregate  (cost=324.62..329.06 rows=89 width=24)
  -> Group  (cost=324.62..326.84 rows=889 width=24)
       -> Sort  (cost=324.62..324.62 rows=889 width=24)
            -> Nested Loop  (cost=0.00..281.08 rows=889 width=24)
                 -> Seq Scan on persons a  (cost=0.00..1.08 rows=8 width=4)
                 -> Seq Scan on income_class b  (cost=0.00..20.00 rows=1000
width=20)


EXPLAIN
```

The execution plans are identical. The results differ only if we want to influence the way the result has to be ordered. If we want the group that occurs most frequently to be displayed first, we can order the result in descending order:

```
SELECT b.label, COUNT(*)
       FROM persons AS a, income_class AS b
       WHERE a.income>b.lower
               AND a.income<=b.upper
       GROUP BY b.label
       ORDER BY COUNT(*) DESC;
```

Now the sort operation is performed differently:

```
label | count
------+------
40k   |   3
50k   |   2
more  |   2
30k   |   1
(4 rows)
```

This way of performing the sort operations also has a significant impact on the execution plan of the query. A second sort operation has to be done to find the result:

```
persons=# EXPLAIN SELECT b.label, COUNT(*)  FROM persons AS a, income_class AS b
WHERE a.income>b.lower AND a.income<=b.upper GROUP BY b.label ORDER BY COUNT(*)
DESC;
```

```
NOTICE:   QUERY PLAN:

Sort   (cost=331.94..331.94 rows=89 width=24)
  -> Aggregate  (cost=324.62..329.06 rows=89 width=24)
       -> Group  (cost=324.62..326.84 rows=889 width=24)
            -> Sort  (cost=324.62..324.62 rows=889 width=24)
                 -> Nested Loop  (cost=0.00..281.08 rows=889 width=24)
                      -> Seq Scan on persons a  (cost=0.00..1.08 rows=8
width=4)
                      -> Seq Scan on income_class b  (cost=0.00..20.00
rows=1000 width=20)

EXPLAIN
```

In the examples in this section, the database always returns values that occur more than zero times. If you look at the list of classifications that can be found in `income_class`, you will see that the list of classes is actually longer than the list of classes to which one or more persons belong.

In statistics, it is sometimes necessary to get a list of all classifications available and not only a list of those where the value is higher than zero.

The problem can be solved by performing an outer join. Normally, a join returns only those values that match certain conditions. For example, `a.id=b.id` returns only rows that can be found in both tables. If you need a full list of all records in one table and want to add just the data that can be found in the second table, you have to perform an outer join.

Here is a simple example of an outer join:

```
SELECT b.label, COUNT(*) INTO temp_1 FROM persons AS a, income_class AS b
    WHERE a.income>b.lower
            AND a.income<=b.upper
        GROUP BY b.label;
```

Now we use the query we used previously, but this time we redirect the result of the query into a table called `temp_1`. The same result can be achieved by defining a view using the same SQL command. Now we perform the outer join:

```
SELECT a.label, b.label
        FROM income_class AS a
            LEFT OUTER JOIN temp_1 AS b
        ON a.label=b.label;
```

The result of the query contains all classifications listed in table `income_class` and all cells that can be found in `temp_1`. Because `temp_1` contains only values that occur more than zero times, we have successfully combined the information:

```
label | label
-------+-------
 10k   |
 20k   |
 30k   | 30k
 40k   | 40k
 50k   | 50k
 more  | more
(6 rows)
```

The previous query returns only the labels. Let's add the data to the labels:

```
SELECT a.label, b.count
       FROM income_class AS a
             LEFT OUTER JOIN temp_1 AS b
       ON a.label=b.label;
```

An empty field is displayed for every record that cannot be found in `temp_1`:

```
label | count
-------+-------
 10k   |
 20k   |
 30k   |    1
 40k   |    3
 50k   |    2
 more  |    2
(6 rows)
```

The result already looks much better. If we want `0` to be displayed instead of nothing, we have to add an additional step to the process:

```
SELECT a.label, b.count INTO temp_2
       FROM income_class AS a
             LEFT OUTER JOIN temp_1 AS b
       ON a.label=b.label;
```

We select the data into a table again. In the next step, we select all records where `count` is higher than `0` and combine it with the `NULL` values. In the query, `NULL` is substituted by `0`:

```
SELECT label, '0' AS count FROM temp_2
        WHERE count=NULL
UNION SELECT label, count FROM temp_2
        WHERE count>0;
```

The table is displayed the way we expect it to be now:

```
label | count
-------+-------
10k   |   0
20k   |   0
30k   |   1
40k   |   3
50k   |   2
more  |   2
(6 rows)
```

Substituting values can be a little painful if you are using plain SQL code, because you can't use control structures such as IF/ELSE to control the output. Writing a small PL/pgSQL is in most cases a faster way than writing complex SQL statements using UNION or other commands.

The following is a simple PL/pgSQL function we can use to substitute values in a column. The first parameter of the function is the row where we want to substitute values. The second parameter defines which string has to be changed, and the third parameter tells the database what to use instead of the string we want to change. If the function finds a NULL value, it is also changed to the string defined by the third parameter:

```
CREATE FUNCTION subst_vals(text, text, text) RETURNS text AS
'
    DECLARE
            result   text;
        BEGIN
            IF      $1 = $2 OR $1 = NULL THEN
                    result := $3;
            ELSE
                    result := $1;
            END IF;
            RETURN result;
        END;
' LANGUAGE 'plpgsql';
```

The function can easily be called to generate the desired result:

```
SELECT label, subst_vals(count, 'a string', '0')
     FROM temp_2;
```

If we want anything but 0 to be displayed instead of a string, we just call the function with different parameters. This leads to the right result:

```
label | subst_vals
-------+------------
10k    | 0
20k    | 0
30k    | 1
40k    | 3
50k    | 2
more   | 2
(6 rows)
```

Classifying the age of a person is a little more complicated than classifying the income, because it can be done only if we have already computed the age of a person. PostgreSQL offers a function called age to find the difference between the current date and the date that has to be processed:

```
SELECT age(birth), * FROM persons;
```

The following table shows how the result is returned by the database:

```
            age             | id | name   | birth      | gender | income
----------------------------+----+--------+------------+--------+--------
31 years 4 mons 17 days 23:00 |  1 | Albert | 1970-01-01 | m      |  35000
28 years 1 mon 14 days 23:00  |  2 | John   | 1973-04-04 | m      |  50000
37 years 6 mons 28 days 23:00 |  3 | Carla  | 1963-10-21 | f      |  32000
18 years 7 mons 28 days       |  4 | Jenny  | 1982-09-21 | f      |  45000
22 years 9 mons 9 days 23:00  |  5 | Hans   | 1978-08-09 | m      |  59000
24 years 11 mons 6 days 23:00 |  6 | Epi    | 1976-06-12 | m      |  21000
41 years 2 mons 27 days 23:00 |  7 | Etschi | 1960-02-20 | f      |  34000
20 years 10 mons 6 days 23:00 |  8 | Bill   | 1980-07-12 | m      |  43000
(8 rows)
```

In general, the age of a person is counted in years; it doesn't make sense to define the age in months, days, and hours. For classification, we need full years instead of the precise time. The round function is defined only for rounding "numeric" fields, and we have to find a different way to generate the result.

Luckily, PostgreSQL provides a function called date_part, which can be used to extract values from the interval returned by age:

```
SELECT date_part('year', age(birth)), * FROM persons;
```

This example shows how the number of years can be extracted from the interval with the help of the date_part function.

```
date_part | id |  name   |   birth    | gender | income
----------+----+---------+------------+--------+--------
       31 |  1 | Albert  | 1970-01-01 | m      |  35000
       28 |  2 | John    | 1973-04-04 | m      |  50000
       37 |  3 | Carla   | 1963-10-21 | f      |  32000
       18 |  4 | Jenny   | 1982-09-21 | f      |  45000
       22 |  5 | Hans    | 1978-08-09 | m      |  59000
       24 |  6 | Epi     | 1976-06-12 | m      |  21000
       41 |  7 | Etschi  | 1960-02-20 | f      |  34000
       20 |  8 | Bill    | 1980-07-12 | m      |  43000
(8 rows)
```

The result of the query can now be used to classify the data. The best way is to use a view:

```
CREATE VIEW view_age_persons AS
        SELECT id, name, date_part('year', age(birth)), gender, income
                FROM persons;
```

The view provides the data in the way we need it for further processing:

```
id |  name   | date_part | gender | income
---+---------+-----------+--------+--------
 1 | Albert  |        31 | m      |  35000
 2 | John    |        28 | m      |  50000
 3 | Carla   |        37 | f      |  32000
 4 | Jenny   |        18 | f      |  45000
 5 | Hans    |        22 | m      |  59000
 6 | Epi     |        24 | m      |  21000
 7 | Etschi  |        41 | f      |  34000
 8 | Bill    |        20 | m      |  43000
(8 rows)
```

The target of the next example is to create a two-dimensional data structure that contains all combinations of age and gender according to the classifications in `age_class` and `income_class`. Before we get to the queries to generate the result, we will have a look at the classification that we will use for the age:

```
SELECT * FROM age_class;
```

We select all records from the table:

```
 id | age_code | lower | upper
----+----------+-------+--------
  1 | age_1    |     0 |     29
  2 | age_2    |    29 |     39
  3 | age_3    |    39 |     59
  4 | age_4    |    59 | 999999
(4 rows)
```

The table contains four classes that we will use to classify the age of a person. To compute the result, we create a view first:

```
CREATE VIEW view_inc_age_1 AS SELECT b.age_code, c.label, COUNT(*)
        FROM view_age_persons AS a, age_class AS b, income_class AS c
        WHERE a.date_part>b.lower
                AND a.date_part<=b.upper
                AND a.income>c.lower
                AND a.income<=c.upper
        GROUP BY b.age_code, c.label;
```

The view contains all combinations of age and `income`, where the amount of people in a class is higher than zero; those classes, where the amount of people is zero, are not displayed yet:

```
 age_code | label | count
----------+-------+-------
 age_1    | 30k   |     1
 age_1    | 50k   |     2
 age_1    | more  |     2
 age_2    | 40k   |     2
 age_3    | 40k   |     1
(5 rows)
```

To make the output fit our demands, we can perform outer joins now to add even values, where the column called `count` contains a `NULL` value. The following performs the operation for the income:

```
SELECT b.label, subst_vals(a.age_code, '', 'none') AS age_code,
               subst_vals(a.count, '', '0') AS count
       INTO tmp_inc_age_2
       FROM view_inc_age_1 AS a RIGHT OUTER JOIN income_class AS b
     ON a.label=b.label;
SELECT * FROM tmp_inc_age_2;
```

The table we created contains the values we expect:

```
label | age_code | count
------+----------+------
10k   | none     | 0
20k   | none     | 0
30k   | age_1    | 1
40k   | age_2    | 2
40k   | age_3    | 1
50k   | age_1    | 2
more  | age_1    | 2
(7 rows)
```

You can see that the values in the empty fields have been substituted by the values we defined in the SQL code. As in the examples before, substitution is done by our PL/pgSQL function called subst_vals.

As mentioned before, statistics will, in most cases, also include those records where the number of persons belonging to a group is zero. We have already shown how these records can be added with the help of outer joins. If the amount of columns we want to compute the combinations for increases and we need a separate table for every column we add, it will become very uncomfortable and very inflexible. An easier and faster way is to use explicit joins and the Cartesian product of columns.

Generating the Cartesian product of two columns is a very easy task, because we only have to write a query with two tables involved without adding a WHERE clause.

The easiest way is to write a query like this one:

```
SELECT age_class.age_code, income_class.label
       FROM income_class, age_class;
```

The result of the command will be exactly 24 lines long, because we have four records in table age_class and six records in table income_class.

The query can also be written differently:

```
SELECT age_class.age_code, income_class.label
       FROM (income_class CROSS JOIN age_class);
```

We use an explicit CROSS JOIN and will combine the output of the query with the records in the view called view_inc_age_1 that we created before. To avoid nasty searching for the definition and the content of the view, we include the definition of view_inc_age_1 again:

```
     View "view_inc_age_1"
 Attribute |  Type   | Modifier
-----------+---------+----------
 age_code  | text    |
 label     | text    |
 count     | integer |
View definition: SELECT b.age_code, c.label, count(*) AS count FROM
view_age_persons a, age_class b, income_class c WHERE ((((a.date_part >
float8(b.lower)) AND (a.date_part <= float8(b.upper))) AND (a.income > c.lower))
AND (a.income <= c.upper)) GROUP BY b.age_code, c.label;
```

Here is the content of the view:

```
 age_code | label | count
----------+-------+-------
 age_1    | 30k   |    1
 age_1    | 50k   |    2
 age_1    | more  |    2
 age_2    | 40k   |    2
 age_3    | 40k   |    1
(5 rows)
```

> **Note**
> The sum of all values in column count is 8.

We combine the content of the view with the Cartesian product of column age_code in table age_class and column label in table income_class:

```
SELECT age_class.age_code, income_class.label, a.count
      FROM (income_class CROSS JOIN age_class)
            LEFT OUTER JOIN view_inc_age_1 AS a
      ON income_class.label=a.label
            AND age_class.age_code=a.age_code;
```

The result of the query will contain 24 records—that's what we expect it to be:

```
 age_code | label | count
----------+-------+-------
 age_1    | 10k   |
 age_1    | 20k   |
```

```
age_1    | 30k    |     1
age_1    | 40k    |
age_1    | 50k    |     2
age_1    | more   |     2
age_2    | 10k    |
age_2    | 20k    |
age_2    | 30k    |
age_2    | 40k    |     2
age_2    | 50k    |
age_2    | more   |
age_3    | 10k    |
age_3    | 20k    |
age_3    | 30k    |
age_3    | 40k    |     1
age_3    | 50k    |
age_3    | more   |
age_4    | 10k    |
age_4    | 20k    |
age_4    | 30k    |
age_4    | 40k    |
age_4    | 50k    |
age_4    | more   |
(24 rows)
```

The sum of all values in column count is 8 again, which is correct. The only problem is that the sum is not displayed in the result—but it can easily be added. We have to add one record to both tables containing the classification shown below:

```
INSERT INTO age_class VALUES (5, 'all', 0, 999999);
INSERT INTO income_class VALUES (7, 'all', 0, 10000000);
```

The two records we inserted into the database match all values that might occur in table persons. If we query the view view_inc_age_1 now, the sums of the various aggregates are returned:

```
age_code | label | count
---------+-------+-------
age_1    | 30k   |    1
age_1    | 50k   |    2
age_1    | all   |    5
age_1    | more  |    2
age_2    | 40k   |    2
age_2    | all   |    2
age_3    | 40k   |    1
```

```
age_3   | all  |    1
all     | 30k  |    1
all     | 40k  |    3
all     | 50k  |    2
all     | all  |    8
all     | more |    2
(13 rows)
```

The view contains the required values, but if we look closer at the second column, we
see that the order of the records does not fit our demands, because the data is returned
in alphabetical order. The sum is therefore not the last record in a block of data.
Sorting works perfectly well for the first column, but if we want the second column to
be displayed correctly, we have to find a way to influence the order of the values.

The easiest way to tell the database the order in which the records have to be returned
is to use a column. Luckily, we have a column called id in both tables that numbers
the records consecutively in the order we need it. If we look at table income_class, we
can see that all comes after more. That's the way we want it to be in the result:

```
id | label | lower |   upper
---+-------+-------+----------
 1 | 10k   |     0 |     9999
 2 | 20k   |  9999 |    19999
 3 | 30k   | 19999 |    29999
 4 | 40k   | 29999 |    39999
 5 | 50k   | 39999 |    49999
 6 | more  | 49999 | 10000000
 7 | all   |     0 | 10000000
(7 rows)
```

A simple SELECT * command, like the one we use to retrieve all data from the view,
will not be enough to compute the result:

```
SELECT a.*
        FROM view_inc_age_1 AS a, income_class AS b, age_class AS c
        WHERE a.age_code=c.age_code
                AND a.label=b.label
        ORDER BY c.id, b.id;
```

We have to join view_inc_age_1, income_class, and age_class, because we need the
ids in income_class and age_class to perform this sort operation. The ids of the
columns are used only for sorting and will not be returned with the data, which is
important.

Note
The column in the ORDER BY clause does not have to appear in the result.

The result looks the way it should:

```
age_code | label | count
---------+-------+-------
age_1    | 30k   |    1
age_1    | 50k   |    2
age_1    | more  |    2
age_1    | all   |    5
age_2    | 40k   |    2
age_2    | all   |    2
age_3    | 40k   |    1
age_3    | all   |    1
all      | 30k   |    1
all      | 40k   |    3
all      | 50k   |    2
all      | more  |    2
all      | all   |    8
(13 rows)
```

The sums of the various aggregates are always displayed at the end. In the last line, you can see that 8 people were counted; that's the sum we have already seen in the previous examples.

Performing very complex operations, as we do in this section, can be dangerous when the amount of data involved in the query increases. When millions of rows have to be processed, it is necessary to look at the execution plan to achieve an acceptable level of performance. The execution plan of the query that we have used before is, in a way, overwhelming:

```
EXPLAIN SELECT a.*
        FROM view_inc_age_1 AS a, income_class AS b, age_class AS c
        WHERE a.age_code=c.age_code
              AND a.label=b.label
        ORDER BY c.id, b.id;

NOTICE:  QUERY PLAN:

Sort  (cost=304288.00..304288.00 rows=987654 width=60)
  -> Merge Join  (cost=58781.93..60029.00 rows=987654 width=60)
       -> Sort  (cost=58712.10..58712.10 rows=98765 width=44)
            -> Merge Join  (cost=45999.97..46135.93 rows=98765 width=44)
```

```
                        -> Sort  (cost=46104.80..46104.80 rows=9877 width=48)
                           -> Subquery Scan a  (cost=44534.10..45274.84
rows=9877 width=48)
                              -> Aggregate  (cost=44534.10..45274.84
rows=9877 width=48)
                                 -> Group  (cost=44534.10..45027.93
rows=98765 width=48)
                                    -> Sort  (cost=44534.10..44534.10
                                       rows=98765 width=48)
                                       -> Nested Loop  (cost=0.00..
                                          31552.19 rows=98765
width=48)
                                          -> Nested Loop
(cost=0.00..
                                             441.08 rows=889
width=28)
                                             -> Seq Scan on
persons
                                                (cost=0.00..1.08
                                                rows=8
width=8)
                                             -> Seq Scan on
age_class
                                                b
(cost=0.00..20.00
                                                rows=1000
width=20)
                                          -> Seq Scan on
income_class c
                                             (cost=0.00..20.00
rows=1000 width=20)
                        -> Sort  (cost=69.83..69.83 rows=1000 width=16)
                           -> Seq Scan on income_class b  (cost=0.00..20.00
rows=1000 width=16)
                  -> Sort  (cost=69.83..69.83 rows=1000 width=16)
                     -> Seq Scan on age_class c  (cost=0.00..20.00 rows=1000 width=16)
```

We have not included the detailed version of the execution plan (this can be done with EXPLAIN VERBOSE), because nobody would understand it.

The main problem with the queries we have shown is that, in general, the process included more than just one step. You have to take into consideration that most operations are based on views. Views are the result of a SELECT statement, and PostgreSQL has to plan and process both operations to compute the result.

If the process is very complex, we not only recommend checking the execution plan. It is also necessary to think about the way a query can be processed, before selecting an algorithm to solve your problem. As a rule of thumb, the best way to find the result is to reduce the amount of data involved in the query as soon as possible. Try to avoid views that have to perform internal sorting with huge amounts of data. You also have to keep in mind that the more tables have to be joined, the more complicated it will be for the planner to find the best way through the query. Defining the order of joins can also help gain a lot of performance.

Another important point is that you should avoid scanning the same table more than once per query. If full table scans have to be performed, your query might slow down significantly, because a lot of additional I/O might have to be done (depending on the amount of data and the way things are cached by the system).

EFEU—The Perfect Tool for Data Warehousing

In the past sections, you explored multidimensional data structures and multidimensional results extensively.

You learned that basically all operations can be done by using plain SQL code. The problem with SQL is that some operations can hardly be performed, or the desired result can be obtained only at the cost of a significant performance decrease. The more complex an operation is, the more performance you can lose, because the execution plan of a query becomes terribly complicated and the optimizer can hardly find the best way through it.

About EFEU

In this section, you learn about one of the most powerful tools for processing extremely huge amounts of data. At the time of this writing, the EFEU package has just been released by Erich Fruehstueck under the terms of the GPL after a decade of development. This is the first book that includes detailed information about EFEU.In the 1980s, Erich Fruehstueck wrote the first prototype of a command-line interpreter in Fortran at the University of Vienna. Like many other computer gurus, he wrote the software just for fun, and at that time he did not know about C and Unix.

In the 1990s, Erich had to work with huge amounts of data for scientific purposes. The problem was to generate attractive reports out of database queries. Because the design and the content of those reports had to be very flexible, he needed an interpreter language fast. The first version of the esh interpreter (*esh* stands for *EFEU shell*) was inspired by PostScript and therefore stack-oriented. Stack-oriented languages can easily be implemented but are not user-friendly. During that time, Erich Fruehstueck was already working with C, so he started working on a C-like interpreter language. The primary target of esh was to evaluate configuration files for C programs. To achieve that target, it is necessary to access C internals directly and to have an easy interface to C library functions.

In 1994, the esh interpreter was ready to be used in a commercial project, a model used to forecast the demand and supply of flats in Vienna. The complex operations of the model could easily be substituted by fast C functions because esh is very close to C.

By this time, many functions were added to the interpreter. The most important feature was the implementation of multidimensional data cubes (Erich calls it *Datenmatrix*; we will call it *data matrix* or *data cubes*). The advantage of data cubes is that they can easily be transposed; you will look closer at that feature in this section.

esh has grown and is now a very powerful interpreter language that enables the programmer to build sophisticated applications. For a long time, esh has been used for scientific purposes and is therefore a very stable piece of software.

The entire package has been written for Unix operating systems and is completely based on ANSI C. All components (Bourne Shell, C compiler, make, GNU Readline, and so forth) needed to run EFEU are included in a Unix system, so EFEU is portable across Unix platforms.

To find out more about EFEU and the esh interpreter, check out `http://efeu.cybertec.at`. If you need additional information about EFEU, feel free to contact us at `office@cybertec.at` or `efeu@cybertec.at`.

(Erich Fruehstueck said: "If I only had something like Python there would be no EFEU." We are happy that there was no Python back in the 1980s.)

Using PostgreSQL and Data Matrices

Because EFEU is so flexible, additional components can easily be added to the esh interpreter. One of the most powerful extension packs is the esh interface to PostgreSQL.

As already mentioned, one of the core features of esh is the capability of working with data cubes efficiently. Before we get to data cubes in detail, let's look at how a connection to the database can be established:

```
#!/usr/bin/env esh

pconfig !
Ident = "test database connection"

//      resources
DBName = NULL
        name of database
Options = NULL
        connect options

//      arguments
:db|DBName
        name of database

//      optional arguments that match regular expressions
/.*=.*/<key>=<val>|Options: append " "
        connect options, where key is host, hostaddr, port, user,
        password, options, tty or requiressl.
!

loadlib("PG");
PG(DBName, Options)
```

> **Note**
> Don't mix up EFEU's data cubes with the datatypes cube provided by a package in
> the contributed section.

The connection is established by the last two lines. The code before provides the
command shell interface for the user.

Let's execute the script without parameters:

```
[erich@duron ex4]$ ./conn1

ÜBERSICHT
        ./conn1 [ --help[=type] ] [ --info[=entry] ] [ --dump[=entry] ]
            [ --version ] [ --debug[=mode] ] [ --verbose ]
            db { key=val }
```

If no parameters are supplied to the program, a help screen is displayed. Some
command-line options, such as --verbose and --help are always defined. This is very
comfortable, because it saves the programmers a lot of work. The following executes
the script with the name of the database and a username:

```
[erich@duron ex4]$ ./conn1 db user=hs
PG = {
        status = ok
        dbname = "db"
        user = "hs"
        pass = ""
        host = NULL
        port = "5432"
        tty = ""
        options = ""
}
```

You can see that the connection to the database has successfully been established, and esh displays some information about the connection.

> **Note**
> The connection to the database does not have to be closed explicitly since this is
> done by esh internally.

It's time to move on to multidimensional data structures. We use the sample database that we used in the section about the C programming interface of PostgreSQL, because it shows very well how things work. To avoid page turning, here is the code:

```
CREATE TABLE "persons" (
    "name" text,
    "birth" date,
    "gender" character(1)
);
CREATE UNIQUE INDEX persons_name_key on persons ("name");
CREATE TABLE "income" (
    "name" text,
    "year" integer,
    "income" integer
);
CREATE INDEX income_name_key on income ("name");

COPY "persons"  FROM stdin;
Albert       1970-01-01      m
John 1973-04-04      m
Carla1963-10-21      f
Jenny1982-09-21      f
Hans 1978-08-09      m
Epi  1976-06-12      m
```

```
Etschi      1960-02-20      f
Bill 1980-07-12      m
\.

COPY "income"  FROM stdin;
Albert      1997    32000
Albert      1998    28000
Albert      1999    30000
Albert      2000    35000
Jon   1998    20000
Jon   1999    40000
Jon   2000    50000
Carla1998    30000
Carla1999    32000
Jenny1999    45000
Jenny2000    45000
Hans  1999    47000
Hans  2000    59000
Epi   1999    25000
Epi   2000    21000
Etschi      1999     30000
Etschi      2000     34000
Bill  1994    41000
Bill  1995    43000
\.

CREATE VIEW pincome
    AS SELECT p.name, p.gender, i.year, i.income
    FROM persons p, income i
    WHERE p.name = i.name;
```

The goal is to write a query that retrieves the number of people of a certain gender in a certain year and to make a data matrix out of it. Before we get to the esh script, let's see what SQL statement we have to use and what the result of that query will look like:

```
db=# SELECT gender, year, COUNT(*)
db-#         FROM pincome
db-#         GROUP BY year, gender;
 gender | year | count
--------+------+-------
 m      | 1994 |    1
 m      | 1995 |    1
```

```
m       | 1997 |     1
f       | 1998 |     1
m       | 1998 |     1
f       | 1999 |     3
m       | 1999 |     3
f       | 2000 |     2
m       | 2000 |     3
(9 rows)
```

Nine records are retrieved from the database. As we have seen in previous sections, no lines are returned where the amount of people belonging to that group is smaller than 1. Again, this might be a problem if you want to generate reports.

With the help of the esh interpreter, the problem can easily be solved:

```
#!/usr/bin/env        esh

/*

NOTE: most functions of mdmat return the object itself,
So
    <create>.mark(<x-axis>).print(<out>, <flags>);
is equivalent to
    mdmat md = <create>;
    md.mark(<x-axis>);
    md.print(<out>, <flags>);
    free(md);
*/

loadlib("PG");

//   creating a new pg object and selecting data
PG pg = PG("db");
pg.query(string !
SELECT gender, year, COUNT(*)
    FROM pincome
    GROUP BY year, gender
!);

//   show data

PrintListDelim = "\t";

mdmat md = pg.mdmat(int, "COUNT", "gender, year")
```

```
iostd << "# \"normal\" output:\n";
md.mark("").print(iostd, "title");

free(md);
close(pg);
```

First we load the PostgreSQL module and connect to the database, which is called db.
Then we run the previous query and create a data matrix object called md. The result
of the query is then assigned to the md object. The mdmat needs three parameters, The
first parameter defines the datatype of the data matrix; the second parameter tells the
esh interpreter which columns contain the data of the query (a list can be passed to the
function). With the help of the third parameter, we define which axis the data matrix
should contain. In general, we pass the names of all columns returned by the query to
the function that are not already listed in the second parameter. iostd prints a string
on standard output. Now we want to display the content of the data matrix; therefore,
we use mark. In our example, the parameter list of the mark" method is empty (we will
have a look at mark in the next examples). The data matrix is written to standard
output without any transformation:

```
[erich@duron ex5]$ ./count3.sh
MD: name="COUNT by gender, year", type=int, dim=2, size=48
# "normal" output:
COUNT by gender, year
1            .
f.1994  0
f.1995  0
f.1997  0
f.1998  1
f.1999  3
f.2000  2
m.1994  1
m.1995  1
m.1997  1
m.1998  1
m.1999  3
m.2000  3
```

One line for every combination of year and gender that can be found in the result is
displayed. No entry of a woman for the year 1997 can be found in the database the
line is printed, because esh makes sure that even lines where the number of records
belonging to that group is 0 are displayed.

7	1994	1995	1996	1997	1998	1999	2000
f	0	0	0	0	1	3	2
m	1	1	0	1	1	3	3

After connecting to the database, sending the query to the server, and creating the data matrix, we want to display the content of the data matrix in a more friendly way.

In the first table, we want the element of the axis called gender to be the columns (x-axis) of the table. Because our data matrix contains two axes (gender and year), there is only one axis remaining for the y-axis.

In the second table, we want the result to be transposed so that the elements of the axis called year will be displayed in the x-axis. The elements of the axis called gender are logically displayed in the y-axis.

You can see that esh offers a simple way to display a data matrix in any way you can imagine. The tremendous power of a data matrix makes esh a great choice when building data warehouses and reports. Up to now we created and displayed data matrices on-the-fly. The next example shows how a data matrix can be stored in a file:

```
#!/usr/bin/env  esh

loadlib("PG");

//      creating a new pg object and selecting data
PG pg = PG("db");
pg.query(string !
SELECT gender, year, COUNT(*)
        FROM pincome
        GROUP BY year, gender
!);

mdmat md = pg.mdmat(int, "COUNT", "gender, year");
md.save("matrix.dat");

free(md);
close(pg);
```

The code of the example is even easier than the earlier scripts. After creating the data matrix, we store it in the file matrix.dat using the save method.

Now that we have successfully created a file containing the data, we want to find out what the file we have just created looks like. Therefore, we use mdfile, one of the commands included in the EFEU core distribution.

The -x flag tells mdfile to display information about the axis of our data matrix:

```
[erich@duron ex5]$ mdfile -x matrix.dat
matrix.dat: int[12=2*6] "COUNT by gender, year"
gender: f m
year: 1994 1995 1997 1998 1999 2000
```

The data matrix contains two axes. The first axis contains the elements m and f, and the second axis contains information about the years 1994 to 1995 and 1997 to 2000. Twelve elements are stored in the data matrix, one for every combination of gender and year.

To retrieve data from the data matrix, mdprint or an esh script has to be used. Here's the mdprint version:

```
[erich@duron ex5]$ mdprint matrix.dat -x gender
##MDMAT    2.0
##Titel    COUNT by gender, year
##Type     int
##Locale   us
##Zeilen   year
##Spalten  gender
2          f          m
1994       0          1
1995       0          1
1997       0          1
1998       1          1
1999       3          3
2000       2          3
```

This command returns the data in the data matrix; -x tells the command to use the elements on gender as columns. If we want the columns to contain information about the various years, we have to use the following command:

```
[erich@duron ex5]$ mdprint matrix.dat -x year
##MDMAT    2.0
##Titel    COUNT by gender, year
##Type     int
##Locale   us
##Zeilen   gender
##Spalten  year
6          1994    1995    1997    1998    1999    2000
f          0       0       0       1       3       2
m          1       1       1       1       3       3
```

The way the result of mdprint is displayed might not fit your demands, because it can hardly be used by other programs, such as Microsoft Excel. Because EFEU has always been used in environments where data had to be exchanged between Windows and Unix systems, Erich Fruehstueck has implemented flexible output functions. In the next example, we want the result to be displayed without header information. A semicolon (;) is used as the delimiter:

```
[erich@duron ex5]$ mdprint matrix.dat -x gender -b -d ";"
2;f;m
1994;0;1
1995;0;1
1997;0;1
1998;1;1
1999;3;3
2000;2;3
```

-d defines the delimiter that has to be used, and -b suppresses the header information.

Data matrices cannot only be created with the help of the esh interpreter. The next example shows how data matrices can be generated out of ASCII text:

```
mdprint matrix.dat -x year | mdread - o.dat
```

This command is a rather unusual way of copying a file. mdprint produces ASCII output we read from the pipe using mdread. mdread takes the ASCII output and makes a data matrix out of it again.

To see whether the input and the output files are equal, we use the mdfile command:

```
[erich@duron ex5]$ mdfile -x matrix.dat o.dat
matrix.dat: int[12=2*6] "COUNT by gender, year"
gender: f m
year: 1994 1995 1997 1998 1999 2000
o.dat: int[12=2*6] "COUNT by gender, year"
gender: f m
year: 1994 1995 1997 1998 1999 2000
```

You can see that the definition of the files does not differ. To make sure that not only the axes are the same, we can use mddiff (see mddiff --help).

Of course, the esh interpreter is not only used to generate multidimensional data structures. The following example shows how cursors can be used in esh:

```
#!/usr/bin/env esh

//    program configuration

pconfig !
Ident = "query data with cursor"

//    resources

DBName = "db"
     name of database
Name = NULL
     name of table
BSIZE = 2
     block size for fetch command
Options = NULL
     connect options

//    options

b:bsize | -bsize:bsize | BSIZE
     set block size for fetch command, default is {BSIZE}
d:name | -dbname:name | DBName
     set database name, default is {DBName}
h:host | -host:host | Options: set {Options} host={}
     set host name
p:port | -port:port | Options: set {Options} port={}
     set port number
u:name | -user:name | Options: set {Options} user={}
     set user name
a:passwd | -auth:passwd | -passwd:auth | Options: set {Options} passwd={}
     set password for user

//    arguments

:name|Name
     name of table
!

//    load shared library

loadlib("PG");
```

```
//   set layout parameters

PrintListBegin = NULL;
PrintListEnd = "\n";
PrintListDelim = "\t";
fmt_str = "%*s";

//   connect to db
PG pg = PG(DBName, Options);
if   (!pg)   exit(1);

//   query data
pg.command("BEGIN");
pg.command("DECLARE tmpcursor CURSOR FOR select * from $1", Name);

for (int k = 1; pg.query("FETCH $1 in tmpcursor", BSIZE); k++)
{
     if      (pg.ntuples == 0)        break;

     printf("# group %d: %d rows\n", k, pg.ntuples);

     for (x in pg)
             iostd << x;
}

pg.command("CLOSE tmpcursor");
pg.command("COMMIT");

//   cleanup
close(pg)
```

First we define the options accepted by the program and the formatting that has to be used. Then we connect to the database and select all data from the table that we defined when starting the program.

In the next step, we create a cursor using a certain block size, which can also be defined when starting the program. The result of the query is written to standard output, and we close the cursor, commit the session, and close the connection to the PostgreSQL server.

Let's start the program:

```
[erich@duron ex4]$ ./xquery

ÜBERSICHT
        ./xquery [ --help[=type] ] [ --info[=entry] ] [ --dump[=entry] ]
              [ --version ] [ --debug[=mode] ] [ --verbose ]
              [ -b bsize ] [ --bsize bsize ] [ -d name ] [ --dbname name ]
              [ -h host ] [ --host host ] [ -p port ] [ --port port ]
              [ -u name ] [ --user name ] [ -a passwd ] [ --auth passwd ]
              [ --passwd auth ] name
```

If we attempt to start xquery with no command-line parameters, esh displays an overview of all command-line parameters accepted by the script.

Now we want the script to query the persons table with a block size of 4:

```
[erich@duron ex4]$ ./xquery --bsize 4 persons
# group 1: 4 rows
Albert   1970-01-01      m
John     1973-04-04      m
Carla    1963-10-21      f
Jenny    1982-09-21      f
# group 2: 4 rows
Hans     1978-08-09      m
Epi      1976-06-12      m
Etschi   1960-02-20      f
Bill     1980-07-12      m
```

The program fetches 4 records at a time from the result and displays them on the screen.

If you need additional information about EFEU and the esh interpreter language, check out http://efeu.cybertec.at or contact office@cybertec.at.

Summary

When dealing with data warehouses, classification and aggregation are essential steps. These important operations can be performed either using plain SQL or in combination with an additional software package, such as the EFEU package by Erich Fruehstueck. The goal of aggregation and classification is to display information in a compact way so that the key information can be seen easily.

CHAPTER **14**

Generating Flash with PostgreSQL and PHP

Modern Web sites are, to a large extent, generated dynamically. Therefore, the content of such Web sites is usually retrieved from a database. Recently, Flash, PHP, and PostgreSQL have become more popular, so consider using PHP and PostgreSQL to generate dynamic Flash movies.

In the beginning, there was nothing. After the golden ASCII age (I guess all of us will remember those wonderful ASCII art artifacts), simple Web sites were built. Since that time, browsers have been used to display Web sites. A few years ago, animation could be done only with the help of those wonderful high-performance Silicon Graphics machines. Times have changed. and now animations can easily be included in Web sites.

Generating graphics can sometimes be quite a burden. Some of you might already have written user interfaces using a text editor instead of a graphical development environment. If so, you discovered that this kind of work can be very tricky and difficult, because you can easily get lost in hundreds of objects and methods.

Now that you want to create animation, not just static graphics, you might think that this is even more difficult. It's not with Flash. Flash provides a lot of power combined with simplicity. Understanding the basic ideas of Flash is easy—and so is building basic Flash animations.

Sometimes, however, building Flash movies might not be enough to satisfy your demands. If you want to create database-enabled Web sites, you might find it useful to create Flash movies dynamically. Therefore, programming interfaces have been implemented for many programming languages, such as PHP, Python, and C/C++.

In this chapter, you take a closer look at one of those interfaces and see how Flash can be combined with PostgreSQL to build even more beautiful Web sites. We will also cover geometric objects, because these are a core feature of PostgreSQL.

This chapter is not meant to be a complete reference of the Ming interface. This information should show what can be done with PostgreSQL and other Open Source tools and give you insight into the topic so that you can start building your own applications with the help of the developers reference.

PHP's Flash Interfaces

Currently, two Flash interfaces for PHP are available: the Shockwave Flash interface and the Ming interface.

The Shockwave Flash interface is built on the libswf module by Paul Haeberli and provides a huge amount of powerful functions for creating dynamic Flash applications. To install the module, libswf has to be downloaded from `http://reality.sgi.com/grafica/flash/` and compiled into PHP. For further information about the installation process, check out one of the PHP mirror sites and the Web site of the module.

The second interface used to generate dynamic Flash is the Ming interface, which was added to PHP in version 4.05.

The Ming interface is the more comfortable one. Another advantage of the Ming interface is that the author of the module provides a large number of examples and easy-to-understand documentation. An important issue, especially for beginners, is that the module can easily be installed. You don't need to compile anything, because a binary version of the required module that you need to run Ming is available on the author's Web site.

For further information about the Ming interface, check out `http://www.opaque.net/ming/`. Ming is entirely written in C and is freely available under the terms of the LGPL (Lesser GPL). In contrast to the GPL, the LGPL is more freely available. It is used as the license for libraries and modules. The module also includes a set of wrappers for PHP, Python, and Ruby.

Simple Flash Examples

Because the Ming module offers a large number of functions and is easy to handle, we use it in this section to show you how Flash can be combined with PostgreSQL.

Before we get into details, let's look at a simple example:

```php
<?php
  dl('php_ming.so');

  # Drawing square ...
  $s = drawsquare(50, 0xee, 0, 0);

  # creating "movie clip"
  $p = new SWFSprite();
  $i = $p->add($s);

  # rotating object
  for($x=0; $x<3; $x++)
  {
    squarerot($p, $i, 5, -4);
    squarerot($p, $i, 10, 4);
    squarerot($p, $i, 5, -4);
  }

  # going to the next frame
  $p->nextFrame();

  # create a new movie object (SWF version 4)
  $m = new SWFMovie();
  $i = $m->add($p);
  $i->moveTo(160,120);
  $i->setName("the_name");

  # setting background and size
  $m->setBackground(0xff, 0xff, 0xff);
  $m->setDimension(320,240);

  # writing header and output
  header('Content-type: application/x-shockwave-flash');
  $m->output();
```

```
# function for creating square
function drawsquare($size, $color1, $color2, $color3)
{
  $s = new SWFShape();
  $s->setRightFill($s->addFill($color1, $color2, $color3));
  $s->movePenTo(-$size,-$size);
  $s->drawLineTo($size,-$size);
  $s->drawLineTo($size,$size);
  $s->drawLineTo(-$size,$size);
  $s->drawLineTo(-$size,-$size);

  return $s;
}

# rotating an object $howoften times
function squarerot($p, $i, $howoften, $angle)
{
  for($j=0; $j<$howoften; ++$j)
  {
    $p->nextFrame();
    $i->rotate($angle);
  }
}
?>
```

Figure 14.1 shows the result.

In the first line, we include php_ming.so. In this case, including the module is necessary because we installed the module but have not added extension=php_ming.so to our php.ini file (see the installation HOWTO). Then we call drawsquare($size, $color1, $color2, $color3) with four parameters. The first parameter defines the size, and the other three parameters define the color of the square.

The eighth line creates an instance of the SWFSprite object. In the next line, the square we created previously is added to the object and we can start rotating it. We want the square to behave like a seesaw (rotating left and right). Rotating is performed by the function squarerot($p, $i, $howoften, $angle) which we implement later in the script. The function needs four parameters. The first two are used to refer to the objects we created before; the first argument tells the function how often the rotation has to be performed. The fourth parameter defines the angle of the various rotations. If you have a closer look at the squarerot function, you can see that the nextFrame() function is called every time the loop is processed. nextFrame goes to the next frame, so the movie is generated.

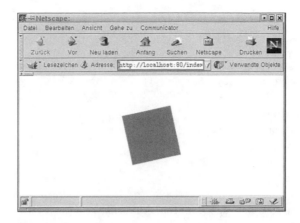

Figure 14.1
A simple Flash example.

After rotating the object several times, we create a SWFMovie() object and add the things we have done up to now to it. Then we move the object to the center of the screen and assign a name to it.

In the next step, we define the color of the background and the size of the animation. After displaying the header for the Flash movie, we output the movie.

The first example shows that drawing with the help of the Ming module is pen-based, which means that many commands draw things relative to the current position of the pen. Because a fully pen-based system would be far too complicated, Ming also provides functions using absolute coordinates. The drawLineTo function, for instance, has a related function called drawLine, which uses relative positioning instead of absolute coordinates.

In the previous example, we drew an animated square. In the next example, we draw two quadratic Bézier curves. We included this example to show you how quadratic Bézier curves can be drawn and how two geometric objects can be added to a scenery:

```php
<?php
  dl('php_ming.so');

  $s = new SWFShape();
  $s->setLine(10, 0xff, 0x11, 0x11);
  $s->movePenTo(30, 30);
  $cx = 0; $cy = 150; $ax = 60; $ay = 140;
  $s->drawCurveTo($cx, $cy, $ax, $ay);
```

```php
$t = new SWFShape();
$t->setLine(10, 0xff, 0x11, 0x11);
$t->movePenTo(30, 30);
$cx = 100; $cy = 50; $ax = 160; $ay = 40;
$t->drawCurveTo($cx, $cy, $ax, $ay);

$m = new SWFMovie();
$m->setDimension(320, 240);
$m->add($s);
$m->add($t);
$m->nextFrame();

header('Content-type: application/x-shockwave-flash');
$m->output();
```

```
?>
```

The result is no Picasso, but it's a good example of drawing curves and adding objects (see Figure 14.2).

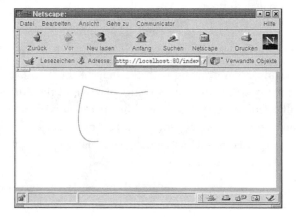

Figure 14.2
Drawing two curves.

Let's have a closer look at the source code of the program. First we create a shape and define the colors of the lines that we are going to draw. Then we move the pen to the required position and define the parameters for the curve that we want to draw. The whole process has to be done twice, because we want two curves to be displayed.

Finally, we create the SWFMovie, setting the size, adding the curves to the instance of the SWFMovie object, and displaying the output.

Before we get to PostgreSQL and Flash, you will see how text can be processed with the help of the Ming module. Knowing how to process text is very important, because most data is displayed as text in real-world applications. In the next example, we want Hello from postgresql.cybertec.at to be moved on the screen:

```php
<?php
  dl('php_ming.so');

  # defining text
  $string = "Hello from postgresql.cybertec.at";

  # creating objects required for text
  $f = new SWFFont("test.fdb");
  $t = new SWFText();
  $t->setFont($f);
  $t->setColor(0xff, 0, 0);
  $t->setHeight(20);
  $t->addString($string);

  # creating movie object
  $m = new SWFMovie();
  $m->setDimension(320, 240);

  # adding text to the movie object
  $i = $m->add($t);

  # setting text to 60 units left and 60 units
  $i->moveTo(100-$t->getWidth($string)/2, 60+$t->getAscent()/2);

  # moving the text ...
  for($j=1; $j<=20; $j++)
  {
    $i->move($j, $j);
    $m->nextFrame();
  }

  # displaying results
  header('Content-type: application/x-shockwave-flash');
  $m->output();

?>
```

Figure 14.3 shows the result.

Figure 14.3
Moving text.

Let's go through the code quickly. First we define the string that we want displayed. In the next step, we create an instance of the SWFFont object. The name of the font we want to use has to be passed to the function in brackets. In our example, we use the font that comes with the Ming source distribution. Additional fonts can be added by using the makefdb utility. The source code of the program can be found in the util directory of the source code. Use make makefdb to compile it:

```
[hs@duron util]$ make makefdb
gcc -g -Wall    -c -o blocktypes.o blocktypes.c
gcc -g -Wall    -c -o read.o read.c
gcc -g -Wall makefdb.c read.o blocktypes.o -o makefdb
```

After defining the font that we want to use for our application, we create an instance of the SWFText object and define the properties of the text, such as font, height, and color. The addString method is used to assign $string to the object.

After those operations related to the text, we create the SWFMovie object, as we did in the previous examples, and add the text to it. With the help of moveTo(), we define the position where the text should be displayed. However, the way the position of the text is computed has to be explained in a more detailed way.

If we want to display the text in the middle of the browser window, we have to use a command such as this:

```
$i->moveTo(160-$t->getWidth($string)/2, 120+$t->getAscent()/2);
```

The center of the window is 160 units right of the left edge of the windows, because
the size of the windows is exactly 320 units. getWidth returns the width of the string,
and we subtract half of that width to find the left position, where the string has to
start. The position of the text on the y-axis is computed the same way, except we use
the getAscent method instead of the getWidth method.

Now that we have the right position of the text in the result, we include a loop to
move the text from the left to the right and from up to down. Finally, we display the
video.

Adding Data to Flash

Now let's get to some PostgreSQL action. The target is to create a Flash movie that
contains the result of a simple query. The idea is simple, but it allows you to build
professional and very impressive Web applications.

We have compiled a small table containing four records that we will use in our sample
program:

```
myflash=# SELECT * FROM persons;
   name    |  profession
----------+---------------
 Alan Cox | kernel hacker
 Etschi   | foodstylist
 Hans     | author
 Falco    | musician
(4 rows)
```

The next application selects all records from this table and makes the lines move from
the upper side of the window to the bottom. The result already looks quite good and
the code is, including all comments, only about 70 lines long. This example shows how
easy it is to build Flash applications with the help of the Ming interface and
PostgreSQL.

Here is the code:

```
<?php
  dl('php_ming.so');

  # connecting to the database
  $dbh=pg_connect("dbname=myflash user=hs");
```

```php
if (!$dbh)
{
  echo ("ERROR: connecting failed");
  exit;
}

# selecting data from the PostgreSQL
$result=pg_exec($dbh, "SELECT * FROM persons");
if (!$result)
{
  echo ("ERROR: cannot failed");
  exit;
}

# creating font and movie object
$f = new SWFFont("test.fdb");
$m = new SWFMovie();
$m->setDimension(320, 240);

# computing number of lines
$num_res=pg_numrows($result);

# processing the data line by line
for ($i=0;$i<$num_res;$i++)
{
  $line=pg_fetch_row($result,$i);

  # creating a new object
  $obj[$i] = new SWFText();

  # setting the object's properties
  $obj[$i]->setFont($f);
  $obj[$i]->setColor(0xff, 0, 0);
  $obj[$i]->setHeight(15);
  $string="$line[0] 's profession is $line[1]";
  $obj[$i]->addString($string);

  # adding the object to the scenery
  $inst[$i] = $m->add($obj[$i]);

  # assigning the starting position
  $ypos[$i]=0-$i*30;
  $xpos[$i]=160-$obj[$i]->getWidth($string)/2;
```

```
    # moving the object to the starting position
    $inst[$i]->moveTo($xpos[$i], $ypos[$i]);
}

# repositioning 101 times
for($count=0; $count<=100; $count++)
{
  # processing the loop for every object
  for($j=0; $j<$num_res; $j++)
  {
    # moving the object and finding the new position
    $inst[$j]->moveTo($xpos[$j], $ypos[$j]);
    $ypos[$j]=$ypos[$j]+2;
    $ypos[$j]=$ypos[$j]%200;
  }
  $m->nextFrame();
}

# displaying results
header('Content-type: application/x-shockwave-flash');
$m->output();

?>
```

Figure 14.4 shows the result.

Let's have a closer look at the code. First we connect to the database—as we showed in the earlier section, "PHP and Flash Interfaces"—and select the data from the table. Then we create the Flash movie and compute the number of lines returned by the query. For every line returned by the query, we create a text object that will be stored in an array called $obj[]. Every object is assigned to the desired properties and added to the scenery. In the next step, we compute the current position of the objects and place the object in the correct position.

> **Note**
> The objects can be assigned to places that are outside the visual area (which means that the coordinates can be negative). This is a very comfortable feature, because it makes programming Flash applications even easier.

After we compile the various objects, we start animating the text. Every object is assigned to a new position 101 times. The position of an object is stored in the arrays $xpos and $ypos. The position of the data in those two arrays matches the order the data is returned by the database. Every time an object is moved, we calculate the new position of the object.

Figure 14.4
Displaying the content of the database.

After displaying the set of objects, we go to the next frame. If the generation of the movie is ready, we display it in the browser.

Flash also supports features such as transparent objects. The following is a slightly modified version of the program we have just discussed. This time, we display only the first column of the result and use transparent objects. We also change the speed of the video. Here's the code:

```php
<?php
  dl('php_ming.so');

  # connecting to the database
  $dbh=pg_connect("dbname=myflash user=hs");
  if (!$dbh)
  {
    echo ("ERROR: connecting failed");
    exit;
  }

  # selecting data from the PostgreSQL
  $result=pg_exec($dbh, "SELECT * FROM persons");
  if (!$result)
  {
    echo ("ERROR: cannot failed");
    exit;
  }
```

```
# creating font and movie object
$f = new SWFFont("test.fdb");
$m = new SWFMovie();
$m->setDimension(320, 240);
$m->setRate(24.0);

# computing number of lines
$num_res=pg_numrows($result);

# processing the data line by line
for ($i=0; $i<$num_res; $i++)
{
  $line=pg_fetch_row($result,$i);

  # creating a new object
  $obj[$i] = new SWFText();

  # setting the object's properties
  $obj[$i]->setFont($f);
  $obj[$i]->setColor(0, $i*30, $i*30, (($i+1)*20)%100 );
  $obj[$i]->setHeight(60);
  $string="$line[0]";
  $obj[$i]->addString($string);

  # adding the object to the scenery
  $inst[$i] = $m->add($obj[$i]);

  # assigning the starting position
  $ypos[$i]=0-$i*30;
  $xpos[$i]=160-$obj[$i]->getWidth($string)/2;

  # moving the object to the starting position
  $inst[$i]->moveTo($xpos[$i], $ypos[$i]);
}

# repositioning 101 times
for($count=0; $count<=100; $count++)
{
  # processing the loop for every object
  for($j=0; $j<$num_res; $j++)
  {
```

```
      # moving the object and finding the new position
      $inst[$j]->moveTo($xpos[$j], $ypos[$j]);
      $ypos[$j]=($ypos[$j]+2)%240;
   }
   $m->nextFrame();
}

# displaying results
header('Content-type: application/x-shockwave-flash');
$m->output();
?>
```

Using transparent objects with Flash is an easy task. Up to now, we have called the
setColor method with only three parameters. Using a fourth parameter is the key to
transparent objects. In the code, the line

```
$obj[$i]->setColor(0, $i*30, $i*30, (($i+1)*20)%100 );
```

sets the level of transparency. Because we do not want all objects to have the same
color, we tell PHP and Flash to make the color of an object depend on the position
($i) of an object in the result. As we mentioned earlier, we also want to set the speed
of the video. Setting the speed means changing the frame rate of the video. This can
be done with the help of the setRate method. In the example, we want 24 frames per
second to be displayed - this is actually a little faster than the default setting.

The movie created by this code is shown in Figure 14.5.

Figure 14.5

An example using transparent objects.

Working with Geometric Datatypes

Up to now we have used PHP and the Ming module for displaying fields that contain ordinary texts. Because PostgreSQL supports a lot of geometric objects and a lot of functions related to those objects, you should combine PostgreSQL and Flash to design applications for displaying geometric data.

PHP can be used as an object-oriented programming (OOP) language. In this section, you explore PHP classes that you can use in combination with Flash and PostgreSQL.

Let's start with a simple example for displaying rectangles stored in a PostgreSQL database. We compiled a small table, which will be used by the program that follows. Here is the data structure of the table:

```
myflash=# \d boxes
          Table "boxes"
 Attribute |  Type   | Modifier
-----------+---------+----------
 label     | text    |
 data      | box     |
 color     | text    |
 trans     | integer |
Constraint: ((trans <= 100) AND (trans >= 0))
```

The table contains four columns. The second column contains the definition of the rectangle. We inserted three records into the table:

```
myflash=# SELECT * FROM boxes;
 label  |        data        |   color   | trans
--------+--------------------+-----------+-------
 first  | (40,40),(10,10)    | 255,0,0   |    80
 third  | (200,180),(30,60)  | 0,0,255   |    10
 second | (150,80),(65,42)   | 0,200,128 |    60
(3 rows)
```

The first column contains a label, and the second column contains the definition of the rectangle. The third column stores the color of the rectangle.

As mentioned earlier, we implemented a class for processing rectangles with the help of PHP. Implementing a class is possibly the easiest way of dealing with geometric objects. Here is the code of the class:

```php
<?php

class box {
        var $x1, $y1, $x2, $y2;
     var $color, $trans;

     # constructor
     function box($a, $b, $c, $d, $e)
     {
             $this->x1=$a;
             $this->y1=$b;
             $this->x2=$c;
             $this->y2=$d;
             $this->color=$e;
     }

     function box($x, $c)
     {
             $search = array("'\s'","'\('", "'\)'");
             $x = preg_replace ($search,"", $x);
             $c = preg_replace ($search,"", $c);

             $array = split(",", $x);

             $this->x1=$array[0];
             $this->y1=$array[1];
             $this->x2=$array[2];
             $this->y2=$array[3];
             $this->color=$c;
     }

     # drawing function
     function draw()
     {

             $c=split(",", $this->color);

             $s=new SWFShape();
             $s->setLine(20, $c[0], $c[1], $c[2]);
             $s->setRightFill($s->addFill($c[0], $c[1], $c[2]));

             $s->movePenTo($this->x1, $this->y1);
```

```
        $s->drawLineTo($this->x1, $this->y2);
        $s->drawLineTo($this->x2, $this->y2);
        $s->drawLineTo($this->x2, $this->y1);
        $s->drawLineTo($this->x1, $this->y1);

        return($s);
    }
}
```

The class is very simple. We implemented two constructors. The first constructor needs five parameters, which are directly assigned to the variables our class has to contain. The second constructor extracts the coordinates of the rectangle from the data returned by the database. Extracting the data from the result of the query is propably the most difficult task, because we use regular expressions to parse and transform the string. All brackets and all whitespace characters are removed from the string so that all further transformations are not hampered.

After the two constructors, a method called draw is implemented. We will use this method to draw the rectangles.

Here is the main program:

```
<?php
  dl('php_ming.so');
  include("class.boxes.php");

  # connecting to the database
  $dbh=pg_connect("dbname=myflash user=hs");
  if (!$dbh)
  {
    echo ("ERROR: connecting failed");
    exit;
  }

  # selecting data from the PostgreSQL
  $result=pg_exec($dbh, "SELECT * FROM boxes");
  if (!$result)
  {
    echo ("ERROR: cannot failed");
    exit;
  }

  # creating font and movie object
  $m = new SWFMovie();
```

```
$m->setDimension(320, 240);


# computing number of lines
$num_res=pg_numrows($result);

# processing the data line by line
for ($i=0;$i<$num_res;$i++)
{
  $line=pg_fetch_row($result,$i);
  $mybox=new box($line[1], $line[2]);
  $s[$i]=$mybox->draw();
  $res[$i] = $m->add($s[$i]);
}
$m->nextFrame();

# displaying results
header('Content-type: application/x-shockwave-flash');
$m->output();


?>
```

First we connect to the database, as we have in the previous examples. We select all records and all columns from table boxes and compute the number of lines returned.

In the next step, we process the result of the query line by line and create an object for every rectangle. The object is drawn and added to the scenery.

Figure 14.6 shows the result.

All three rectangles in the table are displayed.

Sometimes you want your objects to look a bit nicer. In that case, using gradients might be a good choice. Gradients are smooth transitions between colors. To show you how gradients can be used, we changed the draw method:

```
function draw()
{
        $c=split(",", $this->color);

        $s=new SWFShape();
        $s->setLine(20, $c[0], $c[1], $c[2]);

        $g = new SWFGradient();
        $g->addEntry(0.0, $c[0], $c[1], $c[2], 20);
```

```
$g->addEntry(0.5, $c[0], $c[1], $c[2], 90);
$g->addEntry(1.0, $c[0], $c[1], $c[2], 10);

$f = $s->addFill($g, SWFFILL_RADIAL_GRADIENT);
$f->scaleTo(0.12);
$f->moveTo(($this->x1+2*$this->x2)/3, ($this->y1+2*$this->y2)/3);
$s->setRightFill($f);

$s->movePenTo($this->x1, $this->y1);
$s->drawLineTo($this->x1, $this->y2);
$s->drawLineTo($this->x2, $this->y2);
$s->drawLineTo($this->x2, $this->y1);
$s->drawLineTo($this->x1, $this->y1);

return($s);
}
```

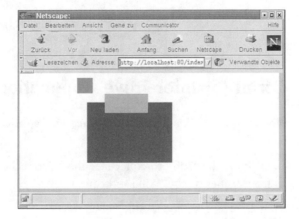

Figure 14.6
Three rectangles.

First we create an instance of the SWFGradient object and add some entries to it. At least two entries have to be added; otherwise, the rectangle will contain only one color. In the next step, we add the fill to the object. In the example, we used SWFFILL_RADIAL_GRADIENT as a flag for the addFill method. If we wanted a linear gradient, we would use SWFFILL_LINEAR_GRADIENT. Figure 14.7 shows the result of the modified draw function.

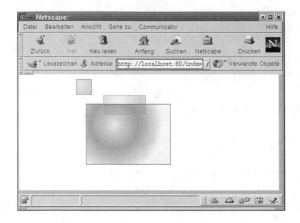

Figure 14.7
Three more beautiful rectangles.

As you can see from this section, it is easy to generate Flash movies with the help of PHP.

Using Action Script for Interactive Applications

Watching movies is great, but it's even better to interact with a movie. In that case, Action Script can be used.

For database developers it can be useful to collect feedback from the Flash movie. The next example counts the number of clicks of a red square.

To store the hits in the database, we add a table called hits:

```
myflash=# \d hits

                           Table "hits"
 Attribute |          Type           |                Modifier

-----------+-------------------------+----------------------- ---------------
--------
 id        | integer                 | not null default
nextval('"hits_id_seq"'::text)
 click     | timestamp with time zone |
 typ       | integer                 |
```

We need two files for interacting with the database. The next file is called index3.php:

```php
<?php
    dl('php_ming.so');

    # creating button ...
    $b = makebutton();

    # creating the movie ...
    $m = new SWFMovie();
    $m->setDimension(320, 240);
    $m->setBackground(0xff, 0xff, 0xff);

    $i = $m->add($b);
    $i->moveTo(160, 120);

    header('Content-type: application/x-shockwave-flash');
    $m->output();

# creating button ...
function makebutton()
{
    $b = new SWFButton();
    $b->setUp(react(0xff, 30, 30));
    $b->setOver(react(30, 0xff, 30));
    $b->setDown(react(30, 30, 0xff));
    $b->setHit(react(30, 30, 30));

    $b->addAction(new SWFAction("getURL('redirect.php', '_blank', post);" ),
SWFBUTTON_MOUSEUP);

    return $b;
}

# reaction ...
function react($r, $g, $b)
{
    global $dbh, $m;

    $s = new SWFShape();
    $s->setRightFill($s->addFill($r, $g, $b));
    $s->movePenTo(-100,-100);
```

```
        $s->drawLineTo(100,-100);
        $s->drawLineTo(100,100);
        $s->drawLineTo(-100,100);
        $s->drawLineTo(-100,-100);

        return $s;
}
?>
```

We create a button and bind certain events to it. The react function changes the color of the square, depending on what is happening. If we click the square, for instance, the color of the square will be blue. addAction defines an action—what to do—when the button is pressed. In this case, we want redirect.php to be called by the Flash movie.

redirect.php opens a connection to the database and inserts the current time into table hits. After that, the user is redirected to Flash again:

```
<?php

        # connecting to the database
        $dbh=pg_connect("dbname=myflash user=hs");
        if     (!$dbh)
        {
                echo ("ERROR: connecting failed");
                exit;
        }

        # inserting clicks into database
        $sql="INSERT INTO hits(click) VALUES(now())";
        $res=pg_exec($dbh, $sql);
        if     (!$res)
        {
                exit;
        }

        # redirecting back to Flash ...
         echo ('<head> <meta http-equiv="refresh" content="0; URL=index3.php">
</head>');

?>
```

The following shows what has been inserted into the database:

```
myflash=# SELECT * FROM hits;
 id |         click          | typ
----+------------------------+-----
 428 | 2001-06-26 10:27:03+02 |
 429 | 2001-06-26 10:27:04+02 |
```

Someone clicked the red square twice; the time stamps of the two events have been stored in the database.

> **Note**
> Redirecting has to be done by the Flash movie; don't include any IF clauses when the events are added to the movie by the PHP file. They won't work, because the movie is displayed when the generation of the movie is over and not before. The interaction with the database is not done by Flash.

The example shows that it is an easy task to build database-enabled Flash applications with the help of PHP. The development of the Ming module will continue, so the Open source community provides a powerful platform for building attractive applications.

A Final Example

This section presents a final example. The following is a simple HTML site that contains images of three people:

```
<html>
<head>
</head>
<body text="#000000" bgcolor="#FFFFFF" link="#0000EF" vlink="#59188E"
    alink="#FF0000">

<b><font size=+1>The final Flash example:</font></b>
<center><p><b>Click your favourite persons</b>
<p><br>

<table BORDER COLS=3 WIDTH="90%" NOSAVE >
    <tr>
      <td><b>Ewald Geschwinde</b></td>
```

```
        <td> <center><b>Etschi Bruckner</b></center></td>
        <td><div align=right><b>Hans-Juergen Schoenig</b></div></td>
    </tr>
    <tr>
        <td><a href="display.php?fname=Ewald&sname=Geschwinde">
                <img SRC="epi.jpg" height=130 width=84></a></td>

        <td><center><a href="display.php?fname=Etschi&sname=Bruckner">
                <img SRC="etschi.jpg" height=130 width=107></a></center></td>

        <td><div align=right>
                <a href="display.php?fname=Hans-Juergen&sname=Schoenig">
                <img SRC="hans.jpg" height=130 width=121></div></td>
    </tr>
</table>

</body>
</html>
```

If we display the HTML code with the help of Netscape 4.77, it looks like Figure 14.8.

If a user clicks an image, display.php is called with the name of the person and the picture.

Every person has an entry in table cybertec; we use this information to generate the movie:

```
myflash=# SELECT firstname, surname, pic FROM cybertec;
   firstname   |  surname   |    pic
---------------+------------+------------
 Ewald         | Geschwinde | epi.jpg
 Hans-Juergen  | Schönig    | hans.jpg
 Etschi        | Bruckner   | etschi.jpg
(3 rows)
```

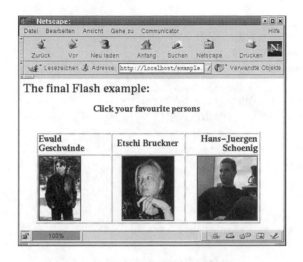

Figure 14.8
Click to see your favourite person in action.

The following is the source code of display.php:

```php
<?php
    dl('php_ming.so');

    # connecting to the database
    $dbh=pg_connect("dbname=myflash user=hs");
    if    (!$dbh)
    {
        echo ("ERROR: connecting failed");
        exit;
    }

    # selecting data from the PostgreSQL
    $sql="SELECT * FROM cybertec WHERE firstname='$fname'";
    $result=pg_exec($dbh, $sql);
    if    (!$result)
    {
        echo ("ERROR: cannot failed");
        exit;
    }
```

```
# creating the movie
$m = new SWFMovie();
$m->setDimension(640, 480);
$m->setRate(12);

# retrieving the data line by line
if      (pg_numrows($result) < 1)
{
        echo ('no results found');
        exit;
}
else
{
        $data=pg_fetch_object ($result, 0);

        $b = new SWFBitmap(fopen($data->pic, "r"));
        $width = $b->getWidth();

        # first pic of Etschi ...
        $i = $m->add($b);
        $i->scaleTo(1.2, 1.2);
        $i->skewXTo(-0.2);
        $i->moveTo(320-$width, 100);

        # second pic of Etschi ...
        $i = $m->add($b);
        $i->scaleTo(1.2, 1.2);
        $i->skewXTo(0.2);
        $i->moveTo(320, 100);

        $i = $m->add($b);
        $i->moveTo(320-$width/2, 100);
        for($n=0; $n<23; $n+=0.1)
        {
                $i->rotateTo($n*8);
                $i->multColor($n, $n, $n);
                $i->addColor(0, 0, 0, -$n);
                $m->nextFrame();
        }
        header('Content-type: application/x-shockwave-flash');
        $m->output();
}
?>
```

As in all the examples, we connect to the database first and query the table to compute the information that we need to generate the Flash movie. We do this with the help of a simple SELECT statement. In the example, we look for firstname. One record will be retrieved and we will use the content of this record for our Flash movie.

After creating an SWFMovie object, we set the size and define the speed of the movie. If the result of the query satisfies our demands, we continue generating the movie; otherwise, an error is displayed. Then we open the picture of the person that the user has clicked. The name of the picture is stored in $data->pic. In the next step, we compute the size of the image; we will need this information later in the script. $i=$m->add($b) adds the image to the movie.

> **Note**
> All transformations of the image are done after adding it to the scenery.

After adding the object to the scenery, we perform basic transformations, such as scaling the picture to the correct size or setting the initial position of the picture. The whole process is done twice, so the picture is displayed two times.

In the next step, we add a third picture to the scenery, perform some rotation, and change the color of the object every time the loop is processed.

Figure 14.9 shows a screenshot of the movie in action.

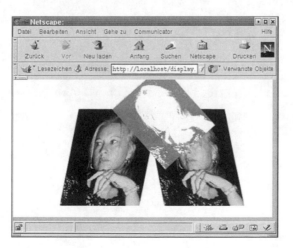

Figure 14.9
Animating the author's girlfriend.

If you want to find out more about the Ming interface, check out
`http://www.opaque.net/ming/`.

Summary

The Ming module is still in development, but it is already very powerful and provides
a pool of functions to generate database-driven Flash movies. In addition, PostgreSQL
supports a geometric database, which can easily be included in Flash movies.

Flash, PHP, and PostgreSQL are a strong team, making your applications even more
powerful.

CHAPTER 15

PostgreSQL Regression Tests

Regression testing is one of the most important methods of proving that PostgreSQL can be run on various platforms.

The Idea Behind Regression Tests

PostgreSQL provides a comprehensive test suite for performing basic server testing. The set of tests performed by the test suite is commonly known as *regression tests* and is distributed with the PostgreSQL source distribution.

The original tests were designed and developed by Jolly Chen and Andrew Yu. Extensive revisions and repackaging has been done by Marc Fournier and Thomas Lockhart. Since version 6.1, the regression tests are maintained for every version of PostgreSQL.

Regression testing is an essential part of developing a database system that is capable of running on multiple platforms, because it is an easy way to perform testing operations and to find out whether PostgreSQL is able to perform basic operations on the tested platform. It gives the development team the chance to find and fix obvious bugs quickly.

Running Tests

The test suite for performing regression tests is distributed with the source code of PostgreSQL and can be found in the src/test/regress directory in the source tree of PostgreSQL. To start the regression test you use the following command:

```
[hs@athlon regress]$ make check
```

PostgreSQL performs a lot of checks and testing. Although a lot of work is done by the test, it takes only a few seconds to complete.

Let's have a look at the test in detail and see what is done by make check -n:

```
[hs@athlon regress]$ make check -n
make -C ../../../contrib/spi REFINT_VERBOSE=1 refint.so autoinc.so
make[1]: Entering directory `/usr/src/redhat/SOURCES/postgresql-
7.1.2/contrib/spi'
make[1]: `refint.so' is up to date.
make[1]: `autoinc.so' is up to date.
make[1]: Leaving directory `/usr/src/redhat/SOURCES/postgresql-
7.1.2/contrib/spi'
/bin/sh ./pg_regress --temp-install --top-builddir=../../.. --
schedule=./parallel_schedule --multibyte=SQL_ASCII
```

A script called pg_regress is started with various parameters. You'll take a closer look at pg_regress later in this section. To execute the test, a temporary server is started. Make sure that the test is not executed as root, because the PostgreSQL daemon must not be started as root.

After executing the regression test, we get the following messages from the test suite:

```
make -C ../../../contrib/spi REFINT_VERBOSE=1 refint.so autoinc.so
make[1]: Entering directory `/usr/src/redhat/SOURCES/postgresql-
7.1.2/contrib/spi'
make[1]: `refint.so' is up to date.
make[1]: `autoinc.so' is up to date.
make[1]: Leaving directory `/usr/src/redhat/SOURCES/postgresql-
7.1.2/contrib/spi'
/bin/sh ./pg_regress --temp-install --top-builddir=../../.. --
schedule=./parallel_schedule --multibyte=SQL_ASCII
============== removing existing temp installation    ==============
============== creating temporary installation    ==============
============== initializing database system    ==============
============== starting postmaster    ==============
running on port 65432 with pid 29536
```

```
============== creating database "regression"      ==============
CREATE DATABASE
============== installing PL/pgSQL                  ==============
============== running regression test queries      ==============
parallel group (13 tests):  name boolean char int2 varchar text float4 float8
oid int8 int4 bit numeric
        boolean              ... ok
        char                 ... ok
        name                 ... ok
        varchar              ... ok
        text                 ... ok
        int2                 ... ok
        int4                 ... ok
        int8                 ... ok
        oid                  ... ok
        float4               ... ok
        float8               ... ok
        bit                  ... ok
        numeric              ... ok
test strings                 ... ok
test numerology              ... ok
parallel group (18 tests):  lseg point path date circle polygon interval
comments inet tinterval time abstime reltime box timestamp type_sanity oidjoins
opr_sanity
        point                ... ok
        lseg                 ... ok
        box                  ... ok
        path                 ... ok
        polygon              ... ok
        circle               ... ok
        date                 ... ok
        time                 ... ok
        timestamp            ... ok
        interval             ... ok
        abstime              ... FAILED
        reltime              ... ok
        tinterval            ... ok
        inet                 ... ok
        comments             ... ok
        oidjoins             ... ok
        type_sanity          ... ok
        opr_sanity           ... ok
```

```
test geometry          ... ok
test horology          ... ok
test create_function_1 ... ok
test create_type       ... ok
test create_table      ... ok
test create_function_2 ... ok
test copy              ... ok
parallel group (7 tests):  create_aggregate create_operator inherit triggers
constraints create_misc create_index
    constraints        ... ok
    triggers           ... ok
    create_misc        ... ok
    create_aggregate   ... ok
    create_operator    ... ok
    create_index       ... ok
    inherit            ... ok
test create_view       ... ok
test sanity_check      ... ok
test errors            ... ok
test select            ... ok
parallel group (16 tests):  select_distinct_on select_into select_distinct
subselect select_implicit union transactions random select_having arrays join
case portals hash_index aggregates btree_index
    select_into        ... ok
    select_distinct    ... ok
    select_distinct_on ... ok
    select_implicit    ... ok
    select_having      ... ok
    subselect          ... ok
    union              ... ok
    case               ... ok
    join               ... ok
    aggregates         ... ok
    transactions       ... ok
    random             ... ok
    portals            ... ok
    arrays             ... ok
    btree_index        ... ok
    hash_index         ... ok
test misc              ... ok
parallel group (5 tests):  portals_p2 alter_table foreign_key rules select_views
    select_views       ... ok
    alter_table        ... ok
    portals_p2         ... ok
```

```
    rules               ... ok
    foreign_key         ... ok
parallel group (3 tests):  limit temp plpgsql
    limit               ... ok
    plpgsql             ... ok
    temp                ... ok
============== shutting down postmaster        ==============


========================
 1 of 76 tests failed.
========================

The differences that caused some tests to fail can be viewed in the
file `./regression.diffs'.  A copy of the test summary that you see
above is saved in the file `./regression.out'.


make: *** [check] Error 1
```

As you can see in the following code, pg_regress has a lot of parameters that you can use to perform the regression test without using the Makefile:

```
[hs@athlon regress]$ ./pg_regress — help
PostgreSQL regression test driver

Usage: pg_regress [options...] [extra tests...]

Options:
  --debug               turn on debug mode in programs that are run
  --inputdir=DIR        take input files from DIR (default `.')
  --multibyte=ENCODING  use ENCODING as the multibyte encoding, and
                        also run a test by the same name
  --outputdir=DIR       place output files in DIR (default `.')
  --schedule=FILE       use test ordering schedule from FILE
                        (may be used multiple times to concatenate)
  --temp-install[=DIR]  create a temporary installation (in DIR)

Options for `temp-install' mode:
  --top-builddir=DIR       (relative) path to top level build directory

Options for using an existing installation:
  --host=HOST           use postmaster running on HOST
  --port=PORT           use postmaster running at PORT
  --user=USER           connect as USER
```

```
The exit status is 0 if all tests passed, 1 if some tests failed, and 2
if the tests could not be run for some reason.

Report bugs to <pgsql-bugs@postgresql.org>.
```

You can see the test suite performs a huge number of tests, but not all of them are always successful, although we have installed PostgreSQL properly and our test system (Red Hat Linux release 7.1 with kernel 2.4.2-SGI_XFS_1.0 on AMD Duron) is capable of running PostgreSQL without any problems. You take a closer look at test evaluation in the next section. First, let's look inside a regression test.

The first step is to create a PL/pgSQL-enabled database and test the basic datatypes. The following code performs a regression test for the datatype `text`:

```
--
-- TEXT
--

SELECT text 'this is a text string' = text 'this is a text string' AS true;

SELECT text 'this is a text string' = text 'this is a text strin' AS false;

CREATE TABLE TEXT_TBL (f1 text);

INSERT INTO TEXT_TBL VALUES ('doh!');
INSERT INTO TEXT_TBL VALUES ('hi de ho neighbor');

SELECT '' AS two, * FROM TEXT_TBL;
```

You can see that the heart of a regression test is a set of SQL commands. In this case, the test is simple and easy to understand, but there are also tests containing a lot more SQL code, such as the following test suite for `rules`:

```
[hs@athlon sql]$ ls -l rules.sql
-rw-r--r--    1 hs        cybertec    24967 Dez  5  2000 rules.sql
```

After checking the rudimentary datatypes implemented in PostgreSQL, the more complex datatypes, such as `lseg` and `timestamp`, are tested. The test suite executes an SQL file for every datatype tested and stores the results in files.

Now that all datatypes have been checked extensively, PostgreSQL checks things such as triggers, aggregates, transactions, and PL/pgSQL. Note that if a test fails, as you saw in the previous regression test, the test suite does not stop working.

All the SQL code needed for the test can be found in the src/test/regress/sql directory in the source tree of PostgreSQL. Feel free to go through the SQL code, because it is a perfect compilation of examples and might save you a lot of time with more complex tasks.

Evaluating Regression Tests

After you successfully execute a regression test, you can analyze the results. To analyze a regression test, it is necessary to know how PostgreSQL finds out whether a test has been successful or not: The result of the SQL statements are stored in files and can be compared with the "correct results" distributed with the test suite. The results are compared by using a simple `diff` command.

Several things can cause a test to fail; you learn about these in the following sections.

Error Messages

Some SQL commands cause the system to raise an error. This behavior is expected, because some SQL commands in the test suite contain errors.

Not all error messages are raised by PostgreSQL, but come instead from the underlying software. The result of a test suite and the expected results are compared with a simple `diff` command. If the two are not 100% equal, the regression test for a specific component fails. In most cases, this does not mean that your system is not able to run PostgreSQL.

Local Differences

The tests should be run in plain C locale. If you are running the tests against a completed installation, this might lead to problems if something different than C locale is used. If you run the test against a temporary installation, this won't be a problem, because the test suite makes sure that the correct settings are used.

Date and Time Differences

The expected results have been generated for time zone PST8PDT (Berkeley, California). Some regression tests are very time zone–dependent, so the results might vary depending on the time zone your system is in.

To set the time zone to the correct value for performing the regression test, you can use this command:

```
[hs@athlon regress]$ export PGTZ='PST8PDT7,M04.01.0,M10.05.03';
```

Sometimes the regression test for `timestamp` can also fail because of underlying libraries.

Floating-Point Differences

Comparing floating-point numbers is always a crucial thing. Depending on the type of microprocessor you have got, the result of a floating-point operation might vary for many reasons.

On one hand, differences can occur because of the way the floating-point unit of your processor works. On the other hand, some differences might occur because of compiler settings, which influence the way floating-point operations are treated. Most differences occur because of differences in the way numbers are rounded.

On AIX-based systems, for instance, it is possible to tell the system how to round floating numbers (check out the RS/6000 docs and the docs of XLC).

In most cases, differences emerging by the rounding algorithm can be found only with the human eye, because the "errors" in the calculations are comparatively small.

Polygon Differences

Geometric datatypes often contain non-integer components. This leads to the same problems discussed in the previous section about floating-point numbers. The errors are comparatively small, so take a closer look at the results when the regression test on your system fails.

Ordering Differences

It might appear that the same data is returned in different order than expected. If no `ORDER BY` clause is used, this can occur easily. Most regression tests do not use `ORDER BY` clauses, so failures might happen.

On some platforms, though, the way data is ordered might vary. Some differences might occur because of a non–C locale setting; other differences might happen because of differences in the underlying function.

In most cases, the results will be the same on all machines, but you have to keep in mind that there might be slight differences. Generally you won't have to worry about the order of your records, because these differences usually won't be significant.

"Random" Testing

In most cases, generating random values is not random. In many real-world applications, deterministic random generators are needed. This might sound strange, but imagine an algorithm that produces huge amounts of data. If the program is used on multiple machines (for scientific purposes, for example), the result of an operation is the same on every machine. Therefore, random generators are, in most cases, deterministic (see man pages of lrand48).

At least one case in the random script is intended to produce random results, and this can cause the regression test to fail because a stochastic value differs from the expected result. If the regression test for "random" never fails even when you execute it many times, you might have to worry.

Summary

Regression testing is an essential part of preparing your database for a production environment. This kind of test is a good way to prove that PostgreSQL works on your platform and that all basic operations are performed correctly.

CHAPTER 16

Extending PostgreSQL's Core Features

PostgreSQL is one of the most flexible databases available—for many reasons. On one hand, PostgreSQL can be used for many purposes. On the other hand, PostgreSQL can easily be extended and provides many programming interfaces, which are designed to extend the core features of PostgreSQL.

In this section, you take a closer look at extensibility. As you have already learned, PostgreSQL is one of the most flexible and most extensible database systems available.

Defining new database aggregate functions or operators is an easy task in PostgreSQL. This section is dedicated to all programmers who need additional functionalities, and to those who just want to have a good time hacking PostgreSQL code.

The key to PostgreSQL flexibility and extensibility lies in the way PostgreSQL treats operations. Information about operations is stored in a set of tables (Oracle calls it a *data dictionary*), so it is an easy task to perform modifications—as long as you know what has to be done.

The advantage of a database-driven system is that the behavior of the database can be changed by almost everyone at runtime. Therefore, prototyping is easy with the help of PostgreSQL.

Two kinds of datatypes are supported by PostgreSQL:

- **Base datatypes**. Base datatypes, such as `int4`, are the fundamental datatypes in PostgreSQL and are those that are also implemented in programming languages such as C.

- **Composite datatypes.** Composite datatypes are built on other datatypes, and therefore additional functions have to be available to tell the database how a datatype has to be used.

Not only datatypes can be added to PostgreSQL. In the next section, you see how other components can be defined.

Adding Functions and an Overview of Programming Conventions

The more complex a database system is, the more important is the existence of rules and conventions to make the code clearer and easier to understand. In the case of PostgreSQL, some basic rules have to be taken into consideration when implementing additional functions. These are primarily important for making the system easier to understand as a whole. Before you get to these calling conventions, let's look at how functions can be implemented.

Writing Simple SQL Functions

Because PostgreSQL is a very flexible software, it is an easy task to add functions to the database. We have already shown how adding functions works with the help of many programming languages (C, PL/pgSQL, PL/Tcl, and so on). Now we will show that it is also possible to implement additional functionalities simply by using "ordinary" SQL code. As you might expect, using SQL for additional functions is just as easy as using any other programming language.

The advantage of functions implemented in pure SQL is that they are extremely portable, because no support for other programming languages is required. Imagine a PostgreSQL system where no support for, let's say, PL/Perl has been implemented. Adding PL/Perl functions to the system requires a recompile of the server, and adding a SQL function can be done without changing anything.

Let's imagine a table called `mynumber` containing a few values:

```
mydata=# SELECT * FROM mynumber;
 a | b
```

```
----+----
 22 |  6
  3 | 12
 55 | 51
(3 rows)
```

Here is a simple function implemented in SQL:

```
CREATE FUNCTION delete_tab() RETURNS int4 AS '
        DELETE FROM mynumber;
        SELECT 1 AS deleted;'
        LANGUAGE 'sql';
```

We simply remove all records from mynumber and return 1. Let's have a look at the function in action:

```
mydata=# SELECT delete_tab();
 delete_tab
------------
          1
(1 row)


mydata=# SELECT * FROM mynumber;
 a | b
---+---
(0 rows)
```

First we select all records from the table to see what the database contains. Then we call delete_tab. 1 is returned and we query the table again. Because the function has been executed successfully, the table is empty now.

Writing C Functions

Implementing really fast PostgreSQL extensions can hardly be achieved by using anything other than C. Because PostgreSQL is entirely written in C, this seems logical. Writing C code is most likely not the fastest way of implementing a feature, but the performance of your functions will not suffer from a lot of overhead that other programming languages (for example Perl or Tcl) will cause.

Normally, user-defined functions are added to PostgreSQL by using a loadable object (shared library). Shared libraries are loaded at runtime (when the function is called the first time) and stay in memory for the rest of the session. Knowing this is extremely important for debugging purposes. If you want to test your extensions with the help of psql, it is necessary to reconnect to the database after recompiling and adding the module to your database. Otherwise, the old object will still be in memory.

Tip
You should always use the full path to the shared library.

Additional functions are not inserted and compiled by PostgreSQL automatically. To add a function to a database, you have to use the CREATE FUNCTION command.

PostgreSQL's C Datatypes

PostgreSQL's C interface supports a large number of datatypes you will need to add additional functions to your PostgreSQL server. The following table lists all datatypes available in C:

SQL type	C Type	Defined In
abstime	AbsoluteTime	utils/nabstime.h
bool	bool	include/c.h
box	(BOX *)	utils/geo-decls.h
bytea	(bytea *)	include/postgres.h
"char"	char	N/A
cid	CID	include/postgres.h
datetime	(DateTime *)	include/c.h or include/postgres.h
int2	int2 or int16	include/postgres.h
int2vector	(int2vector *)	include/postgres.h
int4	int4 or int32	include/postgres.h
float4	(float4 *)	include/c.h or include/postgres.h
float8	(float8 *)	include/c.h or include/postgres.h
lseg	(LSEG *)	include/geo-decls.h
name	(Name)	include/postgres.h
oid	oid	include/postgres.h
oidvector	(oidvector *)	include/postgres.h
path	(PATH *)	utils/geo-decls.h
point	(POINT *)	utils/geo-decls.h
regproc	regproc or REGPROC	include/postgres.h
reltime	RelativeTime	utils/nabstime.h
text	(text *)	include/postgres.h
tid	ItemPointer	storage/itemptr.h
timespan	(TimeSpan *)	include/c.h or include/postgres.h
tinterval	TimeInterval	utils/nabstime.h

Calling Conventions for Functions Written in C

When implementing huge software projects such as PostgreSQL, it is necessary to introduce some sort of convention to make the code clearer and to make sure that programmers can easily keep track of the code and the entire project. Because PostgreSQL is a huge project, conventions for C functions have been introduced.

Two calling conventions are available. Version-0 Calling Convention is the old-style convention, which is still supported for compatibility reasons. A detailed discussion of the old-style convention is far beyond the scope of this book.

Version-1 Calling Convention is based on macros to avoid a lot of complexity for passing arguments and returning results. New-style functions are always defined like this:

```
Datum name_of_function(PG_FUNCTION_ARGS)
```

For dynamically loaded functions, it is necessary to add the macro call to the same source file:

```
PG_FUNCTION_INFO_V1(name_of_function);
```

For internal functions, this is not necessary, because PostgreSQL assumes that all functions are new-style. To retrieve arguments from PG_FUNCTIONS_ARGS, the PG_RETURN_xxx() macro is called, which corresponds to the argument's datatype. The data is returned with the help of a PG_RETURN_xxx() macro call, which also has to correspond with the return value's datatype.

To make the explanation a little clearer, let's look at a simple example. To divide floats, a function called float48div has been implemented in the following:

```
$SRC_ROOT/src/backend/utils/adt/float.c
```

Here is the function:

```
Datum
float48div(PG_FUNCTION_ARGS)
{
        float4          arg1 = PG_GETARG_FLOAT4(0);
        float8          arg2 = PG_GETARG_FLOAT8(1);
        float8          result;

        if (arg2 == 0.0)
                elog(ERROR, "float48div: divide by zero");
```

```
      result = arg1 / arg2;
      CheckFloat8Val(result);
      PG_RETURN_FLOAT8(result);
}
```

PG_FUNCTION_ARGS contains the arguments passed to the function. To extract the first argument from the input, PG_GETARG_FLOAT4 is called. The second argument is retrieved by using PG_GETARG_FLOAT8. The return value is defined as float8. In the next step, the function checks whether a division by zero has to be done. If not, the result is computed and returned using the PG_RETURN_FLOAT8 macro.

Another good example is the time_interval function, which can be found in the following:

```
$SRC_ROOT/src/backend/utils/adt/date.c
```

Let's have a look at the code:

```
Datum
time_interval(PG_FUNCTION_ARGS)
{
      TimeADT          time = PG_GETARG_TIMEADT(0);
      Interval   *result;

      result = (Interval *) palloc(sizeof(Interval));

      result->time = time;
      result->month = 0;

      PG_RETURN_INTERVAL_P(result);
}
```

The input parameter is extracted by using a PG_GETARG_xxx macro again. This time we have to use PG_GETARG_TIMEADT, because this is the macro that corresponds to the required datatype. The macro that is used to return the result of the function also matches the datatype of the return value.

A very important point, when dealing with the previous function, is how the memory required for the return value is allocated: palloc is used instead of malloc.

Rules for Writing C Code

When extending your PostgreSQL server with C functions, some basic rules have to be taken into consideration.

Usually, the header files can be found in `/usr/include/pgsql`. To find out where the header files are installed on your system, you can use the `pg_config` command:

```
[hs@duron Members]$ pg_config  --includedir
/usr/include/pgsql
```

All header files you will need to build PostgreSQL applications can be found in that directory.

When allocating memory, use `palloc` and `pfree` instead of `malloc` and `mfree`, as we showed in the previous section. The advantage of PostgreSQL's onboard memory management tools is that the allocated memory is freed automatically at the end of a transaction. This should help prevent memory leaks.

Your structures have to be "zeroed" using `memset` and `bzero`; otherwise, you might run into trouble, because some functions (hash access method, hash join, and sort algorithm) use the raw bits contained in your structure. Because of alignment padding, initializing the fields of your structure will not be enough.

Include `postgres.h` before `fmgr.h` and any other header file; this should be done for compatibility reasons. `c.h`, `elog.h`, and `palloc.h` will automatically be included by `postgres.h`.

Make sure that your names do not conflict with names in PostgreSQL's executables; otherwise, you will face problems.

Compiling and linking your object files will need special flags so that they can be loaded dynamically. Check out the docs of the compiler on your system to find out more.

Adding Datatypes

PostgreSQL provides an easy interface for adding your own datatypes. In many applications, self-defined datatypes are much more efficient than PostgreSQL's onboard datatypes. Your own datatypes not only speed up your database significantly; they also allow the user to define functions that are not included in PostgreSQL's core distribution. With the help of highly optimized, self-defined datatypes, PostgreSQL can be used in environments that it was not explicitly designed for. There is no need to invent the wheel once again—simply take a PostgreSQL database and add the desired functions to it.

The most efficient way to add new datatypes is to use the C programming language, because C is one of the fastest and most efficient programming languages available.

In this section, we define a simple datatype for PostgreSQL that can be used to store colors. You will see that this is not a difficult task.

The most important components of a datatype are the in and out functions. The in function is used to insert values into the database. The out function is called when a value using the datatype has to be displayed. Besides some SQL code creating the datatype and the function, this is all we need for creating a primitive datatype.

The following lists the content of color.c, which shows the two functions we need:

```c
#include <stdio.h>
#include <pgsql/postgres.h>

/* defining the datastructure "color" */
typedef     struct color
{
    short   r;
    short   g;
    short   b;
} color;

/* function to insert color into database */
color *color_in(char *str)
{
    short r, g, b;
    color *mycolor;

    /* reading the input */
    if      (sscanf(str, " ( %hi , %hi , %hi )", &r, &g, &b) != 3)
    {
            elog(ERROR, "color_in: parse error in %s", str);
            return NULL;
    }

    /* allocating the memory used to store the result */
    mycolor = (color *)palloc(sizeof(color));

    /* setting the minimum value to zero */
    mycolor->r = (0 > r) ? 0 : r;
    mycolor->g = (0 > g) ? 0 : g;
    mycolor->b = (0 > b) ? 0 : b;
```

```
    /* setting the maximum value to 255 */
    mycolor->r = (255 < r) ? 255 : mycolor->r;
    mycolor->g = (255 < g) ? 255 : mycolor->g;
    mycolor->b = (255 < b) ? 255 : mycolor->b;

    return (mycolor);
}

/* function to print colors */
char *color_out(color *mycolor)
{
    char *result;

    /* checking for NULL values */
    if      (mycolor == NULL)
    {
            return (NULL);
    }

    /* allocating the memory used to store the result */
    result = (char *) palloc(37);

    /* assigning the required value to "result" */
    sprintf(result, "(%i, %i, %i)", mycolor->r, mycolor->g, mycolor->b);
    return result;
}
```

Note
Errors in one of the functions related to a datatype can lead to backend crashes.

First we define the data structure of color. This is done by defining a simple struct called color, which contains all components our datatype must have. In our example, we combine three components. The first variable (r) defines the red component of the color. The second component (g) sets the green value, and the third component (b) tells us the amount of blue our color contains.

With the help of these three components, it's an easy task to generate every possible color.

Note
rgb colors are usually used on computers. Printing machines sometime use "ryc" (red, magenta, cyan) colors.

In the next step, we read the input of the function by using `sscanf`, which helps us extract the three components from the input data. The definition of the syntax looks like this: `( %hi , %hi , %hi )`.

We allow only one syntax for our datatype, because this is the easiest way and that's enough for our example (we want the code to be as simple as possible). If you want your datatype to support richer syntax, your `in` function has to be more complex and therefore—in most cases—also slower.

If the string passed to the function by the user does not satisfy our demands, an error is displayed using `elog`. In the example, we want an error to be displayed, which causes the function to quit. If we don't want our function to quit, we would have to use `NOTICE` instead.

In the next step, we allocate the required amount of memory to store the structure. Before we return the result of the function, we make sure that the components of our datatype can contain only values from `zero` to `255`.

The `out` function is even easier than the `in` function. We check for a `NULL` value; if the input does not contain `NULL`, we allocate the memory that we need to display the result and assign the content of the datatype to that memory. Finally, the result is returned as a string.

We compile the code shown as a shared object. As we did in nearly all our examples, we use a simple Makefile:

```
libfoo.so    :        color.c
    rm lib* *o -f
    gcc -Wall -fPIC -c *.c
    gcc -shared -Wl,-soname,libfoo.so.1 -o libfoo.so.1.0 *.o
    ln -s libfoo.so.1.0 libfoo.so.1
    ln -s libfoo.so.1 libfoo.so

    psql mydata < setup.sql
```

The second line does a simple cleanup. In the third line, we compile all C files, and the fourth line makes a shared object of the result. After creating two softlinks, we insert `setup.sql` into the database.

`setup.sql` contains a few lines of SQL code that generate the datatype and drop datatypes having the same datatype as the one we want to insert:

```
DROP TYPE color;
DROP FUNCTION color_in(opaque);
DROP FUNCTION color_out(opaque);
```

```
CREATE FUNCTION color_in(opaque)
    RETURNS color AS '/usr/local/postgres_extpack/libfoo.so'
    LANGUAGE 'c';

CREATE FUNCTION color_out(opaque)
    RETURNS opaque AS '/usr/local/postgres_extpack/libfoo.so'
    LANGUAGE 'c';

CREATE TYPE color (
            internallength=6,
            input=color_in,
            output=color_out
);

DROP TABLE mycolor;
CREATE TABLE mycolor(cfield color);
```

You can see that the functions needed for the datatype can be created just like any other C function. The most critical part of the whole process is the CREATE TYPE function:

The actual creation of the datatype is done by CREATE TYPE. Several parameters are passed to the function. internallength defines—as you might expect—the internal amount of storage needed for a variable using our datatype. input defines the function PostgreSQL should use as the in function of our datatype. output tells the database which out function has to be used. The CREATE TYPE command supports a variety of other parameters; we will deal with some of these later in this chapter.

Let's start the Makefile and see what happens:

```
[hs@duron postgres_extpack]$ make
rm lib* *o -f
gcc -Wall -fPIC -c *.c
gcc -shared -Wl,-soname,libfoo.so.1 -o libfoo.so.1.0 *.o
ln -s libfoo.so.1.0 libfoo.so.1
ln -s libfoo.so.1 libfoo.so
psql mydata < setup.sql
DROP
DROP
DROP
NOTICE:  ProcedureCreate: type 'color' is not yet defined
CREATE
CREATE
CREATE
```

```
DROP
CREATE
```

All CREATE statements have been executed successfully, so it looks as if everything works fine. Let's try it:

```
mydata=# \d mycolor
        Table "mycolor"
 Attribute | Type  | Modifier
-----------+-------+----------
 cfield    | color |
```

The Makefile (it was actually done by setup.sql) has already created a table successfully. Now we want to insert some data:

```
mydata=# INSERT INTO mycolor VALUES ('(0, 20, 0)');
INSERT 119310 1
mydata=# INSERT INTO mycolor VALUES ('(0, 20, 0)'::color);
INSERT 119311 1
```

It seems as if everything is still okay and no errors have occurred. Let's select the data that we have just inserted into the table by using a simple SELECT statement:

```
mydata=# SELECT * FROM mycolor;
   cfield
-----------
 (0, 20, 0)
 (0, 20, 0)
(2 rows)
```

Up to now, all records that we have inserted into the database contained valid components, which means that no number has been smaller than zero and higher than 255. In the in function, these values have to be set to a correct value; let's see what happens:

```
mydata=# INSERT INTO mycolor VALUES ('(-10, 20, 300)'::color);
INSERT 119312 1
```

The record has successfully been inserted into the database; now we query the table again to see what has happened to the record:

```
mydata=# SELECT * FROM mycolor;
    cfield
-------------
 (0, 20, 0)
```

```
 (0, 20, 0)
 (0, 20, 255)
(3 rows)
```

The negative value has been changed to 0, and 300 has been changed to 255, which is the maximum value we allow for a component of a color.

The previous datatype shows impressively how simple it is to extend PostgreSQL's set of datatypes by implementing a simple C function. Some C gurus among you might say that the next code is no efficient implementation of a datatype, because three bytes (instead of six bytes) of storage would be enough to store information about a color. This is certainly true. The reason for our wasteful way of programming is that we want the code to be as simple as possible so that even C beginners can easily understand how PostgreSQL can be extended.

Adding Operators

Adding the datatype is not enough. New datatypes don't support functions yet, because only the in and out functions are defined so far.

We have already defined the datatype itself, but as you can see in the following, our datatype is not very useful yet:

```
mydata=# SELECT * FROM mycolor WHERE cfield='(0, 20, 0)'::color;
ERROR:  Unable to identify an operator '=' for types 'color' and 'color'
        You will have to retype this query using an explicit cast
```

To make the datatype more powerful, we have to implement additional functions and assign them to operators. One of the most important operators for a datatype is the + operator. Without it, there is no way to perform additions. In the following listing, you can see how a prototype of a + operator can be defined for our datatype:

```
/* define + operator */
color *color_add(color *a, color *b)
{
    color *c;

    /* checking for NULL */
    if      ((a == NULL) || (b == NULL))
    {
            return(NULL);
    }
```

```
/* adding the two objects */
c->r = a->r + b->r;
c->g = a->g + b->g;
c->b = a->b + b->b;

/* if a component is > 255 -> set it to 255 */
c->r = (255 < c->r) ? 255 : c->r;
c->g = (255 < c->g) ? 255 : c->g;
c->b = (255 < c->b) ? 255 : c->b;

return c;
}
```

This code is still very simple. We just add the various elements of the datatype and make sure that none of the values is higher than 255. Finally, the result is returned.

Before we can use the operator in combination with the datatype, we have to add the function and the operator to the database. Some things have to be defined:

```
CREATE FUNCTION color_add(color, color)
       RETURNS color AS '/usr/local/postgres_extpack/libfoo.so'
       LANGUAGE 'c';

CREATE OPERATOR + (
       leftarg = color,
       rightarg = color,
       procedure = color_add,
       commutator = +
);
```

We add the function the same way that we have before. Defining the operator is also an easy task. The first argument passed to the CREATE OPERATOR function is the datatype of the left argument; the second argument defines the right argument of the + operator. Because we want to add two colors, the right and the left argument have to be color. If we want to add color and an integer, for instance, we have to change the function assigned to the operator or add a second function for handling int4 + color (instead of color + color). The third object tells PostgreSQL which function has to be used for processing an addition of two colors.

The last parameter is a little more complicated. In case of an addition, it does not matter that we want to compute the result of color1 + color2 or color2 + color1—the result will be the same. Therefore, the commutator of + is +. In other words, the commutator is the operator that has to be used if the statement is written the other way around (color2 + color1 instead of color1 + color2). In case of < and >, the situation is different: a < b is not equal to b < a. If we want to write b before a, the result is b > a. > is therefore the commutator of the < operator. Many operators have a commutator, but not all of them. The - operator, for instance, is not commutative.

The definition of a *commutator* is additional information for optimizing the datatype. Before we get to additional optimization information, let's look at how the + operator can be used for our datatype. here is a simple example:

```
mydata=# SELECT '(0, 20, 255)'::color + '(0, 20, 255)'::color;
   ?column?
--------------
 (0, 40, 255)
(1 row)
```

The two values are added, and our function makes sure that none of the values is higher than 255.

If we want to add NULL to a value, NULL is returned:

```
mydata=# SELECT '(0, 20, 255)'::color + NULL::color;
 ?column?
----------

(1 row)
```

Another important operator is the = operator, which we use to find out whether two values are equal. Without a = operator defined for our datatype, it is not possible to write useful WHERE clauses, because we have to compare values. In the following code, you can see how the = operator has been implemented for our datatype; it checks whether all three components of the datatype are the same. If they are, true is returned; otherwise, the result of the function is false:

```
/* function for "=" operator */
bool *color_abs_eq(color *a, color *b)
{
        bool *retvalue;

        /* checking whether the values are equal */
        if      ((a->r == b->r) && (a->g == b->g) && (a->b == b->b))
        {
                retvalue = 1;
        }
        else
        {
```

```
            retvalue = 0;
    }
    return retvalue;
}
```

To add the operator to the database, we add the function in the shared object, which we have compiled using the Makefile we have shown before. After adding the function, we add the operator and define the left and the right operator, as we did in the previous example:

```
CREATE FUNCTION color_abs_eq(color, color)
        RETURNS bool AS '/usr/local/postgres_extpack/libfoo.so'
        LANGUAGE 'c';


CREATE OPERATOR = (
        leftarg = color,
        rightarg = color,
        procedure = color_abs_eq,
        restrict = eqsel,
        join = eqjoinsel
);
```

We have also included a `restrict` clause in the command. `restrict` helps the optimizer find the right way through a WHERE clause. Four standard restriction estimators are defined:

- eqsql for =

- neqsel for <>

- scalarltsel for < or <=

- scalargtsel for > or >=

> **Note**
> Defining restriction estimators might at first sight seem useless, but it helps the optimizer to find the fastest way through a query. Imagine a query that selects data from a table. With the help of restriction estimators the optimizer tries to guess the amount of rows found or rejected. The information used by the optimizer can be generated by using VACUUM ANALYZE.

Let's have a look at our new operator in action. We insert two records into the database and query the table using a SELECT statement including a WHERE clause:

```
mydata=# INSERT INTO mycolor VALUES ('(53, 66, 0)'::color);
INSERT 120166 1
mydata=# INSERT INTO mycolor VALUES ('(-10, 20, 300)'::color);
INSERT 120167 1
mydata=# SELECT * FROM mycolor;
    cfield
--------------
 (53, 66, 0)
 (0, 20, 255)
(2 rows)


mydata=# SELECT * FROM mycolor WHERE cfield='(0, 20, 255)'::color;
    cfield
--------------
 (0, 20, 255)
(1 row)
```

One of the two records that we have inserted into the database matches the WHERE clause, and therefore it is displayed. If something is wrong with the underlying C function, it is very likely that the backend crashes. Keep this in mind when dealing with datatypes and operators.

After we define the = operator, we want to define the <> operator. Here is the required code:

```
/* function for "<> operator */
bool *color_abs_ne(color *a, color *b)
{
        bool *retvalue;

        /* checking whether the values are equal */
        if      ((a->r == b->r) && (a->g == b->g) && (a->b == b->b))
        {
                retvalue = 0;
        }
        else
        {
                retvalue = 1;
        }
        return retvalue;
}
```

You can see that the C function used for the <> operator is very similar to the function used for the = operator. Now let's have a look at the SQL code that we need to insert the new operator into the database. This time we included a more sophisticated version of the SQL code:

```
CREATE FUNCTION color_abs_ne(color, color)
        RETURNS bool AS '/usr/local/postgres_extpack/libfoo.so'
        LANGUAGE 'c';

CREATE OPERATOR <> (
        leftarg = color,
        rightarg = color,
        procedure = color_abs_ne,
        restrict = neqsel,
        join = neqjoinsel,
        commutator = <>,
        negator = =
);
```

The function is inserted into the database as we did before, but let's take a closer look at the definition of the operator. The `restrict` clause contains `neqsel` this time (according to the four standard restriction estimators we listed previously). The commutator of the operator is <>, because it makes no difference whether we want to compute the result of a <> b or b <> a. Another important parameter that can be passed to the function is the negator. The negator defined the operator, which returns the same result, when the two operands of the statement are swapped. In other words, = is the negator of <>, because NOT (a <> b) is equal to a = b.

Another component of the `CREATE OPERATOR` command shown previously defines the behavior of the database when performing joins. If a `join` clause is provided, the join selectivity estimation function for the operator is defined. In general, `join` clauses make sense only for binary operators that return Boolean. The idea behind a `join` clause is to provide a function that estimates the fraction of rows satisfying a `WHERE` clause. In other words, It helps the optimizer to guess how many rows will most likely have to be omitted and how many rows can be taken from a table. Several types of "join selectivity estimation function" are provided by PostgreSQL:

- `eqjoinsel` for =

- `neqjoinsel` for <>

- `scalarltjoinsel` for < or <=

- `scalargtjoinsel` for > or >=

- `areajoinsel` for 2D area-based comparisons

- `positionjoinsel` for 2D position-based comparisons

- `contjoinsel` for 2D containment-based comparisons

Not only `join` clauses can be used. We have dealt with other parameters before, but PostgreSQL provides even more.

A `HASHES` clause can be used to tell the system that it is okay to use the hash join method for a join based on the operator. If we want to define `SORT` clauses tell the system, that it is allowed to use merge joins.

Now that we have defined the operator, let's look at how it can be used in SQL:

```
mydata=# INSERT INTO mycolor VALUES ('(-10, 20, 300)'::color);
INSERT 120229 1
mydata=# SELECT * FROM mycolor;
    cfield
--------------
 (0, 20, 255)
(1 row)

mydata=# SELECT * FROM mycolor WHERE cfield <> '(0, 20, 255)'::color;
 cfield
--------
(0 rows)
```

There is absolutely no difference between using our <> operator and PostgreSQL's built-in <> operator.

Adding Aggregates

You have learned how to define operators and datatypes. In this section, you explore aggregates. You have already learned the five important aggregate functions (SUM, AVG, MAX, MIN, and COUNT), which are defined for nearly all datatypes in PostgreSQL. These functions are called *aggregate functions* because they summarize the results of a query rather than listing all the rows in the result of the query.

Now that we have defined a new datatype, it might also be useful to define an aggregate function for it. Unfortunately, it is far more complex to write aggregate functions than to write the functions used for the operator, because more than one row is involved in the operation. Full coverage of how aggregate functions can be defined in PostgreSQL is far beyond the scope of this book.

If you want to find out how PostgreSQL's on-board aggregate functions have been implemented, check out $SRC_ROOT/src/backend/utils/adt. In this directory, you can find a lot of files containing a lot of code that make all those wonderful datatypes work the way they do.

Changing PostgreSQL's Rule System

Rules are another fundamental component of PostgreSQL. Rules define the behavior of PostgreSQL and are a very powerful tool.

Using Rules for Changing PostgreSQL's Behavior

In this section, you look at PostgreSQL's rule system and see what can be done with the help of rules. We will not cover all technical details, because this is very complicated and requires a lot of knowledge about PostgreSQL's internals (parse tree, and so forth) The focus will be on aspects that are interesting for users and programmers who want to build more sophisticated PostgreSQL applications.

Let's get right to some practical stuff. To add a rule to the database, the CREATE RULE command has to be used; here is an overview of the command's syntax:

```
mydata=# \h CREATE RULE
Command:    CREATE RULE
Description: Defines a new rule
Syntax:
CREATE RULE name AS ON event
    TO object [ WHERE condition ]
    DO [ INSTEAD ] action

where action can be:

NOTHING
|
query
|
( query ; query ... )
|
[ query ; query ... ]
```

To remove a rule from the database, we use the DROP RULE command:

```
mydata=# \h DROP RULE
Command:     DROP RULE
Description: Removes existing rules from the database
Syntax:
DROP RULE name [, ...]
```

The next example is a prototype of a logging function. The function is simple so that it can easily be understood:

```
#include <stdio.h>
#include <pgsql/postgres.h>
#include <pgsql/fmgr.h>


PG_FUNCTION_INFO_V1(myelog);
Datum myelog(PG_FUNCTION_ARGS)
{
        text       *arg1 = PG_GETARG_TEXT_P(0);

        elog(NOTICE, "%s", VARDATA(arg1));
        PG_RETURN_INT16(1);
}
```

You can see how the logging function has been implemented. First we extract the input and pass the data to the elog function used to add an entry to the logfile. Finally, 1 is returned.

After compiling the code, we add the function to the database and test it:

```
mydata=# CREATE FUNCTION myelog(text) RETURNS int4 AS
'/mnt/data/c/postgres_extpack/libfoo.so' LANGUAGE 'c';
CREATE
mydata=# SELECT myelog('my notice function');
NOTICE: my notice function

 myelog
--------
      1
(1 row)
```

One line is added to PostgreSQL's logfile:

```
2001-07-02 16:12:40 [4241]   NOTICE:  my notice function
```

We have defined a logging function that can be used in combination with PostgreSQL 7.1 or later. For users of 7.0, this function will not work, because fmgr.h and postgres.h were both installed in the include directory but not in 7.1 and up.

Now we create a table called mynumber, using a simple SQL statement:

```
mydata=# CREATE TABLE mydata(a int4, b int4);
CREATE
```

In the next step, we want to define a rule that tells the database to call the logging function every time a value is inserted into table mynumber. The rule for that is very simple; here is the SQL code to create the rule:

```
CREATE RULE notice_insert AS ON INSERT TO mynumber
        DO SELECT myelog('Values inserted into mynumber');
```

If we insert a row into table mynumber, the NOTICE message is displayed:

```
mydata=# INSERT INTO mynumber VALUES('12', '23');
NOTICE:  Values inserted into mynumber
INSERT 120348 1
```

The value has been inserted successfully into the table.

PostgreSQL stores information about rules in a system table called pg_rewrite. We query the table to find out what has been added for the rule that we have just defined, using the following SQL statement:

```
SELECT * FROM pg_rewrite WHERE rulename='notice_insert';
```

The data structure of table pg_rewrite can easily be extracted from the database by using the \d command:

```
mydata=# \d pg_rewrite
        Table "pg_rewrite"
 Attribute  |   Type    | Modifier
------------+-----------+----------
 rulename   | name      |
 ev_type    | "char"    |
 ev_class   | oid       |
 ev_attr    | smallint  |
 is_instead | boolean   |
 ev_qual    | text      |
 ev_action  | text      |
Indices: pg_rewrite_oid_index,
         pg_rewrite_rulename_index
```

Here is the result of the query:

```
 notice_insert | 3         |     120251 |        -1 | f              | <>        | ({ QUERY
:command 1  :utility <> :resultRelation 0 :into <> :isPortal false :isBinary
false :isTemp false :hasAggs false :hasSubLinks false :rtable ({ RTE :relname
mynumber :relid 120251  :subquery <> :alias { ATTR :relname *OLD* :attrs <>}
:eref { ATTR :relname *OLD* :attrs ( "a"    "b" )} :inh false :inFromCl false
:checkForRead false :checkForWrite false :checkAsUser 500} { RTE :relname
mynumber :relid 120251  :subquery <> :alias { ATTR :relname *NEW* :attrs <>}
:eref { ATTR :relname *NEW* :attrs ( "a"    "b" )} :inh false :inFromCl false
:checkForRead false :checkForWrite false :checkAsUser 500}) :jointree { FROMEXPR
:fromlist <> :quals <>} :rowMarks () :targetList ({ TARGETENTRY :resdom { RESDOM
:resno 1 :restype 23 :restypmod -1 :resname myelog :reskey 0 :reskeyop 0
:ressortgroupref 0 :resjunk false } :expr { EXPR :typeOid 23  :opType func :oper
{ FUNC :funcid 120346 :functype 23 } :args ({ CONST :consttype 25 :constlen -1
:constbyval false :constisnull false :constvalue  33 [ 33 0 0 0 86 97 108 117
101 115 32 105 110 115 101 114 116 101 100 32 105 110 116 111 32 109 121 110 117
109 98 101 114 ]
})}}) :groupClause <> :havingQual <> :distinctClause <> :sortClause <>
:limitOffset <> :limitCount
<> :setOperations <> :resultRelations ()})
(1 row)
```

The result of the query shows quite well that rules are a very complex topic in PostgreSQL and are a fundamental and powerful component of the database server. But rules can be used for other purposes. The following is a script called a.sql, which defines two rules. The first rule tells the server to call the logging function. The second rule changes the behavior of the server again and tells the database to do nothing instead of inserting the values defined in the INSERT statement:

```
CREATE RULE notice_insert AS ON INSERT TO mynumber
        DO SELECT myelog('Values inserted into mynumber');

INSERT INTO mynumber VALUES('12', '23');

CREATE RULE notice_redefine AS ON INSERT TO mynumber
        DO INSTEAD NOTHING;

INSERT INTO mynumber VALUES('13', '24');
```

The two rules defined here do the opposite of each other. Let's execute the script:

```
[hs@duron postgres_extpack]$ psql mydata < /tmp/a.sql
CREATE
NOTICE:  Values inserted into mynumber
INSERT 120356 1
CREATE
```

```
NOTICE:  Values inserted into mynumber
 myelog
---------
       1
(1 row)
```

The first INSERT statement is executed and the NOTICE message is displayed on the
screen. Then we add the second rule to the database to make sure that the INSERT
statement is not executed. The NOTICE message is displayed because only the INSERT
statement is replaced. If we query table mynumber, we can see that the table contains
only one value:

```
mydata=# SELECT * FROM mynumber;
 a  | b
----+----
 12 | 23
(1 row)
```

Until now, we have defined rules that call a certain function, such as our logging
function. Now we define a rule used to execute an SQL statement:

```
CREATE RULE notice_insert AS ON INSERT TO mynumber
        DO INSERT INTO mynumber VALUES('1', '2');

INSERT INTO mynumber VALUES('12', '23');
```

The problem with this SQL code is that the rule causes an INSERT statement to be
performed, which also causes an INSERT statement to be performed. The result is an
endless recursion. Luckily, PostgreSQL has an emergency brake implemented, which
quits a recursion after 10 steps (10 has been compiled into the binaries).

If we execute the previous script, the database stops the execution of the code:

```
[hs@duron postgres_extpack]$ psql mydata < /tmp/a.sql
CREATE
ERROR:  query rewritten 10 times, may contain cycles
```

Because the entire process is executed in one transaction, mynumber does not contain
10 values. As you can see in the following, the table is still empty:

```
mydata=# SELECT * FROM mynumber;
 a | b
---+---
(0 rows)
```

Using Rules in Combination with Views

When dealing with views, PostgreSQL's rule system might be essential, because without it some basic operations cannot be performed. In this section, you will see how views can be used efficiently in combination with views.

Let's insert a value into mynumber:

```
mydata=# INSERT INTO mynumber VALUES('1', '2');
INSERT 120373 1
```

As you might expect, the record has been inserted into the table successfully:

```
mydata=# SELECT * FROM mynumber;
 a | b
---+---
 1 | 2
(1 row)
```

Now we create a view that multiplies the values in the table by 2:

```
CREATE VIEW my_view AS
        SELECT a*2 AS c, b*2 AS d
        FROM mynumber;
```

If we query the table, we receive the result:

```
mydata=# SELECT * FROM my_view;
 c | d
---+---
 2 | 4
(1 row)
```

Now we want to update the record in the view by using a simple UPDATE statement:

```
mydata=# UPDATE my_view SET c=6 WHERE c=2;
ERROR:  Cannot update a view without an appropriate rule
```

The UPDATE statement fails, because the database does not know how to treat the tables the view is defined on. A view can be updated only when the user defines a set of rules. Then the database will know what to do when an UPDATE operation has to be performed.

A rule can be defined like this:

```
CREATE RULE view_update AS ON UPDATE TO my_view
        DO INSTEAD
        UPDATE mynumber SET
```

```
        a=NEW.c/2,
        b=NEW.d/2;
```

We tell the database to perform an UPDATE query on table mynumber instead of the UPDATE statement on the view. We set the values in the table to the half of the values that we pass to the UPDATE statement for the view, because the view displays the values in the table multiplied by 2. NEW tells the database to use the value that the view should contain after the UPDATE operation. If we want the old value to be used, we use OLD instead.

Let's perform the UPDATE operation to see whether it works:

```
mydata=# UPDATE my_view SET c=6 WHERE c=2;
UPDATE 1
```

The UPDATE operation has been executed successfully. Let's see what can be retrieved from the view:

```
mydata=# SELECT * FROM my_view;
 c | d
---+---
 6 | 4
(1 row)
```

The values in the view have been changed correctly. Because the view does not contain the data, we query the table that the view is defined on:

```
mydata=# SELECT * FROM mynumber;
 a | b
---+---
 3 | 2
(1 row)
```

The UPDATE query has changed the value in the first column from 1 to 3, which is correct.

Because we do not want to perform only UPDATE operations, we also define rules for INSERT and DELETE statements:

```
CREATE RULE view_insert AS ON INSERT TO my_view
        DO INSTEAD
        INSERT INTO mynumber VALUES(
                (NEW.c/2)::int4,
                (NEW.d/2)::int4);
```

```
CREATE RULE view_delete AS ON DELETE TO my_view
       DO INSTEAD
       DELETE FROM mynumber
       WHERE a=(OLD.c/2)::int4
               AND b=(OLD.d/2)::int4;
```

The rule for INSERT statements is easy. We simply tell the database to insert the values passed to the INSERT statement into the table that the view is defined on. We have to make sure that the result of the division is still an integer value; otherwise, we can't insert the value into the table, because both columns of the table (a and b) are integer fields. In the example, we solved the problem by using a simple cast. A more sophisticated solution would be to use a function that checks whether the result of c/2 or d/2 is a valid integer number.

The rule that we have defined for DELETE statements divides the values of the two columns by 2, casts the result to integer, and deletes the values from the table that the view is defined on.

Let's try to insert a value into a view now:

```
mydata=# INSERT INTO my_view VALUES('12', '10');
INSERT 120400 1
mydata=# SELECT * FROM mynumber;
 a | b
---+---
 3 | 2
 6 | 5
(2 rows)
```

The correct value has successfully been inserted into the table that we are using for our view. Logically, the correct value can also be found when querying the view itself:

```
mydata=# SELECT * FROM my_view;
 c  | d
----+----
  6 |  4
 12 | 10
(2 rows)
```

Let's try to delete records from the table:

```
mydata=# DELETE FROM my_view WHERE c=12;
DELETE 1
mydata=# SELECT * FROM my_view;
 c | d
```

```
---+---
 6 | 4
(1 row)
```

The value has successfully been deleted. To make sure, that the rule works correctly, we try to delete records that don't exist in the table:

```
mydata=# DELETE FROM my_view WHERE c=6 AND d=3;
DELETE 0
```

Nothing has been deleted, so we have proved that the rule does exactly what we want it to do.

Summary

Although PostgreSQL is a powerful database, user-defined functions and operators might have to be implemented. To perform these tasks, PostgreSQL supports easy-to-use programming interfaces.

Rules are a key component when working with views. If the content of a view has to be modified, a set of rules has to be defined to tell PostgreSQL what to do.

CHAPTER 17

Date Calculations

Working with dates is one of the most crucial tasks in the life of a computer programmer. Most operations can be done with the help of modules, but it is still important to have some basic knowledge about working with dates. This chapter guides you through the world of dates and time and shows you how to work with them efficiently in combination with PostgreSQL.

SQL and Dates

When dates are stored in databases, you will soon get in touch with PostgreSQL and simple date and time operations. SQL has to be used. In the next sections, you learn to work with SQL in dates.

SQL, Dates, and Time Zones

When dealing with time and dates, one of the most crucial aspects is time zones. In general, the world has been divided into 25 integer time zones.

Integer means that the difference from one time zone to the other is a multiple of one hour. Some countries have adopted nonstandard time zones. They use 30-minute increments, which can make working with time zones complicated. Each time zone is 15° longitude, as measured east and west from the prime meridian of the world at Greenwich, England. Greenwich, which is a small town near London, is the center of world time. Since 1884, Greenwich has been situated on the prime meridian (0° longitude). Every time zone is defined relative to Greenwich Mean Time (GMT). GMT is the same as Zulu Time. The following table lists all world time zones. The asterisks (*) are an international sign indicating that the time zone marks half-hour steps.

GMT	Zone	Military	Civilian Time Zones	Cities
GMT	Z	Zulu	GMT: Greenwich Mean UT: Universal UTC: Universal Co-ordinated WET: Western European	London, England Dublin, Ireland Edinburgh, Scotland Lisbon, Portugal Reykjavik, Iceland Casablanca, Morocco
GMT+1	A	Alpha	CET: Central European	Paris, France Berlin, Germany Amsterdam, The Netherlands Brussels, Belgium Vienna, Austria Madrid, Spain Rome, Italy Bern, Switzerland Stockholm, Sweden Oslo, Norway
GMT+2	B	Bravo	EET: Eastern European	Athens, Greece Helsinki, Finland Istanbul, Turkey Jerusalem, Israel Harare, Zimbabwe

GMT	Zone	Military	Civilian Time Zones	Cities
GMT+3	C	Charlie	BT: Baghdad	Kuwait Nairobi, Kenya Riyadh, Saudi Arabia Moscow, Russia
GMT+3:30	C*			Tehran, Iran
GMT+4	D	Delta		Abu Dhabi, UAE Muscat Tblisi Volgograd Kabul
GMT+4:30	D*			Kabul, Afghanistan
GMT+5	E	Echo		
GMT+5:30	E*			India
GMT+6	F	Foxtrot		
GMT+6:30	F*			Cocos Islands
GMT+7	G	Golf	WAST: West Australian Standard	
GMT+8	H	Hotel	CCT: China Coast	
GMT+9	I	India	JST: Japan Standard,	
GMT+9:30	I*		Australia Central Standard	Darwin, Australia Adelaide, Australia
GMT+10	K	Kilo	GST: Guam Standard	
GMT+10:30	K*			Lord Howe Island
GMT+11	L	Lima		
GMT+11:30	L*			Norfolk Island

GMT	Zone	Military	Civilian Time Zones	Cities
GMT+12	M	Mike	IDLE: International Date Line East NZST: New Zealand Standard	Wellington, New Zealand Fiji Marshall Islands
GMT+13:00	M*			Rawaki Islands: Enderbury Kiribati
GMT+14:00 Kiritibati	M±			Line Islands:
GMT--1	N	November	WAT: West Africa	Azores, Cape Verde Islands
GMT--2	O	Oscar	AT: Azores	
GMT--3	P	Papa		Brasilia, Brazil Buenos Aires, Argentina Georgetown, Guyana
GMT--3:30	P*			Newfoundland
GMT--4	Q	Quebec	AST: Atlantic Standard	Caracas La Paz
GMT--5	R	Romeo	EST: Eastern Standard.	Bogota Lima, Peru New York, NY, USA
GMT--6	S	Sierra	CST: Central Standard	Mexico City, Mexico Saskatchewan, Canada
GMT--7	T	Tango	MST: Mountain Standard.	
GMT--8	U	Uniform	PST: Pacific Standard	Los Angeles, CA, USA

GMT	Zone	Military	Civilian Time Zones	Cities
GMT--8:30	U*			
GMT--9	V	Victor	YST: Yukon Standard.	
GMT--9:30	V*			
GMT--10	W	Whiskey	AHST: Alaska--Hawaii Standard CAT: Central Alaska HST: Hawaii Standard	
GMT--11	X	X-ray	NT: Nome.	
GMT--12	Y	Yankee	IDLW: International Date Line West	

Some countries do not use the same time for the whole year. Most European countries use winter time and summer time (daylight saving time). Daylight saving time supposedly enables people to use the day more efficiently. IT people usually don't care, because they use the non-daylight hours anyway, to write books or to do some wonderful hacking.

PostgreSQL offers a lot of data types for storing time and dates, and it is important to know how dates, time, and time zones are treated by the database engine. The following sections present a short overview of all datatypes available.

`timestamp``timestamp` is used to store the date and time. `timestamp` is the most precise datatype available; time can be stored up to a precision of 1 microsecond. `timestamp` can store dates from BC 4713 to AD 1,465,001, which should be enough for "ordinary" applications. Eight bytes of storage are required to store a timestamp.

timestamp with time zone

Sometimes it is necessary to store the time zone in combination with a certain date and time. Because an ordinary `timestamp` does not support time zones, PostgreSQL offers a datatype called `timestamp with time zone` to do the job. Both `timestamp` and `timestamp with time zone` need 8 bytes of storage, but because some space is needed to store the time zone, `timestamp with time zone` supports only a smaller range of valid dates. Starting with AD 1903, `timestamp with time zone` can store dates until AD 2037—with a resolution of 1 microsecond.

Inserting a `timestamp` into a table is simple, because PostgreSQL supports ISO-compliant time stamps. To show you how it can be done, we create a table with just one column containing a `timestamp` first:

```
CREATE TABLE showstamp(mystamp timestamp with time zone);
```

The table has been created successfully:

```
                  Table "showstamp"
 Attribute |           Type           | Modifier
-----------+--------------------------+----------
 mystamp   | timestamp with time zone |
```

We can insert a value into the table using the following:

```
INSERT INTO showstamp VALUES('2001-06-25 09:22:12 -8:00');
```

The `INSERT` statement inserts June 26, 2001 into the database. The time is set to 9 o'clock, 22 minutes, and 12 seconds. The time zone is set to PST (Pacific Standard Time).

Let's select the data from the table now. We use a simple `SELECT *` to retrieve the records:

```
performance=# SELECT * FROM showstamp;
        mystamp
------------------------
 2001-06-25 19:22:12+02
(1 row)
```

At first sight it looks strange, but remember that the database displays the time for the time zone you are in currently. At the moment, I am working in Vienna, which is in time zone GMT+1. Because we have summer time in Austria now, we have to use Eastern European time (Eastern Europe is one hour before Austrian winter time). The time zone we are currently in is consequently GMT+2. We have inserted the record in Pacific Standard Time, which is actually 10 hours behind Eastern European time. Therefore 19 o'clock is displayed instead of 9 o'clock. PostgreSQL adds the time zone to the result.

You do not have to worry about time zones on the database level, but it might be a little tricky on the application level. To get around the problem, you use modules, which already exist when you write your own applications.

In the example, we have not defined the amount of microseconds in the `timestamp`. We could have done it the following way:

```
INSERT INTO showstamp VALUES('2001-06-25 19:22:12.32 +2:00');
```

PostgreSQL now adds `32` microseconds to the `timestamp`. Because only a few applications need microseconds, you can omit them when inserting the data into the database.

If you are working with a `timestamp`, you can insert only a date; you do not have to define the time:

```
INSERT INTO showstamp VALUES('2001-03-2');
```

Now the date is set to February 2, 2001. If we query the table, we get the following result:

```
performance=# SELECT * FROM showstamp;
          mystamp
--------------------------
 2001-06-25 19:22:12.32+02
 2001-03-02 00:00:00+01
(2 rows)
```

The time in the second record is set to a default value. In this case, PostgreSQL uses midnight in Central Europe as the default value.

Currently, PostgreSQL offers three ways to define the time zone. The following `INSERT` statements insert the same data into the database:

```
INSERT INTO showstamp VALUES('2001-06-25 19:22:12.32 +2:00');
INSERT INTO showstamp VALUES('2001-06-25 19:22:12.32 +2');
INSERT INTO showstamp VALUES('2001-06-25 19:22:12.32 +200');
```

We perform a simple query to check whether the data in the table is always the same:

```
performance=# SELECT * FROM showstamp;
          mystamp
--------------------------
 2001-06-25 19:22:12.32+02
 2001-06-25 19:22:12.32+02
 2001-06-25 19:22:12.32+02
(3 rows)
```

You can see that it works perfectly well.

`interval`

Sometimes it might be useful to store intervals. The syntax of `interval` can sometimes be a little tricky on the application level, but it is easy to get used to it. PostgreSQL needs 12 bytes of storage to store an `interval`. The precision is 1 microsecond, as it is for "timestamp." The range of valid dates extends from 178,000,000 BC to 178,000,000 AD.

Inserting intervals into a database might be slightly more difficult than inserting a `timestamp`. To show you, how intervals have to be treated, we create a table with one column:

```
CREATE TABLE showinter(mystamp interval);
```

The table has now successfully been created and we can insert some data:

```
INSERT INTO showinter VALUES('1 year 8 months 3 days 12 hours 9 minutes 3
seconds');
```

If the `INSERT` statement succeeds, we can find the record in the table:

```
performance=# SELECT * FROM showinter;
            mystamp
-------------------------------
 1 year 8 mons 3 days 12:09:03
(1 row)
```

If we want to insert 12 hours, 9 minutes, and 3 seconds, we can also do it the following way:

```
INSERT INTO showinter VALUES('12:9:3');
```

If we query the table now, we can see that the record is displayed pretty much the same way that we inserted it:

```
performance=# SELECT * FROM showinter;
 mystamp
----------
 12:09:03
(1 row)
```

Before we get to some additional examples, let's look at the syntax used to define `interval`:

```
Quantity Unit [Quantity Unit...] [Direction]
```

Quantity is an integer value, which can also be negative (for example, 12, 23, and so forth). Units are seconds, minutes, hours, days, weeks, months, years, decades, centuries, or millennia.

Direction can be ago or simply empty. The following example shows how ago can be used:

```
INSERT INTO showinter VALUES('12:9:3 ago');
```

ago tells the database that the value we define in the INSERT statement is negative. If we query showinter after performing the INSERT statement, it looks like this:

```
performance=# SELECT * FROM showinter;
  mystamp
-----------
 -12:09:03
(1 row)
```

date

For many applications, storing a timestamp is overkill and wastes too much space. You can use date to store dates without time. Therefore, the precision is one day. Four bytes of storage are used to store values from BC 4713 to AD 32,767.

You should use date instead of timestamp if you are 100% sure that you will never store time in combination with date, because date requires only half the storage "timestamp" needs.

PostgreSQL supports a variety of methods to insert dates into the database. One way is to use the ISO-8601 format. This format is also used to define the date when inserting a timestamp into the database.

Let's create a simple table:

```
CREATE TABLE showdate(mydate date);
```

Now we can insert June 25, 2001 in various ways:

```
INSERT INTO showdate VALUES('2001-06-25');
INSERT INTO showdate VALUES('June 25, 2001');
INSERT INTO showdate VALUES('20010625');
INSERT INTO showdate VALUES('010625');
INSERT INTO showdate VALUES('June 25, 2001 AD');
```

All these INSERT statements insert the same data into the database. We can easily check this by performing a simple full table scan:

```
performance=# SELECT * FROM showdate;
   mydate
------------
 2001-06-25
 2001-06-25
 2001-06-25
 2001-06-25
 2001-06-25
(5 rows)
```

PostgreSQL also offers two other ways of defining a date. We don't recommend these ways, because they can lead to a lot of confusion. Suppose you want to insert June 5, 2001 into the database. Here are two SQL statements that can be used to do the job:

```
INSERT INTO showdate VALUES('5/6/2001');
INSERT INTO showdate VALUES('6/5/2001');
```

The first SQL statement uses the U.S. style; the second statement uses the European style. You can configure which style to use, but use a syntax that points out clearly whether you mean June 5, 2001 or May 6, 2001.

time [without time zone]

PostgreSQL offers a datatype called time to store a certain time. time without time zone does not store the time zone. The range of values lasts from 00:00:00.00 to 23:59:59.99; in other words, all values from midnight to midnight can be saved by using time. The precision is 1 microsecond again, and PostgreSQL uses 4 bytes of storage.

time [with time zone]time with time zone is similar to time without time zone. The only difference is that time is stored in combination with the time zone. The valid range is therefore from 00:00:00.00+12 to 23:59:59.99–12. Four bytes of storage are used.

Inserting dates into a database is fairly easy. Here are two examples:

```
CREATE TABLE showtime(mydate time with time zone);
INSERT INTO showtime VALUES('12:22:07.04+1');
INSERT INTO showtime VALUES('12:22:07.04');
```

We create a table and insert two records into the table. In the first example, we use Central European time explicitly. In the second one, we do not define a time zone and PostgreSQL uses the default value.

If we perform a full table scan, we receive the following result:

```
performance=# SELECT * FROM showtime;
   mydate
-------------
 12:22:07+01
 12:22:07+02
(2 rows)
```

The table contains two records. The second record uses the default time zone of the system, which, in our case, is Eastern European time.

PostgreSQL offers more methods to deal with time. The next two examples show you how time can be inserted:

```
INSERT INTO showtime VALUES('0:22:07 PM');
INSERT INTO showtime VALUES('122207');
```

Both INSERT statements tell the database to insert 12 o'clock, 22 minutes, and 7 seconds into the database.

Let's check whether the records have been inserted correctly:

```
performance=# SELECT * FROM showtime;
   mydate
-------------
 12:22:07+02
 12:22:07+02
(2 rows)
```

The result looks good—the records are identical.

Special Values and Abbreviations

PostgreSQL supports abbreviations for special dates and times. These abbreviations can be useful and make your software easier to read and easier to understand.

One of the most important values is the "birthday" of Unix systems. In general, the 0 time of a Unix system is set to January 1, 1970. In PostgreSQL, this event is called epoch. Use epoch instead of 1970-01-01 00:00:00+00. The next example shows that there is no difference between the two:

```
CREATE TABLE specials(mydate timestamp with time zone);
INSERT INTO specials VALUES('epoch');
```

We have created a table and inserted epoch into it. Let's perform a simple query:

```
performance=# SELECT * FROM specials WHERE mydate='1970-01-01 00:00:00+00';
 mydate
--------
 epoch
(1 row)
```

epoch is retrieved because it is equal to Unix starting time.

Another important function when working with dates is now. In the next example, now returns the current time. To be more precise, now returns the current transaction time:

```
performance=# SELECT now();
          now
------------------------
 2001-05-12 15:04:15+02
(1 row)
```

In many applications, it might be useful for you to find out today's date. PostgreSQL offers special abbreviations for today, yesterday, and tomorrow. The following shows how these abbreviations can be used in INSERT statements:

```
INSERT INTO specials VALUES('today');
INSERT INTO specials VALUES('tomorrow');
INSERT INTO specials VALUES('yesterday');
```

When we retrieve the data, we can see that PostgreSQL uses midnight as the time:

```
performance=# SELECT * FROM specials;
        mydate
------------------------
 2001-05-12 00:00:00+02
 2001-05-13 00:00:00+02
 2001-05-11 00:00:00+02
(3 rows)
```

If you want to compare dates, you might find the next three abbreviations useful. Sometimes you have to set the time to the latest or the earliest moment available. PostgreSQL offers the appropriate abbreviations:

```
INSERT INTO specials VALUES('infinity');
INSERT INTO specials VALUES('-infinity');
```

We use infinity and -infinity, to define the last earliest moment in the PostgreSQL's time system:

```
performance=# SELECT * FROM specials;
  mydate
-----------
 infinity
 -infinity
(2 rows)
```

Time can also be an undefined value. In this case, you can use NULL or invalid.

When defining dates, the month can be defined as either a number (for example, 1 for January) or a string. Here is a list of all abbreviations accepted by PostgreSQL:

Month	Abbreviation
January	Jan
February	Feb
March	Mar
April	Apr
May	May
June	Jun
July	Jul
August	Aug
September	Sep, Sept
October	Oct
November	Nov
December	Dec

The abbreviations can be used instead of the name of a month. Shortcuts are also available for the day of the week:

Day of the wWeek	Abbreviation
Monday	Mon
Tuesday	Tue, Tues
Wednesday	Wed, Weds
Thursday	Thu, Thur, Thurs
Friday	Fri
Saturday	Sat
Sunday	Sun

Performing Simple Date and Time Operations with SQL

Many of you might already have been in crucial situations where you were not sure how certain operations related to dates could be performed. Sometimes working with dates can be tricky, because you can't find documentation about what is really going on inside a database and how operators are defined for certain datatypes. PostgreSQL offers a good onboard documentation system, but in most cases examples are easier to understand than syntax overviews.

Performing calculations with dates and time has always been complicated. This section presents real solutions for how to work with dates efficiently in PostgreSQL.

Casting is one of the most important tasks when dealing with dates. Currently, PostgreSQL users have a choice of three casting methods.

A function called `cast` can be used to convert one datatype to another. The syntax of `cast` is simple. In the following example, you can see how `timestamp` is converted to `date`:

```
performance=# SELECT CAST(now() AS date);
  ?column?
------------
 2001-05-12
(1 row)
```

The second method is to use the `::` operator. In the next example, we perform the same operation as above, but this time we use the `::` operator:

```
performance=# SELECT now()::date;
  ?column?
------------
 2001-05-12
(1 row)
```

The `::` operator can be used several times per query:

```
performance=# SELECT now()::date::text;
  ?column?
------------
 2001-05-12
(1 row)
```

In this example, we convert the result of `now` to `date` first. After that, we cast the result of the first conversion to `text`.

Sometimes it also is possible to use the name of the datatype that we want to cast a value to as a function. In the next example, we cast the result of now to text using a function called text:

```
performance=# SELECT text(now());
          text
- - - - - - - - - - - - - - - - - - - - - -
 2001-05-12 16:56:39+02
(1 row)
```

One of the most important datatypes when working with dates and times is reltime, which is a limited-range time interval. It also can be called Unix delta time. Every time we add or subtract time or date from a value, we can use the datatype reltime.

In the next example, we want to add 30 days to June 12, 2001:

```
performance=# SELECT '2001-06-12 00:00:00' + ('30 days'::reltime);
        ?column?
- - - - - - - - - - - - - - - - - - - - - -
 2001-07-12 00:00:00+02
(1 row)
```

First we define the timestamp to which we want to add a certain amount of time. Then we define the amount of time we want to add and cast it to reltime. The + operator is defined for timestamp and reltime so the operation can be performed.

If we want to make sure that the datatype of the output is what we want it to be, we can cast the result explicitly. In the next example, we cast the result to timestamp:

```
performance=# SELECT timestamp('2001-06-12 00:00:00' + ('30 days'::reltime));
        timestamp
- - - - - - - - - - - - - - - - - - - - - -
 2001-07-12 00:00:00+02
(1 row)
```

If we look closer at the result of the query, we can see that exactly 1 month has been added, because June is 30 days long. We could have achieved the same result by using a query like this:

```
performance=# SELECT date('2001-06-12 00:00:00' + ('1 month'::reltime));
    date
- - - - - - - - - - - -
 2001-07-12
(1 row)
```

The operations we have just described have been tested on PostgreSQL 7.1. Users of PostgreSQL 7.02 or below might face some troubles with queries such as these. The syntax is right for PostgreSQL 7.02 as well, but PostgreSQL cannot process it correctly. This problem occurs because there is no explicit date+reltime math operator. There is an operator defined for date+int, which assumes that the integer value is counted in days. Additionally, there is a binary-compatible entry for reltime->int. To help you understand what is going on inside the database, here is a short overview of how the error occurs: PostgreSQL 7.02 casts the result of '30 days'::reltime to integer and adds it to timestamp. Seconds should be returned, but the database thinks that it was days and an error occurs. This error shows that working with dates and time is always tricky. You should test a query extensively before you include it in your application. The problem we described previously has already been fixed.

Let's try another query:

```
performance=# SELECT date('2001-06-12 00:00:00' + '30 days');
ERROR:  Bad date external representation 'e'
```

This query fails because PostgreSQL does not know what to do with '30 days'; we have to perform an explicit cast to reltime. In the next example, we perform the same operation that we performed before, but this time we want the result to be displayed as date:

```
performance=# SELECT date('2001-06-12 00:00:00' + ('30 days'::reltime));
    date
------------
 2001-07-12
(1 row)
```

Sometimes people try to add dates, but operations like that don't make sense. Here is a query example:

```
performance=# SELECT date('2001-06-12'::date + '2001-06-12'::date);
ERROR:  Unable to identify an operator '+' for types 'date' and 'date'
        You will have to retype this query using an explicit cast
```

The syntax of the query is okay, but what do we expect as the result of the operation? The result of adding two dates is not defined, so PostgreSQL does not support the + operator for adding two dates.

+ is defined for timestamp + int. In the next example, you can see the result of the addition of two timestamps:

```
performance=# SELECT timestamp('2001-06-12'::timestamp + 1);
      timestamp
------------------------
 2001-06-13 00:00:00+02
(1 row)
```

PostgreSQL simply adds one day. If we try to do the same things we have done with an integer value with `float`, the result is somehow unexpected:

```
performance=# SELECT timestamp('2001-06-12'::timestamp + 1.4);
      timestamp
------------------------
 2001-06-13 00:00:00+02
(1 row)
```

The result is the same when adding 1.4 as when adding 1 (for internal reasons).

The - operator is defined for subtracting two dates:

```
performance=# SELECT date('2001-06-12'::date - '2000-06-01'::date);
    date
------------
 1970-01-01
(1 row)
```

Now we perform the same operation, but cast the result to `timestamp`:

```
performance=# SELECT timestamp('2001-06-12'::date - '2000-06-01'::date);
      timestamp
------------------------
 1970-01-01 01:06:16+01
(1 row)
```

Sometimes, basic arithmetic operations have to be done with intervals. Here is an example:

```
performance=# SELECT interval('3 days') + interval('1 month');
   ?column?
--------------
 1 mon 3 days
(1 row)
```

Adding to intervals is an easy process. You can see from the previous example that PostgreSQL displays the expected result. Now we want to subtract 1 month from 3 days:

```
performance=# SELECT interval('3 days') - interval('1 month');
   ?column?
- - - - - - - - - - - - - - - -
 -1 mons +3 days
(1 row)
```

The result seems a little strange, because PostgreSQL does not seem to calculate the amount of days. If you think about it, you will see the result in a different light. Because a month can have 28, 29, 30, or 31 days, the amount of days cannot be calculated if you don't know how long a month is.

If we cast the result to interval, the output won't change for the reasons we have just described:

```
performance=# SELECT interval(interval('3 days') - interval('1 month'));
   interval
- - - - - - - - - - - - - - - -
 -1 mons +3 days
(1 row)
```

If we add 1 year to the result of this query, the result looks a little better:

```
performance=# SELECT interval(interval('3 days') - interval('1 month')) +
interval('1 year');
   ?column?
- - - - - - - - - - - - - - - -
 11 mons 3 days
(1 row)
```

Now PostgreSQL tells us that the result is 11 mons and 3 days. The number of months can be calculated exactly, because a year always has exactly 12 months.

The next example shows how a simple division can be performed:

```
performance=# SELECT interval('30 days')/10;
 ?column?
- - - - - - - - - -
 3 days
(1 row)
```

As we have expected, the result of the query is 3. But what happens when we divide 1 month by 2?

```
performance=# SELECT interval('1 month')/2;
 ?column?
```

```
----------
 15 days
(1 row)
```

PostgreSQL performs the operation and assumes that a month has 30 days. Therefore the result of the query is 15.

What happens when we multiply 1 day by 60?

```
performance=# SELECT interval('1 day')*60;
 ?column?
----------
 60 days
(1 row)
```

The result is 60 days. PostgreSQL does not display 2 months or something like that for the same reason discussed previously—the number of days in a month is not always the same.

If we multiply 1 month by 13, PostgreSQL displays the result in a great way:

```
performance=# SELECT interval('1 month')*13;
   ?column?
-------------
 1 year 1 mon
(1 row)
```

PostgreSQL not only supports basic arithmetic operations. In real-world applications, it might be useful to find out which one of the two intervals is the higher one. Therefore, PostgreSQL provides a function called interval_cmp:

```
performance=# SELECT interval_cmp(interval('3 months'), interval('4 months'));
 interval_cmp
-------------
          -1
(1 row)
```

interval_cmp returns 1 if the first value is higher, 0 if both values are equal, and -1 if the second value is higher (the cmp function should be defined for every datatype in PostgreSQL to perform join operations).

interval_cmp is not the only function available. PostgreSQL supports many additional functions. If you need a complete list of those functions, use \df interval:

```
performance=# \df interval
```

```
                      List of functions
    Result    |     Function      |        Arguments
 -----------+-----------------+------------------------------
  interval   | interval          | interval
  interval   | interval          | reltime
  interval   | interval          | text
  interval   | interval          | time
  interval[] | interval_accum    | interval[], interval
  interval   | interval_avg      | interval[]
  integer    | interval_cmp      | interval, interval
  interval   | interval_div      | interval, double precision
  boolean    | interval_eq       | interval, interval
  boolean    | interval_ge       | interval, interval
  boolean    | interval_gt       | interval, interval
  integer    | interval_hash     | interval
  interval   | interval_larger   | interval, interval
  boolean    | interval_le       | interval, interval
  boolean    | interval_lt       | interval, interval
  interval   | interval_mi       | interval, interval
  interval   | interval_mul      | interval, double precision
  boolean    | interval_ne       | interval, interval
  interval   | interval_pl       | interval, interval
  time       | interval_pl_time  | interval, time
  interval   | interval_smaller  | interval, interval
  interval   | interval_um       | interval
 (22 rows)
```

PostgreSQL offers a highly developed system for performing date and time operations. We cannot provide a full overview of all functions and operators available in PostgreSQL in this book, but the list of examples should offer a good start for easily adopting pieces of the sample code.

Using Perl—The DateCalc Module

Perl is an efficient programming language originally developed by Larry Wall. It provides a lot of functions and useful modules for solving common and complex problems. One of these modules is DateCalc by Steffen Beyer. It is an excellent supplement to PostgreSQL and provides an easy way to deal with dates and time on the application level.

An Overview

Working with dates is not always done on the database level, because when things get more complicated it might be useful to perform the operations on the application level. When retrieving data from tables, you can easily combine the process with some simple calculations, but in most cases the data returned by the database is used to perform some sort of decision-making on the application level.

The way the date and time are processed depends on the programming language you want to use for your applications. All programming languages offer highly sophisticated modules and libraries for almost all demands. This section shows how date calculations can be done with the help of Perl's DateCalc module, including working with leap years. Keep in mind that DateCalc is not the only module available to work with dates. This book explores DateCalc, because it seems highly developed, widespread, and easy to use.

Perl's DateCalc module can be found on CPAN, the worldwide archive for Perl modules. The package is currently maintained by Steffen Beyer and can be distributed under the terms of Perl itself (Artistic License or the GNU General Public License). DateCalc is based on a C library, which can be distributed under the same terms.

The Current Calendar

The first important calendar used in Europe was the Julian calendar. Initially, the Romans numbered years *ab urbe condita*, which means that the beginning of dates, time, and all other things was the same as the date of the founding of Rome. Today it is said that Rome was founded in 753 BC, but nobody is really 100% sure about that.

The initial Roman calendar was not adequate for an emerging empire, and after the conquest of Egypt in 48 BC Caesar consulted the Alexandrian astronomer Sosigenes about a calendar reform. The adopted calendar was identical to the Alexandrian Aristarchus' calendar of 239 BC and consisted of 12 months, 365 days, and an extra day every fourth year. In the new Roman system, January 1 was the day when the Senate took office. The Roman calendar become very widespread and was even adopted by various Christian churches.

The average length of a year in the Roman system is 365.25 days, but the "mean tropical year" is 365.2422 days long. The error accumulates over the years, and the calendar is out of sync after 131 years.

> **Note**
> The length of the mean tropical year changes slightly every year.

Pope Paul III consulted several astronomers to come up with a solution. On February 24, 1582, he issued a papal bull addressing the issue, which is now called the Gregorian Calendar reform. The most important facts for computer programmers and users of PostgreSQL have to do with leap years.

A year is a leap year if it either is divisible by 4 but not by 100 or is divisible by 400. The year 2004 is a leap year because 2004 can be divided by four but not by 100. The year 2000 was a leap year since 2000 can be divided by 400.

Knowing how the calendar works is important when dealing with dates, because you might lose or gain days if you don't know exactly what to do. Normally, you don't have to worry about it because the job is done by modules; but occasionally you might have to implement a module.

Basic Operations Using DateCalc

To simplify calculations and speed up the process of date calculations, the DateCalc module uses the Gregorian Calendar back to 1 AD. Keep this in mind, when calculating with dates from before the calendar reform.

The DateCalc module offers a huge pool of functions for almost any purpose. In this section, you learn the most important operations that can be done with DateCalc.

Sometimes it is useful to find out how many days in a certain year have passed until a certain month. These operations can be essential when dealing with leap years. DateCalc provides a function called `Days_in_Year` to do the job:

```
#!/usr/bin/perl

use Date::Calc qw(:all);

$year=2001;
$month=2;
$days = Days_in_Year($year, $month);

print "days: $days\n";
```

This program calculates the number of days passed in 2001 until the end of February. If we execute the script, we receive one line:

```
[hs@duron code]$ ./date.pl
days: 59
```

February is a valid month and the program terminates successfully. Let's try the same program with 0 instead of 2 for the month:

```perl
#!/usr/bin/perl

use Date::Calc qw(:all);

$year=2001;
$month=0;
$days = Days_in_Year($year, $month);

print "days: $days\n";
```

As you can see in the next example, the script fails:

```
[hs@duron code]$ ./date.pl
Date::Calc::Days_in_Year(): month out of range at ./date.pl line 7.
```

Every time the DateCalc module faces values that are out of range, an error is displayed and the program quits. Therefore some sort of error handling has to be implemented.

Another important issue is how to include DateCalc into your program. In the previous example, we included all functions the module provides. If you need only one function of the module, it can be useful to include only the required function. In the next example, you can see how this can be done:

```perl
#!/usr/bin/perl

use Date::Calc qw(Days_in_Year);

$days = Days_in_Year(2001, 2);
print "days: $days\n";
```

You can import functions explicitly by enumerating them between the parentheses of the qw() operator. If you want to include all functions, use :all instead.

Another important function when dealing with leap years is Days_in_Month:

```perl
#!/usr/bin/perl

use Date::Calc qw(:all);

$year=2000;
$month=2;
$days = Days_in_Month($year, $month);
print "days: $days\n";
```

The script displays days: 29, because 2000 was a leap year and February had 29 instead of 28 days.

Not every year has 52 weeks. If you want to know the number of weeks a certain year has, a function called Weeks_in_Year can be used:

```
#!/usr/bin/perl

use Date::Calc qw(:all);

$year=2004;
$result = Weeks_in_Year($year);
print "result: $result\n";
```

You can see in the following that 2004 has 53 weeks instead of 52 weeks:

```
[hs@duron code]$ ./date.pl
result: 53
```

The algorithm for calculating leap years is simple. In the following example, we check whether 2004 is a leap year and whether February 29, 2004 is a valid date:

```
#!/usr/bin/perl

use Date::Calc qw(:all);

$year=2004;
$month=2;
$day=29;

$leap=leap_year($year);
print "leap-year: $leap\n";

$check=check_date($year, $month, $day);
print "check: $check\n";
```

leap_year returns true (1) if the specified year is a leap year, and false (0) if it isn't. check_date works the same way:

```
[hs@duron code]$ ./date.pl
leap-year: 1
check: 1
```

What day of the week do we have today? This question can easily be answered by using a function called Day_of_Week:

```
#!/usr/bin/perl

use Date::Calc qw(:all);

$year=2001;
$month=5;
$day=13;

print Day_of_Week($year, $month, $day)."\n";
```

May 13, 2001 was a Sunday:

```
[hs@duron code]$ ./date.pl
7
```

Perl displays 7 as the result of the operation. Sunday is the seventh day of the week. In the Hebrew calendar (the one the Christian calendar is based on), the week starts with Sunday and ends with the Sabbath, which is equal to Saturday. According to Genesis, God rested from creating the world and therefore it can be seen as the last day of the week. In the Middle Ages, Catholic popes declared Sunday as the day of rest and thus the seventh day. Current standards—such as ISO/R 2015-1971, DIN 1355, and ISO 8601—define Monday as the first day of the week.

If we want to know which day of the year May 14, 2001 was, we can use the following program:

```
#!/usr/bin/perl

use Date::Calc qw(:all);

$year=2001;
$month=5;
$day=14;

print Day_of_Year($year, $month, $day)."\n";
```

May 14 is the 134th day of the year 2001. Operations like this might seem needless, but they can be useful when you want to compare dates easily.

Another function mainly used for comparing dates is Date_to_Days, which returns the number of days since January 1, 2001.

Note
Keep in mind that DateCalc supports only the Gregorian system.

If you want to find out which of two dates is the earlier one, you can easily do this by using Date_to_Days:

```
#!/usr/bin/perl

use Date::Calc qw(:all);

if      (Date_to_Days(2002, 8, 9) < Date_to_Days(2003, 12, 31))
{
        print "August 9th, 2002 was first\n";
}
else
{
        print "There seems to be a bug in the module ...\n";
}
```

The output of the program is what we expect:

```
[hs@duron code]$ ./date.pl
August 9th, 2002 was first
```

In Europe, the number of a weeks within a given year is often used to define the period during which certain events such as business meetings are expected to take place. This can be complicated, because if someone tells you that he wants to meet during week number 43, for instance, you will not know precisely what week that is.

Perl offers a function to find out in which week of the year a day occurs:

```
#!/usr/bin/perl

use Date::Calc qw(:all);

$year=2003;
$month=4;
$day=17;

print "Week number: ".Week_Number($year, $month, $day)."\n";
```

April 17, 2001 is in week number 16:

```
[hs@duron code]$ ./date.pl
Week number: 16
```

If you want to find out the date of Monday in a certain week, try the following program:

```
#!/usr/bin/perl

use Date::Calc qw(:all);

$year=2003;
$week=22;

($year, $month, $day) = Monday_of_Week($week, $year);
print "$year-$month-$day\n";
```

May 26, 2003 is the Monday of the week 22 in 2003:

```
[hs@duron code]$ ./date.pl
2003-5-26
```

In many cases, it's useful to calculate the difference between two `dates` or `timestamps`. The next examples focus on how you can add or remove intervals from the date and time:

```
#!/usr/bin/perl

use Date::Calc qw(:all);

$year1=2002;
$month1=3;
$day1=1;

$year2=2003;
$month2=3;
$day2=1;

$Dd = Delta_Days($year1, $month1, $day1, $year2, $month2, $day2);
print "$Dd\n";

$Dd = Delta_Days($year2, $month2, $day2, $year1, $month1, $day1);
print "$Dd\n";
```

The `Delta_Days` function tells us how many days there are between the first and second date passed to the function. `Delta_Days` can be seen as the `-` operator for two dates of the DateCalc module.

```
[hs@duron code]$ ./date.pl
365
-365
```

Delta_Days calculates date2 - date1. Let's look at the first function call in the previous example. The second date is 365 days higher than the first one. In the second example, a negative value is displayed, because the second date is passed to the function before the first date. If both dates are equal, 0 is returned.

Days are very often not enough. If we want to get the difference between two timestamps, DateCalc provides the Delta_DHMS function. Assume a situation where we want to compute the difference between the result of Perl's localtime function and a timestamp. Before we get to the solution of the problem, here is an example of Perl's localtime() function:

```perl
#!/usr/bin/perl

use Date::Calc qw(:all);

($sec1,$min1,$hour1,$mday1,$mon1,$year1,$wday1,$yday1,$isdst1) =
localtime(time);
print "year: $year1, month: $mon1, mday: $mday1, hour: $hour1,
        min: $min1, sec: $sec1\n";
```

Let's see what happens when we execute the script:

```
[hs@duron code]$ ./date.pl
year: 101, month: 4, mday: 13, hour: 16,
        min: 2, sec: 46
```

We executed the script on May 13, 2001. May is the fifth month, but localtime() displays 4 instead of 5 because the function starts counting with 0. 2001 is displayed as 101, because localtime starts to count the years with 1900. To solve the problem, we add 1900 years to $year1 and 1 to $mon:

```perl
#!/usr/bin/perl

use Date::Calc qw(:all);

$year2=2001;
$month2=5;
$day2=13;
$hour2=12;
$min2=25;
$sec2=3;

($sec1,$min1,$hour1,$mday1,$mon1,$year1,$wday1,$yday1,$isdst1) =
localtime(time);
```

```
$year1+=1900;
$mon1++;

($Dd, $Dh, $Dm, $Ds) = Delta_DHMS($year2, $month2, $day2, $hour2, $min2, $sec2,
        $year1, $mon1, $mday1, $hour1, $min1, $sec1);
print "$D1d $Dh $Dm $Ds\n";
```

In the result, shown next, the script performs the calculations successfully and displays the right result:

```
[hs@duron code]$ ./date.pl
0 3 52 59
```

To avoid those nasty troubles with localtime, DateCalc provides a function called System_Clock, which returns the date and time in a format that can be used by the DateCalc module:

```
($year,$month,$day, $hour,$min,$sec, $doy,$dow,$dst) = System_Clock();
```

The difference between localtime() and the time hard-coded in the source code is 3 hours, 52 minutes, and 59 seconds.

If you think that the syntax of Delta_DHMS is a little confusing, because a lot of parameters have to be passed to the function, the result can also be achieved as shown here:

```
#!/usr/bin/perl

use Date::Calc qw(:all);

$year2=2001;
$month2=5;
$day2=13;
$hour2=12;
$min2=25;
$sec2=3;

($sec1,$min1,$hour1,$mday1,$mon1,$year1,$wday1,$yday1,$isdst1) =
localtime(time);

$year1+=1900;
$mon1++;
```

```
@time1 = ($year2, $month2, $day2, $hour2, $min2, $sec2);
@time2 = ($year1, $mon1, $mday1, $hour1, $min1, $sec1);
@diff=Delta_DHMS(@time1, @time2);
print "@diff\n";
```

Simply pass arrays to the functions to make the source code clearer.

Now we want to add time to a certain `timestamp`. For that purpose, we can use a function called Add_Delta_DHMS:

```
#!/usr/bin/perl

use Date::Calc qw(:all);

($sec1,$min1,$hour1,$mday1,$mon1,$year1,$wday1,$yday1,$isdst1) =
localtime(time);

$year1+=1900;
$mon1++;

@time1 = ($year1, $mon1, $mday1, $hour1, $min1, $sec1);

$add_days=30;
$add_hours=0;
$add_min=4;
$add_sec=3;

@addme=($add_days, $add_hours, $add_min, $add_sec);
@time2=Add_Delta_DHMS(@time1, @addme);
print "before: @time1\nafter: @time2\n";
```

We add 30 days, 4 minutes, and 3 seconds to the current time:

```
[hs@duron code]$ ./date.pl
before: 2001 5 13 16 29 33
after: 2001 6 12 16 33 36
```

The operation is simple. In the previous example, we add a full `timestamp` to the given time. If we want to add just full days, DateCalc offers an easier method:

```
#!/usr/bin/perl

use Date::Calc qw(:all);
```

```
$year=2000;
$month=2;
$day=29;

$add=1;

@time2=Add_Delta_Days($year, $month, $day, $add);
print "@time2\n";
```

We add 1 day to February 29, 2000.

```
[hs@duron code]$ ./date.pl
2000 3 1
```

The result is March 1, 2000.

What if we want to perform a subtraction instead of adding days? In the next example, we subtract 1 day from the given date:

```
#!/usr/bin/perl

use Date::Calc qw(:all);

$year=2000;
$month=2;
$day=29;

$add=1;

@time2=Add_Delta_Days($year, $month, $day, -$add);
print "@time2\n";
```

You can see that we added a negative period of time. The result of the calculation is February 28, 2000.

In the examples, we have shown how you can add days, hours, and minutes to a certain time. Of course it is also possible to add or subtract years, months, and days. For that purpose, DateCalc offers a function called Add_Delta_YMD:

```
#!/usr/bin/perl

use Date::Calc qw(:all);

# Input date
$year=2000;
```

```
$month=2;
$day=29;

# To be added
$Dy=1;
$Dm=6;
$Dd=22;

# Computing and printing the result
@time2=Add_Delta_YMD($year, $month, $day, $Dy, $Dm, $Dd);
print "@time2\n";
```

This Perl script adds 1 year, 6 months, and 22 days to February 29, 2001; the result is shown in the following listing:

```
[hs@duron code]$ ./date.pl
2001 9 22
```

For logging, and many other reasons, you might want to know today's date. You have already learned about localtime and System_Clock. These two functions can be used to find out the current date, but DateCalc also offers a function to compute the date only (without current time): Today():

```
#!/usr/bin/perl

use Date::Calc qw(:all);

($year, $month, $day) = Today();
print "$year-$month-$day\n";
```

The function returns three values: one for the current year, one for the current month, and one for the day of the month:

```
[hs@duron code]$ ./date.pl
2001-5-14
```

Today() is used to compute the current date. If we want to find out the current time, we can use DateCalc's Now() function:

```
#!/usr/bin/perl

use Date::Calc qw(:all);

($hour, $min, $sec) = Now();
print "$hour-$min-$sec\n";
```

Here is the output of the script:

```
[hs@duron code]$ ./date.pl
11-54-33
```

In the previous example, the current time is 11 o'clock, 54 minutes, and 33 seconds.

The current date plus the current time can be calculated in many ways. One way is to use Perl's localtime; another way is to use DateCalc's System_Clock. Both functions return a little more information than you might need. If you want to know the current date and the current time without additional information, such as the day of the week, use the Today_and_Now function:

```
#!/usr/bin/perl

use Date::Calc qw(:all);

($year, $month, $day, $hour, $min, $sec) = Today_and_Now();
print "$year $month $day - $hour $min $sec\n";
```

The result of Today_and_Now is a combination of the results of Today and Now:

```
[hs@duron code]$ ./date.pl
2001 5 14 - 11 58 45
```

Calculating Christian feast days can be the most difficult task when dealing with dates, especially if you are working with PostgreSQL. The DateCalc module offers a function called Easter_Sunday. Using the result of this function makes it easy to find out the dates of the most important Christian feast days related to Easter. The following table is an overview of all important dates and their offset to Easter Sunday:

Feast Day	Offset
Carnival Monday	-−48 days
Mardi Gras	-−47 days
Ash Wednesday	-−46 days
Palm Sunday	-−7 days
Easter Friday	-−2 days
Easter Saturday	-−1 day
Easter Monday	+1 day
Ascension of Christ	+39 days
Whitsunday	+49 days
Whitmonday	+50 days
Feast of Corpus Christi	+60 days

If you want to find out the date of Whitmonday in 2002, use the following script:

```
#!/usr/bin/perl

use Date::Calc qw(:all);

$year=2002;

($year, $month, $day) = Add_Delta_Days(Easter_Sunday($year), 50);
print "$year-$month-$day\n";
```

Whitmonday is 50 days after Easter Sunday and therefore the result is the following:

```
[hs@duron code]$ ./date.pl
2002-5-20
```

Dates are not always defined as a number. Sometimes you will face the situation in which you have to convert a string into a number. In the following example, we try to convert September and Wednesday to numbers that we can use for further calculations:

```
#!/usr/bin/perl

use Date::Calc qw(:all);

$month="September";
$day="Wednesday";

print Decode_Month($month)." - ".Decode_Day_of_Week($day)."\n";
```

Because September is the ninth month of the year and Wednesday is the third day of the week, the output shown here is not surprising:

```
[hs@duron code]$ ./date.pl
9 - 3
```

Both functions in the script are highly language-dependent. To find out which language you have selected, try the following piece of code:

```
#!/usr/bin/perl

use Date::Calc qw(:all);

print Language."\n";
```

By default, the language is set to 1, which is English. The core distribution of the DateCalc module supports seven languages (in version 4.3). If you need the complete list of all supported languages, check out the man pages of the module (use `man Date::Calc`), because the number of languages supported by the module is constantly increasing.

Until now, we have always displayed the date as a number. This might not be suitable for your applications, because in most cases it is more comfortable for the user to display the date in a formatted way. In general, two functions are provided:

```perl
#!/usr/bin/perl

use Date::Calc qw(:all);

$year=2002;
$month=4;
$day=26;

print Date_to_Text($year, $month, $day)."\n";
print Date_to_Text_Long($year, $month, $day)."\n";
```

Let's execute the script:

```
[hs@duron code]$ ./date.pl
Fri 26-Apr-2002
Friday, April 26th 2002
```

In the output of the script, you can see the difference between the two functions.

Sometimes you might want to see the calendar of a given month. DateCalc provides a function called `Calendar` to do the job:

```perl
#!/usr/bin/perl

use Date::Calc qw(:all);

$year=2002;
$month=4;

$result = Calendar($year, $month);
print $result;
```

`Calendar` returns a properly formatted calendar. We can use the result of the function directly:

```
[hs@duron code]$ ./date.pl

        April 2002
Mon Tue Wed Thu Fri Sat Sun
  1   2   3   4   5   6   7
  8   9  10  11  12  13  14
 15  16  17  18  19  20  21
 22  23  24  25  26  27  28
 29  30
```

Steffen Beyer's DateCalc module is one of the most powerful pieces of software currently available for Perl. The next section explores how you can build wonderful applications with PostgreSQL, Perl, and DateCalc.

Using DateCalc with PostgreSQL

In this section, we build small database-enabled applications to show you practical solutions with PostgreSQL. First we create a table called `timefield`, where we will try to insert some data with the help of a Perl script:

```
CREATE TABLE mydates(timefield timestamp);
```

The data that you have to insert into a database is often produced by an application. In this case, you need reliable tools to interact with the database. With PostgreSQL and Perl, the DBI module is the most widespread module available; therefore, we will use it in this section.

In general, the main problem when working with applications, modules, and databases is that the format of the data used by the various components is not always the same. Many standards for displaying data have been developed in the past, but for technical reasons interaction is not always as simple as it should be. In this section, you learn about converting data.

Another important decision programmers have to make is which operations will be performed on which level. Simple calculations can be performed by either the database or the application. It depends on you and what you think is better for your application.

Let's get to our first example. We start with a simple program that inserts today's date into the database. An SQL command is created and the data is inserted into the database as `timestamp`:

```
#!/usr/bin/perl

use DBI;
```

```
use Date::Calc qw(:all);

$dbh=DBI->connect("dbi:Pg:dbname=datecalc; port=5432", "hs", "anypasswd") or
        die "can't connect: $!\n";

@time=Today();
$date=Date_to_Text_Long(@time);

$sql="INSERT INTO mydates VALUES('$date'::timestamp)";
print "$sql\n";
$ret=$dbh->do($sql) or
        die "cannot execute ($sql) because of $!\n";
```

After connecting to the database, we compute today's date by using the `Today()` function. Then we convert the date to a string. In this case, we have to use `Date_to_Text_Long`, because the output of `Date_to_Text` would lead to a syntax error in the SQL statement.

If we execute the script, we see the SQL statement passed to PostgreSQL:

```
[hs@duron code]$ ./pg_date.pl
INSERT INTO mydates VALUES('Monday, May 14th 2001'::timestamp)
```

No error has been displayed, so the record has successfully been inserted into the database:

```
datecalc=# SELECT * FROM mydates;
        timefield
------------------------
 2001-05-14 00:00:00+02
(1 row)
```

PostgreSQL automatically uses the default time zone. You have to take care of this when working with DateCalc, because time zones are (at the time we wrote this book) not supported by the Perl module.

In the next example, we use a full `timestamp`, including date and time:

```
#!/usr/bin/perl

use DBI;
use Date::Calc qw(:all);

$dbh=DBI->connect("dbi:Pg:dbname=datecalc; port=5432", "hs", "anypasswd") or
        die "can't connect: $!\n";
```

```
$date=Date_to_Text_Long(Today());
@now=Now();

$sql="INSERT INTO mydates VALUES('$date
@now[0]:@now[1]:@now[2]+02'::timestamp)";
print "$sql\n";
$ret=$dbh->do($sql) or
        die "cannot execute ($sql) because of $!\n";
```

In the next SQL statement, we added the result of the Now() function and the time zone to the SQL statement.

```
INSERT INTO mydates VALUES('Monday, May 14th 2001 14:59:30+02'::timestamp)
```

The statement is inserted into the table properly:

```
datecalc=# SELECT * FROM mydates;
      timefield
-----------------------
 2001-05-14 14:59:30+02
(1 row)
```

Inserting data is not a difficult task. In most cases, you can write a few lines of Perl code to do all the conversions that you need to fit PostgreSQL's demands.

Let's look at some SELECT statements now. The following shows how data can be read from the result of a query:

```
#!/usr/bin/perl

use DBI;
use Date::Calc qw(:all);

$dbh=DBI->connect("dbi:Pg:dbname=datecalc; port=5432", "hs", "anypasswd") or
        die "can't connect: $!\n";

$sql="SELECT timefield FROM mydates";

@row=$dbh->selectrow_array($sql);
($year, $month, $day, $hour, $min, $sec, $zone) = postgres2perl(@row[0]);
print "Result: $year $month $day $hour $min $sec $zone\n";

sub postgres2perl
{
```

```
        return(substr($_[0],0,4),
                substr($_[0],5,2),
                substr($_[0],9,2),
                substr($_[0],11,2),
                substr($_[0],14,2),
                substr($_[0],17,2),
                substr($_[0],20,3));
}
```

We select the only record in the table and store it in @row. The first field contains the
`timestamp`, and we pass the value to a function called `postgres2perl` that we define
next. This function performs simple substring operations and returns the result in an
array. The result of the function is finally displayed by a simple `print`:

```
[hs@duron code]$ ./pg_date.pl
Result: 2001 05 4   14 59 30 02
```

We have even extracted the time zone from the field. Now we can use the data the
way it can be done with the DateCalc module.

The situation is far more complex when working with intervals, because intervals do
not consist of fixed-length components. Depending on the data returned, the structure
of the output might vary significantly. The following is a good example:

```
datecalc=# SELECT '1 century, 2 decades, 1 month, 1 week, 3 days, 2 hours, 1
minute, 2 sec'::interval;


             ?column?
---------------------------------
 120 years 1 mon 10 days 02:01:02
(1 row)
```

The database converts centuries into years and weeks into days, but how does the
output look if we omit some components?

```
datecalc=# SELECT '1 day, 2 hours, 1 minute, 2 sec'::interval;
    ?column?
----------------
 1 day 02:01:02
(1 row)
```

The number of days is now labeled `day` instead of `days` as it was before. PostgreSQL
displays the singular of the word correctly. No information about the amount of years
or months is displayed, because both values are 0. Next we present a prototype of a

script, which converts input data using `interval` as the datatype to a format we can use with the DateCalc module:

```perl
#!/usr/bin/perl

use DBI;
use Date::Calc qw(:all);

$dbh=DBI->connect("dbi:Pg:dbname=datecalc; port=5432", "hs", "anypasswd") or
        die "can't connect: $!\n";

$sql="SELECT '2 year, 1 minute, 2 sec'::interval";

@row=$dbh->selectrow_array($sql);
($year, $mon, $day, $hour, $min, $sec)=interval2perl(@row[0]);

print "years: $year, months: $mon, days: $day, hours: $hour, ";
print "min: $min, sec: $sec\n";

# Converting intervals to variables
sub interval2perl
{
    my $i, @array, $year, $years, $mon, $mons;
    my $day, $days, $hour, $min, $sec;

    my @array=split(/\ +/, $_[0]);
    if      (@array[1]) { ${@array[1]}=@array[0]; }
    if      (@array[3]) { ${@array[3]}=@array[2]; }
    if      (@array[5]) { ${@array[5]}=@array[4]; }

    foreach $i (0, 2, 4, 6)
    {
            if      (@array[$i] =~ /:/)
            {
                    if      (length @array[$i] eq 8)
                    {
                            ($hour, $min, $sec) = split(/:/, @array[$i]);
                    }
                    else
                    {
                            ($hour, $min) = split(/:/, @array[$i]);
                    }
```

```
        }
    }

    return($year+$years, $mon+$mons, $day+$days, $hour, $min, $sec);
}
```

As promised, the script is more complex than the one we used to convert `timestamp`. After executing the SQL code in `$sql`, we call `interval2perl` with the field that we want to convert. At the beginning of the function, we define some local variables that we will need later in the script. In the next step, we split the input data with the help of a simple regular expression. The pattern we use for the split matches one or more blanks in the string. The `if` statements check whether certain fields are defined. The array created by the `split` command might contain up to 7 fields (0–6). Strings, which define the type of the value in the previous field, can be found in position 1, 3, or 5. If field 5, for instance, is defined, we assign the value of the field before to a variable that has the name of the field we are currently accessing. If, for instance, field 1 contains the string `years`, the value in field 0 is assigned to a variable called `$years`. This can be done easily, because Perl supports dynamic variables. Now that we have extracted and processed the strings, we can transform hours, minutes, and seconds. These three values can be defined in position 0, 2, 4, or 6 in the string and can easily be found, because they are separated by a colon.

To make things a little bit more complicated, PostgreSQL does not display the amount of seconds if it is `0`. If seconds are defined, the string is 8 characters long. We have to take this into consideration when splitting the field.

Finally we return the values we have extracted, and now there is only one hurdle left. Some strings might contain singular or plural words, depending on the data in the previous field. We add the variable containing the data of the singular words and the variable containing the data of the plural word. One of the two is always undefined and therefore treated as 0 by Perl.

If we execute the script, we receive the following result:

```
[hs@duron code]$ ./pg_date.pl
years: 2, months: 0, days: 0, hours: 00, min: 01, sec: 02
```

The program has extracted all necessary information from the string and displayed it on the screen.

Converting the date and time used by DateCalc to PostgreSQL is rather easy. The following script shows how it can be done:

```perl
#!/usr/bin/perl

use DBI;
use Date::Calc qw(:all);

$year=2;
$month=3;
$day=32;
$hour=9;
$min=56;
$sec=32;

$interval=&perl2interval($year, $month, $day, $hour, $min, $sec);
print "Interval: $interval\n";

# Converting intervals to variables
sub perl2interval
{
        my $interval="$year years, $month months, $day days, $hour hours, ";
        $interval.="$min minutes, $sec seconds";
        return($interval);
}
```

The script produces a valid `interval`, which can be cast and used by PostgreSQL directly:

```
[hs@duron code]$ ./pg_date.pl
Interval: 2 years, 3 months, 32 days, 9 hours, 56 minutes, 32 seconds
```

We do not have to care about singular and plural words, because PostgreSQL understands both. In the following example, you can see that PostgreSQL does not make any difference in how the data is passed to the database but displays the output correctly:

```
datecalc=# SELECT '2 year, 3 months, 32 days, 1 hours, 0 minutes, 1
seconds'::interval;
            ?column?
---------------------------------
 2 years 3 mons 32 days 01:00:01
(1 row)
```

In general, Perl, PostgreSQL, and DateCalc make a good team. If you want to find out more, check out the man pages of DateCalc.

Analyzing a Time Series

Analyzing a time series is one of the most complicated, but also one of the most interesting, topics. A time series is analyzed for many reasons, but what is a time series and what is it used for?

This section answers this question with the help of an example. In nearly all countries around the globe, people have to pay income tax. Information about people, such as their income and gender, is collected by the state. The data is used for many purposes, including computing the amount of taxes a person has to pay and generating statistics, which are often the bases for political decisions. The collected data is usually stored as a time series, and with the help of special algorithms, it is possible to get a lot of information out of the data. Retrieving statistical information out of a huge amount of data is called *data mining*.

Many books about data mining and algorithms have been written in the past, and it is impossible to provide a full coverage here. This section presents an overview of how a time series can be treated with PostgreSQL and stored efficiently in tables.

Let's create a table called `timeseries` and insert some data. The following creates a labor market table:

```
CREATE TABLE timeseries(id serial, name text, start date, finish date, status
text);
```

The table consists of five columns. The first column is used as the unique identifier of a row. The second column contains the name of the person. Columns three and four define the period of time the person was either employed or unemployed (column five).

```
timeseries=# SELECT * FROM timeseries;
 id |  name   |   start    |   finish   |   status
----+---------+------------+------------+------------
  1 | Paul    | 1989-10-12 | 1999-08-03 | employed
  2 | Paul    | 1999-08-04 | 2001-11-23 | employed
  3 | Jana    | 1970-01-01 | 2002-08-12 | employed
  4 | Jana    | 2002-08-12 | 2002-08-14 | unemployed
  5 | Charles | 1993-03-21 | 1995-10-01 | unemployed
  6 | Charles | 1995-10-02 | 2002-01-09 | employed
(6 rows)
```

We will use this data to perform some operations.

Let's start with a simple example. We want to know how many people were employed on January 1, 2000:

```
SELECT COUNT(*)
        FROM timeseries
        WHERE start<='2000-1-1'::date
                AND finish>='2000-1-1'::date
                AND status='employed';
```

The database will return 3, because all three persons in the database were employed. Things become a bit more complicated if we add one record to the database:

```
7 | Paul    | 2000-01-01 | 2000-01-04 | employed
```

Paul is employed by a second company and is therefore employed twice on January 1, 2000. It depends on what we want to retrieve from the database. If we use this query, the result is 4. If we want to count persons instead of jobs, we use a different query:

```
SELECT COUNT(*) INTO TEMPORARY TABLE temp_1
        FROM timeseries
        WHERE start<='2000-1-1'::date
                AND finish>='2000-1-1'::date
                AND status='employed'
        GROUP BY name;
```

In general, two comparatively easy solutions for the problem can be found, but both consist of two queries. The previous query selects data in a temporary table. Here's what can be found in this table:

```
timeseries=# SELECT * FROM temp_1;
 count
-------
     1
     1
     2
(3 rows)
```

The table contains three records that tell us how often a certain person is employed on January 1, 2001.

The same result can be achieved by defining a view using the same SELECT statement:

```
CREATE VIEW unique_person AS SELECT COUNT(*)
        FROM timeseries
        WHERE start<='2000-1-1'::date
```

```
              AND finish>='2000-1-1'::date
              AND status='employed'
       GROUP BY name;
```

The desired result can now easily be calculated by counting the records in the table or in the view:

```
timeseries=# SELECT COUNT(*) FROM temp_1;
 count
-------
     3
(1 row)
```

The result is, as we expect, 3.

This example shows how quickly simple problems can become very complex. The result of simple queries must always be questioned to make sure that the result is correct. Generating useful data is not a question of being a hardcore SQL programmer. Often it is much more important to know what the data contains and to make sure that you have taken every possible situation into consideration. The biggest problem with data mining is that in most cases people do not know which information has to be extracted from the data. Nearly all questions can be answered, as long as you know what you want to find out.

In the next example, we find all people who were employed after being unemployed. This query leads to an interesting result:

```
SELECT a.name
       FROM timeseries AS a, timeseries AS b
       WHERE a.status='unemployed'
              AND b.status='employed'
              AND a.name=b.name;
```

Two names are returned by the query:

```
  name
---------
 Jana
 Charles
(2 rows)
```

Jana has not been employed after being unemployed. She was employed and lost her job. Because we want to find people who find a job, this query is wrong.

Let's try the following query:

```
SELECT a.name
       FROM timeseries AS a, timeseries AS b
       WHERE a.status='unemployed'
             AND b.status='employed'
             AND a.name=b.name
             AND a.finish<b.start;
```

We have added an additional condition to the query that makes sure that only `Charles` is selected. The person has to be unemployed before being employed; otherwise, the query returns a wrong result.

When executing the SQL command, we receive only one record:

```
  name
----------
 Charles
(1 row)
```

To make sure that everything is right, we select `Charles` from the database:

```
timeseries=# SELECT * FROM timeseries WHERE name='Charles';
 id |  name   |   start    |   finish   |   status
----+---------+------------+------------+------------
  5 | Charles | 1993-03-21 | 1995-10-01 | unemployed
  6 | Charles | 1995-10-02 | 2002-01-09 | employed
(2 rows)
```

You can see, that his employment started exactly one day after his unemployment.

Assume that we want to find out the average number of days that people were employed in a certain year. We perform the query for the year 2002. The easiest way to solve the problem is to write a simple PL/pgSQL function:

```
CREATE FUNCTION avg_days(date, date) RETURNS int4 AS
'
       DECLARE
               v_start date;
               v_end   date;
               result int4;
       BEGIN
               result  := 0;
               v_start := $1;
               v_end   := $2;
```

```
        IF      (v_start < ''2002-1-1''::date) THEN
                v_start := ''2002-1-1''::date;
        END IF;
        IF      (v_end > ''2002-12-31''::date) THEN
                v_end := ''2002-12-31''::date;
        END IF;


        result := result + (v_end - v_start) + 1;
        RETURN result;
    END;
' LANGUAGE 'plpgsql';
```

Normally, dates are not hard-coded in the function, because this would be far too inflexible. Nevertheless, we do some hard-coding here to make the function easier to understand.

Let's have a detailed look at this function. Two parameters have to be passed to the function. The first parameter is the field where the starting time of a period is defined. The second column contains the end of a certain period. After defining and declaring the required variables, we set the starting time of a record to January 1, 2002. The end also needs to be changed. This operation is necessary because we want to perform a subtraction; we want to know only how many days in 2002 a person was employed. Then the result is calculated for a certain record. Finally, we have to increment the result of the subtraction by 1.

> **Note**
> If we have a period that lasts from January 1 to January 2nd, it is 2 days long. If we subtract January 2 from January 1, the result is 1 day. Therefore we have to add one day to the result.

Now we use the function described previously:

```
SELECT id, avg_days(start, finish)
    FROM timeseries
    WHERE start<'2002-1-1'::date
        AND finish>'2001-12-31'::date;
```

All records that do not contain a valid interval have to be removed, which is done in the WHERE clause. Two records will be returned:

```
 id | avg_days
----+----------
  3 |      224
  6 |        9
(2 rows)
```

Jana and Charles were employed in 2002. This query shows the number of days each of the two has been working. If we want to find the average number of days now, we have to add all days and divide it by the number of persons:

```
SELECT SUM(avg_days(start, finish))/
       (SELECT COUNT(*)
               FROM timeseries
               WHERE start<'2002-1-1'::date
                       AND finish>'2001-12-31'::date)
       FROM timeseries
       WHERE start<'2002-1-1'::date
               AND finish>'2001-12-31'::date;
```

In the previous example, we use a subquery to find out how many people are affected. The following shows that the query returns the right result:

```
    ?column?
----------------
 116.5000000000
(1 row)
```

If we look at the execution plan of the query, we can make a critical observation:

```
timeseries=# EXPLAIN SELECT SUM(avg_days(start, finish))/(SELECT COUNT(*) FROM
timeseries WHERE start<'2002-1-1'::date AND finish>'2001-12-31'::date) FROM
timeseries
WHERE start<'2002-1-1'::date AND finish>'2001-12-31'::date;
NOTICE:  QUERY PLAN:

Aggregate  (cost=1.11..1.11 rows=1 width=8)
  InitPlan
    -> Aggregate  (cost=1.11..1.11 rows=1 width=0)
          -> Seq Scan on timeseries  (cost=0.00..1.10 rows=1 width=0)
  -> Seq Scan on timeseries  (cost=0.00..1.10 rows=1 width=8)

EXPLAIN
```

The database has to perform a sequential scan on timeseries twice, so the query is extremely slow. In real-world applications, the problem is avoided by performing all major calculations on the application level. Databases are very fast for searching, but are in most cases not suitable for performing complex operations. If the amount of data that has to be processed becomes really big, you can run into trouble very soon—processing a query that has to do two full table scans will be much too slow.

Another important piece of information is the average time a person has worked in a certain job:

```
timeseries=# SELECT AVG(finish-start) FROM timeseries WHERE status='employed';
        avg
-----------------
 3725.8000000000
(1 row)
```

The SQL code is simple. We just calculate the difference between the beginning and the end and compute the average value. The difference is displayed in days.

PostgreSQL is as good for analyzing a time series as any other database available. Generally, databases are extremely fast for searching and retrieving data, but not for performing complex operations and calculations. Often, things have to be done on the application level to achieve reasonable performance or to keep the code simple. SQL is a language designed to select data and not to do exception handling as it is done with an ordinary programming language. If you need some sort of exception handling, you can use PL/pgSQL; but if you want to build really big functions, PL/pgSQL can be troublesome because it is sometimes hard to debug.

Summary

When building data warehouses and creating statistics, a time series has to be analyzed. Therefore, complex SQL code has to be implemented. In general, all results can be generated by using plain SQL, but the operations—which have to be performed by the database internally—might become complex and slow.

CHAPTER 18

Persistent Database Connections with PHP

Persistent database connections are a core feature of PHP, and they can be used to speed up your applications significantly.

Before we get to some performance tests and an example, let's look at what persistent database connections are and how they can be used.

The difference between a persistent and a non-persistent database connection is, that persistent connections are not closed at the end of a script. If you want to establish a persistent connection to your database, PHP checks whether an identical connection exists. *Identical* means that the name of the host, the username, and the password have to be the same. If no suitable connection is available, a new connection is established.

The advantage of this algorithm is that a lot of connection overhead can be saved by reducing the amount of authentication processes, and therefore the load on your database might be reduced significantly.

Many people who are not familiar with persistent connections think that persistent database connections provide additional functions for user management, session management, or transaction optimization. This is not true. Persistent database connections do not offer additional features. However, a lot of overhead is saved.

To understand persistent database connections, you need fundamental knowledge about how Web servers work. In general, a Web server can interact with PHP in three ways:

- **PHP as a CGI wrapper.** In this case, a PHP interpreter is started for every page that has to be processed. Therefore, persistent connections are not supported, because the instance of the PHP interpreter is destroyed after the page is processed. pg_pconnect can be used, but there is no advantage over using pg_connect.

- **PHP as a module.** In most cases, PHP is used as a module in a multiprocess Web server such as Apache. A parent process controls a set of child processes doing the work. Every time a new request has to be processed, the parent process selects a child process and tells the client process to handle the request. If PHP is used as a module, persistent database connections save a lot of authentication overhead, because every child has to connect to the database only the first time a request is handled. If a second request has to be processed, the child process reuses the same connection it established for processing the first request.

- **PHP as a plugin for a multithreaded Web server**. At the moment, support for ISAPI, WSAPI, and NSAPI is provided by PHP. The behavior is the same as described earlier for the multi-process model.

As mentioned earlier, in most cases PHP is used as an Apache module. This section assumes that PHP is treated as a module.

It is interesting that database connections—whether they are persistent or not—are handled by the same function in PHP. If you look at the file pgsql.c in the source tree of PHP 4.04, you can see this in action:

```
/* {{{ proto int pg_connect([string connection_string] | [string host, string
port
[, string options [, string tty,]] string database)
   Open a PostgreSQL connection */
PHP_FUNCTION(pg_connect)
{
        php_pgsql_do_connect(INTERNAL_FUNCTION_PARAM_PASSTHRU,0);
}
/* }}} */

/* {{{ proto int pg_pconnect([string connection_string] | [string host, string
port [, string options [, string tty,]] string database)
   Open a persistent PostgreSQL connection */
PHP_FUNCTION(pg_pconnect)
```

```
{
        php_pgsql_do_connect(INTERNAL_FUNCTION_PARAM_PASSTHRU,1);
}
```

Persistent and non-persistent connections are handled by the `php_pgsql_do_connect` function. We did not include this function here because it is already quite long and rather difficult to understand. We included the PHP function here, because some of you might find it interesting to see how connections are treated by PHP internally.

Speed Tests

Gaining speed is the most important target when using persistent database connections. This section presents some simple methods to compute how much speed you can gain by using persistent database connections.

The following is a benchmark script for testing the performance gain of persistent database connections:

```php
<?php
# checking time
function gettime()
{
    $tmp = microtime();
    $parts = explode(" ",$tmp);
    $floattime = (float)$parts[0] + (float)$parts[1];
    return $floattime;
}

# processing the benchmark several times
for   ($i=0; $i<5; $i++)
{
    # staring with persistent connection
    $starttime = gettime();
    $connect = pg_pconnect("dbname=db user=hs");
    $endtime = gettime();
    $persistent = $endtime - $starttime;

    # checking non-persistent connection
    $starttime = gettime();
    $connect = pg_connect("dbname=db user=hs");
    $endtime = gettime();
    $no_persistent = $endtime - $starttime;
```

```
    # printing the result
    echo "non-persistent connection took: $no_persistent <br>";
    echo "persistent took: $persistent <br>";
    $gain = $no_persistent / $persistent;
    echo "This is $gain times faster.<br><br>";
}
?>
```

You can use this to find out how much performance you can gain by using persistent database connections.

Let's go through the code quickly. gettime computes the current time we will use to find out how long the authentication process takes. A loop is processed, which establishes a persistent and a non-persistent connection to the database every time the loop is processed. The amount of time needed to connect to the database is measured and compared. We execute the script by using our favorite Web browser:

```
non-persistent connection took: 0.024909973144531
persistent took: 0.00016999244689941
This is 146.53576437588 times faster.

non-persistent connection took: 0.024687051773071
persistent took: 0.00014996528625488
This is 164.61844197138 times faster.

non-persistent connection took: 0.024754047393799
persistent took: 0.00013101100921631
This is 188.94631483167 times faster.

non-persistent connection took: 0.020581007003784
persistent took: 0.00013399124145508
This is 153.59964412811 times faster.

non-persistent connection took: 0.024953961372375
persistent took: 0.00013101100921631
This is 190.47224749773 times faster.
```

The results are extremely impressive—using persistent connections can be up to 190 times faster (in our example). The reason for a result like that seems obvious, because the authentication process of PostgreSQL is far more complex than finding the right connection out of only a few possibilities. We have tested the script several times and the results have always been nearly the same. Only the first time we executed the script led to different results—as discussed in the next section.

Dangerous Side Effects

Persistent database connections might save a lot of connection overhead, which can be a significant advantage—especially when the load on your database server is high. As a rule of thumb, the higher the connection overhead is, the more speed can be gained by using persistent database connections. If you have just a few connections but a lot of queries, which take a long time to be executed, the gained speed will be comparatively low.

But Persistent database connections also have disadvantages. The more connections your database has to handle, the more memory that is wasted to keep backend processes in memory, which are not always working ones. Another problem is that the system cannot only run out of memory, but also runs out of file handles. Normally this happens only on servers with a lot of memory, but you have to make sure that file handles won't be a problem on your system.

Imagine another situation: You have configured Apache to accept 20 connections at a time, and you have told PostgreSQL to handle up to 16 connections simultaneously. Because every Apache process running should have its own backend, you might find yourself in deep trouble soon. Some Apache processes will not be able to connect to the database and errors will occur.

You should also make sure that transactions are committed correctly so that no open transactions will be in the system.

In general, persistent database connections are a good invention, and if they are used correctly, they can help you speed up your database significantly (depending on the type of application you want to run, of course).

Testing Persistent Connections

Before you decide to use persistent connections in a real-world application, you should perform extensive testing. This section explains what you have to take care of and how persistent connections work internally.

Open Connections and Backend Processes

In most cases, theoretical explanations will satisfy the demands of people thinking theoretically. Sometimes, however, it is much easier to show how things work by means of some simple examples. This section is dedicated to all those of you who are looking for some small practical examples of how persistent database connections can be used and how the use of this kind of connection affects the way your system behaves.

Normally, backend processes are terminated automatically at the end of a PHP script (as long as the connection has not been closed manually). Closing a connection means that all memory allocated by the backend process is freed and the garbage will be left on your machine. In case of persistent connections, backend processes stay in memory until a connection timeout occurs. Take a look at the following script:

```php
<?php
        $number=0;

        for($number=1; $number<=5; $number++)
        {
                $db[$number]=pg_pconnect("dbname=mydb");
                if (!$db[$number])
                {
                        echo("connection number $number cannot be
established<br>\n");
                }
                else
                {
                        echo("connection number $number established<br>\n");
                        echo("connection handle:
".bin2hex($db[$number])."<br><br>\n");
                }
        }
?>
```

Our script does nothing else than connect to the same database 5 times. Depending on whether the connection to the database has been established, a message is displayed on the screen. If a connection has been established, we display the number of the connection and a hexadecimal representation of the connection handle. We included this to see whether the connection handles are always the same.

Let's execute the script in our favorite Web browser and analyze the result:

```
connection number 1 established
connection handle: 5265736f75726365206964202331

connection number 2 established
connection handle: 5265736f75726365206964202332

connection number 3 established
connection handle: 5265736f75726365206964202333
```

```
connection number 4 established
connection handle: 5265736f75726365206964202334

connection number 5 established
connection handle: 5265736f75726365206964202335
```

The connection has been established successfully every time the loop is processed. We can also see that the connection handles differ for every connection established. This is not surprising, because we expect a connection handle to be unique.

Now let's see what is going on inside the system:

```
[hs@athlon persistent]$ ps ax | grep post
 2992 pts/2    S       0:00 /usr/bin/postmaster -D /var/lib/pgsql/data -i
 3000 pts/2    S       0:00 postgres: hs mydb [local] idle
 3098 pts/1    S       0:00 grep post
```

We use ps ax (check the man pages of your UNIX system if you are not a user of RedHat Linux) and grep to retrieve all processes related to PostgreSQL. Process number 2992 is the supervisor daemon, which handles the backend processes. Process number 3000 handles an open connection. Only one backend process is open. If we would connect to five different databases, we would also see five backend processes in the process table.

We extracted the list of processes shown after running the PHP script in the browser, which shows that backend processes stay in memory after the execution of the PHP script has been finished.

In the next step, we set the maximum number of connections allowed on the system to 3. This has to be done in postgresql.conf:

```
max_connections = 3
```

Let's see whether the previous script still works if we want to open five connections:

```
connection number 1 established
connection handle: 5265736f75726365206964202331

connection number 2 established
connection handle: 5265736f75726365206964202332

connection number 3 established
connection handle: 5265736f75726365206964202333
```

```
connection number 4 established
connection handle: 5265736f75726365206964202334

connection number 5 established
connection handle: 5265736f75726365206964202335
```

All five `pg_pconnect` commands have been executed successfully again, which means that restricting the number of connections allowed does not affect the number of connections you can open with the same parameters.

The fact that no additional backend processes are started is a significant advantage of PHP, because it might save a lot of memory (this also works with non-persistent connections).

Now that we have tested the script with the following `pg_pconnect` command, one backend process is in memory:

```
$db[$number]=pg_pconnect("dbname=mydb");
```

No matter how often we start the script, there will only be only one active backend process. Now let's change the `connect` string to this command:

```
$db[$number]=pg_pconnect("dbname=mydb user=hs host=localhost");
```

We execute the program again and see whether something has changed in the process table:

```
[hs@athlon persistent]$ ps ax | grep post
 4257 pts/2    S     0:00 su postgres
 4300 pts/2    S     0:00 /usr/bin/postmaster -D /var/lib/pgsql/data/ -i -B 400
 4302 pts/2    S     0:00 postgres: hs mydb [local] idle
 4318 pts/2    S     0:00 postgres: hs mydb 127.0.0.1 idle
```

Now two different backend processes are in memory. Although both connections have been established to the same database for the same user on the same host, the software is not able to figure out whether the two connections are identical, because only the parameters of the `connect` string are compared. Both `connect` strings lead to the same result, but they are not identical, which causes PostgreSQL to create an additional backend process.

Persistent Connections and Transactions

One important—and often misunderstood—point is that *persistent* means that database connections are available for an entire session. Some people think that one `connect` command is enough for making a database connection across multiple PHP files. This is wrong. Because HTTP is not a connection-oriented protocol, database connections are not open during the whole session of a user. They have to be reestablished by every script.

Take a look at this script:

```php
<?php
        echo("<html><body>\n");
        $db=pg_pconnect("dbname=mydb user=hs host=localhost");
        if (!$db)
        {
                echo("connection cannot be established<br>\n");
        }
        else
        {
                echo("connection established<br>\n");
        }

        # creating an empty form
        echo ('<A HREF="transaction2.php/">next screen</A><br>');

        echo ('</body></html>');
?>
```

We establish a connection to the database and display a link on the screen. The next script checks whether the connection is still open:

```php
<?php
        if      ($db)
        {
                echo ('database handle still valid<br>');
        }
        else
        {
                echo ('database handle does not exist anymore<br>');
        }
?>
```

Although only one backend process is in memory during the whole process, the connection handle has to be re-created in the second PHP file.

After a few words about the lifetime of a connection handle, you will have a closer look at persistent database connections and transactions. In general, persistent connections have to be handled like ordinary connections. When dealing with transactions, however, some things have to be taken into consideration.

To show you what you have to take care of, we create a small table called access:

```
CREATE TABLE access(id serial, script text, accesstime timestamp);
```

Take a look at this script:

```php
<?php
        echo("<html><body>\n");
        $db=pg_pconnect("dbname=mydb user=hs host=localhost");
        if (!$db)
        {
                echo("connection cannot be established<br>\n");
        }
        else
        {
                echo("connection established<br>\n");
        }

        $status=pg_exec($db, "BEGIN WORK");
        $status=pg_exec($db, "INSERT INTO access (script, accesstime) VALUES
('1', now())");

        # creating an empty form
        echo ('<A HREF="transaction2.php/">next screen</A><br>');

        echo ('</body></html>');
?>
```

First, we connect to the database and start a transaction explicitly by using the BEGIN WORK command. In the next step, we insert a record into the table. script contains an identification of our script, and accesstime contains the time the database transaction takes place. Our program terminates without terminating the transaction explicitly. Because the backend process will stay in memory, the transaction won't be committed automatically—the open connection (including the open transaction) stays in memory.

After the first site has been displayed, we query the table:

```
mydb=# SELECT * FROM access;
 id | script | accesstime
----+--------+------------
(0 rows)
```

No records can be found in table access because the transaction has not been committed.

If we click the link we have displayed on the screen, we get to the next script:

```php
<?php
        echo("<html><body>\n");
        $db=pg_pconnect("dbname=mydb user=hs host=localhost");
        if (!$db)
        {
                echo("connection cannot be established<br>\n");
        }
        else
        {
                echo("connection established<br>\n");
        }

        $status=pg_exec($db, "INSERT INTO access (script, accesstime) VALUES
('2', now())");
        $status=pg_exec($db, "COMMIT");
        echo ('</body></html>');
?>
```

First, we connect to the database again. This time, we do not start a transaction explicitly, but start with inserting a value into the table. We commit the transaction. Here is the content of table access:

```
mydb=# SELECT * FROM access;
 id | script |       accesstime
----+--------+------------------------
  1 | 1      | 2001-07-11 20:17:17+02
  2 | 2      | 2001-07-11 20:17:17+02
(2 rows)
```

Two records can be found in the table. The first record is also inserted into the database, because PHP continues the transaction in the second script. Unfortunately, we have no guarantee that this is going to happen. If we were working on a highly accessed database, the connection handle generated by the second script might not be assigned to the same backend process, so the INSERT command in the first script would be neglected. Luckily, the connection handle in the second script has been assigned to the same backend process and no data has been lost.

As you can see, dealing with open connections across multiple PHP files is an extremely dangerous endeavor and it should be avoided. Otherwise, the behavior of a program will be stochastic.

Ordinary connections are much safer when dealing with transactions. If we substitute the persistent connection generated with the following:

```
$db=pg_pconnect("dbname=mydb user=hs host=localhost");
```

by an ordinary connection, which can be established to the database by using the following:

```
$db=pg_connect("dbname=mydb user=hs host=localhost");
```

the situation will be slightly different. Because the connection cannot be continued after terminating the first script, only one value will be inserted into the database.

Here is the content of the table:

```
mydb=# SELECT * FROM access;
 id | script |       accesstime
----+--------+------------------------
  1 | 1      | 2001-07-11 20:17:17+02
  2 | 2      | 2001-07-11 20:17:17+02
  4 | 2      | 2001-07-11 20:18:39+02
(3 rows)
```

Record number four has been inserted into the database, but we cannot find record number three in the database. The third record has been silently omitted, but the value of the sequence has increased; this is necessary, because otherwise some values might occur more than once in concurrent transactions.

Summary

In general, persistent database connections are a very powerful component of PHP. A lot of speed can be gained by "recycling" backend processes, which is very important on high-performance Web sites.

Persistent database connections also have disadvantages. In addition to risks concerning the memory usage of your server, persistent database connections can also be a problem, when dealing with transactions, if your code does not contain a perfect transaction handling system.

It's up to you to decide whether persistent database connections are an advantage for your Web site.

CHAPTER 19

Using PostgreSQL and Microsoft Software over the Network

It's not always the software of just one company that reigns over an IT environment. In many office environments, Unix servers have to be connected to office applications. Some powerful tools, such as Samba, are already available and are widespread in the Open Source community to connect a Unix machine to a Windows network. In most cases, databases are connected with a Windows network by using ODBC or some sort of proprietary software offered by many database vendors, such as Oracle. Another possibility is to use Open Source software, such as Perl's DBI interface.

As a rule of thumb we can say that the more Microsoft is involved the more often ODBC is used for database interaction. Especially when dealing with office applications, ODBC especially plays a major role when you're dealing with office applications. Like we have already in Chapter 9, "Extended PostgreSQL—Programming Interfaces," PostgreSQL also offers an ODBC interface. In this section, you look closer at this interface and how it can be used in combination with Microsoft Office and Microsoft Visual Basic.

In most cases, using ODBC is a simple task as long as you are not planning to build extremely complex data structures. This chapter gives you an overview of what can go wrong when using ODBC and how to avoid those problems.

Connecting to MS Office

In this section, you learn how to connect MS Office to PostgreSQL, and about the features and dangers users have to face.

Setting Up the ODBC Driver

The first step you take when working with PostgreSQL and ODBC is to set up the ODBC driver for Windows. ODBC drivers for various databases are usually distributed with Windows. The PostgreSQL driver, however, is not included in the Windows core distribution, so the driver has to be installed manually. Installing the driver is a simple task.

First you download the driver. Check out http://odbc.postgresql.org to download the software. One of the fastest European mirrors is situated at the Technical University of Vienna:

ftp://gd.tuwien.ac.at/db/www.postgresql.org/pub/odbc/versions/

Check out the lastest ZIP file in the full directory and unzip the archive. The ZIP archive contains one Windows executable application that you can start from WinZip. The installation process of the ODBC driver is easy: Click through the install script and answer all questions. You don't have to define a path, because everything is done by the install script (see Figure 19.1).

Figure 19.1
The installation screen.

After installing the ODBC driver on the system, all required files for establishing an ODBC connection to PostgreSQL under Windows are available on the system. The next step is to define the data sources you will need. Click the Start button of your Windows desktop and open the Control Panel. In this menu, you will find an icon for configuring ODBC. Open the tool and look for your PostgreSQL driver. You have to add a data source to access PostgreSQL from your Windows applications.

Figure 19.2 shows how you connect to the database called myodbc on 195.34.147.7.

Figure 19.2
Defining the basic connection parameters.

In this window you can define the basic parameters for your ODBC connection. Now you move on to the Advanced Options (Driver) dialog box (see Figure 19.3).

Figure 19.3
Setting the advanced options.

One of the most important check boxes is labeled ReadOnly. If it is checked, the database cannot be updated, because it is set to read-only mode. Checking this box is a common error if you are not use to connecting to PostgreSQL from a Windows host. Keep this in mind when configuring your system and building applications. All other settings you can configure in this screen are not as important as the ReadOnly flag. Configurations such as query optimizations should be set to the default value. For further information about these settings, check out the documentation of the driver.

The next window shows some additional parameters you can define for your connection. Again, make sure that ReadOnly is not checked (see Figure 19.4).

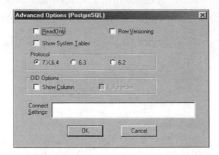

Figure 19.4
Make sure the ReadOnly button is not checked.

Setting up the ODBC driver and defining the data source is an easy task, and in general no significant problems will occur as long as you read what is displayed on the screen by the software.

Using Visual Basic to Connect to PostgreSQL

The first thing you have to do when working with PostgreSQL is connect to the database. In Visual Basic, ODBC is used for interacting with PostgreSQL. In this section, you learn how to connect to the database using ODBC.

The First Contact

Microsoft's Visual Studio is one of those extremely widespread killer applications on Windows. Like MS Office, Visual Studio is a key application providing nearly everything you will need to develop Windows applications—including Visual Basic and a C++ compiler.

After the core distribution has been installed on the system, we have to install the libraries we will need for interacting with the database. These libraries are known as the MSDN libraries and are not installed with Visual Studio (in version 6.0). Because Microsoft provides a simple user interface for setting up the MSDN libraries, it is rather simple to install the required software packages.

Visual Basic is often used to build database applications because there is hardly a programming language in Windows that enables you to develop applications faster. The key lies in the simplicity of the language. No badly used pointers can endanger the programmer and the stability of the software, and not much code has to be written to handle the memory management, as opposed to what is done in C. But Visual Basic also has disadvantages: Many say that the language is far too slow and not suitable for building huge applications.

Why you want to use Visual Basic is always a question you will have to answer. No matter how you decide, it is always worth it to have a brief look at the programming language. We do so in this section.

A Simple Example

To give you a basic idea of how Visual Basic can be used in combination with PostgreSQL and ODBC, we offer a small application. The target of our application is to write a rudimentary SQL client for PostgreSQL. We want to send SQL statements to the server and display the result in the window of our SQL client. The application will be implemented in Visual Basic 6.0.

Before we start writing the source code, we have to add a very important module to the program that we need for interacting with the database. To add the modules to your project, we click Projects and select References in the menu. The module we have to add is called Microsoft ActiveX Data Objects Library (ADODB). In some cases, this module is activated automatically—for example, if we add an ADO element to the toolbox or if you add a DataEnvironment or a DataReport component to your program. We recommend adding it manually so that you can be 100% sure that the module is included. If it is not, you will not be able to compile the project.

After adding the module, the next step is to implement the user interface. Designing a user interface is easy, because Visual Studio has been designed to have strong graphical capabilities (see Figure 19.5).

In the next step, we define the code our script has to execute when the button in the middle of our window is pressed. The code is very simple (see Figure 19.6).

The code calls the Main function, which we have implemented. This function handles all other tasks that have to be done when we click the button.

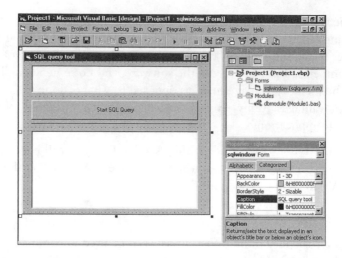

Figure 19.5

Designing the user interface.

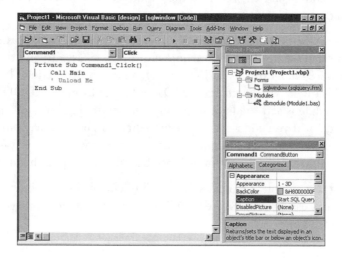

Figure 19.6

Defining what to do when the button is pressed.

Here is the function code of the function:

```
Option Explicit

Sub Main()
    ' declaring variables
```

```
    Set conn = New Connection
    Dim result As Recordset
    Dim i As Integer
    Dim mytext As String
    Dim cols As Integer

    ' connecting to the database and executing  query
    On Error GoTo myend
    conn.open "Data Source = PostgreSQL; Database = mydb; Server =
www.cybertec.at"

    On Error Resume Next
    Set result = conn.Execute(sqlwindow.Text1.Text)

    ' initializing variables and checking amount of columns in result
    cols = 0
    mytext = ""
    While cols >= 0
        On Error GoTo mydisplay
        mytext = result.Fields(cols)
        cols = cols + 1
    Wend

    If cols < 1 Then
        GoTo myend
    End If

mydisplay:
    MsgBox "number of columns found in result: " & cols
    mytext = ""

    ' going through the records returned by the query
    While Not result.EOF
        ' processing all columns and added the value found to the output window
        For i = 1 To cols
            mytext = mytext & result.Fields(i - 1) & "  "
        Next i
        mytext = mytext & Chr$(13) & Chr$(10)
        result.MoveNext
    Wend

    ' adding the data to the output window
```

```
      sqlwindow.Text2.Text = mytext

  myend:
      ' this is the end :)
      conn.close
  End Sub
```

The first line tells Visual Basic to postulate an explicit variable declaration. It is not necessary to use the explicit mode, but we recommend turning it on, because it protects you from using undeclared variables. With undeclared variables, if you have a misprint in your variable name, Visual Basic won't raise an error, but compiles the script anyway. This leads to bugs, which can be very annoying for the programmer.

At the beginning of the `Main` function in this example, we declare several variables that we will need later in the script. The most interesting of these variables are `conn` and `result`. `conn` contains our connection handle. `result` is defined as `Recordset` and contains the data returned by the query. In the next step, we open the connection to the database by using `conn.open`. `Data Source` is set to `PostgreSQL`; this is the name we defined when setting up the parameters of the ODBC connection. We also define the host we want to connect to and the name of the database we want to use. Now we process a `While` loop to find out how many columns are returned by the query. We try to access all columns and stop counting when the column with the desired id cannot be accessed. In case of an error, the script jumps to `mydisplay`, which processes the result of the query line by line and generates a string that we can use for displaying the output in the text box at the bottom of our window.

One crucial point is that we have to add line breaks to the string. On Unix systems, this is usually done by adding a simple \n to the string. On Windows, however, the process is a little more complicated, because \n is not supported by Visual Basic. As you can see in the previous example, we have to use `Chr$(13) & Chr$(10)` to add a line break to our string.

After adding the line break, we use `result.MoveNext` to move to the next record. After processing all records, we display the result of our query in the text field by using `sqlwindow.Text2.Text = mytext`. Figure 19.7 shows our script in action.

Our prototype shows how simple it is to develop rudimentary applications with the help of Visual Basic. With just a few easy-to-understand lines of code, it is possible to implement programs that can readily be used for practical reasons. This is one of the most important advantages of Visual Basic.

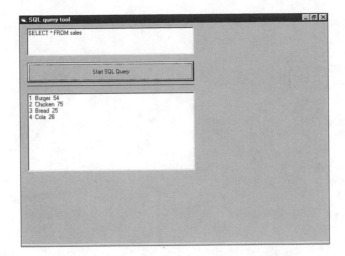

Figure 19.7
Our script in action.

Using PostgreSQL with Microsoft Office

For many years, Microsoft Office has played a major role in desktops. Millions of people around the globe have been using Microsoft's Office package for word processing and table calculations, as well as for building small database applications. Microsoft Office is the commonly used standard, and nearly all other vendors of office suites have included some sort of bridges to MS Office, such as data converters.

Because MS Office is so important in today's IT environments, it seems logical to have a connection from MS Office to host running a PostgreSQL database. In Windows environments, remote databases are usually accessed by using ODBC, similar to the one in the previous section. ODBC is a standard protocol and is supported by all major database platforms.

This chapter is based on MS Office 2000.

An Example Database

Let's get to some real action. We have compiled an example database that we will use in this section. Here is the SQL code:

```
CREATE TABLE supplier(
    "id" int4,
    "name" text,
```

```
        "contact" text
);

CREATE TABLE products(
        "productid" int8,
        "name" text,
        "unit" int4,
        "amount" numeric(9,2),
        "supplier" int4,
        "price" numeric (9,2) CHECK (price > 0),
        "currency" char(3) NOT NULL
);

CREATE TABLE unit(
        "id" serial,
        "description" text
);

CREATE TABLE sales(
        "id" serial,
        "when" timestamp DEFAULT now(),
        "prodid" int8,
        "who" text NOT NULL,
        "amount" numeric(9,2) CHECK (amount > 0),
        "price" numeric(9,2) CHECK (price > 0)
);

COPY "supplier" FROM stdin;
1       Sams    Indianapolis
2       Cybertec        Vienna
3       Acompany        AnywhereCity
\.

COPY "products" FROM stdin;
453465          PostgreSQL developers handbook 1        3243    1       33.99   USD
324324          Python developers handbook     1        2892    1       33.99   USD
324323          Commercial PostgreSQL support  2        0       2       80      EUR
\.

COPY "unit" FROM stdin;
1       piece
2       hour
\.
```

Table `supplier` contains information about the vendors of our products, such as the name and the contact information. In table `products`, we store information about our products. The column called `unit` defines which category a product belongs to. Books are usually sold in pieces; in our example, support activities are sold in hours. `products` also includes the name of the vendor of a product. We store the id of the vendor so that the table `supplier` can be referenced easily. As you can see in the definition of the table, we make sure that the price of a product is higher than zero. This `CHECK` condition helps us make sure that people cannot insert trash into the database. Another important restriction is the constraint set for the `currency` column. We make sure that the user inserts a currency into the table, because the `price` column would be of no use when there is no currency defined.

The `sales` table will be used to store information about the products we sold. If no correct date and time is passed to the database, the result of the `now()` function will be used as the default value. We also make sure that `who`, `amount`, and `price` will contain a suitable value, because we want to know which person has bought how many products and how much these products have cost. If you are planning to build a shop database, make sure that a field that stores the price can be found in the `sales` table; otherwise, you might easily run into trouble when you want to change the price of a product. Don't take the price stored in the `products` table!

After defining the required data structure, we insert a few records into our tables.

Working with MS Access

MS Access is a database system distributed with Microsoft Office and is often used to build small databases that are not accessed by remote machines. Marketing people often say that MS Access is capable of handling network connections, but this is not 100% true, because MS Access is not a real database server like PostgreSQL. It can also be quite painful to torture MS Access with gigabytes of data, because there are some significant restrictions in MS Access that don't allow the user to insert such huge amounts of data into the database. If you have to process huge amounts of data, you might have to split a database into multiple sub-databases to handle the data. An array of sub-databases won't be easy to handle, but with the help of VBA macros, it would be possible to compute a reasonable result. In general, we do not recommend using MS Access for storing huge amounts of data, because there is much better software available for such purposes.

Now we want to connect MS Access to our PostgreSQL database. Therefore, we start MS Access and open a new database (see Figure 19.8).

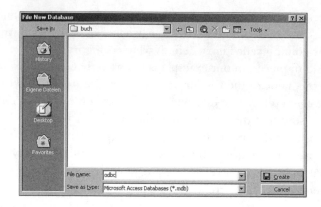

Figure 19.8
Adding a new database.

To access an ODBC data source, we have already defined it. Now we have to define a link to all tables that can be found in our data source. Linking to a table means that we include it in our application, and every change we make is directly sent to the database. To create a link to a table, click File at the top of your MS Access window and select Get External Data. There you can click Link Table to include a table into your application (see Figure 19.9).

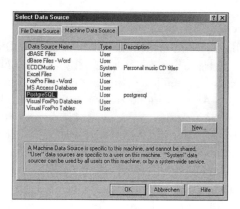

Figure 19.9
Select a data source.

First we have to select the data source that contains the table we want to include. You can see in the figure that quite of lot of data sources are available, because they are predefined. We select PostgreSQL and click the OK button (see Figure 19.10).

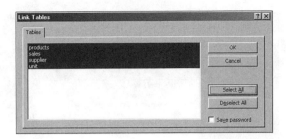

Figure 19.10
Selecting the tables for linking.

Now a list of all tables available in the data source will be displayed. We select all of them and click OK (see Figure 19.11).

Figure 19.11
Linking table by table.

Every table included in our system must have a unique identifier. This is necessary so that Access can distinguish the records. In PostgreSQL, every record has an internal identifier, which is not displayed in the table automatically. The situation is different in Access, so we recommend adding a field called `id` that contains a serial, which is always unique and can therefore be used as a primary key by access. For table products, we use `productid` as the primary key, because a product id must always be unique. After defining the primary key of table products, Access asks for the primary key of the next table and so on. Now that we have included all tables, we can see a complete list of all links available on the screen (see Figure 19.12).

In the next step we want to define the relation model for our tables (see Figure 19.13). Therefore, MS Access offers a powerful and easy-to-use interface. In general, we have nothing else to do than connect the tables with the help of a simple mouse click. Some questions have to be answered about the way the tables have to be joined, but that's all we have to do. Let's have a look at the definition of the relation first.

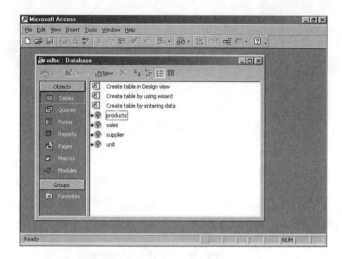

Figure 19.12
Our database contains four tables.

Figure 19.13
Defining the relation.

As you can see in the figure, we want to connect the column productid in table products with column prodid in table sales. At the bottom of the window, you can see that the default type of relation is One-To-Many, which means that one record in table products can have multiple counterparts in table sales. In other words, one product can be sold more than once.

In addition to the relation, we have to define the way the two tables have to be joined. Therefore, we click Join Type, which connects us to a window where we can select one out of three ways to join the table (see Figure 19.14).

Figure 19.14
Select how you want to join the tables.

We define all relations we need for our data model.

> **Note**
> We have already defined all tables and all integrity constraints on PostgreSQL, but
> these settings are not imported into MS Access. Integrity constraints on PostgreSQL
> will only have an effect on the whole matter when inserting or deleting data.

We recommend you define the relations in MS Access as they have been defined in the
PostgreSQL database (see Figure 19.15).

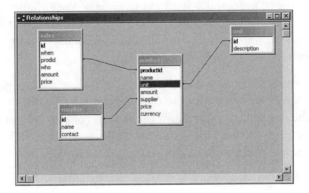

Figure 19.15
The data model.

After we link all tables and define all relations, we have a look at the table products.
Three records are already in the table. Now we want to insert a record: We insert an
additional record for the book Advanced Unix programming to the table. If the price
is higher than zero, the records can be added without any problems.

Let's have a look at the content of the table after inserting the record. We use psql to
see whether the record has been added to the table:

```
myodbc=# SELECT * FROM products;
 productid |              name            | unit | amount   | supplier | price |
currency
----------+------------------------------+------+----------+----------+-------
+----------
   453465 | PostgreSQL developers handbook |   1 | 3243.00 |        1 | 33.99 |
USD
   324324 | Python developers handbook     |   1 | 2892.00 |        1 | 33.99 |
USD
   324323 | Commercial PostgreSQL support  |   2 |    0.00 |        2 | 80.00 |
EUR
   678373 | Advanced Unix programming      |   1 | 2678.00 |        1 | 49.99 |
USD
(4 rows)
```

Four—not three—records can be found in the table now. The new record is added to the table immediately after we press Enter. There are no open transactions in the database system.

Let's look at table sales, which is currently empty. In the definition of the data structure, column id is defined as serial. *Serial* means that if no value is inserted into the table, the value of the serial is used as the value of the column. Inserting into a column that has been defined as serial can be dangerous, because the values in the column might not be unique anymore. The second column in our example has the result of the now() function as the default value.

Now we want to add two records to the table, but we leave the first two fields empty. Surprisingly, MS Access completes the records automatically. In the first column, the next value in the sequence is inserted. If the second column is left blank, the result of the now() function will be added to the records automatically. This is a very comfortable feature, because it enables you to set server-side default values.

As you can see from the following, the values are also inserted into the database automatically:

```
myodbc=# SELECT * FROM sales;
 id |          when           | prodid |   who    | amount  | price
----+-------------------------+--------+----------+---------+----------
  1 | 2001-07-13 10:21:50+02 | 453465 | Reseller | 1000.00 | 33990.00
  2 | 2001-07-13 10:26:26+02 | 799999 | reseller | 1000.00 | 57890.00
(2 rows)
```

If many people are working on one table simultaneously, it might be necessary to refresh the content of the table from time to time. MS Access does not offer a button for that purpose, so we have to open and close the table explicitly to get a refreshed version of the content.

Another step, which is commonly taken when working with databases, is to drop and create tables. Removing a table that is stored in a PostgreSQL database means removing the link; This does not mean that the table is removed from the PostgreSQL database.

It is possible to create and drop tables directly in the PostgreSQL database and not via MS Access.

Working with MS Excel

Data stored in a PostgreSQL can also be included in MS Excel. As you learned in the last section, the data is imported via an ODBC connection.

To import data into MS Excel, select Data | Get External Data | New Database Query (see Figure 19.16).

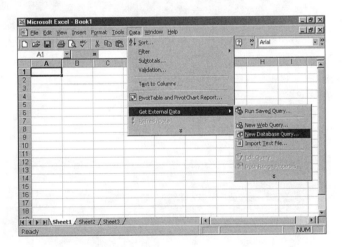

Figure 19.16
Importing data into MS Excel.

In the next step, we define the columns we want to import from the PostgreSQL database.

After selecting the data, we get to the final window, where we have to define what to do with the data. We select Return Data to Microsoft Excel and click Finish. Now the data has been imported into MS Excel.

> **Note**
> We have not created a link. We have imported the data, which means that no changes in the data will affect the data stored in PostgreSQL.

If the data has been imported successfully, the data can be found in the spreadsheet (see Figure 19.17).

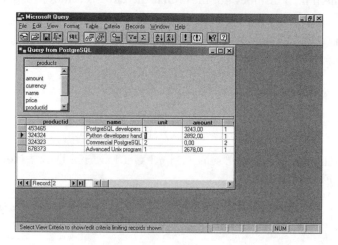

Figure 19.17
The data has been imported.

If we want to edit the data, we have to use Microsoft Query, which is distributed with the MS Office package (see Figure 19.18).

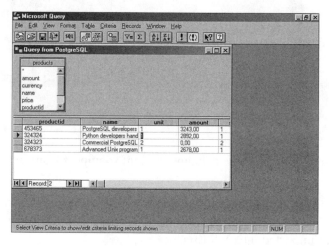

Figure 19.18
Editing data with MS Query.

MS Query offers an easy way to view and modify data. Inserting data that can be modified into Excel is usually done by writing a macro package and a user interface.

In this section you have learned that it is possible to connect MS Excel to PostgreSQL, but it is not the best way to interact with the database.

Working with MS Word

One of the most widespread applications in Microsoft environments is MS Word, a powerful tool for word processing.

In many cases, it is necessary to generate database-driven documents. Like all other office components, MS Word enables you to import data via ODBC. If we want to modify the data in our PostgreSQL database instead of making a simple import, we have to use MS Query or VBA macros instead—as you learned in the last section.

Let's create a simple, database-driven document.

To import the data, we can use the taskbar dedicated for working with databases (see Figure 19.19).

Figure 19.19
Using the taskbar to import the data.

We have to select the data source and the columns as we did in the last section.

After importing the data, we use AutoFormat, as shown in Figure 19.20.

We click through the AutoFormat menu and define all settings for the table. Finally the table is ready (see Figure 19.21).

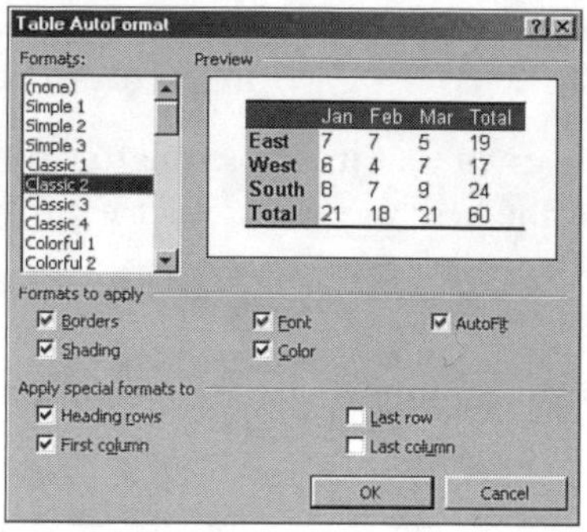

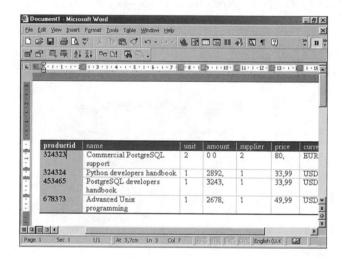

Figure 19.20

Formatting the table.

Figure 19.21

A formatted table.

Using PostgreSQL and MS Office with Huge Amounts of Data

As you learned in Chapter 1, "About PostgreSQL," PostgreSQL is capable of storing gigabytes of data reliably. You can also link huge tables with MS Access or import it to any other office product as well. In our tests, we created a random table with three columns containing 10 million records (about a 200MB ASCII file). In spite of various attempts to link or import the data into an MS Office 2000 product, we did not manage to achieve our target, because all Office products collapse.

Interaction with the database worked well with very small amounts of data, but it was not possible to link or import a "real" database.

Summary

PostgreSQL is capable of interacting with Microsoft products via the ODBC interface. With the help of ODBC, PostgreSQL can be used by Microsoft products as it can with any other database supporting ODBC.

However, when the amount of data increases, problems might occur because MS Office is not capable of handling huge amounts of data.

CHAPTER 20

Drawing Graphs on Unix Systems Using gnuplot and PostgreSQL

It has always been said that Unix and graphics are not a good match. In fact, Unix offers much more than just command shells that aren't user friendly. In this section you take a closer look at a tool called gnuplot, which can be used to generate wonderful graphics on Unix systems (and on Windows systems as well).

About gnuplot

gnuplot was originally designed and developed by Colin Kelley and Thomas Williams in 1986 for plotting functions and datafiles on a variety of terminals. From 1988 to 1989, an alternative version called GnuTex ,which supported LaTex was implemented. Since then, gnuplot has been capable of producing LaTex code. Tex is a text-based layout software, which was originally written by Donald E. Knuth, one of the most famous computer scientists in history. Leslie Lamport finally developed a macro package for Tex that is now known as *LaTex*. With the help of gnuplot and LaTex, you can develop high-quality publications. These days, many famous publishing houses rely on LaTex to produce attractive books efficiently.

In 1989 and 1990, GnuTex and some other implementations of gnuplot were merged into a new release called GNUPLOT 2.0.

Since then, a lot of additional features have been implemented and added to gnuplot, which is now one of the most mature and stable programs provided by the Open Source community. You can use gnuplot in combination with LaTex (the most stable software) to build extremely powerful and stable applications.

gnuplot is included in most Linux distributions. If gnuplot is not installed on your system, check out `http://www.gnuplot.org/` to download the sources.

Using PostgreSQL and gnuplot

In this section, you learn the fundamentals of gnuplot and, after some simple examples, move to PostgreSQL and see how it can be combined with gnuplot to generate database-driven graphics. To start gnuplot, use the following:

[hs@duron hs]$ **gnuplot -background white** `-background` `white` makes sure that the background of the graphs we want to generate is white. After starting gnuplot, we will be in an interactive shell.

Now we can draw graphs by using the `plot` command:

```
gnuplot> plot tanh(x) - cos(x)
```

We want to see the graph of `tanh(x) - cos(x)` (*tanh* is tangens hyperbolicus; *cos* is cosinus). Figure 20.1 shows the result.

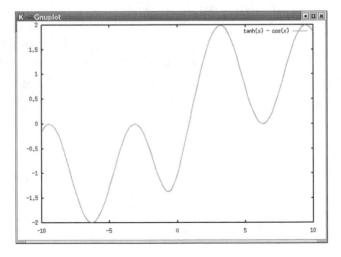

Figure 20.1
A simple mathematical function.

gnuplot finds the best interval for the graph so that only the "useful" part is displayed.

gnuplot provides a large number of functions; you explore the most important ones in this section.

Let's get back to PostgreSQL. We have compiled a small table storing incomes for certain years. We will use this table for the next example:

```
mygnuplot=# SELECT * FROM income;
 year | income
------+--------
 1997 |  24000
 1998 |  26300
 1999 |  26000
 2000 |  29000
 2001 |  32100
 2002 |  32000
 2003 |  32700
(7 rows)
```

The data shown does not have the right format to be used for gnuplot directly; we have to use some parameters when retrieving the data from the table. In this example, we want only the first column to be displayed, so we select only the first column from the table:

```
[hs@duron hs]$ psql -c "SELECT income FROM income" -A -F " " -t mygnuplot
24000
26300
26000
29000
32100
32000
32700
```

The data shown already fits our demands. Let's look at the command-line parameters: -A tells PostgreSQL to use the unaligned table output mode. -F defines the field separator—this option is useful only when multiple columns are returned by the query. -t makes sure that the header is silently omitted.

Now that we have written a shell command, which returns the data in the way we need it, we have to find a way to pass it to gnuplot in order to draw the graph. Luckily, gnuplot supports some easy methods to read the data.

The following shows how we compute the result of the shell command we have shown previously and draw a graph:

```
gnuplot> plot "< psql -c 'SELECT income FROM income' -A -F ' ' -t mygnuplot "
```

The command between the two double quotes is evaluated, and the result is returned to gnuplot, which displays the graph on the screen (see Figure 20.2).

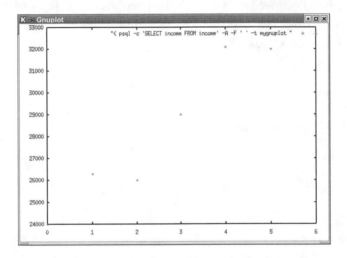

Figure 20.2
gnuplot displays a window containing the graph.

We can see an array of points representing the values in the database.

Up to now, we have created all graphics with the help of gnuplot's shell. This might be a bit of a problem for you when building huge applications. Let's see how the graphics shown previously can be created with the help of one simple Bourne shell command:

```
[hs@duron hs]$ echo "plot \"< psql -c 'SELECT income FROM income' -A -F ' ' -t
mygnuplot \" " | gnuplot -background white -persist
```

We simply pipe the command to gnuplot. All double quotes passed to the program have to be masqueraded using a backslash so that the shell does not mix up the double quotes used for the echo command with the double quotes used for gnuplot.

The -persist flag is necessary; otherwise, gnuplot will close the X windows when the execution of the script is ready. Using -persist makes sure that the window is still alive after gnuplot has terminated.

Having the result displayed in an X window might be nice, but in some cases it is necessary to store the result generated by gnuplot in a file that you can use for further transformation. The following includes a file that contains a short gnuplot script.

First we set the terminal to pbm, which means that a pbm file is generated instead of X11 output. Then we include the command we showed previously:

```
[hs@duron gnuplot]$ cat config.plot
set terminal pbm color
plot "< psql -c 'SELECT income FROM income' -A -F ' ' -t mygnuplot "
```

We start gnuplot with config.plot as the first parameter and redirect the output to a file called graph.pbm:

```
[hs@duron gnuplot]$ gnuplot config.plot  > graph.pbm
```

We can use that file now. If pbm is not our desired file format, we can easily convert the file to jgp or any other format by using a program such as mogrify:

```
[hs@duron gnuplot]$ mogrify -format jpg *.pbm
```

Now we want to change the labels of the graphics we have just generated. The first thing we want to do is to eliminate the ugly string containing psql on the upper edge of the graph. This can be done by using set nokey. The title of the graph should be Income table, and the axis should be labeled with year and income in USD per year. Up to now we have also seen that gnuplot finds the right scale for the graph by itself. In some cases, this might not be what we need, so we define the range of values displayed manually using xrange and yrange.

The following is a file that does exactly what we need:

```
set nokey
set title "Income table"
set xlabel "year"
set ylabel "income in USD per year"

xmax=6
ymin=0
ymax=40000

set xrange [0 : xmax]
set yrange [ymin : ymax]

plot "< psql -c 'SELECT income FROM income' -A -F ' ' -t mygnuplot "
```

We can generate the graph using a simple shell command:

```
[hs@duron gnuplot]$ gnuplot -persist -background white config.plot
```

The result will be the graph shown in Figure 20.3.

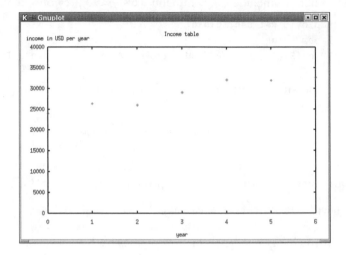

Figure 20.3
Redesigning the graph.

Often it is necessary to plot two independent data sources in one graph—especially when you want to compare data. The following script shows how you can plot two data sources (they contain the same data) in two different ways:

```
set nokey
set grid
set title "Income table"
set xlabel "year"
set ylabel "income in USD per year"

xmax=6
ymin=0
ymax=40000

set yrange [ymin : ymax]

plot "< psql -c 'SELECT year, income FROM income' -A -F ' ' -t mygnuplot" \
            with lines linewidth 3, \
        "< psql -c 'SELECT year, income FROM income' -A -F ' ' -t mygnuplot" \
            with boxes linewidth 3
```

We want a grid to be displayed in the background of our graph. The last four lines of code are responsible for plotting. The first data source is displayed as a line, and `linewidth` is set to 3. The second data source is displayed using boxes. gnuplot makes sure that the two components of the graph are displayed in different colors (see Figure 20.4).

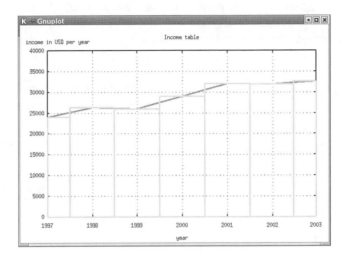

Figure 20.4
Plotting two data sources.

The script plots the graph as we expected it to be, but there are still two problems that have to be solved. We have plotted two data sources, and therefore we have queried the database twice. This leads to two problems: It might happen that the data in the database changes during the execution of the first query, so the result of the second query might differ from the result of the first query. Another problem is that executing two queries takes much longer than executing just one.

Our two problems can be solved easily. To show you how this can be done, we have compiled a table containing the income of males and females:

```
mygnuplot=# SELECT * FROM income;
 year | male  | female
------+-------+--------
 1997 | 24000 |  19200
 1998 | 26300 |  21400
 1999 | 26000 |  21800
 2000 | 29000 |  21000
 2001 | 32100 |  26500
 2002 | 32000 |  26700
 2003 | 33700 |  28200
(7 rows)
```

We use a simple `Makefile` to generate the result:

```
[hs@duron gnuplot]$ cat Makefile
x       :         config.plot
        psql -c 'SELECT year, male, female FROM income' -t -A -F ' ' \
                mygnuplot > file.data
        gnuplot -background white -persist config.plot
        rm -f file.data
```

Let's analyze the `Makefile` first. We select all data from table `income` and store the result of the query in `file.data`. Then we start gnuplot and pass the name of the configuration script to it.

Here is the configuration script:

```
set nokey
set grid
set time
set title "Income table"
set xlabel "year"
set ylabel "income in USD per year"

set yrange[0 : ]

plot 'file.data' using 1:2 with lines linewidth 2, \
        'file.data' using 1:3 with lines linewidth 2
```

The time the image was created is displayed by using `set time`. We don't know the highest income in the database, so we set the lower limit for `yrange`" to 0 and do not specify the upper value. gnuplot will make sure that a suitable border for the upper limit will be used. In the next step, we tell gnuplot to use the first and the second column in `file.data` as the data source for plotting the first line. The second line will be plotted using the first and the third column. Using one `plot` command is enough, because every additional graph is simply added to the list (see Figure 20.5).

The previous examples showed basic tasks that can be accomplished with gnuplot and PostgreSQL. Sometimes it might be necessary to add explanations to the graph so that the reader can easily understand what you want to say. Two components for adding explanations to a graph are essential: arrows and labels.

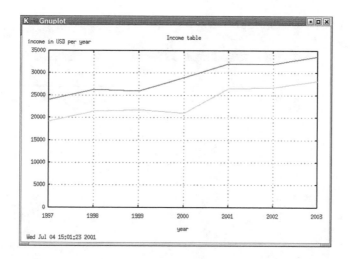

Figure 20.5
Plotting the data in an external file.

In the next example, we added two labels and one arrow to the scenery:

```
set nokey
set grid
set time

set arrow from 1999, 15000 to 2000, 20000
set label "significant changes" at 1998.35, 13000

set label "(c) SAMS" at 2002.3, 2200

set format y "%g$"
set title "Income table"
set xlabel "year"
set ylabel "income"

set yrange[0 : ]

plot 'file.data' using 1:2 with lines linewidth 2, \
        'file.data' using 1:3 with lines linewidth 2
```

First we add the arrow to the graph. As you can see, the coordinates can simply be defined. Then we add the labels to the scenery. The first component that we define for the label is the text we want to be displayed. Then we tell gnuplot where to place it, as we did for the arrow. We start gnuplot with the file shown.

The result can be seen in Figure 20.6.

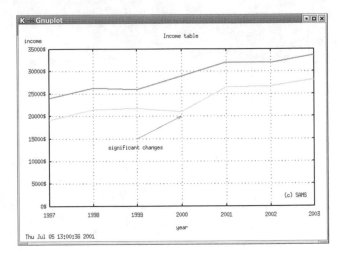

Figure 20.6
A plot including arrows and comments.

For many applications, it is necessary to produce three-dimensional plots. Because gnuplot is a highly developed software, it is also capable of generating three-dimensional graphics.

To show you how such plots can be created, we compiled a table that contains two additional columns, which store the number of people we used to compute the average income (wf is an abbreviation for *workforce*):

```
mygnuplot=# SELECT * FROM income;
 year | avg_male | wf_male | avg_female | wf_female
------+----------+---------+------------+-----------
 1997 |    24000 |     732 |      19200 |       932
 1998 |    26300 |    1412 |      21400 |      1054
 1999 |    26000 |    1930 |      21800 |      1320
 2000 |    29000 |    2065 |      21000 |      1150
 2001 |    32100 |    2163 |      26500 |      1259
 2002 |    32000 |    2254 |      26700 |      1292
 2003 |    33700 |    2620 |      28200 |      1721
(7 rows)
```

The following is the config file for our three-dimensional plot:

```
set nokey
set time

set format y "%g$"
set title "Income table"
set xlabel "year"
set ylabel "income"

splot 'file.data' using 1:2:3 with lines linewidth 2, \
      'file.data' using 1:4:5 with lines linewidth 2
```

Here, we have to use splot instead of plot. Because we have one additional dimension, we have to define three columns containing the data—we select the numbers of the columns according to the order they can be found in the input file.

The screenshot of the plot is shown in Figure 20.7.

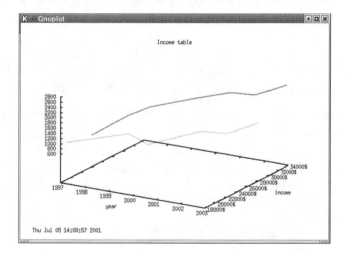

Figure 20.7
A simple 3-D plot.

A Simple LaTex Document

gnuplot has been used in combination with LaTex for many years. Since the days of GnuTex, gnuplot has supported a graphical terminal called *latex*, which produces LaTex code. The code generated can directly be included in LaTex documents. With the help of a programming language such as Perl, it is possible to generate dynamic and very professional-looking reports. Using gnuplot in combination with LaTex has many advantages over other systems:

- **Speed.** LaTex can generate reports with hundreds of pages in a minimal amount of time. gnuplot is implemented efficiently, and a great looking plot can be computed quickly.

- **Power.** LaTex is one of the most powerful text processors available. LaTex has many advantages when you're dealing with a mathematical formula, because Tex was originally designed for laying out formulas.

- **Stability.** For many years, no errors have been found in Tex, although the source code of Tex is one of the most widely read (Tex's source code has often been used for academic purposes). Donald E. Knuth pays a remuneration for every error found in Tex, and the fee is doubled every year. gnuplot is also a very stable piece of software, because the code is already mature and the software has been used for many years.

In this section, we look at a simple application that creates a database-driven LaTex document. Applications like this can easily be implemented and used for reporting purposes because they offer the advantages of stability and speed.

Let's look at our prototype application. We use the following `Makefile` to generate a document named final.ps:

```
x    :        config.plot
     psql -c 'SELECT * FROM income ORDER BY year' -t -A -F ' ' \
            mygnuplot > file.data
     gnuplot -background white config.plot
     maketex.pl
     cat head.tex graph.tex end.tex > final.tex
     rm -f *aux *log *dvi *ps
     latex final.tex
     latex final.tex
     latex final.tex
     dvips final.dvi -o final.ps
```

First we query the database and store the result of the query in `file.data`. Then we start gnuplot with the configuration of the graphics we want to generate. In the next step, we start `maketex.pl`, a short Perl script (we look at this in more depth later). `maketex.pl` creates a file called `head.tex`, which contains the header of the TEX file we will generate and a table containing the data retrieved from the database. Then we take all TEX files (`head.tex` created by `maketex.pl`, `graph.tex` created by gnuplot, and the static file `end.tex`) and make one big file called `final.tex` out of it.

After removing some rubbish, we compile the TEX file to make a DVI file out of it.

> **Note**
> If you want to generate a table of contents, you have to compile the TEX file three times to receive the correct result.

Finally, `dvips` converts the DVI file to a Postscript file. The following, `config.plot`, is the file containing the gnuplot code:

```
set terminal latex
set output "graph.tex"
set nokey
set grid
set time

set format y "$%g$"
set title "Income table"
set xlabel "year"
set ylabel "income"

set yrange[0 : ]

plot 'file.data' using 1:2 with lines linewidth 2, \
     'file.data' using 1:3 with lines linewidth 2
```

The first line sets the terminal to `latex`. This makes sure that the output of gnuplot will contain LaTex code that we can use. The next line tells gnuplot to redirect the output to `graph.tex`. gnuplot uses LaTex's picture environment to display the graph. The result generated by gnuplot can sometimes be quite long and a little bit complicated, so we have decided not to include the LaTex code, which has been generated in this section.

After defining some additional parameters, we define the format of the y-axis' label. If we don't, the label will collide with the graph. In the next step, we define the text the labels should contain and define the y range. With the help of the `plot` command, we display the result.

After running gnuplot, the LaTex code for the graph is stored in graph.tex. The following is the code for maketex.pl:

```perl
#!/usr/bin/perl

# datafile ...
$datafile="file.data";

# opening tex file
open(TEX, "> head.tex") or die
    "cannot open head.tex\n";

# generating header ...
print "Trying to generate tex header ...\n";
print TEX "\\documentclass{article}\n".
    "\\begin{document}\n";

# printing tex code to file
print TEX "\\title{Income statistics}\n";
print TEX "\\maketitle\n";
print TEX "\\begin{abstract}\n";
print TEX "The past few years show a constant increase of male and female ".
    "incomes. Especially in 2001 women's income has increased about ".
    "26 percent compared to the year 2000. .... bla ... bla ...\n";
print TEX "\\end{abstract}\n";
print TEX "\\strut \n\\newline\n";
print TEX "\\begin{center} \n";

# generating a table ...
print TEX "\\begin{tabular}{|r|r|r|r} \\hline\n";
print TEX "Year & Male & Female \\\\ \\hline \\hline \n";

# inserting every line into the table ...
open(DATA, "< $datafile") or
    die "cannot open $datafile\n";
while(<DATA>)
{
    ($year, $male, $female)=split(/\s/, $_);
    print TEX "$year & $male & $female \\\\ \\hline \n";
}
print TEX "\\end{tabular}\n\n";
print TEX "\\end{center} \n";
print TEX "\\pagebreak \n";
close(DATA);
close(TEX);
```

```
# ending script ...
print "tex-header generated successfully.\n";
```

In the beginning, we define the file containing the input data (in our case, `file.data`).

> **Note**
> Every backslash used in the LaTex code has to be defined by using \\ in Perl,
> because one backslash is used for masquerading the second backslash.

It is better to pass the name of this file to the script as a parameter, but we have decided to do some hard-coding to make the code easier to understand. Then the file `header.tex` is opened. We will use this file to store the LaTex code that we will produce. If Perl is not able to create the file, we quit the script.

Now we start generating the LaTex code and generating the required tex header (`\documentclass`, and so forth). After defining the title, we start the `abstract` and add some text to it. This text will be displayed shortly after the title of the document. Then we define a table, which should be displayed in the middle of the page. We open `$datafile` for reading and processing, line by line.

Every line is split into three components (`year`, `male`, `female`) and inserted into the table. This is done with just two lines of code:

```
($year, $male, $female)=split(/\s/, $_);
print TEX "$year & $male & $female \\\\ \\hline \n";
```

`\hline` makes sure that a horizontal line is drawn after every line. If all lines have been processed successfully, the table ends, and we tell LaTex to start a new page using `\newpage`.

Now that head.tex is ready, we can look at the following file, end.tex:

```
\end{document}
```

The file contains just one line, which has to be added to the end of the LaTex document.

Now that all TEX files have been generated by the `Makefile`, the Postscript file is generated. The document will be two pages long. Figures 20.8 and 20.9 show the most important parts of the two pages.

On the first page you can see the title, the date, and the text of the abstract that we have added to our document in maketex.pl. After the text, we can see the table containing the data that we have extracted from our PostgreSQL database.

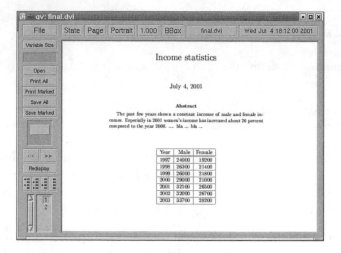

Figure 20.8

The first page of the LaTex document.

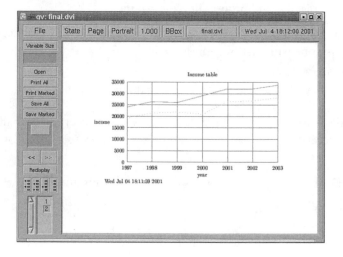

Figure 20.9

The second page of the LaTex document.

The second page shows the graph generated by gnuplot. The line defining the women's income looks different than the men's line, because gnuplot makes sure that the two lines can easily be distinguished.

This example demonstrates how simple, database-driven LaTex documents can be generated with the help of gnuplot and PostgreSQL. You can add applications such as this to a cron job (cron is a tool for starting certain tasks on Unix automatically and periodically) and generate professional-looking reports automatically. No matter how many pages your report contains, LaTex, gnuplot, Perl, and PostgreSQL are capable of handling it easily and reliably.

Geometric Datatypes and gnuplot—A Simple Example

PostgreSQL supports a powerful set of geometric datatypes. Displaying geometric data stored in a PostgreSQL database for many applications might be useful. Drawing database-driven images can be a difficult task, although there is a lot of Unix software available to do the job. Gimp, for instance, provides a powerful ASCII interface to generate and manipulate images from the command line (which is useful for Web applications). You also can use a scripting language in combination with gnuplot to do the job. This section shows you some basic ideas for visualizing geometric data stored in a PostgreSQL database. Let's start with a simple example.

We have compiled a small table containing some points:

```
mygnuplot=# SELECT * FROM mypoints;
 mypoints
- - - - - - - - - -
 (1,0)
 (6,4)
 (-3,-4)
 (3,-4)
(4 rows)
```

With the help of a trivial shell script, we can generate a simple plot. Before we get to the gnuplot code, here is the shell script that we will use to transform the data to the desired format:

```
#!/bin/sh

psql -c 'SELECT * FROM mypoints' -t mygnuplot | sed -e 's/,/ /gi' -e 's/)/ /gi'
-e 's/(/ /gi'
```

First we select the data from table gnuplot. -t makes sure that only the data is returned by the query. In the next step, we use sed (stream editor) to parse the data. We eliminate all brackets and commas so that gnuplot can easily read the input. Then we start gnuplot and use some simple commands:

```
gnuplot> set nokey
gnuplot> set xrange [-10 : 10]
gnuplot> set yrange [-10 : 10]
gnuplot> plot '< /home/hs/geo/plot.sh'
```

The first three lines define some basic properties of the graph, such as the range of values displayed on the x-axis. The fourth line starts our shell script and sends the data to gnuplot. Figure 20.10 shows the display when you run gnuplot.

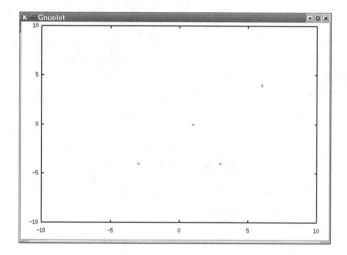

Figure 20.10
Drawing points.

The next example demonstrates how polygons can be plotted with the help of gnuplot. We have already dealt with polygons in Chapter 3, "An Introduction to SQL;" this time we generate a simple prototype of a script that prints all polygons stored in the table in a graph.

We have compiled a small table containing three polygons:

```
mygnuplot=# SELECT * FROM mypolygons;
          mypolygons
------------------------------
 ((-4,2),(3,9),(6,10),(13,13))
 ((4,2),(5,7),(6,12),(9,10))
 ((-4,2),(3,9),(6,0),(3,10))
(3 rows)
```

The following source code is a small script generating a config file for gnuplot:

```perl
#!/usr/bin/perl

use DBI;

# connecting
$connect="dbi:Pg:dbname=mygnuplot;port=5432";
$dbh=DBI->connect("$connect","hs")
     or die "cannot connect to the database\n";

# getting lines
$sql="SELECT * FROM mypolygons";
$sth=$dbh->prepare("$sql")
     or die "cannot prepare statement\n";
$sth->execute()
     or die "cannot execute query\n";

# open gnuplot config-file
open(PLOT, "> config.plot")
     or die "cannot open config file for gnuplot\n";
print PLOT "set xrange [-5 : 15]\n";
print PLOT "set yrange [-5 : 15]\n";

# setting variables and retrieving data
$files=0;
$plotstring="plot";

while   (@row = $sth->fetchrow_array)
{
    $line=$row[0];
    $line=~s/\),\(/\n/gi;
    $line=~s/\(|\)//gi;
    $line=~s/,/ /gi;

    # open file that contains data
    open(DATA, "> $files.data")
            or die "cannot open file $files.data\n";
    print DATA "$line\n";
    close(DATA);

    # generating plot command
    $plotstring.=" '$files.data' with lines linewidth 3,";
```

```
    $files++;
}

$plotstring=~s/,$//gi;
print PLOT "$plotstring\n";
close(PLOT);

# drawing data and cleanups
system("gnuplot -background white -persist config.plot");
system("rm -f [0-9].data");
```

First we connect to the database and send a simple SQL query to the server that retrieves all records in table mypolygons. As you learned in Chapter 9, "Extended PostgreSQL—Programming Interfaces," the SQL query has to be prepared and executed to receive the required result. Then we open the file, called config.plot, that we need to store the gnuplot code:

```
$files=0;
$plotstring="plot";
```

These two lines initialize two important variables. $files contains the number of polygons our graph will contain. $files is also used for generating the temporary file. $plotstring contains the plot command for our graph. Every polygon added to the scenery requires its own entry in the plot command.

After initializing the variables, we start retrieving the data from the query that we have processed before. Every line returned will be transformed to the required format and stored in a temporary file. After that, the polygon is added to the scenery: We extract the line from the result of our query and perform some basic operation such as substituting),(for a linefeed. This is necessary so that gnuplout can distinguish the various points of our polygon. We also eliminate all other brackets by using simple regular expressions.

After adding all components to the graph, we substitute the comma at the end of $plotstring for nothing and write the string to the file. Our config file is now ready and we can execute gnuplot using the file. Before we have a look at the graph, we have included the file config.plot. You can see that the plot command consists of three components, each having its own datafile:

```
set xrange [-5 : 15]
set yrange [-5 : 15]
plot '0.data' with lines linewidth 3, '1.data' with lines linewidth 3, '2.data'
with lines linewidth 3
```

The most important component of our program is the converter that we use for reformatting the output of the database to a format that we can use for gnuplot. Recall that you do this with regular expressions. Lines such as the next one are converted to a file containing multiple lines:

```
((-4,2),(3,9),(6,10),(13,13))
```

Every node of the polygon is transformed to a separate line:

```
-4 2
3 9
6 10
13 13
```

Keep in mind, that the columns of the file should be separated by a blank or a tab; if you use commas, gnuplot will not display the result correctly (if you don't define an input format). Figure 20.11 shows the graph.

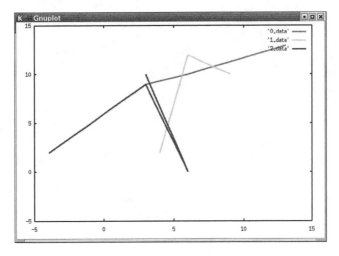

Figure 20.11
Drawing the polygons stored in the database.

Three polygons are displayed, because three records have been retrieved from the database.

As you can see, drawing database-driven geometric objects is an easy task with gnuplot. Of course it is not only possible to implement converters for points and geometric objects. Because gnuplot is flexible and powerful, it is possible to draw almost anything—just try it.

Summary

gnuplot is one of the most powerful and reliable pieces of software available for Unix. In combination with PostgreSQL, you can build powerful and reliable applications.

Software such as LaTex can be used to generate powerful reports, and PostgreSQL's geometric database provides a powerful interface for generating even more professional documents.

Index

Symbols

A

International Organization for
    Standardization (ISO), 453, 477
International Standard Book Number
    (ISBN), working with as datatype,
    453-454
International Standard Serial Number
    (ISSN), 454
Internet, backing up over, 203
interrupting queries, 226
INTERSECT keyword (SELECT
    statement), 99
intersections, calculating, 98
interval data type, 614-615
interval.cmp function, 625
intervals, adding to, 623-624
ISBN (International Standard Book
    Number), working with as datatype,
    453-454
isclosed() function, 95
ISO/ANSI C compilers, 18
isopen() function, 95
ISSN (International Standard Serial
    Number), 454
I/O system and performance, 211, 236-237

J

Java
    history, 372-373
    See also JDBC (Java Database Connectivity)
Java Database Connectivity. See JDBC (Java
    Database Connectivity)
Java Development Kit (JDK), 373
JDBC (Java Database Connectivity)
    API
        commands, 393-396
        exception handling, 391-393
        extensions, 396-399

function, 386-387
    objects, 385-386
    overview of, 385, 399-403
    stored procedures, 396
    transactions, 387-391
applications, 374, 376
components, 374-375
data retrieval, 379-384
data source, 375
database connections, 377-378
drivers, 375-376
installing under RedHat, 376-377
native drivers, 375
SQL, 375-376
JDK (Java Development Kit), 373
join operations, processing, 225
joining
    overview of, 219
    tables, 63-65
joins, 40, 65-68, 84
journaling, 208
jukeboxes, 196, 203-205

K

Kelley, Colin, 691
Kerberos V4, 190
Key Set Query Optimizer (KSQO), 160
Knuth, Donald E., 496, 691
König, Andreas, 315

L

Lamport, Leslie, 691
LANGUAGE command, 134
languages, stack-oriented, 526

P

U